MASTERING™
MAC® OS X

Todd Stauffer

SYBEX®

San Francisco • Paris • Düsseldorf • Soest •London

Associate Publisher: Richard J. Staron
Contracts and Licensing Manager: Kristine O'Callaghan
Acquisitions Editor: Diane Lowry
Developmental Editor: Ellen L. Dendy
Editors: Jim Gabbert, Joseph A. Webb, Marilyn Smith
Production Editor: Elizabeth Campbell
Technical Editors: Marty Cortinas, David Read, Fred Terry
Book Designers: Patrick Dintino, Catalin Dulfu, Franz Baumhackl
Electronic Publishing Specialist: Maureen Forys, Happenstance Type-O-Rama
Proofreaders: Molly Glover, Elizabeth Campbell, Nancy Riddiough, Laurie O'Connell, Nancy Duffy, Nelson Kim
Indexer: Jerilyn Sprotson
Cover Designer: Design Site
Cover Illustrator/Photographer: Sergie Loobkoff

Library of Congress Card Number: 2001086067

ISBN: 0-7821-2581-6

To my grandmother, Martha Morningstar.

Thanks for teaching me some of life's basics,

such as how to appreciate the "little" things,

how to write a thank-you note, and how,

exactly, the ideal kitchen should smell.

—Todd Stauffer

ACKNOWLEDGMENTS

Producing this book took a surprisingly long time for a computer book, thanks in no small part to the constantly mutating schedule of Mac OS X's release. Apple has worked for years to create this operating system, and the end result is something that has changed a great deal since the beginning of this project. In fact, *a lot* has changed a great deal since the beginning of this project, not the least of which was the project itself.

Although many people at Sybex have been part of this effort over the past few years, the last crew shift is the one that's done most of the hard work of putting up with me. Thanks to Ellen Dendy, developmental editor, for being a compass, a quartermaster, and, on occasion, a psychologist doling out small parcels of sanity to those of us (read: me) who desperately needed it. Thanks also to Diane Lowery for early work on managing the book's outline, preliminary chapters, and constant extensions.

Thanks to Elizabeth Campbell and Jim Gabbert for managing the schedule, the pages, and the constant barrage of new files and figures, not to mention my obsessive changes and details, as we got a better picture of what, exactly, Mac OS X would turn out to be. Thanks also to Joe Webb and Marilyn Smith for insightful editing and comments. More thanks to the various technical editors who've worked on this project, including David Read, Fred Terry, and Marty Cortinas. Their input made this book better than it ever would have been if it had relied solely on my own technical knowledge. Lastly, thanks to Maureen Forys, electronic publishing specialist, for her huge help in getting this book to the printer on schedule.

Fortunately, for the really tough bits, the book doesn't rely on me much at all. Two special heroes on this project are Dan Nolen, who authored Chapter 20, and Chris Pepper, who wrote Chapter 22. All those little self-help management books tell you to hire people smarter than you when you need something done right. These guys are both smarter than me and dedicated to knowing more about the innards of Mac OS X and its Unix underpinnings than I could even guess at. I am pleased to have gotten to know them both and called them partners.

I'd be remiss in not thanking Studio B's David Rogelberg and Neil Salkind for helping me secure the opportunity to write this book—even if it was last century when we first started down this particular road. Thanks as always to the rest of the Studio B staff, particularly Sherry Rogelberg, for the checks (and re-checks) that keep me fed and clothed.

Thanks to Liz Stauffer (Mom) for the long conversations, the encouragement, and the Web-production diversions, and to Kathy and C.J. for the love, support, and a much-needed vacation during one of those previously mentioned extensions. Finally, personal thanks to Donna Ladd for putting up with many a long-winded diatribe about how often Mac OS X was changing and how often I was rewriting things and how often I was going to pick up my PowerBook and toss it out a window. She's grown used to this kind of behavior and, yet, continues to put up with me. I'm forever grateful.

CONTENTS AT A GLANCE

CONTENTS

PART III • GETTING THINGS DONE WITH MAC OS X

PART IV • INSTALLING, MAINTAINING, AND TROUBLESHOOTING

18 Peripherals, Internal Upgrades, and Disks   517

19 Fixing Trouble with Applications   543

PART V · ADVANCED MAC OS X TOPICS

22 Terminal and the Command Line   651

INTRODUCTION

A *brand-new operating system.* Although that may seem like the topic of this book, the fact is that Mac OS X took nearly three years to arrive at its current incarnation, and it's based on technology that's been around for a decade and a half. For Mac users, however, it's brand-new, offering perhaps the most advanced consumer platform for computing that has ever been devised.

It's been a bumpy road, but now that Mac OS X is finally here, the result is a satisfying one. Mac OS X offers an improved Finder, a brand-new Dock, and an overall look and feel, called Aqua, that changes the way windows, applications, and graphics appear on-screen. In some ways, Mac OS X fundamentally changes the way that you, as a user, see and interact with a computer. In other ways, Mac OS X is friendly and familiar, offering AppleScript, QuickTime, and other key Apple technologies that have been maturing for quite some time.

Mac OS X is a fully modern operating system that is ready to take Apple's unique hardware to the next level. Gone are many of the problems inherent in older Mac OS versions, including system instability, memory management problems, and some of the networking and peripheral technologies that slowed down the Mac OS for years. Mac OS X has a new printing architecture, new Internet servers, and a new, built-in e-mail client. Many innovations, like Apple's iTools technology and the Sherlock searching capabilities, are more heavily integrated into the OS, making them work together even better.

Mac OS X may require some transition time, particularly for users familiar with Mac OS 9 and earlier versions. Mac OS X offers a different file system, ultimately based on the Unix-like FreeBSD operating system, which can take a little getting used to. It also offers some wonderful new bells, whistles, and honest-to-goodness productivity enhancements. And it offers windows into a whole new world—Unix and Unix-like operating systems—that most Mac users have never encountered but will likely enjoy exploring. Once you grow familiar with this new OS—thanks in part to *Mastering Mac OS X*—you may never want to go back.

What This Book Covers

Mastering Mac OS X is designed to be a comprehensive look at Apple's first release of Mac OS X, particularly aimed at intermediate and advanced users who are comfortable with the idea of a computer operating system. If you'd like to take your knowledge of early versions of the Mac OS or Microsoft Windows (or even Unix and Linux variants) and apply them to this exciting new OS, you've come to the right place. From the basics of the interface to the depths of the Darwin command line (and Unix-like syntax), you'll find that *Mastering Mac OS X* covers most of the topics you need to know to fully exploit your Mac as a workstation, either as a stand-alone computer or in a networked environment.

Mastering Mac OS X is specifically organized as a reference, with parts and chapters divided into topic areas. While you may find it useful to read straight through the text, you certainly don't have to; once you've mastered the basics, you can move directly to a particular chapter to see all you need to know about managing a multi-user system (Chapter 7), setting up a network (Chapter 8), learning AppleScript (Chapter 17), troubleshooting Mac OS X (Chapter 20), or getting around on the command line (Chapter 22), just to name a few.

Mastering Mac OS X covers the first release of Mac OS X, dubbed Mac OS X 10.0. That said, some interim releases have been made available for downloading during the editing phase of the book, and a few of those features are accounted for, particularly those made available in the Mac OS X 10.0.1 and 10.0.2 releases. Subsequent releases, at least in the near future, will likely focus on stabilizing the system and fixing small problems—so you'll find that *Mastering Mac OS X* is a comprehensive look at the OS for quite a while to come. (For important changes, see the Web site addresses at the end of this introduction.)

Here's a quick look at each of the sections of the book:

- In Part I, "The Mac OS X Basics," you'll begin with the basics of Mac OS X, focusing, in many cases, on the differences between Mac OS X, Mac OS X Server, and earlier versions, particularly from the user's point of view. You'll see how to work with and customize the Finder, how to work with native and Classic applications, and how to access the help and search applications in Mac OS X.

- In Part II, "Networks and the Internet," you'll move into topics designed for an administrative-level user of the Mac, including creating and managing users, setting options, and configuring a network. Here you'll also delve into Internet setup for individual Macs or a network of Macs, and you'll see Mac OS X's built-in Mail client, as well as other Internet clients and applications.

- Part III, "Getting Things Done with Mac OS X," focuses on Mac OS X's built-in applications, printing and color issues, multimedia topics, and AppleScript scripting.

- Part IV, "Installing, Maintaining, and Troubleshooting," offers four chapters on setup and troubleshooting, including coverage of peripherals, application troubleshooting, system-level diagnostics, and file maintenance.

- Part V, "Advanced Mac OS X Topics," dives beneath the graphical OS, introducing you to the most advanced parts of Mac OS X—the command line and the built-in server applications. You'll see an in-depth introduction to the Darwin command line and applications, a specific look at remote access and FTP from the command line, and specifics on using and working with the Apache and FTP servers built into Mac OS X. In the final chapter, you'll see a few other add-on Internet services you can work with in Mac OS X, including the QuickTime Streaming Server, file sharing with Microsoft Windows, and a few third-party commercial add-ons for high-end serving.

Conventions Used in This Book

This book uses some conventions and special formatting to easily communicate different commands, ideas, and concepts. Here's a look at some of the formats you'll encounter:

- Items in *italics* are generally terms being introduced and defined. In some other cases, italics are used for variables or placeholders (as in *you@youraccount.com*) that suggest information you need to know or enter to work with a particular feature or application.

- Items in **boldface** are generally commands or text you can type, while lines of programming code, filenames, Internet addresses, and command-line entries appear in a `monospaced font`.

- Menu commands use a right-facing arrow to suggest the menu you should select, followed by the command. For instance, File ➢ Open means to click the File menu in the menu bar at the top of the screen, then click the Open command.

- Keyboard shortcuts often include special symbols and a plus (+) sign between them, such as ⌘+P or Shift+Tab. With keyboard shortcuts, you need to simultaneously press all of the keys indicated, then release them together.

Aside from these formatting conventions, you'll come across a few special callout boxes within the body of the text itself. These boxes are designed to focus your attention on particular issues, depending on the type of box:

 NOTE *Notes* are designed to give you additional information about the current topic or to offer additional insight or definitions. Notes are also used sometimes as cross-references to other topics and chapters.

TIP *Tips* are special add-ons that help you perform the current task faster or give you some other options for working with the current topic. Ideally, you could ignore a tip without risking trouble, but hopefully you'll enjoy them all.

 WARNING *Warnings* are definitely not to be ignored. In most cases, I'll issue a warning only if you could damage files, erase disks, or otherwise perform an irreversible task that you might want to think about twice.

Along with these callouts, you'll also find sidebars throughout the text that are designed to give you more information that's tangential to the current discussion. Again, sidebars can often be ignored, but they may offer interesting or helpful advice for going deeper into a particular topic.

Errata, Extras, and Contact Info

Mac OS X is a moving target, and this book is printed and bound. That doesn't mean it can't breathe, however. For additional information as it becomes available, as well as answers to frequently asked questions (FAQs) and any errata that this book generates, you can visit my special Web site for this book at http://www.mac-upgrade.com/ macosx/. In addition, you can visit Sybex's site at http://www.sybex.com for official updates, addenda, and other information (search for *2581*, which is part of the book's ISBN number).

If you don't find an answer you need after visiting those Web sites, please feel free to send me an e-mail message at questions@mac-upgrade.com. Please include a detailed subject line with your e-mail, indicating whether or not your question is an immediate priority. It can take me a while to reply to every e-mail, but I do my best. Thanks for your patience, and thanks for reading *Mastering Mac OS X*!

PART I

The Mac OS X Basics

LEARN TO:

- Compare Mac OS X to other Mac OS versions available

- Get started with the Mac OS X interface

- Work with files and folders in the Finder

- Explore the basics of your home folder

- Work with native and Classic applications

- Get help and search for items

CHAPTER 1

Mac OS X vs. Mac OS X Server vs. Mac OS 9.x

An *operating system* (OS) is a set of computer instructions that allows the computer to interact with the user and any peripheral devices, such as printers, disk drives, and monitors. Apple Computer's newest operating system, Mac OS X (pronounced as "Mac oh es ten"), is a robust operating system with many behind-the-scenes features that make heavy-duty computing easier and faster. It also offers a new, intuitive interface for browsing files, an integrated e-mail application, and a host of other handy features.

In this chapter, you'll learn how Mac OS X came to be, what its outstanding features are, which version of the Macintosh operating system is best for you, and how you can use your existing Mac applications with OS X.

How Mac OS X Came to Be

For years, the Mac OS (or the Macintosh "system" software, as it used to be called) has been considered the cutting edge of interface design and user friendliness.

But the Mac OS, as innovative as it was when introduced in 1984, has long been in need of a major overhaul in order to make it fully "modern"—it should be as stable and capable as today's computer scientists and programmers can make it. Although the Mac OS has been updated year after year, those updates have continued to be hampered by the original Mac OS design—a design that didn't foresee innovations in OS thinking.

To solve this problem, Apple opted to create a new Mac OS that's built to take advantage of the new thinking and theory. This solution means offering a number of new features that, by necessity, aren't compatible with older Macs and with older Macintosh software. In fact, it means creating an entirely new Mac OS—Mac OS X—that can offer those technological underpinnings in ways that the original Mac OS simply can't.

Mac OS X is based on much of the technology that Apple acquired when it bought NeXT Software, a company launched and run by Steve Jobs from the mid-1980s until 1997. NeXT Software sold an operating system called OpenStep, based on their earlier NextStep, which, in turn, was based on FreeBSD, a Unix-like, open-source operating system. OpenStep was a very modern operating system, featuring many of the advantages that Apple wanted the Mac OS to sport.

There was still a lot of work to do, though. OpenStep had been designed to run on Intel-compatible chips and ran applications that weren't very Mac-like in their interface design. Although OpenStep offered a very attractive graphical interface for applications, it also had a dark side: a Unix command line even more intimidating than the arcane DOS commands that run underneath Microsoft Windows (see Figure 1.1).

FIGURE 1.1

The Unix command line, shown in Mac OS X's Terminal window

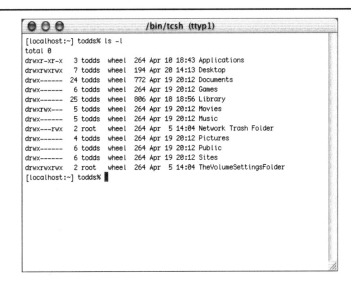

```
● ○ ○                    /bin/tcsh (ttyp1)
[localhost:~] todds% ls -l
total 0
drwxr-xr-x    3 todds   wheel   264 Apr 10 18:43 Applications
drwxrwxrwx    7 todds   wheel   194 Apr 20 14:13 Desktop
drwx------   24 todds   wheel   772 Apr 19 20:12 Documents
drwx------    6 todds   wheel   264 Apr 19 20:12 Games
drwx------   25 todds   wheel   806 Apr 18 18:56 Library
drwxrwx---    5 todds   wheel   264 Apr 19 20:12 Movies
drwx------    5 todds   wheel   264 Apr 19 20:12 Music
drwx---rwx    2 root    wheel   264 Apr  5 14:04 Network Trash Folder
drwx------    4 todds   wheel   264 Apr 19 20:12 Pictures
drwx------    6 todds   wheel   264 Apr 19 20:12 Public
drwx------    6 todds   wheel   264 Apr 19 20:12 Sites
drwxrwxrwx    2 root    wheel   264 Apr  5 14:04 TheVolumeSettingsFolder
[localhost:~] todds% █
```

Apple faced quite a challenge to "port" the OpenStep underpinnings to run on Macintosh hardware. On top of that, Apple spent even more time making the Mac OS X interface similar to the existing Mac interface, while updating and improving it. Throughout this whole process, Mac OS X has also been engineered to support most existing Mac OS 9–based applications.

Mac OS X Features

Because millions of people already rely on the Mac OS as it is, it's important that Apple create a safe, intelligent path for helping to migrate its customers from the old, familiar OS to the new one. Apple's plan is simple: to roll most of the simplicity and friendly design of the original Mac OS—the most recent version being Mac OS 9.1—into Mac OS X, which incorporates the latest "under-the-hood" advances.

So what are these advances? Why is there a need for a new Mac OS? Given the sheer power of today's computer processors, coupled with the complexity of computer applications, it's important that the Mac OS be more robust and include features it hasn't always boasted.

Specifically, Mac OS X is designed to address performance shortcomings in the original Mac OS with the following features: preemptive multitasking, memory protection, dynamic RAM allocation, and a microkernel-based design. With these four fundamental changes, Mac OS X becomes a more modern, less error-prone operating system than its predecessors. In addition, Mac OS X improves on two technologies that have a limited implementation in Mac OS 9.x: multithreading and symmetrical processing.

Perhaps most noticeably, Mac OS X also offers a new interface that builds on the strengths of Mac OS 9.x while incorporating other theories and elements from Open-Step, Linux, and even Microsoft Windows. The result is a visually pleasing interface that makes it easier to navigate a network, work on the Internet, and manage multiple open applications and documents.

What this means for the user is that Mac OS X is a user-friendly operating system that's also very powerful, taking full advantage of modern Macintosh hardware. Mac OS X is applicable to a variety of tasks, including professional graphics and layout, 3-D design and video editing, file sharing, and specialized Internet tasks like serving QuickTime streaming media. That said, Mac OS X is also perfectly well-suited to the home or small-office user, assuming your consumer-level hardware can handle Mac OS X's requirements. Mac OS X is a consumer OS as well as a business one, a fact that's punctuated by Apple's goal of including Mac OS X with all new Macs starting sometime in mid- to late 2001.

So that's what Mac OS X is capable of. Let's take a look at some behind-the-scenes features that make Mac OS X what it is and enable it to take on heavy-duty computing tasks.

 NOTE Throughout this chapter and this book, I'll refer to both Mac OS 9.x generally and Mac OS 9.1 specifically. This has the potential to be confusing, so some definitions are in order. When I'm talking about Mac OS 9.x, I'm referring to the technologies that started in Mac OS 9, continue through Mac OS 9.1, and will likely continue into Mac OS 9.5 or whatever future versions Apple releases. Collectively (along with Mac OS 8.x and even earlier versions), these versions are often called the "Classic Mac OS," to differentiate them from the all-new Mac OS X. When I refer to Mac OS 9.1, however, I'm usually talking about that specific version because it is the release, at the time of writing, that's required for full compatibility with Mac OS X, particularly when both operating systems are on the same Macintosh.

Preemptive Multitasking

Although the Mac OS has had basic *cooperative* multitasking capabilities (which allow more than one application to be running at a time) since Mac System 7 in the early 1990s, the Mac OS has never been updated to embrace a fully "modern," *preemptive* multitasking approach.

In cooperative multitasking, it's up to each individual application to determine how much of the processor's attention it deserves and how much of that attention it's willing to give over to other applications. This system works well when all applications behave. A poorly written application or one that's experiencing errors can get in the way of this multitasking system, making the entire OS less reliable or causing it to hang or freeze, thus forcing you to restart the Mac and possibly lose unsaved data.

With preemptive multitasking, Mac OS X is responsible for telling applications how much time they can get from the processor and how much time other applications get. Working as a traffic cop, Mac OS X can keep an errant application from affecting others that are running at the same time.

Memory Protection

One of the major reasons for an application crash is the accidental processing of garbage input. With any operating system, each launched application generally gets assigned a certain amount of RAM (system memory); that application then can decide how to use the RAM, including where to put its data and instructions. But if one application were to put bad data in a RAM location that actually belongs to another application, that second application may experience errors or crashes when it tries to read that spurious data.

Memory protection in Mac OS X makes it impossible for one application to overwrite another's memory locations. While this isn't exactly a common occurrence in Mac OS 9.x, it's possible, resulting in a less stable system. With memory protection, Mac OS X can keep one crashing application from bringing down other applications, because Mac OS X doesn't allow one application to write to another's memory space.

Dynamic RAM Allocation

Users of previous Mac OS versions know that each application gets a fixed allocation of RAM when the application is started. It's a range that's determined by a setting in the application's Get Info dialog box. (You can see this dialog box in Mac OS 9.x by selecting an application icon and choosing File ➤ Get Info from the Finder's menu, as shown in Figure 1.2.) This fixed RAM allocation system, though, is wasteful because RAM assigned to an open application—even if that RAM isn't being used—is reserved and can't be used by another application.

Unfortunately, many Mac crashes and problems arise from having the Get Info memory settings too low; even though the Mac OS may have more RAM at its disposal, it will give an application only as much RAM as it requests when the application is launched. If the Get Info setting is too low and the application runs out of memory, there isn't much that can be done by the operating system. (Instead, the user has to quit the application, open the Get Info dialog box, and manually increase the memory allocation. Upon relaunch, the application has access to more RAM.)

FIGURE 1.2

*The Memory panel of
the Get Info dialog box
(for Microsoft Excel) in
Mac OS 9.x*

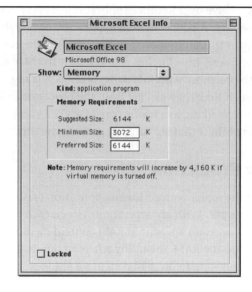

With dynamic RAM allocation, Mac OS X is in charge of dealing with RAM requests from applications. When you launch an application, it will ask for as much RAM as it needs. If that RAM is available, Mac OS X will hand it over. If the application needs more, it can ask for more, and Mac OS X can hand some over. If the application isn't using all that it has been allocated, it can free up that RAM on the fly, and the Mac OS can assign the RAM to another application that needs it.

This approach results in more stability for the system and less hassle for the user: With RAM allocation out of your hands, you can simply launch applications and let Mac OS X figure out how best to allocate memory for those applications.

Multithreading

Another advanced OS feature is *multithreading*, which allows individual applications to create more than one process. For instance, a word processing application might create a thread that's designed to print one document while another thread enables the user to edit another document. In this way, a multithreaded application can be more responsive to user input, with multiple threads within that application accomplishing tasks simultaneously.

Although both Mac OS 9.*x* and Mac OS X offer multithreading, Mac OS X is designed from the ground up to support it, while multithreading support in Mac OS 9.*x* is grafted onto the OS. Not all applications written for Mac OS 9.*x* are multithreaded, for instance, because the approach just isn't as pervasive. Applications written directly for Mac OS X use multithreading as a matter of course.

Symmetrical Multiprocessing

Mac OS X supports Macintosh computers that feature more than one processor (called *multiprocessor systems*). Although Macintosh systems have been capable of dealing with multiple processors in the past, it has always been on an application-by-application basis. (For instance, Adobe Photoshop, a favorite of Macintosh power users, offers a plug-in that supports multiprocessing.) With Mac OS X, the support is built right into the operating system, meaning all tasks and processes can take advantage of multiple processors.

Because the OS has control over managing the different processors, different tasks and threads can be assigned to different processors. This makes the machine more capable and more responsive overall, because more processors are at work and therefore things happen more efficiently. But symmetrical multiprocessing takes this concept even further: You can assign processes and threads *within one application* to different processors, which makes individual applications more responsive as well.

Although multiprocessing hasn't been a hallmark of Apple's hardware designs over the past few years, that changed somewhat in the summer of 2000 with the introduction of dual-processor Power Macintosh G4 models. Although the dual processors are only somewhat useful when running Mac OS 9.*x* (as mentioned, individual applications like Photoshop must specifically support multiprocessing), Mac OS X takes full advantage of multiple processors automatically. So the trend toward multiprocessor Power Macintosh models is guaranteed to continue, with more and more of Apple's desktop computers sporting multiple processors in the near future.

Microkernel Architecture

At the heart of all of Mac OS X's improvements is a *microkernel*—a small mini-OS that works between the Mac OS interface and the physical Macintosh hardware. This microkernel allows for a level of abstraction between the hardware and software; in this way, most of Mac OS X isn't written for a particular piece of hardware, as Mac OS 9.*x* is. That makes the OS more stable and reliable. It also makes it more *portable*, leaving open the possibility that Mac OS X (and later versions) could run on processors other than Motorola's (or IBM's) PowerPC processor, which is the processor type currently shipped in every Macintosh.

The microkernel, called Mach 3.0, is also the traffic cop that manages many of the other features already mentioned: preemptive multitasking, multithreading, and multiprocessing.

What Is Mac OS X Server?

By now, you're probably clear on what Mac OS X is, but you may have also heard of Mac OS X Server and wondered about the differences. Actually, they're reasonably similar—Mac OS X Server simply features more bundled applications and networking capabilities. Mac OS X Server is more expensive, too, because it's designed to be a hub for the activity generated by a workgroup of Mac OS X and Mac OS 9.*x* (and 8.*x*) computers. One Macintosh running Mac OS X Server can serve files, manage the printing, and even serve Internet users, all from the same machine.

Mac OS X Server is essentially a package of server applications and utilities that run on top of Mac OS X. The basic underpinnings—the Mach kernel, the "modern" OS capabilities, and many of the interface elements—are the same for both Mac OS X and Mac OS X Server. Although Mac OS X includes some server applications and utilities in its own right, Mac OS X Server extends those capabilities with high-end add-ons, including these:

QuickTime Streaming Server   QuickTime 4 and higher versions support streaming media—movies and audio clips that play as they arrive, instead of waiting for an entire download to take place before playing. The QuickTime Streaming Server software built into Mac OS X Server allows you to *webcast* such streaming media, making them available to many people at once.

WebObjects   This is another technology brought to Apple from NeXT Software. WebObjects is a network (usually Internet) application development and serving environment, making it easier to create full-fledged e-commerce solutions such as online stores. (For instance, Apple's online store is built and served using WebObjects.)

NetBoot   NetBoot allows Mac OS X Server to boot client machines—iMacs, Power Macs, PowerBooks, and others—directly from a server instead of from that computer's internal hard disk. This feature makes it easier to standardize computers and control them from a central location. It also makes it easier for your personal files to follow you around, because you can actually boot a client computer with your password and then gain access to all your files and custom settings.

Apple File Services   Mac OS X Server can offer file sharing between the server and Macs using typical AppleShare protocols, over either AppleTalk or TCP/IP-based networks. Like AppleShare IP servers, a Mac OS X Server computer can store files and transfer them from the main server to workstations that are logged into the server.

Other Innovations

Besides the basic system advances that Mac OS X offers over earlier Mac OS versions, it also sports a number of new features. These range from advantages brought on by the Unix underpinnings to new features that have been written specifically for Mac OS X. Let's take a look at a quick list, although we'll be exploring these features throughout the book:

New Finder and interface Mac OS X sports a new Finder, based on the Browser interface that was used in NeXT Software's operating systems, including OpenStep. The Mac OS X Finder offers a unique way to browse not only files on your Mac's hard disk but also those that exist over a network—whether it's a local network in your organization or disks and volumes that are available to you via the Internet. The Finder works hand-in-hand with a revamped interface (called *Aqua* by Apple) that offers a simpler, more animated look and feel. The OS also features a new Dock for managing applications and open documents, as well as revamped preferences, menu behavior, and many other changes.

New graphics architecture Called *Quartz,* the graphics architecture is based in part on Adobe's Portable Document Format (PDF). PDF technology allows computers to create documents that can be transmitted to other users and displayed and/or printed correctly, even if those users don't have the same printer, same fonts, or other features of the computer where the document was created. Basing the underlying graphics system on this technology makes it easier for Mac OS X applications to share documents between multiple computers. Likewise, the graphics architecture builds in some sophisticated visual effects like the transparency and text smoothing that's used throughout the Mac OS X interface.

Integrated e-mail client Mac OS X offers Mail, an e-mail client included with the Mac OS, that allows you to send and receive e-mail without launching another application. It also supports system-level technologies, such as adding PDF graphics to e-mail messages and searching your e-mail with Mac OS X's built-in search engine.

Multiuser support Mac OS X requires a login name and password, enabling multiple users to each access a unique desktop, store personal documents and applications, and manage their own Internet connections. Log in with your username, and all your personal preferences are preserved, while your documents and personal applications are secure from other users.

Advanced networking features   Because it's based on TCP/IP, the networking protocol used over the Internet, Mac OS X features a number of networking features, including the ability to network and share files (in various ways) over the Internet. One of these is Apple's AirPort technology, which enables wireless connections between your Macs.

Backward compatibility   With support for *Classic* Macintosh applications, Mac OS X is able to run almost any application that's compatible with Mac OS 9.1. Although these applications aren't given access to full Mac OS X features (such as preemptive multitasking and protected memory), they can be run at the same time that other Mac OS X applications run. This allows you to use older applications that don't offer Mac OS X upgrades or that you can't afford to upgrade for one reason or another.

Which OS for Which User?

The three different, current Mac OS versions—Mac OS 9.1, Mac OS X, and Mac OS X Server—all fit different niches. In some cases, you may need to use all three, especially if you're a system administrator. In others, you may already be committed to using one or another. Although I'd prefer not to encourage you to return your copy of Mac OS X if you're already excited about it, make sure this OS is right for both you and your Mac before you move forward with it.

 NOTE   If your Mac came preinstalled with Mac OS X (either from Apple or from your system administrator or consultant), you can skip the following discussion. Instructions for installing Mac OS X can be found in Appendix A.

If you're looking for an operating system to work as a server for a good-sized workgroup and/or as a high-end Internet server, then Mac OS X Server is probably your best bet. It's the most flexible for a server operating system, featuring the ability to serve content to Mac OS 9.*x* (and earlier) machines, Mac OS X, and even Unix and other operating systems. It acts as a Web server, QuickTime server, and AppleShare server—it's multifaceted and very capable, but it requires some know-how and training.

If you're looking for an operating system for a workstation, such as a computer you're going to use for everyday tasks, then you're probably more likely to consider either Mac OS 9.*x* or Mac OS X. This may be a tougher decision, however.

First, if your Macintosh can't support Mac OS X, then you'll need to run Mac OS 9.1 (or an earlier version of the Mac OS). Mac OS X requires a PowerPC G3 processor running at 233MHz, with a recommended minimum of 128MB of RAM and at least 1.5GB of hard-disk space. If you have an iMac, an iBook, a Power Macintosh G3 or G4, or a PowerPC G3- or G4-based PowerBook (with the exception of the first PowerBook G3 model), you can run Mac OS X.

Mac OS X doesn't officially support earlier Macintosh and "clone" machines that have been upgraded to G3 or G4 speeds using an upgrade card or some other processor upgrade, so you'll want to use Mac OS 9.1 if you have such a machine. In fact, no Macintosh or Mac OS clone machines built before the Power Macintosh G3 are officially compatible with Mac OS X, so you'll want to stick with Mac OS 9.1 in those cases.

 NOTE Actually, some manufacturers of upgrade cards for older Macs do claim compatibility with Mac OS X, especially PowerPC G3 and G4 upgrades that work in Power Macintosh 7300, 7500, 7600, 8500, 9600, and similar models. (These models support a *daughtercard* upgrade that is often compatible with Mac OS X.) Upgrades for Macs that started as Power Macintosh G3 or G4 models are also generally compatible. Check with the manufacturer of your upgrade to see if it claims compatibility. Remember, though, that Apple does not officially support upgraded configurations with technical support, even if the upgrade proves to be compatible. You'll probably need to rely on the third-party upgrade company to update driver software and/or provide answers to your tech-support questions.

If you do have a newer Power Macintosh, iMac, iBook, or PowerBook, you may still find yourself able to make a choice between Mac OS 9.1 and Mac OS X. Which should you choose? The answer depends in part on when you're doing the choosing.

First, you need to decide what sort of "adopter" you are. Mac OS X offers power users and early adopters the opportunity to work with a cutting-edge operating system that offers amazing advantages—all those modern OS trappings that take full advantage of the powerful PowerPC processors in Power Macs.

But that power comes at a price. If you're more interested in working with an established operating system that more consultants know their way around, more application vendors support directly, and more beginning users have navigated successfully, you'll probably want to stick with Mac OS 9.1.

Check out catalogs, Macintosh magazines, and computer stores to see how well Mac OS X is being supported. In the early life of an operating system, there are generally fewer applications designed for that OS. Mac OS X works best with applications designed specifically for it. If you don't see applications on the shelves or in catalogs that perform the tasks you need accomplished, you're probably better off sticking with Mac OS 9.1 for the foreseeable future.

The Applications That Mac OS X Can Run

You'll encounter five different types of applications that Mac OS X can run. Which you choose can affect the performance of not only that one application but also your entire Mac OS X system. So you need to know the types:

Mac OS X applications   These applications are written specifically for the "Cocoa" native portion of Mac OS X. They require no special emulation, and they run directly on top of Mac OS X without modification. Best of all, they take full advantage of multitasking, multithreading, multiprocessor support, and memory protection. An example of these applications is the Mail application included with Mac OS X; it was written from scratch to support Mac OS X.

Mac OS "Carbon" applications   These applications are also native to Mac OS X, and they can take pretty much full advantage of the modern OS underpinnings. They may be a little more limited in their full performance potential, because the Carbon libraries are a stopgap measure for Mac OS 9.x developers who want their applications to run effectively in both Mac OS 9.x and Mac OS X. That said, there's nothing wrong with running a Carbon application every day, all day, if you like. Internet Explorer 5.1 for Mac OS X is an example of a "carbonized" application.

Mac OS Classic applications   These applications are designed to be run only in Mac OS 9.x. Thanks to Mac OS X's ability to run a Mac OS 9.1 environment as an individual process, these applications can also be run in your workspace. This is fine on occasion, but it's not recommended that you rely on Classic applications for all your computing needs. If you have a lot of Classic applications, you should consider sticking with Mac OS 9.1, at least until you've upgraded to Carbon applications.

Java applications   These are applications designed to run on any computer that supports the Java programming language. Mac OS X features an impressive Java interpreter. In general, it's okay to run these applications, although they, too, may not have full access to all the features of the Mac OS. Instead, these applications tend to be more limited in both capabilities and scope, but they generally do what you need them to do.

Command-line applications   Although its use is utterly discouraged by Apple, the fact remains that Mac OS X has a command-line interface (accessed most often through the Terminal application), and it's relatively easy to write and port applications that run from the command line, without a standard Mac graphical interface. If you encounter such an application and wish to run it, you'll definitely need Mac OS X, since it's the only Mac OS that supports such applications. (The Terminal and command-line applications will be discussed specifically in Chapter 22.)

What if you already have a bunch of Classic Mac applications? You'll need to have them upgraded by the software manufacturers, sometimes for a fee. If you're not yet comfortable with that expense, I can't recommend that you upgrade to Mac OS X; even though you can run those applications in Mac OS X, you shouldn't *primarily* run Classic applications using Mac OS X.

 TIP Want to keep track of applications that have been carbonized to work on Mac OS X or certified to work well in the Classic environment? Apple maintains lists of both on its Mac OS X Web site (www.apple.com/macosx/), while VersionTracker (www.version-tracker.com) is a great source for staying on top of both shareware and commercially released software.

Instead, early adopters who are willing to move forward quickly, pay to upgrade applications, deal with limited application choices, and work around a few rough edges are the users who should upgrade to Mac OS X. As developers come on board and more applications are written for Mac OS X, eventually other users—especially those looking for a high-end workstation for graphics, 3-D, publishing, media editing, and Internet production—will also be ready to migrate to Mac OS X.

Bringing Mac OS X and Mac OS 9.x Together

Fortunately, moving to Mac OS X doesn't mean you have to leave all your Mac OS 9.x applications behind. That's because Mac OS X can run a process that emulates the Mac OS 9.1 environment, allowing you to use applications that run specifically on Mac OS 9.x (see Figure 1.3).

The Mac OS 9.1 support in Mac OS X is somewhat limited, since Mac OS X runs the entire Mac OS 9.1 environment (called "Classic") as a single process, as though it were just another Mac OS X application. In other words, individual Mac OS 9.x applications are susceptible to crashes, freezes, and so on, thanks to the lack of memory protection and preemptive multitasking *within* the Classic environment.

Other Mac OS X applications continue to enjoy those features, so if the Classic environment does crash, it shouldn't affect the rest of the Mac OS X system. Instead, you'll be able to just "kill" the Classic process and start over again if you like. But that's the reason you shouldn't rely on Mac OS 9.x applications if you're going to run Mac OS X. Aside from the potential for crashes, the Classic environment can be taxing on a Mac OS X system, causing sluggishness.

FIGURE 1.3

Mac OS 9.1 (the Classic environment) starting up on a Mac OS X system

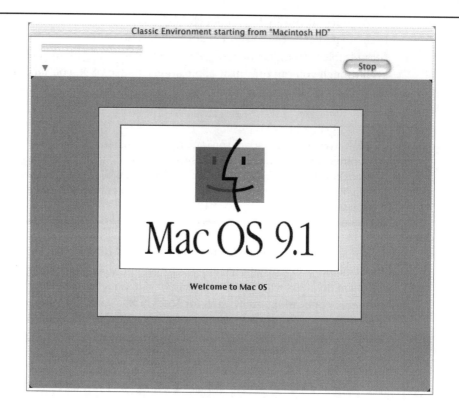

And how about other machines in the office? Mac OS X and Mac OS 9.*x* can work together, side by side, on different machines in harmony. Because both support TCP/IP file sharing and AppleTalk printer sharing, Mac OS X and Mac OS 9.*x* can coexist nicely on the same network. So, even if you have older Macintosh computers sharing a network with your Mac OS X machine, you should have no problem using them together.

What's Next?

That sums it up for this chapter. In Chapter 2, you'll learn the basics of Mac OS X's interface, including the Finder, the Dock, and the way individual items—icons, windows, buttons, and controls—look and work.

CHAPTER 2

The Mac OS X Interface

As discussed in Chapter 1, Mac OS X is a completely new version of the Mac OS. It's based on complicated technical underpinnings, including the Mach 3.0 microkernel, Unix-like FreeBSD technology, and some special new technologies engineered by Apple.

Perhaps the most striking difference, though, is Mac OS X's *interface*. The very way that you relate as a user to the Mac OS has changed dramatically in Mac OS X. From each window's appearance to the way icons work, Mac OS X is different not only from previous Mac OS versions but from most other operating systems that came before it.

Actually, there's a good reason to be excited about these developments. The Mac OS X interface is a colorful and attractive one that is both simple for novice users and powerful for advanced users. If you're making the move from Mac OS 9.1 or an earlier version, you may have an adjustment period ahead of you. Once you're familiar with Mac OS X, though, I think you'll find that it's a pretty effective way to communicate with and use your Mac.

Even with all these changes, Mac OS X doesn't represent a radical departure from computer operating systems in general—parts of the interface will certainly be familiar. What Mac OS X does do is take components from the existing Mac OS, Apple's OpenStep technology (bought from NeXT Software), and a few completely new elements. The idea is to blend some complex OS capabilities with a very simple, friendly, and animated interface that looks a little more like a Hollywood computer screen than one we'd be used to in our offices.

In this chapter you'll look at the different components of the Mac OS X interface and how to interact with them. You'll also see the special menus and menu commands that help you launch applications, change preferences, and configure your Mac. And you'll meet the Trash, which enables you to delete files and folders from your disks. In Chapter 3, you'll go further in depth with the Finder application—Mac OS X's interface to your files and disks.

Startup and Login

When you start or restart your Mac, you'll see the Mac OS go through its startup process, followed by the appearance of the login window. During the startup process, Mac OS X loads system components from the disk and configures hardware components and peripherals according to the preferences you've set (or the default preferences). You'll see small messages below the Welcome to Mac OS X image that show you what's being loaded and configured. Meanwhile, the progress bar creeps across the screen, showing how much longer the startup process will take.

Once the startup process is finished, you'll see the login window. (If you don't see a login window, your Mac may be set to automatically log into a particular user account. This is the default setting if you've created only one user account so far. See Chapter 7 for details on setting automatic login options.) In the login window you'll enter your username and password for the system. Enter your name in the Name entry box and your password in the Password entry box; then press Return or click the Login button.

Logging In: User and Administrator Accounts

Mac OS X introduces a concept that most Unix and Unix-like system users are very familiar with, but that's new to the Mac OS: *user accounts*. Mac OS 9 introduced a Multiple User feature that you may be familiar with, but Mac OS X takes that concept to a completely new level.

The most important difference is that Max OS X is designed from the ground up to be a multiuser environment. That means, generally, that each individual user account gets its own settings and a distinct "home" location on the Mac for storing documents and installing applications. We'll go a little deeper into the home folder concept in Chapter 4.

It also means that Mac OS X actually works best when you create multiple user accounts. Although Mac OS 9.x and earlier versions generally don't need to know your name, Mac OS X creates a personal account and storage space for each user. One reason for that is that Mac OS X makes an important distinction between types of users: regular users and administrators. When you first install Mac OS X and create your initial personal account, you're actually creating an administrator account—one that has quite a bit of power within Mac OS X.

When your named account is an administrator account, you can install applications for all users and make system-level changes in the System Preferences application. If you subsequently create nonadministrator accounts, users of those accounts will be able to make changes only within their own personal folders, thus ensuring that important system files and settings won't get changed or deleted. (Likewise, these regular accounts have limited access to the Mac when they're logged in over a network or via the Internet, making your Mac a bit more secure from the outside world.) You can also, if desired, create additional administrator accounts so that trusted users can have access to settings and special folders.

There's also another account that's even more powerful than an administrator account— the *root* account. The root account is disabled in Mac OS X by default, but it can be activated according to instructions given in Chapter 20. Although you won't often find a reason to use the root account, it can be useful for troubleshooting.

If your login is successful, the login window will disappear and the desktop will begin to load. If the login fails, it's likely because you mistyped your username or password. In that case the login window will appear to vibrate (almost as if it's shaking its head "no"), and the entry boxes will be cleared. Reenter your username and password. If you've forgotten them, you'll need to contact your system administrator and/or log in as an administrator and reset your password. (For more on administrator accounts, see the sidebar "Logging In: User and Administrator Accounts.")

The login window also enables you to restart or shut down the Mac using the Restart and Shut Down buttons. Restarting shuts down the Mac OS and restarts the computer without cutting power to its internals. Shut Down not only shuts down the Mac OS, it also turns the computer off. To start again, press the Mac's power button or the power key on the Mac's keyboard.

Getting Around the Mac OS

When you log into your Mac, your personal workspace is loaded. Your workspace consists of your desktop, your home directory (where your personal files and folders are stored), and the settings and appearance options you've chosen.

Mac OS X is a multiuser operating system, meaning it's designed from the ground up to deal with more than one user. One of the manifestations of this is the personal workspace. When another user logs in under a different username, she will see her own workspace, which has different folders, documents, and settings associated with it. In fact, every user's workspace is unique.

After you've logged into your workspace, the first thing you'll see is the *desktop*. The desktop is the pattern or color behind everything else that's shown on the screen. In a way, the desktop is like an actual desk's top in the real world—it's where you'll spread out your work, access your files, and open your documents. On the desktop, you'll see icons and windows, as well as menus, which appear in the *menu bar* at the top of the desktop.

Windows are areas on the screen where you view information or get work done. You can stack windows on top of one other, move them around the screen, or move them to the Dock, using the Minimize button, for safekeeping until you want to work with them again. In Mac OS X, windows have been redesigned slightly compared to those of previous Mac OS versions. In particular, the Finder window, which appears when you first log into your workspace, offers some very new features in Mac OS X.

Icons are the small pictures, usually labeled, that represent items you can work with on the desktop (or, as you'll see later, in Finder windows). If you're used to Mac OS 9.*x* or Windows 95/98, you'll notice that Mac OS X's icons are set to a larger size by default. The size of the icons can be customized, but the larger icons are designed to be discernible at higher screen resolutions; a typical 17-inch monitor, running at 1024×768 pixels resolution, shows Mac OS X icons well. With earlier Mac OS versions, the icons on such a monitor would have been on the small side.

FireWire HD

Macintosh HD

Network

Open a menu and you'll see the various commands available to you for managing files, formatting your work, or otherwise getting things done in the active application. In Mac OS X, the menus are actually slightly translucent, making it possible for you to see items behind the menus when you pull them down. As in previous Mac OS versions, menus appear at the top of the desktop in the menu bar.

You'll also see the Dock on the desktop, by default. The Dock is a multipurpose region of the workspace that enables you to manage your applications and the Trash. I'll cover using and customizing the Dock in depth later, in the section "The Dock."

Working with Menus

The menu bar holds individual menus, which you'll open to reveal the different commands that are available to you at that particular moment. Each application has its own menus, which will appear in the menu bar when that application is active. Most applications feature File, Edit, and Help menus, but otherwise the menus can vary wildly depending on the tasks and tools available within a given application.

Along with these menus comes one standard menu, called the Apple menu, that always appears on the far-left side of the menu bar. And each application will always have its own Application menu, which will appear right next to the Apple menu. We'll discuss those two special menus in this section as well.

Opening Menus

Each word that appears in the menu bar is the title of a different menu; you'll also occasionally find menus that are labeled with an icon. To open a menu, point the mouse at one of the menu titles and click the mouse button once. That pops the menu open.

Now, you can move the mouse up and down on the open menu to select menu commands. Selected items are highlighted as you roll the mouse over them. In some cases you'll highlight a menu item that, in turn, reveals another menu that pops out to the right of the current menu. (These are called *hierarchical menus*.)

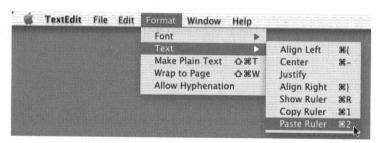

To invoke a particular command, click the mouse button again while that menu item is highlighted. Now, whatever action is associated with that menu command is put into play.

 NOTE If you prefer, you can click a menu title and hold the mouse button down to open that menu, then drag down to the command you want to select. Now, when you release the mouse button while pointing to the menu command, that command is invoked.

As you work with menus, you may notice that some menu commands will appear gray. (The gray text is much lighter than the black text of most menu commands and is more difficult to see.) A *grayed* menu command is simply one that cannot be selected because it's not appropriate or applicable for the current context. For instance, the Save command in a word processor's File menu will be grayed if there are no changes (no typing or editing has occurred) in the document that can be saved to disk.

You'll also notice that many menu commands have letters and symbols associated with them in the menu, usually placed near the menu's right edge. The symbols in those keyboard commands represent the modifier keys you'll find on the Mac's keyboard. The clover leaf (⌘) symbol represents the Command (Apple) key; the up arrow (⇧) represents the Shift key; the caret (⌃) symbol represents the Control key; and the symbol (⌥) represents the Option key.

NOTE These keys are used in combination with other keys to create *keyboard shortcuts,* which enable you to perform basic commands without using the mouse or opening menus. For the most part, these shortcuts help you perform tasks more quickly. For instance, ⌘+Q is used in most applications to quit that application. As you can see, keyboard shortcuts are associated with particular applications, including the Finder. We'll discuss some keyboard shortcuts specific to the Finder in Chapter 3; likewise, you'll see references to keyboard shortcuts throughout the book.

In most applications, on the desktop, and in Finder windows, you can hold down the Control key and click (or click once and hold—it's up to you) to bring up a *contextual menu*. This menu responds to the context of the item or area you're clicking and offers relevant menu items. For instance, Control+clicking on the desktop gives you menu items such as Help and New Folder; Control+clicking a file in a Finder window gives you options such as Open, Move to Trash, and Duplicate. (See Figure 2.1.)

TIP If you have a USB-based mouse that has two (or more) buttons, some Mac OS X native applications will automatically recognize the second mouse button as a Control+click operation, making it easier to pop up contextual menus.

The Application Menu

In the top-left corner of the screen (just to the right of the Apple menu), you'll find another important menu that's always on the menu bar. It's the Application menu, which changes to represent application-specific commands based on the program you're working in. Generally, you'll find Preferences, the Quit command, and the About command in this menu, among others.

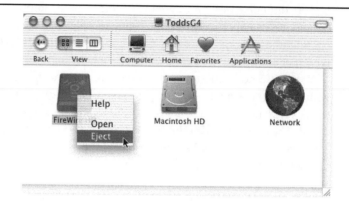

If you've worked with previous Mac OS versions, you'll notice that this Application menu is new. It's in the location where most earlier Mac OS applications placed the File menu, and, to make matters more confusing, it doesn't switch between open applications the way earlier Mac operating systems' "Applications" menu did. This menu is a different animal: It's basically designed to be a central location for application-specific commands, giving programmers a standard way to present some of the application-oriented (instead of document-oriented) commands. (Apple engineers decided that the File menu didn't make sense as the place where you would quit the application or set the application's preferences, because those commands don't have anything to do with "files." So they moved them to the Application menu, where commands that affect the application itself are now stored.)

The Application menu's name changes to reflect the application that you're currently working in. At its most basic, this menu is designed to hold the application-specific commands for the current program—commands such as Preferences, About, and Quit. You'll also find that, in many applications, the Services command appears in this menu. (We discuss the Services command in Chapter 5.)

The Application menu is where you'll find the About command for the active application; this command generally gives you a splash screen with information about the program and its author. Also, you should, by default, find the Preferences command in this menu. Choose Preferences and you'll get a dialog box that includes the major preference settings for this application.

The Application menu also holds some commands that will be familiar to users of past Mac OS versions: the Hide, Hide Others, and Show All commands. These commands can be used to quickly remove the windows of an application from the visible screen (Hide), to hide the windows of all other background applications (Hide Others), or to show all windows for all currently running applications in the background (Show All). To show an application's window(s) again, select that application's tile on the Dock.

 NOTE Using the Hide command isn't the same as minimizing windows. Instead of placing individual windows on the Dock in icon form, the Hide command simply causes the application's menu bar and all its windows to disappear from view.

The Apple Menu

The Apple menu always appears on the far-left end of the toolbar (at the top of the screen) and includes several commands that are grouped there primarily for convenience. The neat thing about the Apple menu is that it's always available, regardless of the application you're working in. That means that you don't have to change to the Finder, for instance, in order to put your Mac to sleep or shut it down. We'll cover the Apple menu in depth in Chapter 3, but note here, for the record, that it's part of the Mac OS X interface and it's always available on the menu bar to do your bidding.

Understanding Icons

Icons come in many shapes and colors, representing a number of different items on your Mac. Each icon represents an item in your Mac's system for managing computer files; for instance, disk icons represent your hard disks, CD-ROMs, or other removable disks you use for storing files. Folder icons can be created and used for organizing and storing your documents and applications; document and application icons represent the actual items you'll be working with on a daily basis.

Some icons are placed automatically on the desktop by the Mac OS, while others are created by you, using application commands. There are also a few different ways to select icons on your desktop and elsewhere.

Selecting and Activating Icons

As you might imagine, icons are easily dealt with using the mouse. If the icons are small representations of items stored on your computer—files, folders, tools—then the mouse acts as your "virtual hand" for picking up and moving those items around on your desktop. But the ability to work with icons using the mouse goes well beyond the metaphor; you'll see that icons can be selected, activated, and otherwise manipulated in many different ways.

On the screen you'll see the mouse pointer—the arrow that's used to point to items on the screen. When the mouse is pointing to a particular item, you can press the mouse button to cause things to happen. Here's what you can do:

Select icons. You select a single icon the way you select anything else with the mouse—point at it with the mouse pointer and click the mouse button once. The icon will usually become highlighted, enabling you to work with it. (You can, for instance, issue a menu command. If an icon is highlighted, that icon will be affected by the menu command.)

 NOTE Highlighted icons are darkened to show that they've been selected.

Activate icons. If you point your mouse pointer at an icon and double-click (click twice quickly) with the mouse button, in most cases you'll activate that item. If the icon represents a program, the program will launch. If the icon represents a document, that document's program will open and the document will be displayed. (Note that items on the Dock are activated with a single click.)

 TIP When you're clicking text in a document window, things work a little differently. Double-clicking text will generally select an entire word. Triple-clicking often selects entire sentences or paragraphs. The occasional application will support a quadruple-click (four quick clicks in a row) to select a large group of text—a paragraph or a page.

Drag icons. If you point at an icon, then click and hold down the mouse button, you can drag that item elsewhere on the screen. (This is particularly true of windows and icons, although other items can also be dragged around.) When you get to the place where you'd like the item to be, you release the mouse button to *drop* the item. (When you hear the phrase *drag-and-drop*, this is the process being referred to.) In document windows, dragging will often quickly highlight the words or sentences as you pass the mouse pointer over them.

 NOTE Mac OS X offers many opportunities for dragging and dropping throughout the interface; for instance, you can pick up an icon and drag and drop it onto the Trash icon, which puts that icon in the Trash. Likewise, you can drag and drop a document icon onto a program icon in order to open that document using that program.

In addition to the basic behaviors, you'll find that Mac OS X offers some modifier keys that work in conjunction with the mouse to perform different tasks. Many of these depend on the context in which you're using the mouse; for instance, while dragging items in Finder windows, you can use the drag modifiers to determine the result of the drag. Here are some of those modifiers:

Command+click   If you hold down the Command (⌘) key while clicking items in a window, you can select multiple items at once. This can be useful for different reasons: opening more than one document at once, moving multiple items to the Trash, or simply arranging the items.

Shift+click   Holding down the Shift key while clicking an item in a window will select all items *between* the currently highlighted item and the item you Shift+click, if those items are arranged in a list or column. (With regular icons, Shift+click works just like ⌘+click.) In an alphabetized list of animals, if you had previously clicked Aardvark (so that it's highlighted) and you now Shift+clicked Zebra, all the animal names in between would become highlighted.

 NOTE This would also work in a text document if you clicked once at the start of a paragraph and then Shift+clicked at the end of it. Note, however, that in other areas where this wouldn't be appropriate—such as windows full of icons that don't really have a "start" and "end"—Shift+clicking acts just like Command+clicking.

Option+drag   In Finder windows or on the desktop, you can Option+drag an icon (or a selection of icons, if more than one has been selected) in order to copy or *duplicate* that item. (More on the duplicate function in Chapter 3, since it's one of the Finder application's responsibilities.) This is done to keep from simply *moving* the icon, which is the default behavior in most cases. When you Option+drag in this way, the mouse pointer gains a small plus (+) sign to suggest that a duplicate command will be given.

 TIP Option+drag has another interesting feature—drag-to-scroll—but it's enabled only in Finder windows and in some applications' document windows. If you have a window that has more in it than is currently shown, you can hold down the Option key. When the cursor turns into a small hand, click and hold the mouse button, then drag the mouse to scroll the window up or down (or side to side if that's an option in that particular window).

Option+⌘+drag   If you modify an Option+drag by tossing in the ⌘ key, you'll create an alias instead of a duplicate when you drop the item. When this function is active, the mouse pointer includes a small, curly arrow.

 NOTE Aliases are more formally introduced in the section "Types of Icons" later in this chapter, and they're discussed in depth in Chapter 4.

Selecting Multiple Icons

I've mentioned that selecting a single icon is simple: Point at it and click once. But what if you need to select more than one icon? If you want to select a group of contiguous icons, you can perform a drag-select: Simply drag a box around the items using the mouse, and all items are selected. Here's how:

1. Begin by placing the mouse pointer at a spot above and to the left of the first icon you want to select. (Actually, you don't have to *completely* enclose an icon to select it, but it's easier that way.)

2. Click and hold down the mouse button.

3. Drag the mouse pointer in a diagonal fashion across all the items you want to select.

4. When your box encloses all the items you want to select, release the mouse button (see Figure 2.2).

When you release the mouse button, all the icons within the selection box will be highlighted. You can now move them as a group (dragging one of the items will drag all the selected items), and any commands you invoke will affect every icon.

FIGURE 2.2

Selecting a group of icons by dragging a selection box

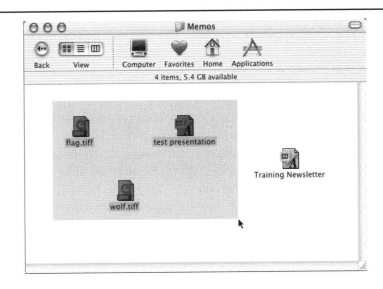

If the multiple icons you want to select aren't next to one another so that they can be easily selected by dragging a selection box, you have another option. If you select icons while holding down the Shift key or the ⌘ key, each new item gets added to your selection while previously selected items remain selected. (Usually when you click a new item, a previously selected item becomes unhighlighted.) So, to select multiple items, simply click each one while holding down the Shift or ⌘ key (see Figure 2.3). You can then move the highlighted icons or issue a command that will affect all of them while leaving others alone.

FIGURE 2.3

You can be more selective when highlighting multiple icons by using the Shift or ⌘ key.

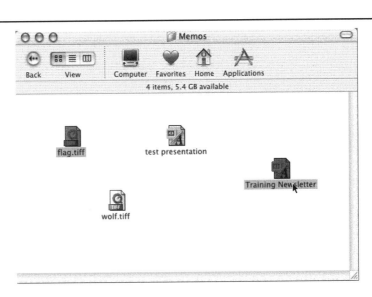

Types of Icons

For the most part, icons are designed to help you see immediately what sort of item you're dealing with. So the icon's picture should give you a strong clue as to what an item does. You'll find icons all over the Mac's interface, including on the desktop, in Finder windows, on the Dock (as tiles), and in toolbars.

Two major types of icons are used for organizing and storing all other icons: disks and folders. Disk icons appear on the desktop when removable disks or network disks are recognized and *mounted* by the Mac OS. CD-ROM and DVD-ROM icons, for instance, appear on the desktop when you insert them in the Mac's CD-ROM or DVD-ROM drive. Folder icons represent directories on your hard disk or on network disks. Folders are used to store and organize other items (all of which are also represented by icons), including document, application, and system files.

Document icons generally look like a piece of paper with a corner turned over, or a variation on that theme. These icons often look quite a bit like the application that created them, or the application with which they are associated. Documents can also be files used by the Mac OS itself, including fonts, preference files, and other items stored in the main System or Library folders on your hard disk.

Application icons are generally the most creative, looking pretty much how the applications' authors want them to look.

System icons vary in their appearance, depending on the parts of the Mac OS that they're supposed to represent. These items are programs and components that help you and applications work with the Mac's hardware and the peripherals attached to the Mac.

Aliases are special cases, with icons to match their capabilities. An *alias* is an "empty" file that points to another file. You can use aliases to conveniently access files that are stored elsewhere. Alias icons generally look like the item they're pointing to—disks, folders, documents, applications, or system components—but you know it's an alias because the icon includes a small picture of a curvy arrow.

Working with Windows

Most of the work you'll accomplish will take place in document windows. And when you interact with the Mac OS (whether you're setting preferences and options or responding to queries by the OS), you'll do that within windows, too. Windows come in a variety of shapes and sizes. Likewise, the typical window has a number of controls you'll encounter.

Parts of a Document Window

Let's begin by looking at the different parts of a standard window. Then you'll see the other, more specialized types of windows you may encounter.

The top of a typical document window looks like Figure 2.4. Although windows will vary in the type of information presented within them, they'll all have these basic controls.

Here are the different parts of the window and how to work with them:

Close button   The red Close button is used to close the window. If the window contains items that have not yet been saved, then clicking the Close button will bring up the Save dialog box (if appropriate) or it will automatically save the changes you've made in the window.

Minimize button   Click the yellow Minimize button to send the open window to the Dock. This removes it from the screen (usually with a fancy animation) and places it on the Dock as an open item. To see the window again, you simply click the item on the Dock and it will return to its last location on-screen.

FIGURE 2.4

The parts of a regular window

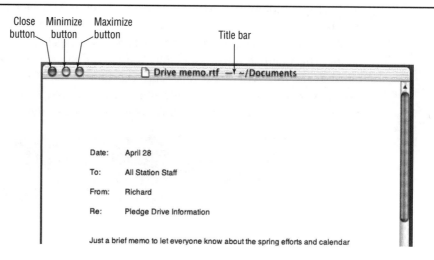

Close button — Minimize button — Maximize button — Title bar

 TIP In most applications, you can use keyboard shortcuts to close and minimize open windows. To close the window (you may be prompted to save the document's changes), press ⌘+W. To minimize a document window to the Dock, press ⌘+M. Also, for a completely useless (but fun) little effect, you can hold down the Shift key while clicking the Minimize button in a document window to see the document minimize to the Dock in slow motion.

Maximize button The green Maximize button is used to grow the window so that it becomes large enough to show as much of its contents as possible. Clicking Maximize will often expand a window to the default "large" size set by the application. Click the button again to return the window to its previous size.

 TIP When your mouse gets near the Close, Minimize, and Maximize buttons, a highlight will appear on them—an X (for close), a – (for minimize), and a + (for maximize). This feature is meant to assist users who cannot discern the colors of the buttons.

Title bar The title bar appears at the top of the window, displaying the name of the window. You can click and drag the title bar to move the window around on the screen. You can also (by default) double-click the title bar to minimize the window, sending it to the Dock.

Scroll bars   The scroll bars appear on the right and bottom sides of the window, but only when there's information in the window that cannot currently be displayed. When the scroll bars are active, they show the scroll arrows and scroll controls to indicate that more information is contained in the window.

 TIP   You can click within an active scroll bar (but not on the scroll control) to scroll quickly through the contents of a window.

Scroll controls   The scroll controls appear when the scroll bars are active. The scroll control can be dragged to show other information in the window. It also changes size to indicate how much more information is not displayed in the window. The larger the scroll control, the higher the percentage of information you can currently see. If you have a very large document, for instance, the scroll control will take up only a small portion of the scroll bar.

Scroll arrows   The scroll arrows appear in active scroll bars. You can use them to scroll through the contents of the window: Simply click the arrow that points in the direction that you'd like to scroll.

Resize area   You can use the resize area to drag the window to a larger or smaller size. Simply point at the resize area, click and hold, and then drag to change the size of the window.

How many of these controls you see depends on a number of factors, including the size of the document and the type of contents being displayed. Likewise, different types of windows offer subsets of these controls, such as dialog boxes that don't offer scroll bars or resize areas.

Types of Windows

When the Mac OS needs more information, you'll see a dialog box window; when it needs to communicate something to you, you'll see an alert box. Likewise, you'll see windows when you attempt to save or open documents and when you open folders in the Finder and elsewhere.

This section takes a look at the different types of windows (aside from the regular windows discussed in the previous section) that you'll encounter.

Dialog Boxes and Sheets

Dialog boxes are windows that are designed to receive information from you. These will often have check boxes, radio controls, menus, entry areas, and sliders.

You'll also encounter a variety of buttons in dialog boxes that enable you to dismiss or alter settings in the dialog box. For instance, if the dialog box has a Cancel button, you can click it to close the dialog box without making any choices or changes. If the dialog box has an OK button, you'll click it to accept whatever information is presented or to move on to another task. Some dialog boxes will have an Apply button that enables you to apply changes you've made without dismissing (closing) the dialog box.

You'll find other buttons in dialog boxes as well, most of which are designed to help you deal with the questions or contents within the dialog box. You may see buttons marked Yes, No, Save, Open, Use Default Settings, Revert, and others. These will all, hopefully, make sense in the context of the dialog box's purpose for being.

Dialog boxes can be *modal* or *modeless*. A modeless dialog box enables you to continue working in the active application's other windows; a modal dialog box requires that you deal with the dialog box before you can continue working in the application or the particular document (you can always, however, switch to a different application).

Mac OS X introduces an interesting behavior for most of its modal dialog boxes: Visually, they're actually a part of the document window they relate to (see Figure 2.5). Apple calls these modal dialog boxes *dialog sheets* or simply *sheets*. This is an interesting interface behavior because it makes it very clear which window needs to be dealt with and why work is being blocked in that document. In these cases, you can still switch to other documents in the application or even use the menu commands in that application—a change from earlier Mac OS versions, thanks to the threaded nature of processes within Mac OS X applications.

In Mac OS X, many dialog boxes have Close, Minimize, and Maximize buttons—an addition that wasn't standard on Mac dialog boxes in the past. You can use these buttons as you would in any other window. Clicking the Close button in a dialog box is the same as clicking Cancel.

FIGURE 2.5

Certain types of dialog boxes, called sheets, "pop down" from the title bar of the document window.

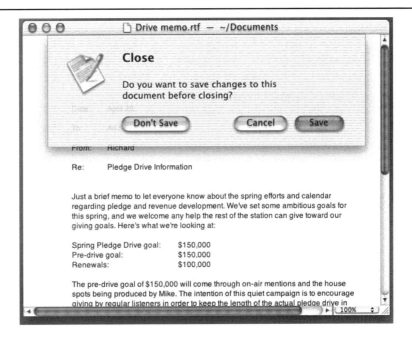

Alert Boxes

Alert boxes are a special subset of dialog boxes that are designed specifically to tell you when something is happening in an application or part of the Mac OS that requires your attention. Most of the time, these will be error messages, although they may be messages telling you something else that's important or asking you to switch to another open application or process. Most alert boxes simply have an OK button; click it to dismiss the alert.

Palettes

Generally, palettes are floating windows designed to hold tools that you need for working in the current application. Mac OS X also features many different types of *inspectors,* which are floating palettes designed to offer information about items in the Finder or in an application.

One of the significant features governing palette windows is that they always stay "on top," meaning other windows can't cover them up. Palettes usually have only a Close button, a Minimize button, and a title bar. (They appear to have a Maximize button as well, but that button isn't active in a palette window.)

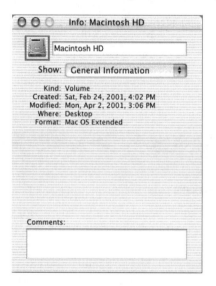

Layering Windows

When you have just one window open, you'll always be able to see its controls and manipulate it immediately. But if you have more than one window open, the windows become layered upon one another. The window in the *foreground* maintains its detail, but windows in the *background* lose some of their characteristics—for instance, scroll bars lose their color, and the title bar darkens somewhat, as shown in Figure 2.6.

The foreground window is said to be the *active* window. To make another window active, click it once. If the window is in the current application, that window simply switches to the foreground and the previous window is moved behind it. If you click a background window that belongs to a different application, that application's menu will appear as the window comes to the foreground.

FIGURE 2.6

Background windows don't show as much detail and color as the active window.

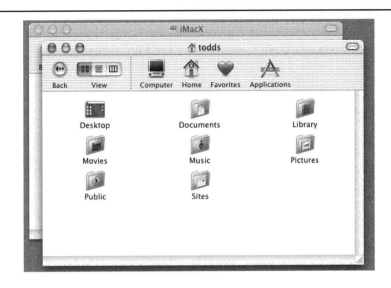

 TIP Want to move a background window without making it active? Hold down the Command (⌘) key and drag the window to move it around while it remains in the background.

Controls within Windows

As detailed earlier, windows have their own distinct controls that enable you to manipulate them on-screen and view their contents. Within windows of all types, however, you'll see a number of different controls. You'll use these controls to make choices and offer necessary information within application programs, system components, and utilities. Besides typing, selecting these controls with the mouse is the primary way you'll interact with your Mac and your Mac's programs. Figures 2.7 and 2.8 show these controls.

Here's what each control enables you to do:

Icon toolbar Some Mac OS X windows offer an icon toolbar that enables you to quickly access different commands or options. The System Preferences application, Mail application, and Finder all have icon toolbars. You can also customize most of these toolbars by dragging icons to and from them.

FIGURE 2.7

Some of the controls you'll find in Mac windows

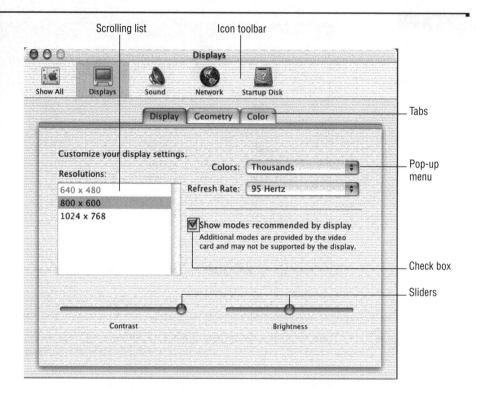

FIGURE 2.8

Some additional controls you'll encounter in Mac windows

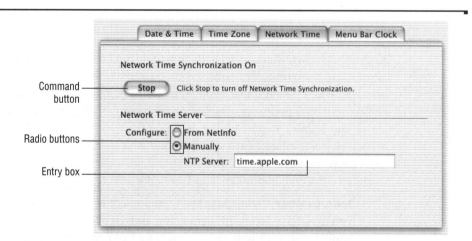

Tabs   Tabs are used to enable more than one screen of choices to appear in a single dialog box. A tab makes it possible to group similar choices so that one huge dialog box with scores of choices isn't necessary. Click a tab to view its grouping of controls and options.

Check box   Click in the check box to place a check mark, which turns that option on. If there's already a check mark in the check box, click the box to remove the check mark, thus turning the option off.

Pop-up menu   Click the menu to open it and reveal its options; then click again to select one of the options.

Radio buttons   Use these controls to select one of several options presented. They're a little like presets on a radio dial, in that they allow you to make only one choice from a number of options.

Slider   Drag the selector along the slider to configure the setting.

Command button   Click the button to put the command into action. In some windows, this command will be "OK" for accepting an action or "Cancel" for stopping an action. You'll also often find that these buttons toggle between Start and Stop or between On and Off.

Entry box   Click in the entry box to place the insertion point; then enter information by typing.

Scrolling list   Select an item from the list using the scroll arrows or scroll control. In many scrolling lists you can hold down the ⌘ key to select more than one option, or the Shift key to select a range of options.

Disclosure triangle   Click the triangle to reveal additional information (which will cause the triangle to point downward). If the triangle's information is already revealed, click the triangle again to hide the additional information.

The Trash

The Trash is unique among the icons you'll find in Mac OS X: It's always there on the Dock, it has a very specific task, and it can't be removed. It's also the main way that you'll delete items in the Mac OS.

To delete an item, drag it from the desktop or from a Finder window and drop it on the Trash icon. You'll see the Trash icon change; as you're hovering over it, it darkens a bit. When you release the mouse button, you've "thrown away" the item. Once you've dropped the item on the Trash icon, you'll see the icon change so that wadded-up paper appears in the picture of a trash can. This tells you that there are items in the Trash.

 TIP In the Finder, you can also move items to the Trash by selecting an icon and pressing ⌘+Delete on the keyboard.

Not all items are deleted immediately when you drag them to the Trash, although some are, such as items on network volumes and, in some cases, items that you drag to the Trash while the Trash is being emptied. For the most part, items remain in the Trash until you empty the Trash using a special command in the Finder. If an item is to be deleted immediately, however, you'll see a warning alert box that reminds you that the item will be deleted immediately.

Because most items stay in the Trash, it's possible to open the Trash and retrieve items you've thrown in there. (Fortunately, there are no coffee grounds or eggshells in this particular trash can.) To open the Trash, double-click its icon. A window appears, showing you the items that have been dragged and dropped on the Trash previously, as shown in Figure 2.9.

FIGURE 2.9

Opening the Trash reveals items that have been tossed there.

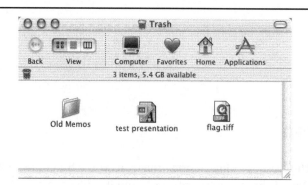

To retrieve items, simply drag them out of the Trash window to the desktop or to another open Finder window. (You'll find that some items can't be dragged directly to the desktop from the Trash—you'll need to drag them to an open Finder window instead.)

To delete items in the Trash permanently, you'll *empty* the trash. Items deleted in this way can't be retrieved through the Finder and may be gone for good. (Some disk utilities can recover deleted files in an emergency, but otherwise they can't be easily retrieved.) So you should think carefully and be sure before you empty the Trash.

To delete items in the Trash, choose Empty Trash from the Finder's Application menu—the menu called Finder. (If you're not currently working in the Finder, you'll need to switch to it by clicking once on the desktop area or the Finder tile on the Dock.) You'll see an alert box warning you that emptying the Trash is permanent. If you're sure you want to proceed, click the OK button. The items in the Trash will be deleted.

 TIP If you'd like to skip the warning alert box, you can hold down the Option key while selecting Special ➤ Empty Trash. Also, you can use the keyboard sequence Shift+⌘+Delete to empty the Trash while the Finder is active.

The Dock

Another of Mac OS X's new features is the Dock, which is used in place of many traditional Mac OS elements, including the old Applications menu (used for switching between applications) and the Launcher. The Dock is an innovative and simplified approach to the tasks it accomplishes: launching often-used items, switching between applications, and managing documents. Experienced Mac users may find that the Dock takes some getting used to—it seems too simple at first glance, but that doesn't attest to its full power (see Figure 2.10).

FIGURE 2.10

The Dock is a deceivingly simple-looking part of the Mac OS X interface.

By default, the Dock appears at the bottom of the screen with a number of prein-stalled *tiles*—Apple's name for the Dock's icons. The default tiles include the Finder, Mail, System Preferences, Clock, and Sherlock, among others. You'll also find the Trash on the Dock, and if someone else administers your Mac, you may find tiles for other applications there—your word processors, Web browsers, terminal emulators, or anything else you need to access quickly.

In fact, the Dock is designed to show you five different things. (This is part of the Dock concept that seasoned Mac users may have to get used to.) Those things are:

Application aliases   Besides the aliases placed on the Dock by default, any application's icon can be dragged to the Dock, which creates a tile for that application that can be clicked for convenient launching. In fact, many appli-cations will install their own tile on the Dock when you run their installer program.

Running applications   Whether or not an application's alias is on the Dock already, its tile will appear there after it has been launched. That makes it possible to monitor and switch between all of your running applications using the Dock interface.

Document or folder aliases   You can also place on the Dock aliases to doc-uments or, for that matter, aliases to folders. When clicked, a document alias will launch the original document and its associated application; a folder alias will open that folder in a Finder window.

 NOTE   If the document is associated with a Classic application, the Classic environment will also launch (if necessary) in order to display that document in the Classic application.

Dock Extras   You can place these icons on the Dock so that you may more easily check the status of certain items or quickly change settings. The Dock Extras folder inside the main Application folder holds a few of these. Click on a Dock Extra icon, and a menu appears, enabling you to use that Extra.

Minimized document windows   When you minimize a document win-dow within an application, it will appear separately on the Dock, making it eas-ier for you to return immediately to that document. Note, by the way, that *document window* is defined loosely here; any window within a running applica-tion that has its own Minimize button will appear on the Dock if you click that button. (For instance, some applications offer dialog boxes that you can mini-mize to the Dock.)

NOTE Microsoft Windows users and Unix/Linux users (especially those who have used KDE or an OpenStep-like window manager) may not require as much time to get used to the Dock as Mac users will. In some ways, the Dock is similar to the Windows taskbar, especially when it comes to managing open applications and documents.

On the Dock is a small, vertical dividing line, which visually separates the application side of the Dock from the document side. On the left side of that line is where the tiles for application aliases and running applications are found; on the right side of the Dock is where document aliases and minimized document windows appear. Application tiles can't appear in the document space, and vice versa. The Trash, which is really just a special folder tile, always appears on the far-right side of the Dock.

Using the Dock

Among the Dock's primary purposes is its role as a launcher. By default, you can launch an application on the Dock by pointing to its tile and clicking once. When you click, you'll see the tile bounce up and down (again, by default) to indicate that the application is starting up. After a few seconds, you should see the application's menu pop up on the top of the screen.

Once you have an application running, you can use the Dock to switch to and from that application. Simply point the mouse at a running application's tile and click once; that application comes to the front, and you can begin to work in it.

TIP Want to switch to an application while simultaneously hiding all others? Hold down ⌘+Option while clicking the application's tile on the Dock.

How do you know if an application is running? Actually, a closer look at the Dock reveals a couple of indicators that are important to using it effectively (see Figure 2.11):

Mouseover names   Pass the mouse over the tiles on the Dock, and the names of the items will appear immediately above their icons. While it's not always possible to determine what an item is simply from its cute little tile, the combination of tile and name should give you a good idea.

Running indicator   If an application has been launched and is currently running, you'll see a small arrow beneath its tile. This indicator is there to let you know that the application has already been launched. Now, if you click that tile, you'll switch to the application.

TIP You can use the keyboard to switch between open applications: ⌘+Tab will take you from left to right along the running applications on the Dock, and ⌘+Shift+Tab will take you through them from right to left. Note that this skips document windows that are on the Dock, switching only between active applications.

Mouseover name

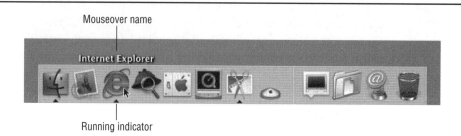

Running indicator

Dock items feature one more little trick: Each of them offers menu commands that will pop up directly over the item's tile. Click and hold the mouse button on a tile to see the menu commands that are available to you. Every tile has a menu; active applications can be quit from their tile, active document windows can be selected, and so on.

Note that this is the technology behind Dock Extras, too. Clicking a Dock Extra brings up a menu that lets you quickly change settings or check the status of whatever that Extra governs, such as changing your screen resolution.

This also works for folders that you place on the Dock, giving you a convenient way to quickly access documents or open a particular folder in the Finder. For instance, if you place your home folder on the Dock, you can reach five levels deep into the subfolders inside your home folder to quickly access your personal stuff.

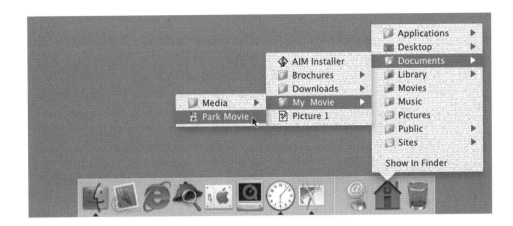

Finally, it's important to note that many Dock items are *active*—they can change to show you different bits of information. For instance, the Mail icon can include a small number (when the Mail application is running) that tells you how many new messages are waiting for you. QuickTime movies that are playing when you minimize them to the Dock will continue to play in icon form.

Setting the Dock's Preferences

The more icons you have on the Dock—of any variety—the more it gets filled up. As it fills, it reaches toward the ends of the screen; and when it gets there, the icons start to get smaller. This can eventually make the icons hard to read.

The solution is in the Dock Preferences dialog box. Choose Dock ➢ Dock Preferences from the Apple menu in the top-left corner of your screen. This launches the System Preferences application and displays the Dock options, shown in Figure 2.12.

FIGURE 2.12

The Dock options in the System Preferences application

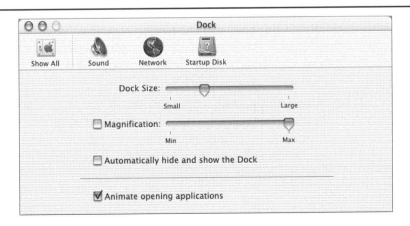

Now you'll see a few settings you can make that relate to the Dock:

Dock Size   Use the slider to change the size of the Dock, sliding between Small and Large. Note that you can make the Dock only as large as will currently fit, given the number of tiles on the Dock. (Once you have enough tiles to fill the screen, the tiles automatically become smaller to accommodate more.)

 TIP   You can also change the size of the Dock using only the mouse. Point the mouse to the dividing line between the application side and the document side of the Dock. The pointer should change to a two-sided arrow. Now, hold down the mouse button and drag the mouse upward to make the Dock bigger, or drag it downward to make the Dock smaller.

Magnification   Turn this on (by clicking its check box), and an interesting thing happens: Now, as you run the mouse pointer along the Dock, each tile will be magnified so that you can see it more easily. This feature makes it possible for you to have more items on the Dock than you can comfortably see; when you mouse-over the tiles, their true purposes will be revealed. Notice also that if the Magnification slider isn't set to a larger size than the Maximum tile size, there's no magnification when the tiles are already at their Maximum level.

Automatically Hide and Show the Dock   Turn this option on, and the Dock will appear only when you move the mouse all the way to the bottom of the screen. When you pull the mouse pointer away from the bottom (to move it around in applications or documents), the Dock will disappear below the bottom of the screen, invisible until you move the mouse to the bottom again.

Animate Opening Applications   If this option is on, application icons will seem to bounce up and down as they're starting up, to indicate that they've been launched successfully. You can turn this behavior off if you find it distracting or annoying, or if you feel it slows your Mac down slightly.

Adding and Removing Dock Items

The Dock probably won't be of much use to you as a launcher if you can't make your own decisions as to what items you want to put there. Of course, you can—and it's actually quite simple.

If you have a document, folder, or application that you'd like to add as a tile on the Dock, simply drag that item's icon out of a Finder window (or off the desktop) and down to the Dock. (Remember that applications go to the left of the dividing line and documents go to the right. Dock Extras may be dragged to either side of the Dock.) When you've dragged the icon to the Dock, you should notice some space open up; it's showing you where the tile for this item will appear if you release the mouse button. (Notice also in the following graphic that the original Transmit icon is still in its Finder window, suggesting that the application itself hasn't been moved or altered.)

You can drag the item to different locations on the Dock if you'd prefer that it appear in another place. Once you've found your chosen spot, release the mouse button, and a tile for that item is created.

By doing this, you're simply creating an alias to the document, folder, or application. It isn't *moved* to the Dock, so the original item will still be stored in your folder in the same place it was before you dragged its icon to the Dock.

Once you've got an alias on the Dock, you can drag it around on the Dock to change its location, or you can remove it altogether. To move an item, point to it with the mouse, then click and drag the item's tile. You'll be able it move it left and right on the Dock until you find the location you like.

To remove a tile, simply drag it up and off the Dock. With the icon hovering over the desktop, release the mouse button. You'll see a small, animated puff of smoke to show that the alias is being removed from the Dock. This doesn't erase or otherwise alter the original file or folder; it simply lets you know in a cute way that the alias has been removed from the Dock.

TIP If you add a folder to the Dock, you'll notice that it's just a plain folder icon; the folder can be tough to differentiate if, say, you add a *second* folder. The trick is to give the folder a unique icon to make it stand out on the Dock. You can change an item's icon using the Get Info command in the Finder. See Chapter 3 for details on changing an item's icon.

What's Next?

So those are the basics of the Mac OS X interface—how to get around, how to select things, and how some of the key elements of the Mac OS X work. In Chapter 3, you'll learn more about the Finder, including how to create, move, and duplicate items, how to use and customize Finder windows, and how to use the Apple menu's special commands, including Sleep, Shut Down, and Log Out.

CHAPTER <u>3</u>

The Finder and the Apple Menu

When you log into Mac OS X, you're presented with your workspace, where you'll access applications, save documents, and manage files. As a user on a Mac OS X system, you get your own home folder, which is given the same name as your username; it holds Documents, Desktop, and Public folders, among others.

Along with those folders, the home folder stores your own set of personal preferences. Because your personal preferences are stored there, any application you run can have unique settings that remain the way you set them, even if other users also run that application. You could, for example, launch Internet Explorer, set a home page, and then log off the Mac. Later, if other users log on, launch Internet Explorer, and change their home-page settings, your settings aren't affected. All your preferences are stored in your home folder (specifically, in the Library folder within your home folder).

Personal preferences also extend to your entire workspace environment. If you drag a folder out to the desktop, it's *your* folder and *your* desktop—another user won't see it there when they log in. If you set your display to a resolution that's different from that of another user's settings, the system will switch back and forth according to whether you or the other user logs in. Even the way the Dock is arranged, the Alert sound you choose, and the mouse speed you set are all uniquely your own. Your settings are stored in your personal home folder, where no one (except someone with your password) can change them.

 NOTE Actually, an administrator could conceivably delete some of your settings or change your password and log in as you. But in normal activity, your workspace is your own.

In this chapter, you'll get a quick introduction to the Finder. Then you'll see how to work within Finder windows and to change their settings, as well as how to use the Finder's special Go menu to quickly access certain folders and disks. After that, it's on to working with icons in the Finder—copying, moving, and getting information about items. Finally, you'll see the Apple menu, where you'll find special options, a Recent Items menu, and commands for putting the Mac to sleep, logging out of the Mac OS, or shutting down the Mac.

Working with the Finder

The Finder is a utility program that is always loaded by Mac OS X, appearing whenever you log into your account. You can't quit the Finder as you can quit most applications. It's a permanent fixture in your workspace, designed to help you access and manage your files, folders, and applications. Even while you work in other programs, the Finder is in the background, waiting to help you manage the workspace. Just click the desktop color or pattern behind your open windows, and you're returned immediately to the Finder.

When you switch to the Finder, its windows enable you to view your disks, folders, and files. Here, you can create, rename, and delete folders, and you can move items between folders. Using menu commands in the Finder application, you can duplicate items, create aliases, and get additional information about items.

Most of all, the Finder is designed to help you manage your personal files and folders while enabling you to access other resources connected to your computer, including secondary hard drives, removable media, and networked drives.

If you're an experienced Macintosh user, you might know that the Mac OS has offered a Finder since the operating system's debut in the mid-1980s. Mac OS X, however, has a completely updated Finder application, based in part on some of the technology Apple acquired in OpenStep. The Finder window, for instance, is an almost entirely new animal. It features a toolbar across the top for quickly accessing important folders, a Back button that works a little like a Web browser's Back button, and a special Columns view that's new to this version. You'll see all of those—including a good bit about customizing the Finder window—in this chapter.

The Mac OS X Hierarchy

If you're a seasoned Mac user, perhaps the most important thing to realize about Mac OS X is the fact that its files are arranged very differently than in Mac OS 9.1 or earlier. Earlier Mac OS versions offer very little structure on the hard drive, allowing you to store documents, applications, and other files pretty much anywhere you want, with certain exceptions, such as the System Folder.

Mac OS X, because of its Unix-like, multiuser underpinnings, requires a little more structure. All users of the Mac OS X system—even if only one user account exists—have their own place on the hard drive (or on a network, in some configurations) where documents, preference files, e-mail databases, personal applications, and many other interesting tidbits are stored.

The added structure segments the Mac OS X file system into folders and files that a user should work in and into folders and files that are best left completely ignored. Again unlike Mac OS 9.1 and earlier, the exact location and format of certain files is necessary for Mac OS X to operate correctly. Therefore, a regular user account is allowed access only to certain parts of the file system.

The structure also makes it possible for certain shortcuts to allow you to use the Finder to move quickly to your documents, applications, and your home directory. I'll explain more about that later in this chapter.

For starters, though, we need to take a look at the basic Mac OS X file-system hierarchy. Figure 3.1 shows you the basics of a typical Mac OS X folder hierarchy.

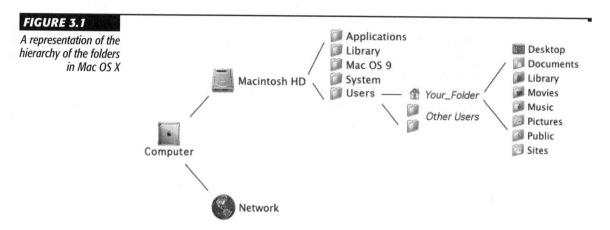

FIGURE 3.1

A representation of the hierarchy of the folders in Mac OS X

The most basic level of the files system is the Computer, which you can access by clicking the Computer button in a Finder window. When you do so, you'll see the hard drives, any mounted removable media (like CD-ROMs or Zip disks), and Network disks (via File Sharing) that the computer has to offer.

Open up the main startup disk where Mac OS X is installed, and you'll see five basic folders: Applications, Library, Mac OS 9, System, and Users. (You'll also see a Mac OS 9.1 "System Folder" and an "Application (Mac OS 9)" folder if you installed Mac OS X over Mac OS 9.1.) The Library folder holds a number of application-related settings and system files, including fonts, preferences, and logs for your applications. The System folder holds the hierarchy of folders and files used to get Mac OS X up and running. (If you're the administrator for your Mac OS X machine and/or network, you'll dig deeper into the Library and System folders, as discussed in Chapter 7 and later chapters.)

The Applications folder is designed to hold applications accessible by all users on your Mac. You'll find a number of applications are already installed there by the Mac OS X installer. To learn more about installing new applications in the Applications folder, see Chapter 7.

Within the Users folder, you'll find the home folder for each individual user, where a person can store documents, personal applications, and program settings or data, like mailboxes and downloaded files. Users (aside from an administrator) cannot change or move the contents of another user's home folder.

The Lingo of Hierarchy

Files on Mac OS X disks are generally stored hierarchically, meaning you'll have folders that include subfolders that include subfolders, and so on. The enclosed folders are called *child* folders or *subfolders*, and the enclosing folders are called *parent* folders.

An example might be your home folder in Mac OS X. The folder is given the same name as your username, and (by default) it has the subfolders (child folders) Documents, Library, and Public, among others. The parent folder for these subfolders, then, is your home folder. (In my case, the home folder might be called "todds.")

Likewise, your home folder has a parent folder, called Users. The Users folder's parent is the *root* folder on the hard disk, which is usually represented by the Mac OS X disk icon when viewed in a Finder window. (The root folder may also be called "Macintosh HD" if Mac OS X was installed over a previous version of the Mac OS.) This series of relationships creates a *path* in the hierarchical storage system on your Mac. The path might be represented as `Macintosh HD:Users:todds` in typical Macintosh notation, or as `/Macintosh HD/Users/todds/` in Unix-style notation.

In Mac OS X, the hierarchy extends all the way back to the computer that you're working on, as represented in the toolbar of each Finder window by the Computer icon. Selecting the Computer icon shows you the disks connected to that computer. At the Computer level, you'll also see a Network icon, which can be used to browse any items connected to your Mac via a network connection.

Within each home folder, you'll find other folders—Documents, Library, Public, and others. Although it isn't mandatory to store documents in the Documents folder (you can store them anywhere within your home folder), you'll find that doing so can be convenient, because Finder windows can offer quick-access buttons to take you directly to Documents and the other folders.

The Finder Window

With past Mac OS versions, you would generally double-click a disk icon on the desktop to open a folder window for that disk. Then, to get at a subfolder, you'd double-click its icon. Within that folder, you could work with the icons or double-click yet another subfolder in the folder window, burrowing deeper and deeper. You can do the same in Mac OS X, but it isn't always the most efficient way to access a file.

Mac OS X introduces a new method via its revamped Finder window (see Figure 3.2). The Finder window reflects a fundamental shift in the way disks, folders, and files are managed in the Mac OS. It helps you move quickly to different parts of a large file system—one with many folders and subfolders where items may be hiding. Likewise, the Finder window makes it easier to see networked disks and volumes.

FIGURE 3.2

The Finder window, by default, shows icons in a single window.

The Finder window offers three different views—Columns, Icons, and Lists. How you view the Finder window may be a matter of personal preference, but you may also discover that certain views are more productive than others for certain tasks.

NOTE The name *Finder window,* new to Mac OS X, may sound familiar to Macintosh users. Apple wanted to suggest that it really isn't very different from the Finder in older Mac versions. It's also sometimes called the *Browser*, which is what its predecessor was called in OpenStep and NextStep.

Open a Finder window

To open a Finder window, select File ➤ New Finder Window in the Finder's menu or press ⌘+N. A Finder window appears. If you already have a Finder window open, a second Finder window will open.

You can open as many Finder windows at a time as you like. Doing so is one way to copy and move files between folders (more on that later in the section "Working with Icons"). You can then close Finder windows by clicking their Close buttons or by selecting a window and choosing File ➢ Close Window from the Finder menu.

 TIP You can use the Window menu in the Finder to switch between different Finder windows quickly. Also, remember that you can click a Finder window's Minimize button if you'd like to place it out of the way on the Dock.

Browse in the Finder Window

By default, the Finder window opens in *Icon* view, meaning the window is filled with the current folder's icons. If you've just logged in, you're likely looking at the icons in your home folder.

You can treat these icons as you would any icons in windows or on the desktop, as described in Chapter 2. You can single-click an icon to select it, drag-select multiple items, and so on. You double-click a document or application to launch it, and you double-click a folder to view its contents.

Double-clicking a folder doesn't open a new Finder window; instead, the entire Finder window changes to show that folder's contents. (This is different from Finder behavior in past Mac OS versions.) If you'd prefer to open a new window with the folder's content shown, hold down the ⌘ key while double-clicking the folder icon.

 TIP You can reverse the way windows open in the Finder when you click a folder icon, making it a little more like Mac OS 9 and earlier. For details, see the section "Changing Finder Window Behavior" later in this chapter.

You might notice that the Finder window in this view works a little like a Web browser. When you double-click a folder icon, you'll go "forward" to that folder's contents, similar to when you click a link in a Web-browsing application. To move back, click the Back button—the left-facing arrow. To go back to a particular folder in the hierarchy of folders that you've opened, use the folder menu just above the window's content area.

Back

At the top of the Finder window, you'll see the name of the folder currently being viewed. This title bar also hides a secret little capability: If you hold down the ⌘ key and click the folder name, you'll see a pop-up menu that enables you to select any of the parent folders of this current folder.

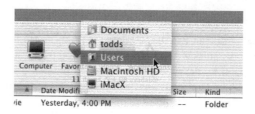

 TIP It's also worth noting that the small folder icon next to the folder name in the title bar is an active element. You can drag that folder icon to the desktop or to another Finder window if you'd like to move the entire folder to another location on your hard disk (or copy it to another disk). You can also drag the icon to the Dock if you'd like to add the folder as a tile.

The Finder Window Toolbar

One of the new features of the Finder window is the row of buttons at the top of it, arranged in what's called a *toolbar*. Most of these buttons are just shortcuts to different parts of the hierarchy, provided for convenience, to help new users, and to make diehard Unix fans roll their eyes. Figure 3.3 shows these icons.

FIGURE 3.3

The Finder window's toolbar

Most of these buttons are self-explanatory. Computer takes you to the lowest level of the hierarchy, where you can see the drives, removable media, and network connections that are attached to the Mac. The Home button is a shortcut to your home folder. Applications takes you to the system's Applications folder.

The Favorites button takes you to your Favorites folder, which is also found in your home folder. It's the folder with aliases to items that you've deemed a *favorite*. How do you make something a favorite? Use either the File ➢ Add to Favorites command (discussed later in this chapter) or the Add To Favorites button found in Open and Save dialog boxes (see Chapter 4).

The three small View buttons allow you to change the way you view the window. From left to right, they're the Icon, List, and Columns view buttons.

 TIP   You can customize the toolbar to show items that you'd prefer to have quick access to. See the section "Customizing the Finder Toolbar" later in this chapter.

The Status Bar

In a Finder window, you'll see some statistics and information that tell you a little about the folder you're viewing and the disk that the folder is stored on. At the top of the window's content area, just below the toolbar, you'll see the *status bar,* which tells you how many items are in the current folder and how much space remains on the current disk.

If you don't see the status bar, you can toggle it on by selecting View ➢ Show Status Bar. Conversely, you can remove the status bar by selecting View ➢ Hide Status Bar.

At the far left of the status bar, you'll also see a small icon that tells you what your privileges are for the current folder. Each user account has certain privileges that allow different levels of access to folders on local or networked disks. For instance, only administrator accounts have the ability to change files (or *write* files) within certain system-level folders such as the Applications and Library folders. As a regular user, you'll have the ability to write files to your personal folders, execute files from public folders (such as the Shared folder inside the Users folder), and read files from some others.

If you see an icon that looks like a pencil with a line through it, you don't have *write* privileges for the folder. So you can't change its contents or alter anything within it. If you see items in the folder, however, you do have *read* privileges—you can launch applications or view documents in the folder. You can't change documents unless you use a Save As command to save a copy of the document to a folder for which you do have write privileges. If you don't see a pencil icon and you can see folders, then you have both read and write privileges.

TIP See Chapter 4 for more on setting permissions for your personal folders and Chapter 5 for more on the Save As command.

Use the Columns View

Why switch views? The Columns view is a powerful way to peer into your Mac's mounted disks. The view is a significant innovation, part of the design adapted from OpenStep.

The Columns view, in a nutshell, allows you to see and think of the disk as hierarchical. Instead of moving back and forth one folder at a time, you can use the Finder window to see three, four, or five levels of the folder hierarchy at once. And all you have to do is select View ➤ As Columns or click the Columns button in the Finder window's toolbar. Figure 3.4 shows the Finder in Columns view.

  TIP The number of columns you can see in Columns view depends in part on your display's resolution. The higher the resolution, the more columns you'll be able to see in a Finder window. Chapter 4 discusses changing display resolution.

FIGURE 3.4

In Columns view, you get a better view of the hierarchy of folders.

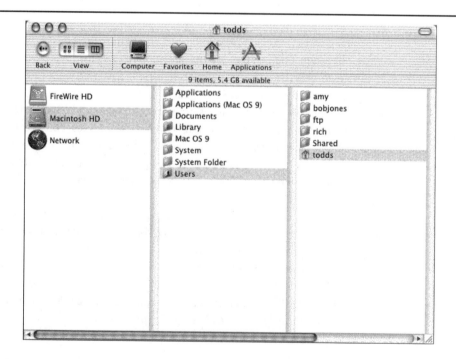

In Columns view, clicking the Computer button sets the first column to show any disks connected to your Mac, both internally and externally, including any active removable disks (such as a Zip disk or a CD-ROM). Then, if you click a disk icon, for instance, all the subfolders on that disk appear in the next column to the right. If you click once on one of the subfolders, its items appear in the next column, and so on.

To select a disk, folder, application, or document, click it once in *any* of the columns. In the next column to the right, you'll see either the folder's contents or, in the case of nonfolders, some information about that item (see Figure 3.5). In some cases, images or QuickTime-compatible files can show a preview of themselves right in the Finder window.

To view a different disk or folder, you can select a folder, disk, or item in any of the visible columns. Doing so changes your location on the disk, revealing the contents or information of the item selected. This can take some getting used to, because clicking in earlier columns (those to the left) will completely change what appears in later columns (those to the right). If you're looking at your home folder, for instance, and go back a few columns and click the main System folder, the entire character of the Finder window will change, showing you the contents of the System folder.

If you have quite a few columns open (because you've dug deep into a particular folder hierarchy), you'll notice that the window has a scroll bar and arrows running across the bottom of the window. You can scroll to see previous columns.

FIGURE 3.5

For nonfolders, you can view a little information or even a preview.

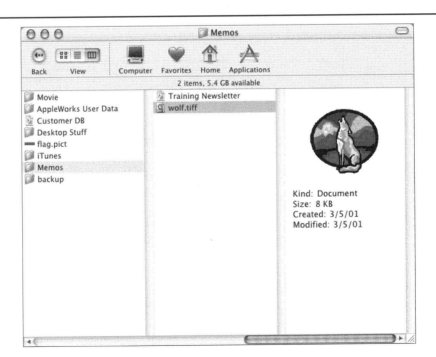

If you'd like to see more columns in the window, drag the resize box (at the bottom-right corner of the window) to make the Finder window larger. The larger the Finder window, the more columns you can see.

Of course, as with the As Icons view, you can use all the buttons in the Finder window's toolbar (Home, Applications, Favorites, and so on) to move directly to your home, documents, applications, or favorites folder simply by clicking the corresponding button. Likewise, you can use the Back button to move backward through the choices you made to get to where you are. So, if you clicked your home folder and then clicked the Sites folder, clicking the Back button will return you to your home folder (see Figure 3.6).

FIGURE 3.6

Click the Back button, and the open column (top image) is closed (bottom image).

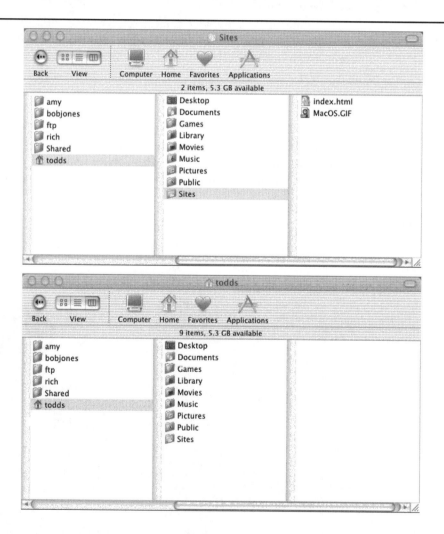

Change to List View

Another view you can use in the Finder window is the List view, which you can set by choosing View ➢ As List. List view replaces the columns or icons of the default view with a listing of the items on a particular disk or in a folder, as shown in Figure 3.7. The List view is generally best suited to folders that include many, many files—usually documents—about which you'd like the most information possible. The List view can be sorted by name, date modified, size, or other variables that other views can't be sorted by. (The view can be sorted by only one variable at a time.) You can then find files more easily and quickly.

FIGURE 3.7

The List view shows you the contents of a disk or folder with columns of information.

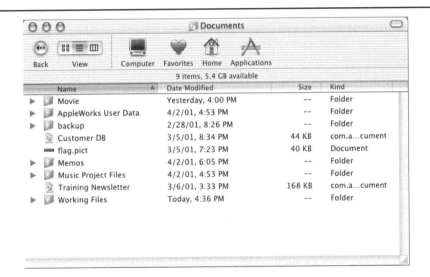

If you double-click a subfolder while in List view, the window switches to a view of the subfolder's contents. Using the Back button returns you to the parent folder. As with the Icon and Columns views, you can hold down the ⌘ key while double-clicking a folder icon in order to open a second Finder window containing the subfolder's contents.

The List view's greatest strength is probably its ability to show more than one folder's contents at a time. Click the disclosure triangle next to a folder in the list, and that folder will reveal its contents. Notice that the subfolders list is indented somewhat to show at a glance that it's a subfolder (see Figure 3.8).

The List view is pretty flexible in its presentation of subfolders. For instance, you can have more than one subfolder revealed, as is also shown in Figure 3.8. Further, subfolders needn't have the same parent in order to be revealed—you can see subfolders within other subfolders as long as you have enough space on the screen to reveal them. If you run out of screen space, you can use the up and down scroll arrows to see more folders and files in the hierarchy.

 TIP Want to move an item from a revealed subfolder to its parent folder that's currently displayed in the Finder window's List view? This can be a little tricky. You need to drag the item from its subfolder to the area just below the Name column heading—you'll see the entire folder become outlined in light gray. That suggests that dropping the item will place it in the parent folder. (In Figure 3.8, for instance, you could drag the file Product Demo up to the top of the folder area, very near the Name column head. When the gray outline appears, release the mouse button, and Product Demo will be moved up to the Documents folder.)

FIGURE 3.8

Clicking disclosure triangles allows you to see the contents of a folder and a subfolder simultaneously.

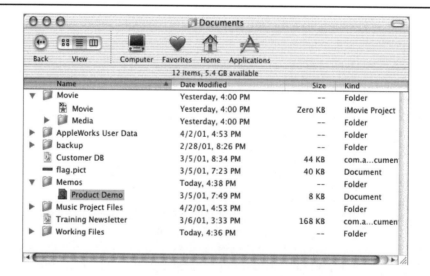

The List view can be sorted. Click any of the column heads (Name, Date Modified, Size, or Kind), and you'll see the list sorted by that column's criterion. If you'd like to change the order of the sort, simply click the column's name again and the sort order will change (see Figure 3.9).

You can change the size of the columns by placing your mouse pointer on the line that divides two columns. The mouse pointer changes to a line with arrows pointing left and right. Click and hold the mouse button, then drag to resize the column. Release the mouse button when you're happy with the width of the column.

FIGURE 3.9

Click a column title to sort by that column (the example here is sorted by Kind). The column name can be clicked again to change the sort order, indicated by the small triangle in the column heading.

Sort-order indicator

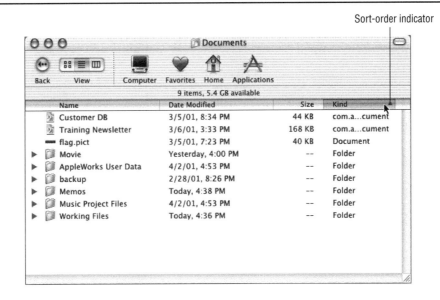

To change the order of columns, point at a column name and then click and hold the mouse button to drag that column to another part of the window. When you drop the column name, that column is placed in that spot, and other columns are reordered accordingly.

 TIP One nice trick in the List view is to move directly to an item in the list. How? Just start typing the first few characters of its name. If you have a folder named "Memos" that you want to select, just start typing **Mem**, and the selection will jump to folders with those letters. Although this is most effective when the List view is sorted alphabetically, it works regardless of the sort order. (The trick works in Icon view, too.)

Arrange Icons (in Icon View)

If the icons in a Finder window have become a bit haphazard, you can clean them up easily. Select the window you want to organize (you don't need to select the icons) and then choose View ➤ Clean Up. The icons will be placed on a grid and separated by a minimum distance to make them easier to view (see Figure 3.10).

You can also choose to arrange icons alphabetically, if you'd like. Select the window you want to arrange and then choose View ➤ Arrange by Name. The icons will be cleaned up (again, by an invisible grid that keeps the icons a certain distance apart) and alphabetized.

FIGURE 3.10

On the left, a messy Finder window; on the right, it's all cleaned up.

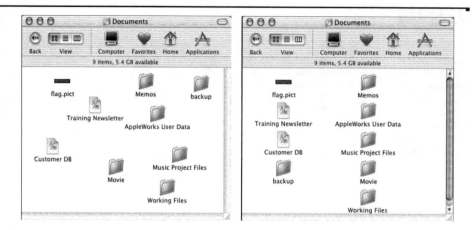

View Options

As you've seen, the Finder window offers a number of methods for viewing and arranging the contents of a folder. To help get a handle on all these different view options and behaviors, the Finder application offers a command that enables you to set some basic preferences for how folders look and behave.

Mac OS X can store preferences for folders individually. You may have already noticed that one folder can be set to a List view while another is set to an Icon view, for instance, and each time you return to a folder, its most recently set view is displayed. (With Columns view, however, once you set the Finder window to view columns, it stays that way.) Likewise, you can set both global preferences for how List view and Icon view windows will look and individual preferences for each window.

You can set the viewing preferences in the View Options palette. With the Finder active, select View ➢ Show View Options from the menu (see Figure 3.11).

By default, most folders will have the Use Global View Preferences option selected, meaning the particular folder is set up to use the global view preferences, whether it's Icon view or List view.

The View Options palette (which actually takes the name of whatever folder is currently selected in the Finder window) has two tabs: Window and Global. On the Window tab, you'll make choices for the current folder window that's open in the Finder. Select the Global tab, and you can choose system-wide settings for how windows will appear.

If you choose Window, you'll see either the Icon view settings or the List view settings, depending on which view the current window has active. In other words, if the Finder window is currently in Icon view, then the preferences in the View Options window will be those that are relevant for Icon view.

FIGURE 3.11

The View Options
window lets you set
options globally or for
the current window.

If you choose the Global tab, you'll see the View menu, which enables you to
choose whether you want to alter global settings for Icon view or List view. Choose
either Global Icon or Global List from the menu. The rest of the options will change
according to your selection, as detailed next.

Icon View Settings

If you're choosing the options for an Icon view, you have four settings: Use Global
View Preferences, Icon Size, Icon Arrangement, and Folder Background.

The first option you'll see lets you determine whether or not this window will use
any custom settings. If a check mark appears next to the option Use Global View Preferences, the rest of the settings will be dimmed. Thus, the window will use whatever
options have been set globally for Icon view windows. Select this option only if you
don't want special settings for the particular window.

If you don't have a check mark next to the Use Global View Preferences option,
you can set individual preferences for the window using the remaining controls (see
Figure 3.12).

For Icon Size, you'll see a simple slider control. Drag the selector back and forth on
the slider to change the size of the icons that appear in this particular folder window.

In the Icon Arrangement section, you have three options:

None   Choose this option if you don't want to do anything to the arrangement of icons.

FIGURE 3.12

The Icon View settings

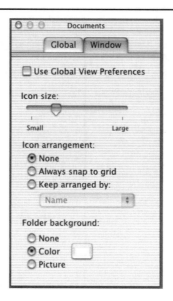

Always Snap to Grid   Select this option to force icons into a grid-based alignment whenever you drop them in the window.

Keep Arranged   This option places icons in a grid alignment and automatically arranges the window by the criterion you select in the pop-up menu. Your choices for arranging the window are by name (alphabetically), by the creation or modification date, by the size of the file or folder, by the kind of item, and by the item's label.

In the Folder Background section, you have three options:

None   Choose this option if you don't want any special background for the folder.

Color   When you select Color, a small button appears. Click the button to show the Color Picker, which enables you to choose the background color. (See Chapter 5 for more on the Color Picker.)

Picture   Choosing Picture brings the Select button to the screen. Click Select and an Open dialog box appears, enabling you to locate an image file that you'd like to use as the background of the folder. You would then locate the appropriate file and click OK in the Open dialog box. Your selected image would then appear as the background in the current folder.

List View Settings

If you're choosing the options for a folder that's in List view, you'll have some settings that are different from those in Icon view, including what columns will appear and how the date and size of items will be shown. Figure 3.13 shows the View Options dialog box for a List view.

FIGURE 3.13

The View Options dialog box for a folder in List view shows options different from those for Icon view.

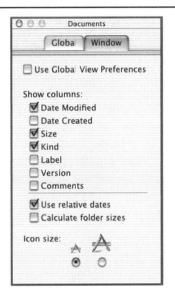

Again, the first option you'll see enables you to determine whether or not the window will use any custom settings. If a check mark appears next to the option Use Global View Preferences, other settings will be dimmed. The window would then use whatever options have been set globally for Icon view windows.

If the option Use Global View Preferences is unchecked, you'll see other options:

Show Columns   Choose each column that you'd like to see in the List view by placing a check mark next to its entry.

Use Relative Dates   Select this option to enable date entries that are relative to the current date, as in "Yesterday at 9:16 P.M.," as opposed to month, day, and year.

Calculate Folder Sizes   Turn this option on, and folder sizes (for subfolders in the window) will be calculated and displayed. Displaying folder size can slow down the appearance of items in the window, which is why you can turn it off.

Icon Size   Choose the size for the icons in List view.

Global Settings

Regardless of which folder window is open in the Finder or even the type of listing (Icon or List) that's displayed, you can alter the global settings for both Icon and List views at any time, using the View Options window. Click the Global tab, and you'll see a pop-up menu called View. Then select the settings you'd like to alter—either Global Icon settings or Global List settings.

Next, edit the settings to taste. They're exactly the same options outlined in the previous two sections, "Icon View Settings" and "List View Settings." When you're done, close the View Settings window by clicking its Close button. The global settings should take effect immediately, so that any folder that's been set to Use Global View Preferences will be changed when you next visit that folder.

Customizing the Finder Toolbar

As noted earlier, one of the major additions to the Finder's capabilities in Mac OS X is the new toolbar, which can be used to quickly move you to your home, Applications, and other important folders. What's even more impressive about the toolbar, however, is how customizable it is. You can change the icons on the toolbar, add important items to it for quick access (or for easy drag-and-drop), or remove the toolbar altogether—which not only hides it but reverts the Finder to behavior that's more familiar to users of early Mac OS versions.

Dragging Items to the Toolbar

The easiest way to customize the toolbar is to simply drag folders to it from either the desktop or the Finder window itself. This enables you to add a folder that you'd like to access often or even to add a document or application that you'd like to be able to launch with a single, quick click. To add an item, simply drag it to the toolbar area; if you drag the item between two existing items, a gap will open up to allow you to drop it there.

What this essentially does is place an *alias* to the item on the toolbar. You haven't moved the item anywhere—it still resides in the same place on your hard disk as it did before. But you now have an easy click or drag-and-drop target, which can add a bit of convenience. For instance, you might place your Documents folder on the toolbar so that you can quickly drag and drop items to that folder without opening a second Finder window. And, when you click that Documents folder once, it will open up immediately in the Finder window, giving you another convenient shortcut.

 TIP You can put applications on the toolbar, too, making for easy little drag-and-drop targets. If you have an application that you're often dragging items to—the StuffIt Expander application, TextEdit, or Preview, for instance—it could be nice to have the application right there on the toolbar. Of course, you can drag and drop to the Dock as well—so you can avoid cluttering up your Finder window toolbar with icons.

If you want to remove an item from the toolbar, simply drag it from the toolbar to somewhere else on the screen (for instance, the desktop area). As long as you don't drop the item back in the toolbar area, it will disappear from view when you release the mouse button. Nothing will be deleted—only the icon will be gone. (You can even drag the icon to the Trash, and nothing but the icon will be deleted. The icon will not remain in the Trash, however.) The original item will still be where it always has been on your hard disk.

Changing the Toolbar

Besides dragging items to the toolbar, you can also go in for more wholesale changes. Select View ➤ Customize Toolbar, and you'll see the Finder window change to its Customize screen, as shown in Figure 3.14.

Now you can drag any of these items up onto the toolbar to add them. Note that the icons represent more than just locations on your hard disk; you can add an Eject button for ejecting disks, a Path button for navigating parent folders, and even a separator line to help organize the toolbar. You can also drag items already on the toolbar to other locations—for instance, put the View buttons on the right side, or rearrange the items that are already on the toolbar. Here's a fully customized example:

FIGURE 3.14

All-out customizing of the toolbar happens on this screen.

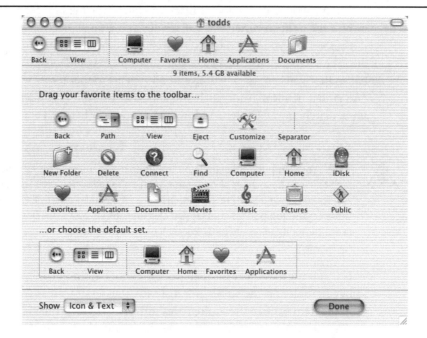

The Customize screen also offers a small pop-up menu in the bottom-left corner where you can choose how you'd like the tools in the toolbar to appear. By default, both icon and text are shown. You can also choose Icon Only or Text Only if you'd like to squeeze a few extra buttons onto the toolbar.

 TIP Want the standard toolbar back? Just drag the default set from the bottom of the Customize screen up to the toolbar area, and it will replace any custom tools you've added.

When you've finished customizing, click the Done button. You'll be returned to the Finder window, now complete with your new toolbar.

Changing Finder Window Behavior

You don't like the toolbar? Or you don't like the whole Finder window concept? You can remove the toolbar and, in the process, change the way Mac OS X's Finder windows act.

At the top right of every Finder window is a small, oval button. Click it once and the Finder toolbar disappears. (You can also select View ➤ Hide Toolbar.) The result is a plain window that can still be viewed in Icon, Columns, or List view.

Hide Toolbar button

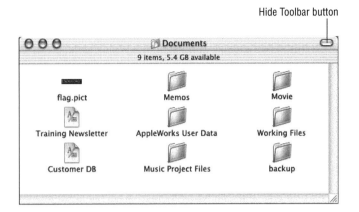

One other important thing has changed about this window, though. Double-clicking a folder inside it will now open that folder in a *new* Finder window—one that still doesn't have a toolbar. If you're familiar with older Mac OS versions, you'll note that this is exactly how folders work in those older versions of the Finder. It's something I like to call "dig mode."

 TIP When you're in dig mode, you can hold down the Option key while double-clicking a folder if you'd like the parent folder's window to disappear when the new folder's window appears. (This reduces folder clutter, and it's another holdover from older Mac OS versions.)

To return the Finder window to its default behavior, click the oval button again or select View ➢ Show Toolbar. The newfangled Mac OS X Finder window will return in all its glory.

 NOTE If you double-click a hard disk or removable disk icon that appears on your desktop, the resulting Finder window, by default, will automatically appear without a toolbar and will act with this older-Finder behavior. (If you try this and see a Finder window with a toolbar, click the Hide Toolbar button, close the window, and double-click the hard-disk icon again.) That's done so that old Mac hands can feel comfortable digging into the hard disk exactly as they're accustomed to doing. If you don't see hard-disk icons on the desktop, you may need to change a preference setting in the Finder Preferences dialog box; see the section "Finder Preferences" later in this chapter.

The Go Menu

The Finder offers a menu that's new to users of previous Mac OS versions: the Go menu. In some ways, the Go menu has taken over some of the Apple menu's functions in earlier Mac OS versions. If you're used to Microsoft Windows, you'll see that the Go menu has some similarities to the Start menu (see Figure 3.15).

FIGURE 3.15

The Go menu in action

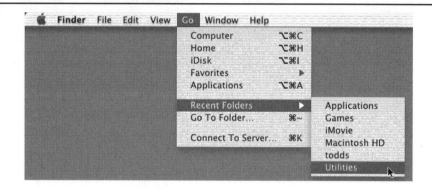

Hidden within the Go menu are a few important and disparate tasks, such as these:

Folder presets The Go menu includes commands that exactly mirror the toolbar buttons in a Finder window. Select Go ➢ Home, for instance, and the front-most Finder window (if one isn't open, a new window will appear) will switch to a view of your home folder. (You can also get to the home folder by pressing Option+⌘+H anywhere within the Finder application.) Other options include Computer (Option+⌘+C) and Applications (Option+⌘+A).

iDisk Choose the iDisk preset to open your iDisk (assuming you have an active Internet connection) based on the settings in the Internet pane of the System Preferences application. (See Chapter 11 for more on iDisk.)

Favorites Instead of simply switching to your Favorites folder (which is what the Favorites button on the Finder window's toolbar does), you can use the Go ➢ Favorites menu to access your favorites directly. Simply select an item in the menu, and it's launched (if it's an application or document) or, if you're selecting a folder, its contents are displayed in the front-most Finder window. If you'd like to view the Favorites folder, select Go ➢ Favorites ➢ Go to Favorites or press Option+⌘+F.

Recent Folders   When you select a recently used folder in the Recent Folders menu (Go ➤ Recent Folders), you move directly to it. Once selected, that folder's contents are displayed in the front-most Finder window.

Connect to Server   Choosing Go ➤ Connect to Server or pressing ⌘+K opens the Connect to Server window, which enables you to connect to Apple File Protocol or some Web-server computers over a network. (You'll read more about this in Chapter 8.)

Go to Folder   When you select Go ➤ Go to Folder or press ⌘+~ (which is actually ⌘+Shift+`), the Go To Folder dialog sheet appears in the front-most Finder window, where you can type a *path statement* to a particular folder. A path statement describes the entire hierarchy of a folder's location on the hard drive. Enter this statement, click Go, and the front-most Finder window will change to that folder if it's found (see Figure 3.16).

FIGURE 3.16

The Go To Folder dialog sheet

Interestingly, the Go To Folder dialog sheet allows Unix-like command syntax to creep into the Finder. This is actually quite convenient, though, if you know what you're doing.

You've seen in this chapter that a hierarchy of folders exists on your disks and digging into them creates a path, which is shown in the Icon bar. The path has an equivalent in the text-based, Unix-like underbelly of Mac OS X. Essentially, each folder name is separated by a slash (/), with another slash at the beginning to represent the "root" of a disk. For instance, say you've opened your Mac hard disk's Users folder and then the todds folder. The text-based shorthand in Figure 3.16 would take you directly to that folder (in the front-most Finder window) when you click Go.

TIP   You can use two special shortcuts in the Go To Folder entry box. The first is that leading forward slash (/) already mentioned. Enter it by itself and press Return, and you're taken immediately to the first level of your Mac's root folder on the startup disk. The other is the tilde (~). Enter it and press Return to be taken immediately to your home folder. You can build on the tilde if you like, as in (~/Documents/Newsletters/) to get to folders within your home folder.

Working with Icons

Once you've figured out the Finder and the many options for its windows, you're ready to do more than just look through your disks and folders. Using the menu commands in the Finder (or keyboard combinations in conjunction with the mouse), you can create folders, duplicate items, and move items between folders. I'll also discuss some other Finder commands, like using the Info window to get information about an item or using the Add to Favorites command.

Create a Folder

Before creating a folder, you must first decide where to put that folder. Begin by selecting the disk or parent folder where you'd like the new folder to appear. In a Finder window, click the parent folder once in a column or double-click it to open it in an Icon or List view.

Then select File ➤ New Folder or press ⌘+Shift+N. The new folder appears with its name highlighted, ready for editing. Type in the folder's name. When you've finished typing the name, press Return or click once outside the text area. Once named, the folder may jump to another location in the Finder window if you've previously chosen to arrange the folders by name, date modified, or some other criterion.

Rename Items

You can rename items, folders, and even disks, depending on the account you're using and your access privileges. For instance, ordinary users can easily rename items and folders within their home folders. Only a user with administrative privileges, however, can change folder names for most folders on the system (not that you'd necessarily want to, because renaming some system folders can cause trouble).

To rename an item for which you have write privileges, select the item in a Finder window. Click once on the name (not the icon) of the item and then wait a few seconds. The name of the item becomes highlighted, and you can type a new name or use the arrow and delete keys to edit it.

Items can just as easily be renamed in List view or Columns view. The process is the same—click the name (not the icon) and wait a few seconds. Then edit to taste.

NOTE Item names can be up to 255 characters long and shouldn't begin with a period (.). Note that names longer than about 31 characters, however, may be difficult to work with, both in Finder windows and in earlier Mac OS versions, particularly if you're dual-booting between Mac OS 9.1 and Mac OS X.

When you're naming or renaming documents and applications in Mac OS X, you should be careful to maintain the filename extension that ends the name of the file. The extension is usually three or four letters after a period, and it tells the Mac OS what type of file it is—a document associated with a particular application. I'll discuss extensions in more depth in Chapter 5.

 WARNING Although you'll see the importance of filename extensions in Chapter 5, it's worth noting here that you shouldn't ever add a filename extension to a folder's name. Doing so could cause it to no longer look or act the way a folder should. (You can rename such a folder without the extension, however, and it will revert to folder-like behavior.)

Duplicate Items

Duplicating an item creates a separate copy of the item. Once created, the duplicate can be used separately from the original. If you duplicate a document, for instance, you now have a separate copy of the document that you can edit and save.

To duplicate an item, highlight it in a Finder window or on the desktop. Then choose File ➢ Duplicate or press ⌘+D. A new, identical item appears, with the word "copy" appended to the end of the name. Two items can't have the same name if they're stored in the same folder—hence the appendage. You can then rename the duplicate, if desired, or move it to another location.

Move Items

You can move items between Finder windows or, in many cases, between a Finder window and the desktop area. Moving an item means you simply change its location from one folder to another on the same disk. (When you move a file to another disk, it's actually duplicated without the word *copy* appended.) After a successful move operation, the document will no longer be available in its original location.

You can move files and folders from one Finder window to another Finder window or between folders in a Columns or List view. To move an item, simply drag it from one window to another or from one part of a columns or list window to another. (See Figures 3.17 and 3.18)

FIGURE 3.17

Moving items from one Finder window to another Finder window

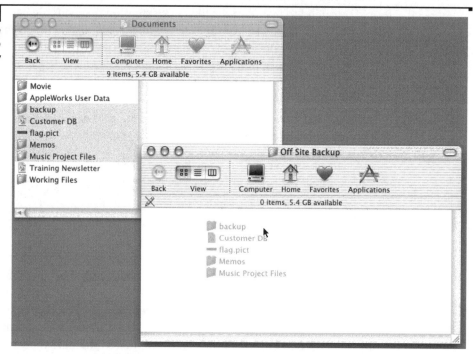

FIGURE 3.18

Moving from one folder to another in Columns view

When you're moving an item, avoid dropping it on another program or file; doing so may launch both of the items. (As detailed in Chapter 5, you can open a document for editing by dropping the document's icon on an application icon.) You can, however, drop items on a folder icon; the action will store that item within the folder. In any view (List, Icon, or Columns), a folder becomes highlighted if you drag an item to it. If you release the mouse button while the folder is highlighted, the item will be stored within that folder.

Images

Copy Items

The two methods just described allow you to create a copy of an item and move it to a new folder. Using the Duplicate command and a move, you could place a copy of an existing item in a new folder.

Of course, the Mac OS can make it easier for you. If you'd like to copy an item using a simple mouse movement, you can. Simply perform a drag-and-drop while simultaneously holding down the Option key. You'll see the mouse pointer change so that it includes a plus sign (+), which is the indicator that a copy is in progress.

In this drag-and-drop method, the word *copy* isn't appended to the duplicate item's name. Since two items can have the same name in two different folders, it isn't necessary to automatically change the name.

The plus sign also appears when you're dragging items from one disk to another, because the Mac OS won't allow a move between two disks. It requires that you copy between disks.

If you're copying reasonably large files or folders with a number of items in them, you may see a dialog box. The Progress dialog box tells you how many items are being copied and approximately how much time is remaining. You can click the disclosure triangle to see more exact statistics.

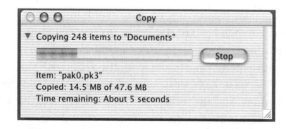

The Progress indicator may also include an alert message if you need to attend to something before the copy can take place. For instance, you may see an alert if an item or folder has the same name as the item or folder you're attempting to copy. (You need to decide whether to overwrite that item or folder or return to the original and rename it before copying.) You may also encounter an alert if you don't have the correct privileges for copying items to or from a location you're working with.

Show Info about Items

The Finder includes a component, called the Info window, that allows you to learn more about items. The Info window lets you look at an item's information and statistics. Via the Info window, you can also set privileges for an item, determining who can access it and under what circumstances.

General Information

To see an item's information, select it and choose File ➢ Show Info. You'll see the General Information screen, as shown in Figure 3.19.

If you like, with the Info window open, you can select a different item in a Finder window or on the desktop, and the Info window will change to show information about the newly selected item.

For any selected item, you can rename it in the entry box where the name is shown (assuming you have correct access privileges to rename it). Simply click in the entry box and edit the name. Press Return or click outside the entry box when you've finished editing.

If you're viewing the information for a folder and you have write privileges for that folder, you can click the Locked option to lock it. The folder then can't be moved to another location, including the Trash. (It can, however, be unlocked and moved or renamed by other users with write privileges for that folder.)

When you're viewing the Info window for a document, you'll see both a Locked option and a Stationery Pad option. A locked document also won't be edited by applications. When loaded in an application, the locked document will be *read-only*, meaning the application can't save edits to the file. If you turn on Stationery Pad, the file becomes Mac OS Stationery, or a template for documents, as opposed to a document itself.

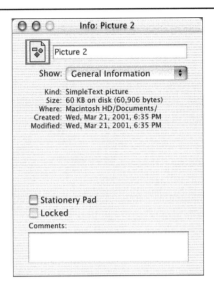

FIGURE 3.19

The Info window shows general information about items you select in the Finder.

If you happen to be viewing information on a Carbon application (one that is capable of running in both Mac OS X and Mac OS 9.1), you'll see another check box on the General Information screen: "Open in the Classic environment." When this option is turned on, the application will be launched as a Classic application instead of as a native Mac OS X application.

TIP The General Information window offers a hidden ability. Select the icon next to the name of the item, and it becomes highlighted. You can then use the Edit ➢ Copy command to copy that icon. You can also use the Edit ➢ Paste command to replace that icon with the contents of Mac OS X's Clipboard. These Edit commands enable you to change the look of an item's icon by first copying an item elsewhere (for instance, copying a downloaded custom icon out of an Info window or copying an altered icon graphic from a graphical application) and then pasting that copied icon in the Info window.

Privileges

In the Info window's Show menu, you can select Privileges to choose the privileges for that item. Privileges determine who can access a particular folder or file in a multi-user and networked environment (see Figure 3.20).

Setting privileges to secure your personal files is discussed in more detail in Chapter 4, and setting privileges as an administrator is covered in Chapter 7.

Other Options

Depending on the type of item you're viewing, the Info window may offer other options in its Show pop-up menu. Each of these options allows you to view different aspects of the item and, in some cases, make changes or choose more options:

Application   Choose Application from the pop-up menu, and you can select the application used to launch the document. This option is available only when you're viewing a document. You can either launch the item with its default application or choose another with the A Specific Application option. (I'll say more about this in Chapter 5.)

Preview   Choose Preview from the pop-up menu to see a preview of the selected document. Images or multimedia files will appear in *thumbnail* view (a smaller version of the original that lets you see its contents quickly) in the Info window. Text-based documents will show some of the text in the document, if the Info window is capable of rendering it.

Eject Disks

Another type of icon we haven't discussed much is the disk icon, which appears whenever you insert a removable disk into a drive that's attached to your Mac. That includes CDs or DVDs that you place in your Mac's built-in disk drive, as well as other disks you may have for removable drives connected via FireWire, SCSI, USB, or some other technology. (Disk icons also appear whenever you mount a *disk image* file, as discussed in Chapter 4.) You can use these icons to access the folders and files stored on the external disk, just as you would use the icon for your main hard disk. (Likewise, by default, hard-disk icons representing your internal hard disk(s) also appear on the desktop.)

When you've finished working with a removable disk, there's a special command for ejecting it from its drive so that you can work with another disk. Switch to the Finder, select the disk's icon (either in the Computer folder in a Finder window or on the desktop), and choose File ➤ Eject. That should cause the disk's icon to disappear from the desktop and pop out of its drive.

There's another way to accomplish this: Drag the disk's icon to the Trash tile in the Dock. This may seem disconcerting at first, but I promise that you won't be deleting anything on the disk; in fact, the Trash icon changes to show you that you'll be ejecting the disk from your computer. Drop the disk's icon on the Trash tile, and it will disappear from the desktop and pop out of its drive (if it's a removable disk).

 NOTE You can also eject hard disks, which is a good idea if you'd like to disconnect a hard disk that's connected via FireWire or USB. Eject the disk's icon, then unplug the external drive; that way, you can be sure the drive isn't currently in use when it's disconnected. Apple warns against ejecting *internal* disks, however. Although Mac OS X won't allow you to eject your startup disk, you can sometimes eject disk volumes that are *partitions* on the startup disk. If you do that, you may cause your Mac to become unstable. It's best to leave hard disks on the desktop, even if you're not using them.

Finder Preferences

You can modify some characteristics of the Finder application, the background desktop, and the Finder window through the Finder Preferences dialog box. To open this dialog box, switch to the Finder application and then select Finder ➤ Preferences (see Figure 3.21).

FIGURE 3.21

*The Finder Preferences
dialog box*

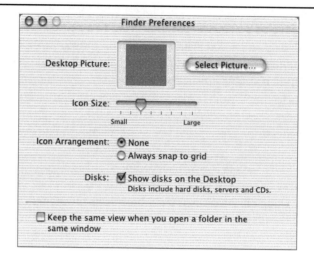

In the Finder Preferences dialog box, you'll see the following options:

Desktop Picture If you'd like to use an image as the background for your Mac's desktop, click the Select Picture button. In the Choose A Picture dialog box, select the image you'd like to use. You can choose one of the Apple-provided images that appear in the Desktop Pictures folder, or you can choose one of your own in JPEG, GIF, or TIFF format. The ideal background image is the same size (in pixels) as your Mac's screen resolution—most likely 800×600 or 1024×768, at a minimum. The exception is an image that's actually only a single, simple color. The image would then need to be only a few pixels in size; the Mac OS will *tile* the image (repeat it over and over again) to create the entire background.

 WARNING If you're working with Mac OS X 10.0, avoid other image formats for desktop pictures. In my experience, choosing the wrong picture type can result in a kernel panic—a massive Mac OS X crash!

Icon Size This slider control enables you to choose the size of icons that appear on the desktop. It won't affect icons in Finder windows—only those that have been dragged to (or otherwise appear on) the desktop.

Icon Arrangement Here you can select whether or not you'd like icons on the desktop to snap to a grid.

Show Disks on the Desktop   This option replicates earlier Mac OS behavior: When you put a CD, Zip disk, AppleShare volume, or other removable disk in the appropriate drive, an icon for that disk will appear on the desktop if this option is selected. Hard disks attached to the Mac at startup will also appear on the desktop. If this option is turned off, disk icons won't appear on the desktop; instead, they'll be visible only when you click the Computer icon in a Finder window's toolbar.

Keep the Same View...   This option, when turned on, will force a new folder window to open in the same view as the current Finder window, regardless of the new folder's previous View Options settings. (For instance, if you're currently viewing a folder in Icon view and you open a subfolder that's set to List view, it will open in Icon view if this setting has been turned on.)

When you're done with the Finder Preferences dialog box, click its Close button to dismiss it.

The Apple Menu

Introduced briefly in Chapter 2, the Apple menu is a convenient way to access a few commands and shortcuts from wherever you happen to be working on your Mac. Instead of requiring you to switch back to the Finder to accomplish some tasks, the Apple menu is always in the upper-left corner, ready to be selected regardless of the application you're using.

Users familiar with the Apple menu from Mac OS 9.1 and earlier versions will note that Mac OS X's Apple menu is a bit more limited (see Figure 3.22). It can't be customized with new aliases or commands, as can the old Apple menu. It does offer access to Recent Items, however, as well as some often-used preference settings. And, new in Mac OS X, this is where you'll go to put your Mac to sleep, restart it, shut it down, or log out of your user account.

Top of the Menu

Open the Apple menu, and you'll immediately see two very specific commands: About This Mac and Get Mac OS X Software. They do very different things. The About This Mac command opens a small window that tells you the current version of Mac OS X, the amount of RAM you have installed in your Mac, and the type of processor that's installed. To dismiss the About This Mac window, click its Close box.

The Get Mac OS X Software command will launch your Web browser and (if you're connected to the Internet or set up to automatically connect) load a special Web site that Apple has designed to help you locate and download software and software updates for Mac OS X.

FIGURE 3.22

The Mac OS X
Apple menu

Preferences

The Apple menu gives you quick access to a number of preference settings, including a fast way to launch the System Preferences application and to change some basic Dock behaviors. Open the Apple menu, and you'll see the following commands:

System Preferences   Select this command to launch the System Preferences application, where you can make basic decisions about how your Mac will operate and behave (discussed in Chapters 4, 7, and elsewhere).

Dock ➢ Turn Magnification On/Off   This option toggles on Dock magnification, so that tiles in the Dock are magnified when you point to them with the mouse.

Dock ➢ Turn Hiding On/Off   This option toggles Dock hiding, which causes the Dock to conveniently disappear at the bottom of the screen. When you point the mouse at the bottom of the screen (and wait a second), the Dock pops back up for you to use.

Dock ➢ Dock Preferences   Select this option to quickly launch the Dock pane of the System Preferences application.

Location   The Location menu is used to change between different saved *location sets* of Network and Internet settings. These are discussed in Chapter 9.

Recent Items

The Recent Items menu enables you to quickly access the five applications and five documents that you've worked with most recently. You'll find that this is handy; for instance, when you start working for the day, you'll often want to open an application and document that you were working with the previous afternoon (or, if you're like me, late last night). If it's one of the most recent applications or documents, you should be able to find it in this menu, thus avoiding a hunt through your home folder or hard disk.

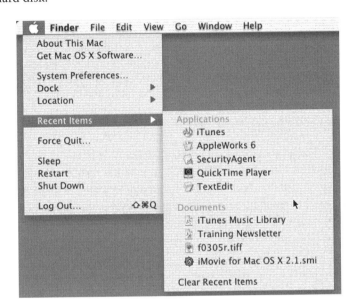

If you want to clear the Recent Items menu so that none of the items on it are there the next time you check, select Clear Recent Items from the menu. Any new applications and documents you launch will appear on the freshly cleaned Recent Items menu.

Force Quit

The Force Quit command launches the Force Quit palette window, which you can use to cause an errant application to shut down immediately. You should do this only when the application in question has frozen, hung, or crashed, since the Force Quit command causes that application to quit immediately, without saving any changed data. See Chapter 19 for more on using Force Quit.

Sleep

The Sleep command is used to put your Mac into the special sleep mode. Sleep is a low-power mode that keeps power trickling to some of the components, including RAM. Anything you're working on (open documents and applications) can be left active while the Mac is in sleep mode. When you wake the Mac up (by pressing a key or the spacebar, or clicking the mouse), your open documents and applications will be unchanged.

NOTE If you're using a PowerBook or iBook, sleep mode is automatically invoked if you close the screen while the Mac is still operating. (On some Mac models, you'll then see a pulsating indicator light that almost suggests that the Mac is "snoring" as it sleeps. It's cute.) Opening the screen will wake the Mac from sleep mode. Most modern Power Macintosh and iMac models can be put into sleep mode by pressing the power button on the front of the Mac. (Don't hold the power button down too long, however, since that may reset the Mac.)

The advantages of the Sleep command are pretty obvious. The Mac uses very little power while sleeping, but you can get back to work quickly when you wake the Mac up. The major disadvantage, however, is that it leaves your personal account signed into Mac OS X. If you walk away from your Mac, others have access to your personal files, settings, and home folder by simply pressing a key on the keyboard. If that's a risk, it's best to log out.

TIP As you'll see in Chapter 12, you can set your personal keychain to lock itself when your Mac enters sleep mode. This can help secure your private passwords if other folks gain access to your Mac after it has been put into sleep mode.

Restart

The Restart command in the Apple menu is used to shut down Mac OS X and immediately send the Mac through the startup process again, without actually powering down the internals. When you choose this command, all open applications are told to shut down by the Mac OS; in all cases, you should be given the opportunity to save any changed data in your applications. Then the Mac OS itself will go through its shutdown process. When it's done, the Mac will immediately start up again (complete with the startup chime).

This is useful when you've installed a driver or a utility application that requires the Mac to go through its startup phase in order to be recognized. It's also useful if you want to boot into a different operating system (such as Mac OS 9.1) that you've selected from the Startup Disk pane in the System Preferences application.

TIP You can also restart your Mac from the login screen. Choose Apple ➢ Log Out, then click the Restart button.

Shut Down

If you'll be gone for a while and you don't need your Mac running, you can choose Apple ➢ Shut Down, or select Apple ➢ Log Out and then click Shut Down. In either case, applications and documents will be closed. Then, after you're logged out, the Mac OS will shut itself down and then shut down your Mac. To power the Mac back up, press its power key or power button, depending on the model.

The advantages of shutting down Mac OS X are that the computer won't use any electricity and no one will be able to access it while you're away. The disadvantage is that no low-level applications—like Web or file sharing—will run on a shut-down Mac. Although it may be common to shut down Macs used as home or office workstations, Macs used as servers or lab machines are likely to be shut down much less often.

NOTE Shutting down your Mac isn't really recommended on a day-to-day basis, because Mac OS X does quite a bit of important behind-the-scenes maintenance (maintaining and erasing log files, for instance), sometimes scheduled for night or other times when the Mac is idle. If you're simply leaving for the rest of the day, you should consider logging out of your Mac and/or putting it into sleep mode. Ideally, you should shut down your Mac only if you'll be gone from your Mac for a full day or longer.

Log Out

The Log Out command shuts down all your active applications and documents. If you have unsaved changes to any documents, you'll be asked if you want to save them. After any such documents are saved and all open applications are successfully closed, you're logged out. The Mac OS makes a note of the fact that you're no longer using the Mac and returns to the Login prompt discussed in Chapter 2. Another user can then log in.

You don't have to shut down the Mac after logging out. It will automatically go into a power-saving mode after a few minutes of inactivity. (This has the advantage of allowing Web and file-sharing access to continue, even though no user is currently logged in.) If you do want to shut down, though, you simply click the Shut Down button. You can also restart the Mac if desired. Some application installations and preferences require that the Mac be restarted before they can take effect.

What's Next?

In this chapter, you saw how the Mac OS X Finder enables you to manage your icons, as well as how the Apple menu can be useful for quick commands and shortcuts. In Chapter 4, you'll see specifically how to manage your home folder and personal workspace, including the setting of file and folder privileges, working with aliases, and setting your personal preferences.

CHAPTER **4**

Managing Your Desktop: Setting Privileges and Preferences

FEATURING:

When you start up your Mac, you may or may not see a login screen that asks for your username and password. If you're just beginning to use Mac OS X in a home or small-office setting, your Mac may have only one user—the user account you created when you first configured Mac OS X using the Setup Assistant. That user account is an administrative user, and, by default, the account is logged into your Mac automatically whenever you start up the computer. (You can change this, as detailed in Chapter 7.)

If you do see a login screen and your administrator has given you a username and password, you are likely a regular user on a multiuser Mac. You'll have a home folder and access to your personal documents, but your ability to alter other files on the Mac will be limited.

Mac OS X is designed, ultimately, to support multiple users, all with their own personal usernames and passwords. This multiuser approach is useful for two reasons. First, it makes it possible for different users to have completely different preference settings and to maintain a personal workspace that's completely separate from other users' workspaces. Second, these user accounts prevent users from gaining access to the entire Mac's file system, so that only special administrator accounts can change important system files.

Mac OS X has a rigid, hierarchical system of folders and files that aren't supposed to be moved much, especially at the lowest levels. The system is in stark contrast to Mac OS 9.1 and earlier versions; to some degree, even Microsoft Windows allows a bit more freedom of movement. In one sense, then, users of other operating systems might be frustrated with having to work with files in only certain folders like the home folder, the Applications folder, and a few others.

In another sense, though, the structure implemented by Mac OS X is good. Behind the shift is the idea that a single user is no longer alone on a computer. Before, the particular user on the Mac was irrelevant to its operation. Now, if there is more than one user, everyone can log into the computer, enabling them to access their own personal space on the Mac OS X system. Once logged in, you'll have access to your own files and preferences, as you've seen in Chapters 2 and 3.

You'll also have your own home folder, where you can store documents, install applications, and otherwise organize your presence. And, if your Mac is connected to a network, you can use your login to access other resources elsewhere on that network.

 NOTE This chapter discusses working on your Mac as an individual user—it's tailored to discuss issues that affect all users. If you are an administrator for your Mac (either as the primary user for a home machine or as the dedicated administrator in a office environment), see Chapter 7 for more on creating individual user accounts for the people who need to use or access your Mac. Chapter 7 also covers the responsibilities that an administrator has on a Mac OS X machine.

Working from "Home"

For day-to-day work, your base of operations in Mac OS X is the home folder, which gives you a location on the Mac OS X system to store files and control other users' access to them. Also, the home folder enables you to store preferences and applications that make your workspace unique.

You can access your home folder quickly by clicking the Home icon in the Finder toolbar or selecting Go ➤ Home in the Finder's menu. The home folder is named for your username and is stored in the Users folder on your Mac.

Inside the home folder, you'll find four important folders by default: the Desktop folder, Library folder, Public folder, and Sites folder (see Figure 4.1). You'll also see some other folders available for convenience: the Documents, Movies, Music, and Pictures folders.

FIGURE 4.1

A sample home folder

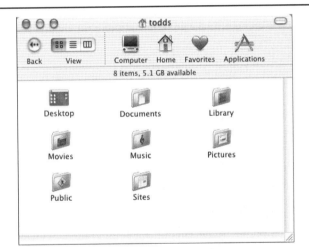

 NOTE You can't rename your home folder, although you're free to create folders within your home folder and name them as you please. (I, for instance, have created an Applications folder and a Games folder, where I store programs that I don't necessarily need to share with other users on the Mac.) You shouldn't rename, move, or delete the existing folders within your personal folder (like Desktop or Library), because the Mac OS and your applications require them as named.

Your Desktop Folder

The Desktop folder is a representation of the items that appear on your desktop—in the background behind Finder windows and other applications. If an item is placed in this folder, it will appear on the desktop. It may seem a bit redundant to have both this folder and the actual desktop area, but the folder is there for a reason. It's an easy way to quickly access desktop items from within an Open or Save dialog box. If, for instance, you need to open an item that's on your desktop from an Open dialog box, you simply navigate to your home folder, open the Desktop folder, and then select the item.

Your Documents Folder

You can actually store documents anywhere that you'd like in your home folder—again, the Documents folder is there as a convenience. Using the Go menu in the Finder, a Documents icon in the Finder toolbar (if you customize it to include a Documents icon), or shortcuts in Open and Close dialog boxes, you can quickly maneuver to your Documents folder.

Store all your documents in your Documents folder, and you'll also make it easier to back up your Mac; you'll know where all your documents are at all times. In this way, Mac OS X can be a major improvement over older Mac versions, where documents could be stored all over the place, with no particular system to their organization.

The Documents folder, by default, is also designed so that only you can read and write to that folder; others users, when logged into the Mac, won't be able to see items you place in the Documents folder. This is an important distinction from your home folder, which does allow Read access to other users of your Mac. (See the later section "Managing Privileges" for more details on read and write privileges.)

Your Public Folder

Mac OS X creates a folder in your home folder called the Public folder, which is used for a very specific purpose. If you'd like to share files with others who have access to your Mac OS X computer, you can drag items to your Public folder. By default, the contents of your Public folder are available to any user who is logged into your Mac, either via a direct user account or over a network connection.

You'll also find that you can access the Public folders that are in other users' home folders, even if you can't access their other folders and files. And all Public folders have another special folder inside them—the Drop Box folder (see Figure 4.2). If you drop a file into another user's Drop Box, only that user will be able to see and access the file.

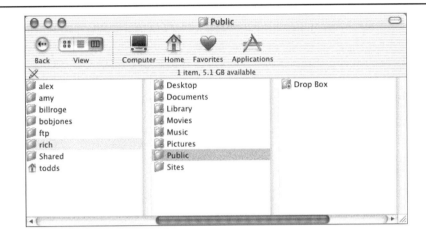

FIGURE 4.2

A Drop Box folder appears inside each user's Public folder.

NOTE You can also see in Figure 4.2 how *privileges* work: The folders with the minus sign on them tell me that I don't have access to folders in the "rich" home folder from my account. I can't open them, read files from them, or write files to them. More on privileges later in the section "Managing Privileges."

Your Library Folder

The Library folder isn't really for day-to-day use, but it's worthwhile to know what's in there. In general, the Library folder holds general preferences, data files, and other settings files required by your applications. Remember, whenever you launch an application—even if it's in the main Applications folder on the hard disk—you get your own preferences and settings for that application. Those preferences files are stored, predictably enough, in the Preferences folder inside your Library folder.

Besides preferences and data files, you'll find some other interesting subfolders within your Library folder. For instance, the Fonts folder is a repository for any personal fonts you'd like to install. Once installed, these fonts will be available in the applications that you use, but they won't appear in other users' Font panel. This can be convenient if you like to work with certain fonts but don't want (or don't have permission) to install them in the main Library folder on your Mac's hard disk.

The Mail folder inside your Library folder holds information about your different POP or IMAP accounts. (See Chapter 10 for more on the Mail application and checking e-mail accounts.) The Mailboxes folder, inside your Mail folder, is where all of your actual sorted mail is stored.

What's most interesting about the Mail folder is how easy it makes it to back up your e-mail. Just copy the Mail folder to a removable disk or otherwise put this folder into your regular backup rotation. If you ever need to restore your e-mail files, you just copy the backup folders back into your Library folder. Otherwise, don't worry about them. (Also, don't move them!)

I'll discuss later some of the other folders in your Library folder, including Favorites (later in this chapter), Internet Search Sites (in Chapter 6), Scripting Additions (in Chapter 17), and Preferences (in various chapters, including Chapter 19).

The Sites Folder

The Sites folder is where you can store HTML documents and images for your own personal Web site. If Web Sharing is turned on, others can access your Web site via a Web browser, using a combination of the Mac's hostname, domain, and your user-name, as in `http://mac1.mac-upgrade.com/todds/` or `http://192.168.1.3/todds/`. Turning on Web Sharing and making Web sites available via your Mac is discussed in Chapter 24.

Managing Privileges

One of the more important home-folder tasks you'll be responsible for is assigning *privileges*. When you assign privileges, you determine which users have the ability to read or write to files within your folders. Whenever a user (whether a local user or one accessing your Mac over a network) attempts to access a particular folder on the Mac OS X system, the OS takes a look at the privileges allowed by the owner of that folder. If the user has permission to access the folder or, more likely, if the user is an administrator and you've given the administrator group permission to access the folder, then the OS will let the user access the folder.

 WARNING There is one difference between a local user and a network user, as far as the Mac OS is concerned. Over Mac OS X's File Sharing, remote users with administrator accounts can generally see files (and often "read" them by copying them elsewhere or launching them in an application) in your folders, regardless of the privilege level that you've set. And, if another administrative user boots your Mac into Mac OS 9.1, that user will have access to all your files; permissions in Mac OS X don't restrict users in Mac OS 9.1. So note for the record that storing files with certain privileges isn't always completely secure, particularly if other users have administrator access on your Mac.

You are the owner of your home folder and any subfolders you create within it—so you alone determine who gets access to them. Using the Show Info command in the Finder, you can set four access levels for any or all of your folders:

- With *Read Only* access, a user can open the files or documents within a folder but cannot save documents in that folder, copy files to it, or delete files in it. Read access also makes it possible for other users to launch applications that you've stored in your file folders.

- With *Write Only* access, also called *Drop Box*, the user can save and copy items to the folder, but cannot see or open items already in the folder.

- With *Read and Write* access, the user has full access to the folder.

- A fourth option, *None*, means the user does not have permission to access the folder at all.

To set privileges for one of your folders, select it in a Finder window and choose File ➢ Show Info or press ⌘+I. In the Info window, select Privileges from the Show pop-up menu, and you'll see the privileges options (see Figure 4.3). You'll then be able to set the privileges for the owner, a user, the "wheel" or "staff" group (administrators), and everyone.

 TIP By default, Mac OS X sets most of your home subfolder privileges to "None" for all users except yourself. When you create a new subfolder in your home folder, however, it will be assigned Read Only access for other users. (Indeed, any time you create a new folder within your home folder, it receives the same privilege settings as its parent folder.) If you don't want other users to have read access to your newly created subfolder, it's important to change the privileges for that folder immediately.

Most likely, you won't want to change the privileges for the owner of the folder, because that's you. You can, though; open the menu and select a different privilege level.

In the group section, you can change the privileges for the wheel or staff group, which simply means anyone on the Mac who is an administrator. (Some automatic functions are also considered part of the wheel group; so if you want installer applications and other such utilities to have access to a folder, set that access here.)

Besides setting privileges for the owner and the wheel/staff group, you can also do so for everybody else on the system. For instance, you may want everyone on the system to be able to read files, but only members of the wheel group to have Read and Write access. You can set up that scenario (or other similar scenarios) by selecting the Read Only level for the Everybody entry. Just open its Privileges pop-up menu and select that level.

FIGURE 4.3

The Privileges options
for a folder in my
home folder

 WARNING When you set a level for Everybody, it applies to anyone with access to the system. It's generally wise to not assign full Read and Write access to Everybody, since limiting privileges will keep your files (and your Mac OS X system) more secure from mischief or mistakes.

Finally, once you've chosen privileges for a folder, you may decide that you want all subfolders of the folder to have the same privileges. Instead of setting them individually, you can click the Copy button to copy the same privilege settings to all the folders enclosed by the current folder.

 WARNING Think carefully before invoking the Copy command for the subfolders, since previously set subfolder privileges will be negated.

When you've finished setting privileges, click the Info window's Close button. Your changes will then be made, and new privileges will be set.

The Shared Folder

Mac OS X offers another special folder that any user, regardless of account type, can access. The Shared folder inside the main Users folder is designed to allow all users on the Mac to easily access files that should be made public to them all. For instance, if you have created a particular memo or report that all users of this Mac should be able to access, you can store that document in the Shared folder. Other users can then read that document and save any changes they make to the Shared folder, if desired.

You'll find other uses for the Shared folder, too. I store MP3 music files in the Shared folder so that they can be accessed by different users on my Macs who decide to launch iTunes. And often when I download a third-party application or game, I put it in a Downloads folder that I've created within the Shared folder so that others can access it without being forced to spend the time downloading that item again.

It's important to note the privileges that are assigned to items you move to, or create within, the Shared folder. In most cases, you (as owner) will have Read and Write privileges, while all other users will have Read Only privileges. This is often okay, but sometimes you may wish to change the privileges for items you save in the Shared folder so that other users have Read and Write privileges. This is particularly true if you've created a folder within the Shared folder; if you don't change the privileges to Read and Write for Everybody, then other users will not be able to save items within that folder.

Installing Personal Applications

Mac OS X lets you install applications for your personal use within your home folder. Doing so is useful when an application won't be of interest to the rest of the users on your Mac, or when you don't have an administrator's account, which would allow you to install system-wide applications. Generally, applications are installed in the main Applications folder so that they will be available to all users. (If that's your goal, see Chapter 7.) In more controlled environments, such as computer labs and work settings, installing personal applications in the home folder can be a convenience.

In your home or small office, you may not find it all that useful to install personal applications in the home folder. But certain situations may still lend themselves to that type of installation—for instance, if you have a financial program that you don't want the kids to launch and play with from their own personal accounts.

 NOTE Remember, other users can still launch applications in your home folder and/or a subfolder if those users have Read access to the folder.

To install an application, you'll need to find and launch the program's installer. If the program is on a CD or other removable media, it should be easy to install. Simply skip down to the "Installer Applications" section. If the application is one that you've downloaded from the Internet, you'll need to first unarchive the downloaded file.

Opening Archives

Most applications that you download for Mac OS X will be in one of two forms. The easier to deal with is the StuffIt archive file, which can be unstuffed using the StuffIt Expander application included with Mac OS X. (It's in the Aladdin subfolder of the Utilities folder, which is in the main Applications folder.) The other type of archive, a Unix *TAR* archive, is only slightly more complex because it may or may not be compressed with the GZIP format.

An *archive* is a file that's created for storage or transfer of a group of files or an application and its associated support files. Archives are often created from entire folders or folder hierarchies and can include many different files. Using a special application, all the folders and files are turned into a single archive file to make them easier to track, name, and transmit over the Internet or a similar network.

 NOTE Files, including archives, will often be compressed before they're transmitted over the Internet. Using a sophisticated algorithm, the compression tool is able to remove redundant information from the file, making it smaller but unusable until it is expanded again. See Chapter 11 for more on downloading and dealing with compressed files.

You can generally tell how an archive has been stored by its filename extension. StuffIt archives (which are both archived and compressed) will have a .sit filename extension. TAR archives compressed with GZIP will have a .gz (or sometimes .tgz or .tar.gz) extension, and TAR archives not compressed with GZIP will have a .tar extension. GZIP files, regardless of whether they've been archived with TAR, may have a .z extension. Thus, if an archive has been compressed, you'll likely see a filename extension like .sit, .tar, .gz, .z, or .tgz.

The easiest way to decompress any of the types of compressed files is to simply drag the file to the StuffIt Expander utility. (StuffIt Expander is located in the Utilities folder inside the main Applications folder on your hard disk.) Once the file is expanded, you'll likely see one of three formats: the full application (which you can simply double-click to begin using), a disk image (which you can double-click to mount), or an installer application.

 NOTE You can also double-click an archive to expand it by using the default application, which is usually StuffIt Expander. Occasionally, doing so will launch the Classic version of StuffIt Expander, however, instead of the Mac OS X native version. The Classic version can have trouble expanding some archives, particularly TAR and other Unix-style archives. In this case, the best solution is to drag the archive to the Mac OS X version of StuffIt Expander.

A disk image is a file that acts like a removable disk. Once you double-click the image file, a disk icon appears on your desktop. This disk icon works just like a removable disk such as a Zip disk or a CD. (You also "unmount" a disk image icon in the same way: Drag the disk icon to the Trash. Note, however, that dragging the disk image *file* to the Trash—the one with the .img or .dmg extension—will place the file in the Trash for deletion.)

Once the disk icon is mounted, you can double-click the disk icon, and you'll see its contents appear in a Finder window, as shown in Figure 4.4.

FIGURE 4.4

After double-clicking a disk image file (the file with the .dmg extension), a disk icon appears, along with the image's contents, in a Finder window.

If the contents of the disk image include an installer application, double-click the installer. Often, though, the disk image will simply contain a full version of the application (and any other necessary files) that you can drag to your home folder or a subfolder within your home folder. Now the application is installed and ready to run.

Installer Applications

If you have an application that installs itself with an installer application, you can begin simply by double-clicking the installer. There are actually a few different types of installers. A package installer will most likely end with the filename extension .pkg, and, when double-clicked, it will launch Mac OS X's built-in installer application. (This installer is commonly used with Mac OS X–only applications built in the "Cocoa" environment.)

Click the Install button, and the installer will step you through the process. You'll select a destination folder (most likely the Applications subfolder of your home folder) and otherwise customize the installation. Once the installation is completed, you should be able to access the new application by double-clicking it in your home folder or using any of the other methods described in Chapter 5.

A common third-party installation program, the Installer Vise application, is particularly popular for shareware applications and Carbon applications that can be installed for either Mac OS 9.1 or Mac OS X. If you see such an installer, shown in Figure 4.5, know that you have the option of selecting a destination for the installation. From the Install Location menu, choose Select Folder. In the Choose A Folder dialog box, choose the folder within your home folder where you'd like the application installed.

Once you've selected a location, click the Install button to begin installing the application. When the installer is finished, a new Finder window should appear, showing you the installed application. Double-click its icon to begin working with it.

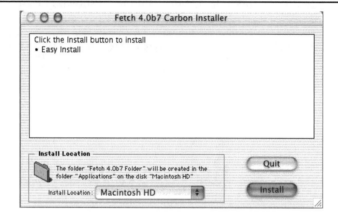

Using Aliases

Once you begin working with applications and documents, you'll be able to more fully appreciate the power of *aliases,* those special icons that I've only hinted at so far. Aliases are empty files—little more than icons, really—that the Mac OS uses to reference another item. For instance, all items that appear in your Favorites folder are aliases (assuming you've created Favorites, as discussed in the section "Working with Favorites" later in this chapter).

Aliases allow you to access a particular file from more than one place in the hierarchy of your folders. If you'd like to have an icon for accessing a particular document or folder from the desktop, you can create an alias there. Or, if you wanted to create a folder for a particular project and wanted to include the necessary applications and documents in the same folder for convenience, you could employ aliases (see Figure 4.6).

Consider the example in Figure 4.6. You wouldn't want to actually move the applications to the project folder because you're likely to want to use them for other projects. Also, moving applications around in Mac OS X can sometimes keep them from working properly. But you can use aliases in your own folders to represent those items. When you launch the alias, it finds the original item and executes it for you.

FIGURE 4.6

You can create a project folder that uses aliases for documents and applications.

Aliases offer another advantage. When you delete an alias, you're simply deleting the empty file, not the original document. So you can delete aliases without worrying about accidentally deleting important folders, documents, or applications.

 TIP You can create an alias of an item located elsewhere on a network (via Apple File Protocol or Mac OS X File Sharing). When you launch the alias, the network connection will be accessed, if possible. If the connection isn't up, you'll see a dialog box that allows you to log into the network volume to access the item. An alias offers a convenient and quick way to access often-used items stored on a network volume.

Create an Alias

If you've read Chapter 3, you know how to create a duplicate. Creating an alias is really no different except for the Finder command. To create an alias, simply select the item you'd like to create an alias of and then choose File ➢ Make Alias from the Finder menu or press ⌘+L.

Drive memo.rtf   Drive memo alias.rtf

By default, the alias will include the word *alias* at the end of its name to differentiate it from the original file. (Remember, files must have unique filenames if they're stored in the same folder.) The alias icon will also include a small curving arrow. The name of the alias will be highlighted so that you can immediately type in a new name, if desired. You can now move, duplicate, or copy the alias to any other folder or disk where you have access privileges.

You can also create an alias by holding down modifier keys as you drag an item to a new folder. When you drag an icon while holding down the Option and ⌘ keys, you're indicating to the Mac OS that you don't intend to copy or move the item but to create an alias. While you're holding down the modifier keys, you'll see a small curved arrow appear as part of the mouse pointer to indicate that you're creating an alias.

When you release the mouse button, the alias is created in the folder to which you've dragged the item. The alias will not have the word *alias* appended to its name because you are creating it in a location different from the original file. It will, however, have a small curved arrow as part of its icon.

 TIP Once an alias is created, you can rename it without affecting the link to the original. So if you make an alias of the file Letter to Dan and change the name of the alias to Letter to Sue, double-clicking the alias will still launch Letter to Dan.

Locate the Original

The Finder includes a command that makes it easy to locate the original file that an alias is pointing to. Select the alias and choose File ➤ Show Original in the Finder or press ⌘+R. The original item's parent folder will open, and the original item will appear on-screen in the front-most Finder window.

Select a New Original

Although you can select a new original for an alias at any time, the main reason for doing so is a *broken* alias. An alias can break—that is, it can no longer locate the original—for a variety of reasons: The original was deleted, the alias was moved to a network disk, the original was on a removable disk that's no longer available, or the privileges for a folder changed.

If an alias stops working, it's conceivable that you could fix it. Select the alias and choose File ➤ Show Info. In the Info window, click the Select New Original button.

(The button's label doesn't seem to strike the Apple engineers as a paradox, so that's its name. See Figure 4.7.) The Fix Alias dialog box then appears.

The Info window enables you to select a "new" original file for a broken alias.

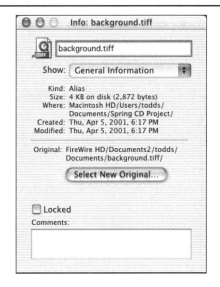

In the Fix Alias dialog box, locate the file that you want the alias to point to. Once you've selected that item, click the Choose button. The alias will now launch that new item (even if it's the *old* item that you've managed to track down) whenever it's double-clicked.

Working with Favorites

Mac OS X makes extensive use of *Favorites*. Favorites are quite simple. They're sort of aliases in disguise. Once you've defined a Favorite, you can then access it via the Go ➤ Favorites menu in the Finder, the Favorites button in Finder windows, and the Open dialog box in most Mac OS X native applications. You'll find that once you've set up your personal Favorites, it's much easier to move quickly to specific folders and items throughout Mac OS X.

Adding a Favorite in the Finder is easy. Select an item on the desktop or in a Finder window and then select the File ➤ Add to Favorites command (see Figure 4.8) or press ⌘+T.

FIGURE 4.8

*Adding a Favorite from
the Finder*

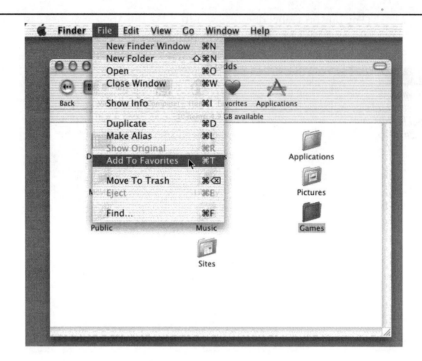

An alias to the selected item is created and automatically stored in the Favorites folder within your personal Library folder. You can then access that Favorite quickly in a number of ways. You can click the Favorites button in a Finder window's toolbar to see it directly. You can access it through an Open or Save dialog box, as discussed in Chapter 5. Or you can access it directly from the Finder by selecting Go ➢ Favorites and then selecting the individual Favorite from the menu that appears.

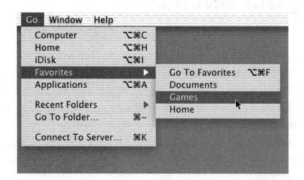

If the Favorite you select is a folder, that folder is opened in a Finder window. If the Favorite is an application, that application is launched. If the Favorite is a document (or, for instance, a URL file, which is technically a document), the associated application is launched and that document is loaded or otherwise accessed by the application. (Again in the case of a URL, you'd be taken directly to the associated Web site. See Chapter 11 for more on URL documents and accessing the Web.)

The easiest way to edit your Favorites is to open the Favorites folder by selecting Go ➤ Favorites ➤ Go to Favorites from the Finder's menu or clicking the Favorites button in a Finder window. Once there, you can copy aliases to the Favorites folder to add them as Favorites, or you can delete the aliases from that folder to remove them as Favorites.

Setting User Preferences

Another aspect of managing your personal workspace is setting preferences that affect it. The System Preferences application is, one could argue, somewhat poorly named because it offers options that affect both the entire system (including all users—to be set from an administrator's account) and only your personal workspace. We'll talk about that second category here.

To set the preferences in System Preferences, launch the application. The quickest way is to select System Preferences from the Apple menu. Or, most likely, a System Preferences tile is already on your Dock, waiting to be single-clicked. If you don't find it there, System Preferences can also be found in the main Applications folder. Once it's launched, you'll see the main System Preferences window (see Figure 4.9).

System Preferences work a little like control panels in past Mac OS versions. (They work much like the Control Panel in Microsoft Windows as well—perhaps even more so than earlier Mac OS control panels.) Each icon represents what Mac OS X calls a *pane*, which is used to change different settings. When you select a given pane's icon, the window changes to show that pane and allow you to make choices.

The only part of the window that doesn't change is the toolbar at the top, which includes the Show All icon as well as a small tray of icons that you can change. If you have a pane that you access more often than some other panes, you can drag its icon from the main window up to the toolbar. If there's room for that icon, it will be added. (If no room exists, you'll have to drag an icon out of the toolbar before you can add another.) You can also drag the icons around in the toolbar to rearrange them.

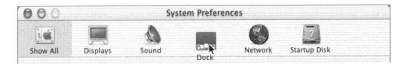

FIGURE 4.9

*The System
Preferences window*

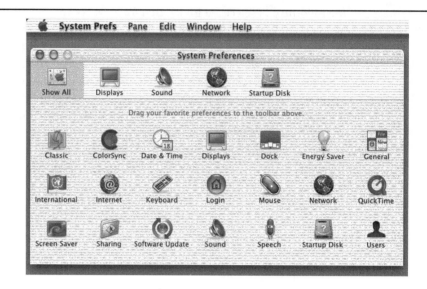

To remove an icon from the toolbar, just drag it out of the toolbar. When you release the mouse button, the icon will disappear in a puff of smoke. (Don't worry—it's still in the Show All list. It will simply be removed from the toolbar.)

Administrator Settings

Note that not every item allows you to edit the settings. In some cases, settings can be changed only by the root account. In those panes, you'll see a small padlock icon that indicates that you can't edit items in the window. The Preferences screens that are disabled for user editing are Date & Time, Energy Saver, Network, Sharing, Startup Disk, Users, and portions of the Login pane.

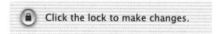

If you know the administrator's password or your account has administrator privileges, however, you can edit these items. Simply click the padlock icon and enter an administrator's account name and password. Then click OK. If Mac OS X recognizes the login as a valid administrator's account, you'll have the ability to edit those options. (System administrator settings will be covered in Chapter 7.)

User Settings

If you're logged into a regular (nonadminstrator) user account, you can still work in a number of System Preferences panes, and these preferences will affect only your personal workspace. Among the Mac OS Preferences panes you can control are Classic, ColorSync, Displays, Dock (discussed in Chapter 2), General, International, Internet, Keyboard, Login, Mouse, QuickTime, Screen Saver, Sound, and Speech. I will cover some of these panes in more depth in later chapters; however, I'll take a brief look at them here.

Classic

The Classic pane allows you to select the disk volume (from the Select A Startup Volume list) to be used for starting up the Classic Mac OS environment. (Mac OS X uses Classic to run older Macintosh applications. See Chapter 5 for details.) You can also determine whether or not Classic should be started up when you log in. If you choose to turn on "Start up Classic on login to this computer," the Classic environment will launch and operate in the background once you log in, leaving less of your system RAM available for Mac OS X native applications. The advantage of background operation is that you won't encounter any delays when starting up an application that requires Classic; the disadvantage of leaving Classic running in the background is that your entire Mac may run much more slowly when Classic is active, particularly if you don't have a great deal of RAM installed.

You can also Start, Restart, and Force Quit the Classic environment from within the Classic pane; these and the Advanced options are covered in more depth in Chapter 19.

ColorSync

The ColorSync pane enables you to create and manage ColorSync profiles for your various devices, including your monitor and printer. ColorSync is Apple's technology for ensuring that monitors, printers, proofers, and graphics applications all have a fixed idea of what a color is, so that a color on your screen, for instance, is the same as the final output on a printed document. I'll discuss ColorSync in much more detail in Chapter 14.

Displays

The Displays pane enables you to choose the resolution for the Mac's display. Using the Display tab in this pane (see Figure 4.10), you can choose your own resolution, color, and refresh-rate settings.

FIGURE 4.10

Changing your display's settings in the Display pane

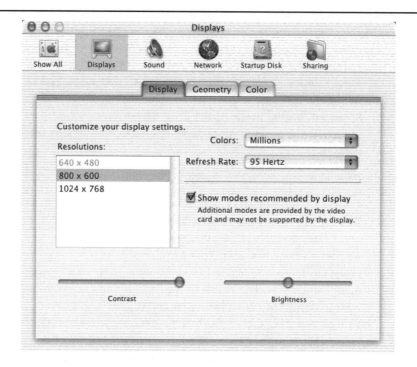

Before changing these settings, however, be sure you know what your monitor can handle. Here's a quick discussion:

Resolutions In the Resolutions scrolling list, you can select the resolution at which you'd like the screen displayed. Resolution is measured in pixels wide by pixels high, with a pixel representing a single dot, or *picture element*, on the screen. Switching to a larger resolution allows you to see more items on the screen at one time (often described as more *screen real estate*), but it makes each item—icons, text, etc.—appear smaller. Larger monitors are suited to larger resolutions (for instance, 20-inch monitors look good at 1024×768 or 1152×870), but you should choose a level that's comfortable for your personal viewing.

TIP Choosing a very high resolution may limit the number of colors you can choose in the Colors menu and lower the maximum refresh rate you can choose in the Refresh Rate menu. If you'd prefer to see more colors (for instance, you'd like to choose millions of colors, but you can't) or a higher refresh rate, try lowering your resolution.

Colors The Colors menu enables you to determine the overall color *palette* available to applications and the Mac OS. By this, I mean the number of *potential* colors available for displaying images on the screen. The more colors, the crisper and "truer" the images, especially with photographs and movies.

Refresh Rate The Refresh Rate menu enables you to choose the number of times per second that a CRT display is updated, or refreshed. The more often the display is refreshed, the clearer the overall screen image will appear. If your screen appears to flicker, you might do well to select a higher refresh rate, if one is supported. (Note that Refresh Rate is not an option if you have an LCD flat-panel display connected to your Mac.)

 WARNING Selecting an unsupported resolution and/or refresh rate for your monitor could potentially damage the monitor. For best results, leave the Show Modes Recommended by Display option turned on unless you're sure that an unrecommended option will work correctly.

If your display is an Apple-branded model (or you're using a Mac with a built-in display such as an iMac, iBook, or PowerBook), you may see other options in the Displays pane. At the bottom of the Display tab, you may see two sliders: a Contrast control and a Brightness control. You can use these sliders to change contrast and brightness for the monitor. (My general monitor advice: Bump the contrast all the way up to maximum, but slide the brightness back a bit from the maximum setting until things look good. A very high brightness setting can wear out your monitor over time.)

You may also see a Geometry tab, which you can select to change the exact position and shape of the image on your screen. Select one of the radio buttons, then use the on-screen buttons to change the height, width, pincushion, shape, and so on. If you mess things up and don't like the shape of your display's picture, click the Factory Defaults button.

 NOTE You may also see a Color tab, which is used for calibrating your monitor's Color-Sync profile. This process is discussed in Chapter 14.

Mac OS X can support two (or more) monitors connected to the same computer. If you have two Mac OS X–compatible video cards installed in your Mac and two monitors connected, on each monitor you'll see Display options where you can opt to change each individual screen's resolution, color, and refresh settings.

NOTE Some PowerBook G3 and all PowerBook G4 models can support dual monitors. If you connect a monitor to the PowerBook's external VGA port, you may be able to configure both displays separately, particularly with newer models. Older PowerBook G3 models only *mirror* output to a second monitor (e.g., for presentations), which doesn't require additional setup. (iMac DV and later iMac models can also mirror video output.)

If Mac OS X detects two or more compatible displays and display circuitry, you'll also see a new option: On the "main" screen (the one with the System Preferences window on it), there will be an Arrange tab in the Displays pane. Select that tab, and you'll see an interface that shows representations of both (or all) of your screens. By dragging the screens around, you can determine which will have the menu bar (making it the startup and main screen) and which screen will be on which "side," as far as the mouse pointer is concerned. Once you have the screens arranged properly, you should be able to move the mouse naturally from one screen to the other as though you were dealing with one very wide display.

 NOTE Are the screen representations on the Arrange tab different sizes? If so, the difference simply indicates that each monitor is running at a different resolution—for instance, one at 800×600 and one at 1024×768. If you can, switch them to the same resolution for best results (although this isn't mandatory).

General

The General pane enables you to choose some appearance and behavior options for Mac OS X's windows and menus. At the top of the panel, you can select Appearance. By default, the color choices are Blue and Graphite.

The Blue appearance settings cause scroll bars and buttons to appear blue (or aqua) in color, whereas the Graphite appearance tones that down to a more subtle gray. Graphite is deemed better for graphic artists and designers whose judgment of colors in photo, multimedia, or page-design programs may be affected by the additional color that the aqua scheme adds to windows and scroll bars. You can also choose a personalized Highlight color for how the selection area in menus and applications will look.

Finally, at the bottom of the General pane, you can select how scroll bars behave when you click them.

International

The International pane holds a number of options for determining how your Mac deals with languages, dates, times, and numbers. You can set the keyboard mapping from within this panel so that international keyboards (non–U.S. English keyboards) map keystrokes to the appropriate letters.

Unlike previous versions of the Mac OS, Mac OS X offers built-in support for multiple languages. (Early versions had to be localized for particular languages and regions.) Click the Language tab in the International panel, and you're given the opportunity to choose a preferred language for application menus and dialog boxes. For instance, native French speakers might choose to drag Français over English in the Languages list box so that applications that support both French and English display the French commands and text, but applications that don't support French show their English-language commands and text. Figure 4.11 shows an example where French is selected as the primary language.

 NOTE You may need to log out and log back in before changes to your language options take effect, especially to see changes in the Finder or System Preferences.

FIGURE 4.11

With French moved to the top of the Languages list box, many, but not all, commands and items are in French.

The Date, Time, and Numbers tabs can each be used to set preferences for how you'd like dates and times to be represented on-screen and in applications. Each of these tabs has a pop-up menu, where you can select a particular, predetermined region. This is the easiest way to switch to the generally accepted settings for your area of the world.

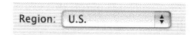

Once you've chosen a region, you can tweak the settings yourself, if desired. For instance, if you prefer a different month/day/year ordering, select the Date tab and make those changes. For different separators between hours and minutes, select the Time tab and change settings there.

Finally, the Keyboard Menu tab allows you to enable more than one keyboard layout or input method so that you can configure Mac OS X to work with your particular keyboard or nonstandard input device (such as a Dvorak keyboard layout). Place a check mark next to the items that you might want to use. A new menu item, called the Keyboard menu (but labeled only with the flag or icon of the current keyboard layout) will then appear as a permanent fixture on the Mac OS X menu bar. You will thus be able to switch between different keyboard layouts at any time.

For more detailed options on keyboard-layout behavior on the Keyboard Menu tab, click the Options button. Using the check boxes, you can determine which keyboard shortcut will switch the available keyboard layouts. You can also choose whether or not changing to a different keyboard layout will automatically change you to an international font layout.

Internet

The Internet settings are definitely something you can change, but I'll cover them in detail in Chapter 9. For now, know that the Internet pane is where you can store an e-mail address, a Web home page, and server information so that your Internet applications have a central location where they can find Internet-related settings. It's also a place to sign in or configure your iTools account, which is discussed in Chapter 11.

Keyboard

In the Keyboard pane, you can select some basic options for how your Mac responds when you press a key. Move the slider below Key Repeat Rate to determine how quickly a key will repeat once the repeat mode has kicked in. Move the slider below Delay Until Repeat to determine how long the Mac OS will wait while you hold down a key before it goes into repeat mode. Once a key starts repeating, the character you've pressed repeats on-screen without requiring you to lift your finger.

Login

Open the Login pane, and you'll find options on the Login Items tab that you can change. (The Login Window tab requires an administrator password.) Using the check boxes, you can determine whether or not each item should be hidden when it launches. (Items in the list will always launch unless they're removed, but you can opt to have them launch in the background, hidden from view, until you select them in the Dock.) These items can be applications or utilities (such as the CPU Monitor) that you like to be greeted with every time you log into your Mac, as shown in Figure 4.12.

 TIP You can also drag the items up and down the list to determine the order in which Login items load at login.

FIGURE 4.12

After adding some items to the Login Items tab, you can click their check boxes to hide them at login.

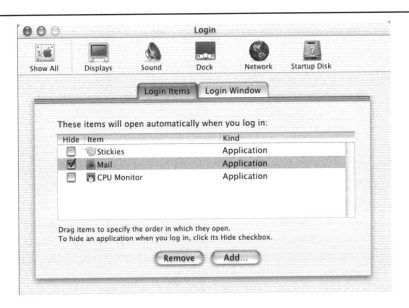

To add items that launch automatically when you log in, click the Add button. This displays an Open dialog box where you can locate and select applications that you'd like to have run at the beginning of your sessions. (You can also drag and drop applications or documents from Finder windows into this list, if desired.)

To remove an item from the list, select it and click Remove. Now that item won't launch when you sign into your account.

Mouse

Open the Mouse pane to change the way your mouse behaves. Two sliders appear: Tracking Speed and Double-Click Speed. Move the Tracking Speed slider to change how quickly your mouse moves across the screen. Move the Double-Click Speed slider to determine how much time can pass between the two clicks of a double-click and still have the Mac OS recognize it as such (instead of as two single clicks). You can use the small test area to try your double-clicking prowess.

QuickTime

The QuickTime pane enables you to set certain options concerning how movies are played in your Web browser (on the Plug-In tab), what connection speed QuickTime should report to distant QuickTime servers (on the Connection Speed tab), and what keys you have enabled to access secured QuickTime content (on the Media Keys tab). QuickTime settings are discussed in detail in Chapter 15.

Screen Saver

The Screen Saver pane enables you to set options for Mac OS X's built-in screen saver. In theory, a screen saver prevents a monitor from burning in a particular screen image that appears on the screen for too long. (You may have seen the effect on older ATM displays at your bank.) But modern CRT and LCD screens don't suffer from burn-in, so screen savers are really designed more for entertainment and, in the case of Mac OS X, for additional password security.

On the Screen Savers tab, select from the list the screen saver you want to use. The item "Custom Slide Show" is a special case—it will use images you place in your personal Photos folder (inside your home folder) to create a custom screen saver. Once you've selected a screen saver, you can click the Configure button to see any options for a particular screen-saver module, and you can click the Test button to see a module in action.

Select the Activation tab, and you'll see a slider that enables you to determine how much idle time should pass (without the keyboard or mouse being touched) before the screen saver starts. At the bottom of the Activation tab, you can turn on the "Use my user account password" item if you'd like to be prompted for your password whenever the Mac "awakes" from the screen saver (that is, whenever a key is pressed or the mouse is moved while the screen saver is displaying). This can be a convenient security measure to have in place; when you get up from your Mac, you can activate the screen saver (or allow it to activate automatically), and no one, ideally, will be able to access it until you're back with your password.

So how do you activate the screen saver? Aside from waiting the amount of time specified on the Activation tab, you can use a hot corner for the screen saver. Click the Hot Corners tab, then click to place a check box on one of the corners of the screen image. Now, whenever you move the mouse pointer to that corner of the screen (and leave it there for a second), the screen saver will launch into action immediately.

 TIP You can also click twice on a corner check box on the Hot Corners tab to place a minus sign in the check box. That means that moving the mouse to that corner will prevent the screen saver from kicking in.

Sound

Open the Sound pane to change the sound settings on your Mac. Here's what you can set (see Figure 4.13):

System Volume   Set the volume using the speaker-icon slider. Volume is increased as you move the slider to the right. Note also the Mute option, which you can turn on to mute the speaker volume.

Balance   You can use the left/right slider under the volume slider to change the balance between two speakers.

Alert Volume   The Sound pane has a separate control for the volume at which alerts (error or other attention-getting tones) play.

Alert Sound   From the scrolling list, choose the alert sound you'd like.

Speech

The Speech pane enables you to select a few options for the Text-to-Speech and Speech Recognition technologies. On the Text-to-Speech tab, you can select a voice that you'd like your Mac to use when it talks; Fred, Bruce, Kathy, and Victoria are the most humanlike, but the others are fun to listen to. Once you've selected a voice, you can choose the rate at which it speaks (certain speeds can sound more natural) using the Rate slider, and click the Play button to hear a sample. The Speech Recognition tab gets a bit more complex, so it's best left for Chapter 16, where Text-to-Speech is also discussed in more depth.

FIGURE 4.13

The Sound section of Mac OS Preferences lets you set the volume, balance, and alert sounds.

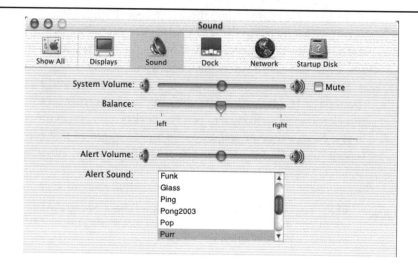

What's Next?

In this chapter, you saw a number of options associated with working in your own home folder and setting preferences that govern your personal workspace. In Chapter 5, you'll move on to working with documents and applications, including launching them, installing applications, and using some of the commands found in nearly all Mac OS X applications. You'll also see how to launch and work with applications that run in the Classic environment of Mac OS X.

CHAPTER <u>5</u>

Using Native and Classic Applications

I n Chapter 2, you saw the different items that the Mac OS uses to create an interface for applications; and in Chapter 3, you saw a special application, the Finder, that's used to manage your disks, folders, and files. Ultimately, though, the Mac OS and the Finder are both designed to help you get something done with your Mac, not just manage its files. You'll get those things done in *application* programs, which are computer programs that you apply toward some task or goal. Most often, you'll use applications to create, edit, and save documents.

In this chapter you'll see how to get started with applications and what the standard methods are for opening and saving documents to your disks. You'll learn some of the basic controls found in most *native* Mac OS X applications, including menus and commands that are common to all applications written specifically for Mac OS X. Later, you'll take a look at the Classic environment that enables you to run *Classic* Mac applications (those designed for Mac OS 9.1 and earlier versions), and you'll see the issues and trade-offs involved in using such applications.

Launching an Application or Document

Computer programs are designed to help you accomplish a task, whether it's creating a written document, tabulating figures, tracking items, or communicating with other people. That's why they're called *applications*—you're applying the program's tools toward a specific end result. In most cases you use an application to work with a document, which you can create, edit, open, and save. This document management is so fundamental to the operation of a computer that the operating system itself actually handles a lot of the work of opening, saving, printing, and so forth.

Applications need to be *launched* before you can work with them. When you launch an application, you're telling the Mac OS that you want to work with that application's tools. The Mac OS responds by creating a portion of system memory for the application and loading portions of that application from the hard disk into system memory. The application then begins running, often showing you a "splash screen" that tells you the application's version number and gives credit to the programmers; it then, for native Mac OS X applications, places that application's menu commands on the menu bar, representing the *Application menu*:

There are two basic ways to launch an application: directly or by launching an associated document. Launching a document is more convenient if you're interested in working with that particular document. You'll launch an application directly if you want to create a new document or if the application isn't designed to work with documents.

Launch an Application Directly

If you'd like to launch an application directly, you'll generally do that in one of three ways:

Launch the application's icon.   In a Finder window or on the desktop, locate the application's icon and double-click it with the mouse. You can also select the icon and choose File ➢ Open or press ⌘+O.

Launch an application's alias.   If you come across an alias to the application on the desktop or in a Finder window, you can double-click that alias, or you can select the alias and choose File ➢ Open or press ⌘+O.

Select the application via an interface shortcut: the Dock, the Finder's Go menu, or the Apple menu.   If you have the application on the Dock, or if it's available in the Go menu or in the Go ➢ Favorites submenu, you can choose it from one of those places to launch it quickly. You can also relaunch recently used applications, using the Apple menu's Recent Items menu.

In most cases any of these methods should result in the application launching and appearing on your screen. If you launch an alias, you may run into trouble if the alias can't locate the original application (see Chapter 4). Also, if you're running low on memory, you may run into errors or other trouble when attempting to launch an application.

 NOTE   If you attempt to launch an application that's already running, you will most likely be switched to that application. Very few applications will open more than one *instance* of themselves.

Launch a Document

If you have a particular document you'd like to work with, you can launch the document itself, and its associated application will launch along with it. There are three basic ways to do that:

Double-click the document or an alias to the document.   This will launch the document and the application that the Mac OS believes to be associated with that document type. It won't always launch the correct application (or at least the application you're wanting to launch), but you can change that behavior as detailed in the next section, "Edit a Document Association."

Select the document from the Go or Recent Items menu.   If the document is listed in the Go ➤ Favorites menu, you can select it to launch the document and its associated application. If the document has been used recently, it may also appear on the Recent Items menu in the Apple menu, where you can select it to launch it again.

Drop the document icon on an application icon or tile.   You can drag a document icon to an application icon (or an application's tile in the Dock) to launch it. Only certain applications can accept dragged documents; when you hover over the application icon with the document icon, you should see the application icon become highlighted (see Figure 5.1). If it does, then the application will accept the dragged document and attempt to display it. If the application does not become highlighted, then it can't open that document (or at least it doesn't recognize it as a document that it can open).

The application will become high-lighted to signify that it can accept the dragged-and-dropped document.

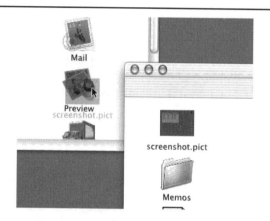

Edit a Document Association

Sometimes a document won't be associated with the correct application, or, in some cases, it won't be associated with any application at all. If that's the case, you can manually associate that document with an application. That will allow you to open the document with the selected application in the future.

You set a document association using the Info window in the Finder. Select the document in the Finder and choose File ➤ Show Info or press ⌘+I. The Info window appears. Select Application from the Show pop-up menu, as shown in Figure 5.2.

Managing Multiple Applications

You've already seen that Mac OS X is a powerful operating system that allows you to *multitask,* or run multiple applications, in a very efficient way. The manifestation of that multitasking is the Dock, where you can switch between running applications.

If you've launched one application and you're ready to launch another, you can do so just as you did the first. Switch to the Finder (click on the desktop background or the Finder's tile in the Dock), and double-click a second application or drag and drop a document onto a second application. You can also double-click another document to launch its associated application, or you can select another application in the Dock, Go menu, or Recent Items menu.

Once you have multiple applications running, you can use the Dock to switch between them, as discussed in Chapter 2. You can also press ⌘+Tab and ⌘+Shift+Tab to cycle forward and backward, respectively, through all running applications.

You can run as many applications as your Mac's system memory will allow. Each application requires a certain minimum amount of memory (determined by the application itself) to be active, so each application takes away from the total available system memory. Once the Mac OS reaches a certain limit, you won't be able to launch additional applications.

Before your Mac refuses to run more applications, though, it will probably already have reached a performance limit. Because Mac OS X makes extensive use of *virtual memory* (a scheme that allows the hard disk to be used as a temporary memory-swapping location), the more applications you have open, the more the Mac OS will have to access the hard disk. The hard disk is much slower than RAM, so those accesses tend to bog down the system, especially as you switch between applications.

If you notice a slowdown and you have quite a few applications open, try quitting one or two of them to see if your Mac speeds up. If quitting the applications speeds things up—but makes it tougher for you to get your work done—then your Macintosh may be a prime candidate for a RAM upgrade.

FIGURE 5.2

The Info window can be used to associate a document with a particular application.

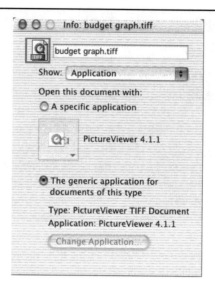

To associate the document with an application, you can choose either a specific application (the first radio button) or the default application for this file type (the second radio button). If you select the "specific application" radio button, you can then click the icon menu to select a new application to associate with this document.

If the application you want to associate with this document doesn't appear on the menu, you can select Add Application from the menu. Now you'll see the Add Application dialog box (which acts just like a standard Open dialog box), allowing you to locate the application you'd like to use. When you find it, highlight that application in the dialog box and click Add. (If you can't highlight the application you want to use, select All Applications from the Show menu at the top of the dialog box.)

When the Add Application dialog box closes, you're returned to the Info window; there you'll see that the chosen application is associated with this document. Close the Info window. Now, double-clicking that document will launch it using the application you've selected.

Global Document Settings

In many cases you may decide that you want a particular type of document to be launched by a particular default application. For instance, the Mac OS launches Rich Text Format (RTF) documents using TextEdit by default. You may, however, prefer to use a word processing application such as AppleWorks to launch your RTF documents. If that's the case, changing the association for each individual document would be tedious.

Fortunately, you don't have to do that. You can change the way particular document types are launched, using the Info window. Here's how:

1. Select a document that is of the type you'd like to reassociate. For instance, if you want all RTF documents to launch in AppleWorks instead of TextEdit, select an RTF document.

2. With the document highlighted, choose File ➤ Show Info from the Finder menu or press ⌘+I. The Info window appears.

3. Select Application from the Show menu.

4. Select the radio button next to "The generic application for documents of this type."

5. At the bottom of the Info window, click the Change Application button.

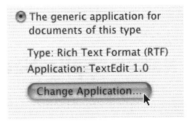

6. The Choose Application dialog box appears. Locate the application that you'd like to associate with the selected document type and select it. If you can't select the application (because it's dimmed in the window), choose All Applications from the Show menu at the top of the Choose Applications dialog box. If you're viewing All Applications, the Choose Applications dialog box lets you know

whether the Mac OS believes that the selected document type can or cannot be handled.

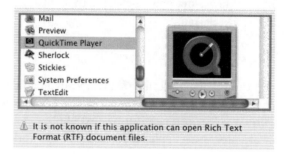

⚠ It is not known if this application can open Rich Text Format (RTF) document files.

7. Once you've highlighted the application you want to use, click Choose. That application is now the default application for the selected type of document.

Remember that only documents that are set to the Generic Application setting will respond to this change; others that have been manually set to open in a specific application will still open in that other application. Still, this is a quick and easy way to change the behavior of most documents of a certain type if you'd like to begin using a different default application.

NOTE One particular problem you may run into are documents that are associated with Classic applications when a native Mac OS X application might be a better choice. If you make a habit of changing the generic application for documents to native applications (for instance, changing image file associations to Preview or another native application), over time Mac OS X will learn more and more to launch native applications.

Documents in Native Applications

Once you have your applications launched, you're ready to create and edit documents. If you've already launched a document, you can probably jump right in and begin using the application's tools. If you simply launched the application, you may need to start a new document or open an existing document to begin editing it. And once you've gotten some work done, you'll want to save your document to the disk in order to preserve your hard work.

Some applications, when launched directly, will create a new document. If a new document is what you wanted, you can begin working in it—typing, drawing with the mouse, selecting items, or doing whatever that application is designed to do. (As noted in the later section "Save a Changed Document," it's a good idea to save a document soon after you begin working in it.) If you encounter an application that doesn't automatically create a document, look for a File ➤ New or File ➤ New Document command. (In most applications you can also press ⌘+N to create a new document.)

In Mac OS X, there are two distinct types of Open and Save dialog boxes that you'll encounter, since the Mac OS supports diverse types of applications. The "native" dialog boxes are those that appear when you're working with applications that run directly on top of Mac OS X—the Carbon and Cocoa applications. The other type of dialog box is that which you'll encounter when working with Classic applications; I'll cover that type later in the section "Running Classic Mac Applications."

Open an Existing Document

If you have an application in which you'd like to edit an existing document, you'll use the application's Open command. In nearly all applications, that's File ➤ Open. (You can also press ⌘+O in most applications.) Now, what you see next depends on the type of application you're using.

NOTE If you're familiar with Mac OS 9.1 or earlier, you might be interested to know that Mac OS X will allow you to switch to a different application even if an Open dialog box is currently on the screen. In earlier Mac OS versions, Open dialog boxes are often (although not always) *modal*, requiring you to finish using the box before you can access other applications. In Mac OS X, however, you can switch to a different application, then switch back to finish working with the Open dialog box, if desired.

If your Open dialog box looks similar to Figure 5.3, then your application is using the native Mac OS X–style dialog boxes. These dialog boxes tend to be a bit simpler to use, especially if you're a fan of the Finder's Columns view.

At the very top of the Open dialog box, you'll see one or two pop-up menus, depending on the application. The Show menu (which doesn't always appear) is used to restrict the *types* of files that are presented in the dialog box; an application can optionally enable you to view only the documents that work with that application, for instance, helping you to cut down the clutter a bit.

The From menu is a quick navigation tool for moving directly to recent and Favorite folders. If you've stored a particular folder as a Favorite or if you've recently visited another folder in an Open dialog box (or a Finder window), you'll see that folder listed here so that you can return quickly to it.

FIGURE 5.3

The Mac OS X Open
dialog box

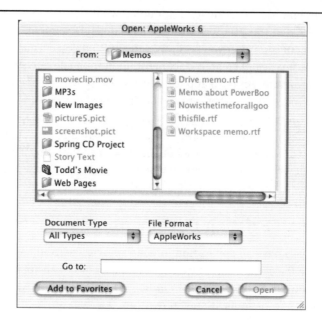

The rest of the dialog box works almost exactly like the Finder's Columns view. In the left-most column, select a folder to view. That folder's listing appears in the next column to the right, where you can select another folder or an item. Keep selecting folders until you've found the item you want to open, and then click Open.

 TIP You can enter a path statement, such as **/users/todds/** or **~/documents**, in the Go To entry box to move quickly to a particular folder. The tilde (~) symbol is a shortcut for your home folder.

Below the Go To entry box, you'll find an area where applications will add their own individual options to the dialog box, allowing you to make choices specific to that application. You'll find pop-up menus, check boxes, and other controls here, depending on the application.

At the bottom of the window, you'll find an Add to Favorites button, which you can use to add a selected item to your Favorites folder. Otherwise, you can click Open to open the selected document or Cancel if you want to dismiss the dialog box without opening a file.

Save a Changed Document

Whether you've created a new document or you're editing an existing one, you should save that document almost immediately after making any changes, then continue to save often. Saving a document writes the content of that document to the hard disk or other disk that you're using for storage. This stores the document in a permanent state for future use. Saving regularly also provides security in case of a system failure or application crash.

With Mac OS X, you'll see two different types of Save dialog boxes, depending on how the application has been designed. In most cases you'll see a dialog sheet—a Save dialog box that's connected to the document you're working on. In other applications, you'll see a more typical-looking dialog box that's similar to the Open dialog box. Most of the time, these dialog boxes will be accessed by selecting File ➢ Save or File ➢ Save As from the application's menu bar.

 TIP You can also press ⌘+S in most applications to invoke the Save command. Some applications enable Shift+⌘+S for the Save As command.

Mac OS X's native Save dialog box is a slightly different animal from the Open dialog boxes we've seen. The first time you invoke the Save command, you'll see this special Save dialog box, actually called a *dialog sheet.* Instead of popping up like any of the others we've seen so far, this one "opens up" in an animated way from the window's title bar, as shown in Figure 5.4.

FIGURE 5.4

Saving with the Mac OS X Save dialog sheet

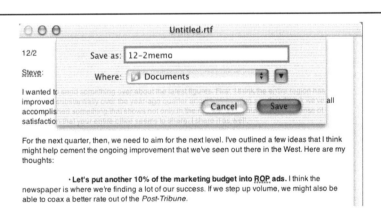

There's actually a good reason for this: It makes it absolutely clear which window's contents you're about to save. Simply enter a document name (filename) and choose a destination folder from the Where menu.

You don't see the destination folder you want to use? In that case, click the down-arrow button. That reveals the rest of the dialog box, which you'll notice is similar to the Mac OS X Open dialog box. You can use the columns to navigate to the destination folder (see Figure 5.5).

 TIP The Save dialog sheet enables you to create a new subfolder, if you like, for storing this document. Select the folder (for instance, Documents) where you'd like to create the new subfolder. Now, click New Folder. In the small dialog box, enter a name for the folder and click Create. Now that folder is created and automatically opened so that you can save your document in it.

Enter a filename in the Save As entry box. The filename may contain up to 256 characters and should not, in most cases, include a three-letter extension code (instead, the application you're using will likely add this on its own). In general, it's best not to begin filenames with nontext characters, and you should definitely avoid starting a filename with a period (.) or a hyphen (-). You may use a hyphen in the middle of a name, and, in fact, Mac OS X will automatically change any slashes (/) to hyphens if you try to type them. Slashes are strictly disallowed because they're used to indicate folders in path statements.

FIGURE 5.5

Once you've clicked the down-arrow button, the full, columnar dialog sheet is revealed.

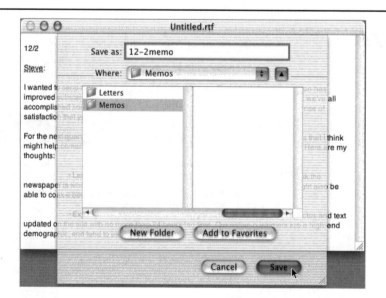

The Mac OS X Basics

 NOTE Although a filename can be up to 256 characters, it's best to limit the number to 31 if you'll be working with the file in both Mac OS X and Mac OS 9.1, or if you intend to send the file to someone who uses an older Mac version. Older Mac versions (and some Classic applications) are limited to working with filenames of 31 characters or less. And besides, shorter filenames are usually easier to see in Finder windows.

Once you've entered a filename, press Return or click the Save button. Your document will be saved. If you decide not to save, click the Cancel button.

Save Again

After you've saved your document for the first time, you're still not done with the Save command. Instead, you should save your work at regular intervals while you're working in the application. As you're typing, editing, drawing, or otherwise working with a document, you'll want to save any changes you've made so that, in case of an application crash or a computer failure, you'll still have all your recent changes.

To save as you work, simply select File ➤ Save or press ⌘+S. After you've named the file for the first time, this command no longer brings up the Save dialog box. Instead, it simply saves the changes you've made to the file, updating it to the current state of the edited document.

Save As

If you're working in a named document and you'd like to save it using a different name and/or save it to a different folder or disk, you'll choose the File ➤ Save As command instead of the Save command. This instructs the application to display the Save dialog box, even though you've already given the file a name. Now you can select a new name and/or a new folder in which to store the document. When you've named it and pressed Return, the new copy is saved.

Note that using the Save As command does two things. First, any changes you've made since you last saved the original document will not appear in the original document, only in the new copy. For instance, if you saved a document called Letter, typed the words *Dear Mom*, immediately chose the Save As command, and saved a new document called "Mom Letter," then the words *Dear Mom* would show up only in the document "Mom Letter."

Second, the Save As command leaves the *newly named* document open in the application for editing, not the previous document you were working in. When you Save As, the original document you were working in is still available on the disk, but you're no longer editing it. Instead, you're editing the copy you just created.

Save by Closing

If you've been working in a document that either has never been saved or has changes that haven't been saved, you'll see a small dot in the window's Close button when you mouse up to it to attempt to close the document window. This is one indicator that you have changes that need to be saved.

Clicking the Close button (or pressing ⌘+W to close the window) will cause a dialog sheet to appear (again, animated from "under" the menu bar), asking if you want to go ahead and save changes. If you do, click Save.

Now, if you've previously saved the document, any changes will be saved automatically and the document window will close. If the document is still untitled, the Save dialog sheet will appear, enabling you to name the document and determine where it will be stored.

Document Window Layering

Mac OS X has an intriguingly deviant way of working with document windows, particular for users familiar with Mac OS 9.1 and earlier. Imagine this scenario: You're working in TextEdit, writing a report, and you decide to switch to Internet Explorer to view a Web site. (In our scenario, Internet Explorer is already running, and it has multiple windows open.)

If you switch to Internet Explorer by selecting its tile in the Dock, all of the Internet Explorer windows come to the foreground, most likely obscuring your TextEdit document window in the background. (The TextEdit document window doesn't disappear, minimize, or hide, but you probably can't see it.)

TIP Actually, you can cause the foreground application to hide when you select another application's tile in the Dock: Hold down the Option key while clicking the Dock tile.

But besides clicking the Internet Explorer tile in the Dock, there's another way to bring an Internet Explorer window forward: clicking part of that window in the background. If you can see one of IE's windows behind your TextEdit document window, and you click it, that IE window will come to the foreground and Internet Explorer's menus will take over the menu bar.

Interestingly, however, *only* that clicked IE window will appear on top of the TextEdit window—the other open IE windows will remain in the background. This is what's odd about window behavior in Mac OS X. In earlier Mac OS versions, clicking one document window of a background application brings all of that application's windows to the foreground, just as selecting an application's tile in the Dock does in Mac OS X.

So what do you do? The behavior isn't particularly good or bad; rather, it's just something to get used to, particular for old Mac hands. If you need to see all document windows for a given application (or some buried document window that you can't manage to click in the background), then select the application's tile in the Dock.

Working with Native Applications

You've already seen how to launch applications and how to save and load documents within your applications. Now let's move on to some standard features you're likely to encounter in applications written specifically for Mac OS X. These applications use special APIs, or *application programming interfaces*, that are built into the Mac OS. Because of that, you can be reasonably assured that all Mac OS X applications will use these dialog boxes, or very similar controls with a minimum of alterations.

What am I talking about? Specifically, the special commands that appear in the Application menu, along with the Print, Page Setup, Colors, Font, and Spelling dialog boxes and palettes, are all standard for Mac OS X applications, so you'll encounter them often, particularly in native applications written specifically for Mac OS X.

The Application Menu

As discussed in Chapter 2 and elsewhere in this book, every application has its own Application menu that appears on the left side of the menu bar (just to the right of the Apple menu) at the top of the screen. The name or icon of the menu changes based on the application that's currently active on-screen. In each Application menu you'll find some commands that are specific to that application, including the About command, Services menu, Hide/Show commands (discussed in Chapter 2), and Quit command.

 NOTE Because the Application menu changes for each application, you'll notice that whenever I tell you to access a command in the Application menu, it will be in the form *Application menu ➤ command*. In those references, *Application menu* is simply a placeholder for whatever the current application's Application menu is named.

About Command

The Application menu ➤ About command is present in all applications. It's used to tell you something about the application, generally by showing you a splash screen. On this screen you'll see the name of the application, the version number, and usually some information about the programmers (or company) who created the application. Most About windows have a Close button that you can click; in some cases, the About window may be a dialog box that includes an OK button that you can click when you've finished learning about the application.

Services Menu

In the Application menu of most programs you launch (including the Finder), you'll find a Services menu. This special menu is designed to enable you to access the commands of other applications from within the current application. The idea with the Services menu is that you're feeding data from the current application to another application for processing. So you usually have to select or highlight something in the current application before the commands in the Services menu will become active.

For instance, by default you can access commands from the TextEdit application via the Services menu of almost any other Mac OS X application. If you highlight some text and choose Application ➤ Services ➤ TextEdit ➤ Open Selection, the selected text will then be opened in TextEdit.

Other applications, when installed, can add items to the Services menu, which then makes that application's "services" available system-wide. Just remember that you usually need to highlight or choose a compatible item in the current application, such as an image or a selection of text, before a command in the Services menu will become activated.

Hide and Show Commands

As discussed in Chapter 2, the Application menu is also where you'll find the Hide Application, Hide Others, and Show All commands. The Hide Application command can be used to hide all of an application's windows, the Hide Others command will hide all *other* applications' windows, and the Show All command will display every open window of every open application.

Quit Command

To quit the current application, select Application menu ➢ Quit. Most applications will display dialog boxes if you have any unsaved changes in open documents. Then those documents will be closed, and the application will terminate, handing its portion of memory back to the Mac OS.

Page Setup and Print

Before you print for the first time in any Mac OS X application (or any time you need to change some basic settings), you should open the Page Setup dialog sheet. Select File ➢ Page Setup to see this standard dialog sheet, which offers a few basic options (see Figure 5.6).

At the top of the Page Setup dialog sheet, you'll see the Settings menu, where you can choose Page Attributes to see the basic options for a page or choose Summary to see a summary of your current selections.

FIGURE 5.6

The Page Setup dialog sheet

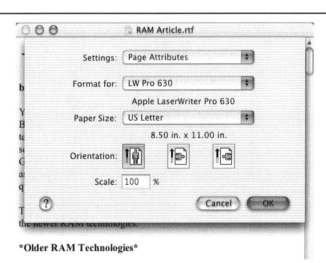

In the Format For menu, select the printer whose options you want to change. All printers currently installed via the Print Center (see Chapter 13) are available in this menu.

If you've selected Page Attributes in the Settings menu and you've chosen a printer in the Format For menu, you can now select, from the Paper Size menu, the type of paper you'll be printing to. Then click the button that represents the orientation you'd like the printer to use when printing to the paper. Finally, you can enter a percentage at which you'd like the page to be printed—for instance, entering **90** results in the page being scaled and printed at 90 percent of its actual size.

Once you've left the Page Setup dialog sheet (by clicking OK), you can head to the Print dialog sheet to actually print the document. With the document active on your screen, select File ➢ Print from the application's menu. That brings up the Print dialog sheet.

From the Printer menu at the top of the dialog sheet, you can choose the printer you'd like to use. Once you've made that selection, the dialog sheet may reconfigure itself slightly for that printer; in most cases, what changes are the options available in the unlabeled pop-up menu, which by default shows Copies & Pages, as shown in Figure 5.7.

For basic printing, simply enter the number of copies you'd like to print, your decision about collating those copies, and the range of pages within your document that you'd like to print. If desired, you can pull down the Options menu (it doesn't have a label, but it's the menu that defaults to Copies & Pages) to see other options for your particular printer. For instance, depending on the printer model, you may be able to choose different quality levels, different graphics printing options, or the option to print more than one document page per sheet of paper.

*The standard
Mac OS X Print
dialog sheet*

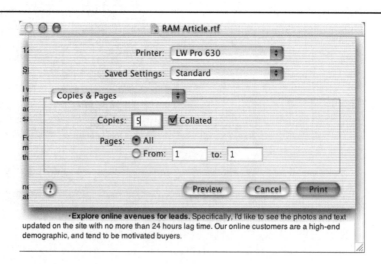

Once you've set all the options you care to set, you can click the Preview button to see a full-screen representation of how the printed output will look. Or just click the Print button to send the document to the printer and begin the printing process.

 NOTE Printing is discussed in much more detail in Chapters 13 and 14, including information on setting up printers and installing driver software. Chapter 13 also takes a closer look at the options in the Print dialog sheet.

The Colors Palette

Many applications will call upon you, at some point, to choose colors for your documents, so the Mac OS provides a standard Colors palette that you'll use for choosing. Actually, "Colors palette" has two meanings: Not only does the Colors window enable you to choose from a "palette" of color choices, it's also officially a floating *palette window*, which will appear over other windows in the application (see Figure 5.8).

Most of the time, you'll bring up the palette by selecting a Colors or Show Colors menu command; in text editors, for instance, it'll be under Format ➢ Fonts ➢ Colors. Obviously, fonts aren't the only elements that can be colorful, so you'll find the Colors palette popping up fairly frequently. It's fairly easy to use, although it offers some interesting and complex options.

FIGURE 5.8

The Colors palette, showing the color wheel tool

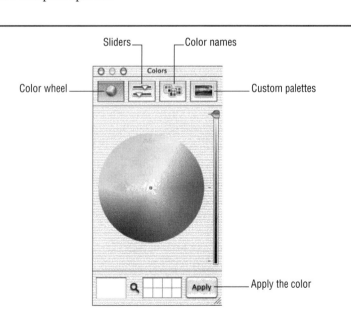

In essence, the Colors palette is simple: You pick a color and click Apply to apply it to the selection in your application. What's a bit more complicated is how you pick the colors. First, you select the type of controls you'd like to use:

Color wheel   The color wheel allows you to pick a color by simply clicking on it with the mouse. Once the color is selected, you can use the slider control on the right side of the window to darken or lighten the color.

Sliders   Click the Sliders button and you're shown a second row of buttons, representing the different types of approaches you can use for selecting a color. Shown, from left to right, are the grayscale, RGB (red-green-blue), CMYK (cyan-magenta-yellow-black), and HSB (hue-saturation-brightness) controls.

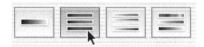

Color names   In this one, you can select exact colors by their name or other label. By default you can access system colors and "Apple" colors, but you can also customize the name by pulling down the List menu and choosing Open. That makes it possible to add other lists (for instance, Pantone colors) that are appropriate for your project. (You'll likely find that professional graphics applications and utilities offer lists that are compatible with the Colors palette.)

Custom palettes   By default, this button leads to a Spectrum tool, which simply allows you to select a color using the mouse. Other palettes can be loaded into the control, however, by selecting the Palette menu and choosing the New from File option. Once loaded, you can use a custom palette created for your project, for Web development, and so on.

So, once you've decided *how* you're going to select the color, the next step is to select the item in your document to which you want to add the color (if it isn't already selected) and click the Apply button. Then, if you're done with the palette, you can click its Close button.

   TIP   At the bottom-left corner of the Colors palette is a small box where your selected color appears. You can drag that color to one of the smaller eight boxes to save the color as a favorite color. Later you can quickly click one of those colors and then Apply. It's a handy way to store your favorite colors for quick access while you're working.

The Font Panel

Many document-centric applications also include the Font panel, which enables you to preview and fine-tune your selection of fonts in the document. You'll usually find the panel under Format ➢ Fonts ➢ Font Panel, or a similar command. This panel is shown in Figure 5.9.

 NOTE You won't see the full Font panel shown in Figure 5.9 unless you first drag the small resize box at the bottom-right corner of the Font panel. By default, you're shown a smaller version of the panel that fits better on low-resolution displays.

Changes to your selected font are made on the fly in your document windows. Select a new family, typeface, or size, and you'll immediately see it reflected in any highlighted text on your document page.

Choosing a Font

Choosing a font is actually fairly simple. Begin by selecting a collection (you'll likely choose All Fonts unless you've created collections in the past), then choose a font family. That will cause a list of typefaces to appear, which you can choose from. After selecting the typeface, you can choose the point size of the font, or you can enter a size in the small entry box that's above the scrolling list of sizes.

So what are all these things? The word *collections* is a Mac OS X term. Collections allow you to collect different fonts in different arrangements, making them easy to manage.

FIGURE 5.9

The Font panel gives you a standard window for choosing fonts.

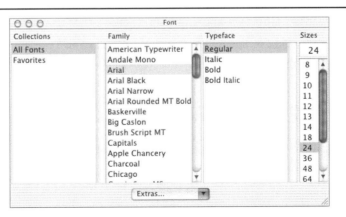

The *font family* is a group of typefaces with the same basic design—for instance, Helvetica or Times. The *typefaces* are variations on the font family theme—for instance, Helvetica Oblique (italic) or Helvetica Bold Oblique (bold italic).

After you've selected the font you want to use, you can select Add to Favorites from the small menu at the bottom of the panel, if desired, or simply click the panel's Close button. That will close the window, and you can get back to editing.

 NOTE Fonts and font technology are discussed in more detail in Chapter 14.

Using Favorite Fonts

If you've been adding fonts to your Favorites collection by choosing Add to Favorites from the Extras menu in the Font panel, you can access those favorites by selecting the Favorites collection in the Collections column of the Fonts panel. Now you'll see a list of your favorite fonts, enabling you to select them quickly.

Check Spelling

The spelling tools are also common across many Mac OS X applications, allowing the most basic programs to include a spell-checking feature, if desired. This is also handy because whenever an application uses the built-in Spelling dialog box, you'll have access to your personal dictionary, which you may have already trained to understand the spelling of new words.

In applications that support the Spelling dialog box, you'll have three special commands in the Edit menu:

- Edit ➢ Spelling ➢ Spelling opens the Spelling dialog box.

- Edit ➢ Spelling ➢ Check Spelling as You Type, if turned on, causes misspelled words to appear in the document window with a red underline. This can be handy for helping you notice immediately and at-a-glance if you've misspelled something.

- The Edit ➢ Spelling ➢ Check Spelling command is useful only if you don't have the As You Type option turned on. In that case, choosing Check Spelling will cause the next misspelled word (after the insertion point) in the document to be highlighted. The misspelled word won't *stay* highlighted once you resume typing. (This option is really designed for people who are annoyed by the colorful underlining created by the Check Spelling as You Type option.)

Of course, just the highlighting of misspelled words may not help, which is why the Mac OS offers the Spelling dialog box. If you don't know how to spell a word, you can consult the dialog box. Select Edit ➤ Spelling ➤ Spelling, and the Spelling dialog box appears (see Figure 5.10).

FIGURE 5.10

*The Spelling
dialog box*

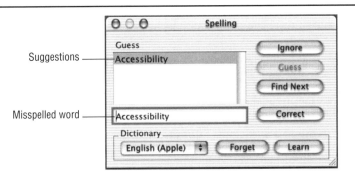

In the Spelling dialog box, click the Find Next button to find the first word that the application has noted as misspelled. The panel offers its guesses for the word's actual spelling in the Guess scrolling list. If you see the correct spelling, select it in the list and click the Correct button.

You can also correct the word yourself by editing the misspelled word in the entry box just below the Guess list. Then click the Correct button to change the spelling in your document.

Once you've corrected this word, or if you simply intend to ignore it, click Find Next again. The Spelling panel will move on to the next word. When no more words are found, the Spelling panel can't find any more words that it believes are misspelled.

At the bottom of the panel, you'll find the dictionary controls. In the pop-up menu, you can select from the different languages and language dialect dictionaries, if you have more than one installed on your Mac. The Forget and Learn buttons are used to add words to, or remove them from, the dictionary.

If, while spell-checking, the Spelling panel comes across a word that you know is correctly spelled, click the Learn button. (For instance, the dictionary doesn't know the word *iMac* even if you've typed it correctly.) Clicking the Learn button adds that word to the dictionary.

If you add a word that actually is not spelled correctly—or if you notice that the Spelling panel seems to pass over an incorrectly spelled word—you can do something about that. In the Spelling panel, enter the word in the entry box below the Guess menu. Now, click the Forget button. That particular word will be "forgotten" by the dictionary and, in the future, will be flagged with a red underline when it's spell-checked.

Running Classic Mac Applications

As we discussed in Chapter 1, Mac OS X is a completely new Mac OS built on a different foundation from Mac OS 9.1 and earlier versions. Although Mac OS X is designed to run best with applications written specifically for it (the native applications), it offers a compatibility mode that allows it to run some applications designed for Mac OS 9.1 and earlier versions.

In fact, Mac OS X is capable of running three different types of applications. (Actually, a fourth type, Java applications, works similarly to hybrid applications, but few are available for Mac OS X at the time of writing.) Here are the types:

Native applications   A native Mac OS X application, also called a Cocoa application, runs directly within the Mac OS X environment. When you double-click the application, Mac OS X creates a memory partition for it, loads its menu bar, and presents you with the application.

Hybrid applications   These applications, also called Carbon applications, are designed to run either in Mac OS 9.*x* or Mac OS X. These applications run the same way as native Mac OS X applications, except that they can also run within the Classic environment. And you'll notice that these applications can behave a bit differently than Cocoa applications, sometimes, for instance, displaying a slightly different Save dialog box instead of a Save sheet that's attached to the document's toolbar.

Classic applications   Classic applications are those designed exclusively to run in Mac OS 9.1. (Such an application may have been written initially for an older version of the Mac OS, but it needs to be fully compatible with Mac OS 9.1 to work in the Classic environment.) Although Classic applications appear to run from within Mac OS X, the truth is that an entire Mac OS 9.1 environment—the Classic environment—is launched first, in its own Mac OS X process, and then the Classic application launches within the Classic environment. Classic applications are easy to spot, because they use different menu fonts, dialog boxes, and window controls that are reminiscent of earlier Mac OS versions.

Although native applications are the best to choose in terms of performance and reliability, hybrid applications also run efficiently and productively within the Mac OS X environment. They also have the advantage of being easier for developers to create, since they can be built for both the Mac OS 9.1 and Mac OS X environments simultaneously.

Classic applications are less efficient than the other two types, in that they don't take full advantage of Mac OS X. The Classic environment also requires quite a bit of RAM (after all, an entire instance of Mac OS 9.1 is launched along with the Classic application), and the Classic environment can be responsible for system-wide slowdowns. Because of that, I recommend that you work with native Mac OS X applications whenever possible. When it's not possible, though, Mac OS X can launch Classic applications in two ways: You either double-click the Classic application to load the Classic environment and the application, or you launch Classic first via System Preferences and then launch the Classic applications at your leisure.

 TIP Because Carbon applications can, by definition, run in both Mac OS 9.1 and Mac OS X, you have the option from within Mac OS X to launch a Carbon application in either the native environment or the Classic environment. To access this option, select a Carbon application in a Finder window and use the File ➢ Show Info command. In the Info window, note that on the General Information screen there's an option, Open in the Classic Environment, that you can turn on by clicking to place a check mark. Once turned on, this application will run as though it were a Classic application the next time it's launched.

The Classic Environment

You can launch the Classic environment in one of two ways. The first way is to simply launch a Classic application, following any of the steps discussed earlier in the section "Launching an Application or Document." When a Classic application is launched, the Mac OS automatically loads the Classic environment. In essence, the Mac OS is loading a "transparent" version of Mac OS 9.1. Instead of switching between Mac OS 9.1 and Mac OS X, you'll continue to do all your work within Mac OS X. The transparent Mac OS 9.1 code, however, sits in the background and makes it possible for the Classic application to run correctly.

When a Classic application is first launched, you'll need to wait for a minute or two while the transparent Mac OS 9.1 code is launched. The indication of this process is a small window and a progress bar, which shows you the Mac OS 9 transparent environment being launched (see Figure 5.11).

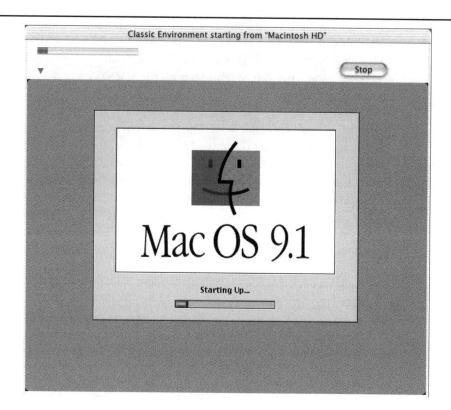

The Classic window includes a disclosure triangle, which you can click to reveal the startup screen for Mac OS 9.1. You can also click the Stop button in the window to stop the launching of the Classic environment.

The other way to launch the Classic environment is from within the Classic pane of the System Preferences application. There you'll find options that enable you to launch the Classic environment at any time by clicking the Start button. You can also opt to have Classic start up whenever you log into your Mac. (These options are discussed in more detail in Chapter 19.) The main reason for launching Classic from the System Preferences application is to avoid waiting for the environment to load whenever you want to use a Classic application. The disadvantage of this method is that it leaves the Classic environment open in the background, where it can use precious system memory and sometimes slow down your Mac's overall performance.

Once launched, the Classic environment can actually be used to run more than one Classic application at once. Simply locate a Classic application and double-click it in the Finder. The application launches, appears in the Dock, and will seem to work much like a native application. There are some differences, but they're more cosmetic

What System Folder Should You Use?

The Classic environment requires a valid Mac OS 9.1 System Folder in order to start up correctly. So you'll need to have Mac OS 9.1 installed on your Mac in order to use Classic applications.

If you'd like to change the System Folder (or disk volume) that's used to launch the Classic environment, you can. Open the System Preferences application and select the Classic icon. Now, on the Start/Stop tab, select the volume you'd like to use to start up the Classic environment. Note that you can also elect to have Classic start up when you log into the Mac; this takes a little extra time at login, but subsequent launches of Classic applications happen much more quickly.

But the fact that you can have more than one Mac OS 9.1 System Folder and select which to use from within Mac OS X suggests a question: Should you have more than one System Folder? The short answer: It depends.

If you plan to work primarily within Mac OS X, using the Mac OS 9.1 System Folder almost exclusively from the Classic environment, then having only one Mac OS 9.1 System Folder should work fine. You can tweak that System Folder (see Chapter 19) to work well within the Classic environment. Then, hopefully, you can pretty much forget about it.

If you plan to do a lot of dual-booting between Mac OS 9.1 and Mac OS X, you may want to consider having two Mac OS 9.1 System Folders. This is especially true if the System Folder that you use for actually starting up in Mac OS 9.1 has a number of system extensions or other drivers that don't work well in the Classic environment. (An example would be a lot of peripherals or gaming drivers that aren't supported in the Classic environment.) After all, the simpler and less cluttered your System Folder for Classic is, the more reliably the Classic environment will run. If you have a simpler System Folder for Classic and a more complex one for booting into Mac OS 9.1, you'll probably have better luck with the stability of both.

The only real problem with two System Folders is that Mac OS 9.1 applications and control panels tend to store preferences within the active System Folder. So, when you change a setting or preference in the Classic environment, that setting won't be reflected in the other System Folder if you subsequently boot into Mac OS 9.1. It's a trade-off, but one you'll have to balance, particularly if you decide to be a power user of Mac OS 9.1 and X.

Appendix A covers your installation options as well as the tools for dual-booting between Mac OS 9.1 and Mac OS X.

than functional: You may notice different dialog boxes, different window controls, and a few different conventions used by the Classic Mac environment. For instance, you'll notice that dragging the window of a Classic application shows only the outline of the window while it's dragged; dragging a window in Mac OS X shows the entire window as it's dragged.

If you started the Classic environment by launching a Classic application, you won't need to specifically shut the Classic environment down; it automatically shuts down after you quit the last Classic application. If necessary, you *can* quit the Classic environment, especially if a Classic application has crashed or has become unresponsive. You also do this from the Classic pane of the System Preferences application. Make sure the Start/Stop tab is selected, then click either the Stop button or the Restart button.

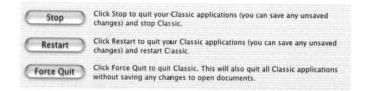

Restarting is the same as shutting down, only Classic starts back up immediately upon successfully shutting down. This is useful if you're having intermittent problems in the Classic environment or if a Classic application has just crashed or encountered an error. Unlike Mac OS X's native applications, a problem with one Classic application can cause other Classic applications to exhibit problems (or even crash or quit); so after any sort of Classic crash, it's a good idea to restart the Classic environment.

Note that you can also use the Force Quit command in the Classic pane or on the Apple menu to shut down the Classic environment. This command can be used when the Restart and Shut Down commands don't appear to be effective, particularly after a crash within the Classic environment. This is a choice of last resort, however, since you'll lose unsaved data in any open Classic applications.

 NOTE If you start the Classic environment from the Classic pane in the System Preferences application, then you *do* need to specifically shut it down, if desired. Again, you can shut it down by clicking Shut Down in the Classic pane. The environment is also shut down automatically when you log out of your account.

The Application and Apple Menus

Aside from the look and feel of many of the windows and menu items, two other obvious vestiges of earlier Mac OS versions appear when you're running a Classic application: the Classic version of the Application menu and the Apple menu. If you're familiar with Mac OS 9.*x*, you'll recognize these menus right away.

The Classic Apple menu (see Figure 5.12), which appears on the far left (the same place where the Mac OS X Apple menu appears), is a repository of aliases and shortcuts to many Mac OS 9.1 applications, control panels, and tools. It's different from the Mac OS X Apple menu, which is more limited. In fact, many of those control panels can be accessed and their values changed, with the results affecting only the Classic environment. For instance, you can use the Internet control panel, accessible from Apple menu ➢ Control Panels, to change default Internet settings for Internet applications that run in the Classic environment.

FIGURE 5.12

The Classic Apple menu, accessible when a Classic application is front-most

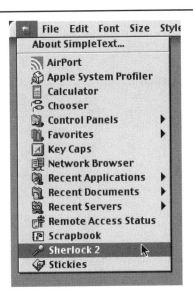

You'll find that the Classic Apple menu offers some other quick-access options, such as Recent Applications, Recent Documents, and Recent Folders. Each option holds (by default) the 10 items you've most recently accessed in that category. In many cases, even items you've accessed outside the Classic environment show up in these menus.

TIP As with Mac OS 9.1 and earlier, you can open the Apple Items Folder, located inside the active System Folder (the one you're using for the Classic environment) to see the items that are slated to appear on the Apple menu. If you copy items (or aliases) into that folder or remove items from it, they'll appear on or disappear from the Apple menu, respectively.

On the other side of the Classic menu bar, you'll see the Mac OS 9.1 (and earlier) version of the Application menu. This menu is somewhat similar to the Application menu that appears on the *left* side in native Mac OS X applications. Like the Mac OS X Application menu, the Classic Application menu has the name of the current application (and/or its icon), and the menu enables you to hide the current application (using the Hide Application command) or hide all other applications that are running (using the Hide Others command).

In other ways, though, the Classic Application menu (see Figure 5.13) is different, as it's really the precursor to the Dock's application-switching capabilities. Open the menu and select one of the applications listed, and you're switched to that application, just as though you had selected the application in the Dock.

FIGURE 5.13

The Application menu in Classic is really an application switcher— sort of a precursor to the Dock.

Classic's Application Dialog Boxes

Besides the different look and feel and the additional menu items, the Classic environment also offers slightly different dialog boxes within Classic applications. If you're familiar with Mac OS 9.*x*, these Classic dialog boxes won't pose much of a challenge to you. If you're new to the Mac with Mac OS X, however, you may begin to find the proliferation of different-looking dialog boxes and applications a bit troublesome. Don't worry—although they look different, they do, for the most part, act similarly to dialog boxes in Mac OS X's native applications. In this section we'll take a quick look at some of the differences.

Classic's Open Dialog Boxes

Although most Open and Save dialog boxes in native Mac OS X applications (those that employ either Carbon or Cocoa technology) use the columns-inspired interface discussed earlier in this chapter, Classic applications continue to use dialog boxes that look exactly like their Mac OS 9.1 counterparts. These dialog boxes can vary somewhat, since the Mac OS has a few different interfaces available to programmers. (As the Mac OS engineers have improved the Open and Close dialog box templates, they've left older types available in order to retain compatibility with older applications.)

One of the more common types is called Navigation Services, and it's the dialog box interface that you'll see in more recent versions of Classic applications. So, if you're working in a Classic application and select File ➢ Open, there's a good chance you'll see either the standard Mac OS Open dialog box shown in Figure 5.14 or the Navigation Services Open dialog box shown in Figure 5.15.

NOTE   Why Navigation Services? When Apple was updating the Mac OS to Mac OS 8.5, it introduced this new type of dialog box designed to improve the way you access files in future Mac applications. At the time, these dialogs were called "Navigation Services" to differentiate them from the earlier style of dialog box, as well as to underscore the fact that they offered a lot more flexibility for accessing files. Outside the Classic environment, though, it's a moot point, since Mac OS X introduces its own style of Open and Save dialog boxes based on the Finder window's Columns view.

FIGURE 5.14

The standard Mac OS 9.1 (and earlier) Open dialog box

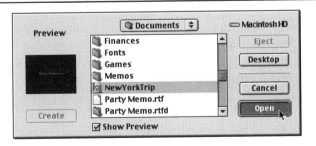

FIGURE 5.15

The Navigation Services Open dialog box

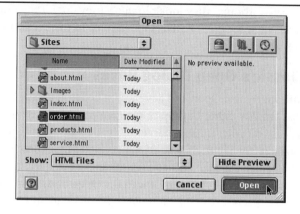

The standard Open dialog box is fairly straightforward—you locate a file in the hierarchy of folders, select the file, and click Open to open it. (You can also double-click the file name in the list of files.) To move back to a parent folder, you can use the pop-up menu at the top of the dialog box.

The Navigation Services dialog box isn't very different, although it does offer a bit more flexibility. Within the dialog box, you can click the disclosure triangle to reveal a subfolder's contents. The other major differences are the small menu buttons at the top-right corner of the dialog box. From left to right, these are the Shortcuts, Favorites, and Recent menus.

In the Classic environment, these buttons vary in their usefulness. Using the Shortcuts button, you can bring up a menu that shows you the main hard-disk volumes, removable drives, and network drives that are connected to your Mac. Select an item in this menu, and you're taken to it immediately.

The Favorites menu includes an Add to Favorites command that enables you to select an item in the dialog box, then select the command. When you next open this Favorites menu, you'll see that favorite. On the far right, the Recent menu can be used to access items and folders that you've selected recently in this or other Navigation Services dialog boxes. Note, however, that these Recent and Favorites menus don't have any relationship to the same menus in Mac OS X; if you add an item to the Favorites here, it isn't added to the Favorites you can access via the Go menu in the Finder.

TIP Need to see more files or folders? You can also drag the Navigation Services Open dialog box to make it larger, using the resize control at the bottom-right corner of the window. You can't resize a regular Mac OS 9.1 dialog box, however.

You may also see a Show pop-up menu in some Open dialog boxes, which allows you to choose what sort of documents you'd like to see in the Open dialog box. You can use this menu if you're not seeing the document you want (in that case, you might choose Show Readable Documents or Show All Documents), or you can use the menu to limit the number of items you're seeing in the Open dialog box.

Some dialog boxes include a Show Preview button, which enables you to view a small preview of image and text documents. Click the Show Preview button to see the preview pane. Now, when you select a document that has a compatible format (image, Internet, and some text files), you'll see a preview of that document here in the Open dialog box.

Once you find the document you'd like to open, highlight it and click Open. If the document is compatible with your application, the document should load in that application and appear on-screen.

If you don't find the document you want, or if you'd like to dismiss the dialog box for some other reason, click Cancel.

Classic's Save Dialog Boxes

The first time you save your document from within a Classic application, you'll see one of two Save dialog boxes—either the standard Mac OS 9.1 Save dialog box (see Figure 5.16) or the Navigation Services Save dialog box (see Figure 5.17).

Again, the standard Save dialog box is fairly straightforward, while the Navigation Services dialog box has a few additional options that make the dialog work like the List view in a Finder window. Using the tools in the dialog box, locate the folder where you'd like to store your document. When you find the folder, give the file a name in the Name entry box.

When saving in the Classic environment, you're limited by the dialog boxes to 31 characters for filenames, and you should not, in most cases, include a three-letter extension code (instead, the application you're using will likely add this on its own if one is needed). In general, it's best not to begin filenames with nontext characters, and you should definitely avoid starting with a period (.) or a slash (/). (You can't use a slash anywhere within the name.)

FIGURE 5.16

The Save dialog box in many earlier Classic applications

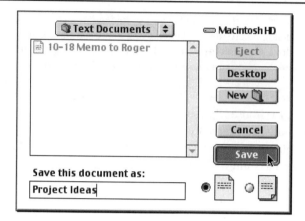

FIGURE 5.17

The Navigation Services Save dialog box

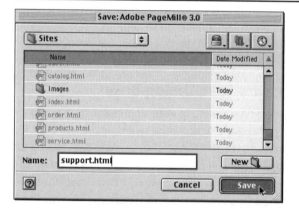

 NOTE In some cases you may opt to add a three-letter filename extension to a document you create in a Classic application, particularly if you intend to send that document over the Internet or to use it later with a native Mac OS X application. This is particularly true if the document you're creating is being saved in a standard, cross-platform format, such as a Plain Text (.txt), Rich Text (.rtf), or Word (.doc) file, or in an image-file format, such as TIFF (.tif), GIF (.gif), or JPEG (.jpg).

You may also find application-specific options below the Name entry box. Many applications, for instance, allow you to choose a format for your document if that application supports more than one document format. Likewise, you'll usually find a New Folder button, which you can use to create, within your selected folder, a new subfolder where you can save your document.

When you've entered the filename and made your optional choices, press Return or click the Save button. Your document will be saved.

If you choose a filename that already exists in the selected folder, an alert box appears, asking you if you want to replace the existing document with the one you're saving. If you do, click Replace. Otherwise, click Cancel and either rename the file you're saving or choose a different location.

Classic Printing

Whenever you attempt to print from within a Classic application, the Classic environment will again present you with dialog boxes that look a little different from those you're accustomed to. In fact, before you can print at all from a Classic application, you'll need to configure a printer from within the Classic environment's Chooser. (This is discussed in Chapter 13.) Once you have the printer configured, you can access the Page Setup and Print commands from within a Classic application.

Select File ➤ Print Setup from within a Classic application, and you'll see a Page Setup dialog box that looks somewhat like Figure 5.18. In this dialog box you can select the basics that were discussed previously in the section "Page Setup and Print." These include page attributes such as the paper type to print to, the orientation of the final printed output (whether the page should be printed vertically or horizontally for wider output), and the percentage at which the final printout should be scaled. You may also find that the Options pop-up menu (which defaults to say "Page Attributes") hides some other option screens, including options specific to the selected printer.

FIGURE 5.18

The Page Setup dialog box from a Classic application

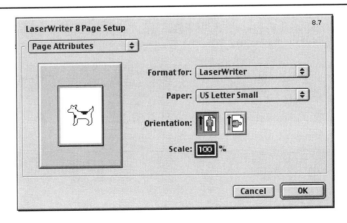

Once you have the Page Setup dialog conquered, you can select File ➤ Print to bring up the Print dialog box. This one, unlike the native Mac OS X Print dialog box, will be different depending on the printer that has been selected; many printers have different driver software and, hence, different Print dialog boxes. Figure 5.19 shows a fairly common Classic Print dialog box—it's the dialog box that's based on the Laser-Writer 8 driver. This is the printer driver used by many PostScript-compatible printers, even if the printers aren't manufactured by Apple.

FIGURE 5.19

The Print dialog box for a LaserWriter-compatible printer

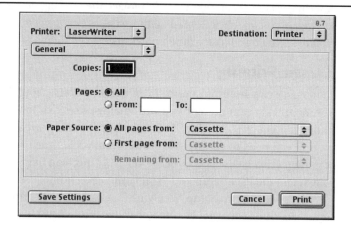

At its most basic, the Print dialog box enables you to enter the number of copies you want to print and which of your document's pages (inclusive) you want to send to the printer. You can also select the paper source if your printer has multiple paper trays or loading options.

In the untitled options pop-up menu (by default, it has the name *General*), you may have many, many more options to choose from, depending again on the printer driver you're using. For LaserWriter-compatible printers, options include the ability to select when to print a document, how color matching will work, whether to print a coverage page, and how many document pages will be printed on each sheet of paper.

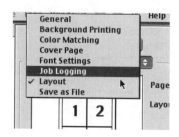

Once you've made all your selections, you're ready to print. (If you'd like to save the settings changes you've made for use in future printing sessions, click the Save Settings button. Now the driver will reflect these settings the next time you print from a Classic application.) To print, click the Print button. Your print job is sent to the printer.

In many cases another Classic application, the Print Monitor (see Figure 5.20), will be launched when you send a document to the printer. The Print Monitor enables you to manage your print jobs. Select the name of a print job (if you have more than one) and click Cancel Printing to clear that document from the Print Monitor and stop printing temporarily. Or you can select a print job and click Set Print Time to schedule that job for a later date. When all documents are finished printing, the Print Monitor quits on its own. (It will also quit if you chose to shut down or restart the Classic environment, after it asks you whether you'd prefer to print documents before shutting down or saving the documents until the next Classic session.)

FIGURE 5.20

The Print Monitor enables you to manage print jobs in the Classic environment.

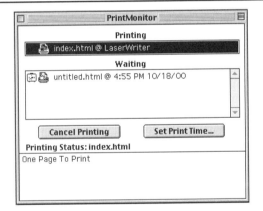

What's Next?

In this chapter you saw how to launch and work with applications and documents, both in Mac OS X and within the Classic environment. In the next chapter you'll see how to get help from the Mac OS and many Mac OS X native applications via the standard Help menu. You'll also learn how to use Sherlock to search local disks and the Internet for files, people, and other tidbits of information.

CHAPTER <u>6</u>

Getting Help and Searching with Sherlock

lthough Mac OS X certainly is a departure from earlier Mac OS versions, it also incorporates some of the familiar staples from Mac OS 9.1 and earlier versions. Two of those are the Help Viewer and Sherlock, the Mac's comprehensive search tool.

Both of these tools were designed to be as straightforward as possible for users and easy for application developers and other third parties to integrate the tools into their own products. The Help Viewer, for instance, uses a standard Web-like interface and HTML-based help files, making it familiar to most users and developers alike. The Sherlock application is a bit more involved, but Apple has made it easy for third parties to allow their Web sites to be searched from within Sherlock.

In this chapter, you'll look at both the Help Viewer and Sherlock, including not just ways to use the tools but also ways to install add-ons for those tools.

Viewing Help Documents

In past Mac OS versions, a number of different ways existed to get help. If you've used Mac OS 9.1 or earlier versions, you may be familiar with Balloon Help and earlier types of Help systems, like the Apple Guide system. And, in fact, you may still encounter those systems occasionally in a Classic application (see the section "Help in Classic Applications" later in this chapter). Mac OS X focuses almost exclusively on the Help Viewer as its conduit for help information, making it a one-stop shop for finding out about both the Mac OS and applications (especially Cocoa and Carbon applications) written directly for Mac OS X.

The Help Viewer is very similar to a Web browser, so if you've surfed the Web, you'll find that you're reasonably comfortable with the Help Viewer interface. Figure 6.1 shows the Help Viewer.

The Help Viewer features instructional text, images, and illustrations to help you understand concepts. The viewer has underlined links that work just like hyperlinks in a Web browser. Click a link once and you're taken to a related article, or the Help Viewer automatically locates documents on that topic. (In some cases, the Help Viewer will download a help document from a special Apple server on the Internet, but most of the time documents are stored on your Mac's hard disk.) Other links activate Apple-Script commands, which can cause other applications to open automatically or settings in the Mac OS to be made for you.

Again like a Web browser, the Help Viewer has Forward and Back buttons (in the bottom-right corner) to enable you to move back and forth between previously accessed screens. At the bottom left, the Help Viewer has a Home button (the question mark) that will take you back to the main Help Center screen.

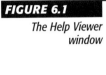

FIGURE 6.1

The Help Viewer window

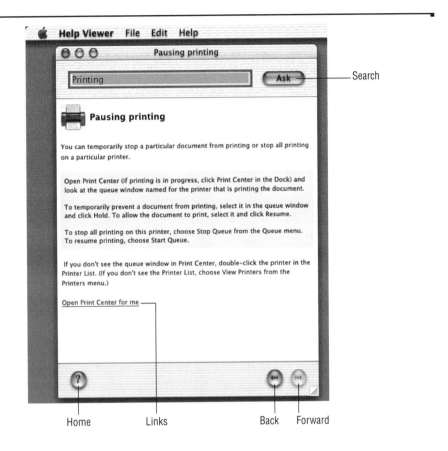

At the top of the Help Viewer window is a search entry box, where you can enter keywords to search help documents. Once your keywords are entered, click the Ask button to initiate the search. (I'll have more on searching in the section "Help by Keyword.")

Accessing the Help Viewer

The Mac OS has a fairly simple, straightforward Help system, and you can access it quite a number of ways. The Finder and most other applications written specifically for Mac OS X include a Help menu, where you'll find at least one Help command. The command name includes the name of the application (e.g., Mail Help in the Mail application), in most cases. In the Finder, the command is Help ➤ Mac Help. In the QuickTime Player application, the command is Help ➤ QuickTime Help.

 TIP Currently in Mac OS X, the Help key on extended keyboards doesn't work. However, you can often press ⌘+? (⌘+Shift+/) to get help, both in the Finder and in many applications.

Another way to access the Help Viewer is through the Help button, located in many different places throughout the interface, including Print dialog boxes and settings windows. What's more, these quick links are usually *contextual*, meaning the link takes you directly to a help topic of interest, not just a general index of help topics. The Help button should be obvious—it's a small, round button with a question mark inside it.

A third way to access the Help Viewer is via a contextual menu entry. Hold down the Control key while clicking the mouse button on an object in the Finder (or elsewhere in many other native Mac OS X applications), and a contextual menu will appear. Included in that menu will be a Help command, which you can select to access help documents relevant to the application and items you're working with at that moment.

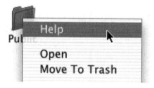

Help by Topic

In many cases, accessing the Help Viewer takes you directly to a page on the topic that you're seeking. In some other cases, though, you may decide to browse a particular application's help or look through a number of different articles to learn more about a procedure or feature. You would then start at the top level of an application's help topics and click a topic link to view related help documents.

Most applications that use the Help Viewer have a main index page that includes topic listings down the left side of the screen (see Figure 6.2). In the case of Apple's own help documents, most of these links are actually built-in search phrases—when you click one of the links, some predetermined search keywords are plugged into the Help Viewer's search box.

FIGURE 6.2

Many applications have a main contents page with predefined search topics on the left.

Articles that match the search criteria appear on a results-listing page, enabling you to click to view an article that looks interesting. You may also see a More Results link at the bottom of the results listing. Click that link and you'll see another series of help articles that may be of interest.

If you click one of the results listings, more than likely you'll immediately view the help document in the Help Viewer window. In some other cases, however, you may see a dialog box, indicating that a help document needs to be downloaded.

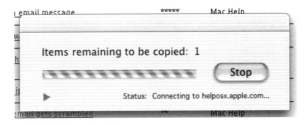

If so, the Help Viewer will be accessing a special Apple-run server on the Internet that stores up-to-date help articles for Mac OS X. If you don't have an Internet connection active, your Mac may attempt to connect to your Internet service provider automatically. If a connection isn't possible, you'll have to skip that help document; click the Stop button.

As you're browsing, you can use the Back button to return to a previous screen or the Forward button to move forward again. The Home button takes you to the Help Center, where you can start over by clicking the link to a particular application's Help system.

 NOTE Many of the applications included with Mac OS X—including Mail, Preview, Grab, and even Sherlock—have help documents stored within the Mac Help system. In other words, don't despair if you don't see a separate entry in the Help Center for these applications. Just access the Mac Help system to learn more about the included applications.

Help by Keyword

If you have a good idea what you want help with and you'd prefer not to browse for that help, you can search for it directly. Open the Help system for a particular application using one of the methods described earlier in the section "Accessing the Help Viewer." If you'd prefer to search all Help systems at once, click the Home button in the Help Viewer to bring up the Help Center listing. At the top of the Help Viewer, enter a keyword or two that describes the topic on which you'd like help. If you have more than one keyword, separate the words with just a space and then click the Ask button to begin the search.

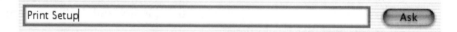

Once you've clicked Ask, you'll see a results page listing the help documents that the Help Viewer found. Clicking one of the titles will open that help document (or, as noted in the previous section, it will cause that help document to be downloaded from Apple's Internet help server). You'll also notice, as shown in Figure 6.3, a "dot-rating" system; that's Help Viewer's way of showing you how relevant it thinks each article is to your search. The more relevant the document according to Help Viewer, the more dots you'll see.

FIGURE 6.3

A results listing page in the Help Viewer

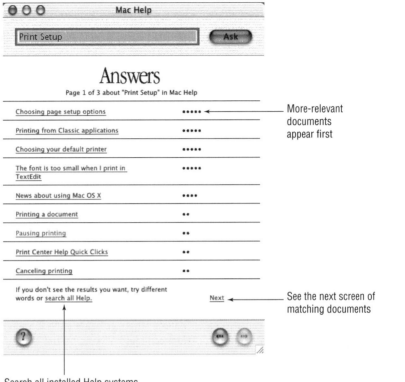

Mac Help

Print Setup — Ask

Answers

Page 1 of 3 about "Print Setup" in Mac Help

Choosing page setup options	•••••
Printing from Classic applications	•••••
Choosing your default printer	•••••
The font is too small when I print in TextEdit	•••••
News about using Mac OS X	••••
Printing a document	••
Pausing printing	••
Print Center Help Quick Clicks	••
Canceling printing	••

More-relevant documents appear first

If you don't see the results you want, try different words or search all Help.

Next — See the next screen of matching documents

Search all installed Help systems

If you don't see a document that helps you, the Help Viewer offers three additional options. First, you can click the Next link at the bottom of the page to see another page of possible matches, although they will be those that the Help Viewer deems less relevant. The Help Viewer isn't always right, so go ahead and check the less-relevant results.

Your second option is to click Search All Help. By default, only the currently selected Help system is searched, unless you enter keywords while accessing the Help Center listing. But by clicking Search All Help, you'll see documents in other Help systems (perhaps the AppleScript Help system or an application's own Help system) that match your keywords.

If that still doesn't work for you, you can use special symbols to create *Boolean* search phrases. A Boolean search phrase is made up of keywords and the words *and, or,* or *not.* For instance, "Printer and USB" is a Boolean search phrase that will find pages with both the words *Printer* and *USB.* "Printer or USB" would find pages that include either of the two terms. "Printer not USB" would locate pages that do include *Printer* but don't include *USB.*

In the Help Viewer, these phrases must be put together with symbols instead of *and, or,* and *not.* The plus sign (+) stands for *and,* an exclamation point (!) for *not,* and a vertical line (|) for *or.* For example, the following tells Help Viewer to search for documents that have the word *Printer* but not the word *USB*:

Printer ! USB

You can also use brackets to enclose parts of the Boolean phrase. The following tells Help Viewer to search for documents that include either *Printer* or *Scanner* but not *USB*:

(Printer | Scanner) ! USB

Also, it's worth noting that, by default, words entered without Boolean symbols are always assumed to be "or" searches, meaning you don't need to enter the "or" symbol if you're simply typing two or three keywords.

 TIP You can also enter "natural-language" queries in the search box, such as "How do I install a USB printer?" or "How can I find a friend on the Internet?" As far as I can tell, natural phrasing offers no advantage over targeted keywords (such as "USB printer" or "search Internet"), but you can try it as another approach to brainstorming your keywords.

Installing Help Documents

In most cases, help documents should be installed for you by the Mac OS installer or application installers. If for some reason you have a help document that hasn't been properly installed, you can install it in one of two places.

Help documents for the entire Mac OS X system (all users) are stored in the main Library folder in the Help subfolder, which is located in the Documentation folder. (That's the /Library/Documentation/Help folder.) If you have a valid Help Viewer system file (with the filename extension .help), you can drag that file to this folder. The next time you launch the Help Viewer, the new Help system will be recognized.

You also have a personal Documentation folder (inside the Library folder in your home folder), where you'll find the subfolder Help. If desired, you can install Help system files there, where they can be accessed only by you when your user account is logged in. Other users will not be able to see the Help system you've installed. (This may be your only option, by the way, if you don't have an administrator's account.)

Other Documentation Systems

Although the Help Viewer is the main retrieval system for getting help in the Mac OS, you'll find documentation in other forms as well. The most common type is probably the Read Me file, a file that's usually included in any new application's folder.

The Read Me file can vary from a simple document telling you a little about the program and/or programmer to a complex set of instructions, bug alerts, and other issues that have to do with the application. Read Me files are usually Plain Text files that can be read in TextEdit, although they may also be RTF (Rich Text Format, which TextEdit can also display) or PDF documents (display these in Preview, Adobe Acrobat, or another PDF-capable application).

 NOTE PDF stands for Portable Document Format, a special document format designed to make formatted documents display in a standard way on multiple computer platforms. Creating and working with PDF documents is discussed in Chapter 14.

Applications aren't strictly limited to the Apple Help system for their own help documents, so it's also possible that you'll find help documents stored in an application's folder in PDF format or RTF format. Either type of file can be printed out and used as a hard-copy manual (see Figure 6.4).

FIGURE 6.4

Here's a user's manual in PDF format.

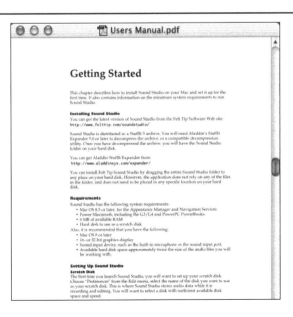

Of course, application developers are free to write their own Help systems or, in some cases, use updated versions of older Mac OS Help systems. For instance, REALBasic (a program that enables you to develop Basic-language applications) has a Mac OS X–compatible version that uses a Help system that resembles the Apple Help system in Mac OS 9.1 (see Figure 6.5). While it's a fairly easy system to grasp (it has Web browser–like controls, using sort of an HTML frames interface), it's a bit different from the standard Apple help. Likewise, many application developers (especially those who develop Internet applications like Web browsers and e-mail programs) opt for HTML-based Help systems that actually use a Web browser instead of the Help Viewer.

FIGURE 6.5

The REALBasic Online Reference system uses a Web browser-style Help system.

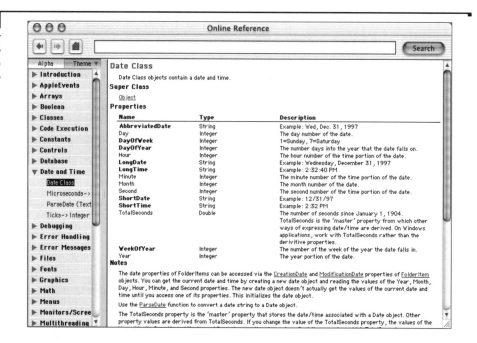

 TIP Working in the Terminal application? Commands and programs in the Unix-like environment of the Terminal have their own Help system, called "man" (manual) pages. Type **man xx**, where the *xx* is the name of the command you're trying to learn more about. See Chapter 22 for details on using the Terminal.

Help in Classic Applications

Classic applications don't have access to the Mac OS X Help Viewer and don't place their help documentation within its control. Instead, you'll use Mac OS 9.1's equivalent Help system, which is similar in many ways to Help Viewer. It's HTML-like, using links and Back, Home, and Forward buttons to get around.

To access a Classic application's Help system, pull down its Help menu and select the Help command. The application name will precede "Help" (for instance, QuickTime Help). Figure 6.6 shows a sample of the Help system used by Classic applications.

FIGURE 6.6

The Classic Help viewer

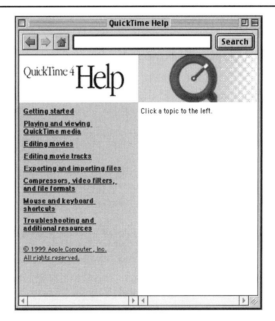

Aside from the Help command, you might encounter some other types of earlier Mac OS Help systems. The Apple Guide system, for instance, was a popular way to add help to Mac OS applications in the mid-'90s. If you're using Classic applications written during that time (or Classic applications that haven't had their Help system updated, since the Apple Guide will still work in Mac OS 9.*x* and earlier versions), you may see a Guide entry in the Classic application's Help menu. Select that entry, and you'll see the Guide window appear, as shown in Figure 6.7.

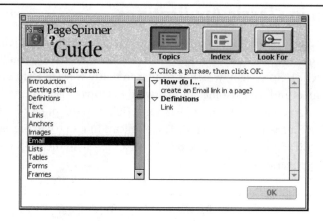

The Apple Guide system was a bit more complex than the current Help Viewer approach. Although some of the controls work like a Web browser, the Guide is a more active Help system. Using AppleScript and other technologies, it guides you through basic tasks, working a little more like the Assistant that helps you configure Mac OS X after an installation. (Assistants and wizards are also popular in productivity applications like Microsoft Office or AppleWorks.)

If you encounter a Guide, simply walk through the suggested steps, using the arrow buttons. You'll notice in some cases that the Guide will perform tasks automatically for you. You'll also find that the main Topics window offers an Index view and a Search view, enabling you to move quickly to any topic that interests you.

NOTE Apple Guide is a nice system for help. It fell out of favor with Apple primarily because it's hard for application developers to implement (at least, harder than HTML pages or the Help Viewer approach). Therefore, it wasn't used by nearly as many developers as had been hoped.

While working in Classic applications, you'll likely encounter at least one other type of standard help—the venerable Balloon Help. It was Apple's first real Help system for the Mac, and, although limited in scope, it was fairly effective during its time. (Clearly, it still is, at least in Classic applications. A Balloon Help feature doesn't exist in Mac OS X applications.)

Balloon Help works by being turned on and off. Select Help ➢ Show Balloons from the menu of a Classic application, and you've turned on Balloon Help. Then move the mouse over a button, command, or portion of a window that you don't understand. If a Balloon Help resource was written for that item, a small, cartoon-like balloon pops up to tell you about the item.

Perhaps the most persistent complaint about Balloon Help is that, when it's switched on, balloons pop up continuously as you work (or any time you move the mouse to an item with a Balloon Help resource). So most folks turn off Balloon Help after they've learned what they needed to know. Select Help ➢ Hide Balloons to turn the feature off.

Finally, as with applications native to OS X, Classic applications can have Help systems written or implemented by the application developers. For instance, Figure 6.8 shows Adobe PageMill 3.0's Help system, which uses QuickHelp, a popular third-party Help system that has also been used by Classic versions of Palm Desktop and earlier AppleWorks and ClarisWorks implementations. If you encounter such a system, just hold your breath and dive in. In most cases, it will resemble a Web browser and/or be reasonably similar to the Help Viewer—so it should make sense almost immediately.

Introducing Sherlock

In Mac OS 8.5, Apple introduced Sherlock, an exciting, new approach to searching for items on your Mac, on a local network, and on the Internet. Updated slightly for Mac OS X, Sherlock continues to offer three fundamental capabilities that you'll probably use from time to time. It can search the filenames and attributes of files on your Mac (or network), the text *within* text-based documents on your Mac or network, and a myriad of Internet-based sites.

FIGURE 6.8

Classic applications can have their own Help systems, generally similar to a Web browser interface.

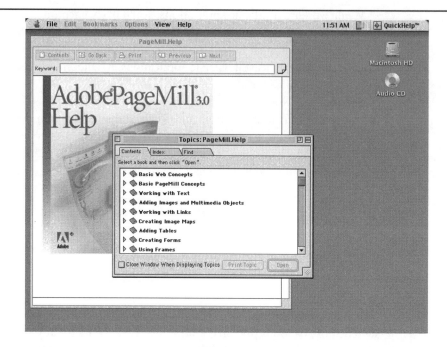

The Internet option includes the ability to search at major portal sites (such as Yahoo, GoTo, Excite, and HotBot), e-commerce sites (like Amazon, eBay, EyeWire, and Virgin Megastore Online), or people sites (for example, ClassMates.com and World-Pages.com), along with other sites, such as the Apple Web site and those sites under News and Reference.

Sherlock offers the items for searching via what it calls *channels*. You'll see them along the top of the Sherlock window. Select one, and you can change the type of search you conduct from within Sherlock (see Figure 6.9).

Sherlock is an application separate from the Finder, but it's also fairly well integrated. You can launch Sherlock by clicking its tile on the Dock, double-clicking its icon in the Applications folder, or, from the Finder's menu, selecting File ➢ Find (or pressing ⌘+F).

Once Sherlock is up and running, you can select a channel, select the items you'd like to search in the Listing pane, enter some keywords in the Keyword box, and then click the magnifying glass. Items found show up in the Listing pane; selecting them once, in most cases, results in a little information or a preview of that item in the Information, or Info, pane (see Figure 6.10). Sherlock is usually that easy to use—not that you can't go a little further in depth, as I will in the next few sections.

FIGURE 6.9

The Sherlock interface offers different search types via channels. Shown is a search using popular Web search engines.

Internet channels

Files channel

Keyword box

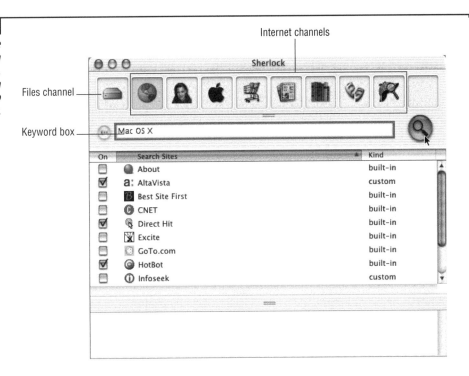

FIGURE 6.10

After a successful search, you'll see in the Listing pane items you can select.

Listing pane

Information pane

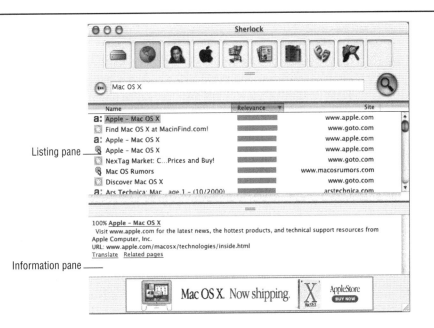

Searching Your Disks and Folders

Before the Sherlock utility got the name Sherlock, it was called Find File and was used primarily to search the local disk and connected network volumes for files either by name or another file criterion, such as the size, modified date, or file type. When Internet searching capabilities were added, the utility was renamed Sherlock and touted as one of the most striking features of the Mac OS. The ability to search for files remained.

Sherlock in Mac OS X enables you to search for files in three different ways. You can search the names of the files on attached disk volumes, looking for a match to the keyword you type. You can search *within* text-based documents for keyword(s) you specify. And you can create a custom search that looks for files based on a variety of criteria.

The Files Interface

To begin any type of search destined to find files on your hard disk or elsewhere on your local network, you click the Files channel icon in the Sherlock window. The window will reconfigure itself to show the Find Files interface. You'll see a Keyword box and three radio buttons beneath it: File Names, Contents, and Custom. Which radio button you choose dictates how Sherlock will search for files.

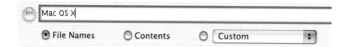

Below those radio buttons, in the Listing pane, you'll see the disk volumes (both local disks and networked disks) that you can search. (Your home folder will also be in this list by default.) When you initiate a search, you'll checkmark the box next to each volume you want to search.

For file searches, the search-sites list is easily modified. Open a Finder window and locate a particular folder, for instance, that you'd like to include in the search. Then drag that folder from the Finder window into the Listing pane and drop it. The folder is now one of your search-site options. By turning off the check boxes next to other disks and folders, you can designate only a particular folder, if desired, to quickly search it. (Dragged folders are also automatically indexed, which is important for searching the contents of files, as discussed later in the section "Searching Contents of Files.")

 TIP You can also add folders to the Listing area using the File ➢ Add Folder command in Sherlock, which enables you to locate folders via an Open dialog box.

When you've completed a search (completing the different types of searches is discussed in the next three sections), a list of located items replaces the search sites in the Listing pane. (This, in my opinion, is a weakness of Sherlock's design, because it can be confusing. The alternative, however, is having a second window for a "results list," which Apple abandoned in earlier Sherlock versions in favor of a single window.) Select a search item, and the path to that item (its place in the hierarchy on your disk or a network disk) is revealed in the Info pane.

Items can be double-clicked in the Info pane, and they'll be launched as if they were double-clicked in a Finder window. (If you double-click a disk or a folder, it will be opened in a Finder window.) You can also drag items from the Sherlock window into a Finder window or onto the desktop if you'd like to move or copy them (assuming you have the correct file privileges). You can even double-click a folder that appears in the Info window to see the folder's contents in the Finder, even if that folder isn't the main item you were searching for (for example, if it's a parent folder).

If you want to perform another search, you may need to get back to the search-sites list. (If you want to search exactly the same folders and volumes you selected before, you can simply enter new keywords and click the magnifying glass.) To return to the search-sites list, click the Back button just to the left of the Keyword Entry box. You'll see the list of disk volumes and/or folders appear once again in the Listing pane.

Searching Filenames

If your plan is to search for files by name, that's easily accomplished. Select the File Names radio button, place a check mark next to the volume(s) or folder(s) you want to search, and then enter a keyword or, more likely, a partial filename in the Keyword box. Then click the Search button—the magnifying glass.

 NOTE The keyword search is not case sensitive, so entering "mac OS X" will find files that have "MAC OS x" in the name, or some such permutation. The search is sensitive to the location of the words and spaces, so entering "Mac OS X" as the keyword phrase will not find a file named "macosx.doc", for instance.

In a file search, the results can range dramatically from folders to documents to entire disk volumes. You'll see the results appear in the Listing pane; selecting one of the results will display in the Info pane its path in the hierarchy of drives and folders (see Figure 6.11).

FIGURE 6.11

Here's a list of results with the keywords Mac OS X in the filename.

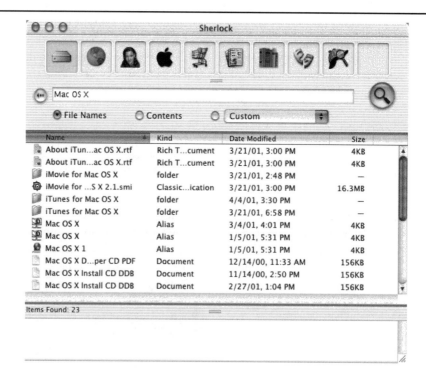

TIP Of course, you'll get better results from some keywords than from others. The key is to think clearly about the correct keyword or partial filename to use. Sherlock can attempt to find nearly anything. A search for ".doc" might help you find all the Word documents on your disk (or in a particular folder), but the result might also be hundreds of files. If the list is too long, think of a unique part of the file's name that you're searching for and then enter that as the keyword.

Searching Contents of Files

Select the Contents radio button, and you can search within text files for particular keywords or phrases of keywords. Most documents that have text—Plain Text documents, RTF documents, and even PDF documents and some proprietary word processing documents—can be content-searched. The drive or folder, however, must be indexed before Sherlock can find keywords inside text documents.

When you index a drive or folder, Sherlock creates a database of significant keywords that it finds in text-based documents it can read. Then, during a search, it cross-references that database with your keywords and then locates relevant files on the disk (or in the selected folder). So it's fairly simple for Sherlock to take a look at your keyword, check its database, and then head out to the selected volume to make sure relevant files are still there. The alternative—having Sherlock look through every text file on your drive or in a folder every time you search—would be slow, to say the least.

Besides needing to index a drive or folder, you need to do so relatively often if you want a search to be up-to-date. Fortunately, Sherlock makes both indexing and reindexing relatively painless.

You can immediately see whether or not a volume has been indexed by looking at its entry in the Listing pane. In the Index Status column, you'll see when the volume was last indexed, assuming it has been.

       Macintosh HD   Can't index

       todds   Indexed Sun, Apr 8, 2001, 6:50 PM

To index a drive or folder, select that item's name (so that it's highlighted, along with its icon) in the Listing pane and then select Find ➤ Index Now. You'll see the index begin to build, as reflected in the Index Status column. Indexing can take a while, depending on the number of files stored on the volume. If the index hasn't been updated in a while, you can head back to the Find menu and select Index Now again.

NOTE You can't index the main startup disk for Mac OS X because you won't have read/write permission for the entire disk. If you want to search items stored there, it's best to drag your Documents folder (or other folders) to the Sherlock window and to index the folders individually.

Once a folder or volume is indexed, you can place a check mark next to it in the Listing pane, enter a keyword or phrase that you'd like to find within those documents, and click the Search button (the magnifying glass). After a few seconds, you should see a list of matching files—all text documents—appear in the Listing pane. As with other such results, you can double-click the document to launch its application and access the file, or you can drag it from the Sherlock window into a Finder window.

 TIP Select Sherlock ➤ Preferences to see Indexing Options. You can use the check boxes to determine whether Sherlock should index items automatically. Click the Languages button to view the Languages dialog box, where you can determine which languages Sherlock should be prepared to index within your documents. The fewer the languages, the faster the searches.

Building Custom Search Phrases

Ready to dig in and really find something? The Mac OS categorizes each file and folder on your attached volumes in many different ways, including by the date it was created, the date it was most recently modified, and the size of the file or the amount of storage space it requires on disk. These items (along with a host of others) can all be turned into search criteria if you choose to customize your search. And customizing is really rather painless.

To begin, click the radio button next to the Custom menu, select that menu, and choose Edit from it. The More Search Options dialog box appears, as shown in Figure 6.12.

Okay, so the dialog box looks a little intimidating at first. But it's actually quite easy to use. All you are really doing is building small search phrases in the More Search Options dialog box and using check boxes, pop-up menus, and entry boxes to narrow the search down.

FIGURE 6.12

The More Search Options dialog box

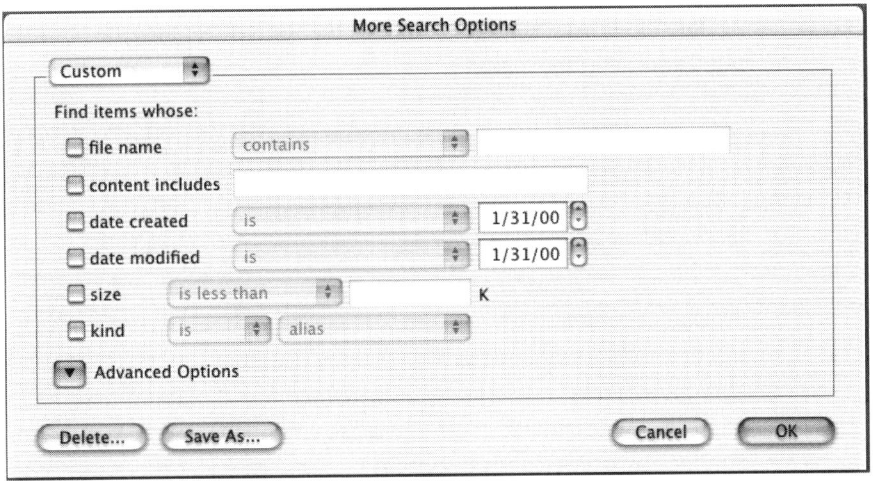

Choosing Criteria

To begin building your search phrase, you select a single criterion. The first two criteria, File Name and Contents Includes, are permutations of the other two types of file searches: Name and Contents. Place a check mark next to the File Name entry, leave the pop-up menu set to "contains," and enter a keyword. The search performed will be very similar to the type of search described back in the section "Searching Filenames."

Notice, though, that the search phrase here is slightly more powerful, because you can use the pop-up menu to change the way in which filenames are searched in the selected volume. Pull down the menu, and you'll see options like Starts With, Ends With, Is, Is Not, and Doesn't Contain. You can customize a filename search so that, for instance, the phrase reads as follows:

The search would then be much more targeted: You would see only results where the name of the file begins with "Mac OS X."

But what about the negative options, like Is Not and Doesn't Contain? How can they be useful? After all, the likelihood that you would need to search for all files in a particular volume or folder that *aren't* named something is reasonably slim. But a negative option is powerful when used in conjunction with other criteria, such as Date Created or Date Modified. Place an additional check mark next to one of those options and build another phrase, as in:

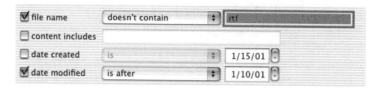

This search will find files that don't contain the .rtf extension and that have been modified since January 10, 2001. Such a search is useful in backing up certain files to a removable disk or in finding a misnamed file. (It should have had .rtf in its file-name, but you know it doesn't because you misnamed it. So you can find the file with Sherlock by using Doesn't Contain.)

The more creative you need to be to find a file, the more useful More Search Options can be. Here's a quick look at each of the options and a sense of what you can do with each:

File Name   This entry is useful for customizing the standard filename search.

Content Includes   This option is exactly the same as the search option described in the earlier section "Searching Contents of Files," except that it can be used in conjunction with other types of criteria. Thus you can search, for instance, for all files that have ".Memo" in their name (by turning on the File Name criterion) and that include the keyword "Nancy."

Date Created   Search for files or volumes created on, after, or before a certain date, or within a range of dates.

Date Modified   The Mac OS also keeps track of the date when any document file, folder, or volume is modified, so you can base your search on that date as well. You could thus limit searches to the files most recently worked with, or you could search for files that *haven't* been modified in quite some time. The option is very useful for backup or archiving purposes.

Size   Search for files that require more (select Is Greater Than) or less (select Is Smaller Than) than a certain amount of storage space, in kilobytes.

Kind   Are you looking for a particular type of file, or are there certain files you'd like to exclude? Use the Kind criterion, selecting either Is or Isn't and a particular type. For instance, you could build the phrase "kind is alias" on the Kind line and specify "filename contains Mac OS X" on the File Name criterion line. The result would be only aliases with "Mac OS X" in their names.

Advanced Options

If you're looking at the More Search Options dialog box and you don't see the criterion you want to use in your file search, there may still be hope. Select the Advanced Options triangle button. The More Search Options window expands, showing you quite a few additional search criteria (see Figure 6.13).

FIGURE 6.13

Click the Advanced Options triangle, and suddenly you have a major dialog box to contend with.

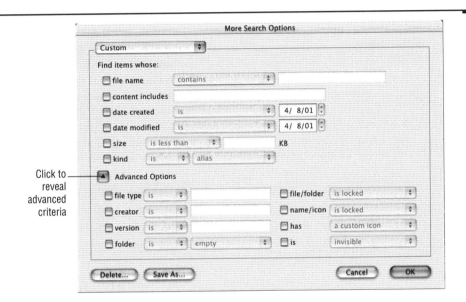

You can add each of these criteria to your overall custom search in the same way you selected basic options. Place a check mark next to the item you want to use and then use the pop-up menu and (if appropriate) the entry box.

Some of the Advanced options are a bit complex, but there is a trick to them. All of them (with the exception of the Invisible criterion) are items that would appear in the Info window if the item were selected in a Finder window and the command File ➤ Show Info were selected. So, if you want to explore the options further, check out a few files in the Info window. Here's a quick list:

File Type The Mac OS stores a special four-character file-type code for many different types of document files, which you can search for. (File types can be found, in many cases, by selecting a representative document, invoking the File ➤ Show Info command, and choosing Application from the Show pop-up menu.) Examples are PICT (for a Macintosh Picture file) and MOOV for a QuickTime movie.

Creator   Creator is another special, internal code used to signify the application that created a particular document.

NOTE   File Type and Creator are holdovers from earlier Mac OS versions. Mac OS 9.1 and earlier created files with both a *resource fork* and a *data fork*, and File Type and Creator are stored in the resource fork. (If you're familiar with older versions of the Mac OS, you'll remember that the Mac OS seems to know intuitively what a file is, even without a special filename extension on the end of it.) Mac OS X doesn't rely on these codes, although it can recognize and work with them. Just realize that these criteria are really useful only when you're searching files created in Mac OS 9.1 and earlier.

Version   Applications and some component files (particularly those for older Mac OS versions) can have a special version number assigned to them, which you can see in the Info window when viewing the application. You can enter that number in the entry box to find an application with a particular version number, such as 3.3.

Folder   You can use this criterion to search for folders based on whether or not the folder is empty, mounted, or shared.

File/Folder Is Locked   Select Locked or Unlocked to search for a file or folder that is one or the other. (This criterion simply refers to whether the item's Locked check box is checked in the Info window.)

Name/Icon Is Locked   Certain system-level files and folders can have their name or icon locked so that they can't be inadvertently changed by users.

Custom Icon   Select this option if you'd like to view items that do or do not have a custom (nonstandard) icon. The items include folders or files that have icons you've changed, as discussed in Chapter 4.

Visibility   This last option enables you to find items that have been marked invisible (so that they don't appear in Finder windows) via a special application or a tool in the Terminal.

TIP By default, in Mac OS X, files or folders that begin with a period (.) are invisible. If you'd like to make a file or folder invisible, you can use the Terminal application to do so, by renaming the file with a period.

Saving the Search

If you've created a search in the More Search Options dialog box that you'd like to keep and use again, you can save it. Not only does keeping the search save you from entering criteria again, it also adds the search to the Custom menu in the main Sherlock window. So to invoke the search again, you won't even have to open the More Search Options dialog box.

To save, click the Save As button in the More Search Options dialog box. You'll see a small Save Custom Settings dialog box appear. Give the settings a name and click the Save button.

 NOTE If you need to edit the saved search, select Edit from the Custom menu in the main Sherlock window. In the top of the More Search Options dialog box, you'll find a small pop-up menu that you can use to switch to the saved search. Edit to taste and click the OK button to store the changes.

After saving the search, you will be returned to the Sherlock window, where you can select the search from the Custom pop-up menu and then click the magnifying glass to begin searching.

Need to delete a custom search? Select the Delete button in the More Search Options dialog box, and you'll see the Delete Custom Search Settings dialog box. Select a search to delete and then click the Delete button.

Putting the Search into Play

If you elect not to save the search, simply click OK in the Advanced Search Options dialog box. You'll be back in the Sherlock window, where, in small letters in the Info pane, you'll see the criteria you've selected for the search. You can also type text in the Keywords area, which will add to the description in the Info pane.

Find items whose file name contains "downloads", is invisible

Finally, click the Search icon (the magnifying glass). The search begins, and any items that are found will appear in the Listing pane.

Accessing Internet Search Sites

Although Sherlock is strong in searching for and within files on disks connected to your Mac, another side to its personality makes it even more powerful—it's ability to search Internet sites. In fact, all of its other channels are devoted to different ways that it can search the Internet and present results.

 TIP Wondering what a channel's name is? The icons are cute, but a name can be helpful. Just point the mouse at one of the channel icons at the top of the Sherlock window, and its name will pop up in a small box below the icon.

Searching the Internet is very easy with Sherlock. Although it has many different channels and appears to have many different ways to search, you really search all the channels in the same way:

1. You select the Web search engines or Web sites that you want to search in the Listing pane.

2. You enter keyword(s) in the Keyword Entry box, and you click the Search button (the magnifying glass).

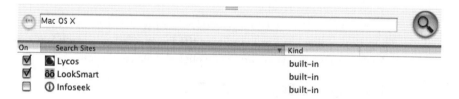

3. The resulting "hits" appear in the Listing pane.

4. When you select one of the result entries, a preview of that item or page will appear in the Info pane.

5. If you double-click one of the results in the Listing pane (or if you click a hyperlink in the Info pane), that page is launched in your Web-browser application.

The only major difference between the search channels is in the way the results are shown. Sherlock offers four basic results-listing types: Web searching, people, news, and shopping. I'll take a look at each in turn.

NOTE To search the Internet with Sherlock, you need to be connected to the Internet. (In some cases, accessing Sherlock's Internet capabilities will cause your Mac to attempt to connect.) If you're not sure how to connect to the Internet yet, see Chapter 9 for details.

Searching and News Channels

Select the Internet, Apple, or Reference channel, and you'll be searching for Web pages. Your ultimate goal is to find an article or page somewhere on the World Wide Web that has a topic similar to the keywords you enter to describe it. Perhaps what's most important is the relevance of the search, which is front and center in the results list (see Figure 6.14).

With Web searches, the results in the Listing pane show the name of the page, the relevance of the site to your keywords (according to Sherlock, which looks for how often the words appear in the target page and how close to one another they are), and the site in question. You can re-sort the listing, if desired, by clicking one of the headings (Name, Relevance, or Site) in the Listing pane.

FIGURE 6.14

Search on an Internet channel and then select one of the results. A quick summary appears in the Info pane.

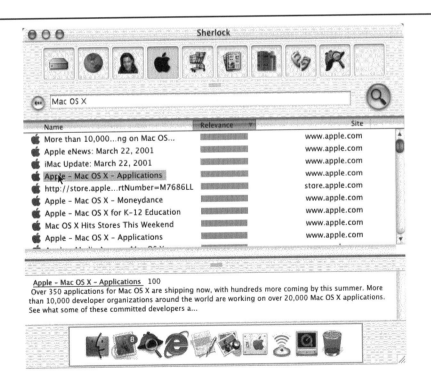

TIP When searching for Web sites, you can use plus (+) signs and minus (–) signs to help target your search. A plus sign means you definitely want the results to include that keyword, and a minus sign means you definitely do *not* want the results to include that keyword. So the term "Steve Jobs" looks for pages that have either word in them. "Steve -Jobs" looks for pages that have "Steve" but not "Jobs." "+Steve Jobs" looks for pages that have "Jobs" in them, but only if they also have "Steve" in them.

I've included the News channel in this section. I couldn't bear to give it its own section title because it's different in only one way, really, from a Web-search listing: A News search site will return results that include a date column, ideally letting you know when the story was published or posted on the Web.

Investor rally s...h shares soaring	4/5/01	news.search.com
Internet bond-t...s bottoming out	4/4/01	news.search.com
Case: AOL doesn't need rate hike	4/3/01	news.search.com
Parts makers st...y tech slowdown	3/29/01	news.search.com

The People Channel

Search sites on the People channel enable you to look for ordinary people—not just celebrities who show up all over the place in regular Web search engines. With these People channel search sites, you can retrieve multiple listings for common names ("Jack Smith") and start to narrow them down. In many cases, the search engines will even help you find an e-mail address or a phone number.

In fact, that's what makes them different. Perform a search, and you'll see a name, e-mail address, and phone number, if they can be found.

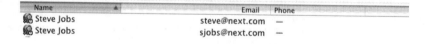

Name	Email	Phone
Steve Jobs	steve@next.com	—
Steve Jobs	sjobs@next.com	—

 NOTE When you're searching for people, you'll almost always do fine just entering their first and last names (a middle initial can help, too, although it will limit the results you see). If you don't succeed that way, some search sites will also work with "last name, first name" as in "Jobs, Steve."

The Shopping Channel

Select the Shopping channel, and you'll see some popular sites. Shopping is one of Sherlock's most heavily touted features, especially in early keynote addresses that introduced the application. Why? Because whenever you search for a product using one or more of the search sites on the Shopping channel, you'll get results in the Listing pane that include availability and price.

Name	Price	Availability	Site
APPLE MACINTOSH iMAC DV 400/64/DVD/BLUE	US $635.00	10/30 08:04	cgi.ebay.com
APPLE MACINTOSH iMAC DV 400/64/DVD/BLUE	US $660.00	10/30 07:41	cgi.ebay.com
APPLE iMAC DV 400/64M/10G/DVD/USB/56k LI	US $660.00	10/30 07:44	cgi.ebay.com

This availability date might not seem like much until you realize that Sherlock can search auction sites such as eBay and Amazon Auctions on the Internet. For auctions, the availability information tells you when the auction will end. That makes Sherlock a great tool for quickly pricing Internet auction items, even from multiple auction sites at once.

 NOTE When you're searching shopping sites, you'll sometimes find that tailoring your keywords to a particular site will help you get better results from that site. For instance, eBay is a stickler for the order of words. (For example, "iMac Bondi" will not find listings that have "iMac" and "Bondi" in different parts of the title.) Other shopping sites will find listings with keywords in any order, though, so feel free to experiment.

Adding Search Sites to Sherlock

Besides providing a collection of included search sites in Sherlock, Apple has also made it easy for third parties to create their own search sites. Apple-related Web sites, shopping sites, and others have taken heed, creating search-site files that can be added to Sherlock. These small files define the type of search (such as Web search, shopping, news, or people) that the third party wants associated with its site, as well as some other important parameters to help Sherlock talk to the search engine. You can then download the small search-site file and install it. (These files will usually have the .src filename extension.)

 TIP You can create a new channel in Sherlock, if you like, by selecting Channels ➢ New Channel. You can also use My Channel (the channel with the Sherlock hat and magnifying glass icon) to add your own search sites, if desired.

You can find search-site files at the sites themselves (as you're surfing around, especially at Mac-related sites, look for a link that lets you download such a file) or at Apple's Sherlock pages (`www.apple.com/sherlock`). Once you've downloaded the plug-in, you can install it in one of two ways:

- The easy way is to select the channel into which you'd like to add the site, then choose Channels ≻ Add Search Site. In the Open dialog sheet, locate the plug-in file and click Add. The new search site is added to the current channel. (You can delete the original SRC file if you want, because it has been copied to your Internet Search Sites folder.)

- The hard(er) way to add a site is to manually copy the SRC file to your personal Internet Search Sites folder, located in the Library folder inside your home folder. Drag the search file either to the My Channel folder or to a folder representing a channel of *related* search types (for instance, don't drag a Web search-site file to a Shopping channel). Once the site is added, you should be able to access it immediately in Sherlock.

What's Next?

In this chapter, you learned how to access Mac OS X's Help system and other Help systems, including Classic and third-party approaches. You also saw how to search local volumes and Internet search sites using Sherlock. In the next chapter, you'll learn many of the tasks that go along with being an administrator of your Mac, including creating user accounts, assigning passwords, installing applications, managing file privileges, and determining system preferences.

PART II

Networks and the Internet

LEARN TO:

- *Manage users and administrative responsibilities*

- *Connect to remote networks*

- *Enable File Sharing between Macs*

- *Connect to the Internet*

- *Read, write, and manage e-mail*

- *Access the Web and FTP*

- *Use Apple's online iTools*

CHAPTER **7**

Being the Administrator: Users and Settings

Because Mac OS X is designed from the ground up to be a multiuser operating system, it's going to require a little extra vigilance if you're the person who manages the system. In the Mac OS X system, an administrator is required for a number of tasks, including creation of user accounts, installation of applications for all users, and some fairly regular maintenance tasks. We'll discuss some of these tasks throughout the book; issues ranging from networking to disk maintenance have components that require an administrator's intervention.

In this chapter I want to talk about the administrator account itself, along with special issues that require you to log in using an administrator's account. Then you'll look at the process of creating user accounts, setting privileges and managing your hard disks and resources, installing applications, and setting system-level preferences. Even if you're the only person who uses your Mac, you might want to take a quick look at this chapter, as it will set the groundwork for discussions in later chapters that require some knowledge of an administrator's responsibilities and privileges.

The Administrator Basics

When you first install Mac OS X (or the first time you turn on a Mac that has Mac OS X preinstalled), it asks you to create the initial user account. That account is automatically given administrator responsibilities and privileges, which means that you can write to many of the main folders on your Mac's hard disk, such as the Applications and Library folders. Likewise, you can set many of the system-level preferences in the System Preferences application without first entering an administrator's password—those panes are automatically "unlocked."

As we'll see in the section "Creating and Editing Users," other user accounts can also have administrative ("Admin") access, making it possible for others to install applications or drivers and make system-level preference changes. We'll see many of those options later in this chapter.

The extra power granted Admin users means that such users should take care to avoid leaving their account logged in at a Mac that sees a lot of traffic—in an organizational or Mac lab setting. One solution is to turn on the password features of the Screen Saver pane in the System Preferences application, so that if you do get up, your password will be required to unlock the screen saver. But it's best to remember to keep your Admin password well hidden and to log out of an Admin account whenever you'll be leaving a Mac that others could access; the file privileges of an Admin account could allow a neophyte or reckless user to cause some damage to applications, drivers, and settings.

For the record, an Admin account is different from the *root* account, or what is often called the *superuser* account in Unix circles. The root account has universal file-system privileges—it can change any file on your Mac. It can also see hidden files and folders, and it can make changes to any preferences setting. By default, however, the root account is disabled in Mac OS X. Although this isn't customary in most Unix iterations, it was deemed wise by Apple's engineers, who apparently decided that beginner and intermediate Mac users should be shielded from the root account at all costs. After all, one false move (renaming or deleting the wrong file in the system hierarchy, for instance) could render your Mac useless.

In general, there isn't much reason to use the root account, even as an advanced user; Admin accounts have enough power and privileges to perform most of the tasks you need to accomplish. In some cases, you may need to re-enable the root account to do some very low-level troubleshooting, as well as some system administration that's discussed in the final chapters of this book. So, enabling the root account is discussed in Chapter 20. In this chapter, though, I'll stick to discussing the Admin accounts.

Administrative Folder Privileges

One of the issues discussed in Chapter 4 is the idea of read and write privileges, and how you can change them within user folders. The rest of the folders throughout the Mac OS X system are also, in some ways, defined by which user accounts have privileges to access the folders. The most important folders, for instance, can be altered (written to) only by the root account.

The second level of importance goes to any user with administrative authority. Once a person is made a member of this Admin group, that individual can alter some basic system-level settings folders and files. (Adding a user to the Admin group is discussed in the section "Creating and Editing Users" later in this chapter.)

So, let's take a look at the various root-level folders to get an idea of who has access to what.

Root-Level Folders

Chapter 3 discussed the basics of the Mac OS X file system, including a quick look at the root-level folders that appear in a standard Mac OS X system: the Applications folder, Users folder, Library folder, System folder, and Mac OS 9 folder. Don't let the term *root-level* fool you, by the way. This use of "root" doesn't mean "root account" but rather that these folders are the first level of folders on a typical Mac OS X startup disk. In Mac OS X's path parlance, these would be represented as /Applications and /Library, for instance. The initial slash (/) is referred to as the *root level* of the disk.

In both Chapter 3 and Chapter 4, you'll find a lot of information about the Users folder (and particularly, each user's home folder), where most users' account privileges enable users to alter and affect the makeup of their individual folders. The other folders on the Mac, however, tend to be accessible only by Admin accounts (see Figure 7.1).

 WARNING The Admin account grants you the power to rename some important folders, which you should avoid doing. Don't rename root-level folders or subfolders within them, such as those in the Library hierarchy or the Utilities folder inside the Applications folder. Doing so can adversely affect your applications and even the Mac OS itself.

The Applications folder is where you, as an administrator, can install applications for all users on the Mac to use. While regular users can only read and launch applications in this main Applications folder, an Admin account can install, move, or delete applications in this folder.

The System folder is accessible by Admin accounts, but only the root account (if enabled) can delete items from it or move items to it. In fact, Mac OS X is designed so that the System folder should be accessed very rarely, since many of the system settings and drivers for Mac OS X actually reside in the root-level Library folder, not the System folder. Ideally, the System folder should be accessed only by Apple installers and updaters. (That's not to say you won't occasionally delve into the System folder—but only very rarely for troubleshooting tasks as discussed in Part IV of this book.)

FIGURE 7.1

The root-level folders

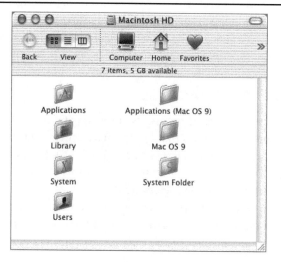

The Library folder at the root level is the main repository of system-level preferences and settings files for applications, including items like Fonts, ColorSync profiles, and system-level help files. Likewise, you'll access subfolders that store preferences, settings, and plug-ins or other support files for system-level applications and even server programs. Unlike the System folder, which can be altered only by Apple installers and the root account (or users who know the root password, if the root account has been enabled), the root-level Library folder and its subfolders are accessible by anyone with an Admin account.

 WARNING By default, all users have read and write privileges for the Mac OS 9.1 System Folder, and only the root account can change this. If you've enabled the root account, it may seem tempting to assign limiting privileges to the Mac OS 9.1 System Folder, but doing so could affect your users' ability to run the Classic environment. A user must have read and write privileges for the Mac OS 9.1 System Folder in order for the Classic environment to launch.

Determining Privileges

So, by default, the Admin-level accounts can write to the Applications folder and Library folder. The implications of this are fairly obvious: Admin-level users have the privileges they need to install system-level applications (those that all users on this particular Mac can access) and even to troubleshoot the support files of applications in the Library folder. When it comes to altering low-level Mac OS settings, however, you'd have to enable the root account or, more appropriately, rely on Apple's installers and utilities.

If you want to see this for yourself, select one of the folders (such as Applications, Library, or System) and use the File ➢ Show Info (or ⌘+I) command to view that folder's attributes. In the Info window, select Privileges from the Show menu. Now you'll see the sharing levels for the folder. As shown in Figure 7.2, the "system" account has ownership of the Applications folder (along with read and write privileges). The Admin group also has read and write privileges, while all other users have read privileges only (making it possible for them to launch applications, but not alter the folder's contents). Note that the Admin group is sometimes referred to as the "wheel" group for some folders and resources.

 NOTE In Mac OS X, administrative users belong to both the wheel group and the Admin group. The groups are technically different: The wheel group is used to store users who are allowed to gain "superuser" access at the Terminal command line. That said, the only difference you'll see in day-to-day use is that some folders grant the wheel group privileges and some grant the Admin group privileges (sometimes apparently at random).

FIGURE 7.2

The privileges associated with the root-level Applications folder

Users' Home Folders

Users' home folders actually work a little differently from the other folders, because they don't have the system account as their owners; a home folder is owned by the individual user, who is free to set permissions as discussed in Chapter 4. That means that even Admin-level users generally have only read access to a user's folder and sub-folders unless that user has specifically given the Admin group or wheel group read and write access.

For the Users folder itself, only read permission is given to the Admin or wheel group (see Figure 7.3). Even with an Admin account, you can't manually alter the contents of the Users folder. You can, however, add and manage users using the Users pane in the System Preferences application, as you'll see later in the section "Creating and Editing Users."

You should also note that within the Users folder, the Shared folder has a different privileges profile by default. The Shared folder grants read and write privileges to everyone, making it a safe place for users to copy files that all other users should be able to access freely.

Likewise, each user has a Public folder (inside each user's home folder), where everyone, regardless of account type, has read permission. Inside that folder is a Drop Box folder, where everyone has write privileges, but not read privileges. That makes it possible, for example, for a user to send a file to Gwen by placing it in her Drop Box folder, but disallows users other than Gwen from seeing (and launching or copying) what has been placed in that folder.

FIGURE 7.3

*The Privileges settings
for the Users folder*

Volume Privileges

If you have additional disks or volumes (other than the startup disk) attached to your Mac, you may also wish to check the privileges set for those volumes. By default, the root level of attached disks can have wide-open privileges, particularly disks originally created and formatted with an earlier Mac OS version. If you highlight a disk icon and select File ➢ Show Info in the Finder, you may find that all users have read and write privileges. If that's okay, you can leave the settings that way; otherwise, you may wish to change the privileges for that disk so that the volume is read-only or offers no access to users.

If you'd prefer that users have access only to certain parts of an attached volume, you can dig into the volume and assign privileges to individual folders. Set the Everybody Else setting to Read & Write for those folders, while setting others to Read Only or None.

You may notice that folders created on external volumes will sometimes have "unknown" as the group instead of the Admin or wheel group. This makes it difficult to assign a folder on the volume so that administrative users have different access privileges from regular users. This can't be changed easily without heading to the Terminal window and the command line. See Chapter 22 for details on changing a particular item's group using the chgrp command.

You'll also notice that the Info window for external volumes includes another option, "Ignore privileges on this volume." Apple notes in its technical documentation that this option is for a very specific situation. If you've been forced to delete and reinstall Mac OS X on your Mac, and newly created users are having trouble accessing the external volume, this may be because the permissions on that disk were mapped to the previous user accounts, and the newly created users aren't being recognized. The quick fix is to turn on "Ignore privileges on this volume," thus granting access to all users. If you do so, you should make sure you don't have important or private files stored on that volume, since this is a fairly unsecure approach to sharing.

Creating and Editing Users

Admin accounts are the only accounts that can create (add) and edit users on the system. To add users to a particular Mac, launch the System Preferences application, then choose the Users pane (see Figure 7.4).

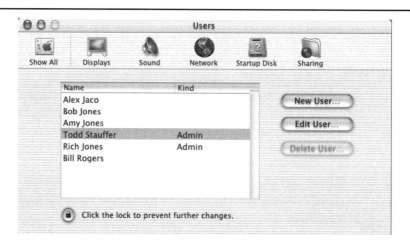

If you're currently logged into a regular user account, you'll need to *authenticate* as an Admin user by entering a username and password for an account that has Admin status. Then you can edit or add a user.

To do so, click the padlock icon in the bottom-left corner of the window. In the dialog box that appears, enter your username and password (if you have Admin status). If your username, password, and Admin status are recognized, the padlock icon will change from locked to unlocked.

Now you're ready to add, edit, or delete a user account from the Mac OS X system.

Creating a User

Once you have full access to the Users pane, you can add a user by clicking the New User button. Doing so brings up the New User window, shown in Figure 7.5.

 WARNING Apple warns that you shouldn't use "root" as a Short Name when creating a user. If you need to enable the root account, do so using the instructions in Chapter 20.

FIGURE 7.5

The New User window

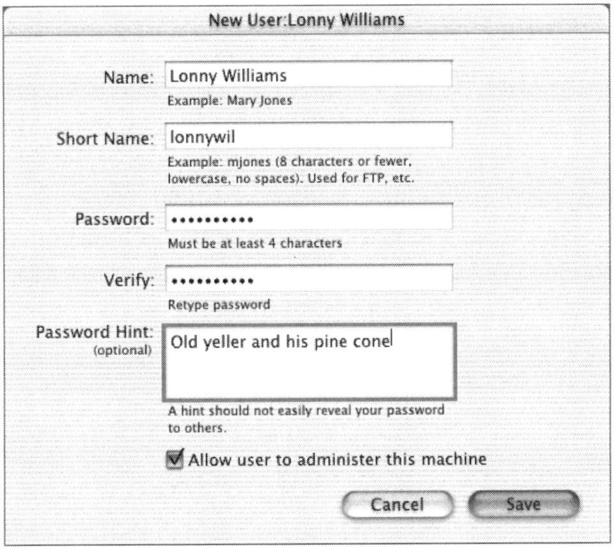

New User:Lonny Williams

Name: Lonny Williams
Example: Mary Jones

Short Name: lonnywil
Example: mjones (8 characters or fewer, lowercase, no spaces). Used for FTP, etc.

Password: ••••••••••
Must be at least 4 characters

Verify: ••••••••••
Retype password

Password Hint: Old yeller and his pine cone
(optional)

A hint should not easily reveal your password to others.

☑ Allow user to administer this machine

Cancel   Save

Here are the items you should fill in to create a new user:

Name   In the Name entry box, enter the full name (first and last) of your user.

Short Name   In the Short Name box, enter the username you'd like to assign to this user, assuming you don't like the default that Mac OS X assigns. Note that a user can actually use either the Name or Short Name to sign into Mac OS X, but the Short Name, which is limited to eight characters, can be used in any application that requires a shorter username (especially FTP, Telnet, or other applications used to access the Mac from a different computer).

Password   Enter this user's password. Remember that passwords are case sensitive.

Verify   Retype the user's password to verify that it was typed correctly the first time.

Password Hint   This entry box enables you to optionally enter a hint that the user can use to remember the password. A hint can be a little dangerous, because it shouldn't reveal the password or help others guess it. The hint should definitely not be a code that could be broken by rearranging letters or numbers.

 NOTE   For password hints to be useful to your users, you have to turn on the Show Password Hint option in the Login pane, as discussed later in the section "System-Level Preference Settings."

Allow User to Administer This Machine   Selecting this option places this user in the Admin group, which, as noted in the previous section "Administrative Folder Privileges," gives that user the ability to install applications and alter settings in the root-level Library folder.

When you've finished entering all this information, click the Save button to create and save the new user's information. That user will now appear in the Users pane, and a new home folder will be created for the user in the root-level Users folder.

Playing with Passwords

There's an interesting issue when it comes to assigning passwords in Mac OS X. In most cases you want to encourage two things about passwords—that they be as long as possible and that they be as "unguessable" as possible. In Mac OS X, however, as with many Unix-derived OSs, only the *first* eight characters of a password are used to authenticate. So you should encourage your users to create eight-character passwords with nonwords, numbers, and text, such as "ham455sq." (Remember that passwords are case-sensitive.)

Note that it's also possible to create a user who doesn't have a password, making that account easy to sign into and work with. This isn't recommended, especially in any organizational setting or in any situation where your Mac is directly connected to the Internet. (Even over a phone line, this could be unsecure, allowing others access to your Mac.) If, for some reason, you do want to do this, simply leave the Password and Verify entry boxes blank. (I'd absolutely recommend *not* giving this account administrator privileges.) When that user logs in, no password will be required.

Editing a User

If the user account in question already exists, you can edit that user's information, giving you the opportunity to rename the user, change the user's password, or alter the user's Admin status. To do so, you may need to enter the administrator's password by clicking the locked padlock icon. (If the icon appears unlocked, then you're ready to edit.)

Highlight the user in the Users pane and click Edit User. You'll see that user's window appear. Now, edit the portions of that user's profile that you'd like to change, including the long name, password, or Admin status. When you're done, click Save.

 NOTE Although these entries are the same as those you use to create a new user, note that Mac OS X doesn't allow you to change the short name of a user in the Edit User window. If your user requires another username, you'll need to create a new user account and move that person's personal files to the newly created user folder.

Removing a User

Although removing a user isn't in any way more difficult than adding or editing the user, it's not something you'll want to do hastily. Once you remove a user, you can't re-add that user easily. Instead, you'll need to re-create the user (with the same username and password, if desired), then manually copy files from the user's old home folder to the new home folder. When you delete a user, the contents of that user's home folder aren't removed—they're simply reassigned to an administrator. So the files are intact, but the user's settings, preferences, and any Library additions (personal fonts or printers, for example) will need to be reinstalled. It's best, therefore, to remove users only when you're fairly sure they won't be reaccessing your system and requiring the same workplace settings.

To remove a user, simply select that user in the Users pane and click Delete User. You'll then see an alert box asking if you really want to delete the user. You'll also see a list of usernames that are in the Admin group, to whom you can assign the privileges for the removed user's home folder. Select an Admin user from the list, then click the Delete button.

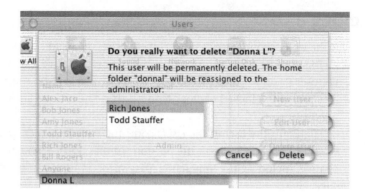

Once you've deleted the user, the account will no longer appear in the Users pane. The user's home folder will still be found in the root-level Users folder, although its privileges will now be assigned to the selected Admin account. The word *deleted* will also be appended to the user's folder.

You can't really reinstate the user now, but you can re-create the user by clicking New User in the Users pane and walking through the steps of creating the user. Then, once the user is created, you can copy files or subfolders (such as the Documents folder) from that user's disabled folder to the user's new Drop Box folder, enabling the user to again gain access to old files and to place them elsewhere in the user's folder.

TIP Placing files or folders in a user's Drop Box automatically makes that user the owner of the items, which can be convenient because you'll probably want the user to have full read and write access to the restored items.

Installing Applications

To install applications that all users of the Mac OS X system can use requires that you log in to an account with Admin status. You can then install applications in one of two ways: You can drag applications (or folders that include applications) to the Applications folder, or you can use an installer application to install the applications.

Installing by Dragging

If you've logged in using an Admin account, you can simply drag an application file to the Applications folder. You can also, if you wish, drag a folder that contains an application to the Applications folder. Because the Admin group has privileges to write to the Applications folder, anything you drag to the folder will be placed there, such as the Transmit and AppleWorks applications shown in Figure 7.6. Such applications become available to all users on the Mac, because all user accounts have read access for the Applications folder.

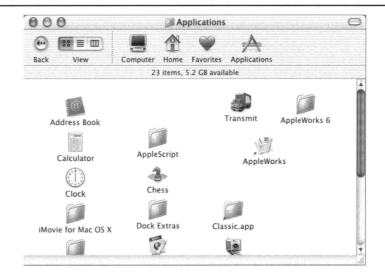

FIGURE 7.6

Transmit and AppleWorks were installed by dragging them into the Applications folder.

If you drag an application's folder to the Applications folder, it's also a good idea to create an alias to the actual application if you plan to store it in that folder. (You can see this in Figure 7.6, where I've dragged the AppleWorks folder into the Applications folder, then created an alias to the AppleWorks application that's inside that folder. You can tell it's an alias because of the small, curved arrow that's part of its icon.) The alias makes it easier for users to find and double-click the application icon without wandering into the application's folder and subfolders. Remember that the alias and the folder will need to have slightly different names, because no two items in the same folder (in this case, the Applications folder) may have the same name.

Problematic privileges are another thing to watch out for when dragging applications around. When you're dragging an application from your home folder to the Applications folder to relocate it there, you'll probably need to change the privileges for the application (or the application's folder, if relevant). For instance, open the Info window for that particular application or folder and make sure "Everybody" is set to read-only privileges; otherwise, some of your users may not be able to launch the application. If you are setting privileges for a folder, you should also copy those privileges to all enclosed folders using the Copy command in the Privileges portion of the

Show window. (In some cases you may need to set an application's folder to Read & Write for everyone, particularly if there's a subfolder in that folder where the application needs to store temporary files.)

That said, if you'd like to set an application or application folder so that only Admin users (those in the Admin or wheel group) can access the application, that's possible and might be useful if you have certain applications that only Admin-level users should access. Set the application or application folder so that only the wheel or Admin group (whichever is listed) has read and write privileges and that the Everybody entry is set to None.

Installing via an Installer Application

Most applications that come on a CD-ROM or similar distribution mechanism will include a special installer application. This is also true of some downloaded applications, especially those from Apple and other commercial developers. In fact, some downloaded applications are stored as *disk images*, a special type of archive that appears to mount on the desktop like a removable disk.

When you double-click the disk image file (which will usually have a .img or .dmg filename extension), you'll see the file "mount" on the desktop as though it were a disk. Then, if you double-click that disk icon, the application or an application installer will appear in that disk's Finder window (see Figure 7.7). Note that if you've set the Finder application so that it doesn't mount removable disks on the desktop (in the Finder ➤ Preferences dialog box), then you'll see the mounted disk image after clicking the Computer button in a Finder window.

 NOTE See Chapter 14 for more on using Disk Copy and disk images.

FIGURE 7.7

The download resulting in a disk image, which, when double-clicked, "mounts" as though it were a removable disk

In other cases, especially if you've downloaded the file from the Internet, you'll need to decompress the application's archive file, then copy the application to the Applications folder.

Using the Package Installer

If the result is not an application (or a folder in which the application is stored), it's possible that it's a package file (especially if it has a .pkg filename extension). When you double-click the package file, you'll see the Package Installer, an Apple application that developers can use to install their own applications. In many cases, the Package Installer will require a password (see Figure 7.8). If your user account has Admin status, you can enter your own account name and password. Click the padlock to authenticate.

 WARNING Some Mac OS X developers (notably StepWise, at www.stepwise.com) warn about problems with the Package Installer, particularly in early versions of Mac OS X. You should realize that authenticating the Package Installer is a potential security risk. It's possible that the package could do harm—purposefully or accidentally—to system-level files in the main System folder, Library folder, or elsewhere on your Mac. So you should authenticate the Package Installer only when you're dealing with packages from Apple or from other reliable third-party application developers.

PART
II

Networks and the Internet

FIGURE 7.8

Here I'm trying to install an application that requires an administrator password.

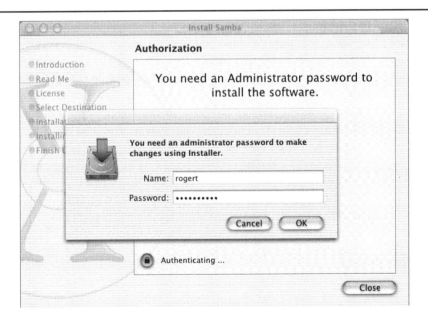

Once you've been authenticated, you're ready to begin the installation process. The installer will walk you through the process of selecting a destination (the volume where you'd like the application installed) and customizing the installation, if you have that option. (Some installations don't allow for customized installation.) If the Customize button is available, click it. You'll see options that enable you to select which parts of the application you'd like to install and which parts you'd like to skip.

Once you've made your choices, click the Install button. The installation will take place, with a progress indicator crawling across the screen to prove it. When the installation is complete, you'll be asked if you'd like to quit the installer or, in some cases, restart your Mac. Click the appropriate choice.

 NOTE You may also encounter other types of installers, from developers other than Apple. If they don't have an authentication option, they may allow you to install the application only if you've logged into an Admin account. Note also that many installers include an Uninstall option that can be helpful if you subsequently decide to remove the application from your Mac.

System-Level Preference Settings

In Chapter 4, I detailed the settings via the System Preferences application that regular users have access to, enabling them to customize their personal Mac OS X session. Along with those settings come a few others that can be accessed only by users who belong to the Admin group. These particular settings affect the Mac at a system level—the disk it starts up from, its networking settings, the file-sharing state, and others. Although some of these will be explained in depth in later chapters, let's take a quick look here at the settings that require an administrator's password.

To access these preferences, launch the System Preferences application by clicking its tile in the Dock or by double-clicking its icon in the Applications folder. Then you'll see all the System Preferences panes, including those that I'm discussing here: Date & Time, Energy Saver, Login, Network, Sharing, Startup Disk, and Users. By default, you won't have to authenticate as long as you're signed into an Admin account; if you're signed into a regular account, you'll need to authenticate with a valid Admin username and password.

NOTE A number of other utility applications require authentication, and most of them are covered elsewhere in this book, including the NetInfo Manager (Chapter 20) and Disk Utility (Chapter 18).

Date & Time

It may seem odd at first, but the Date & Time settings within the Mac OS can be altered only by an administrator. The reason for this is simple: Many parts of the Mac OS and some applications rely heavily on the clock and calendar being correct; if they are changed, it can affect everything from automated tasks to the way e-mail is received and sorted. Because of this, and the fact that Date & Time offers some Internet-related settings, these preferences are padlocked away for nonadministrative users.

The Date & Time pane offers four different tabs: Date & Time, Time Zone, Network Time, and Menu Bar Clock. Once unlocked, the Date & Time tab can be used to select Today's Date (by clicking on the calendar interface) and the Current Time (using the up and down arrows next to the digital time readout). Note that these can't be set if Network Time Synchronization has been turned on.

On the Time Zone tab, you can select your current locale and time zone, which include special areas of differentiation. For instance, choose a time zone near the eastern coast of the U.S., and you can individually select "U.S.A.—Indianapolis" from the pop-up menu, which tells your Mac to note the differences in that locale's observation of daylight savings time. You can also, obviously, choose the country where your Mac is located to force its clock to follow national timekeeping guidelines.

On the Network Time tab (see Figure 7.9), you'll see controls that enable you to set your Mac's clock automatically using a network time server. These are special computers that are synchronized to atomic clocks in an effort to make a standard, exact time available on the Internet. Click the Start button to turn on Network Time Synchronization, and, in the Network Time Server section of the tab's panel, choose how you'd like it synchronized. You can either select Manually and enter the address of a time server (Apple's default address is `time.apple.com`) or select From NetInfo if your network has a NetInfo server in place.

On the Menu Bar Clock tab, you can determine whether or not you want the menu bar clock (in the top-right corner of the Mac's screen) to be displayed, and you can also set some options for how it's displayed.

PART

II

Networks and the Internet

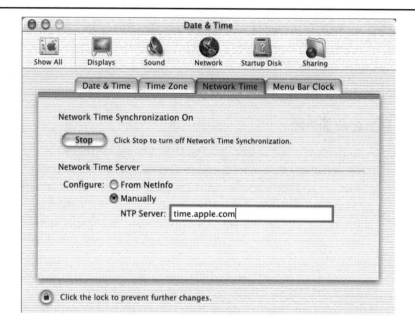

Energy Saver

In the Energy Saver pane, you can set how long the Mac should wait while it's inactive before it automatically activates sleep mode. To set this, use the slider control to choose the amount of time, in minutes, before an idle Mac will put itself into sleep mode.

You can also, if desired, set separate timings for turning off the display and spinning down the hard disk, by placing check marks next to those options and using the sliders to set time limits. Note that the time limits must be *less than* the main sleep setting, since there's no point in having the display enter sleep mode *after* the entire Mac (including the display) has entered sleep mode!

Login

The Login pane is only half administrator-controlled—the Login Window tab requires a password in order to change items.

On the Login Window tab, you can click the Automatically Log In option to force the Mac to bypass the initial Mac OS X login window and default to a particular user account and password.

You can also turn on the option to disable the Restart and Shut Down buttons if you'd like to prevent users from restarting or shutting down the Mac. This can keep the machine somewhat more secure, especially in a computer lab setting, as it makes it more difficult for a user to boot the Mac into an earlier Mac OS version or to use a system CD.

 NOTE Why does restarting give power? If a user restarts the Mac, inserts a CD-ROM with a valid System folder on it, and presses the C key on the keyboard, the Mac will start up from that CD-ROM and give the user some less-than-secure access to the Mac, especially if the CD holds Mac OS 9.1 or earlier. Likewise, if you restart while holding down the Option key on a dual-boot Mac OS X system, the Mac can be restarted in Mac OS 9.1, again giving the user access to other users' document files as well as portions of the Mac OS X System folder. Disabling the Restart and Shut Down buttons makes it harder to restart the Mac from the login window, although the Restart and Shut Down commands are still active when a user is logged in. So, make sure you remind your users to log out when they've finished working.

You can turn on the "Show password hint after 3 attempts to enter a password" option if you'd like users to see password hints (which are set in the Users pane) when they're having trouble. And you can select a custom authenticator if you have one installed that you'd prefer to use. (Authenticators are stored in the System/Library/Authenticators/ folder.)

 NOTE The authenticator is simply the system used to compare an entered username and password against the database to determine if the user is valid on the system. If you prefer, for some reason, to use an authenticator other than Mac OS X's built-in Kerberos authentication, you'll need to install it first, then select it here in the Password pane.

Network

The Network pane offers extensive administrator-only controls that govern how the Mac will behave on both a local network and the Internet via Ethernet, modem, or other interfaces, such as AirPort wireless networking, that you may have installed. You assign TCP/IP (Transmission Control Protocol/Internet Protocol) characteristics on the TCP/IP tab and basic AppleTalk settings on the AppleTalk tab. All these options and settings will be discussed extensively in Chapters 8 and 9, but if you already have an awareness of how TCP/IP and AppleTalk work, you can open the Network pane and begin changing things.

PART

II

Networks and the Internet

Sharing

Like the Network pane, the Sharing pane requires an Admin account before changes can be made. Here you can determine a number of different settings, including whether or not File Sharing is turned on (making it possible for others to access this Mac via Apple File Services). You can also turn on Web Sharing, FTP access, and remote login (SSH) access. All these options are discussed later in this book. (File Sharing is covered in Chapter 8, remote login is in Chapter 23, and Web Sharing and FTP are in Chapter 24.)

Startup Disk

In the Startup Disk pane, you can choose what disk (or what System folder, if you have multiple folders on a particular disk) should be used to start up the Mac. This pane enables you, primarily, to dual-boot between Mac OS 9.1 and Mac OS X installations by choosing the appropriate folder or volume (see Figure 7.10). You may also have the choice of selecting a network volume if your local network supports Net-Boot, giving you the ability to boot a Macintosh from a network server.

To change startup disks, all you have to do is select, from the pane, the startup folder you'd like to use. When you restart the Mac from the login window or via the Apple menu's Restart command, the Mac will use the selected folder for its startup files.

Users

The final pane that requires Admin access, Users, is where you create, edit, and delete user accounts, as discussed earlier in the section "Creating and Editing Users."

FIGURE 7.10

The Startup Disk preferences pane

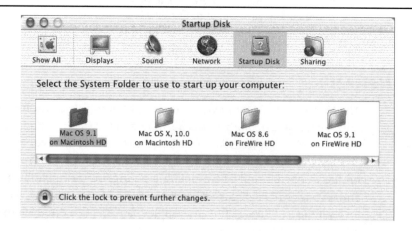

What's Next?

In this chapter you saw some of the tools and responsibilities for administrator accounts. In Chapter 8, you'll move on to networking issues—both connecting to remote servers (as a user) and making network connections available to users (as an administrator). In that chapter you'll see how to configure TCP/IP and AppleTalk connections, how to enable File Sharing, and how to access remote network volumes over a wide area network or via the Internet.

PART

II

Networks and the Internet

CHAPTER 8

Accessing Network Volumes and Sharing Files

Want to connect to another computer to share files? If you've got more than one Mac in your home, office, or organization, chances are that you'd like to connect in order to share files—as well as share printers and other resources. Fortunately, that's easy to do in Mac OS X.

Mac OS X enables you to access individual Macs using personal File Sharing capabilities, which place a folder or hard disk from a remote computer directly on your desktop to be accessed via the Finder.

You can access remote disks and volumes via other protocols, including Apple File Protocol volumes, which are common if you're using AppleShare IP or Mac OS X Server on your server computer, and Network File Services (NFS) volumes, which are fairly common if you're dealing with Unix server computers. Doing so, you can perform a whole host of tasks, including sharing files, backing up to a central location, sharing printers, accessing central databases, and even accessing your Mac remotely.

In this chapter, you'll see how to create a *local area network* (LAN) for sharing files and other resources like printers. (A LAN is differentiated from a *wide area network*, or WAN, in that a WAN is a group of more than one LAN. The Internet is an example of a WAN.) The chapter includes a discussion of the technologies behind networking as well as a look at the various protocols and standards for networking. You'll also see how you can connect two or more Macs, whether they're running Mac OS X, Mac OS 9.*x*, or a combination of both.

If your Macs are already connected, move down to the later sections that cover connecting to an AFP (Apple File Protocol) server or Web server. Later, you'll see how to access more permanent server networks like those served by AppleShare IP or Mac OS X Server.

Putting Together a Network

The term *network* refers to two or more computers (or other devices, such as printers) that are connected via some form of cabling or wireless solution. For Macs that support Mac OS X, that's either Ethernet cabling or AirPort wireless connections. (All modern Macs have Ethernet support built in, whereas AirPort is an add-on for the latest models of iMac, Power Macintosh, iBook, and PowerBook.)

Then, once wired together, the computers use a common protocol to communicate—in the case of Mac OS X, it's the Transmission Control Protocol/Internet Protocol (TCP/IP). TCP/IP routes data between the computers in an orderly way, making sure packets of data leaving one Mac arrive at the other. Although TCP/IP is commonly thought of as the protocol used on the Internet, it's not used exclusively for

Web browsing and e-mail. In fact, it's the basis of all networking between Unix-based computers, which include Mac OS X, thanks to its FreeBSD-based underpinnings.

Once a protocol has been established, services can be made available via that protocol. The most common service for a typical office network is file sharing, which, in the case of the Mac OS, can be made available via Apple File Protocol (AFP) over TCP/IP. The service makes it possible for Mac OS X and earlier Mac versions to share files via the protocol commonly called "AppleShare over IP." As with earlier versions of the Mac OS, you can log directly into a Mac that has File Sharing active, mounting its disk (or a volume that represents the shared item on that Mac's disk) directly on your desktop or in a Finder window.

You can also use NFS (Network File Services) over TCP/IP to create permanent network connections between Mac OS X machines or between Mac OS X and Unix machines. The remote volume would then be permanently available in the /Network/Servers folder on your Mac.

You can also use two services generally associated with the Internet: FTP (File Transfer Protocol, used for transferring files) and HTTP (Hypertext Transport Protocol, used for serving Web pages and files), to share files and information. These are covered in more depth in Chapters 11, 23, and 24, but it's worth noting here that you can use them between local machines just as easily as you can use them over the Internet.

I'll take a close look at all these elements and how they work together to build a network.

Ethernet Connections

By far the most common method used to connect computers in a network is Ethernet. In the past, Macs have also been connected via other types of cabling, including LocalTalk and TokenRing standards. These days, all Macs come with Ethernet built into the computer, including all models that are compatible with Mac OS X. All Macs also use the *unshielded twisted-pair* (UTP) standard of Ethernet cable, not the older, obsolete 10base2 (or *coaxial*) standard.

Twisted-pair cabling can be used between Macs that support three different Ethernet speed standards: 10baseT, 100baseT, and Gigabit Ethernet. All three standards can use the same type of UTP cable (UTP Category 5 cable) to make the connection. UTP Category 5 cable resembles the telephone cable you'd use to connect a telephone to a wall jack, but Ethernet cable is thicker with a larger connector (RJ-45) on each end. The cable works with all Ethernet port speeds, so you can use it to connect your Macs regardless of whether they support 100BaseT or Gigabit Ethernet. (The earliest Mac OS X–compatible models are limited to 10BaseT, but they're still compatible, just slower.)

PART II

Networks and the Internet

You can't simply connect Macs to one another directly using standard Cat 5 cable. Instead, you need to use an Ethernet *hub*, which is a special device designed to act as a central connecting point for all the Macs in your LAN. The cost of a hub ranges from as low as $50 to many hundreds of dollars, depending on how many connections the hub supports and whether or not it's *managed*—that is, whether it actively moves data from one port to the other. (Unmanaged hubs simply replicate data from one Mac on all the ports, which is less efficient.)

Each length of UTP cabling is connected between a port on the hub and the Ethernet port on the side (or back) of the Mac. Once two or more Macs are connected to the hub, you're ready to configure the TCP/IP protocol and enable the Macs to communicate.

 NOTE You can connect *only two* Macs (or two devices, like a Mac and an Ethernet-capable printer) using a special cable called a *crossover cable.* It is Cat 5 Ethernet cable, but the wires inside are crossed to create the appropriate connection for sharing data. The cabling isn't ideal for long-term networking. But if you're simply connecting two Macs to share data quickly or you're connecting a single Mac to an Ethernet-based printer, a crossover cable will work fine. The configuration is the same; you simply don't need a hub.

AirPort Connections

Mac OS X supports another type of network "cabling," if I can stretch the term a bit. AirPort is a wireless technology, enabling Macs to share data without requiring them to be cabled together; instead, data is transferred via a wireless radio connection. Air-Port is actually Apple's name for a technology otherwise known as the IEEE 802.11 standard.

Other manufacturers have cards and devices that are compatible with the IEEE 802.11 standard as well, making it possible for you to upgrade other non-AirPort-capable Macs with third-party cards and upgrades. Older PowerBooks, which can accept PC Card–based IEEE 802.11–compatible expansion cards, are prime candidates for such an upgrade. Of course, all PowerBooks made in 2000 or later support AirPort.

In AirPort's current implementation, AirPort-enabled Macs can share data with Macs that are up to 150 feet (46 meters) away, assuming those Macs have AirPort capabilities installed and activated. In most Macs, you need to first install a special

AirPort card (offered for $99 by Apple), if the Mac can support it. The following Mac models support AirPort:

iMacs   The iMac DV series introduced in 1999 can accept an AirPort card, as can all iMac DV, DV SE, and DV+ models made since then. Since early 2001, all iMac models have been updated to accept an AirPort add-on card.

iBooks   All iBook models can accept an AirPort card.

PowerBooks   The PowerBook G3 2000 (FireWire) and PowerBook G4 models include a slot for an AirPort card; others can accept an IEEE 802.11 PC Card expansion device, although they may require a PC Card that is specifically Mac OS X–compatible.

Power Macintosh   Only the Power Macintosh G4, G4 Cube, and later models can accept an AirPort card. However, the Power Macintosh G4 (PCI Graphics) model, offered for a limited time in the fall of 1999, doesn't support AirPort.

If you're working with a Mac that has an AirPort card installed, the next step is to consider how that Mac will be connected to the network. Like Ethernet connections, AirPort connections generally work with a hub, although the hub doesn't have to be a special hardware device. Any Mac running AirPort Software Base Station software can act as a hub for other wireless Macs. For instance, an iMac DV could act as a hub for other wireless Macs if it's running the AirPort Software Base Station. (At the time of writing, the AirPort Software Base Station works only for Macs running Mac OS 9.*x*. Presumably, a Mac OS X version is in the works; check www.apple.com/airport/ for details.)

Hardware hubs are available for AirPort connections, however, particularly the (similarly named) AirPort Base Station from Apple. This UFO-looking hardware device offers an Ethernet port as well as AirPort capabilities and a built-in modem, making it not only a wireless hub (connecting multiple wireless Macs) but also a wireless-to-wired hub, making it possible for both Ethernet-based and AirPort-based Macs to communicate with one another.

 NOTE   As with Ethernet, two AirPort-enabled Macs can network directly—without wires!—in order to exchange files. All you have to do is configure the AirPort software correctly, as detailed in the later section "Selecting Your AirPort Network."

What About Sharing with Windows?

This chapter focuses on two types of file-sharing networks—AFP and NFS. Although these common protocols cover both the Macintosh and Unix worlds, one big chunk of the computing world is left out of this equation—Microsoft Windows. So, how do you share files with Windows users? You've got a few options:

Samba serving   You can install Samba, an open-source server that enables you to turn a Mac OS X machine into a Windows file server. Samba will allow Windows users to connect to your Mac using the tools built into Windows. Installing Samba is discussed in Chapter 25.

Windows 2000 Services for Macintosh   Windows 2000 includes an option to turn on Apple File Services of TCP/IP, which makes the Windows 2000 server look like it's a standard AFP server. If you have a Windows 2000 server on your LAN, you should be able to access it directly from your Mac as described later in the section "Accessing Remote File Servers."

Dave from Thursby Software   Dave (www.thursby.com) is a third-party solution that allows your Mac to sign into Windows machines for file sharing.

PCMacLAN from Miramar Systems   PCMacLAN (www.miramarsys.com) is another third-party utility that enables a Windows 95/98/NT/2000/Me computer to log into a Mac OS 9.x or Mac OS X computer or server that has File Sharing enabled.

The TCP/IP Protocol

The Transmission Control Protocol/Internet Protocol is the basis of all networking between Mac OS X machines (and between Mac OS X machines and other computers), primarily because it's the basis of all networking between Unix machines. In fact, TCP/IP serves as the foundation of the Internet for pretty much the same reason— Unix machines were the early basis of the Internet (and remain largely so today). If the Internet had begun as a huge global network consisting completely of Macs, it might have been based on AppleTalk instead.

In fact, AppleTalk was the main networking protocol for Macs since the beginning of the Mac in the mid-1980s, and arguably remains the most popular protocol for Macs running Mac OS 9.1 and earlier (especially for smaller networks). The Mac OS had begun to migrate away from AppleTalk, however, because TCP/IP is more efficient and faster, even for Apple's traditional File Sharing capabilities. Mac OS 9.x, for instance, includes File Sharing over IP capabilities, which makes it possible to share files between Mac OS 9.*x* (and Mac OS X) machines using the TCP/IP protocol instead of AppleTalk.

Mac OS X makes file sharing over TCP/IP mandatory, since the operating system doesn't support AppleTalk or any other option for file sharing (unless you install another protocol using a third-party solution—for instance, Samba, which enables Windows computers to connect to your Mac, as discussed in Chapter 25).

Still, because Mac OS X includes the ability to connect to Apple File Protocol over a TCP/IP, the only real difference compared to older-style Mac networking comes in the way you configure your Mac. If you're familiar with AppleTalk networking, you'll see that File Sharing over TCP/IP tasks, such as mounting servers using the Network Browser, are similar to Mac OS 9.*x*.

 NOTE Mac OS X does support the AppleTalk protocol, but only for printing. All file sharing is done using TCP/IP.

TCP/IP is the main protocol you'll use for networking. But what is it? Actually, it's two different protocols—the Transmission Control Protocol and the Internet Protocol. TCP is a protocol for sending data, while IP is a protocol for making sure data gets to the right place. It's like an envelope and the post office. TCP is an envelope that wraps up data, and IP is the postal service that makes sure the envelope gets to the right person.

More to the point here, TCP/IP is something that needs to be set up on each Macintosh that will be part of your network, and for each networking port—Ethernet, AirPort, and so on—that your Mac supports. You'll find settings for TCP/IP in the Network pane of the System Preferences application, as shown in Figure 8.1.

 NOTE When you install Mac OS X (or when you start a new Mac with Mac OS X preinstalled), the Startup Assistant asks you for TCP/IP configuration information. So it's possible that your Mac is already properly configured. If that's the case, you can skip this section and move on to later sections regarding starting up File Sharing and accessing network volumes. If your network settings weren't configured properly at installation time or you've added a new network interface, you'll need to configure TCP/IP.

| CHAPTER 8 • ACCESSING NETWORK VOLUMES AND SHARING FILES

FIGURE 8.1

Here's what the TCP/IP tab in the Network pane looks like when you are configuring an Ethernet port.

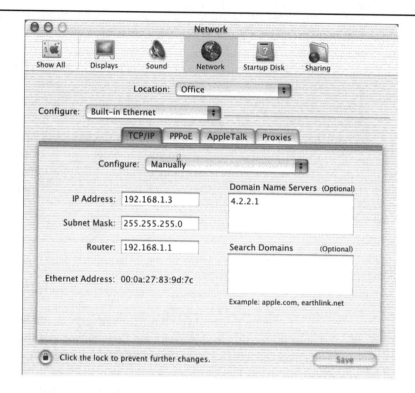

Configuring TCP/IP

In order to configure TCP/IP, you need to know a little about your network. First, you need to decide what type of network interface(s) you have and, following from that, how your network addresses are assigned. Next, you'll need to determine what factor, if any, the Internet will play in your TCP/IP configuration. Then, you may need to know some specifics concerning your network, including arcana such as the IP address, subnet mask, and other necessary evils.

NOTE Before you configure TCP/IP, you'll need to either log into Mac OS X using an administrator (Admin) account or click the padlock in the Network pane and enter an Admin account name and password. You can't alter the Network configuration without an administrator's password.

Selecting the Port

If you have more than one networking port in your Mac, you need to begin by selecting the appropriate port for configuration. Each Ethernet or AirPort card that's installed in your Mac constitutes a port, so for each networking port you can assign individual TCP/IP addresses. (The Network pane is also used to set up your modem, if you have one, for TCP/IP access. That's discussed in Chapter 9.)

Why have more than one networking port? You may want to use different ports at different times—for instance, any AirPort-enabled Mac will, by default, also have Ethernet built in. With two ports configured, you could switch back and forth between types of networks when, for instance, you take your PowerBook from one office to another.

You might also want to have more than one network port to access two different networks at once. As an example, you might want your Mac to access an Ethernet network and an AirPort network simultaneously, in order to share data between an iBook (via AirPort) while connecting to a wired LAN via Ethernet.

 NOTE If you have an AirPort-capable Mac, you'll be choosing between multiple ports because all AirPort-capable Macs have Ethernet built in as well. If you only want to use AirPort, you can select No Connection for the Ethernet port, so that it won't need to be configured. (You can configure it later, if desired, to connect to an Ethernet network.)

You select the port that you're going to configure using the top Configure menu in the Network pane. (This menu, above all the tabs, is where you can select from Ethernet and, if installed, Modem and AirPort options.) Note, as shown in Figure 8.2, that the options change according to the type of port you're configuring; AirPort options are slightly different from the Ethernet options shown in Figure 8.1.

 NOTE In most cases, Ethernet and AirPort hardware devices are automatically recognized by the Mac and noted in the Configure menu. If you don't see a card that you believe is correctly installed, see Chapter 19 for details on installing cards and driver software. Also see the section "Advanced Settings" later in this chapter, as the particular port in question may have been turned off.

So, to begin configuring a networking port, you should select it in the Configure menu. Once it's selected, make sure you've clicked the TCP/IP tab. Now you're ready to enter TCP/IP information.

FIGURE 8.2

The TCP/IP tab for an
AirPort connection

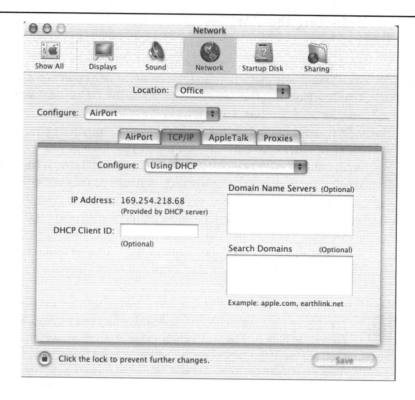

Selecting the Type of Configuration

If you don't know much about TCP/IP setup, that may be okay; you may not need to
dig into the arcana of IP addressing. In some cases, you'll simply select a configuration method and leave it at that. In other cases, though, you'll have to enter all the
addresses manually. Mac OS X gives you a few different choices, including Manually,
Using DHCP, and Using BootP.

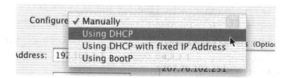

Here's a look at each choice for addressing:

Manually Select Manually if you intend to give the Mac a fixed IP address
and if you otherwise need to specify the particulars of your network setup, as
directed by your network administrator. If you select Manually, you'll need to

enter the IP Address, subnet mask, and so on. (See the section "Configuring TCP/IP Manually" later in this chapter.)

Using DHCP   The Dynamic Host Configuration Protocol is the more popular way to configure TCP/IP automatically these days, especially on networks of personal computers. Server computers (such as Macs running Mac OS X Server) or special router devices that include DHCP server functions can manage DHCP. If you have a DHCP server or router on your network, select Using DHCP from the Configure menu. The server will automatically configure your Mac.

 TIP   If you don't have a DHCP server or router, DHCP can still be valuable. As long as you're not worried about Internet access using the selected Ethernet port, you can use DHCP to create a local network automatically. Select Using DHCP on all your Macs that are connected by Ethernet. Then, after a short delay while the Macs look for and fail to find a DHCP server, addresses will be assigned automatically, making it possible for you to share files between the Macs, using File Sharing. Note also that DHCP is the most often used choice for AirPort networks that include an AirPort base station.

Using DHCP with Fixed IP Address   With this option, your Mac will use a DHCP server to retrieve all TCP/IP settings except the IP address, which you can enter manually. This is a nice compromise when you have a DHCP server available, but you want to make sure this Mac always has the same IP address (for instance, when you want to make Internet services such as Web Sharing available from this Mac).

Using BootP   If your network offers a special BootP (Bootstrap Protocol) server, you can use it to configure your Mac's TCP/IP settings automatically. Select Using BootP from the Configure menu, and you won't need to enter any other addresses or information. Note, however, that if you don't have a BootP server on your local network, your TCP/IP configuration will not be completed correctly. BootP is especially common if you're using a Mac OS X server on your LAN.

Now, if you've selected an automatic type of TCP/IP configuration (and you don't need to specify DNS addresses, which are discussed in the following section), you can click the Save button in the Network pane to apply the changes to your TCP/IP settings. (You may need to enter DNS addresses.) You can then close the System Preferences application and, with any luck, begin using your new network settings immediately. (Occasionally, a restart seems to be necessary, but in most cases changes to network settings are immediate.)

Configuring DNS

Both the automatic and manual approaches to TCP/IP settings optionally give you the opportunity to enter DNS (Domain Name Service) information for your Mac. Whether you need DNS entries depends on how your LAN in configured; when in doubt, consult your network administrator. If you're configuring TCP/IP using the Manually option, DNS settings are likely required; for all other options, you probably don't need the settings unless your network administrator tells you that you do. Here are the settings:

DNS Addresses   These IP addresses are those of DNS computers, which translate text names (for example, www.mac-upgrade.com) into numerical IP addresses. DNS servers are designed so that they automatically update when a domain name is moved or added somewhere on the Internet. Web browsers and other Internet applications reference the DNS servers most often to determine the proper IP address associated with an Internet domain name entered by the user.

Search Domains   Enter local domain names in this entry box so that Internet applications don't have to request information from a DNS server. In most cases, these local domain names are those that are assigned to your local network. On my network, I might enter **mac-upgrade.com**. Then, if I type **toddsmac** into the address box in a Web browser (or if someone else on my network types it), TCP/IP will first look in Search Domains and attempt to access toddsmac.mac-upgrade.com.

Configuring TCP/IP Manually

If you've selected Manually from the TCP/IP tab's Configure menu, you'll need to dig into each of the TCP/IP settings and enter them by hand. (As you type, you can press the Tab key to move to the next entry box.) Here's a look at the different addresses:

IP Address   The IP address is the unique address number, in the format *xxx.xxx.xxx.xxx*, that's assigned to a particular node (networked device, whether a computer or other device) on a TCP/IP network. The exact nature of the IP address depends on the type of network you're creating. For instance, if your Mac has a direct connection to the Internet (without a router or firewall), you must have a unique IP address so that you can be differentiated from other servers on the Internet. But the Internet isn't the only type of TCP/IP network—you can have a private IP network for only small groups of computers, if desired.

 TIP   If you're selecting the IP address on your own and you're creating a private network, you should use the common private IP address ranges. Use the format 192.168.1.x within the range 192.168.1.2 through 192.168.1.254. Note that the 1 address and the 255 address are generally reserved addresses.

Subnet Mask   The subnet mask is a special number used to help your Mac understand what *class* of network you're operating on. In most cases (home, small office, or direct Internet connection), you're operating on a class C network, which means, essentially, that only the last of the four numbers in a given IP address differentiates the machines on your network. (For example, on a class C network, only the numbers 2 and 254 in the addresses 192.168.1.2 and 192.168.1.254 are significant for differentiating between the two local Macs.)

The subnet mask uses the number 255 to indicate that a portion of the IP address isn't relevant and 0 to indicate that it is. So, most small networks use the subnet mask 255.255.255.0 to indicate that the last number in the Mac's IP address is the one that's relevant to the local network. (For instance, if I have a Mac that has the IP address 192.168.1.3 and the subnet mask is 255.255.255.0, the Mac knows that all devices with an address 192.168.1.*x* are in the local network. If the subnet mask is 255.255.0.0, then the local network includes machines with an address 192.168.*x*.*x*.) The likelihood is that you'll use 255.255.255.0 unless you're told differently by your Internet service provider or your organization's network administrator.

Router   The router address is the IP address of the routing device that provides access to any larger networks that the LAN might be connected to. For instance, if your LAN is connected to the Internet via an Internet router, the IP address for that router is entered here. If you don't have such a router, you don't need a particular number here—the .1 address of the current subnet (e.g., 192.168.1.1) will suffice.

After you enter all the settings, you can click the Save button in the Network pane to make them your current TCP/IP settings. Your changes should take place immediately—in almost all cases, no restart is required.

 NOTE   Before you finish with a manual TCP/IP configuration, you will probably also wish to configure DNS manually, as discussed in the previous section.

Selecting Your AirPort Network

If you've been configuring TCP/IP for an AirPort connection, you have another step before you're ready to begin sharing files. With AirPort selected in the Configure menu of the Network pane, select the AirPort tab. Now, in the Preferred Network menu, select the local AirPort network that you'd like to connect to. If necessary, you should also enter that network's password.

PART

II

Networks and the
Internet

If you don't see an entry in the Preferred Network menu, it's likely that your Mac isn't detecting an AirPort base station. You'll need to make sure that the base station is turned on and that your Mac is within range of the base station. If you still can't seem to connect, you may need to check the AirPort card inside your Mac to make sure it's installed properly. (It's also possible that the AirPort card is turned off; see the next section for details.)

Internet Connect

You have two ways to manage your AirPort connection and, in fact, to change the setting in the AirPort tab of the Network pane without actually opening the System Preferences application. These methods are via the Internet Connect application and the Signal Strength Dock Extra.

The Internet Connect application is discussed more thoroughly in Chapter 9, where you'll find that it's used for modem-based connections to the Internet as well as some DSL connections. It can also be used to configure AirPort, however, regardless of whether that AirPort connection involves the Internet. Launch Internet Connect by double-clicking its icon in your main Applications folder, then select AirPort from the Configuration menu to see the AirPort options. (If you don't see all of the configuration information, click the triangle button to the right of the Configuration menu.)

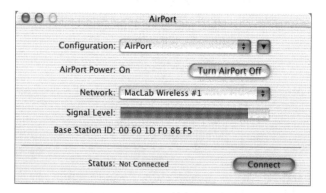

You'll see two items in the window that you can use to manage your AirPort connection. First, you can click the Turn AirPort Off button to turn off power to the Air-Port card. This can be important for PowerBook and iBook users who are using battery power while not connected to an AirPort network—the AirPort card drains battery power whenever it's on. If the card is currently off, the button changes to Turn AirPort On, which you can click to send power to the card.

Second, in the Network menu, you can choose to connect to a different AirPort network, if one is detected. When you select a different network, a dialog sheet will usually appear, asking for that network's password. Enter it and click OK. Now you should see that network selected in the Network menu and the signal strength for the connection noted on the Signal Level indicator.

If the AirPort network you want to join doesn't appear automatically, you can select Other from the Network menu to enter the name and password of the network. Click OK and check the Internet Connect window for the signal level. If no signal is indicated, you may have configured the connection incorrectly, you may be too far from the AirPort base station, or your AirPort card may not be installed properly.

You can also choose to connect to a computer-to-computer network if you have two Macs with AirPort cards that you'd like to connect without an AirPort base station acting as a hub. To do this, you'll choose one computer to act as a host to create the network. On the host Mac, launch Internet Connect and select Computer to Computer Network from the Network menu. In the Computer To Computer dialog box that appears, enter a name for the network and a password in both the Password and Confirm entry boxes. Select a channel (or leave the default channel active). Click OK, and the network is created.

Now, on the other Mac, launch Internet Connect and select the newly named network in the Network menu. You'll be asked for the password for this network; enter the password you just assigned on the host Mac and press Return, and you'll be connected. You can now share files by turning on File Sharing on one of the Macs and using the Connect To Server window to log in from the other Mac, as discussed later in this chapter.

 WARNING Whenever AirPort is active and File Sharing, Web Sharing, FTP, or Remote Login is turned on, you're opening yourself up to a slight security risk. It's possible that someone else with AirPort capabilities could access your Mac and gain guest access (if not full user access), enabling them to peruse your Public folders and place items in users' Drop Box folders. Since AirPort has a range of 150 feet or more, you might have no idea that your Mac is accessible. When you're not specifically connected to an AirPort network, it's best to turn AirPort and/or servers in the Sharing pane off—particularly if you're mobile with an iBook or PowerBook. (The AirPort card drains power from the notebook's battery, anyway, so it's good to turn it off when not in use.) And even when you *are* connected to an AirPort network, you should consider whether you really need to have servers in the Sharing pane active; if not, turn them all off, just to be safe.

Signal Strength Dock Extra

Another way to manage your AirPort connections (and alter the AirPort tab's settings automatically, without opening the Network pane) is to use the Signal Strength Dock Extra, which may appear on your Dock automatically if you start up your Mac with an AirPort card installed. (If not, you can drag the Signal Strength Dock Extra to your Dock from the Dock Extras folder inside your main Applications folder.)

The most basic function of the Signal Strength tile is to show you the strength of your current AirPort connection. If your Mac is connected to an AirPort network, you'll see orange lines indicating how strong that connection is; the more lines, the stronger and more reliable the connection. If you aren't seeing any lines, you'll need to make sure you're connected properly. If you're seeing only a few lines, you may need to move closer to the AirPort base station.

But the Signal Strength tile does more than indicate the strength of your connection. Click the Signal Strength tile once, and you'll see a menu of options. You can select any AirPort networks that are in range (they'll show up automatically in the menu), or you can connect to a network that doesn't appear by selecting Other and entering information about that network.

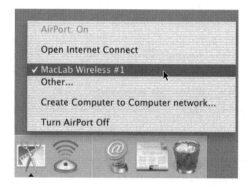

You can also select Create Computer to Computer Network if you have two AirPort-equipped Macs that you'd like to connect to one another for swapping files. Select Create Computer to Computer Network on the Mac that you'll use as a host, then set up the connection just as described in the earlier section "Internet Connect." You'll note that once you've set your Mac up as a computer-to-computer host, the Signal Strength tile icon changes to two iMacs pointed at one another.

Advanced Settings

The Network pane offers advanced settings that you may wish to dig into at some time, particularly if you find yourself configuring multiple ports for your Mac and using a variety of different connections. Choose Advanced from the Configure menu in the Network pane, and you'll see the Advanced screen, shown in Figure 8.3.

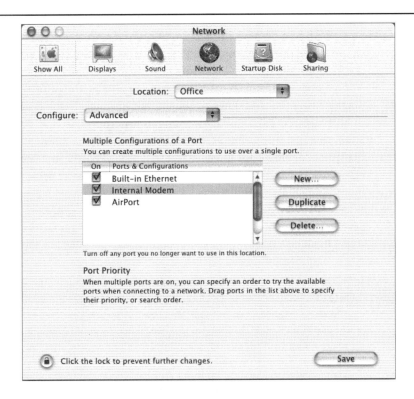

FIGURE 8.3

The Advanced options of the Network pane

The Advanced options enable you to do three things: You can turn ports on and off, you can create multiple configurations for a particular port, and you can set port priority.

To turn a particular port on or off, click the check box next to that port's listing. Without a check in the check box, the port is off; it won't appear in the Configure menu until it's turned on again.

Turning ports on and off is most useful in situations where you'd like multiple configurations for the same port. For instance, you can create two different configurations for your built-in Ethernet port—one using DHCP and one where you enter its TCP/IP settings manually. Then you can turn off one of those configurations and turn on the other when necessary.

To create another configuration, select the port you'd like to duplicate and click the Duplicate button. You can then give the new port configuration a name in the dialog sheet that appears. Click OK, and that new port will appear in the list. That entry will also appear in the Configure menu, allowing you to configure it as desired. You can also opt to create a completely new port by clicking New, then entering a name and choosing the port from the Port menu in the dialog sheet that appears. Now you'll have a new port configuration that starts out with blank settings. Select it in the Configure menu and configure away. To delete a port configuration, select it in the list and click the Delete button.

If you have multiple ports listed, you can change the priority of those ports by dragging them up and down in the list. For instance, if you drag AirPort above Built-in Ethernet in the list, any networking (or Internet) task that you attempt will be attempted first using AirPort, then, if unsuccessful, via Built-in Ethernet. This is particularly convenient for Internet access; if you have Internet access via both your Ethernet and AirPort connections, you may want to give top priority to the higher speed by dragging it above the others.

When you've finished making changes to the configurations and priority, click Save in the Network pane. Then select one of the configurations from the Configure menu to alter that configuration, if desired.

NOTE Although these Advanced settings are handy, they're generally useful only in limited circumstances, where your Mac has more than one static network connection to choose from. If you find that you're often switching your networking connections because you're moving your Mac from place to place (for instance, from your office to your home, where the networking and/or Internet connections are different), then you may want to use the Location Manager for those changes. The Location Manager is discussed in Chapter 9.

File Sharing

With TCP/IP configured, the next step in your network configuration is to determine whether you want File Sharing turned on. File Sharing in Mac OS X is actually a form of Apple File Protocol, similar to Personal File Sharing over IP in Mac OS 9.x. In a nutshell, turning File Sharing on enables users at Macintosh computers running Mac OS X or earlier to access portions of your Mac's hard disk (and other connected disks) by "mounting" those volumes on their desktop.

A network that employs this sort of file-sharing approach is called a *peer-to-peer* network, because each computer is a potential server. If you want a file from Julie's computer, you log in to that computer, enter your password, and then gain access and begin transferring files. If Julie wants access to your computer, she gains assess in the same way, assuming that you've turned on File Sharing.

NOTE The other type of network besides a peer-to-peer network is a *client/server* network. With client/server networks, a central server computer is the only (or primary) repository for shared files. In some cases, you'll still log onto the server, especially if it uses AFP. (For instance, a Mac OS X Server computer can be used as a central AFP server for a group of Macs, with each running Mac OS 8.*x,* Mac OS 9.*x,* or Mac OS X.)

A remote user logs in through the Connect To Server window discussed briefly in Chapter 3 (and later in this chapter in the section "Connecting to AFP Servers"). The remote user must have a valid account on your Mac—the same type of user account you saw how to create back in Chapter 7. If a valid account doesn't exist, the user can still access your server as a guest, with access only to the Public folders on your Mac.

 NOTE Actually, a user with a Mac running Mac OS 8.1 or higher can sign into your Mac if File Sharing is enabled. In versions prior to Mac OS 9, the user may need to enter your server's IP address in the Chooser by selecting AppleShare, then clicking Server IP Address.

Once logged in, users can select volumes or folders that will then appear on their desktops. The users can then read from and save to your disk. What the user sees depends on the type of permissions granted to the user's account. With an Admin account, the user can see and access:

- That user's own home folder
- Most of the Mac OS X startup disk, including other users' Public folders
- Any other attached hard disks or removable disks

If the user has a normal user account, the only items that will accessible to that user will be:

- That user's home folder
- The Public folders of all users on the computer

Note that regular users are a bit more limited than with earlier versions of the Mac OS, which enabled them to access virtually any portion of the Mac they wanted.

Guest users don't require a username or password and are given access only to Public folders. With Mac OS X, security is paramount, so regular and guest users are limited to accessing Public folders during remote connections.

PART

II

Networks and the
Internet

Security Issues with File Sharing

Any time you decide to make your Mac available for remote connections and file sharing, you're introducing a possible security risk. After all, a remote user may be able to guess or crack a valid username and password on your Mac, thus gaining access to your files. Here are a few security issues to ponder:

- Consider carefully before turning on File Sharing on any Mac with a publicly available IP address—that is, any Mac with a static (or otherwise direct) IP address on the Internet that isn't situated behind a firewall. Although it's convenient to access remote volumes across the Internet, you should take into account that anyone might be able to access the files on your Mac. (After all, there's no easy way to disable the guest account.) See Chapter 9 for more on securing your Macs from others on the Internet.

- Anyone can access the Mac via its guest account, giving an unauthorized user the opportunity to access Public folders. Mac OS X allows guest access by default—it can't be turned off. So you should warn your users that others might be able to access items in their Public folders, and not to place sensitive files in them. (Also, users should be warned that an unauthorized user could conceivably put items in their Drop Box folder—even a virus, worm, or other damaging application or document.)

- Turning on File Sharing in Mac OS X may give some users (particularly Admin accounts) unfettered access to any external volumes (such as an external disk drive) that are attached to your Mac. In general, this shouldn't be a problem—you should trust your users with Admin accounts. If it *is* a problem, consider assigning those users regular accounts (you can turn off Admin status in the Users pane of System Preferences). Also, if you wish, you can use the Show Info command in the Finder to change the permissions for sensitive folders on those external volumes. (See Chapter 7 for more, and remember that users must have read/write access to the Mac OS 9.1 System Folder that you use for the Classic environment.)

Turning On File Sharing

If you think you'd like to turn on File Sharing, it's easy enough to do. Here's how:

1. Open the System Preferences application.

2. Select Sharing.

3. In the Sharing pane, unlock the administrator's padlock, if necessary. (You can't change the File Sharing state without an administrator's password.)

4. Under File Sharing Off, click the Start button.

That's it. You'll see a message indicating that File Sharing is starting up. Once it meets with success, you'll see the section change so that it's called File Sharing On, and the button will read Stop (see Figure 8.4).

FIGURE 8.4

After you click the Start button, the Sharing pane will indicate that File Sharing is on.

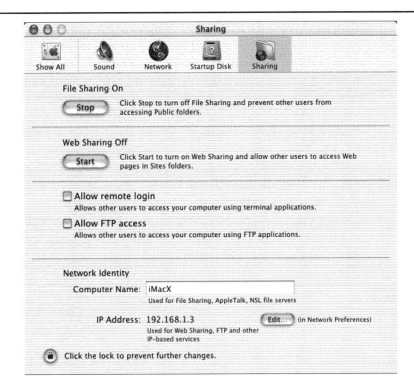

PART

II

Networks and the Internet

 NOTE Wondering about the settings for Web Sharing, remote login, and FTP access? Remote login is covered in Chapter 23; Web Sharing and FTP are covered in Chapter 24.

Naming Your Mac

By default, remote users will be able access your Mac for file sharing using its IP address in the Connect To Server window (or, for earlier Macs, in the Network Browser or Chooser). But you'd probably also prefer to give your Mac a unique name that users can see in their Connect To Server or Network Browser window.

To name your Mac, enter a name in the Computer Name entry box in the Network Identity section of the Sharing pane. If you don't give your Mac a computer name, remote users will be able to access the computer only as an IP address. (Note also that the Sharing pane shows you the correct IP address in the Network Identity section; so you'll know what IP number to give out if you need to.)

Turning Off File Sharing

Turning off File Sharing is about as easy as turning it on. In the Sharing pane, click the Stop button that appears under the section head File Sharing On. That begins the process of turning off File Sharing. If no users are currently connected, you'll see the button change to Start and the section head change to File Sharing Off, indicating that remote users can't access File Sharing anymore.

If users are currently connected to your Mac via File Sharing, you'll see another dialog box (see Figure 8.5) where you can enter the number of minutes that File Sharing should wait before disconnecting users. In the text area, you can enter a message that remote users will see. If you enter 0 in the Minutes entry box and click OK, users will be immediately disconnected, and they will see a message stating that the server unexpectedly closed down. Otherwise, users will see a warning message when you click OK, telling them how many more minutes they have. Then they'll be disconnected automatically once the time is up.

FIGURE 8.5

If you shut down File Sharing while users are connected, you're given a chance to warn them.

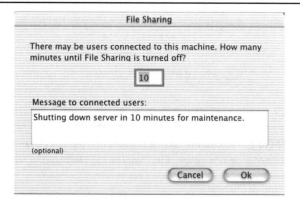

 NOTE If you simply log out of your account on your Mac, users can continue to access the Mac via File Sharing. If you restart or shut down the Mac, however, remote users will receive an error message and will no longer be able to access items on your Mac. Once your Mac is up and running again, they'll be able to log in once more.

File Sharing over IP (Mac OS 9.*x*)

Mac OS 9–based Macs can also share files with Mac OS X machines, but only if the File Sharing over IP option is turned on. (Otherwise, the Mac is using AppleTalk for its File Sharing connection, and Mac OS X doesn't support AppleTalk for file sharing—only for accessing printers.) The Mac OS 9.*x* machine must also have a valid TCP/IP configuration that makes it part of the same subnet as the Mac OS X machine, connected via Ethernet or AirPort. Of course, you can also access the Mac OS 9.*x* machine via a fixed IP address on the Internet if it is so configured.

If all the stipulations are met, you can configure the Mac OS 9–based machine to share its files. In the File Sharing control panel (Apple menu ➢ Control Panels ➢ File Sharing), turn on the Enable File Sharing Clients to Connect over TCP/IP option and then click the Start button to start up File Sharing on the Mac OS 9.*x* (see Figure 8.6). Once File Sharing has started, you'll be able to connect with a valid username (if you have an account in the Mac OS 9.*x* machine's Users control panel) as a guest.

Accessing Remote File Servers

Whether or not you've decided to turn on File Sharing, once you have your Mac connected to others via either Ethernet or AirPort and you've entered correct settings for your TCP/IP connection, you're ready to access remote servers. Of course, you'll need to have remote servers to access. In this section, I'm talking about servers that you

PART

II

Networks and the Internet

FIGURE 8.6

The File Sharing control panel in Mac OS 9.x enables you to share files over TCP/IP.

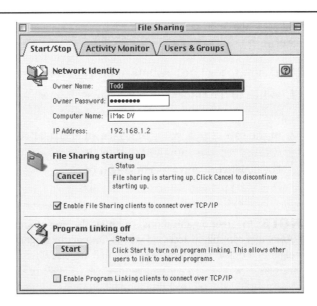

access via the Connect To Server window—that is, servers that you need to actively log into so that the server's volume appears on your desktop. That means one of three possibilities:

- Another Mac OS X machine with File Sharing turned on
- A Mac OS 9.*x* computer with File Sharing over IP activated
- A server computer that's running an AFP file-server application, such as Apple-Share IP (running on Mac OS X or earlier), Mac OS X Server, or some Windows NT servers

You can also use the Connect To Server window to connect to some types of Web servers. I'll cover logging into Web servers in this section as well.

Connecting to AFP Servers

If you have an AFP server on your local network that you'd like to access, it's easy enough to do. You'll use the Connect to Server command in the Finder to log into that server with either a guest account or a username and password. Once you've successfully logged into the remote Mac, the folder or disk that you're accessing will appear on your desktop.

 NOTE The Connect To Server window in Mac OS X is similar to the Network Browser found in Mac OS 9.*x*, but there's an important difference: To enter the exact IP address of a remote server, you need to select Connect to Server from the Shortcuts button menu in the Network Browser. (In Mac OS X's Connect To Server window, you can enter an IP address in the Address entry box.)

Here's how to log into a remote Apple File Protocol volume:

1. Switch to the Finder and select Go ➢ Connect to Server. You can also press ⌘+K to launch the Connect To Server window.

2. In the listing area, you should see an entry called Local Network. This is a *neighborhood* representing AFP servers that are part of your local subnet. Open the Local Network entry by clicking it once.

 NOTE In larger organizations, you may also see other neighborhoods outside of your subnet that can still be accessed via the Connect To Server window. Select one of the other neighborhoods to seek remote servers that are elsewhere on your WAN.

3. Now you'll see a listing of active AFP servers. Select the name of the machine that you'd like to access and click Connect.

Connect to Server

Choose a server from the list, or enter a server address

At: 🖳 PowerBook G3

🖳 Local Network
- 🖳 G3_X
- 🖳 iMacX
- 🖳 PowerBook G3

3 items   Searching...

Address: afp://192.168.1.2

Add to Favorites   Cancel   Connect

4. You'll now see the "connect to" dialog box where you can enter the username and password you'd like to use to access the remote volume. You must have a valid user account and password on the remote system in order to successfully access the remote volume with appropriate user privileges. If you don't, you can select the Guest radio button to access the remote server as a guest. (If the remote server doesn't accept guests, the Guest radio button will be "grayed out," or not selectable.) Once you've entered a name and password or selected Guest access, click the Connect button.

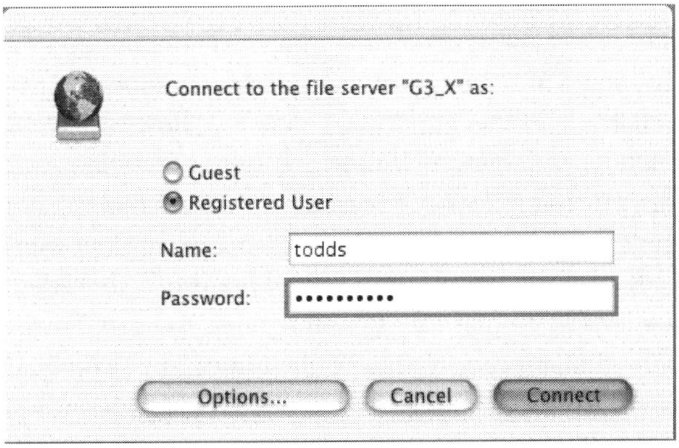

Connect to the file server "G3_X" as:

○ Guest
● Registered User

Name: todds

Password: ●●●●●●●●●●

Options...   Cancel   Connect

5. Once connected, you'll see a listing of the volumes to which you have access privileges. In the case of an administrator account, you'll generally see the main volume of the remote Mac listed, along with mounted removable disks and your home folder. For more limited accounts, you'll see only your account's home folder and the names of other users, representing their Public folders. To access a volume, select it and click OK; you can also double-click the name of a volume.

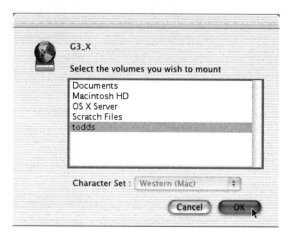

 TIP You can select more than one volume by holding down the ⌘ key while clicking additional volume names. Then click OK to mount all of them.

Once you've successfully logged in, the remote volume(s) will also appear on your desktop, ready to be double-clicked and accessed. (This is true unless the Finder Preferences have been set so that mounted volumes don't appear on the desktop.) Further, you'll also see any attached volumes appear in the main Computer listing that's available in Finder windows. Figure 8.7 shows three volumes mounted and displayed in Finder windows, including the user's remote home folder (in the figure, the home folder is "todds").

It's worth noting that when you access another user's Public folder, you have read access, but not write access, to any items in that folder. In other words, you can't save files directly to that user's Public folder. You can, however, save files to the Drop Box folder that appears in each Public folder. The Drop Box folder offers you write access but *doesn't* give you read access, as a security precaution. If you have a file that you'd like to share with the user, copy it to that user's Drop Box.

FIGURE 8.7

Three remote volumes have been mounted and accessed.

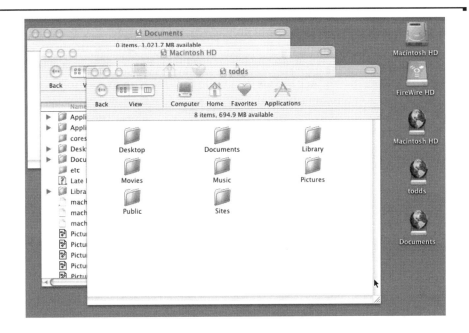

If you've signed in with a valid user account, you have full access to your own home folder on that remote machine. You can copy files to and from your home folder, your Documents folder, or your Public folder, as desired.

 TIP The Connect To Server window has an Add to Favorites button that you can use to add a particular server (when selected) as a Favorite. You can then access that Favorite by selecting it from the At menu at the top of the Connect To Server window. You can also access servers to which you've recently connected via the At menu.

Connecting for Servers via URL

The Connect To Server window enables you not only to choose servers on your local network but also to log into remote AFP servers by directly entering the server's URL. You do that in the Address box at the bottom of the Connect To Server window.

In fact, as shown in the preceding image, this is one way to log into your iDisk (one of Apple's iTools offerings, discussed in Chapter 11). You could also enter a numerical IP address or a text URL for any AFP server with a static address on the Internet, including, of course, your own Mac if you're accessing it from the road. Note that for AFP servers, you begin the URL with `afp://` followed by the IP address or host and domain name.

Along with signing into AFP servers, you can use the Connect To Server window to log into some Web servers and gain access to the their root folders (where the Web files are stored), if you have an account that has the proper permissions to do so. In general, you can access only specific types of Web servers that offer WebDAV (Web-Based Distributed Authoring and Versioning) services. WebDAV, put succinctly, is a type of Web server that improves on the HTTP model by giving both read and *write* access to authorized users. In most cases you'll need to enter an IP address manually to access a WebDAV server. Enter it in the Address entry box, starting with `http://` and finishing with the WebDAV server's IP address or host name and domain. Then click Connect.

Connecting via Alias

Mac OS X offers another way to shortcut the steps required to log into a server: You can create an alias of a mounted server volume. After you've disconnected from the server and want to access it again, you can double-click the alias you've created. You will then see a login window that lets you bypass the Connect To Server window completely.

Login Options

If you've logged into a few remote servers by now, you may have noticed that the "connect to" dialog box (where you generally enter your username and password after selecting a remote server) includes an Options button. It enables you to set a few preferences for how your password is sent, for adding the password to your keychain, and for changing your password on the remote server, as long as you know the current password. Here are those options:

Add Password to Keychain Turn this option on if you'd like the password for this connection to be added to your keychain. In the future, your password will be automatically entered in the Connect window (as long as your keychain is available and open). Also, if you access a particular volume on that server by double-clicking an alias or selecting a favorite, you won't be asked for your password at all—the volume will mount immediately. See Chapter 12 for more on keychains and the Keychain Access application.

Allow Clear Text Password   With this option on, your Mac is able to send an unencrypted password in order to connect to a remote server. If security is paramount, you can turn this off; however, some servers may not be able to accept encrypted passwords.

Warn When Sending Password in Clear Text   If the Allow Clear Text Password option is on, you can also turn this option on so that an alert dialog box appears when a password is sent unencrypted.

Click the Save Preferences button if you've made changes that you want to save.

The Options dialog also gives you the opportunity to change your password on the remote server, if desired. In the interest of security, it's a good idea to change your password on a regular basis.

 NOTE   In my experience, Mac OS X won't allow you to change the password for your user account remotely; it must be done on-site through the Password pane of the System Preferences application or by that Mac's administrator. When connecting to Mac OS 9.x–based servers and most server-based file sharing (such as Mac OS X Server and AppleShare IP), you can change your password remotely.

To change your password, realize that you must first have entered your username correctly in the Connect window. Then, after clicking Options, click the Change Password button. You'll see the Change Password dialog box. Enter your current password in the Old Password entry box. Then enter the new password you'd like to use in the New Password and Confirm Password entry boxes, typing them exactly the same each time. Finally, click OK (see Figure 8.8).

PART

II

Networks and the Internet

FIGURE 8.8

Changing your remote password

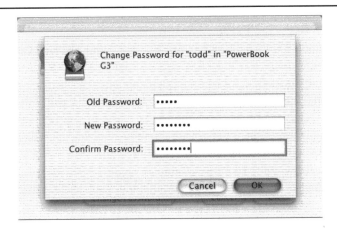

Disconnecting from AFP and Web Servers

However you managed to log into a remote-server volume or folder, logging out is fairly easy. First, you should close any documents or applications accessed on the remote server. Next, drag the remove server's icon from your Mac's desktop to the Trash icon in the Dock. You'll notice that the Trash icon changes to the Eject icon; release the mouse button to drop the server icon on the Eject icon. Your Mac will no longer be connected to the server.

Alternatively, you can select a server icon that's either on the desktop or in a Finder window (for example, when you're viewing the Computer window in a Finder window) and select File ➢ Eject from the Finder's menu. Finally, you can Control+click (or right-click, if you have a two-button mouse) on a remote server volume and select Eject from the contextual menu.

Working with NFS Servers

So far I've dealt exclusively with the type of server that you log in to and off of whenever you feel the need to share files. Using AFP and Web protocols, you mount these servers on your desktop, open them up, do your business, close them, and drag them to the Trash. Mac OS X supports another approach, too, using the Network File System (NFS), that is one way to mount server volumes in Unix and Unix-like operating systems.

Creating the network mounts is a task for a system administrator because it can get a bit complicated and it isn't a standard service offered by Mac OS X. (Other Unix operating systems offer NFS sharing, as does Mac OS X Server.) But accessing an NFS server volume couldn't be simpler. Figure 8.9 shows how. All you have to do is access the Network item at the Computer level of your Mac's folder hierarchy. Then select Servers and you'll see all mounted NFS servers. Select a server and you'll see a listing of the volumes for that server.

FIGURE 8.9

Mounted NFS servers will usually appear under the Network hierarchy in the Servers folder.

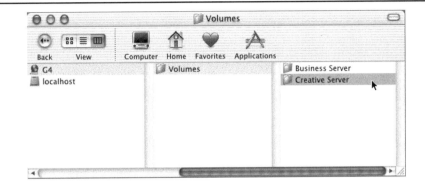

These servers act pretty much as if they were an extension of your Mac's hard disk—in fact, the Macintosh interface is designed to make them appear to be just that. Instead of logging in to and out of the server volumes, they're always there. Your Mac OS X username and password grant you access and determine your privileges.

Like local folders, you can have a range of permissions on NFS volumes, from read-only to read/write to write-only. Your network administrator determines the permissions and exactly which volumes or folders will show up. The Mac looks for the NFS network mounts whenever it is restarted, and, for all practical purposes, the mounts are permanent. The icons don't appear and disappear; if a server happens to be down for maintenance, you'll see an error message when you attempt to access it.

 NOTE Adding NFS mounts using Mac OS X is tough because OS X hides the tools (and it requires some advanced knowledge of NetInfo Manager)—but it is possible. A shareware tool, NFSManager, can help; it's available at www.bresink.com/osx/ on the Web.

What's Next?

In this chapter you learned how to configure your Mac for network access via Ethernet or AirPort connections. You also saw how to turn on File Sharing so that remote users can connect to your Mac. And you saw how to connect to remote servers, whether they are Apple File Protocol servers, WebDAV servers, or mounted NFS volumes. In Chapter 9, you'll learn how to configure your Macintosh—or a LAN of computers—for Internet access.

PART

II

Networks and the Internet

CHAPTER **9**

Accessing the Internet

Mac OS X is an operating system more at home on the Internet than most, with its Help system, the Sherlock searching system, and the System Update technology, which can regularly check for updates to Mac OS X and Apple's applications. And that doesn't even consider the fact that Mac OS X has an Internet browser, a Mail application, and a whole host of other applications that can access—and even serve files—on the Internet. Unless you have a drop-dead security reason for keeping your Mac off the Internet, getting Internet access is probably one of your top priorities.

How you access the Internet depends on the type of connection that you've secured and paid for via an Internet service provider. If you have a modem and a dial-up connection, you'll use the Internet Connect application that's included with Mac OS X.

If you have a cable modem or DSL (digital subscriber line) connection—common ways to connect from homes and small offices these days—you'll configure them using the Network pane in System Preferences. (For some DSL implementations you'll also use the Internet Connect application, with which you can initiate some PPP-over-Ethernet connections.) Finally, if you're on a local area network (LAN) that has direct access to the Internet, you needn't do much more than simply tweak your TCP/IP settings, although you may want to add special hardware if you have a small LAN that needs Internet access to all its computers.

Once you've gotten connected, you can move on to a discussion of TCP/IP in the Classic environment (what will and won't work and what to do about it). Then it's on to setting your Internet preferences in the Internet pane of the System Preferences application. The Internet preferences are used as a central repository of your default settings—the Web browser you like to use most, your favorite e-mail application, your home page, and, if you've signed up, your username and password for Apple's iTools service.

Dial-Up Internet Access

If your Mac has a modem and you want to use it for Internet access, the Internet Connect application is your built-in choice. You'll need an Internet service provider (ISP) that offers PPP access and either dynamic or static IP addressing service (either will work). PPP stands for Point-to-Point Protocol, and it's the standard way to create a TCP/IP connection over a phone line. Internet Connect does just that—it creates the connection over the phone line, making it possible for you to run Internet applications over a modem-based Internet connection.

If you're familiar with PPP connections in past Mac OS versions, you might also be interested to know that Mac OS X tracks different TCP/IP settings for your modem and other ports, such as Ethernet or AirPort, that are used for networking. So you don't have to change the TCP/IP settings in order to use a modem for Internet access; you simply choose the modem's settings and forget about them. Then you can use the Internet Connect application to initiate your modem connection.

Setting Up Your Modem and TCP/IP

For Internet access over a modem, your first step is to set up TCP/IP and other settings for your modem connection. You'll likely need whatever information your ISP has given you regarding the connection, including how TCP/IP should retrieve its settings for your modem (using PPP, manually, or otherwise) as well as your username, password, and other vital information regarding the dial-up connection. Then you'll be ready to configure your Mac's modem in the Network pane.

Launch System Preferences and select the Network icon. Choose your modem (most likely Internal Modem, although you may see other entries if you have an external USB or PC Card–based modem) from the top Configure menu in the Network pane. Now you'll see the TCP/IP, PPP, Proxies, and Modem tabs, which you can use to set up your modem-based Internet connection (see Figure 9.1).

FIGURE 9.1

The Network pane when configuring a modem connection

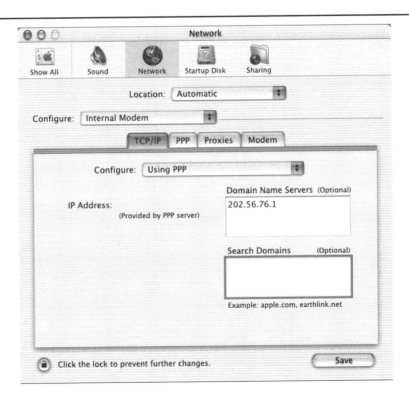

The TCP/IP Tab

To begin, make sure the TCP/IP tab is selected, then choose the type of configuration your ISP has specified for the connection; as mentioned, it's most likely Using PPP, unless you have a fixed IP address, in which case you might use Manually. If you choose Manually, you'll need to enter an IP address, subnet mask, and router address, again as specified by your ISP. (These are discussed in more detail in Chapter 8.) Also, if your ISP tells you to, you should enter IP addresses for your DNS servers in the Domain Name Servers entry box; press Return to separate each entry if you have more than one.

The PPP Tab

Next, select the PPP tab and you'll see entry boxes for setting up the connection information for your PPP dial-up account. It's here that you'll enter the phone number, account name, and password, among other items (see Figure 9.2).

FIGURE 9.2

The PPP tab of the Network pane when configuring a modem connection

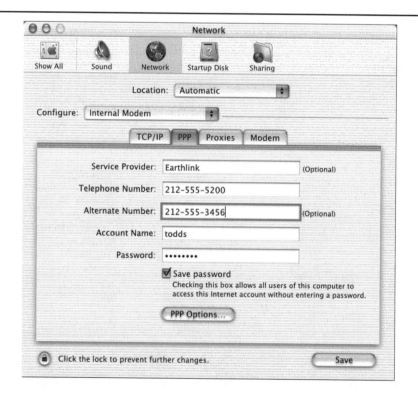

To set up your PPP account, you'll need to get some information from your ISP regarding that account and then enter it in the Internet Connect window. Here's an explanation of the information you'll enter on the PPP tab:

Service Provider   This is the name of your ISP. It isn't mandatory, but it can be helpful for identifying this setup if you happen to have more than one dial-up account.

Telephone Number   What number will you be calling to initiate the Internet connection? On the PPP tab, you'll need to enter everything that needs to be dialed for the connection, including long-distance 1s and area codes, if necessary.

 TIP   Need to dial special codes or numbers? You can enter them with commas to cause your modem to pause before it completes dialing. For instance, if you're calling from a hotel room and need to dial a 9 for an outside line, you could enter **9,555-1234** or **9,,1-800-555-6450** as the phone number. Your modem would pause after each comma to allow the phone system to catch up with the dialing; more than one comma lengthens the pause. In fact, you could even enter something like **1010555,,1-212-555-0345** if you needed to enter a special long-distance code first.

Alternate Number   If your ISP offers other numbers in your area, you can enter one here. This number will be dialed if a connection doesn't succeed using the first number.

Account Name   The username for your Internet account as assigned by the ISP.

Password   The password that's associated with your Internet account. (Note that the PPP tab includes an option that you can turn on so that the password is "remembered" every time you sign on. Otherwise, you'll have to enter it each time you connect to the Internet via Internet Connect.)

The PPP tab also offers a special PPP Options button, which you can click to see a dialog sheet that offers advanced PPP options. At the top of the dialog sheet are the Session Options. Most of them are self-explanatory; you can elect to have a prompt appear after a certain amount of idle time, or you can automate the disconnect process. One important setting is "Connect automatically when starting TCP/IP applications." By default, this option is turned off, but having it turned on can be handy. If you'd prefer to have your Mac automatically dial its modem whenever you access an Internet application

(Mail, Internet Explorer, Sherlock's Internet channels, and so on), then check this option to turn it on.

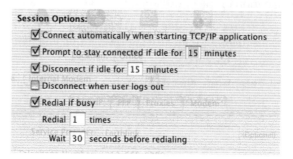

At the bottom of the dialog sheet, you'll see Advanced Options, most of which you shouldn't have to alter unless your ISP or a technical support representative suggests it. Just know that the options are found by clicking the PPP Options button on the PPP tab of the Network pane.

NOTE One of these settings, Use Verbose Logging, may be of slight interest to you, particularly if you're having trouble with your Internet connection. When turned on, the Internet Connect log records more information than the default setting. You can see the log in the Internet Connect application by selecting Window ➢ Connection Log.

When you've finished changing options, click OK in the dialog sheet. Now you're ready to move on to the Proxies tab.

The Proxies Tab

Proxy servers are intermediary servers that are used to either increase performance or filter the sites that are available to your Mac. For instance, a company might use proxy servers to intercept Web requests and determine whether a requested Web site has already been viewed by someone else in the company and is thus available in a cached version on a local server. The site can then be sent to your Mac more quickly. Likewise, an elementary school might use proxy servers to disallow access to unapproved Web or FTP sites.

Reasonably few dial-up connections use proxy servers, but if you find that your connection is one of them, you can set those proxy servers on the Proxies tab. Click the check box next to the server type, then enter an address in that server's entry box.

Proxy servers can also have a unique port number, which you should enter in the Port entry box on that server's row.

If you have particular hosts and domains that should bypass the proxy server, enter those in the entry box at the bottom of the tab's screen, separating them by pressing Return.

The Modem Tab

Before you can dial out and create your Internet connection, you'll need to tell the Network pane a little something about your modem. You do that by selecting the Modem tab (see Figure 9.3).

Here's a look at the options:

Modem   Use the Modem pop-up menu to choose the type of modem that's installed in (or external to) your Mac. If you don't have one of the models specifically listed, you can choose Hayes Compatible to get basic modem capabilities. (If you have an external modem from a third party, you may need to install that modem's Mac OS X driver using an installer made available by the manufacturer.)

FIGURE 9.3

*The Modem tab in the
Network pane*

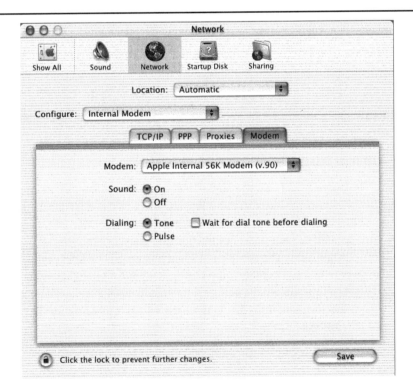

NOTE Modem configuration files are stored in the Modem Scripts folder inside the main Library folder on your hard disk. If you don't have Admin privileges, you can store a modem configuration file in the Modem Scripts folder inside your personal Library folder, located inside your home folder.

Sound   Select On if you'd like to hear the modem's connection tones through your Mac's speaker. Interestingly, in Mac OS X 10.0, this option has no effect—you can't hear an internal modem's tones in this version of Mac OS X. Future versions will very likely enable the modem's sounds.

Dialing   Select Tone or Pulse, depending on the type of phone line to which you've connected the modem. (Pulse is used only for rotary-service lines that don't support touch-tone dialing. Few of these are left, although you may still have one in a very rural area.)

Wait for Dial Tone before Dialing   This option causes the modem to first attempt to detect a dial tone on the line before it begins dialing the ISP's number. Having this option turned on isn't mandatory, and turning it on can cause the modem to be confused by "stutter-tone" features such as phone-company voicemail. But it can be used to detect when the phone line is in use (for instance, when someone is talking on another extension) and to stop the modem from dialing if it can't detect a dial tone.

Once you've made these choices, you've finished configuring your modem in the Network pane. Click Save and close the System Preferences application, if desired. You're ready to move on to Internet Connect to establish your connection.

Connecting via Internet Connect

If you've entered all the preferences and settings for your PPP service and modem in the Network pane, you're ready to connect to the Internet. Verify that your phone line is connected to your modem, then open the Internet Connect application, which is located in your main Applications folder.

Establishing the connection is easy: Click the Connect button in the Internet Connect window. Internet Connect will dial your modem, showing you a small Status line telling you what's happening. Once your PPP server has been contacted and the connection established, you'll see the window reconfigure slightly, showing you connection statistics.

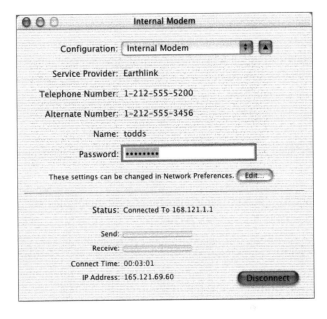

The window tells you a number of things about your connection, including small indicator bars that show activity (the Send and Receive bars), the length of time you've been connected for this session, and your current IP address. (The IP address won't change if you have a fixed IP address, but it will change if you have a dynamic address.)

The Internet Connect window hides some additional information about the connection by default. Click the triangle button next to the Configuration menu to see the full Internet Connect window.

There isn't much you can do on this expanded screen except change your password (if necessary) or enter it if you opted not to save your password in the PPP tab of the Network pane. If you see a setting that looks incorrect, click the Edit button to automatically launch the PPP tab of the Network pane, where you can change settings.

 NOTE You can actually quit the Internet Connect application if you like, and your PPP connection will remain up and running until it times out (many ISPs will disconnect the connection after a certain amount of inactivity) or until you relaunch Internet Connect and disconnect.

Disconnecting from PPP

To disconnect your PPP session, click the Disconnect button in the Internet Connect window. You'll see the Disconnect status indicator momentarily; then you'll see the full PPP window, and the status will indicate Idle.

Note that logging out of your Mac OS X account does not necessarily disconnect the Internet connection—it will remain up and running for as long as your ISP allows an inactive connection to stay connected. (This is one of the options in the PPP Options dialog sheet that you can access from the PPP tab of the Network pane.) Another user can log in and immediately begin using Internet applications, if desired. The connection is terminated, however, if you shut down or restart your Mac.

High-Speed Connections

More and more people are moving from modem-based Internet connections to *broadband* connections, which is simply a catchword for any Internet connection that has reasonably high speed. Technologies for such high-speed connections include DSL technologies, cable modem technologies, and direct connections like frame relay or T1 and T3 connections. Phone companies (and ISPs working in conjunction with phone companies) commonly provide DSL, while cable TV companies provide cable connections. Other types of connections (T1, T3, and frame relay) are commonly found in businesses or large organizations that can afford the dedicated lines and hardware required to complete the connections.

NOTE Another type of subscription technology, ISDN (Integrated Services Digital Network), is still common in some locales. ISDN is somewhat similar to DSL service, although it's slower (in most implementations) and requires additional hardware and software. Both provide Internet access over phone lines; however, ISDN requires that a special digital phone line be installed, while DSL offers a high-speed Internet connection over your existing phone line. Phone companies and most consumers prefer DSL, but ISDN remains the only option in some areas, especially rural areas in the U.S.

Most of these high-speed technologies are "always on" Internet connections that are really just a form of wide area networking. Just as you can use TCP/IP settings to configure a LAN, you can also use TCP/IP settings—and the correct boxes and wiring—to access computers at your phone company, cable company, or ISP. This creates the high-speed connection, making it possible for you to launch and use Internet applications, such as Web browsers and e-mail programs, to access Internet servers.

How exactly you set up Mac OS X for high-speed access depends on the type of service you have and how it's implemented. In some cases your approach to completing an Internet connection may be very similar to completing a modem dial-up connection, using special settings in the Network pane and the Internet Connect application. This is especially true if your Internet connection requires a PPP-over-Ethernet connection (PPPoE), which is common for many DSL implementations. Some ISDN connections also require the Internet Connect application, particularly those that are set up with the Using PPP setting on the TCP/IP tab. If your connection requires PPPoE, you'll need to follow the special setup instructions in the later section "PPPoE Connections" to get up and running on your connection.

 NOTE Cable, ISDN, and DSL hardware devices are often called "modems," even though they don't technically *mo*dulate and *dem*odulate, as phone-line modems do. (Cable modems are a bit more like phone modems than DSL and ISDN modems, which are nothing like phone modems. Say that three times fast.) They're called modems simply because it's a convenient marketing term meant to suggest "a small box that gets you on the Internet."

In other cases, setup is as simple as entering an IP address for your router in the Network pane of the System Preferences application. Most cable modems, for instance, don't require special setup or a dial-up application such as Internet Connect, but they do require particular TCP/IP settings in the Network pane of the System Preferences application.

This presents an interesting problem. If you have a local area network, you need to set up your Macs so that they can access the other Macs on your network. Often you'll do this either by configuring Built-in Ethernet to use the DHCP (Dynamic Host Configuration Protocol) or by manually setting the Ethernet ports on your Macs to a series of private IP numbers in the 192.168.1.*x* range. (This is discussed in more detail in Chapter 8.)

If you have such a LAN and your Mac has only one Ethernet port, then changing your TCP/IP settings to access the Internet could mean interrupting your ability to share files on your LAN. The solution is to either install a second Ethernet adapter to be used exclusively for the Internet device or install a *router*, which is a device that can send Internet data to all computers on your LAN. (See the later section "Internet Access for Local Networks" for more details.)

Direct Ethernet Connections

In the meantime, if you have a direct connection to the Internet via your Ethernet port, configuration should be fairly simple. Open System Preferences, click the Network icon, and select an Ethernet port from the Network pane's main Configure menu; then click the TCP/IP tab in the Network pane. (You may select either the Built-in Ethernet port or another Ethernet port if you have an internal Ethernet card installed and you want to use it for Internet access.) At this point, you may need to click the padlock icon and enter an administrator's username and password in order to edit these settings. Now you're ready to edit the TCP/IP settings (see Figure 9.4).

FIGURE 9.4

TCP/IP settings for an Ethernet port

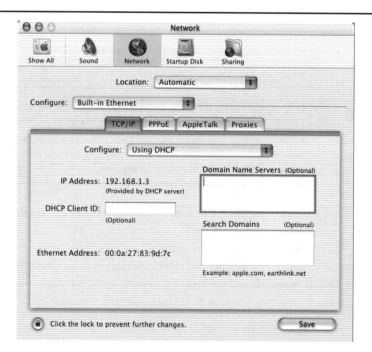

Testing Your Connection with Network Utility

You can also test your connection using Network Utility, which, on current Mac OS X installations, is included in the Utilities folder inside the Applications folder. Network Utility gives you access to `ping`, `traceroute`, `lookup`, and other Internet-related commands that are commonly used to test connections.

Select Ping from the pop-up menu, for instance, to see if you can successfully contact outside servers. (You enter `www.apple.com` in the entry boxes at the top of the Ping tab's screen, then click Ping to begin pinging. If you see repeated lines that say "*xx* bytes from...," that means that your connection is working.)

Likewise, you can use `lookup` to make sure your DNS server addresses are correct. Choose Lookup from the pop-up menu, enter an Internet server address in the entry boxes at the top of the window, and click Start. After a moment, you should see an entry that shows you the IP address for the domain name you entered.

Experiment with the others. `Whois` looks up and shows you a particular domain's registration details. `Finger` looks up a particular e-mail address to see if it has a "finger" record attached to it (which gives personal info about that person). `Traceroute` traces the route of a packet of data from your computer to a remote computer, showing you all the Internet points through which the packet passes. For more on Network Utility, see Chapter 20.

PART

II

Networks and the Internet

For the next step, configure TCP/IP according to your ISP's instructions. How you do that can vary depending on your ISP:

- If your ISP uses DHCP to assign IP addresses, select Using DHCP from the Configure menu. Then move down to the Domain Name Services entry box and enter the DNS address(es) for your connection if your ISP requires this. (If not, you can leave this entry box blank.)

- If your ISP requires you to enter the TCP/IP configuration manually, choose Manually from the Configure menu. Now, enter an IP address, subnet mask, router, and other information as required by the ISP. For manual settings, the router address is important to get right, as it tells your Mac where to locate the router device that will feed it TCP/IP data.

Once you've entered your settings, you should click the Save button on the Network pane, then close the System Preferences application. Now you can launch an

Internet application to ensure that your TCP/IP settings are correct and the broadband connection is functioning correctly. If you see a Web page or you successfully access your e-mail application, it's likely that things are now working. If not, dive back into the documentation from your ISP and ensure that you've set TCP/IP correctly.

PPPoE Connections

PPP-over-Ethernet, as the name suggests, is similar to a dial-up modem connection, except that it takes place via your Ethernet port instead of using your modem and phone lines. Unlike some Ethernet-based Internet connections, a PPPoE connection isn't "always on," but rather must be initiated before the Internet connection can be used.

If you have a DSL modem or a similar Internet device that uses PPPoE protocols, you have some special setup considerations in the Network pane. Once those settings are made, you'll then use the Internet Connect application to complete your PPPoE connection.

The PPPoE Tab

Begin by selecting your Ethernet port from the Configure menu in the Network pane. (If you have multiple Ethernet ports, select the port that's connected to your Internet modem or gateway device.)

 NOTE Turning on PPPoE automatically changes your TCP/IP settings to Using PPP. Again, if you're using this Ethernet port for a LAN connection, you cannot also use it for a PPPoE connection. You'll need to either install a second Ethernet adapter card (if your Mac will support one) or add an Internet router, discussed in the later section "Internet Access for Local Networks." If you install a router, note that you'll likely use that router to configure your PPPoE connection, not the Network pane.

Select the PPPoE tab (see Figure 9.5). At the top of the tab's screen, you'll see the option Connect Using PPPoE. Click the check box to turn on that option. The Service Provider entry box is optional—you can enter your ISP's name if you'd like. The PPPoE Service Name box is reserved, however; enter something in that box only if your ISP instructs you to.

Then, in the Account Name entry box, enter the account name that your ISP assigned you; in the Password box, enter the password you were assigned. If you'd like to save this password (so that you don't have to enter it later in the Internet Connect application), turn on the Save Password option.

FIGURE 9.5

The PPPoE tab is where you'll configure your PPPoE account information.

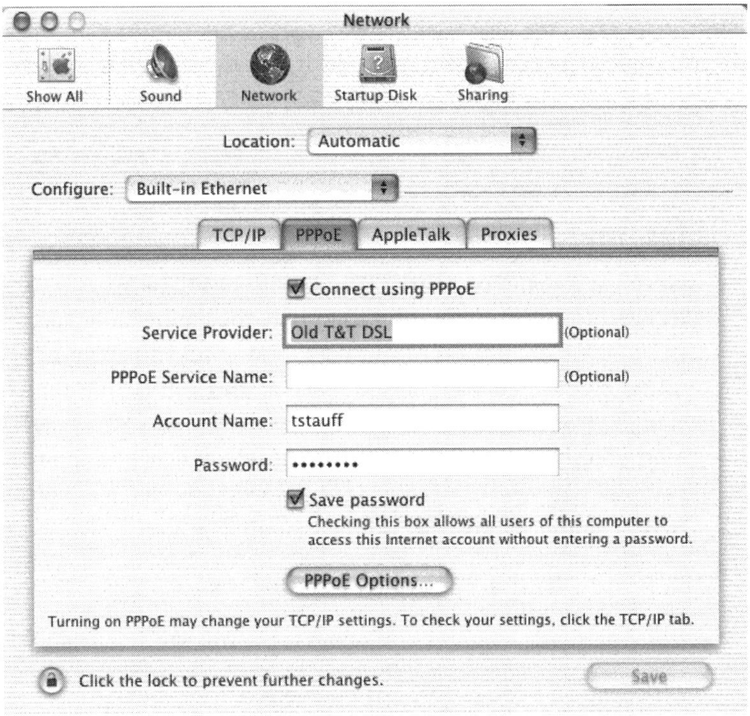

The PPPoE tab also offers a PPPoE Options button. Click this button, and you'll see a dialog sheet appear with two sets of options, Session Options and Advanced Options. In the Session Options, you can choose how often your Mac will remind you that you're connected and/or how much idle time will elapse before your Mac automatically disconnects you. You can also select how the Mac will disconnect as you log out of your account. By default, the option "Connect automatically when starting TCP/IP applications" is turned off, but you may want to turn it on. This enables your Mac to initiate the PPPoE connection whenever you launch an Internet application (Mail, Internet Explorer, or an Internet channel in Sherlock) without first requiring you to establish the Internet connection using the Internet Connect application.

In the Advanced Options, you can turn off "Send PPP echo packets" if your ISP suggests this, and you can turn on "Use verbose logging" if you'd like more detailed logging of your connections. (This log can be accessed via the Internet Connect application by choosing Window ➢ Connection Log.) When you're done in the dialog sheet, click OK.

NOTE You may need to switch back to the TCP/IP tab to add domain name servers if your ISP requires you to enter them manually. Also, if your Internet connection requires proxy servers, use the Proxies tab as discussed in the section "Setting Up Your Modem and TCP/IP" earlier in this chapter.

Internet Connect

Once you've entered your PPPoE settings in the Network pane, you can switch to the Internet Connect application to initiate the connection. Launch Internet Connect (it's in the main Applications folder) and select your Ethernet port from the Configuration menu. Now you can simply click the Connect button to initiate the connection. If your DSL (or similar) modem is turned on and properly connected to your Mac, you should quickly see the Status line indicate a connection; also, the Internet Connect window will change to show Send and Receive indicators, as well as the length of time connected and the current IP address.

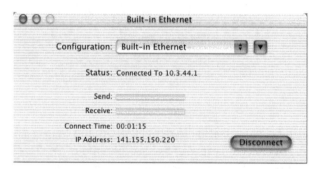

If you'd like to see more information about your connection, or if you need to enter your password, click the triangle button next to the Configuration menu. That opens up the Internet Connect window to reveal your username, password entry box, and other details.

To disconnect, simply click the Disconnect button. You should quickly see the Status line return to Idle.

AirPort Connections

If your AirPort network includes an AirPort Base Station, the Base Station may be configured to route Internet access to your Mac's AirPort card. Usually the Base Station will connect automatically whenever you attempt to access an Internet application. If you

HIGH-SPEED CONNECTIONS | **257**

don't seem to be receiving Internet data over AirPort, open Internet Connect. Select Air-Port from the Configuration menu, and you should see a Connect button at the bottom of the Internet Connect window; click the Connect button to force the Base Station to dial its internal modem or otherwise initiate your Internet connection. To disconnect the Base Station, click Disconnect. (Note that you don't always have to disconnect the AirPort Internet connection. Other Macs using AirPort can also connect and disconnect the AirPort Internet connection, and the AirPort Base Station itself will usually disconnect after a certain number of idle minutes, depending on its configuration.)

Creating Multiple Locations

Mac OS X has another feature that I've only touched on until now but that is very relevant for both Internet access and regular TCP/IP network configuration. It's the Location menu at the very top of the Network pane.

By default, your location is set to Automatic, and you can really create only one set of TCP/IP and other settings for each of your installed ports—Ethernet, modems, and AirPort, if you have them. (You can get around this by digging into the Advanced settings from the Configure menu, but that's a complicated solution.) By creating different locations, however, you can actually have completely different sets of settings for your ports, and switch between them easily.

For instance, if you have a PowerBook or iBook that you frequently carry from work to home, you probably need to change some settings in order to access the Internet in those two different places. At work, you may have a direct Ethernet connection that requires certain settings for the Built-in Ethernet port; at home, you might use a DSL modem that requires different settings. Instead of changing the settings in the Network pane by hand every evening and morning, you can create a location instead.

To create a location, select the Location menu at the top of the Network pane and choose New Location. In the dialog sheet that appears, type a name for this location, then click OK. Now you'll see the Location menu indicate that new location, and you'll notice that all of your port settings are blank—ready for you to fill in information for this new location.

Now, select a port in the Configure menu and configure it as desired for this location. If you're creating the Home location and you're setting up your Built-in Ethernet port for DSL connections, you'll probably dig into the PPPoE tab, which wasn't necessary for your Work location, and so on.

PART
II

Networks and the
Internet

Once everything is configured, you can use the Location menu to add more locations, or you can switch between them using the Location menu. Now you can quickly change between entire sets of Network settings without altering or retyping constantly.

 NOTE A location isn't just about TCP/IP settings; each location can have different AppleTalk, PPP, and proxy settings—and anything else you can set in the Network pane. And they don't have to vary dramatically; you could create Dallas and Houston locations, for instance, where the only difference is the local phone number on the PPP tab.

There's another trick to creating locations: You don't even have to open the Network pane to switch between them! Open the Apple menu, select Location, and you'll see all of your created locations appear in the menu.

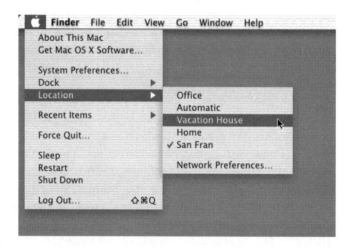

Now, whenever you move your Mac (or whenever you want to change to a different set of network settings), you can simply select a new location in the Apple menu, and your network settings will change immediately.

Internet Access for Local Networks

Okay, so your problem is that you have a broadband networking solution—a DSL modem, cable modem, or something similar—but you also have a LAN and you're sharing files using TCP/IP. Your ISP tells you that TCP/IP needs to be set one way, but that means your Mac will no longer be configured to access other Macs on your local network. Two solutions present themselves.

First, you could install another networking port in your Mac, by adding either an Ethernet card or an AirPort card (if your Mac supports AirPort). Most likely, your ISP is requiring an Ethernet port for the broadband connection, so adding another Ethernet port would be necessary if you want to use Ethernet for your LAN. If it's okay to use AirPort for your LAN, you could stick with one Ethernet port and one AirPort port, with your file sharing being conducted exclusively over AirPort.

Second, you could install and use a hardware router between your broadband modem and your LAN. The router would then become responsible for negotiating Internet data between all the Macs on your network and the ISP. Let's take a look at each option in turn.

 WARNING Some ISPs (particularly for cable and DSL modems) require that you pay for each computer on your LAN that receives Internet access, and they may enforce that policy strictly. If you intend to share a single broadband connection with multiple computers, check with your ISP to see if an Internet router is considered "legal" or if the ISP charges extra for using such a device.

PART

II

Networks and the Internet

Configuring Multiple Ports

If you install a compatible Ethernet or AirPort card in your Mac, and Mac OS X recognizes it, you'll have an instant solution to the problem of getting both Internet access and LAN access using TCP/IP. You'll connect one of the ports to your LAN, while connecting the other port to your broadband Internet device or modem, by simply selecting the ports in the Network pane's main Configure menu and configuring them accordingly.

Here's what you do:

1. Shut down your Mac and install the additional networking card.

2. Restart your Mac and log in. If necessary, install any software drivers required by your networking card.

3. Once the networking card is working, open System Preferences, open the Network pane, and, from the Configure menu, select the networking port (e.g., Built-in Ethernet) that you plan to use for your Internet connection (it should

correspond to the Ethernet or AirPort device that's actually attached to your broadband modem). Configure that port according to your ISP's instructions, including domain name server entries, if necessary.

4. Next, from the Configure menu, select the networking port that you plan to use for your local network (e.g., PCI Ethernet Slot J11), as shown in Figure 9.6. (If it's an Ethernet port, it should be connected to your Ethernet hub.) Configure the port so that you can properly access your local network; see Chapter 8 for details.

Now you've got two active networking ports that are configured for accessing both the Internet and your LAN. You should now be able to click the Save button in the Network pane and immediately begin using both your LAN and your Internet connection. (If your Internet connection requires that you connect via Internet Connect, you'll need to do that before working with any Internet-enabled applications.)

 NOTE In my experience, such a wholesale change to the Network pane will occasionally not work immediately after closing the System Preferences application. If you're having trouble, you may need to restart your Mac before the settings will take full effect.

FIGURE 9.6

I'm configuring my second Ethernet port, which will be used to connect to my LAN.

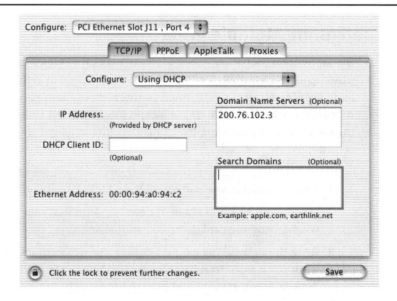

Using a Router

The discussion above enables you to use two Ethernet ports (or an Ethernet port and an AirPort) to gain access to both Internet data and a local LAN. But what if you need Internet access for your entire LAN? The solution in that case is an Internet router. Such a device sits between your Internet connection and your Ethernet hub, moving data from the broadband device to your entire network. Some routers are also integrated Ethernet hubs, enabling you to connect multiple computers directly to the router. The router then forwards IP data from the Internet connection (usually a broadband modem) to your entire LAN.

 TIP It's also possible to have *software* routers that run on your Mac and offer Internet access to the rest of your LAN. At the time of writing, no such routers are available for Mac OS X, but popular versions for Mac OS 9.x are available from Vicomsoft (www.vicomsoft.com) and Sustainable Softworks (www.sustworks.com).

Besides simply forwarding IP data, routers can offer security settings, enabling you to create a *firewall* between your network and the Internet. One scheme, *network address translation* (NAT), is common to most of today's consumer Internet routers. NAT translates your public IP address into private addresses on your LAN, making it much more difficult for outsiders on the Internet to access one of your Macs directly. Some routers also offer "virtual server" features, which automatically reroute server requests to a particular computer on your LAN, while denying other requests. And some even offer access control features, which enable you to deny your own users access to particular Web sites or domains.

You configure the router as specified in its documentation; then, with it connected to your Ethernet hub to which your Macs are also connected, you can configure the Macs to access that router. Most hardware routers are platform-independent, so they'll work with Macs, PCs, Unix machines, and most any other computer. Figure 9.7 shows an example of a router configuration screen; note that it's being accessed via a Web browser.

Configuring your router is beyond the scope of this book, so follow the instructions that came with it. Once the router is set up, however, there are two ways to configure your Macs to access the router and, hence, the Internet:

- Most routers act as DHCP servers, assigning IP addresses to the Macs on your LAN. If you've set up your router to serve DHCP, you can simply select Configure ➢ Using DHCP in the TCP/IP tab of each Mac's Ethernet port that you want to be configured automatically.

- With most routers you can also, if you like, assign fixed IP addresses in the private range to your Macs. If you elect to do this (by selecting Configure ➢ Manually in the TCP/IP tab), you'll need to enter the router's IP address in the Router entry box. You may also need to configure a domain name server address (or addresses) to access Internet sites successfully.

In either case, once you've finished setting your TCP/IP addresses and options, close System Preferences and restart your Mac. When you sign back in, your LAN-based Macs should have access, through the router, to the Internet.

The AirPort Base Station

The AirPort Base Station device, offered by Apple, is a hybrid router and wireless hub for AirPort-based networks. If you don't need Internet access, you can use the Base Station simply to connect multiple AirPort-based Macs in a wireless network. You can also opt to use the Base Station as an Ethernet-to-AirPort router by connecting an Ethernet cable to the *uplink* port on an Ethernet hub or switch. In that way, the Base Station can be used to make both AirPort and Ethernet-based Macs appear on the same TCP/IP network, so that files can be shared among them all.

Finally, the Base Station can also be used as a router for Internet access. By connecting a broadband modem to the Base Station's Ethernet port, you can give Internet access to all of your AirPort-based Macs. The Base Station must be configured to do this, and, at the time of writing, the Base Station cannot be configured from within Mac OS X.

Instead, you'll need to dual-boot into Mac OS 9.1 and run the AirPort Setup Assistant from there. Configure the Base Station according to the Assistant's instructions (see Chapter 18 for more about this). You begin by setting the Mac's TCP/IP and Remote Access control panels with the settings the Base Station will require; then you use the Assistant to transfer those settings to the Base Station. Once the settings are transferred, the Base Station is no longer reliant on the Mac's settings—it can access the Internet on its own, either via its built-in modem or via a broadband connection, whenever an AirPort-equipped Mac requests a connection.

AirPort software updates appear at www.apple.com/airport/, and Apple will presumably have a Mac OS X–compatible update available at some point in the future.

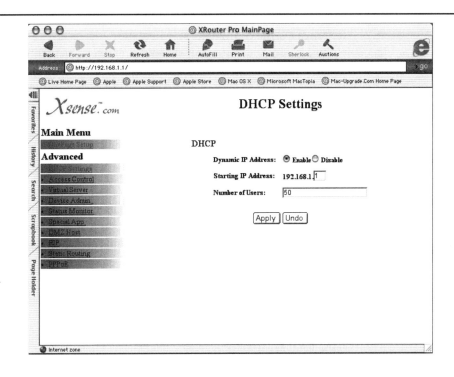

FIGURE 9.7

The XRouter Pro from MacSense (www.macsense. com) offers a Web-based configuration for options such as DHCP serving, PPPoE setup, and firewall options.

TCP/IP in the Classic Environment

You can access the Internet within the Classic environment without any trouble, for the most part. The idea is to treat the Classic environment as if it were simply another Mac OS X application. If you need to connect to the Internet using a Classic application, you'll want to establish your Internet connection first, particularly if you use the Internet Connect application for your connections. Once the Internet connection is established, you should be able to launch the Classic application and begin accessing online resources.

If you have a direct connection to the Internet, including a broadband connection like DSL or a cable modem, using Internet applications within Classic is even easier. Once TCP/IP is properly set up in System Preferences and you've successfully accessed the Internet from Mac OS X, launch a Classic Internet application and test your connection from within the Classic environment.

This system works because the TCP/IP control panel in Mac OS 9.1 has been modified to work in a Classic configuration, where the panel receives TCP/IP settings directly from Mac OS X, as shown in Figure 9.8. (You can view this control panel by launching a Classic application, then choosing Control Panels ➤ TCP/IP from the Classic Apple menu.) By default, you can't alter any of these settings, since they're set by Mac OS X. You should avoid changing this configuration by, for instance, using File ➤ Configurations in the TCP/IP control panel's menu.

Classic applications can't speak directly to your Mac's modem, so modem-based applications like America Online can't be run from within the Classic environment. If you need to use AOL, and a Mac OS X native version isn't yet available, you'll need to dual-boot into Mac OS 9.1 to launch AOL. The only exception to this rule is using AOL's "bring your own access" plan, where you connect to AOL over a TCP/IP connection. In that case, you can establish your Internet connection in Mac OS X, then launch AOL and configure it to use TCP/IP to connect to the service. From there you should be able to access AOL without trouble.

TIP Although they are outside the scope of this book, you shouldn't have trouble understanding modem-based Internet connections from within Mac OS 9.1, if you boot into it. Use the TCP/IP control panel to select PPP and configure it for your connection—it's somewhat similar to the options you'll see in the Network pane. Then use the Remote Access control panel, which has similarities to Internet Connect, to dial your ISP and enter an account name and password.

FIGURE 9.8

The Mac OS 9.1 TCP/IP control panel has a special Classic configuration that's used when a Classic Internet application is active.

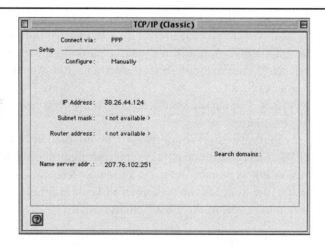

Setting Internet Preferences

Although Internet applications tend to manage their own preferences, Mac OS X includes a central place where a number of such settings can be stored: the Internet pane in System Preferences. If you enter Internet-related data here, you won't have to repeatedly enter, say, a new home page for your Web browser if you switch to a new program or version. In fact, information related to e-mail, the World Wide Web, and Internet newsgroups can all be stored as Internet preferences. This central repository can be accessed by any Internet application, and preferences you set here can automatically be entered in those applications when they're launched. Ideally, that means that you won't have to enter this information again whenever you install and use a new Internet application of some kind. (Practically speaking, you'll still sometimes need to fill in a few preferences if you install new Internet programs, but not as often.)

The Internet pane also enables you to enter your Apple iTools account information, making it accessible to other applications—and the Mac OS—automatically. Entering iTools information in the Internet pane gives you the ability to access the iTools features automatically from different places within the Finder and other applications, such as Mail.

To set your Internet preferences, launch System Preferences and click the Internet icon. You'll see the window reconfigure to show the Internet pane, starting with the iTools tab.

The iTools Tab

PART

II

Networks and the Internet

On the iTools tab, you're asked to enter your iTools member name and password. Once entered, these items can be used automatically by the Mac OS and applications to access your iTools account; for instance, the Go ➤ iDisk command in the Finder can automatically launch the iDisk that's associated with the account entered on the iTools tab.

If you don't have an iTools account, you can click the Free Sign Up button to launch your Web browser and begin signing up for iTools at Apple's Web site.

The Email Tab

| iTools | Email | Web | News |

Default Email Reader: Mail

☐ Use iTools Email account

                                                     Examples

Email Address: rich@mycorp.com   psmith@mac.com

Incoming Mail Server: mail.mycorp.com   mail.mac.com

Account Type: ○ POP ● IMAP

User Account ID: rich564   psmith

Password: •••••••••

Outgoing Mail Server: smtp.localaccess.net   smtp.mac.com

Select the Email tab and you'll have quite a few default settings you can make regarding your e-mail applications and your primary e-mail account. (Note that the Email tab doesn't offer settings for more than one account; if you have more than one, you'll need to set it up within your e-mail application.)

There are two basic ways to use this tab. The first way is simply to click the Use iTools Email Account check box if you've already entered a member name and password on the iTools tab. Now, all necessary e-mail information is entered automatically on this screen, and you won't have to do anything special to begin using the Mac.com e-mail account. (In fact, Mac OS X's Mail application will also automatically configure itself to use your Mac.com account the next time it's launched.)

The other way to use this screen is to manually enter information about your primary e-mail account. Here's a look at the settings:

Default Email Reader   Select the e-mail program that you'd like to set as the default. The default e-mail reader is (usually) launched automatically when you click a Web link that includes an e-mail address, or when other e-mail issues come up. If you don't see the e-mail application you want to use, choose Select from the menu. An Open dialog box will appear, enabling you to locate the program you want to use.

Email Address   This is often referred to as your "reply to" address, because it's the address that others will see when you send them an e-mail message.

Incoming Mail Server   Enter the address for your default incoming e-mail server.

Account Type   Choose your primary e-mail account's type: POP (Post Office Protocol) or IMAP (Internet Message Access Protocol).

User Account ID   Enter the e-mail account's username. Note that this isn't *always* the name portion of the e-mail address that you entered at the top of this screen, although it usually is. For instance, you might sign into an account using the ID *rich564*, even though your address is rich@mydomain.com. In fact, this is fairly common; to the outside world, you have a nice, streamlined e-mail address, but to your ISP, you're just one of many account names.

Password   Enter the password for your e-mail account. You can leave this blank if, by default, you want to enter your password whenever you check e-mail in your e-mail application.

Outgoing Mail Server   Enter the address for your outgoing e-mail server, often an SMTP (Simple Mail Transfer Protocol) server.

 TIP   Do you have different ISPs for Internet access and e-mail? It happens. Note that your SMTP server generally needs to be associated with the ISP through which you have your access, not the ISP through which you have your e-mail account. For instance, I primarily access the Internet via Verizon's DSL service, but my e-mail account is with another provider. I use Verizon's SMTP server, though, because that's the service I'm using to connect to the Internet. (If you use an SMTP server to which you're not directly connected, you'll often get error messages that keep you from sending e-mail.)

The Web Tab

iTools	Email	Web	News

Default Web Browser: Internet Explorer ⬍

Home Page: http://www.mac-upgrade.com

Search Page: http://www.excite.com/apple/

Download Files To: /Users/rich/Desktop   Select...

On the Web tab, you can use the Default Web Browser pop-up menu to select the Web browser that you'd like to assign as the system-wide default, which means that any Internet shortcuts or Web addresses that you click in non-Internet applications will *usually* launch in that default browser. (It doesn't always work, because browser brands, like Democrats and Republicans, have a tendency to lean toward their own on occasion. Sometimes when you click a hyperlink in a Microsoft application, that page loads in Internet Explorer, regardless of the preferences you've set here.)

In the Home Page entry box, enter the Web address for the Web page that you'd like to use as your default home page. In the Search Page entry box, enter the Web address for your favorite search engine. (Some, but not all, Web browsers actually pay attention to these entries. The Search Page entry is often ignored because of commercial relationships forged by the big browser companies that tend to direct you toward their preferred search engines. Ah, capitalism.)

 TIP You can cut and paste Web addresses from your Web browser's address bar into these entry boxes. That can be particularly helpful with some of those long, winding Web addresses.

In the Download Files To entry box, you can enter a path to the folder on your Mac's disk where you'd like downloaded files to be saved. If you're not into typing path statements, click the Select button and use the Open dialog box to locate the folder where you'd like to store files you download from within Internet applications.

The News Tab

The final tab, the News tab, enables you to enter preferences for reading Internet newsgroups. Internet "news" isn't really news in the CNN sense, but rather discussions by groups of Internet users. Newsreaders are programs that enable you to participate in online discussion boards, sending and reading messages on a variety of topics. Here's a look at the options:

Default News Reader   Select a newsreader application from the pop-up menu. Although Mac OS X's Mail may appear as an option, you can't actually read newsgroups with it; if you have Outlook Express installed, it can be used for newsgroups.

News Server   Enter the Internet address of your news server computer.

Connect As   Choose whether you should connect as a Registered User (with a username and password) or as a Guest. Some news servers don't require authentication, enabling you to access them anonymously. To do this, choose Guest.

User Account ID   If you've chosen Registered User, enter your user account name in this entry box. It's most likely the same as the user ID you use to log into your ISP, if your ISP runs your e-mail server.

Password   Enter the password associated with the User Account ID you just entered.

PART

II

Networks and the
Internet

What's Next?

In this chapter, you saw how to configure Mac OS X for Internet access, whether you're using a modem and phone line or a higher-speed broadband connection. You also saw how to use Internet applications in the Classic environment and how to configure the Internet pane with common Internet addresses and preferences.

In the next chapter, we'll move on to an in-depth look at the Mail application that's included with Mac OS X. You'll see how to send and receive mail as well as how to read, respond to, and forward messages. You'll also see advanced techniques for managing, storing, and automating various e-mail tasks.

# CHAPTER 10

Managing Mail with the Mail Application

Mac OS X features a built-in mail client, called simply Mail, that enables you to access both Internet e-mail and, if properly configured, local e-mail between multiple users on the Mac OS X system. Mail also offers a number of features for managing, storing, and searching through all the e-mail you receive.

Mail allows you to deal with multiple accounts, including both POP (Post Office Protocol) and IMAP (Internet Message Access Protocol) accounts; the latter enables you to store your mail on a mail server, downloading messages only when you need to read them. You can also create automatic filters and set advanced preferences to automate the retrieval and filing of incoming messages. As you'll see, Mail is a nice, sophisticated program, especially considering that it's free.

Setting Up Your Mail Account(s)

In order to get much done with Mail, you're going to need to set up your Internet e-mail accounts. Mail can handle four different types of accounts easily: POP, IMAP, Unix, and Mac.com, the account that's included with an iTools membership.

A POP mail account is the standard, offline approach to e-mail. When you access your POP e-mail account, you download all messages from a receiving e-mail server computer to your Mac, where the messages are processed by Mail and displayed in the Inbox. By default, e-mail is left on the server computer, but you can change the default so that the mail is deleted from the server once you've accessed it. The mail server computer can be on your network (perhaps running on another Mac OS X machine), or your Internet service provider may manage it.

With an IMAP account, more of your e-mail storage and access is done on the server. Instead of immediately downloading incoming messages to Mail, you view the message titles, search them, and organize them while they're still on the server. Thus, you can maintain your e-mail on a remote server, yet access all your mail—even mail that has been read, categorized, and stored in folders—in any IMAP client. If you have such an account, you can use Mail to access it.

Note that POP is an offline solution (you download your e-mail and read it at your leisure), whereas IMAP is an online solution—you have to be connected to the server to retrieve your mail. Although a POP account is probably the more convenient choice for modem-based users, anyone with an "always-on" Internet connection (such as a LAN-based connection, a service like DSL, or a cable modem) should at least consider an IMAP account, assuming your ISP or administrator can provide one. The main advantage of IMAP is that you can access the account from different locations and different computers, since both new and saved messages are left on the server.

Mac.com accounts, in fact, are IMAP accounts, at least when configured automatically by Mac OS X and Mail. If you'd like a Mac.com account, you'll need to sign up for iTools, as described in Chapter 11. You can then use your Mac.com e-mail address together with Mail to read, reply to, and manage your mail. (Note that unlike some corporate and institutional IMAP accounts, you do need to download and file your Mac.com e-mail in separate folders, called mailboxes, in the Mail application. That's because you have a limited amount of storage space you can use on Apple's servers. But messages left in your Inbox can still be accessed from other IMAP clients or other computers, as desired.)

Finally, Unix accounts are accounts you can create if you're in a networked Unix environment where mail is sent to your local machine instead of being held at a central POP or IMAP server computer.

POP and IMAP Account Information

Most e-mail accounts you'll manage in Mail are either POP or IMAP accounts. If you're not sure whether you have POP or IMAP, ask your Internet service provider or your system administrator. Once you know, you'll just need a little additional information, which you enter at setup. Here's the information you'll need to get from your ISP or system administrator:

Incoming Mail Server Address This is the mail server's name or address. In most cases, it will be in a form such as `mail.myserver.net`, `pop.myserver.com`, or `imap.myserver.com`.

Username or Account ID You'll need to know the username you've been assigned for your e-mail account.

Password You'll need to enter the password that's been assigned to your mail account.

Outgoing Mail Server Address This is the server address for outgoing messages, often called an SMTP (Simple Mail Transport Protocol) server address. The address is often (though not always) different from the address of your incoming mail server; sometimes it's in the form of `smtp.myserver.net`. It may also be in the form of `smtp.myserviceprovider.net` if you're accessing an e-mail account that isn't managed by your ISP. For instance, if you're accessing your office POP account, but you're currently on the road using your Earthlink account to access the Internet, you'll use Earthlink's SMTP server instead of your office's SMTP server.

Creating Your First Account

Before you can get started with Mail, you've got to enter information for at least one e-mail account. This can be done in one of two places—in the Internet pane of the System Preferences application or in the Mail Setup window that appears when you first launch Mail. The only difference is this: If you enter an account in the Internet pane, it becomes your *default* account, meaning that other Internet applications will have access to that information and could conceivably configure themselves to use that account for e-mail. So, if you're not sure which e-mail account you'd like to be your default, you might opt to simply start up Mail and enter an account from there.

 NOTE If your only e-mail account is an iTools Mac.com account, you'll need to configure it in the Internet pane; the Mail Setup window doesn't give you the option of easily creating a Mac.com account. See Chapter 11 for details on signing up for iTools and entering your Mac.com e-mail account information in the Internet pane.

If you've opened Mail and haven't already created an account, you'll likely see the Mail Setup panel window on-screen (see Figure 10.1). This special panel is designed to make your setup as easy as possible the first time around if you have a standard POP or IMAP account. (If you're working on the Mail tab of the Internet pane in the System Preferences application, you'll note that the options are almost exactly the same as they are in the Mail Setup window.)

FIGURE 10.1

Setting up your first e-mail account

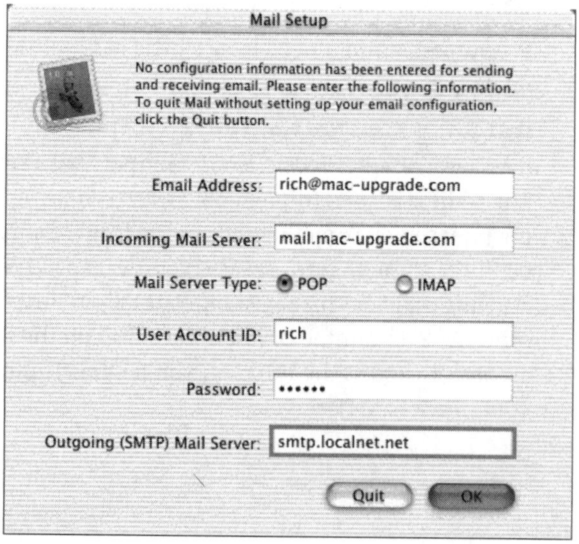

Mail Setup
No configuration information has been entered for sending and receiving email. Please enter the following information. To quit Mail without setting up your email configuration, click the Quit button.

Email Address: rich@mac-upgrade.com

Incoming Mail Server: mail.mac-upgrade.com

Mail Server Type: ● POP ○ IMAP

User Account ID: rich

Password: ••••••

Outgoing (SMTP) Mail Server: smtp.localnet.net

(Quit) (OK)

Here's how to create the account:

1. First, realize that it can be helpful to sign on to the Internet (if you use Internet Connect for your Internet connection) before launching Mail. When you've finished entering your e-mail information, Mail will attempt to connect to your account and immediately download any waiting e-mail. If you're not connected, you'll get an error message.

2. If you haven't already launched Mail, do so by clicking its tile in the Dock or double-clicking its icon in the Applications folder. The Mail Setup panel will appear if you haven't previously set up an e-mail account.

3. In the Email Address entry box, type the e-mail address you're going to use for this account. Note that this is the address that others will use to send you e-mail (for instance, you@yourcompany.com, even if you sign into the account using an address such as accountname@yourserviceprovider.net or something similar).

NOTE In some cases your *actual* e-mail address is different from the e-mail address you give out to friends and family. For instance, you might have an e-mail address such as bob@mac-upgrade.com, even though your actual e-mail account is bob245@mail .myisp.net. In the Mail Setup panel, the Email Address entry box is for your public e-mail address.

4. In the Incoming Mail Server entry box, type the address for your incoming mail server, as specified by your ISP.

5. Choose the type of mail server (POP or IMAP) by clicking the appropriate radio button.

6. In the User Account ID entry box, enter your account ID or username for accessing the mail server. (This may be different from your e-mail address. For instance, you might have an account where your username is bob245, even though you receive mail at the address bob@mac-upgrade.com.)

7. In the Password section, enter your mail account password.

8. In the Outgoing (SMTP) Mail Server entry box, enter the address of the SMTP server you want to use with this account. The SMTP server address is often (but not always) different from that of the incoming mail server.

After clicking OK, Mail will automatically attempt to connect to the Internet and verify your e-mail settings. If you use Internet Connect for a modem-based connection and that connection isn't currently active (or if you otherwise don't yet have a working Internet connection), you'll get an error message. If you know your Mail

PART

II

Networks and the Internet

account settings are correct and you'd like to continue despite the error message, click the Continue button.

Once Mail connects successfully to your e-mail server, it will download your incoming e-mail (if you have a POP account and any e-mail is waiting for you) or will otherwise open your account for access (if you have an IMAP account). Then you'll see Mail's viewer window, with your Inbox displayed. If your main interest is simply accessing a single Internet e-mail account, you're done.

 TIP If you need further configuration, want to add more e-mail accounts, or have special settings or circumstances for your e-mail, see the section "Creating and Editing Accounts" later in this chapter.

Accessing Your E-Mail

Once you've set up your initial Internet account, you're ready to begin reading and replying to incoming e-mail. In this section you'll see a quick overview of how to read messages, reply to them, and compose new messages. If you've worked with Internet e-mail applications in the past, you can probably skip this section and move straight to the section "Managing Your E-Mail," where I'll detail the unique features in the Mail application. For now, though, I'll cover just the quick basics.

Retrieving Your Mail

 By default, Mail automatically checks (and, for POP accounts, downloads) your mail every 5 minutes, as long as it is running. It also, while active, updates the Mail icon in the Dock so that you can quickly see whether you have new messages. (The number in the red circle represents how many new messages are in your Inbox.)

The automatic checking is convenient for some but can be something of a problem if you have a dial-up connection to the Internet, so you may want to change the setting. (See the later section "E-Mail Checking Options.")

If you've turned the automatic option off or if you'd simply prefer to check manually, all you have to do is click the Get Mail button in at the top of the viewer window. You'll see a spinning-arrow indicator on the Status line (the line just below the toolbar), showing that messages are being checked.

If you have new messages, you'll see the messages appear in the message list at the top of the viewer window.

 TIP If you'd prefer, you can also select Window ➤ Activity Viewer to display the Activity Viewer window. The Activity Viewer will give you a more exact sense of what's going on as your mail is being checked and, if found, downloaded.

Reading Incoming Mail

As mentioned earlier, immediately after you enter information about your e-mail account, Mail will bring up the viewer window (see Figure 10.2) and display your Inbox, along with any messages that have been received. Reading messages in this interface is really very simple. All you have to do is click an e-mail in the top pane of the window (the *message list*). The bottom pane of the window (the *message area*) changes to display the text of the selected message. On the far right (by default) is the *mailbox drawer,* where the Inbox and personal mailbox folders are stored. If you can't see new messages, make sure the Inbox mailbox is selected. (If you have more than one account, make sure the correct Inbox is selected.)

FIGURE 10.2

The viewer window shows your incoming mail and the text of the selected message.

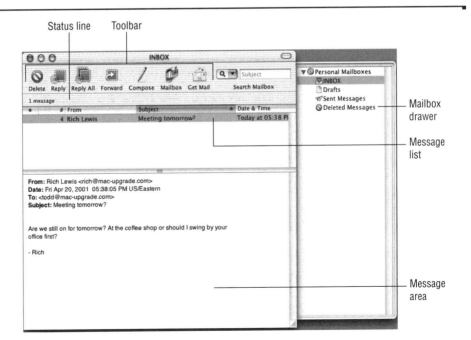

You can also double-click a message in the message list to view it in a separate window. When you've finished viewing the message, you can click one of the buttons in the message's toolbar (Delete, Reply, Reply All, Forward, or Print), or you can click the Close button in the window to close the message.

NOTE You can customize how e-mail looks in the message area. Select Mail ➢ Preferences, and you'll see the Mail Preferences dialog box. Select the Viewing icon to see options for viewing, including whether or not you want to automatically download attachments and how much header detail (the details of the To, From, and routing information for the message) should appear. Then click the Fonts & Colors icon if you'd like to change the fonts and sizes used for the message list and message area. Here you can also decide how quoted text should appear. (As you exchange replies to messages back and forth with your recipient, the colors can change to denote different "levels" of reply—earlier replies will have a different color.)

While viewing a message, there's another little trick you can perform: You can add the sender of the message to your Address Book. This can be convenient for finding that sender later and sending messages to that person. To add a sender to your Address Book, highlight the message in the viewer window or double-click the message to view it in its own window. Now, select Message ➢ Add Sender to Address Book. That user's name and e-mail address will be stored in the Address Book, for later retrieval. (Chapter 12 discusses the Address Book in detail, including more information on using it with Mail.)

Replying to a Message

You can reply to an incoming e-mail message by selecting it in the list and clicking the Reply button. A new window appears, allowing you to compose your response. Note that the window already has the recipient's e-mail address filled in for you. Simply type your reply above the quoted portion of the message that appears in the message area (see Figure 10.3).

NOTE If the original message was sent to other recipients besides you, you can send your reply to all of them if desired. You can actually do so in two ways. In the viewer window, select the message in the message list and click the Reply All button instead of clicking Reply. Or, if you've already clicked Reply, you get another chance—another Reply All button is at the top of the reply-composition window. Click that button, and any additional recipients of the e-mail message will be added to the Cc line.

FIGURE 10.3

Replying to a message

By typing an e-mail address on the Cc line, you can send a courtesy copy of an e-mail to another user. (In fact, receiving a courtesy copy is the same as receiving a regular e-mail except that the recipient's address appears on the Cc line.)

Once you've finished typing your reply, click the Send button (it looks like a paper airplane) to send the e-mail reply to its recipients. If you're connected to the Internet, the message will be sent immediately. If you aren't connected to the Internet, see the later section "Sending Your Message" for details on what happens.

Forwarding a Message

If you're reading a message that you want to send to a recipient who didn't see it the first time around, you can select the message in the viewer window and then click the Forward button. Doing so creates a message with the contents of the original plus the line "Begin forwarded message." The To address line is blank for you to fill in the e-mail address for the person to whom you're forwarding the message. (As with a reply, you can use the Cc line for additional addresses, separated by commas, if desired.) Once you've entered all the addresses (and you've typed a note in the message area, if desired), you can click the Send icon (the paper airplane) to send the message.

PART

II

Networks and the Internet

Creating a New Message

If you'd like to create a new message, that's done just as easily. Click the Compose button (it looks like a pencil) in the viewer window, and a New Message window appears (see Figure 10.4). Enter an Internet e-mail address on the To line and then a subject for your message on the Subject line. (Note that once you enter a subject line, the name of the window changes from New Message to whatever you've typed as the subject of the message.) If you'd like to send a courtesy copy to another user (or users, separated by commas), you can enter e-mail addresses on the Cc line.

FIGURE 10.4

Composing a new message

Then enter the text of your message in the message area. When you're done, you can click the Send button to send the message on its way.

Sending Your Message

A new message, a reply, and a forward all get sent the same way—you click Send in the composition window. Unlike some other e-mail applications, Mail doesn't have an option that enables you to "send later"—at least, not from the composition window.

If you aren't currently connected to the Internet but you want to create messages or reply to e-mails and then gather your messages for later delivery, you have an option. Select Mailbox ➤ Go Offline from the Mail menu. That enables you to work in offline mode. When you next click the Send button, you'll see a message saying that Mail can't connect to the server. You'll be asked if you want to save the message for later delivery. Click OK.

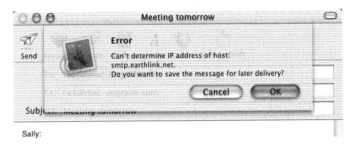

The message will then be stored in a new personal mailbox (a folder) called To Be Delivered. The next time you send a message, the messages in the To Be Delivered mailbox will also be sent. (To access the mailbox drawer, click the Mailbox icon in the viewer window. Also, see the later section "Managing Your E-Mail" for more on working with different mailboxes.)

So what happens if you're not connected to the Internet, you're not in offline mode, and you still attempt to send a message? For a while, nothing—the message may disappear for a few seconds, as if sent. Eventually, the message will reappear and you'll see an error message similar to the one shown in the preceding graphic, giving you the choice of saving the message for later delivery. If you click OK, the message will be stored in the To Be Delivered mailbox.

Saving a Message

If you haven't finished composing a message or reply and you'd like to save it for later, you can do so easily. With the composition window front-most, select File ➢ Save as Draft from the Mail menu or press ⌘+S. The message, in its current state, is saved to the Drafts mailbox, accessible in the mailbox drawer.

Once the message is saved, you can close the composition window if you've finished working on the message for now, or you can continue typing. (Note that, in this case, the Save as Draft feature can be used to save multiple versions of a message if you'd like to be able to revert to an earlier draft.)

If you've closed the composition window and want to subsequently work on the saved message, you can return to the message by selecting the Drafts mailbox and then either double-clicking the message or selecting it once and choosing File ➤ Restore from Draft. Then edit the message and click Send to send it as usual.

Managing Your E-Mail

Once the e-mail starts coming in, you'll feel the need to manage it more effectively. You'll do that by filing the messages in different *mailboxes* (Mail's word for folders) of your design. Mail allows you to customize how you view items in your mailboxes, including the Inbox mailbox that appears on-screen when you access your account. I'll focus on the tools for managing e-mail in the second part of this section.

The Inbox Window

A good deal of your time in Mail will be spent in the Inbox mailbox of your POP or IMAP account. It's there that you'll see new messages in the message list, as well as those that you haven't yet answered, filed, or deleted.

If you're not currently viewing the Inbox, you can switch to it by opening the mailbox drawer (click the Mailbox icon in the toolbar) and then selecting the Inbox icon that you'd like to use. As shown in Figure 10.5, it's possible to have two or more Inbox mailbox folders, particularly if you have both IMAP and POP accounts.

FIGURE 10.5

The viewer window, with an Inbox selected

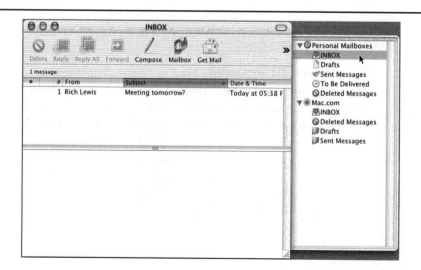

Customizing the Toolbar

Many basic commands can be accessed via the toolbar in the mailbox window. Many of these commands have already been covered in the section "Accessing Your E-Mail," and the rest of them will be discussed in more detail in this section.

If you'd like, you can customize the toolbar in a way that might seem familiar if you've done any customization in Finder windows—it's the same drag-and-drop system. Choose View ➢ Customize Toolbar, and a large dialog sheet pops out from the viewer window's title bar (see Figure 10.6). To customize the toolbar, drag items from the dialog sheet to the toolbar. You can also drag the separator to the toolbar, and you can drag items around on the toolbar to rearrange them.

If you'd like to return the toolbar to its original set, drag the default set of icons at the bottom of the dialog sheet to the toolbar.

In the Show menu at the bottom of the dialog sheet, you can choose whether the toolbar buttons should appear as icons, text, or both. When you've finished customizing, click the Done button to dismiss the dialog sheet.

FIGURE 10.6

Customizing the Mail toolbar

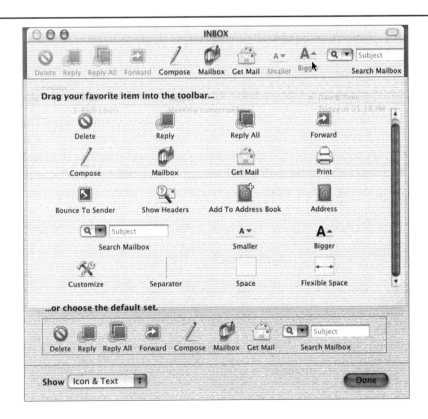

The Message List

The message list in Mail offers quite a bit of information about each e-mail message. A new message shows a small bullet, the *read indicator*, at the far left of the listing, which tells you that the message is unread. The indicator likely means that you've *never* read the message, but it may also mean that the message has been *marked* as unread, as I'll discuss in the section "Marking and Deleting Messages." For now, though, assume that a bullet at the left-most edge simply tells you the message has not been read.

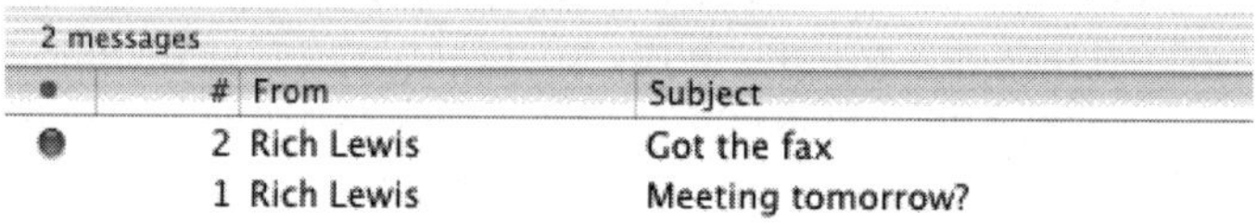

To the right of the read indicator, you'll see the name of the sender of the message. If the sender has entered a name in their e-mail program, the name you'll see will usually be the sender's full name. If they haven't, you'll see the sender's e-mail address.

Next, you'll see the subject of the message, which the sender entered when composing the message to you. To the right of the subject is the approximate date and time that the message was sent.

Aside from these columns, you can display a few optional columns, if desired. Select View ➢ Show Message Numbers, and you'll see a column of numbers appear to the left of the From column. Each incoming message is numbered by Mail; you can therefore view them in the order they were downloaded. The download order can sometimes be different from the date-and-time order because the date represents when the message was sent (and it may have been sent from a different time zone, or it may have taken longer than another message to arrive at your mail server computer).

Select View ➢ Show Message Sizes, and another column appears, this time to the far right of the message list. The column shows the amount of disk space each message consumes.

All these elements are shown in Figure 10.7.

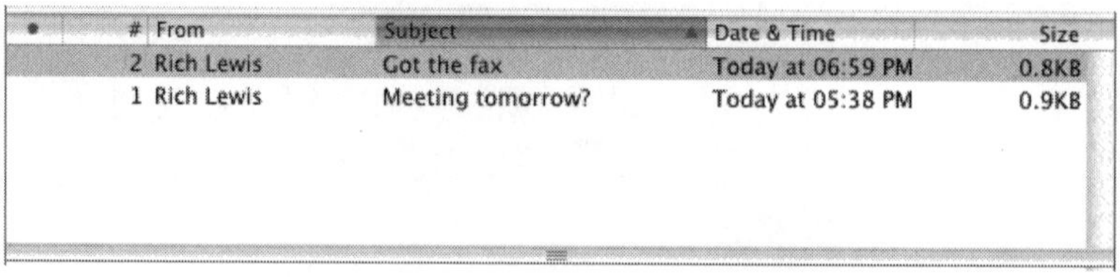

FIGURE 10.7

Elements of the message list

Sorting the Message List

With all these different criteria available in the message list, you may find reason to sort the display using one of them. After all, it would be nice to view the list differently at different times. You might want to view in order of date sent, for instance, or view messages sorted alphabetically by the name of the sender.

It's easy enough to do. Simply click a column title in the message list, and you'll see the list resorted according to that column's entries.

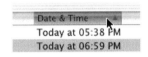

To reverse the order of the sort, just click the column title again. For instance, if you want to see names from *Z* to *A* or dates from the past to the present, you can click the column title to reverse the sort order. You'll see a small triangle in the active column title. It's pointing up when the sort order is reversed.

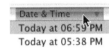

The same commands appear in the View ➤ Sort menu, if you'd prefer to use a menu command. In the Sort menu, select the type of sort you'd like to perform—By Number, By Date & Time, By Sender, By Subject, By Size, or By Read Status. The message list will change to reflect your new choice. You can also switch the sort order by choosing View ➤ Sort ➤ Ascending or View ➤ Sort ➤ Descending, as appropriate.

Showing and Hiding Messages

The Mailbox menu offers a number of commands to change the type and number of messages that appear in the message list. The commands can be useful if you need to cut through the clutter of messages in order to find those that are important. Here are some of the options:

>**Show Deleted Messages**   Select View ➤ Show Deleted Messages to cause messages marked as deleted (but not yet *compacted,* as discussed in the later section "Marking and Deleting Messages") to reappear in the message list. Deleted messages are grayed in the message list to help you identify them. Once selected, the command becomes View ➤ Hide Deleted Messages.

NOTE The Show Deleted Messages command is active only if you've turned off a special option in the Mail Preferences window. See the later section "Marking and Deleting Messages" for more on how messages are deleted.

Focus on Selected Messages   The View ➤ Focus on Selected Messages command allows you to selectively hide the majority of the messages in your mailbox. Select only the messages you want to see in the list, using the ⌘ key to select more than one message, if desired. Then, invoke the command. Only the highlighted messages will be shown in the message list, making them easier to deal with (see Figure 10.8). When you're finished dealing with those messages, you can view the whole list again by selecting View ➤ Show All Messages.

Show All Headers   The Message ➤ Show All Headers command displays in the viewer window the full Internet headers for any selected messages. The headers contain all the routing information required for a message to get from its creator to you, the recipient. Once selected, the command changes to Message ➤ Show Filtered Headers, which you can select if you feel you're getting a little too much information.

Marking and Deleting Messages

You've seen different ways to view the messages in the message list, but you'll also find a number of commands that change the status of the messages. When you select a message to read it, for instance, you're automatically changing that message to a *read* status. You can change that, though, if you'd like to mark it *unread* so that it appears with a bullet point and is considered not yet read by the program. You can also change the status when it comes to deleting and undeleting messages, as shown in this section.

FIGURE 10.8

Select messages in the message list (left) and choose the Focus command; your message list changes to reflect only those messages (right).

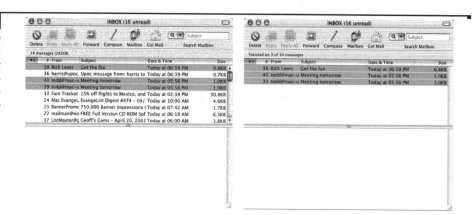

TIP If you hold down the Control key and click a message in the message list (or click the right mouse button on some two-button USB mice), you'll see a contextual menu that enables you to quickly delete a message or mark that message as read, as described next.

Read/Unread

You mark a message as read by selecting it in the message list. (The Mail application doesn't actually watch you to see if you're reading the message, because it trusts you.) Once a message is selected in the message list, its new-message bullet disappears and the message becomes "read." (That means it won't show up with other unread messages when you sort by Read Status in the View ➢ Sort menu, for instance.)

If you'd like to change a particular message back to an unread status, select it and choose Message ➢ Mark as Unread. The message will then have new-message status again, meaning the bullet reappears and the message will appear again if the Hide Read command is invoked.

Delete/Undelete

There are a few different ways that deleting messages can work. The default behavior is to have a message, when deleted, move to the Deleted Messages mailbox folder. All you have to do is select a message in the message list and press the Delete key or choose Message ➢ Delete. The selected message is moved to the Deleted Messages mailbox folder, where you can forget about it. If you decide you want the message back, open the Deleted Messages mailbox, then drag the deleted message back to the Inbox mailbox. After a message has been in the Deleted Messages mailbox for a month, that message is deleted permanently.

But you can change this default setting in the Mail Preferences window. Select Mail ➢ Preferences. In the Mail Preferences window, select the Viewing icon. Now you have some choices you can make regarding the way items are deleted.

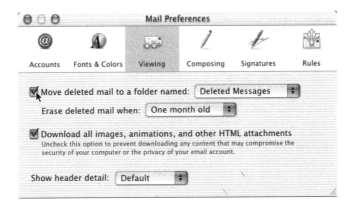

In the first menu, you can choose different mailbox folders to use—Deleted Messages, Deleted Items, or Trash—whichever you're most comfortable with. In the "Erase deleted mail when" menu, you can choose how long a message will wait in the specified mailbox folder before it's deleted permanently.

If, however, you turn off the "Move deleted mail to a folder named" option altogether (i.e., remove the check from the check box), you'll get a different behavior. Now, instead of moving to another folder, the deleted messages will simply be marked as deleted and hidden from view. These messages will then wait around until you *compact* the mailbox, which *permanently* deletes messages that are marked as deleted.

So, if you've turned off the "Move deleted mail..." option and you're working again in the viewer window, you delete a message like this: Select the message in the message list and click the Delete button in the button bar. Alternatively, you can press the Delete key on the keyboard after selecting a message; you can also select more than one message while holding down the ⌘ key, if desired, before invoking the Delete command. Once a message has been deleted, it will either disappear from the message list (by default) or continue to appear in the message list, but grayed, if the Show Deleted Messages command has previously been chosen from the Mailbox menu, as shown here:

| 2 | Rich Lewis | Got the fax | Today at 06:59 PM |
| 1 | Rich Lewis | Meeting tomorrow? | Today at 05:38 PM |

To "undelete" a message, the Show Deleted Messages command must be invoked (otherwise, you can't see the deleted message in order to select it). Select the message and choose Message ➢ Undelete. (You can also press Shift+⌘+U while the message is selected.) The message will reappear in the message list, now ungrayed.

Compact the Mailbox

If you'd like to permanently remove messages that have been marked as deleted, you can compact the mailbox. Compacting removes the messages permanently, much like emptying the Trash in the Finder does away with files that have previously been thrown away.

To compact the mailbox, choose Mailbox ➢ Compact Mailbox or press ⌘+K. Note that you aren't asked to confirm this operation—the message(s) are immediately removed from the Mail application's database and cannot be retrieved.

Rebuild the Mailbox

Mail offers a special command that allows you to rebuild a mailbox that's seen a lot of activity. Because the Mailbox is based on a single database file, that database file can experience corrupt or fragmented entries over time. If you experience trouble or if accessing the Mailbox has simply slowed down considerably, the Mailbox ➤ Rebuild Mailbox command can recover lost or damaged messages. You'll sometimes find that rebuilding the desktop will return deleted messages to an undeleted state as well as make the Mailbox more efficient and, in many cases, reduce the storage space it requires.

 WARNING   It's a good idea to have a backup of your Mail folder (inside your personal folder) before performing a rebuild operation, in case something goes wrong during the rebuild process. Of course, it's a good idea to always have a backup of your mail and other important files, as detailed in Chapter 21.

Using Multiple Mailboxes

Once you've gotten more than a few messages in your Inbox, you'll be ready to create new mailbox folders for storing your mail. Mail allows you to create multiple mailboxes, open them to see their messages, and move messages between different mailboxes to organize them. Most of this is done through the Mailbox panel.

The mailbox drawer is the center of mailbox management. Through this drawer you'll create mailbox folders, move mail between them, and delete messages. To open the mailbox drawer, select View ➤ Show Mailboxes from the menu or click the Mailbox icon on the button bar. The mailbox drawer appears, cleverly sliding out from the left (or right) side of the viewer window (see Figure 10.9).

PART

II

Networks and the Internet

FIGURE 10.9

The mailbox drawer, at the far right of the window, enables you to view, open, and manage your mailbox folders.

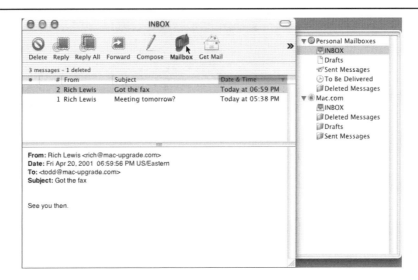

In the mailbox drawer, you'll see entries for each of your e-mail accounts, if you have more than one. Click the disclosure triangle next to the account that you'd like to access, and you'll see an Inbox entry for the account. Selecting the entry will enable you to view that account's Inbox in the viewer window.

NOTE When you add new POP e-mail accounts to Mail, you can decide whether the mail for each will come into a single Inbox (the one listed under Personal Mailboxes) or whether mail will come into separate Inboxes for each account. See "Create or Edit an Account" later in this chapter for details.

Click the disclosure triangle next to Personal Mailboxes to see your personal mailboxes, which you can use to organize your e-mail. You may see a few mailboxes that have already been created, such as Drafts (for saved messages in progress), Sent Messages (copies of messages you've sent), and, in some cases, To Be Delivered (if you've ever had a message that wasn't successfully sent the first time you tried).

In addition to these mailboxes, you can create your own. To create a new mailbox, first click the Personal Mailboxes entry in the mailbox drawer and then select Mailbox ➢ New Mailbox. The New Mailbox window appears.

Enter a name for your mailbox and then click OK. The new mailbox appears in the mailbox drawer.

Select the new mailbox in the mailbox drawer, and you'll see the viewer window change to show the contents of that mailbox. You can then read, manage, and search through mail in that mailbox, just as you can with the Inbox. Of course, you'll need some messages in that box first.

To transfer messages, switch to the Inbox (or switch to another mailbox where you have messages). Then, in the message list, select a message you'd like to transfer. (You can use the ⌘ key while selecting multiple messages in the message list.) With message(s) selected, choose Message ➢ Transfer and then select the mailbox to which you'd like to transfer the message(s).

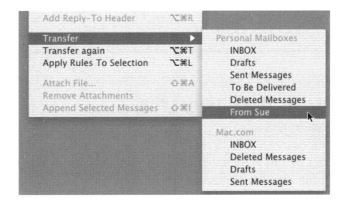

You can also drag and drop messages from the viewer window to a particular mailbox when the mailbox drawer is open. Simply select the message (or multiple messages) and use the mouse to drag it (or them) to the destination mailbox in the mailbox drawer.

You can create a special type of mailbox that includes subfolders, if you like, to help manage mail further. In the mailbox drawer, select either Personal Folders or the e-mail account where you want to create the special mailbox, then choose Mailbox ➢ Create Folder. Enter a name for the parent folder, then a slash, then the name of the subfolder you're creating. For example, you could enter **Business/Memos** to create a mailbox called Business that includes a subfolder called Memos. You could then create additional subfolders within the mailbox, such as **Business/Projects** and **Business/Budgets**.

 NOTE Note that you can't create subfolders for a mailbox folder that already exists. For instance, if Business already exists, you can't create subfolders within Business without deleting the Business mailbox folder first. Also, in my experience with Mail 1.0, you need to quit and relaunch Mail to see new mailbox subfolders.

To delete a mailbox, select it in the mailbox drawer and then select MailBox ➢ Delete Mailbox. The mailbox disappears, along with any messages in that mailbox, so make sure that's something you really want to do. (You should move the messages to another mailbox first if you want to save the messages but delete the mailbox.)

 TIP Want a third way to transfer items? Hold down the Control key, point the mouse at a message, and click the mouse button. (If you have a two-button USB mouse, you can use the right mouse button instead of holding down Control.) You'll see a contextual menu. Select Transfer and the mailbox to which you'd like to transfer that message. This method will also work if you have highlighted multiple messages (using ⌘+click) and you perform the Control+click maneuver on any of the highlighted messages.

Rules and Automatic Filing

Does your Inbox fill up in a hurry? One way to deal with that is to tell Mail that you'd like certain incoming messages—those, say, from a particular person or with a particular keyword in the subject line—to automatically be filed in one of your personal mailboxes. You can do so fairly easily.

To implement automatic filing, you need to create a *rule*. A rule is a simple test applied to each incoming message. It follows the form "if *part of the message* contains *a keyword,* then transfer the message *here.*" You can have multiple rules, and each message will be tested against each rule in turn. When a message meets the criteria of one of the rules, then the message is automatically transferred to one of your personal mailboxes. If the message gets by all of the rules, it's left in your Inbox. If a message meets the criteria of two or more rules, it will be moved according to the first rule it matches.

You'll create the rules in the Rules section of the Mail Preferences window. Select Mail ➢ Preferences, and the Mail Preferences window appears. Click the Rules icon. Then you'll see the Rules window, where you can set up the automatic behaviors (see Figure 10.10.)

Here's how to set up a rule:

1. Click the Create Rule button to create your first rule. A dialog sheet appears with the rule's default name highlighted so that you can type your own name for the rule, if desired.

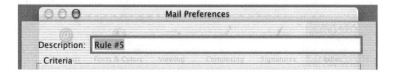

FIGURE 10.10

The Rules section of
Mail Preferences
enables you to set up
rules for automatically
filing incoming e-mail.

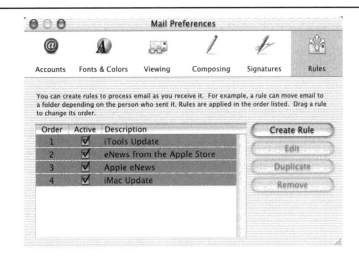

2. Set up the rule using the menus and text boxes. To begin, move to the Criteria section and use the first menu to select the e-mail-header field that you'd like to search (e.g., To, From, or Subject). Then, in the second menu, choose how you'd like to search that header field.

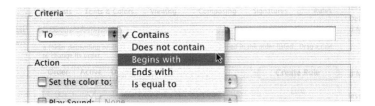

3. Enter a keyword (or even a few letters) against which the header will be compared. If you enter the word *upgrade,* for instance, then only messages that contain (or begin with, end with, etc.) that word in the selected header field will be processed.

NOTE You've got to be as exact as you can when you enter a keyword. Enter *upgrade,* for instance, and you'll get messages that have *upgrade* in the selected field, as well as permutations like *upgrades, upgraded,* and so on. If, however, you select Contains from the second menu and then enter *up,* you may or may not get what you bargain for—fields that include words as diverse as *supper, upright,* and *cupboard.*

PART
II
Networks and the
Internet

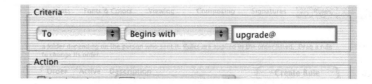

4. Now, choose the actions that you'd like taken if the criterion specified is matched. Place a check mark next to each action that you'd like taken, then use the corresponding menu to determine how, exactly, that action will be accomplished. (For forwarding the message, enter a valid e-mail address in the entry box.)

5. Click OK in the dialog sheet.

That's it—the rule is now active. You're returned to the Rules screen in Mail Preferences, where you can create a new rule, if desired. You can also drag the rule that you just created to another part of the rule list if you'd like to change that rule's order; the higher the rule, the sooner it's applied to each incoming mail message.

If you'd like to remove the rule, you can select it in the rule list and click the Remove button. The rule is removed instantly. If you'd like to simply turn the rule off (so that it isn't used to process incoming e-mail) but not delete it, click the check mark in the Active column next to the Description in the rule list. Without the check mark, that rule is off and won't process incoming e-mail.

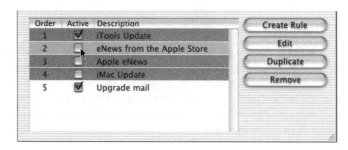

Searching Mailboxes

By default, you'll come across two different, unrelated ways to search within Mail. The Find Text command, accessed via Edit ➤ Find ➤ Find Text, enables you to search for text within a particular e-mail message while you're reading or composing that message. This works like the Find and Replace feature in most Mac OS X applications: Enter a term in the Find entry box of the Find Panel, then click Next to find the next occurrence of that term. You can also enter a term in the Replace With entry box (assuming you're searching a message that you're composing) and click Replace to replace the found term with the "replace with" term.

The other search feature, accessed through the small Search Mailbox entry box in the Mail toolbar, allows you to search the message *headers* in a particular mailbox. You begin by selecting the type of header that you'd like to search—Subject, To, or From—by clicking the small pop-up menu next to the Search Mailbox entry box. (The menu has only a small magnifying glass as its icon, but you'll see the options when you click it.) Then, type a word (or part of a word) into the Search Mailbox entry box, and you'll immediately see the number of messages in the mailbox begin to diminish. This indicates that the message list is showing only messages whose headers include the word or letter combination that you typed.

The search term should be something fairly unusual, such as a keyword that would be in the subject of the message or part of the name (or e-mail address) of the person who sent you the message you're seeking. As you type, the list of messages will slowly dwindle until, hopefully, you're viewing one or a few of the messages you want to see (see Figure 10.11).

It's nice to be able to quickly whittle down the messages in your Inbox by name or subject, but what if you want to search more deeply? You can use the Search Mailbox entry box to search *within* messages in the currently selected mailbox (including the Inbox or one of your Personal Mailboxes) and to display any messages that include the keyword you type.

PART

II

Networks and the Internet

FIGURE 10.11

As you type a search keyword, the number of found messages dwindles.

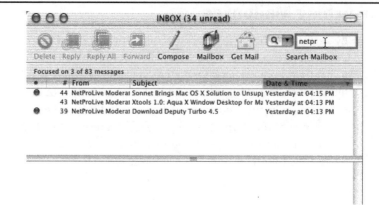

To search the full text of messages (including the headers) in a selected mailbox, all you need to do is select Any from the Search Mailbox menu (the tiny pop-up menu next to the Search Mailbox entry box) and then start typing in the Search Mailbox entry box. Enter a word or phrase that you'd like to search for in your messages—something fairly uncommon that's likely to be found in only a limited number of messages. Avoid articles (a, an, the), prepositions (of, for, over), and other very common words. (See the sidebar for additional searching hints.)

 TIP The Mail application searches for words similar to those you enter, so you'll get best results if you enter the simplest form of the word. For instance, entering *sleep* will find results that include *sleepy, sleepiness,* and so on.

You'll notice that the results of your search are altered automatically as you type different words or change the options in the menu. The results appear in the message list, ranked in order of *relevance*. Mail weighs the number of appearances of your keyword (and their proximity, if you enter more than one), coming up with a relevance ranking. Messages with higher ranks are shown toward the top of the list (see Figure 10.12).

FIGURE 10.12

When you're searching a mailbox, the listing includes a relevance rank for each found message.

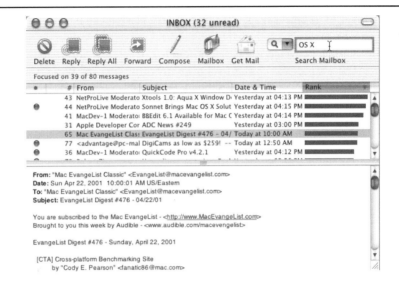

Advanced Searching: The Power of Boolean

If you'd like to search your messages a little more exactly, you're ready to create a Boolean search statement. Boolean statements are simply those that include *and, or,* or *not* between two (or more) search words. By using one or more of these words, you can put together a more powerful search query.

Here's how it works:

Steve and Jobs   This phrase limits the results to messages that contain both words.

Steve or Jobs   Using the word *or* broadens the results to include messages with either word (or both words).

Steve not Jobs   *Not* limits results to messages that include the first word but not the second.

Not only can you use these keywords, but you can also use parentheses to help narrow the search down. *Steve and (Jobs or Wozniak),* for instance, garners results that include both *Steve* and either *Jobs* or *Wozniak* (or both). Using parentheses, you can structure the statements like algebra problems, coming up with creative ways to search powerfully.

Advanced Sending and Attachments

Earlier, I covered the basics of sending, receiving, and replying to messages. In Mail, these basics are similar to almost any other Mac- or Windows-based e-mail program.

In this section, though, you'll take a closer look at the message-composition window, getting deeper into the options you have for composing and sending messages. In addition, you'll look at the process of attaching files—documents or file archives—to your e-mail messages so that you can transmit them over the Internet.

The Composition Window

Whether you're replying to a received message or composing a new one, the composition window offers some sophisticated options. Earlier in this chapter, you saw how to address messages for your users in the To and Cc lines of the composition window.

The composition window offers a few other significant options, however, enabling you to create more advanced, colorful, and better-spelled messages. Figure 10.13 shows this window.

Mail's composition window is really pretty straightforward. The buttons across the top enable you to send the message, append quoted text, access the Address Book, access Favorites, or attach a file.

Notice that in the body of the text, by default, misspelled words appear underlined in red as you type. You'll likely find this feature helpful, but you can also turn it off by selecting Edit ➢ Spelling ➢ Check Spelling as You Type. This will remove the check mark next to the menu entry, indicating that spelling will *not* be checked as you type. (You can still use the other spelling tools, discussed later in this section.)

Working with the Address Book

The Address Book is a separate application that's included with Mac OS X. It's covered in more depth in Chapter 12, including its features that enable you to use it with Mail. It's worth noting here, however, how the Address Book may affect your work in the composition window.

The first thing you may notice is the *autocomplete* feature in Mail, where addresses that have been stored in the Address Book will automatically be completed as you type the first few letters of a name or e-mail address in a To, Cc, or other header line. For instance, typing **Ste** might cause the address "Steve Jobs <steve@apple.com>" to fill in on that header line automatically. If that's the address you wanted to enter, you can simply press Tab to move to the next entry box; if it's not the address you wanted to use, keep typing to finish the address you started. Once you get used to this feature, you'll find it very handy for often-typed addresses.

> To: Rich Lewis <rich@mac-upgrade.com>

You can also open the Address Book quickly to add names to your header entry boxes. Click the Address button in the toolbar to open the Address Book. Locate a person you'd like to add to your message, then drag and drop that person's icon from the Address Book window to one of the entry boxes (To, Cc, or Bcc if you'd added a Bcc line) to add that address to your message.

Blind Courtesy Copy

As discussed earlier, entering an address on the Cc line in the composition window doesn't really cause the message to be sent differently than to a To recipient. The courtesy copy suggests "for your information," and all recipients see the Cc entry. Ideally, Cc recipients need not respond to the message.

A blind courtesy copy (Bcc) is different. In this case, Bcc recipients still receive a copy of the message, but other recipients won't see any e-mail addresses you place in

PART

II

Networks and the Internet

the Bcc field; in fact, your regular recipients won't even know the message has been sent to the Bcc recipients. Although it may seem impolite to send messages secretly, it can be useful in a number of circumstances.

In an organizational setting, you may want to send a blind courtesy copy of a message to a colleague or your supervisor. For instance, if you're sending a reply to a customer and you'd like your manager to see the message, you can include the manager's e-mail address in the Bcc line. That way, the manager sees the message but the customer doesn't know that the manager has seen your reply.

The Bcc line can be important for privacy. Any address entered in the Bcc line is kept private, so you can use the Bcc line to send a message to multiple recipients without revealing their e-mail addresses to one another. For instance, if you're sending the same e-mail to multiple customers (or to a group of friends to invite them to a party), you can enter each of their addresses (or an entire Address Book *group*, as discussed in Chapter 12) on the Bcc line so as not to reveal their e-mail addresses to the rest of your recipients.

 NOTE When a recipient replies to your message, none of your Bcc recipients will appear in their e-mail program, even if they invoke a Reply to All command. Only To and Cc recipients are responded to when a Reply to All command is used.

To add a Bcc line to your message in the composition window, choose Message ➤ Add Bcc Header from the menu. A Bcc line appears where you can enter e-mail addresses for your blind-courtesy-copy recipients.

Reply To

In some cases, you may wish to send your e-mail messages with a different Reply To address so that recipients' responses will go to a secondary location. Although you set the Reply To address whenever you create an e-mail account (it's in the Email Address entry box), you can still change the Reply To address on an individual basis when you're sending a message. From the composition window, select Message ➤ Add Reply to Header to add a Reply To line, then enter the e-mail address you'd like your users to see in their From header line.

To:	rich@mac-upgrade.com
Cc:	sally@mac-upgrade.com
Subject:	Meeting on Saturday
Bcc:	roger@spys.r.us.com
Reply To	custserv@mac-upgrade.com

Mail Format

By default, e-mail messages are sent as Rich Text messages, meaning the messages can include special formatting, fonts, colors, and other elements that you generally have at your disposal when you're using different applications, like word processors. Although Rich Text makes for more interesting-looking messages, they can't be displayed correctly by some e-mail programs and computing platforms.

Mail also has the capability of creating messages in Plain Text, and you can switch between Rich Text and Plain Text as desired. Rich Text, in Mail, refers to the MIME format, whereas Plain Text means ASCII. (MIME means Multipurpose Internet Mail Extensions, which is a standard system for augmenting e-mail messages with Rich Text and formatting, as well as attachments. ASCII is the standard computer-independent standard for exchanging basic-text characters.) To change the format in which a current message will be sent, select Format ➢ Make Plain Text or Format ➢ Make Rich Text (as appropriate).

 TIP If you want your new messages to be in Plain Text by default, you can set that in the Preferences panel. Choose Preferences from the Mail menu and then select the Composing icon. You can choose the default message format—Plain Text or Rich Text—from the Default Message Format menu. You can also choose some other behavior, such as turning on the option "Use the same format as original message" in the When Replying To Messages section.

Change Font Style

To change the font style in your e-mail message, you'll first need to set the mail type to Rich Text, if you haven't already done so. Then you can select text and use the Format ➢ Font command menu to change the text to bold, italic, underline, and so forth.

PART

II

Networks and the Internet

For more options, choose Format ➤ Font ➤ Show Fonts. This brings up the Font panel (which should be familiar if you've read Chapter 5), as shown in Figure 10.14. You can also click the Fonts button in the composition window's toolbar to open the Font panel.

FIGURE 10.14

The Font panel

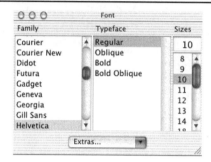

You can change the font either before or after typing. To change the font before typing, simply open the Font panel, select a font, and begin typing in the composition window.

You can also highlight text that has already been typed and select a new font in the Font panel. As soon as you make your choice, the change is made.

 WARNING Because not all computers have the same fonts, your message may not appear in your recipients' e-mail application with the same font you selected. If you're sending to other Mac OS X users, they should be able to see the message as you intend. For other users, you should avoid special fonts and only use very common fonts like Helvetica, Arial, and Times.

Change Colors

When editing a Rich Text e-mail, you can change the color of the text by opening the Colors panel and choosing Format ➤ Show Colors (or by clicking the Colors button in the composition window's toolbar). As with fonts, you can either choose a color first and then type, or highlight text and choose the color. As shown in Figure 10.15, the Colors panel offers a bit of complexity.

FIGURE 10.15

The Colors panel
in Mail

PART

II

Networks and the
Internet

Actually, the Colors panel offers many of the standard color tools built into
Mac OS X (and discussed in more detail in Chapter 5). Basic usage is simple:

1. Highlight the text for which you want to change the color, unless you're going
   to simply "turn on" a color for any new text you type.

2. Click in the Color Wheel area to choose a color.

3. Click the Apply button. The chosen color is applied to the selection (or, if no text
   was selected, the color is activated so that new words are typed in that color).

Format Text

Aside from font and color, you can also change the alignment of elements in the message. Select a paragraph (or simply place the insertion point within a paragraph), and
you can choose Format ➤ Text and then an alignment command—Align Left, Center,
Align Right, and Justify.

Check Spelling

As noted, spelling is automatically checked as you type. (If you've turned off the feature, you can select Edit ➤ Spelling ➤ Check Spelling to have the misspelled words
highlighted in the window.) But when you find a misspelled word that you don't
know how to spell correctly, you may need to consult the Spelling panel. To open
the Spelling panel, select Edit ➤ Spelling ➤ Spelling. The panel appears, as shown in
Figure 10.16.

FIGURE 10.16

The Spelling panel

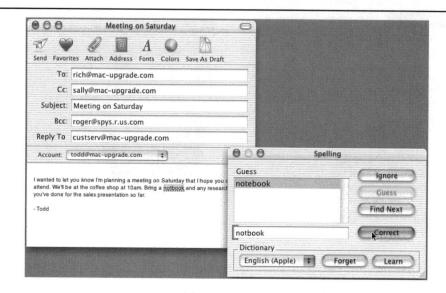

When opened, the Spelling panel will select the first misspelled word and display suggested new spellings in the Guess list. If you see the word you meant to type, select it from the list and click Correct. If you'd like to correct the word yourself, you can type its replacement in the text area next to the Correct button and then click the Correct button to change the spelling in your message. If the word is correctly spelled, you may want to teach it to Mail so that Mail won't mark the word as misspelled in the future. Click the Learn button at the bottom of the Spelling panel.

Once corrected, or if you simply intend to ignore this word, click Find Next. The Spelling panel will move on to the next word it believes is misspelled. When no more words are found, Mail thinks that your message is correctly spelled. As with other common application panels, the Spelling panel is discussed in more depth in Chapter 5.

Adding a Signature

It's common with Internet e-mail to include a signature block at the end of your e-mail messages, usually including your name, e-mail address, associated Web site, and perhaps a favorite quote, information about your business, or a little bit of bragging. (For instance, I tend to include a few of the books I've published.) With Mail, you can create a standard signature that's attached to all your messages, or you can set up multiple signatures if you'd like to switch between them. (Again, as an example, I have signatures that include my phone and fax number that I send to people who need that information, but my other signatures include just my Web site for when I'm not interested in revealing my more personal information.)

To set up a signature, you'll open the Mail Preferences dialog box (Mail ≻ Preferences) and select the Signatures icon. You'll see an empty list of signatures and four buttons: Create Signature, Edit, Duplicate, and Remove (see Figure 10.17).

FIGURE 10.17

Creating a new signature

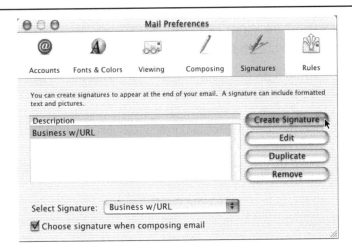

To create a new signature, click the Create Signature button. Then you'll see the Edit Signature dialog sheet. Give the signature a name in the Description box and then enter a few lines in the text box below. When you're finished editing the signature, click OK. Then you'll see the signature added to the signature list.

You can then use the Select Signature menu to determine which will be the default signature. Once selected, that signature will be added to all e-mail messages you send out.

 NOTE The Select Signature menu offers two other options: Sequentially and Randomly. If you've created multiple signatures simply for the sake of variety, choose one of these options to get a different signature with each message.

If you'd like to choose the signature for each message as you create it, turn on the "Choose signature when composing e-mail" option. Now, whenever you're composing a message, you'll see a new menu in the composition window.

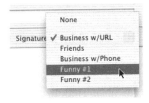

PART

II

Networks and the Internet

To edit or remove a signature, select it in the signature list and click the corresponding button. You can also select an existing signature and click the Duplicate button to create a new signature that's similar to the signature that's highlighted. When you've finished creating and editing signatures, close the Mail Preferences window.

Sending Attachments

As you've seen so far, e-mail is designed primarily for sending text messages back and forth between users. If you plan to transfer other types of files, you may want to use FTP, as discussed in Chapter 11.

But it is possible and common to transfer files via e-mail, and it can often be a convenient way to get files to a specific individual. You do that by *attaching* a file to your e-mail message before sending it. Unfortunately, by default, the Internet e-mail protocols are really not designed to transfer files; rather, they are designed primarily to transfer Plain Text documents. In order to be transferred, then, attached files must be *encoded*, a process that changes a *binary* file into a text, or *ASCII*, file. The file is then added to the e-mail message and sent along as though the entire e-mail message were just regular text. Once the message arrives at its destination, the receiving mail client needs to decode the attachment and turn it back into a binary file. In most cases, this is done easily by the client application.

Mail encodes messages using the base64 (or MIME) format, which is generally compatible with most other platforms (Microsoft Windows, Mac OS 9) and e-mail programs. Although other formats exist (including AppleDouble, BinHex, and uuencode, among others), Mail doesn't support them.

 TIP It's often advisable to compress a file before sending it as an attachment. File compression is discussed in Chapter 11.

When you're ready to attach a file to an outgoing message, click the Attach button in the composition window or choose Message ➤ Attach File. An Open dialog sheet appears in the window, enabling you to locate the file you'd like to attach. Find it, select it, and click Open. You'll then see a small document icon appear at the bottom of the message you're composing. That indicates that the document is attached, ready to be sent. When you send the message, the attachment will go along for the ride.

Subject:	The memo

Bob:

Here's the memo I sent around today. Hope you feel better soon!

- Todd

Drive memo.rtf

NOTE Don't see an icon? If you attach an image file that Mail can recognize, the actual image appears in the window instead of an icon.

Want to attach other e-mail messages to your message? Although you can forward messages using the Forward button in the viewer window's toolbar, there's a more convenient way to attach multiple e-mail messages to a message you're creating in the composition window. First, return to the viewer window and select one or more messages in the message list. Now, click the composition window to make it active, then choose Message ➢ Append Selected Messages. The messages will appear at the bottom of your composition window, enabling you to send them quickly to your recipients.

Receiving Attachments

Receiving attached files is even easier than sending them. When you open a message that includes an attachment, you'll see a document icon, usually at the bottom of the message. That icon represents the attached document. Simply click the icon's name (it's in blue text, much like a Web link) to launch the document. You can also drag the icon to a Finder window or to the desktop to save it.

Creating and Editing Accounts

The basic account information taken by Mail when you first launch the program is adequate for many needs, but you can customize quite a bit in Mail, including setting up additional e-mail accounts. To see the options available to you, select Mail ➢ Preferences. Then you'll see the Mail Preferences window (see Figure 10.18).

FIGURE 10.18

The Mail Preferences window displaying Account options

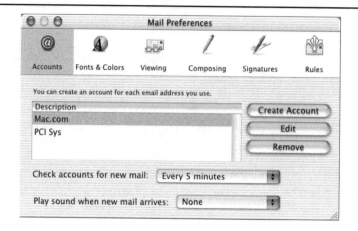

Along the top of the Mail Preferences window, you'll see icons that enable you to select the preferences you want to change. To add e-mail accounts or change preferences for e-mail accounts that already exist, click the Accounts icon. On the Accounts screen, you'll see a list of e-mail accounts that have been created. That list should include any Internet and/or Mac.com accounts that you've set up using Mail or the Internet pane of the System Preferences application.

E-Mail Checking Options

Below the list of accounts on the Accounts screen, you'll see global options for automatic or manual e-mail checking (you can see them in Figure 10.18). If you have a dial-up Internet connection or you don't want Mail to check your e-mail account(s) automatically for some other reason, select Manually from the "Check accounts for new mail" menu. Your e-mail will then be checked only when you invoke the Get Mail command.

If you do want e-mail to be checked automatically, you can choose a frequency from the "Check accounts for new mail" menu—Every Minute, Every 5 Minutes, Every Hour, and so on.

Also, you can use the "Play sound when new mail arrives" menu to select a sound from the standard OS X alert sounds if you'd like one played whenever new mail arrives in your Inbox.

Create or Edit an Account

The processes for creating and editing accounts are very similar. To create a new account or edit an existing account, open Mail Preferences (Mail ➤ Preferences) and select the Accounts icon. For a new account (so that you can access more than one Internet e-mail account from within Mail), click Create Account. To edit an existing account, select the name of the account you want to edit, and click the Edit button. Then a pop-up dialog sheet will appear with the Account Information tab selected, as shown in Figure 10.19.

On the Account Information tab, you'll have access to the basic e-mail account settings that Mail asks for when you first launch the application. (For a new account, these items will be blank.) You can enter or change the name of the account in the Description entry box, which can be whatever you want—it's just Mail's designation for the account. You can also enter or change the type of account (using the Account Type pop-up menu), as well as the host name of your mail server, your e-mail account username, and your password.

Click the Account Options tab, and you'll see a series of additional options that you can alter, if desired. The options available depend on the type of account you're creating.

FIGURE 10.19

The Account Information tab of the Mail Preferences dialog sheet

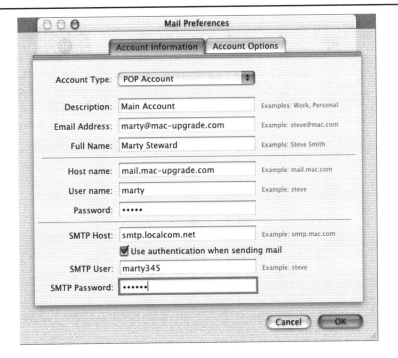

For a POP account, you can set the following options:

Enable this account   When turned on, this account is active in Mail.

Include this account when checking for new mail   This option is interesting. If you've set Mail to check for new messages automatically (see the earlier section "E-Mail Checking Options"), turning off this option means that mail is checked only when its Inbox is selected in the Mailbox panel and you click the Get Mail button. If you've set Mail to check new accounts manually, however, turning this option off makes it so that you cannot check for new mail in this account at all. If you don't seem to be receiving mail, make sure you haven't unchecked this option.

Delete messages on server after downloading   When selected, messages that you download into Mail are deleted from the server. If this option is off, the messages are left on the server. If you subsequently retrieve your mail (or if you retrieve your mail from a different e-mail application), those messages can be downloaded again.

Show this account separately in mailboxes drawer   If you'd like this account to have its own Inbox and set of personal mailbox folders, select this option.

Download messages from this account into folder   Turn on this option, and the "Show this account separately..." option is turned off. In this case, the account won't be shown separately, and incoming messages will appear in the mailbox folder that you choose from the pop-up menu.

Prompt me to skip messages over __ KB   When you enter a number in this entry box, Mail will ask you if you want to skip any messages larger than the number of kilobytes indicated. (For instance, if you enter 50, any messages over 50KB will result in a dialog box asking if you want to skip the message.) The option can be helpful if you want to decide when to download larger messages and messages with attachments.

Connect to server using port __   If you connect to your mail server using a nonstandard port, you can enter that number here.

Account directory   Enter (or edit) the path to the folder you'd like to use for the particular e-mail account, if you prefer to use a path that's different from the default.

If you're setting up an IMAP account (or a Mac.com account, which uses IMAP), you'll see a slightly different list of options:

Enable this account   When turned on, this account is active in Mail.

Include this account when checking for new mail   This causes a list of e-mail messages to be retrieved whenever you launch Mail or whenever Mail automatically checks for new mail.

Compact mailboxes when closing   With an IMAP account, messages that you choose to delete aren't deleted from the server immediately; instead, they're marked for deletion and then deleted whenever you compact a particular mailbox. This option allows you to automatically do away with messages marked for deletion every time you close Mail.

Message caching   Use the pull-down menu to select whether or not messages will be stored on your Mac when you check for mail (Cache all messages locally), when you read the message (Cache messages when read), or never (Don't cache any messages). *Caching* a message means the message is saved on the Mac's hard disk so that it can be accessed more quickly. If you'd prefer that your e-mail not be saved to the local machine (usually for security purposes), select "Don't cache any messages."

Connect to server using port __   If you connect to your mail server using a nonstandard port, you can enter that number here.

Account directory   Enter (or edit) the path to the folder on your Mac's hard disk that you'd like to use for this e-mail account. Generally, this is created for you by Mail, but you can edit it if you'd prefer to use a different folder.

When you're done configuring the account, click OK in the dialog sheet; then click the Close box in the Mail Preferences dialog box if you've finished setting options. If you created a new account, you'll also see that account listed in the Mailbox panel back in the main viewer window. You can access a new account just as you did your first account.

NOTE   Once you've added more than one account in Mail, you'll see a new option in the composition window—an Account menu. You can use this menu to choose the account from which you want to send the message. By default, replies that you create are sent from the account they were initially sent *to*, but you can change that by using the Account menu when you're composing the reply.

What's Next?

In this chapter, you learned about Mac OS X's built-in Mail application. You saw the basics of creating an e-mail account, retrieving e-mail, replying, and composing new messages. You also saw how to dig deeper into the Mail application in order to manage your messages with mailboxes, automate the filing of messages, format Rich Text messages, and work with attachments.

In Chapter 11, you'll move on to Web browsing in Mac OS X using Internet Explorer and other Web browsers. You'll learn about FTP, the protocol for transferring files over the Internet, as well as important issues such as encoding and compressing files. Finally, Chapter 11 covers iTools, Apple's Internet-based applications that enable you to store and transfer files online, set up a Mac.com e-mail account, and create your own Web pages using the Homepage tool.

CHAPTER **11**

The Web, FTP, and iTools

As you might expect from a fully modern operating system, Mac OS X is built for the Internet. Not only is it relatively easy to get your Mac set up for Internet access and wired for reading and sending e-mail, but the OS also includes a number of other built-in and bundled applications designed specifically for the Internet. Among those is Microsoft Internet Explorer, the default Web browser included with Mac OS X. Internet Explorer is a full-featured Web browser that's capable of pretty much any Web site you throw at it.

Along with a Web browser, you'll want to know something about FTP—the File Transfer Protocol—and the applications that enable you to transfer files online. You can transfer files in a number of ways, not the least of which is using a shareware FTP program to move files to remote servers.

And, whether you download files via your Web browser or an FTP program, you'll probably need to decode and decompress those files from their archive file formats—the type of files you can send over the Internet—into usable file formats for your Mac. That's easily done with StuffIt Expander or other tools built into Mac OS X.

Finally, Apple offers iTools, a group of online applications designed for use by every Mac OS X user. The iTools suite includes online storage (a personal space on the Internet for you to store and swap files), a Mac.com e-mail address, and HomePage, which enables you to create your own Web page without extensive knowledge of HTML or Web-development tools.

Browsing the Web with Internet Explorer

Mac OS X includes Microsoft Internet Explorer for Mac OS X, a "carbonized" version of the popular Internet Explorer 5.1 for Macintosh. Internet Explorer (IE) is a very capable Web browser with a number of different features worth exploring in depth. Although this chapter won't cover them all, you'll see the basics of browsing, storing, and organizing favorites, working with Internet shortcuts, and accessing advanced Web media content by installing and using browser plug-ins.

Because Internet Explorer is a carbonized application and not a fully native Cocoa application, you may find that it's a bit slow in some operations—particularly when you're working with multiple Web pages or downloaded files at once. You may wish to try other Web browsers to see if another third-party option suits you better. Early contenders are OmniWeb from Omni Group (www.omnigroup.com), iCab for Mac OS X (www.icab.de), and some early testing versions from the Mozilla project (www.mozilla.org), the open-source version of Netscape's browser code. Other browsers, including official releases from Netscape and other third parties, are sure to follow as Mac OS X gains in popularity.

Some early users of Mac OS X have reported that Internet Explorer in the Classic environment runs faster than the carbonized version! If you like IE's features but find that IE 5.1 doesn't perform well for you, you might try running IE in the Classic environment. If you've installed Mac OS X over Mac OS 9, you'll find Classic versions of Internet Explorer and Netscape Navigator in the Internet folder inside the Applications (Mac OS 9) folder on your hard disk. In my experience, Classic browsers can be fairly snappy over a broadband connection, but rather slow over a modem connection.

Hypertext Basics

We begin, however, at the beginning, with the basics of Internet Explorer. Start up your Internet connection (if you have a PPP or PPP-over-Ethernet connection) and click the Internet Explorer icon in the Dock. (You can also double-click the Internet Explorer icon in your Mac's main Applications folder.)

Once IE is launched, you'll see the home page that's specified in the Web tab of the Internet pane in the System Preferences application. (See Chapter 9 for details on changing this option.) If you haven't changed the default home page, what you're likely looking at is the Apple Excite home page, which offers news, weather, sports, and lots of other information, and is constantly updated. Every time you open a new window in IE, it will default to this page.

Getting around on a Web page is fairly simple—you click underlined hyperlinks within the text, which causes a new Web page to be accessed and displayed in the browser window. You'll also find that images on the Web page can also be links, so that clicking them loads a new page in the browser. Figure 11.1 shows an example of a page with both images and text that are hyperlinks.

 TIP When you're using Internet Explorer, it gives away the fact that you're pointing the mouse at a link. When the mouse pointer turns into a pointing hand icon (the index finger is extended on the little hand icon), that means that the item underneath the pointer is "clickable." Click the mouse button once to load the associated Web page.

Internet Explorer offers you a few different ways to modify that clicking behavior for opening new pages. Hold down the Command (⌘) key while clicking a link (or an image), and the resulting Web page will be displayed in a new window. Hold down the Control key while clicking a link (or use the right mouse button if you have a two-button mouse), and you'll see a contextual menu that offers you a number of different choices regarding that link.

PART II

Networks and the Internet

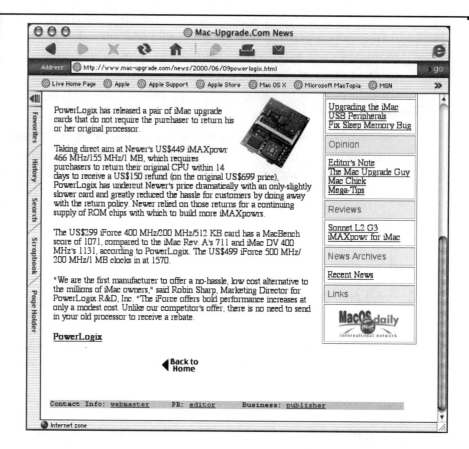

These options include Open Link in New Window, which does the same thing as ⌘+clicking the link. Download Link to Disk downloads the linked Web page; instead of displaying it in a browser window, it's saved to your Mac. Copy Link to Clipboard copies the Web address of that link to the Mac's clipboard, enabling you to paste it into another document elsewhere. Add Link to Favorites adds the selected link to Internet Explorer's list of favorite Web sites, as discussed later in the section "Managing Favorites."

Understanding URLs

You'll note that I just mentioned Web addresses. What are they? Every page or document on the Web has a specific address, which is a combination of the protocol used to access that page or document, the Internet address of the server computer where that document is stored, and the exact path, on the server computer, where the document is located. All these items come together to form a Uniform Resource Locator, or URL, which is the basis of document retrieval on the Web. Take, for example, this URL:

```
http://www.fakecorp.com/index.html
```

The URL is made up of three components. The protocol is `http://`, which tells the receiving application (in this case, Internet Explorer) that the document we're looking for is to be retrieved using the HyperText Transfer Protocol, which is standard on the Web. That protocol could also be `ftp://`, which would tell the program to access the server using the File Transfer Protocol. (More on FTP later in this chapter.)

The second part of the URL is the Web server's address—I've discussed server addresses in Chapters 8, 9, and 10 as well. This could be either a textual host name and domain name (`www.fakecorp.com` in the example above) or an IP address (such as `192.168.1.4`).

Finally, the URL ends with a path statement to the exact document that you want to access. It can be as simple as `index.html`, which would point to a document with that name in the main Web directory of the server, or something more complex, such as `/news/2001/02/14.valentine.html`. Whatever it is, you may already recognize it from the discussion of path statements in Chapter 3; it's simply a path throughout a hierarchy of folders to the document in question.

 NOTE Documents on the Web don't have to be HTML documents (those that end with `.html`). You can access all sorts of documents, from Plain Text (`.txt`) to graphical images (`.jpeg` and `.gif`) to QuickTime movies (`.mov`). In fact, almost any sort of computer document can be transferred over the Web; if your Web browser can't display the document on its own, it will usually give you the option of saving the document to your Mac's hard disk so you can open it with another application.

When you're viewing a Web page, each hypertext link has a URL associated with it. When you click the link, that URL is fed to the browser, which then begins the process of locating the document and downloading it to your Mac so it can be displayed in the browser window. But you don't have to click a link to access a particular URL—you can also enter one directly. You do so in the Address box toward the top of the Internet Explorer window. Enter a URL, then press Return or click the Go button to attempt to access that Web document.

PART
II

Networks and the
Internet

TIP You'll notice that Internet Explorer will attempt to auto-complete addresses that are similar to URLs that you've typed in the past. If auto-complete is successful, press Return to reload that page. If it isn't, just keep typing. If IE encounters more than one match, it will appear in a small window below the Address box; click one of the links to load the associated page.

The Toolbar

Above the Address bar in Internet Explorer you'll find the toolbar, where a number of commands can be accessed quickly. Many of these are standard items found in most Web browsers, while a couple of them are unique to IE. Here's a look at the basic toolbar:

What do these buttons do? Here's a quick look:

Back   The Back button enables you to click quickly to the previously visited page. Click and hold the mouse button on the Back button (or right-click it), and you'll see a menu of recently visited pages.

Forward   If you've just clicked Back, you can then click Forward, which returns you to a page from which you've gone back. (The button isn't always active.)

Stop   If the current Web page is still in the process of downloading to your Mac, you can click the Stop button to stop it from finishing. Internet Explorer will display as much of the page as it managed to download.

Refresh   This causes the current page to be reloaded in Internet Explorer. This is useful if it didn't load completely the first time or if the page is updated frequently (as are many commercial news sites) and you want to see the latest version.

Home   This button takes you to your home page, which is the page that loads initially whenever you launch Internet Explorer or open a new IE window.

AutoFill   This is a special Internet Explorer function that automatically fills in form fields (entry boxes) with personal information that you've stored in IE. You'll encounter many form-based pages on the Web that need your name, address, phone number, and so forth (assuming you want to give them out). AutoFill can be used to streamline that data-entry process.

Print   This is the same as choosing File ➤ Print from the IE menu. Click and hold the mouse button on the Print icon to see a pop-up menu where you can also select Print Setup and Preview commands.

Mail   This opens the default e-mail program. If you click and hold the mouse button while pointed at the Mail icon, you'll see other options, too.

Aside from these functions, the toolbar can be altered to offer quick access to many other functions. Select View ➤ Customize Toolbars, and you'll see the browser change to a page that includes more tool icons. Drag one of the icons up to the toolbar, and it's automatically added. To remove an item from the toolbar, Control+click its icon and select Delete from the pop-up menu.

Managing Favorites

As you surf the Web using Internet Explorer, you'll probably come across pages that you'd like to revisit in the future. Instead of forcing you to write down each URL that you deem worthy of tracking, IE offers its own Favorites feature—not unlike the favorites elsewhere in the Mac OS—which enables you to save references to pages you'd like to remember. You can then access those pages via the Favorites menu in IE's menu bar. (If you're working with another browser, you'll likely find this feature called "bookmarks," which is the generic term for saving references to Web pages. Microsoft, of course, likes to be different.)

To save a page as a favorite, first load the page in the main browser window, as you would any Web page. Now select Favorites ➤ Add Page to Favorites from the IE menu bar. The current page is saved to the list of pages that appears when you access that same Favorites menu. They appear in chronological order, so the most recently added page appears at the bottom of the menu.

If you'd like to move that favorite around, you can do so. Select the Favorites tab on the left side of any open browser window (see Figure 11.2). This displays a list of all your favorites (a mirror image of the Favorites menu) and enables you to edit them. You can drag a favorite around in the list to change its order, for instance.

To delete a favorite, select it in the list and click the Delete button in the Favorites list. You can also select the favorite and press the Delete key on your keyboard, or you can drag the favorite from this list directly to the Trash on the Dock. (Note that doing so doesn't actually place it in the Trash folder—the favorite is deleted immediately.)

 NOTE   Selecting a favorite in the Favorites tab pane can be a bit of a, well, pain, because single-clicking a favorite will open it in the browser window. The easiest way to select the favorite is to drag-select, as though you were selecting more than one icon in a Finder window. Place the mouse pointer just to the left of the favorite, then click and drag the mouse across the favorite until it's highlighted. Now you can drag it around.

FIGURE 11.2

You can use the Favorites tab on the side of Internet Explorer's window to manage your favorites.

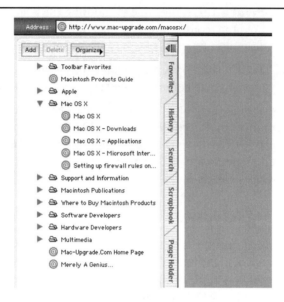

You can drag the favorite to any of the folders that appear in the list; drop the favorite on the folder icon to store it inside that folder. Folders in the Favorites list correspond to submenus in the Favorites menu, so adding a favorite to one of the folders adds it to the corresponding submenu in the Favorites menu. You can delete a folder in the same way that you delete individual favorites, but you should realize that you'll delete all the favorites inside that folder as well.

To create a new folder, click the Organize button. A menu appears, where you can choose New Folder. When you do, the folder appears in the list, ready for its name to be edited. Edit the name and press Return on the keyboard. Now you can drag favorites to the newly created folder, and they'll appear not only in that folder but also in the corresponding submenu that you've created in the Favorites menu.

One special folder is the Toolbar Favorites folder, which holds the favorites that appear on the IE toolbar, just beneath the Address bar (by default). If you'd like to add or delete favorites from the Toolbar Favorites, open that folder and add or remove favorites. You can also drag and drop favorites to and from the Toolbar Favorites directly, as shown here:

History and Other Tabs

You may have noticed that, along with Favorites, a few other tabs run down the left side of the browser window. Select one, and out pops the associated pane, scooting the Web page you're viewing over to the right a bit. (You can click the same tab again to close the tab control and return your page to the full width of the browser window. For instance, if the Favorites tab is active, click it again to hide the Favorites pane.)

The History tab corresponds to items that appear in IE's Go menu. Internet Explorer tracks all the pages you've recently accessed, so, if desired, you can go back to a page you've visited recently. The quickest way to do so is to access the Go menu and select the URL. (Note that pages you've visited in recent days show up in hierarchical menus below the current day's history.)

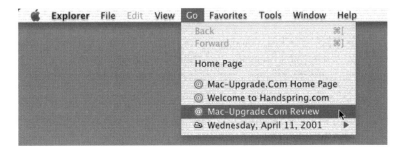

If you click the History tab in any browser window, you can also quickly access pages in your history; just click once on a page to reload it. You can also delete items from your history by selecting them and pressing the Delete key on your keyboard. Likewise, you can drag an item from the History list to the Mac's Trash icon on the Dock. It's deleted immediately, not stored in the Trash folder.

 TIP Want to decide how many sites should be tracked in your History? Select Edit ➤ Preferences and click Advanced. Toward the top of the window, you'll see an entry for History; enter a number in the entry box. Click OK in the dialog box to store your choice. You can find more information about the preferences in the later section "IE Preferences."

Another tab on the left side of the window is Search, where you can search the Web using controls that IE makes available to you. Click the Search tab, and the Search Assistant appears. Enter keywords in the entry box and click the Search button. Results appear in the Search pane; when you click one, the associated Web page loads in the main viewer portion of the window. To begin a new search, click the New Search button. To customize the search, click the Customize button. The Customize Search Settings dialog box appears, allowing you to select how you'd like to search. For instance, you can select Use One Search Service for All Searches and then select the service you'd like to use. Click OK in the dialog box to set your preferences.

The Scrapbook tab reveals the Internet Scrapbook, where you can add text clippings, images, and other multimedia elements that you find on Web pages. To add an image to the Scrapbook, simply drag it from the main browser window to the Scrapbook pane. To add a Web page, just click the Add button in the Scrapbook pane. To delete an item from the Scrapbook, click and hold the mouse button on that item until the contextual menu appears; then select Delete. To rename an item, click and hold the mouse button on that item; in the contextual menu, select Edit Name.

 TIP You can also organize the Scrapbook by clicking Organize and adding folders or divider lines. Drag items to folders to store them inside.

The final tab, Page Holder, opens a pane where you can store a single Web page. While you're viewing (in the main browser window) the page you want to store, click Add. Now you can click links on the stored page, and the results of those links will appear in the main browser window. This is a great way to quickly move through a list of links on a particular page without constantly clicking the Back button.

Subscribing to Sites

IE has a special feature that enables you to *subscribe* to a site, which means simply that IE will periodically check the site for changes since your last visit. If changes are noted, IE will let you know that by placing a special check mark icon next to the subscription favorite in the Favorites menu. IE also downloads the subscribed page into the browser cache so that it loads quickly the next time you visit it.

To subscribe to a page, open the page in the main browser window, then select Favorites ➤ Subscribe. In the dialog box that appears, click the Subscribe button.

Downloading Files

Sometimes you'll have the option of clicking a hyperlink that will download a file to your Mac; this is an HTML or multimedia file that isn't necessarily designed for reading by a Web browser or an associated application. Instead, most such downloads are either document files or application archives that you can then use to install an application on your Mac. The download might even be a Mac update that you've downloaded from Apple. (As mentioned earlier, you can also download any link by clicking and holding on the link until a contextual menu appears, then selecting Download Link to Disk.)

When you click a link to a downloadable file, that file appears in the Download Manager, which pops up automatically. (If you don't see it, select Window ➤ Download Manager.) The Download Manager then tracks the file as it's downloaded.

File	Status	Time	Transferred
✓ KeyspanUSAdriver...	Complete	< 1 minute	247 KB
✓ Igniter_3.1.1_Dri...	Complete	< 1 minute	2.2 MB
✓ OmniWeb-4.0cf3.d...	Complete	About one minute	3.0 MB
✓ Fetch_4.0b7_Carb...	Complete	3 Minutes	2.9 MB
✓ Samba_for_OS_X_...	Complete	< 1 minute	3.7 MB
✓ Sound Studio 1.5.4...	Complete	< 1 minute	491 KB
✓ Journal-2.0Pre1.d...	Complete	< 1 minute	132 KB
⬤ pagespinner-302-...		< 1 minute	401 KB of 1.9 MB, 54 KB/sec

You can view an information window about a download by double-clicking it in the Download Manager. The Location entry shows you where the file was stored on your disk; the Address box shows you the original URL that was used to access the file. If the download of that item is currently in progress, you can click the Cancel button to stop it. If the download didn't complete properly (or if you need to download it again), you can click the Reload button in the information window.

NOTE Need to install an application? See Chapter 5 for installing personal applications and Chapter 7 for details on installing system-wide applications.

Internet Shortcuts

Mac-Upgrade.Com.url

With most Internet applications, including Internet Explorer, you can drag a URL out to the desktop (or to a Finder window) in order to create a *shortcut* file to that URL. Now, double-clicking the shortcut will launch that URL in your browser window (or,

PART

II

Networks and the
Internet

if you've used another type of Internet application, the shortcut will launch in that application).

The problem is knowing what to drag. In IE, either you can drag the small @ icon that appears next to a URL in the Address bar, or you can highlight the address itself and drag it to the desktop. Likewise, you can drag a link out of the History, Favorites, Scrapbook, or Toolbar Favorites onto the desktop to create a shortcut.

 TIP You can also drag URLs directly to the Dock (on the documents side only), if desired, where they will be represented by an icon that looks like an @ symbol that's attached to a coiled spring.

Archiving Web Sites

Internet Explorer has the ability to actually save and archive entire Web sites—or portions of those sites—for you to browse at your leisure. This can be useful in a number of settings, especially situations where you plan to be out of contact with the Internet for a certain amount of time, but you'd like the opportunity to read a particular Web site.

Creating a Web archive can be time consuming, however, depending on the speed of your connection and the options you choose. And the larger the Web site you archive, the more disk space it will require. Still, it's a great idea if you need to take your PowerBook or iBook on a plane or down to the local café and you'd appreciate having a particular set of Web pages along with you.

To create a Web archive, open the *root* Web page of the site you'd like to save. You may need to think about this a bit, because Internet Explorer will archive the site in terms of the *layers* of that site—meaning, it will dig into all the linked pages and graphics on the site, down to a certain point, and attempt to save as many layers of the site as you specify. This may require that you know at least a little about how the site is organized, which is something you might want to explore before you create your archive.

Once you have the page open in your browser, select File ➤ Save As from the Internet Explorer menu. In the Save dialog box, choose a location for the Web archive to be stored. Now, from the Format menu, select Web Archive. Next, click the Options button. You'll see the Site Download Options dialog box appear.

In the Options dialog, place a check mark next to all the items that you'd like to download as part of the archive; to save time, you can elect not to download images, sounds, and movies. If you select Download Links, you can use the Levels Deep menu to choose how many "levels" of links IE should explore and save. It's also best to leave Skip Links to Other Sites turned on to avoid having IE follow links at the archived site to other servers, causing a potential explosion in the amount of downloading required.

Click OK, then click the Save button back in the Save dialog box. IE creates an archive of the site, storing it in the location you've chosen.

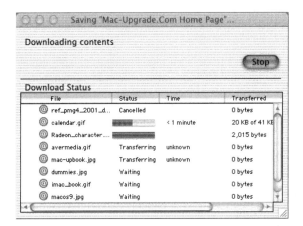

Once stored, you can access the Web archive by choosing File ➤ Open File from the IE menu. Now, locate the stored Web archive in the Open dialog box, select it, and click Open. You'll be able to view the saved site in your browser.

PART

II

Networks and the
Internet

NOTE The Save As command also gives you the option of saving the current page as HTML Source (so that it can be loaded into a Web browser again with much the same formatting) or as Plain Text (making it readable in TextEdit or a similar application). If you'd like to save the page in either of these formats, give the page a name in the Save dialog box, select a location for it, select either HTML Source or Plain Text from the Format menu, and then click Save.

Web Browser Plug-Ins

Web browsers are good at handling some types of data—particular text formats and a few graphic image formats. But they're not designed to deal with some other types of data, such as QuickTime movies, Macromedia Flash animations, and RealPlayer streaming audio and video. And yet, some browsers manage to handle these things very well. How? By using plug-ins.

A *plug-in* is a special snippet of a computer code that a Web browser can use to extend its knowledge of how to work with and play back certain types of data. When the browser encounters a particular command (the EMBED or OBJECT command, to be exact), it looks for the plug-in that's being requested by that command. If it finds it, it gives over part of the browser window to that plug-in, so that the data can be displayed right there within the Web page.

One example of this is the QuickTime plug-in, which comes with Mac OS X. (That's why QuickTime movies can play back in IE, even though, as I just mentioned, IE doesn't technically know how to display them on its own.) QuickTime movies can be embedded in Web pages by Web developers, so that they appear right there as part of the page itself (see Figure 11.3). A basic Macromedia Flash Player plug-in is also included with Mac OS X. (For later versions of the Flash Player plug-in, check www.macromedia.com.)

For multimedia files other than QuickTime movies and Flash animations, you'll need to download and install the appropriate plug-in file. These files are stored in /Library/Internet Plug-Ins/ on the main level of the Mac's disk. If you have a plug-in that you'd like Internet Explorer to work with, drag that plug-in to this folder, then restart Internet Explorer. (Or direct the plug-in's installer application to this folder, if necessary.)

NOTE If you don't have Admin privileges, you can store plug-ins in the ~/Library/ Internet Plug-Ins/ folder—the one located inside your home folder.

FIGURE 11.3

*Here's a Web page
with a QuickTime
movie embedded in it.*

If you need to set preferences for a plug-in, it will likely enable you to do so
through a contextual menu. Click and hold the mouse button on an image that's created by a plug-in (on the QuickTime movie or Flash animation, for instance).

 NOTE Plug-ins are different from *helper applications,* which are secondary applications
designed to work with a Web browser to display certain types of data. See the next section,
"IE Preferences," for more on helper applications.

IE Preferences

Internet Explorer offers quite a few preferences you can set to tweak the way the program behaves both on and off the Internet. Though we don't have space to go into all
of them, a few highlights stand out that we should discuss. For starters, you can open
Internet Explorer preferences by selecting Edit ➢ Preferences from the IE menu. That
reveals the Internet Explorer Preferences dialog box, shown in Figure 11.4.

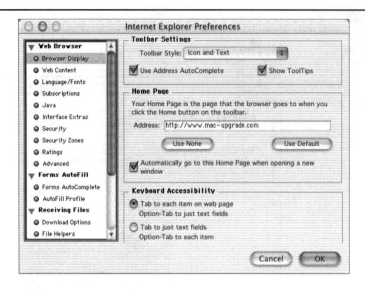

The left side of the dialog box works much like many "tabbed" interfaces that you'll find elsewhere in Mac OS X applications: Select one of the topics, and the options on the right side of the dialog box will change to reflect it. Here's a look at what each entry does:

Browser Display   This entry gives you a series of settings for how the browser's interface works. At the top, you can select whether the toolbar shows icons, text, or both, whether ToolTips appear (small pop-up descriptions when you mouse-over the buttons in the toolbar), and whether Address AutoComplete is active (IE attempts to complete addresses automatically as you type them in the Address bar). Below that, you can change the URL for the home page that IE uses, and you can determine whether or not the home page loads every time you open a new window. Finally, in the Keyboard Accessibility section, you can decide how the Tab key will work. (The Browser Display settings are shown back in Figure 11.4.)

Web Content   This entry enables you to determine how each page's content will look in the browser window, and offers quite a few options for whether images, animations, sounds, and other multimedia elements should be allowed to play or display. At the bottom of the dialog box, you can choose whether active content—scripting—should be enabled or disabled. Scripting and plug-ins are generally secure, but you can disable them if you notice that your browser crashes often or if you find that plug-ins and scripted pages slow down your browser display.

Language/Fonts If you want to see Web pages in languages other than English, you can add an entry to the top of this dialog box in the Language section. Default fonts, sizes, and character sets can be selected in the Fonts and Sizes section.

Subscriptions You can set options for how often your subscriptions are checked and how you're notified of changes.

Java Here you can enable Java, choose the type of error messages you want to see, and set other advanced Java options.

Interface Extras This one just has a few basic radio buttons that let you decide how IE selects text in the Address entry box and how it interacts with other applications.

Security The Security preferences let you decide what alerts and error messages should appear when you've visited secure and nonsecure pages. In the Certificate Authorities section, you can manage the certificate authorities that you're willing to trust, if you have any opinions on the matter.

Security Zones These options enable you to set limits for the sites that Internet Explorer can visit. If you have young children or otherwise want to limit sites that can be visited, set the Zone to Trusted Sites and click the Add Sites button to add the sites that you want to allow. You can also choose a security level for each zone, which determines how "paranoid" IE will be when it sees potentially damaging content (scripts and programming that could be suggestive of virus behavior, for instance).

Ratings Use these tools to add a third-party rating system to the browser. You'll usually do this to filter objectionable content for younger viewers.

Advanced The Advanced preferences let you set options for history, cache, multiple connections, and offline browsing (see Figure 11.5). In the Cache section you can choose how often a particular page will be updated and how large a cache of stored documents and images IE should keep on your hard disk. Pages stored in the cache can be accessed again more quickly because they're on your hard disk, not the Internet. You can reload the document from the Internet at any time, though, by clicking Refresh in the browser window.

Forms AutoComplete Using these options, you can add items that you'd like to be auto-completed as you type them into forms. For instance, if you enter "4563 Morningstar Drive" as one of the listings, whenever you begin typing "4563" into a form in a Web page, the rest of the address will be "auto-completed" by IE.

FIGURE 11.5

The Advanced settings include options for how history, cache, and offline browsing work.

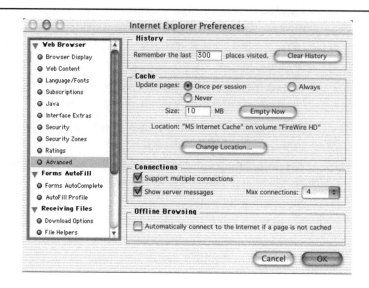

AutoFill Profile   Here you can enter the personal information for the Auto-Fill features offered by IE. Now, when you see a form that requires personal information, you can click the AutoFill button in the Toolbar to quickly add all your info.

Download Options   Click the Change Location button to select a location for downloads that IE completes. In the Download Destination section, you can determine whether to download files to the fixed destination folder, or to folders determined by helper applications. The other options enable you to determine how many downloads can happen at once, how many downloads should be remembered by the Download Manager, and which downloads should be decoded once they're completed.

File Helpers   Here you can determine what application is to be used with a particular type of file that's encountered on the Web. You can use these options to change the current relationship or to add new document types and associate them with your applications. To associate a document type, select it in the list and click Change. You'll see the Edit File Helper dialog box (see Figure 11.6), where you can determine how the file should be saved and what application should be used to "handle" the document. When you're done, click OK. If you want to add a file type, click Add. You'll see the Add File Helper window, with similar options, except that you'll need to fill in the file type, filename extension, and MIME type.

FIGURE 11.6

Use the Edit File Helper
dialog box to deter-
mine how a specific
file type will be
treated.

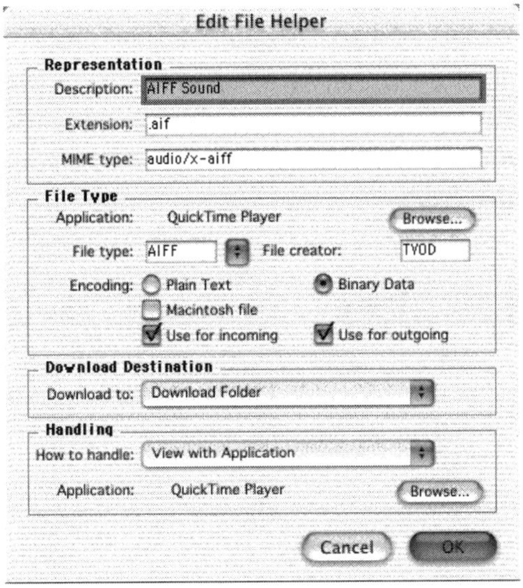

Edit File Helper

Representation
Description: AIFF Sound
Extension: .aif
MIME type: audio/x-aiff

File Type
Application: QuickTime Player   Browse...
File type: AIFF   File creator: TVOD
Encoding: ○ Plain Text   ● Binary Data
☐ Macintosh file
☑ Use for incoming   ☑ Use for outgoing

Download Destination
Download to: Download Folder

Handling
How to handle: View with Application
Application: QuickTime Player   Browse...

Cancel   OK

TIP MIME stands for Multipurpose Internet Mail Extension, and it's a method by which multimedia data can be identified over the Internet. See www.hunnysoft.com/mime/ for information on different MIME types and other helpful hints.

Cookies Using these settings, you can track the cookies that have been accepted by IE, and you can set future cookie acceptance options. (*Cookies* are small data files that Web sites can store on your hard disk to track your visits to the site. Cookies are generally harmless, but some surfers choose to turn them off for maximum privacy.) Select a cookie and click Delete to get rid of it, or click View to see information about it. From the When Receiving Cookies menu, select how you'd like IE to deal with cookies.

Protocol Helpers These preferences show you the different types of Internet protocols and enable you to select helpers, if desired, for each type. Highlight a particular protocol and click Change to change the helper application that's used to display data from such a server.

Proxies If your system administrator has configured Internet access so that you must use a proxy server, enter that server's address here.

Site Passwords If you've chosen to have IE store your name and password for a site, you can edit those settings here.

E-Mail General   Set the basics of your e-mail address and SMTP host. (These will be updated automatically from the Internet pane in the System Preferences application, if you've entered them.)

When you've finished setting preferences, click the OK button on the Internet Explorer Preferences dialog box. Your settings will be remembered and put into action by Internet Explorer.

Accessing FTP Sites

File Transfer Protocol, or FTP, is one of the major mechanisms, along with HTTP, the Web protocol, for transferring files over the Internet. In fact, FTP is often preferred over HTTP, for both reliability and speed.

In order to use FTP for transferring files, you need two things. First, you need a program that's capable of connecting to an FTP server. Second, you need a valid FTP server to connect to. Fortunately, both of those are easy to come across.

For instance, Internet Explorer offers some support for the FTP protocol. You can easily access FTP servers for downloading files, including servers that require a username and password. Simply enter the URL for the FTP site in the Address box at the top of the browser window, then click Go or press Return.

Once you've logged into an FTP server, you can open folders by selecting their links in the browser window; then, once located, you can download files the same way. Downloaded files are then managed by the Download Manager and stored on your hard disk like any other downloaded file.

Using an FTP Client

FTP is about more than just downloading files—you can upload them, too. (*Uploading* simply means sending files from your Mac to the remote server.) You'll find this handy for accessing remote computers with Unix and Unix-like operating systems, since they often have FTP server capabilities built in. FTP is the standard for sharing files on remote computers across the Internet, whether the remote computer is a public FTP server designed to handle thousands of connections or an individual computer that has a built-in or third-party FTP server running.

For instance, one of the ISPs that serves my Web site is located across the country, so I regularly log into my Web server computer via an *FTP client*, an application that's designed to access an FTP server and send or receive files. I can then access the Web folder, upload new files for displaying Web content, and rename or delete others. It's similar to file sharing between Macs, except that you don't use the Connect to Server box and Finder windows—you use a third-party application.

 TIP Actually, there is an FTP client built into Mac OS X, but it's not a graphical client. FTP can be accessed from within the Terminal window in Mac OS X. See Chapter 23 for details on the Terminal window and associated FTP commands.

A number of FTP clients exist for the Mac OS, including the venerable Fetch (www .fetchsoftworks.com), a popular Mac application for many years that has recently been updated for Mac OS X. Other FTP clients include the popular Interarchy (previously Anarchy) from Stairways Software (www.interarchy.com) and Transmit (www.panic.com).

FTP clients enable you to log into remote FTP servers using your username and password; then they work a little like the Finder to help you maneuver the remote file system. (In Fetch, for instance, choose File ➤ New Connection to open the New Connection dialog box, where you'll be able to input a host server address along with your username and password. See Figure 11.7.) Once you find the file you want to download, select the Get File command within any FTP client (or, in a graphical client such as Fetch, drag and drop the file from the FTP client's window to the desktop or a Finder window).

FIGURE 11.7

*Signing into an FTP
site with a user
account and password
using Fetch*

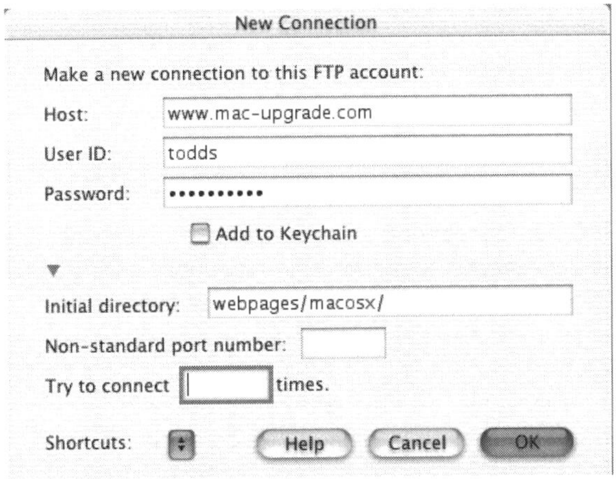

New Connection

Make a new connection to this FTP account:

Host: www.mac-upgrade.com

User ID: todds

Password: •••••••••

☐ Add to Keychain

▼

Initial directory: webpages/macosx/

Non-standard port number:

Try to connect   times.

Shortcuts: [⬍]   (Help) (Cancel) (OK)

If you're uploading files, you can generally do so by locating the destination folder on the remote server, selecting the file you want to send, and using the Put File command to upload that file. In some FTP clients it's even easier—just drag and drop the file from your desktop or a Finder window to the remote directory. The file will be uploaded (you'll probably see a progress indicator in the FTP window or in a dialog box).

File Encoding and Archiving

FTP is a binary file transfer protocol, meaning, unlike with e-mail attachments, you aren't required to encode a file before you send it using an FTP program. That doesn't mean encoding isn't a good idea, at least in some cases. The process of encoding files enables them to preserve any important OS-specific features in the files; this is particularly important for dual-fork files created in Mac OS 9.1 and earlier. You'll find that your FTP application (if you're using a graphical client such as Fetch or Interarchy) can encode such Mac files in the MacBinary format before you send them.

If you're sending files from a Mac OS X machine to another, or to a Unix-based server, there's less concern for encoding. That said, you'll often want to *archive* files—turning multiple files or folders into a single archive file for easy transfer—and *compress* files to make them smaller for quicker transfer. You can decompress most archives using StuffIt Expander, which is included with Mac OS X. If you're sending files via FTP, however, you may wish to create your own compressed archives. You can do that with DropStuff, a program available from the same people who produce StuffIt Expander, Aladdin Systems (www.aladdinsys.com).

Drag a file, group of files, or a folder to the DropStuff icon. Once dropped, DropStuff launches and begins creating an archive, a single file that includes all the files you've dropped on the application. It also compresses that archive in the StuffIt format, making it smaller for quicker transfer via FTP. Once completed, you'll have a new archive (called archive.sit) that includes all the files and folders you dropped on DropStuff. You can now send that file to anyone you'd like via FTP.

 NOTE DropStuff is *shareware*, which means that it works when you download it, but you're expected to register the software by paying a fee if you find it useful. Aladdin Systems currently charges $30 for the registration code.

To decompress the file, your recipient will need StuffIt Expander or a similar program that can handle the StuffIt format. StuffIt Expander is preinstalled on most Macs and Mac OS X–based machines, so it's usually safe to send a StuffIt archive to a Mac user. Programs to decompress StuffIt archives also exist for Microsoft Windows–based computers, although StuffIt is not the most popular archive format on Windows machines. (Aladdin Expander, also available for free from Aladdin Systems, is the Windows version of StuffIt Expander.) Instead, you might want to use an application on your Mac that can create archives in the PKZIP format, which is most popular on Windows machines. One such application also comes from Aladdin—DropZip, also shareware for $30.

 NOTE For sending to non-Mac Unix-based computers, you'll probably want to use a different format: TAR (usually GNUTAR, with a `.tar` extension) for creating the archive, and ZIP (GNUZIP, with a `.zip` or `.z` extension) for compressing the archive. Mac OS X includes Terminal-based tools for creating Unix archives, as discussed in Chapter 22. You can also use the popular OpenUp (`www.stepwise.com/Software/OpenUp/`) and ColdCompress (`www.stepwise.com/Software/ColdCompress/`) tools to work with these Unix-style compression and archiving formats.

Apple's iTools

PART

II

Networks and the Internet

Apple offers Internet-based tools to extend the functionality of Mac OS X and help you create a presence on the Internet. You can use some or all of Apple's iTools, depending on your level of interest. These are all Internet-based applications, enabling you to easily perform some Internet-based tasks from your Mac.

Here's a quick look at the tools that Apple offers:

Mac.com Email   You can use iTools to create your own e-mail account within the Mac.com domain, proclaiming to one and all that you are a Mac user. You access the Mac.com e-mail from your own e-mail application (such as the Mail application), making it easy to work with.

iDisk   iDisk gives you an area on Apple's Internet servers where you can store files remotely. This is great for transferring documents from one Mac to another, accessing files while you're traveling, or simply backing files up to a secure location away from your home. (That way, if your computer got damaged, some of your data could still be secure, which might be more important and valuable than the computer itself.) iDisk is well integrated into the Finder and elsewhere throughout the Mac OS, including Open and Save dialog boxes.

HomePage   If you want to create your own personal Web page but don't want to learn a lot about HTML and Web publishing, that's easily accomplished with the HomePage tool. Plus, HomePage helps you create Web pages that display images, QuickTime movies (such as those created with Apple's iMovie), and other multimedia files you've created on your Mac.

 NOTE Apple currently offers another iTool, called iCards, that enables you to send Internet-based greeting cards. It's easy to walk through and available to anyone, even non-Mac users, so it isn't covered here. (Unlike the other tools, it doesn't require you to log in before you can use it.)

To begin the process, you need to sign up for iTools service from Apple's Web site. Visit www.apple.com and click the iTools link at the top of the screen, or visit http://itools.mac.com/ directly (see Figure 11.8). (You can also begin this process by clicking the Free Sign Up button on the iTools tab of the Internet pane in the System Preferences application. Likewise, you can sign up when you're initially configuring your Mac after installing Mac OS X.) On the sign-in screen, select the option to create a new account (currently the button that says "Free sign up," but the ever-changing Web could see that altered in the future). Now you'll enter personal information, select your username and password, and so on. Remember that your username will be part of your Mac.com e-mail address, so choose it carefully.

FIGURE 11.8

The iTools sign-in screen

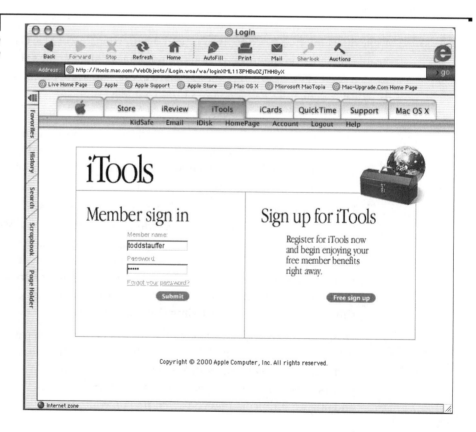

Once you've created your account, you can sign in at any time at `itools.mac.com`. Enter your username and password in the Member Sign In section of the screen, then click the Submit button. If you've entered your information correctly, you'll see the main iTools screen, where you can select the tool you want to work with.

 TIP You may find it convenient to add your iTools information to the Internet pane of the System Preferences application. With the Internet pane open, click the iTools tab. Now, enter your username and password. This makes it possible for you to automatically use iTools in a number of situations, including the option to choose your iDisk in the Finder's Go menu, in Finder window toolbars (if you've customized them to include the iDisk icon), and in Open and Save dialog boxes.

Mac.com Email

Mac.com Email isn't really an online tool as much as it's simply a new account for your existing e-mail program. If you've successfully signed in to a new iTools account, you have a Mac.com address automatically: *username*@mac.com. All you have to do to begin sending and receiving e-mail from that account is to add it in your e-mail application. (Chapter 10 shows you how to create a new account in the Mail application.)

If you're configuring your Mac.com e-mail account in a third-party e-mail application, you'll need to know a few simple addresses:

E-mail address *username*@mac.com, for example, toddstauffer@mac.com. The *username* portion is the member name that you use to sign into your iTools account.

Account name *Username*. Again, it's the same member name you use to sign into iTools.

Mail password The same password you use to sign into iTools.

POP server `mail.mac.com`

SMTP server For this one, use the SMTP server offered by the ISP that gives you access to the Internet.

If you access the iTools home page, log in, and then select the Mac.com screen, you'll see a few additional options for dealing with your Mac.com mail—for instance, you'll see an option that enables you to forward your Mac.com mail to another account. You can also set an auto reply, which notes received messages and sends an automatic reply to the senders, usually to let them know that you're out of town or otherwise not responding to e-mail for some length of time. You'll still be able to retrieve your e-mail and reply personally when you return.

 TIP If you've entered your iTools information in the Internet pane of the System Preferences application, your Mac.com e-mail account can be automatically set up to work with Mac OS X's Mail application (in this case, as an IMAP account). Click the Mail tab in the Internet pane and turn on the option Use iTools Email Account. Your Mac.com information will automatically be added. The next time you launch Mail, you'll be able to access your Mac.com e-mail account immediately.

iDisk

The iDisk tool gives you an area on Apple's Web servers where you can store (for free) up to 20MB of files. In addition, you can purchase additional space. The advantage of online storage is twofold: First, you can access it from any compatible Mac, regardless of where you are. Second, your iDisk is an extra layer of security for important data, enabling you to store documents off-site in case something catastrophic happens to your Mac. If my office went up in flames, for instance, I could still access some of the important work documents that I tend to store on my iDisk. To me, that data is worth more than the computer, and it may be the same for you if you work with your Mac or use it for important household or organizational tasks.

Logging into and out of iDisk

toddstauffer

You can log into your iDisk in a few different ways. The first way is from the iDisk page on the iTools server. Sign into the iTools server and click the iDisk link at the top of the page. You'll see the Open My iDisk button. Click that button, and the iDisk is mounted on your desktop. In fact, that's probably the coolest part of the way iDisk works—it actually appears right there on your Mac's desktop, like a remote server volume, even though it's on Apple's server computers.

The second way is to simply select Go ➢ iDisk from the Finder's menus. This command will automatically attempt to log into the iDisk that's associated with the iTools settings in the Internet pane of the System Preferences application.

If you haven't entered an account in the Internet pane of System Preferences, of if you'd prefer to log into a different iDisk (one associated with a different username and password), you'll need to take other steps to log into your iDisk. Here's how:

1. In the Finder, select Go ➢ Connect to Server.

2. At the bottom of the Connect To Server window, enter the URL **afp://
idisk.mac.com** and press Return.

3. In the Connect To File Server dialog box that appears, enter your iTools username in the Name entry box and your iTools password in the Password entry
box. Then click Connect.

4. You'll see the Select dialog box, where you choose your iDisk volume. Select it
and click OK. Your iDisk should appear on your desktop, just like any other
remote server volume.

When you've finished working with your iDisk, you can sign out of it by either
dragging its icon to the Trash on the Dock or selecting the icon and choosing
Special ➢ Eject, or Control+clicking (or right-clicking) the icon and choosing Eject
from the contextual menu.

NOTE If you leave your iDisk on the desktop but don't work with it for a few minutes,
you'll see alert boxes appear after a period of inactivity. Eventually, if you don't use your
iDisk again, it will log itself out, removing the icon from your desktop. Just sign in again to
use it.

Using Your iDisk

Your iDisk works like any network or removable disk volume: Just drag and drop items
from Finder windows to the folders in the iDisk. You'll notice that you can drag files
only to the folders on the iDisk—you can't save items on the main level. Also, you can
create folders only within the folders—you can't add a new folder at the main level.

When you drag a file to one of the folders, you may notice something else about
your iDisk: It can be slow. This is especially true if you have a modem-based or other
low-bandwidth Internet connection. This is simply a fact of life—your iDisk is just
like any other server on the Internet, and your ability to copy files to and from it
depends completely on the speed of your Internet connection.

When you're copying files to your iDisk, it's also important to consider which
folder you're copying to. Your iDisk offers individual folders for very particular types
of files, depending on what you plan to do with them.

The Documents folder is where you can store your personal documents for backup
or for accessing from a different Mac, while the Public folder is where you can place
files that you wish to share with other Internet users. Anyone with Mac OS 9 or
higher who knows your iTools member name can access your Public folder and download files from it.

Upstream vs. Downstream Speeds

Many broadband connections, especially DSL and cable modems for home users, can have two speeds: *upstream* and *downstream*. The downstream speed is usually faster, and it's the one you'll encounter more often, while downloading Web pages, images, files, and anything else you might be accessing on the Internet. The upstream speed is the speed of your connection when you're *sending* files.

Depending on your type of connection, your uploading speed might be considerably slower than your downloading speed, because ISPs assume that, in general, users send much less data to the Internet than they receive from the Internet. If the slow upstream speed is too much to bear, you might discuss higher speeds with your ISP (particularly for DSL accounts); they may have a more expensive option that improves speed in both directions.

The Music, Movies, and Pictures folders are used with the HomePage tool; place AIFF and MP3 files in the Music folder, QuickTime movies in the Movies folder, and JPEG or GIF images in the Pictures folder. The Sites folder is where HomePage stores the Web pages it creates. As noted in the next section, you can also store HTML documents and other files in the Sites folder if you'd like to use your iTools account for Web serving.

 TIP Apple can add folders to your iDisk at any time, sometimes just to help you organize things and at other times to add new features. For instance, Software is a special folder that's not really on your iDisk—it's an alias to a repository of shareware and freeware archives that Apple has stored on its servers. You can use this folder to access both Apple software updates and popular third-party applications. Just drag them to your desktop, home folder, or another folder on your disk, and they're downloaded from Apple's servers.

HomePage

The HomePage tool enables you to create your own Web page (or a site consisting of multiple pages) using some novice-level editing tools. HomePage offers basic templates that you step through, typing text and adding images and QuickTime movies that you've stored in the appropriate folders on your iDisk. To begin using HomePage, click the HomePage link at the top of any iTools screen.

A walk-through of the HomePage tool is beyond the scope of this book, but it's sufficient to say that it's easy enough to use. You begin by selecting the type of page you want to create in the Create A Page section; options range from photo albums and iMovie "theater" screens to resumes, classroom pages, and team sports newsletters. Once you've selected a theme, HomePage will walk you through the process of entering information and selecting multimedia files that you've uploaded to your iDisk.

Once created, your Web page is stored in the Sites folder on your iDisk, and you (and others) will access your Web page at `http://homepage.mac.com/username/`, where *username* is your exact iTools member name. Typing `http://homepage.mac.com/toddstauffer/` into a Web browser brings up my page, for instance; typing `http://homepage.mac.com/steve/` brings up Steve Jobs's page.

 TIP If you happen to know a little HTML, you can create your own Web pages and upload them to your Sites folder on your iDisk. Internet users will then be able to access your pages at `http://homepage.mac.com/username/page.html`. Note that if you create a page called `index.html`, it will load automatically if no other page is specified in your personal site's URL (for example, just `http://homepage.mac.com/toddstauffer/` will load the document `index.html` stored in my Sites folder).

What's Next?

In this chapter you learned how to surf the Web with Internet Explorer, including many of its management and customization features. You also saw how to access File Transfer Protocol servers using third-party graphical FTP client applications. And you saw Apple's iTools online applications that give you online storage, help you create a Web site, and offer access to a special Mac.com e-mail account for all Mac users.

In Section III, "Getting Things Done with Mac OS X," you'll move on to see many of Mac OS X's built-in applications and capabilities, including accessory programs, printing, PDF creation, QuickTime movies, audio and speech technologies, and the AppleScript scripting language.

PART III

Getting Things Done with Mac OS X

LEARN TO:

- *Use Mac OS X's bundled accessory applications*

- *Configure printers and print your documents*

- *Create PDF documents, manage fonts, and configure color matching*

- *Work with QuickTime movies and multimedia*

- *Play CDs, MP3 audio, and DVD movies*

- *Automate your Mac with AppleScript*

CHAPTER **12**

Using Mac OS X's Bundled Applications

Mac OS X comes bundled with quite a few applications and utilities. While many of these applications are designed to help you with particular tasks covered in other parts of this book (for instance, the Mail application in Chapter 10 and Disk First Aid in Chapter 21), others are designed to stand on their own and help you accomplish tasks.

In earlier versions of the Mac OS, these were often called Desk Accessories; other operating systems (like Microsoft Windows) include their own folders full of accessory applications. Mac OS X doesn't really have a formal name for them, but "accessory applications" will do fine; these are bonus applications that can be used to customize your Mac or otherwise make the time spent with your Mac a little more useful.

In this chapter I'll cover these accessory applications, some of them in detail. You'll also see some of these applications pop up in other chapters, but you can return here to learn exactly what those applications do and perhaps to see some preferences and commands within those applications.

Address Book

Address Book might seem a bit redundant if you happen to use the Palm Desktop software, Microsoft Entourage, or another application that helps you manage people and addresses. But if you don't have one of those applications, you'll find that Address Book is a useful accessory application. And it has a hidden strength—integration with the Mail application.

Address Book is located, by default, in the main Applications folder. Locate and double-click the Address Book icon to launch the program. Once it's launched, you'll see the main Address Book window, as shown in Figure 12.1.

You'll notice right off that Address Book is similar in design to the Mail application and even, to some extent, the Finder window. It has a toolbar across the top of the window, where you'll find often used commands; these command buttons can be customized using the View ➢ Customize Toolbar, just like the toolbar buttons in Mail and the Finder.

Like Mail, Address Book has a Search entry box that can be used to quickly locate particular individuals in the names listing area. The Search entry box is a little limited; it searches only the name entry for each person and shows you matches as you type letters. It's a quick way to whittle the list down to certain names, but doesn't enable you to search through entire records for other information.

The Show menu, just below the toolbar, is used to focus different categories of people that you can create and design. Choose All from the menu to see all people in your address book, or choose a particular category to see people you've assigned to that category. (You assign categories as you create and edit people, as I'll discuss in the next section.)

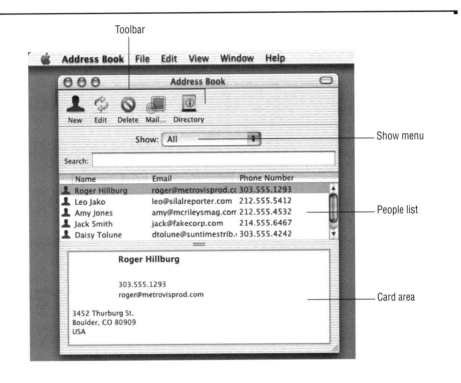

FIGURE 12.1

*The main Address
Book interface*

Toolbar

Show menu

People list

Card area

Below the Search box is the People list, where each individual person stored in
Address Book is listed. When a listing is selected, you'll see the corresponding contact
information in the card area at the bottom of the Address Book window.

Adding and Editing People

You can add people in one of two ways—either from within Address Book or by
switching to Mail, selecting an e-mail message, and choosing Message ➢ Add Sender
to Address Book. If you add a person via Mail, only the name and e-mail address are
stored for that person in Address Book—you'll have to select the entry in the people
list and click Edit (or select Edit ➢ Edit) to add other information.

To create a new person, click the New button in the toolbar or select File ➢ New
Person. The untitled address card window appears, enabling you to enter information
for that user (see Figure 12.2). Enter a name and address, and use the pop-up menus
to select any other information you'd like to store, including e-mail addresses, phone
numbers, and so on. Note that you can add more than one e-mail address, if desired,
but only the first e-mail address listed will be used for things like adding that person
to a group or sending that person an e-mail from the Mail application.

PART

III

Getting Things Done
with Mac OS X

FIGURE 12.2

Editing a person in the address card window

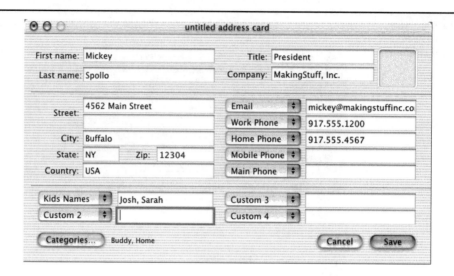

 TIP At the top-right corner of the address card window is a small box. You can drag an image file (from the desktop or from a Finder window) to that box in order to add a picture of the person, if desired. In fact, you can drag any compatible image file—an animal, a background pattern—if you'd like a little variety in your address cards.

Toward the bottom of the address card window, you'll find four custom entry boxes that you can use to store information that Address Card hasn't anticipated. Pull down one of the menus and choose Edit to change the custom entry names; a dialog sheet appears where you can edit each of the four custom field labels.

At the bottom of the address card window, you can click the Categories button to open the Categories dialog sheet. Click to check each of the categories to which you'd like to add this person.

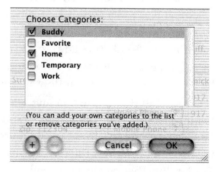

To add an additional category, click the plus (+) button at the bottom of the dialog sheet, then edit the name of the category in the Choose Category list. To remove a category, highlight that category by clicking its name, then click the minus (–) button. Click OK in the dialog sheet when you've finished choosing categories.

When you've finished editing the address card, click Save. That person is now added to your address book and, when you select that person in the people list, the card's information will appear in the card area of the Address Book window.

To edit the address card for a person you've already created, select that person in the people list and click the Edit button in the toolbar or choose Edit ➢ Edit.

Deleting People

To delete a person from your address book, select that person in the list and click the Delete button in the toolbar. This will immediately delete the person. Be warned—there's no retrieving the person's data (unless you've backed up your Address Book database file). The person is not moved to the Dock's Trash, and no warning alert box appears—so avoid clicking the Delete button by accident, if you can help it.

 TIP The Address Book files are located in a folder called Addresses.addressBook, in the Addresses folder inside your personal Library folder. It's a good idea to back this folder up occasionally. Don't move items out of this folder, however, as doing so may affect Address Book's ability to track your people in the future.

Sending a Mail Message

If you'd like to quickly send a message in Mail to one or more of the people in your address book, first select the recipients in the people list. (You can use the ⌘ key to select multiple people. Note also that the selected people must have e-mail addresses as part of their entry.) Once you've selected everyone to whom you want to send the message, click the Mail button in the toolbar or choose Edit ➢ Compose Mail. A new Composition window will appear in Mail (you may have to wait for Mail to launch if it isn't already running), and the selected addresses will appear in the To field of the message.

 TIP If you want to add people to other address boxes in the Composition window (the Cc or Bcc field, for instance), drag that person's icon from the Address Book people list to the target address box in an open Composition window.

Adding a Favorite

You can designate individuals as Mail favorites, making it easy to quickly address messages to those people from within Mail. Select a person in your people list and choose Edit ➤ Add to Favorites. Now, in a Composition window within Mail, you can click the Favorites button in the toolbar to reveal the Favorites drawer. In the drawer, you'll find all the people you've added as favorites; highlight a name and click the To or Cc buttons to add the desired recipient to the message.

Creating a Group

A group is used primarily to put individual recipients together so that you can send e-mail messages to the entire group at once rather than having to type in individual addresses. Address Book gives you two ways to create a group—the easy way and the hard way. If you already have some of the people for your group entered into Address Book, you can take the easy route: In the Address Book people list, select each person you'd like to add to the group, then choose File ➤ New Group from Selection. If, however, you'll be building the group from scratch, simply choose File ➤ New Group. You'll see a blank version of Figure 12.3.

In either case, an untitled address card window appears, but it's a little different from the address card window for an individual person—this address card will be for an entire group of people. At the top of the address card window, enter a name in the Group Name entry box and a description, if desired, in the Description entry box. Then click the Categories button if you'd like to see the Choose Categories dialog sheet.

If this group doesn't include all the e-mail addresses that you want it to, you can enter addresses manually. Type e-mail addresses in the Add Address entry box and press Return or click Add (see Figure 12.3).

If you have other people in your address book that you'd like to add to the group, you get a second chance to do that. You can add an address to the group list by simply dragging the person's icon from the main Address Book window to the list of e-mail addresses directly under the Add Address entry box. Dragging people to a group doesn't remove them from the main Address Book people list—it simply copies their e-mail addresses to the group you're creating. (If a person has more than one address, only the first address entered on that person's address card is added to the group.)

Once you've created a group, it can be used to address an e-mail message in Mail, just as you use a regular entry to address an e-mail message. Simply drag the group's icon from the Address Book window to an open Composition or Reply window in Mail. Drag the icon to one of the address boxes in the Mail window: To, Cc, or Bcc. Then, when you drop the group's icon, all of the associated e-mail addresses are added to the message.

FIGURE 12.3

You can type e-mail addresses directly into a group to add them.

 TIP It's best to address a group on the Bcc line, so that every recipient of the message isn't shown every e-mail address in the group. This ensures the group's privacy while avoiding an annoying situation where each recipient has to scroll through a long list of e-mail addresses before the recipient can read your message.

Importing Contacts

If you have an address book from another application that you'd like to import into the Address Book application, you can do that—with varying levels of success, depending on the application you're exporting from.

In my experience, Address Book works best with contacts that have been exported from Microsoft Outlook Express. In Outlook Express, choose File ➢ Export Contacts, then choose a location to save the file on your hard disk.

In other applications, you may need to experiment. The fewer fields you try to export, the better. With Palm Desktop, for instance, I've had some success exporting just the first name, last name, one phone number field, and the e-mail field. In whatever application you're using, save your exported contacts in tab (or tab and return) delimited format, which creates a text file. (You may also have more luck importing the file into Address Book if you name it with a .txt extension.)

Once you have the contacts exported from your previous application, choose File ➢ Import in Address Book. Use the Open dialog box to locate the file, then click the Open button. You'll see Address Book work to import the contacts, if it's able to. Scroll through the people list to see if names appear to have been added correctly.

Address Book also has limited support for the *vCard* standard—virtual address cards that are gaining some popularity for trading via e-mail. If you receive a vCard as an e-mail attachment, or if you're working with an application that can export contacts as vCards, then you have another way to add contacts to Address Book. Simply drag a vCard to the Address Book window and drop it in the people list, and that contact is added. (As a bonus, all the vCard fields are recognized by Address Book, so there's no need to retype a person's info.)

Finding an Address on the Internet

Address Book offers you the ability to look up people directly on the Internet by consulting an LDAP (Lightweight Directory Access Protocol) server. Such servers are readily available (and some are already entered as preferences in Address Book), making it easy to search for e-mail addresses and other personal information related to individuals.

To search for someone on the Internet via Address Book, click the Directory button in the toolbar. This opens the LDAP Directory Search window, shown in Figure 12.4. All you have to do to search is enter the information on which you'd like to search. For instance, to search based only on the last name, type in the Last Name entry box and press Return. Although it's less common, you can also type in the Email Address entry box and press Return to perform a "reverse lookup" of sorts, where you can see which person belongs to a particular address.

An icon appears next to each entry in the LDAP Directory Search window, so you can drag that entry from the window to the people list in the currently open Address Book. (You can also drag one of these entries directly to the To or Cc entry box in a Mail Composition window, if desired.)

To customize the search engines used for the LDAP lookup, select Address Book ➢ Preferences. This opens the Address Book Preferences window, which shows a listing of LDAP servers (see Figure 12.5). You can add to the listing by clicking the Add Server button, or you can highlight a server and click Remove Server. You can also click in the Use column next to a particular server name to toggle on or off, indicating whether or not that server will be accessed when you enter criteria in the LDAP Directory Search window.

FIGURE 12.4

Here's a sample lookup of a particular individual.

NOTE In Mac OS X version 10.0.2 and earlier, WhoWhere doesn't seem to work and can cause long delays if selected. If you have a later version, you might try enabling WhoWhere.

FIGURE 12.5

The Address Book Preferences dialog box is all about LDAP server addresses.

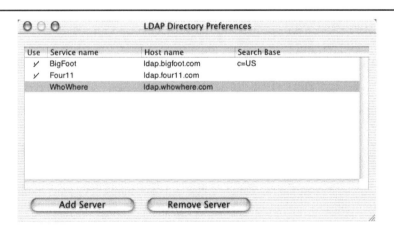

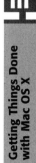

Apple System Profiler

The Apple System Profiler is one of those applications that you'll learn more about in later chapters, but it's worth introducing in this one. The Apple System Profiler is designed to tell you some important, low-level things about your Mac, including the processor and memory installed in your Mac, the peripheral devices that are attached, and the applications that are installed. You'll find that Apple System Profiler is a useful utility to access when you want to know something in particular about your Mac.

The Apple System Profiler is located in the Utilities folder inside the Applications folder. Double-click it in a Finder window to launch the application. Once it's launched, you'll see the Apple System Profiler window, as shown in Figure 12.6.

FIGURE 12.6

The Apple System Profiler

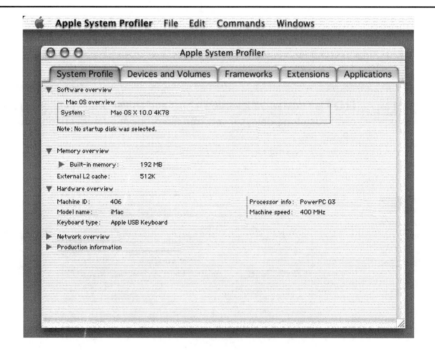

The Apple System Profiler has five different tabs where you'll find information about your Mac. Click a tab to view its offerings:

System Profile On the System Profile tab, you'll find a Software Overview showing information about Mac OS X and the startup disk, a Memory Overview with information about installed RAM, and a Hardware Overview, where you'll see information about the Mac and its processor. You'll also see a Network Overview entry, where you can find information about any network ports this Mac has; and you'll see Production Information, where you'll find low-level information about the Mac, such as the internal ROM (read-only memory) chip version number and other important information.

Devices and Volumes   On the Devices and Volumes tab, you'll find information about external peripherals connected to your Mac via USB, PCI, SCSI, ATA, and other system buses that connect devices to your Mac.

Applications   On the Applications tab, you'll find a listing of applications that Apple System Profiler finds on all attached and mounted storage volumes. You can select an application to see information about that application in the information area at the bottom of the Apple System Profiler window.

The other two tabs are less useful to individuals but might prove useful to a troubleshooting technician if you're ever talking to one on the phone. Frameworks shows some of the low-level system components that are installed on your Mac, including the name, components, and version number. The Extensions tab shows the kernel extensions (mainly device drivers) that are installed. As noted in Chapter 18, you'll occasionally install your own kernel extensions, but it's rare (and will always require an administrator's password).

As you're viewing items in the Apple System Profiler, you'll notice that some items have disclosure triangles next to them. These generally disclose additional information about a particular topic or device. For instance, click the disclosure triangle next to Hardware Overview on the System Profile tab to see information about the Mac and its processor. Likewise, you can click the disclosure triangle next to a particular storage volume on the Devices and Volumes tab to see information about that volume, such as its capacity and whether or not it's ejectable.

Apple System Profiler has one other major capability: It can generate a report (for viewing or printing) that includes some or all of this information. Select File ➤ New Report, then select the items you want included in the report in the New Report window. When you're done, click OK to generate the report.

The resulting report will appear in its own window (it's called "ASP Report" and shows the current date), which you can scroll through or print, if desired. At the top of the ASP Report window, you can also decide whether the report should be formatted as a text document or as an Apple System Profiler document. A text document might be more convenient for copying and pasting the report into an e-mail message.

 TIP In fact, you can also save the report and e-mail it as an attachment, which might be requested if you ever call a customer support hotline to discuss problems with your Mac or its software. Once you've e-mailed the report to the technical service representative, the rep will know more about your Mac and what's installed on it, perhaps offering better solutions to your problems.

Calculator

Mac OS X comes with a Calculator accessory application (see Figure 12.7) that can be used for some basic arithmetic. Calculator is found, by default, in the main Applications folder.

The application is designed to work well with the number pad on an extended Mac keyboard, with all functions mapping exactly to the keys on the keypad.

 TIP Late-model PowerBooks and iBooks offer numeric keypad capabilities when you press the Fn key while pressing keys on the right side of the keyboard that represent the numeric keypad (look at the small numbers on the U, I, and O keys, for instance). If you don't press the Fn key, you'll end up typing letters and punctuation.

FIGURE 12.7

Mac OS X's Calculator

The Calculator can add, subtract, multiply, and divide. To clear the display, click the C button or press Clear on your Mac's numeric keypad.

Chess

Just as the name suggests, Chess is Mac OS X's version of the classic board game. Double-click the Chess application in the Applications folder to begin playing by moving your pieces on the board. You can begin a new game by choosing Game ➤ New Game, and, if you don't finish playing, you can save a game by choosing Game ➤ Save Game—in the Save dialog box, choose a folder for the game and give it a name, then click Save. Later, you can open it using Game ➤ Open Game.

In the Move menu, you'll find my favorite command—Move ➤ Hint. It will give you a suggestion for your next move by highlighting a piece on the board, then highlighting the square to which you should move the piece. Other commands in the Move menu let you see the most recent move and take back your most recent move (using ⌘+Z, which is commonly the keyboard shortcut for Undo commands).

In the View menu, you can choose whether you'd like to play on a two- or three-dimensional chessboard.

Chess also has voice commands enabled by default, using Mac OS X's Speech Recognition technology. In my experience it doesn't work terribly well, but it's something to play with. See Chapter 16 for more detail on Speech Recognition, including more on Chess's implementation of the technology.

 TIP Choose Chess ➤ Preferences to see the Preferences dialog box, where you can turn off Speech Recognition or choose how you'd like to play in the Game menu. You can also choose how difficult you'd like the game play to be using the Level slider.

Disk Copy

Disk Copy is a small Mac OS X utility used to mount disk image files. A *disk image file* is a data file that's capable of looking and working as though it were a removable disk, as long as it's "mounted" by Disk Copy. Disk image files are useful because they're compressed and archived (similarly to, for instance, StuffIt archive files), but they work in a way that's familiar to most Mac users—just like a removable disk.

Disk image filenames generally end with .img or .dmg extensions. (Self-mounting images end with .smi and don't require Disk Copy.) To mount a disk image, just double-click the image file, which will automatically cause Disk Copy to launch. If this doesn't work (double-clicking a disk image file will occasionally attempt to open that disk image in the Classic environment), you can launch Disk Copy first, then drag the image file to the Disk Copy window.

Once you've activated a disk image document, Disk Copy will begin the process of verifying the file. You can either wait until the file is verified, or you can click Cancel to cancel the mounting or click the Skip button to skip the verification process and mount the image immediately. (You should verify each new disk image at least once, but if you subsequently mount the same image, you're probably safe in clicking Skip.)

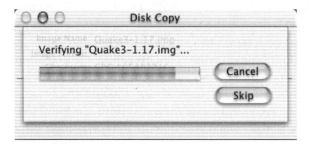

Once the verification process is complete, the verified disk image will be mounted—it pops up on the desktop as though it were a CD-ROM or similar removable disk. Double-click the mounted disk image to open a Finder window and work with the files stored on the disk image.

When you've finished working with the mounted disk image, you can unmount it by selecting its icon, then choosing File ➤ Eject. You can also drag mounted disk images to the Trash to unmount them. (Note that dragging the disk image *file* itself to the Trash will place that file in the Trash for future deletion, so be sure that's what you want to do.)

Most, but not all, disk images are read-only. Occasionally you may work with a disk image that offers some additional space for you to store files within the image file, but in most cases you can only read files from a disk image, not save files to one. That's one reason that disk images are primarily used as archive files for installers and to transfer applications across the Internet.

 NOTE In Mac OS 9.x, you can use Disk Copy to create disk image files, although, at the time of this writing, this capability is not available in the version that ships with Mac OS X. It may be available in future releases. You can launch the Classic version of Disk Copy inside the Utilities folder in the Applications (Mac OS 9) folder and create disk images from there using the Image ➤ Create New Image command. A disk image created in the Classic Disk Copy can still be mounted using Mac OS X's native Disk Copy at a later time.

Grab

Grab is an application that enables you to take *screen shots*—pictures of the current state of your Mac—then save those screen shots as image files. In essence, a screen shot is just a picture of the screen, saved as a standard image-file document. In fact, Grab is the program I've used throughout the writing of this book to produce the screen shots you see as figures and graphics in the book.

You can use screen shots for a variety of purposes. It can be useful to take a screen shot when you need to show a particular screen to a technical support person. You can take a screen shot to teach others how to use a particular application or setting. You can take a screen shot of a Web page to remember how it looked at a given time (after all, Web pages can change quickly). You can even take a screen shot of the high score you've achieved in a game so you can brag to friends.

Whenever you need to take a screen shot, just start up Grab, which you'll find in the Utilities subfolder of the Applications folder. When you launch Grab, you won't immediately see any windows—just menu items. Grab offers you four different commands that you can use to take a screen shot; all these commands are found in the Capture menu:

Selection   Select Capture ➢ Selection, and Grab will display a pointer that you can use to draw a rectangle around the item on-screen that you'd like to capture as an image file. (The item must fall outside the Selection Grab window.) The selection mouse pointer also includes a small box that shows you the X and Y coordinates of the mouse pointer, just in case that's helpful. After you've dragged a rectangle around the item you want to capture, release the mouse button and the image appears in Grab.

Window   Select Capture ➢ Window, and Grab will enable you to capture a single window that appears on-screen (other than the Screen Grab window). Just click the window (it can be pretty much any type of window: a document window, a dialog box, an alert, a palette), and Grab will create an image of only that window.

 NOTE   Although Capture ➢ Window is an option in Grab, I have never seen it work in the version of Grab that ships with Mac OS X at the time of writing. Hopefully it will be implemented in a future version of Grab.

Screen   Choose Capture ➢ Screen, and Grab will take a screen shot of the entire screen immediately after you click outside the Screen Grab window.

Timed Screen   Select Capture ➢ Timed Screen, and Grab will enable you to take a screen shot of the entire screen, but with a twist: You'll have 10 seconds after you click the Start Timer button in the Timed Screen Grab window to arrange things on-screen before the screen shot is snapped. This option gives you the ability to select a particular window, highlight items, open menus, and perform other tasks, within the time allotted, in order to accomplish more "active" screen shots. I use this option for most of the screen shots you see in the book, especially those where a menu item is being selected or an item is being dragged.

In each case, selecting a screen shot command doesn't immediately cause the screen shot to take place. Instead, you'll first see the Grab dialog box, giving you instructions according to the command that you chose. (Each dialog box has a slightly different name, such as Timed Screen Grab or Selection Grab, depending on the command.) For instance, the Selection Grab dialog box offers a Cancel button so that you can cancel the selection grab, while the Timed Screen Grab dialog box offers both a Cancel button and a Start Timer button, which you click to begin the timer.

Once you've successfully taken the screen shot, you'll be switched back to the Grab application, where a document window will appear, complete with the screen shot you just took (see Figure 12.8). Now you can choose to save the document or discard it. To save it, select File ➢ Save. In the Save As dialog sheet, find the folder where you'd like to save the image, give the image a name, and click Save. (You don't need to add a filename extension, since .tiff, for "tagged image file format," is added for you. Grab saves all screen shots as TIFF image files.) If you don't want to save the screen shot, click the image's Close box, then select Don't Save from the Close dialog sheet that appears.

Want to view a Grab image once it's been saved? Double-click it in a Finder window, and it should launch Preview and display itself. If not, you can also drag a screen image document to the Preview icon (in the Applications folder) to display it in the Preview application.

One feature you might want control over as you take screen shots is the way the mouse pointer appears on-screen. By default, Grab doesn't display the mouse pointer in screen shots. Select Grab ➢ Preferences, though, and you can customize how the mouse pointer will look (or whether it will appear at all).

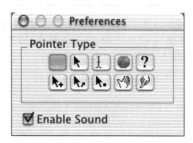

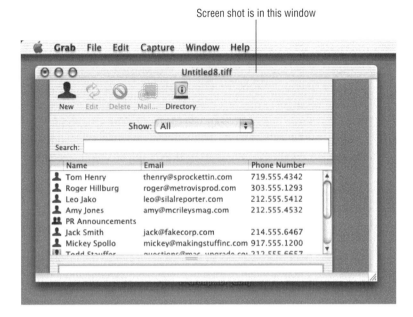

Screen shot is in this window

*Don't let this image
confuse you. I've used
Grab to create a
screen shot of an
Address Book window.*

Select the blank button if you don't want any mouse pointer to appear on-screen; otherwise, select the button that corresponds to the pointer that you'd like to see on-screen when the screen shot is taken. (Note that you can force Grab to change the mouse pointer to any of these options, even if the mouse pointer wouldn't normally look this way at the time that the screen shot is taken.)

Also note that you can turn the sounds on and off in the Preferences window, just in case you decide you don't want to hear Grab's shutter sound every time a screen shot is "taken."

 NOTE In Grab, select Edit ➢ Inspector to see a small inspector window that shows a little detail about the active screen shot document (if there is one).

Image Capture

This sample application works with certain models of still digital cameras to download images from the camera to your Mac via a USB connection. It also features the ability to automatically process those images as they're downloaded if you turn on the Automatic Task feature and select a task from the pop-up menu.

If you have a compatible camera, it will appear in the Camera menu; select it, and you can then make other choices in the window. For instance, in the Hot-Plug Actions section, you can choose what will happen when you plug your camera into a USB port on the Mac in the future. In the Download Folders section, you can either choose to use the Pictures, Movies and Music folders in your home folder or to choose Select a Download Folder and click the Select button to locate that folder.

With a camera connected, click the Download All button to immediately begin downloading all images from the camera to the selected folder. If you'd prefer to choose the images to be downloaded, click Download Some, then select the specific images you want to download in the dialog box that appears.

 NOTE Image Capture is compatible with a limited number of digital cameras and devices, although Apple is presumably working to increase that number. See the Web page `http://til.info.apple.com/techinfo.nsf/artnum/n58827` (Tech Info Article #58827) for more on devices that are compatible with Image Capture.

Key Caps

Key Caps is something of a one-trick pony—it's a small application designed to help you determine what combination of keystrokes is necessary to cause a particular character to appear on-screen. Key Caps can be used to view most of the nonstandard characters available in any of the fonts on your Mac. Launch Key Caps by double-clicking its icon in the Utilities folder inside your main Applications folder.

Once the application is launched, you'll see the main Key Caps window; it's simply a reproduction of your Mac's keyboard, along with an entry box that shows characters as you type them. You can type anything on the keyboard, and it will appear on-screen. You'll also notice that every time you press a key, that key's representation in the Key Caps window is highlighted at that same moment.

Key Caps shines, though, when you press one or more of the modifier keys on your keyboard: Control, Option, Shift, or ⌘ (Command). Try pressing one or more of these and you'll see that the Key Caps window changes to show you what characters are available when you're pressing these modifier keys. In the next example, I'm holding down the Option key.

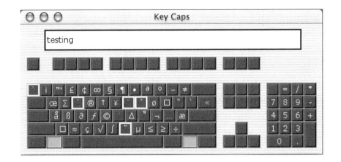

You may notice that some of the keys are outlined. These represent a special case, called *dead keys*. These keys add diacritics (accents, tildes, macrons) to other characters. You press a dead key combination first, then you type a character that can be modified by that particular combination. (For instance, in most fonts you can type Option+N to create a tilde, then type the character *n* on its own. The result: ñ.)

Key Caps doesn't only show you what's possible when you're pressing modifier keys, it also shows what's possible within each of the different fonts that are installed on your Mac. Select any font from the Font menu, and you'll see Key Caps change slightly so that it represents that font. Now, when you press modifier keys, you'll see the extra characters that are available from within that font.

You can use what you've learned from Key Caps (for instance, that pressing Shift+Option+K when the font Times is active results in a small Apple logo) as you're typing in other applications. You can also type the special characters you need in Key Caps, then use the command Edit ➢ Select All to select all of your typing, then Edit ➢ Copy in Key Caps to copy the typing to the Mac OS Clipboard. Now you can switch to the application in which you want the special characters and use the Edit ➢ Paste command in that application.

Keychain Access

Keychain Access is a utility application used to manage your personal keychain. A *keychain* is a special database, protected by a single password that's used to store a group of other usernames and passwords. It's a convenient way, for instance, to store passwords that you use for secure Web sites and remote servers—or even passwords such as your bank PIN number and other information you'd like to store securely on your Mac.

Once you've entered these other passwords in Keychain Access, all you have to remember is your main keychain password. When you enter that password, you "unlock" your keychain, which means you can then view the stored account names and passwords. You can even access some of those resources—if they happen to be Internet URLs or network volumes—with a single click. (See Chapter 8 for a discussion of accessing network volumes via your keychain.)

By default, a keychain is created for you when your Mac OS X account is initially created, and that keychain has the same password as your original Mac OS X account login password. So, when you first launch Keychain Access, by double-clicking its icon in the Utilities folder inside your main Applications folder, you'll likely see your keychain appear in its own window, as shown in Figure 12.9.

FIGURE 12.9

The Keychain window

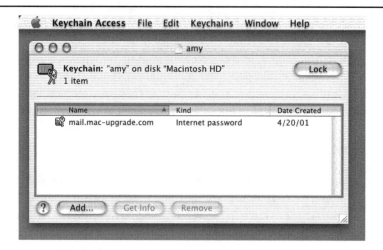

You may also see items that have already been added to the keychain—for instance, when you opt to save an e-mail account password in Mail, that account password is saved in your keychain. Likewise, if you've signed up for iTools, you may see that password on your keychain.

 NOTE If an administrative user has changed your login password, you may find that your keychain password is different from your login password. If that's the case, and you've never changed your keychain password in the past, then you need to use your *original* login password to access your keychain. You should then change it to your current login password by selecting Edit ➤ *Keychain Name* Settings. (*Keychain Name* will be replaced by the actual name of your keychain.) In the Change Settings dialog box, click the Change Password button.

Add to Your Keychain

Want to add an item to your keychain? There are two basic ways to store passwords on your keychain. The first way is via another part of the Mac OS, for instance, the Connect To Server window, discussed in Chapter 8. You may also find commands in some third-party Internet applications, such as some popular FTP applications (Fetch, discussed in Chapter 11, can add passwords to the keychain). Using a command from within those applications, you may be able to automatically add usernames and passwords to your keychain.

The other way is completely manual. When you add an item this way, you're really just creating a record of the resource, username, and password. This is actually pretty flexible for storing any sort of password that you'd like to keep secure; you can even enter your bank's ATM PIN or the combination for your gym locker if you like. The whole point is that you can store these little bits of information, but the information can be accessed only by someone who knows your master keychain password.

In the main keychain window, click the Add button. Now you'll see the New Password Item window, shown in Figure 12.10.

FIGURE 12.10

The New Password Item window

In the New Password Item window, you can manually enter a name, account name, and password that you'd like to store in your keychain. For instance, you can enter a Web site's name or URL, an account name, and a password. Or you could enter **Bank ATM** as the name, skip the Account entry box (or enter your bank account number, if you'd like), and enter a password. In some respects, it really doesn't matter. If you happen to enter a URL as the name, and a valid user account and password, you may be able to sign into the Internet site automatically. In many cases, though, what you enter here is really just personal information that you'd like to secure with your keychain password.

PART

III

Getting Things Done
with Mac OS X

NOTE If you enter a URL in the Name entry box, you'll create an Internet password item, which can be used to automatically access and log into that Internet site (under certain circumstances). To create an Internet password item, remember to type the correct protocol as part of the URL, as in `http://www.mac-upgrade.com` instead of simply `www.mac-upgrade.com`.

When you've finished entering details for this particular password item, click the Add button. Now you'll see that item appear in the main keychain window.

Access a Password Item

Can't remember a particular username or password? If you've stored it as an item on your keychain, you can access that password item and retrieve both the account name and the password. Begin by opening and unlocking your keychain (that is, launch Keychain Access and enter your keychain password if prompted). Now, with your keychain's main window open, you should be able to double-click any of the entries, or you can select an entry and click Get Info.

In the Get Info window (the window is actually given the same name as the password item, "Apple Store" in the example shown here), you'll see your account name and some other information about this password item. You can view the password itself, if you like, by clicking the View Password button. You will probably see your password appear immediately in a small dialog box. Click OK to dismiss the dialog box. Then click the Close button in the Get Info window to dismiss it.

In some cases, you won't immediately see the password dialog box; instead, you'll see the Confirm Access to Keychain dialog box. This is just another checkpoint that pops up in the Mac OS to confirm that an application is authorized to automatically access your keychain. (This happens in other places, too, such as the Connect To Server window and some Internet applications that attempt to access the keychain.)

Click the Allow Once button if you'd like Keychain Access to decrypt the password and display it only this one time; click Always Allow if you'd prefer the password to be visible whenever you click the View Password button for this item. Click Deny if you don't want to allow Keychain Access to access your keychain. (You're not likely to choose this now, but you may encounter it in another application where you do want to deny the application access to your keychain.)

If an item is an Internet password, you'll see another option in the Get Info window—the Go There button. Click this button, and Keychain Access will launch your default Web browser (or another type of Internet application, if appropriate) and will attempt to log into that Internet server using the username and password you've supplied. Whether or not this is successful depends on the type of security used by the remote site. If the site takes advantage of HTML's built-in security capabilities (that is, if it pops up a dialog box in the Web browser or FTP application that asks for a username and password), the username and password will be passed on and you'll likely be signed in securely. If the Web site uses an internally created security scheme, you probably won't be logged in automatically. Still, you can use the Internet password item to help you remember the URL, username, and password for that particular resource.

Remove an Item

To remove an item from your keychain, highlight that item in the main Keychain window and click the Remove button. You'll see an alert box asking if you really want to remove the item. If so, click OK. (If you have second thoughts, click Cancel.) Once you click OK, the item is removed and there's no getting it back. (You'll need to re-create it.)

Lock and Unlock Your Keychain

Whenever you plan to leave your Mac idle or whenever you feel that it's important to secure your passwords, you should lock your keychain. Locking the keychain simply forces you to enter your main keychain password again to access the individual keychain items. You can lock your keychain immediately by clicking the Lock button in the main Keychain window or by selecting File ➢ Lock *Keychain Name* or File ➢ Lock

All Keychains. (In the Lock command, *Keychain Name* is replaced by the current keychain's name, as in File ➤ Lock "Todd's Keychain".)

 WARNING Keychain Access actually presents an interesting security problem. By default, your keychain is always unlocked whenever you're logged into your Mac (assuming your keychain password and Mac OS X account password are the same.) That means that anyone who gains access to your account can also see those prized passwords that you've hidden in your keychain. Knowing this, it's important to be vigilant about locking your keychain either manually or automatically by using one of features detailed in this section.

If you lock the keychain but leave it open, you'll see a new view of the main Keychain window:

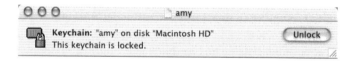

To unlock the keychain, click the Unlock button and enter your keychain password in the alert box that appears. Click OK, and your keychain is unlocked once again.

 NOTE Your keychain is automatically locked when you log out of your user account on the Mac or at certain other times, such as when you shut down the Mac.

Each keychain can also accept some individual settings that govern automatic behavior; in other words, you can tell your keychain to lock itself, if desired. Select Edit ➤ "*Keychain Name*" Settings from the Keychain Access menu. (*Keychain Name* is replaced in the actual command with the name of the current keychain, as in Edit ➤ "amy" Settings.) The Keychain Settings dialog box appears:

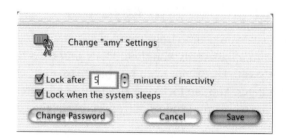

This dialog offers two options for automatically locking your keychain. In the Lock after ___ Minutes of Inactivity option, you can turn on the option and select the number of minutes the keychain should stay open (without any activity) before it becomes locked again. In the Lock When the System Sleeps option, you can choose to have your keychain lock itself automatically whenever the Mac sleeps—whether that sleep setting happens automatically or results from you actively putting the Mac into sleep mode.

 WARNING Closing Keychain Access doesn't necessarily lock any unlocked keychains. If you have an automatic setting active (such as Lock after 5 Minutes of Inactivity), that setting will still be in effect if Keychain Access is closed. Otherwise, you need to explicitly lock your keychains before quitting Keychain Access.

Managing Multiple Keychains

Whenever a user account is created on your Mac, that user also gets his or her own keychain. So, unless you've decided to dispense with Mac OS X's Users feature, there's no need for you to personally create individual keychains for different users.

But you may decide to create additional keychains that help you manage your own passwords and user account names. For instance, you might have one keychain that enables you to access network volumes and secure Web sites, while another keychain is designed simply to hold your bank and credit card PINs. The advantage of this system is that anyone who does happen to gain access to one of your keychains won't necessarily get access to all of them (especially if you use different passwords for each keychain).

To create an additional keychain, choose File ➢ New Keychain. A small Create Keychain dialog box appears; enter a name for the keychain and click Create or press Return. Next, enter a password (twice, pressing the Tab key between each and typing it the same way each time) and click OK or press Return. If your passwords are correctly typed, you'll see another new Keychain window, where you can manage the new keychain.

You can lock an individual keychain by clicking the Lock button in its respective window. You can also lock all keychains at once by choosing File ➢ Lock All Keychains. To close a particular keychain's window, select that window and choose File ➢ Close Window. (You can also click the window's Close button.) And, as noted, each keychain has its own Edit ➢ *Keychain Name* Settings command to determine if and when it locks automatically.

PART

III

Getting Things Done
with Mac OS X

If you have multiple keychains, another menu comes into play—the Keychains menu. Here you can switch between your keychains, quickly opening any that aren't unlocked. Also, you can choose a different default keychain, if desired. (The default keychain is used to store password items that are generated by other applications or utilities, such as the Connect To Server window or a keychain-enabled Web browser.) To change the default, switch to that keychain's main window first, then select Keychains ➤ Make "*Keychain Name*" Default, where *Keychain Name* is the actual name of the selected keychain, as in Keychains ➤ Make "Todd's Keychain" Default.

Preview

Preview is Mac OS X's built-in viewer application, designed to display image files and PDF (Portable Document Format) files. Double-click a compatible image file, and Preview will launch automatically and display the image, as shown in Figure 12.11. (Preview can display TIFF, PICT, JPEG, GIF, Windows BMP, and PDF documents.) If you want to launch Preview directly, you'll find it in the Applications folder.

FIGURE 12.11

Displaying an image in Preview

Preview is a simple program in terms of the commands it offers, but it's good at what it does. Preview offers a few controls you can use while you're viewing an image, including these:

Display ➢ Actual Size (⌘+A)   Select this command to return the image to its full, actual size, even if that size is larger than the screen can show. (This command is particularly useful if you've previously used one of the other Display commands to change the size of the image.)

Display ➢ Zoom In (⌘+up arrow)   Zoom in on the image so that more detail can be seen.

Display ➢ Zoom Out (⌘+down arrow)   Zoom out from the image to show more of it at once. (If an image doesn't fill the screen and you choose Zoom Out, you'll effectively make the image appear smaller.)

Display ➢ Zoom to Fit (⌘+=)   This causes the image to zoom to a level that fills the screen exactly.

Display ➢ Rotate Left (⌘+L) and Display ➢ Rotate Right (⌘+R)   These commands cause the image to be rotated 90 degrees in the selected direction.

Display ➢ Flip Horizontal and Display ➢ Flip Vertical   These commands cause the image to be flipped horizontally (creating a mirror image) or vertically (creating an upside-down image).

Remember, too, that the Preview application is used to display PDF documents, which can often be made easier to read by changing the zoom level. And other commands exist in Preview for dealing with PDF documents, which, unlike most image files, sometimes consist of multiple pages. For instance, the commands Display ➢ Page Forward (⌘+right arrow) and Display ➢ Page Backward (⌘+left arrow) are used to move back and forth within a PDF file.

You can use the File ➢ Save As command to save an image file to another location, but note that images saved in Preview are automatically saved as TIFF documents.

 NOTE   Preview is also used by the Mac OS as the main mechanism for previewing documents before you print them. This ability, coupled with Mac OS X's built-in support for PDF, makes it possible to create PDF documents from nearly any Mac OS X application. See Chapter 14 for more details on using Preview for printing and for PDF creation.

PART

III

Getting Things Done
with Mac OS X

Stickies

If you've used an earlier Mac OS version, you're probably familiar with Stickies, an application that enables you to type quick notes into "sticky note" windows. You can leave these notes displayed on your screen to help you remember things or keep track of small blocks of text (see Figure 12.12).

Once you've launched Stickies (located in the main Applications folder), you can use the File ➤ New Note command to create a new note on the screen. Then drag the resize control in the bottom-right corner of the note window to change its size. You can customize the color of the note by selecting a color from the Color menu. As you type, you can also use standard font controls to change the look and feel of the fonts in your note.

TIP Highlight some text that's formatted in a way that pleases you, then choose Note ➤ Use as Default from the Stickies menu bar. Now, all new notes will have these same font settings the moment you begin typing in them.

FIGURE 12.12

The Stickies application lets you jot down quick notes and leave them hanging around on-screen.

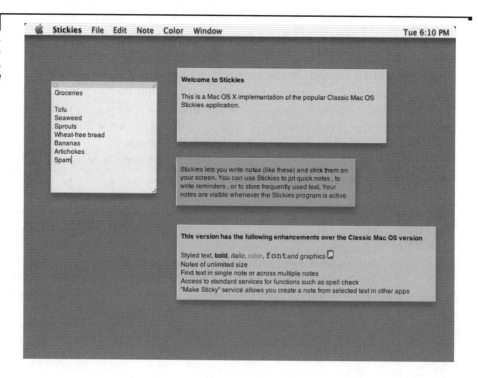

You can add an image to your note by dragging and dropping the image file onto an open note window. (The image is placed at the point in the note where the insertion point is placed; so if you want to move the image, you'll need to move the insertion point, then redrag the image file into the note window.)

To save changes in all your notes, select File ➢ Save All.

When you close a sticky note (by choosing File ➢ Close or by clicking the note's Close box), you're really deleting it. Stickies will display an alert box that asks if you'd like to save the note. If you click Save, you'll see the Export dialog box, where you can enter a name, select a folder, and choose the format for the saved version (Plain Text or Rich Text Format). Once you've made your choice, click Save.

You don't have to close sticky notes to get them out of the way—Stickies offers a special way of dealing with overlapping notes. Click the Minimize button in any note's title bar (it's over on the far-right side), and something interesting happens: The note collapses to show only the title bar. This is actually familiar to users of previous Mac OS versions, which offered window shade controls instead of Mac OS X's minimize-to-Dock feature. (You can also double-click the title bar of a note to get the same effect.) Stickies holds onto that window shade feature and augments it by using the first line of your note as the title that appears in the collapsed note's title bar, as shown here:

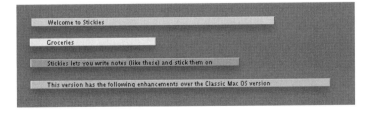

To reveal a note again, just double-click the title bar.

Stickies offers some other standard text application features, such as an Edit ➢ Check Spelling command. Also note that Stickies offers you the ability to print the front-most sticky note (File ➢ Print Active Note) or all notes (File ➢ Print All). When you choose Print All, notes are printed so that they fill an entire piece of paper instead of printing to separate pages.

 TIP You can import sticky notes from previous Mac OS versions if you happen to have an early Stickies document file. Choose File ➢ Import Classic Stickies, then locate the Classic Stickies document file (called "Stickies file") in the Open dialog box. By default, Mac OS 9.x stores Stickies files in the Preferences folder inside the System Folder.

TextEdit

TextEdit is Mac OS X's text editor. It's both a Plain Text and a Rich Text editor, meaning it can be used for a variety of functions, ranging from basic text editing—editing configuration files, HTML (HyperText Markup Language) documents, and other "plain text" documents—all the way up to basic word processing functions. To launch TextEdit, you can either double-click a Plain Text or Rich Text document, or you can double-click the TextEdit icon in the main Applications folder.

Most of the time, Rich Text documents have an .rtf filename extension, and Plain Text document have either no filename extension or a .txt filename extension. If you double-click a Rich Text document, you'll be able to view and edit it in Rich Text; if you double-click a Plain Text document, TextEdit will enable you to view and edit that document in Plain Text mode.

Creating a Rich Text Document

If you launch TextEdit from its application icon, it opens a blank window, which, by default, enables you to create a Rich Text document. Type in the window, remembering that you don't need to press Return at the end of each line—press it only at the end of a paragraph. As you're typing, you can use the Format ➢ Font menu to change the look of your fonts (including the Format ➢ Font ➢ Font Panel command to launch the Font panel). Figure 12.13 shows a Rich Text document in progress.

TIP You can drag and drop images into TextEdit documents from Finder windows or from some other open document windows. Remember that the image appears at the insertion point, so you'll want to click on the portion of the document where you want the image to appear before you drag it into the TextEdit document window.

FIGURE 12.13

Creating a Rich Text document

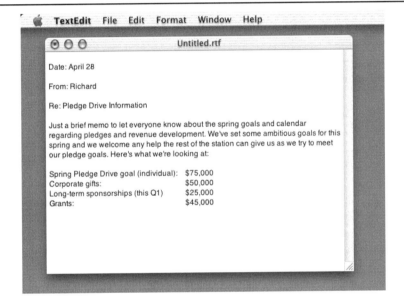

When you're editing a Rich Text document, you're free to change font sizes, font faces, and other settings at any point, including within a single sentence. You can also use the Format ➤ Text submenu of commands in order to align paragraphs of text:

Format ➤ Text ➤ Align Left   Aligns all text at the left margin of the page.

Format ➤ Text ➤ Center   Centers text on the page.

Format ➤ Text ➤ Align Right   Aligns all text at the right margin of the page.

Format ➤ Text ➤ Justify   Aligns text on both sides, so that there are no "jagged" left or right edges. This makes the page look similar to a newspaper column.

TextEdit also includes the Format ➤ Text ➤ Show Ruler command, which will display a ruler in the top of the document window. This ruler can be used to set tab positions, change alignment, and change the spacing between lines of text; and you can choose to lock a paragraph so that individual lines of text can't have different line spacing. The commands Format ➤ Text ➤ Copy Ruler and Format ➤ Text ➤ Paste Ruler can be used to copy and paste ruler settings between different documents.

In a Rich Text document, you can also choose Format ➤ Allow Hyphenation, which enables TextEdit to hyphenate larger words at the ends of lines of text to keep the page from becoming unbalanced by large gaps at the right margin. (If you have your paragraphs justified, it's particularly important to turn on hyphenation to prevent TextEdit from stretching the spaces between words on some lines of text.) TextEdit also offers you the Format ➤ Wrap to Page option, which causes the document to be viewed as if it were on the printed page. Once selected, this option changes to Format ➤ Wrap to Window, which is the default behavior. The "wrap to page" approach is best when you're creating documents that you plan to print.

When you save a Rich Text document, you'll need to save it as either an RTF (Rich Text Format) file or an RTFD (RTF that supports graphics) format. You don't have to do anything special to do that; simply choose File ➤ Save or File ➤ Save As and give your document a name in the Save As entry box. It will be saved with the filename extension .rtf if the document contains only text or .rtfd if the document includes images.

Creating a Plain Text Document

When you're working with Plain Text documents, you'll find that you have fewer options than with Rich Text. You can't add images, for instance, and you don't have as much freedom with fonts and alignment. (Though you can select a font, all text in that document must be the same font and size, and you can't change the alignment or line spacing of text.)

 NOTE   "Plain Text" is how you'll often see text files referred to within Mac OS X. Plain Text is also commonly known as ASCII text, as it refers to a set of characters laid out in the American Standard Code for Information Interchange. ASCII documents, unlike any other types, are generally readable by any computer, even if that computer runs a command-line MS-DOS or Unix operating system without the capability of displaying Rich Text or other graphical documents.

Still, it's important to be able to work with Plain Text documents, because these documents are the heart of a number of machine-readable technologies. For instance, many configuration and preference files, such as those found in your personal Library folder in your home folder, are Plain Text files, and must be maintained as Plain Text in order for the Mac to be able to read and use them. Likewise, files such as HTML documents—those readable by Web browsers—must be saved as Plain Text via TextEdit. If you inadvertently save such a document as Rich Text, it will likely be useless as a configuration or HTML file.

By default, new documents in TextEdit are Rich Text documents. You can change that by selecting Format ➢ Make Plain Text or by pressing Shift+⌘+T on your keyboard. This causes the document to switch to Plain Text mode; now, certain formatting options will be disabled in TextEdit, and when you go to save the document, it will be saved as Plain Text. In fact, you can use the Format ➢ Make Plain Text command even if you've already begun editing in Rich Text mode. Figure 12.14 shows the document that was created for Figure 12.13, but now switched to Plain Text format.

 NOTE In Figure 12.14, you'll see that the document appears in an Untitled window. Whenever you switch from Plain Text format to Rich Text format (or vice versa), TextEdit will place the altered document in an Untitled window so that you can save the document in its new format. It has to, really, because a Plain Text document can't be saved with an .rtf filename extension or it will be confused by applications as a Rich Text document.

FIGURE 12.14

The document has been switched to Plain Text format.

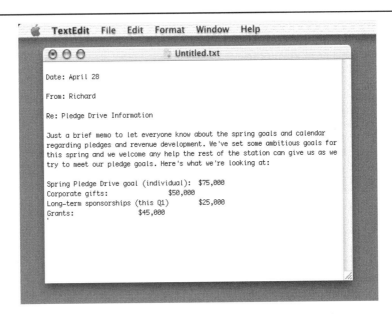

Most of the time, when you work with configuration and other Plain Text documents, you'll find it useful to set the document so that it wraps to the window (Format ➤ Wrap to Window) and that there is no hyphenation (Format ➤ Disallow Hyphenation).

When you save a Plain Text document, TextEdit doesn't automatically append `.txt` to the document's name, although this is generally a good idea. Even Mac OS X applications will react better if the `.txt` extension is part of a Plain Text document's name. If the document is something other than a Plain Text file (a configuration file or an HTML document), you should give it an appropriate filename extension so that it's recognized. For instance, an HTML document should have the filename extension `.htm` or `.html`, Mac OS X preference files often have the extension `.plist`, and many configuration files have no filename extension.

What's Next?

In this chapter you saw a number of the accessory applications that are included with Mac OS X to perform various functions, including managing addresses and e-mail contacts, editing text, taking screen shots, and viewing image files. In the next chapter, you'll see how to install and set up a printer (and printer driver), configure your applications for printing, and print documents from Mac OS X and Classic applications.

CHAPTER 13

Printing in Mac OS X

Mac OS X relies in most cases on a new, sophisticated printing engine for both simple and complex printing tasks. With the right driver software and connection cables, you can easily add a basic ink-jet or laser printer to your individual Mac. Or, if you have a workgroup of Macs and PCs, you can add a more sophisticated network printer that multiple computers can access. How you go about doing this depends on both your printer and your printing needs.

How your printer works also depends in large part on the *printer driver* software that you use for the printer. The driver software tells the Mac OS how to communicate with the printer, including options and preferences that enable you to configure the printer's particular options and unique capabilities. As Mac OS X becomes more widely accepted, printer drivers will be written and rewritten to support a variety of printers. Mac OS X itself also comes with some basic drivers for popular printers, so that even if your printer manufacturer hasn't yet released a Mac OS X–compatible driver, you'll at least have some basic printing functionality.

Printers are set up and managed in the Print Center, a new application in Mac OS X. If you're familiar with earlier versions of the Mac OS, you'll notice that the Print Center incorporates the functionality of both the Chooser and the PrintMonitor (or, with later Mac OS versions, the desktop printer icons). That is, you both set up and manage your printer with the Print Center.

When it comes to actually printing your documents, though, you'll find that the process should be familiar. In all your applications (at least those that support printing), you'll find a Page Setup dialog box and a Print dialog box, where you can configure options for how your final document will look. We'll examine all those in this chapter, along with the basics of the Preview feature, which enables you to see your document on-screen before it's printed. And, you'll see how to configure certain compatible printers for printing from the Classic environment.

Then, in Chapter 14, you'll see some advanced issues related to printing documents, including creating PDF documents, installing and customizing fonts, and dealing with color and color matching in Mac OS X.

Connecting and Configuring a Printer

Mac OS X supports two basic types of printers: PostScript printers and non-PostScript printers. In order to recognize a printer, Mac OS X must have software installed, called a printer driver, that's designed to help the Mac OS locate and communicate with that printer.

Most PostScript printers are easy to configure, partly because the Mac OS already has a PostScript printer driver built into it. So you first connect a PostScript printer, then open the Print Center and look for the printer. Once a printer is recognized by the Print Center, it can be assigned a PostScript Printer Description (PPD), which tells the built-in PostScript driver what makes this particular printer different from other PostScript printers. You'll then see different options in the Page Setup and Print dialog boxes for that printer, thanks to the PPD.

Other printers are different, because the Mac OS includes only basic non-PostScript printer drivers for a limited number of printers. For these printers, which are often ink-jet printers and some low-end lasers that use the PCL printer language instead of Post-Script, you'll have to install a printer driver first in order to use all the features of that printer. Then, once the driver is installed, you can open the Print Center and locate the printer. You won't have to assign a PPD to that printer, though, because the driver tells the Mac OS what's unique about that printer, which will be reflected in the Page Setup and Print dialog boxes.

What Printers Does Mac OS X Support?

The easiest printers to use with Mac OS X are PostScript printers that connect via either USB (Universal Serial Bus) or Ethernet. (FireWire is also supported, although I've seen only a few FireWire-based printers so far.) Such printers are generally supported right out of the box, with only minor tweaks necessary (for instance, a PPD file) to get a good deal of functionality from the printer. These aren't the only printers supported—just the easiest.

The next easiest type of printer to use with Mac OS X is a USB-based laser or ink-jet printer that uses PCL (Printer Control Language) as the basis of its print engine. PCL is the most popular printer language for Windows-compatible printers, and it has become very popular with the latest USB-equipped Mac printer models. Nearly all USB-based ink-jet and many USB-based laser printers marketed for the Macintosh use PCL to print the page. The only real issue that this causes Mac users is the necessity of installing a PCL printer driver in order for the Mac to talk to the printer. (As mentioned, Mac OS X includes some basic drivers that may enable you to perform basic printing.) This is true for Mac OS 9.x and earlier as well as for Mac OS X.

At the time of this writing, it appears that common printer models that won't be supported by Mac OS X are those that use QuickDraw technology to render the page. This includes a number of printers made by Apple in the past, including the ImageWriter, Personal LaserWriter (some models), and StyleWriter models.

Will these printers ever be compatible? It's possible. In most cases where Apple leaves out support for legacy applications, some enterprising company comes along and adds in the capabilities. There is a point of diminishing returns, however, and low-end ink-jet printers cost $100 or less these days. With prices like that, users of much older printers (especially ink-jet and impact dot-matrix models) are encouraged to upgrade.

PART

III

Getting Things Done
with Mac OS X

Installing Drivers and PPDs

The first issue for any printer is to make sure you have the right software to get the printer and Mac OS X to communicate. For PostScript printers, this generally means a PPD from the printer manufacturer. (If you have an Apple PostScript printer, Apple includes PPDs for most models.) You then install the PPD file either by running the manufacturer's installer application or by copying the PPD to the PPDs folder in the main Library folder. This folder (shown in Figure 13.1) is found at `/Library/Printers/PPDs/` on your main startup disk.

NOTE Installing PPDs and printer drivers requires an administrator account, because the software must be written to the main Library folder (so that all users can make use of the drivers and PPDs). However, your personal Library folder also has a Printers folder, where you can install drivers and PPDs for local printers if you don't have access to the administrator account. Those printer drivers will be available only when you're signed in to your account.

FIGURE 13.1

The PPDs folder, where PPD files for your PostScript printers are installed

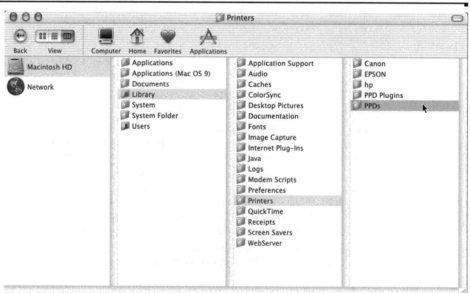

If your printer requires a driver, you'll almost certainly install it using an installer made available by the printer's manufacturer. As Mac OS X ages and gains popularity, more printer drivers are being released by printer manufacturers to enable you to use existing printers with Mac OS X. While many of these drivers aren't as fully featured as their Mac OS 9.*x* counterparts, the features will likely improve over time. Check your printer manufacturer's Web site often for updates.

In fact, you may not even be forced to look around for the drivers—Apple has been making them available occasionally both online (`www.apple.com/downloads/macosx`) and via the Software Update utility, which you can access via the Software Update pane in the System Preferences application. If Software Update reports that new drivers are available from your printer manufacturer, you can download and install them automatically using Software Update.

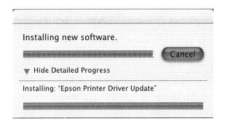

Printer drivers are stored in the folder /Library/Printers/, generally in their own folders or folders named for the printer manufacturer. In Figure 13.2, for instance, you can see drivers that have been preinstalled for HP Deskjet ink-jet printers.

FIGURE 13.2

Printer drivers are stored in the Library folder on the main startup disk.

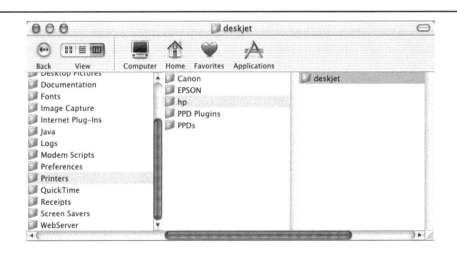

PART

III

Getting Things Done with Mac OS X

Once your printer driver or PPD is installed, you can move on to physically connecting the printer to your Mac or network, if it isn't already connected. Then you can launch the Print Center and begin configuring the printer.

Types of Printer Connections

One issue that's important to the configuration of your printer is how, exactly, it's connected to your Mac. The way your printer is connected has a direct bearing on how the printer is accessed in the Print Center. Here's a look at the options:

USB   If a printer offers a USB connection, you'll connect that printer directly to your Mac, via a USB port on the side of the Mac or on a USB hub. In most cases, this sort of printer can't be made available over a network connection. USB devices are hot-pluggable, so you should be able to connect your printer to your Mac at any time. USB-based printers can be either PostScript printers or non-PostScript. PostScript printers require a PPD, and non-PostScript printers require special driver software. Then, open the Print Center, and the printer should be accessible.

AppleTalk   An AppleTalk printer is usually connected to your Mac via Ethernet. The printer can be plugged directly into your Mac's Ethernet port using an Ethernet crossover cable, or the printer can be connected to an Ethernet hub that your Mac is also connected to. If you have the printer connected to a hub, there's the added advantage that the printer is now available for all Macs (indeed, all computers, if they're compatible with the printer) on that network. For an AppleTalk-based printer connection to work correctly, you must turn on AppleTalk in the Network pane of the System Preferences application (see Figure 13.3) of each Mac that will access the printer. Most AppleTalk-based printers are also PostScript printers, so they don't require special driver software.

NOTE   If the printer is connected to an Ethernet hub that is also connected to an AirPort Base Station or similar AirPort router, you can access it from your AirPort-enabled Mac as well. (In the Network pane of System Preferences, select AirPort from the Configure menu, then use the AppleTalk tab to turn on AppleTalk access over the AirPort connection.) Likewise, you'll find special "bridge" devices that connect LocalTalk-based PostScript printers to Ethernet ports and networks offered by companies such as Farallon (www.farallon.com).

Line Printer (LPR)   Mac OS X can also support a Line Printer (LPR) connection, which is a TCP/IP-based connection to a network printer that's generally connected via Ethernet. Some printers can act as line printers on their own, while others require a printer server to manage their spool files. If your printer supports an LPR connection, you'll need to know the IP address of the printer and whether or not it requires that you use a local spool. The advantage of this setup, if your printer supports it, is that you don't have to enable AppleTalk in order to print.

With software installed and the printer connected, you're ready to move on to the Print Center and to configure the printer.

FIGURE 13.3

If you have an AppleTalk-based network printer, it should be accessible once you've activated AppleTalk.

Configuring in the Print Center

The Print Center is a catchall utility in Mac OS X that actually performs two different major tasks with regard to printing: setup and management. In previous Mac OS versions (including the Classic environment), setting up a printer was handled in the Chooser, and managing print jobs either in the PrintMonitor or via a desktop printer icon. In Mac OS X, all of that management is done through the Print Center.

NOTE Desktop printing isn't possible in the Classic environment, but if you boot into Mac OS 9.1, you can access your printer via a desktop printer icon. You can, however, use the PrintMonitor in the Classic environment, as you'll see later in this chapter.

Add a Printer

We'll focus on managing print jobs later in this chapter; for now, it's time to configure the printer. If you've connected the printer to your Mac (or your network of Macs) and installed the proper drivers or PPD files, you're ready to launch Print Center. Do so by double-clicking its icon in the Utilities subfolder of the main Applications folder. If you haven't set up a printer previously, the first thing you'll see is a dialog box asking if you'd like to set up a printer:

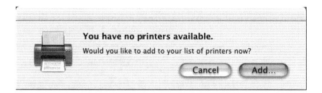

> **You have no printers available.**
> Would you like to add to your list of printers now?
>
> Cancel   Add...

Click the Add button, and a sheet appears from the title bar of the Printer List window (see Figure 13.4). Here is where you'll select the type of printer. You begin by selecting the type of printer connection from the pop-up menu. By default, you'll see Directory Services listed; if a listing of printers appears in the window, your network administrator has set up a Directory Services listing for your printers. Simply select the printer you want to use and click Add.

If your printer has been preconfigured on a large network, you may find it on the Directory Services menu. This simply means that your network administrator has made the printer visible via either NetInfo or LDAP services databases. Your Mac has queried the server's database, found a network printer, and made it available to you for easy selection. Select the printer and click Add.

Otherwise, select the type of connection you're using for your printer from the pop-up menu: AppleTalk, USB, or LPR Printers Using IP.

Once you've selected the type of connection, any recognized printers will appear in the listing below. How you select the printer depends on the type of connection:

> **USB**   If you've chosen USB, you'll see any printers connected to your Mac via its USB ports (assuming a driver has been installed for the printer). Select the printer you want to use, then click the Add button.

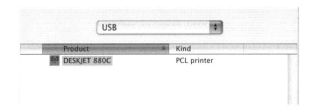

AppleTalk If you've chosen AppleTalk from the menu, you'll see any printers that are currently connected to your Mac via AppleTalk, including any printers found on the local network. If you have multiple AppleTalk zones, you'll see a second pop-up menu from which you can select the zone where you'd like to look for the printer. (Printers can be placed in different zones using AppleTalk routers. Selecting the correct zone makes it easier for you to avoid using an AppleTalk printer that isn't convenient—on another floor or in another building within your company. If you have a home or small-office network, however, you likely don't need to worry about AppleTalk zones.) Once that zone is selected, you should see the printer; select it and click Add.

FIGURE 13.4

Using the Add Printer sheet to add an AppleTalk printer

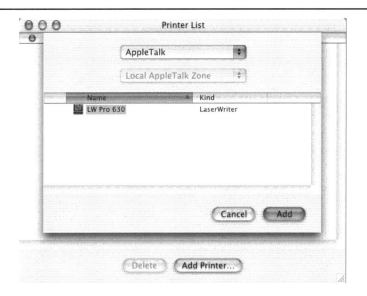

LPR Printers Using IP If you choose LPR Printers Using IP (see Figure 13.5), the printer isn't automatically recognized; instead, you enter the printer's IP

PART

III

Getting Things Done
with Mac OS X

number in the LPR Printer's Address entry box. (If the printer or print server has its own host and domain name, e.g., `printer1.mac-upgrade.com`, you can enter that instead.) If the remote printer or print server has its own queue, leave the Use Default Queue on Server option checked; if you want a local queue, uncheck that option and enter the name of a queue in the Queue Name entry box. Finally, select the PPD to use with this printer from the Printer Model menu. (If the model isn't listed and the printer is PostScript, you can choose LaserWriter or Generic for basic functionality.) Click Add to add the printer.

 TIP In the Printer Model menu, at the very bottom, is a Choose command. Select it if your printer model isn't listed but you've downloaded a PPD for your printer. You'll see an Open dialog box that will enable you to locate the PPD file and add that description.

FIGURE 13.5

Adding an LPR printer using the Add Printer sheet

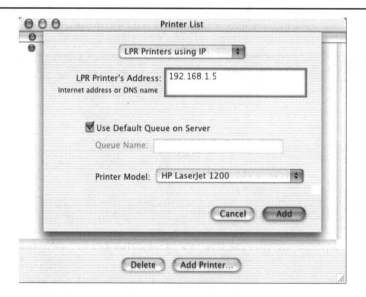

Managing the Printer List

Once you've added a printer, you're returned to the Printer List, where you can now see all the printers to which your Mac has access. Double-click a printer, and you'll see that printer's queue, where you can manage individual print jobs. (More on the printer queue in the section "Managing Print Jobs" later in this chapter.)

The Printer List enables you to select a default printer—the printer that's selected automatically when you or your users attempt to print a document. (It's also the printer used by applications that have a Print One Copy command or a similar command that bypasses the Print dialog box.) In the Printer List, the default is indicated by a small round dot next to the printer in the listing.

	192.168.1.5	lpr host
	DESKJET 880C	PCL printer
●	LW Pro 630	LaserWriter

To change the default, select a new printer's name in the Printer List, then choose Printers ➤ Make Default from the Print Center's menu bar. The selected printer will become the default.

To delete a printer, select that printer in the Printer List and click the Delete button. The printer is immediately deleted, unless it has active print jobs. If you attempt to delete a printer while it has jobs active, you'll see an error message and you'll need to wait until the printer is finished printing; or you can cancel active print jobs before deleting the printer.

Printing Your Documents

Once you have your printer or printers installed and recognized by the Print Center, you're ready to move on to the actual act of printing from your applications. This is a two-step process. The first step, Page Setup, is where you'll select some overall options for how you'd like to print to your printer; specifically, you'll choose the type of paper and the orientation of the output. Then, every time you print a document, you'll use the Print dialog box (or, in some cases, a Print *sheet* interface that pops out of the document window's title bar) to configure the individual print job, including settings like the number of copies, page range, and printer-specific options.

Page Setup

The first time you visit an application, and occasionally after that, you'll want to visit the Page Setup dialog box by selecting File ➤ Page Setup (see Figure 13.6). This dialog box (or a dialog sheet in some applications, such as TextEdit, shown in Figure 13.6) offers basic options that govern how documents within that application will be printed. In general, these include the paper size you plan to print to, the orientation of the printed page, and the scale at which the page will be printed.

FIGURE 13.6

*The Page Setup dialog
sheet enables you to
set Page Setup options
for each application.*

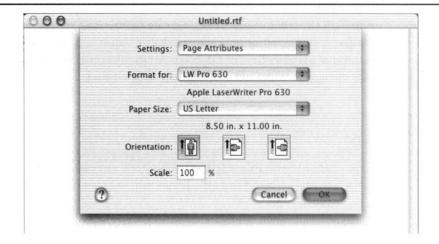

Note the Format For menu in the Page Setup dialog box. This menu enables you to select the printer for which you'd like to select Page Setup attributes. It enables you to quickly choose from among printers that you've already added in the Print Center. You can also choose Any Printer in the Format For menu if you'd like all your printers to have the same basic Page Setup settings.

At the top of the Page Setup dialog is the Settings menu, which enables you to switch between the different panels of information in the window. (By default, the menu reads Page Attributes.) To switch between different setup options, select an item from this menu. By default, you'll likely see only Page Attributes and Summary. Depending on the printer driver and/or PPD you've installed, however, you may see additional options here. (Note that selecting Summary simply gives you a quick listing of all your current settings.)

With Page Attributes selected, you can set a few different parameters:

Paper Size   Select the size of paper that the application should be prepared to encounter in the printer. (You'll also have to load that paper and tell the printer, in the Print dialog box, where to find that particular type of paper, if necessary.) The standard settings include US Letter, US Legal, international paper sizes, and standard envelope sizes. Note that different printer drivers and PPDs will change these options to any other specific paper sizes that are supported by that printer.

Orientation   Orientation refers to how the document should be printed on the page. The default option is Portrait, which prints a page that is longer than it is wide—the typical orientation. Click the middle button for Landscape, which prints a page that's wider than it is long (ideal for ledger books or other columnar output). The third button sets the printer to print in Reverse Landscape, which simply flips the Landscape output by 180 degrees.

Scale   Enter a number in the Scale entry box that represents the percentage at which you'd prefer to print the document. A document that's larger than your currently selected paper size, for instance, might be printed at 75% or smaller in order to fit on the page.

Once you've set your options, you can select Summary from the Settings menu to see a summary of the settings you've chosen. If everything looks right, click OK in Page Setup to set your choices and dismiss the dialog box.

 NOTE As mentioned, each application's Page Setup dialog box is a separate entity. So you should select Page Setup in each of your applications to make document setup choices whenever necessary.

Print

When you've set up a printer, configured it, and made your choices in Page Setup, you're ready to print. Printing is accomplished via the Print dialog box, which you access in nearly all applications by choosing File ➢ Print or pressing ⌘+P. (You'll also find that many applications with icon-based toolbars offer a Print icon that you can click to quickly open the Print dialog box.) When you've selected the Print command, you'll see either the Print dialog box (see Figure 13.7) or the Print sheet, which pops out from the document window's title bar.

FIGURE 13.7

*The Print dialog sheet,
which appears in
native (Cocoa)
Mac OS X applications*

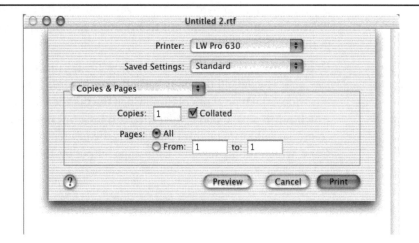

Mac OS X offers this standard Print dialog box/sheet interface element to application developers and those who develop drivers for printers. In almost all cases, you'll find that the dialog box works in a standard fashion, with typical settings located in familiar places. At the same time, though, the Print dialog box can be extended by programmers so that you can access the special features of the application's printing ability as well as the built-in special features of the printer.

To begin, note that one feature, new to the Mac OS in Mac OS X, is perhaps long overdue for experienced Mac OS users: the ability to select the printer you want to use from within the Print menu. Instead of heading back to the Print Center or some other application in order to activate a printer, you can simply select it in the Print dialog box. You do so by selecting the desired printer in the Printer pop-up menu:

Also in the Printer menu, you can select Edit Printer List if you don't see the printer you'd like to choose. When you select Edit Printer List, the Print Center application is launched and brought to the front so that you can configure or add more printers.

Below the Printer menu is the Saved Settings menu, where you can access previously saved sets of Print dialog settings. As you'll see, you can set a host of settings in the Print dialog box (number of copies, quality settings, special layout options) and then save those settings with a particular name. Once named, you can access that set of choices in the Saved Settings menu, making it quick and easy to change from one set of choices to another.

The next menu is the untitled panel menu, which likely shows the default Copies & Pages selection. This pop-up menu is used to access both the standard and optional panels of printer options. Here's a quick look at the standard options available in most Print dialog boxes:

Copies & Pages   In the Copies & Pages panel, you enter, in the Copies entry box, the number of copies of this document that you'd like printed. If you'd like those copies collated (so that all pages of the first copy are printed in their entirety before the next copy is printed), turn on the Collated option. Then, for the Pages option, select either All or From. If you select From, enter the range of pages in the current document that you'd like to have printed. (The range is inclusive, so if you want the last page that prints to be page 7, for instance, then enter **7** in the second entry box.)

Layout   In the Layout panel, you choose how many document pages should appear on a single sheet of paper, if more than one, what order they should be printed in. (You may find it useful to print more than one page at a time on a piece of paper, either to create a "thumbnail" representation of a longer document or to conserve paper for drafts or notes that you're printing for your own use.) In the Pages Per Sheet menu, choose the number of document pages you want to print on each printed sheet of paper. Then select the icon that represents the Layout Direction you'd like the multiple pages to take on the page—this is the flow of document pages on the printed piece of paper. Finally, from the Border menu, select the type of line you'd like to use to separate each document page that appears on the printed sheet.

Paper Feed   Standard on many printers, especially PostScript laser printers, is a panel that enables you to select the cassette or tray from which the paper should be retrieved when you print. Using the radio buttons, you can select All Pages From, then choose a tray from the pop-up menu. The other selection, First Page From, enables you to select the first page from one tray (or the manual feed) and the remaining pages from a different tray.

Quality or Print Modes Many ink-jet printers offer a Quality or Print Modes panel, where you can select the quality setting for printed output. In most cases you'll simply select from options such as Draft, Normal, and Fine. You may also be able to select paper types (normal, photo paper) so the printer knows how densely to print pages and images.

Error Handling For PostScript printers, you can determine how PostScript errors are reported—either they're ignored or a report is generated. You can also tell the printer how to handle an out-of-paper error, either by switching to another cassette or displaying an alert message.

Application Specific The application you're printing from has the option of adding panels to your Print dialog box, enabling you to select from options the application developer wants to specify. For instance, a particular application may offer you options such as printing only part of the document (text but not images), printing documents in a particular sequence, setting an internal quality level, and so forth. If an application offers such choices, you'll likely see a menu item in the panel menu with the application's name. (For Internet Explorer, for instance, options include printing a header or footer and how Internet Explorer should print large Web pages.)

Summary Select this panel to see a listing of all the options as you've set them thus far.

Save Custom Setting Select this option, and the Print dialog will save your current settings as the Custom set. Now you can select Custom from the Saved Settings menu in the future to return quickly to these settings.

Have you made all your choices? If so, you have only two options left. You can click the Print button, which sends the print job to the Print Center. You can then move on to the section "Managing Print Jobs," assuming you feel the need to manage this print job. (If you don't, just move on to other tasks until your document prints.)

Before you click the Print button, however, you also have the option of clicking the Preview button, which causes your document to appear in a preview window (see Figure 13.8). In fact, it appears in a new window in the Preview application.

 TIP Before clicking Preview, you should use the Save Custom Setting option to save any changes you've made to the settings in the Print dialog box up to this point. When you preview a document, the dialog sheet is closed and any changes you've made to settings will be lost if you haven't saved them.

The fact that Mac OS X uses the Preview application to show you the document before it's printed is something that we can take advantage of in a number of ways, which I'll mysteriously leave for coverage in Chapter 14. (The upshot is that the Preview command actually creates a PDF file from your printed document, which you can save, archive, distribute, and even print later without even returning to the original document.)

FIGURE 13.8

Previewing your document before printing

PART

III

Getting Things Done with Mac OS X

In the meantime, if the preview looks good, you've got two choices for how you print the document. First, you can use the File ➤ Print command in the Preview application to print the document. Second, you can switch back to the application you were printing from (quit Preview and select the document window or the original application in the Dock) and then choose File ➤ Print to display the Print dialog again. Choose Custom from the Saved Settings menu (if appropriate), then click Print in the dialog box to print your document.

Managing Print Jobs

Once you've sent a document to the printer, management of that document is taken over by the Print Center application. The Print Center enables you to manage each printer's *queue*, the lineup of documents waiting to be printed. If you need to change the order of documents as they print, halt the printing of a document, or suspend printing to a particular printer, you'll do that from within Print Center. Print Center isn't launched automatically when you print, so you'll need to locate it in the Utilities folder of the main Applications folder and double-click its icon. (If you print often, you'll probably want to drag the Print Center to the Dock to create a Dock tile for it.)

The Print Center's Printer List shows you immediately if items are printing by displaying each printer's status in the Status column.

If all is going well, the status of your selected printer will be shown as "Printing"; if the printer's queue has been stopped, the status could be "Stopped"; and if there's a problem with the printer, the status will be "Error." In the Printer List, you can select a printer and use the Print Center's Queue menu to stop the queue (Queue ➤ Stop Queue, if items are currently printing) or start it again (Queue ➤ Start Queue).

To open a particular printer's queue (thus revealing all the currently printing and waiting documents), double-click the printer in the Printer List, or select a printer and choose the Printers ➤ Show Queue command. That printer's queue appears, as shown in Figure 13.9.

At the top of the printer queue window (each window's actual title is the name of the printer), you'll see the name of the currently printing document. Beneath that is the status area, where you'll see where, exactly, the printer is in the process—sending data, processing the job, and so on. If the printer reports an error (it's out of paper, there's a paper jam, etc.), you'll see that in the status area as well.

FIGURE 13.9

Managing documents in the printer's queue

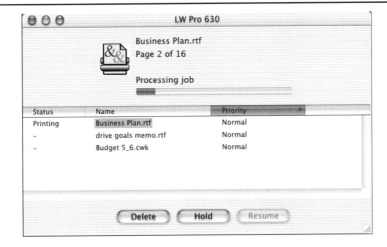

In the job list, you'll see each print job as it has been added to this printer's queue. Using the job list, you can manage each print job:

- Select a job, and you can click the Hold button (or select Queue ➤ Hold Job) to keep that job from printing. Other jobs behind it will now take priority and move up in the job list. After you hold a job, you can resume printing it by selecting it in the job list and clicking Resume (or selecting Queue ➤ Resume Job).

- To remove a job from the queue, select it in the job list and click Delete (or select Queue ➤ Delete Job). You can select multiple jobs, if desired, by holding down the ⌘ key while clicking them.

NOTE Although the queue window shows a priority column, you can't change the priority of print jobs in Mac OS X 10.0. Presumably, a future version will enable you to drag and drop print jobs to reprioritize them. Likewise, print jobs cannot be dragged between different printer queue windows, although this feature might seem useful. (Apple has stated this issue is a technical note, which suggests that the company may make the feature available in a future version.)

PART

III

Getting Things Done
with Mac OS X

You don't always have to be in the Print Center to manage jobs; sometimes, if there's a problem, Print Center will pop up an alert dialog and ask you for guidance. If Print Center encounters an error while you're working in other applications, you're likely to see something like this:

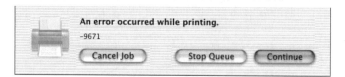

You can make your choice in the alert dialog (choose Cancel Job or Continue), or you can click Stop Queue so that you can return to the Print Center (and/or the actual printer) to investigate.

Printing from Classic

Printing in Classic applications in Mac OS X is a little different from printing in Cocoa and Carbon (that is, native-running) applications. For one, printing from Classic is a little more limited. Although most AppleTalk-compatible PostScript printers will allow you to print from Classic, other printers may be touch and go, because the Classic environment doesn't access printers directly.

In some cases, a printer driver (such as the driver for an ink-jet printer) that works for printing in Mac OS 9 doesn't necessarily work for printing in the Classic environment. And for printers that do work, you'll need to configure the Classic environment to use them.

With others—particularly USB-connected PCL printers—you may be able to separately configure the printer driver within the Classic environment and successfully print to it. At the time of writing, HP has made it clear that this is the case for some of its Mac-compatible USB ink-jet printers.

Otherwise, you'll find that the Page Setup and Print dialog boxes for PostScript printers are similar to their Mac OS X counterparts (if a little less capable) in the Classic environment. Dialog boxes for USB-based printers are a bit different, as you'll see later in this section.

 NOTE With the current version of Mac OS X (and available drivers and technology), you can't print to serial-port printers that use the older QuickDraw language for printing. To use such a printer, you'll need to boot into Mac OS 9.1.

The Chooser

In order to print from Classic applications, you need to access the Classic Chooser application. To do so, launch any Classic application. Once Classic is launched, open the Apple menu (on the Classic menu bar) and select Chooser. The Chooser appears (see Figure 13.10).

 TIP You can also launch the Chooser directly by opening the System Folder that you use for Classic, then opening the Apple Menu Items folder. Inside, you'll find the Chooser icon. Double-click the Chooser icon to launch the Classic environment and the Chooser application.

FIGURE 13.10

The Chooser is where you set up a printer for Classic printing.

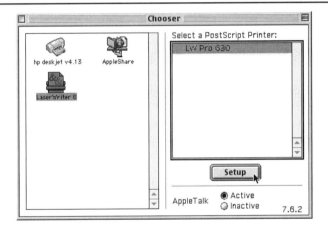

On the left side of the Chooser, you'll see icons that represent, in most cases, printer drivers. If you haven't installed any additional printer drivers for the Classic environment, you'll see only the LaserWriter 8 driver. When you select an active printer driver, the right side of the window will light up with either a list of compatible printers or a port you can choose in order to access that printer.

Support for non-PostScript printers in Mac OS X varies from manufacturer to manufacturer. If your printer manufacturer supports printing from Classic, you need to download drivers from the manufacturer's Web site and run an installer application. Ideally, you should boot into Mac OS 9.1 (don't forget to select the System Folder that you use for Classic, if you have more than one Mac OS 9.1 System Folder installed),

PART

III

Getting Things Done
with Mac OS X

then run the installer that you've downloaded. Then, open the Chooser and configure the printer by selecting its driver on the left side and the printer connection on the right. You may even wish to test the printer by printing from an application in Mac OS 9.1. Then, boot back into Mac OS X to configure the printer in the Classic environment.

If you've installed an ink-jet driver that can work from the Classic environment, select it from the left side of the Chooser window. On the right side of the window, you'll see the connection options—most likely USB. Select that connection and click the Configure button to configure the printer.

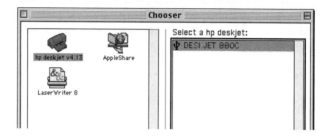

For PostScript printers, select the LaserWriter 8 icon, as shown in Figure 13.10. Now, the right side should change to a listing of recognized PostScript printers. (If you don't see the printers, you may not have AppleTalk turned on. Click the On button in the AppleTalk portion of the Chooser window.)

Select the printer you want to use, then click the Setup button. You'll see a small status window. If you have the option, click either Auto Setup (which will automatically configure the printer) or Select PPD. In the Select The PostScript Printer Description File dialog box, locate the name of the printer you're using and click Select. If you don't see the exact printer, you can choose LaserWriter for basic functionality.

NOTE PPD files for the Classic environment are stored in the System Folder that you use for the Classic environment. If you installed Mac OS X over Mac OS 9, you'll find those PPDs in /Mac OS 9/System Folder/Extensions/Printer Descriptions/.

Once you've set up the printer, click the Close box in the top-left corner of the Chooser window to close it (or select File ➤ Quit). The Chooser closes and you're ready to print.

Classic Page Setup

Choose File ➤ Page Setup in any Classic application, and you'll see the printer's Page Setup dialog box. In the Classic environment, both the Page Setup and Print dialog boxes vary much more widely than they do in Mac OS X. In some cases the Classic versions of these dialog boxes offer more options than do the native Mac OS X counterparts. Figure 13.11 shows a typical Page Setup dialog box for a PostScript printer.

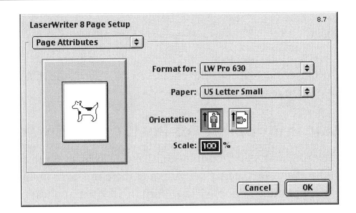

The first thing you might notice about Page Setup in the Classic environment is that the dialog box is completely *modal*—you can't move it or do anything else at all (in the Classic environment) while the dialog box is on the screen. This is how dialog boxes often work in Mac OS 9.1 and earlier versions, and it's one of the reasons for the development of modeless dialog boxes and dialog sheets in Mac OS X. Within the Classic environment, you'll need to complete your work in the dialog box before you can do anything else. (If you want to use the Dock to switch to another Mac OS X application, though, you can do that.)

Like Page Setup in Mac OS X native Page Setup, the Classic Page Setup dialog box offers different panels that are accessed via an untitled pop-up menu. By default, you'll see the Page Attributes options, where you can select which printer you're formatting for (in the Format For menu), what size paper you're printing to (in the Paper menu), the orientation, and whether or not documents should be scaled before they're printed.

Unlike the native Mac OS X Page Setup dialog, you'll find another option in most LaserWriter 8–based Classic Page Setup dialog boxes: PostScript Options. Select PostScript

Options from the pop-up menu, and you'll see a slew of choices you can turn on to affect how items print on your PostScript printer.

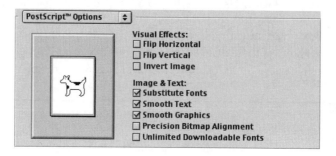

Once you've made your choices in the Page Setup dialog, click OK to dismiss it. Now you're ready to print.

Classic Print Dialog for PostScript Printers

Printing to PostScript printers in Classic is similar to printing in the native Mac OS X Print dialog box, partly because they share the same use of PPD files (at least, for Post-Script printers). Choose File ➢ Print in a Classic application or press ⌘+P to bring up the Print dialog box, shown in Figure 13.12.

FIGURE 13.12

The Classic Print dialog box

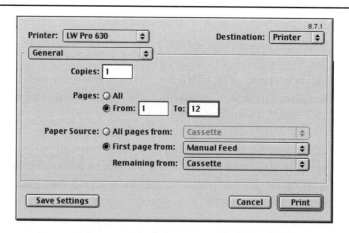

Like the native Mac OS X Print dialog box, the Classic version has quite a few options available from the unlabeled pop-up menu (by default, it's called "General"), especially when you're dealing with PostScript printers. Some of them are similar: General (similar to Copies & Pages) offers settings for the number of copies to print, the range of pages to print, and the paper sources. Layout is another familiar option, where you choose how many document pages will print on each sheet of paper.

You'll also find some other panels that vary somewhat from the Print dialog box in native Mac OS X applications. Here are some of those, which you can select from the unlabeled pop-up menu:

Background Printing   This panel lets you decide whether or not the document will print in the background, enabling you to continue your work in the application. In Mac OS X, this isn't an option; documents are always printed in the background. In Classic, a document will print more quickly if it prints in the foreground, but you'll get control of the application more quickly if it prints in the background. If you elect to print in the background, you can also choose to have it print at a particular time or priority level.

Color Matching   Here you can select whether or not you want the document to print in color (assuming that's an option with your printer) and, if so, what ColorSync profile to use. (More on ColorSync in Chapter 14.)

Cover Page   On this panel you can choose whether or not a cover page (which offers details on the print job) should print before or after your document prints.

Font Settings   Here you can decide on certain options regarding fonts and PostScript printing. Annotate Font Keys means that comments are added to PostScript output. In the Font Downloading section, you can choose which type of font should be downloaded to the printer, whether or not fonts should be downloaded if needed, and whether they should be turned into a special type of font called a *hinted Type 42* font.

 NOTE   Type 42 fonts are TrueType fonts that are converted to this special format for printing on PostScript printers that recognize Type 42 fonts. The quality is better, but not always as compatible with PostScript interpreters.

Job Logging   This panel has two sections. In the top section, you can determine what happens in case of a PostScript error: nothing, a screen report, or a detailed report. In the Job Documentation section, you can determine whether a full copy of the PostScript file will be saved (Generate Job Copy) or just a log entry (Generate Job Log). If you choose one of those options, you can then choose the Job Documentation Folder on the right side of the panel.

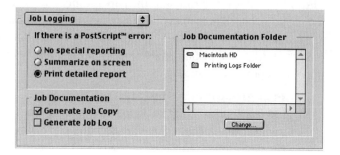

Paper Handling   You can choose how the printer responds when it's out of paper.

Save As File   By default, you can save a PostScript print job as a file—either as a job file or as an encapsulated PostScript document. If you've installed Acrobat software, you can also save print jobs as PDF files. In the Save As File section, select the options for saving to the particular file type you're interested in creating.

 NOTE   The Save As File options come into play only if you choose File from the Destination menu in the top-right corner of the Print dialog box. Selecting File changes the Print button (in the lower-right corner of the Print dialog box) to a Save button, telling you that you'll be saving a file instead of printing it when you click the button.

Your particular printer (or, more specifically, the PPD file) may offer special settings such as Imaging Options and Printer Specific Options. Consult your printer's manual and make your choices in those panels, if they're available.

At the bottom-left corner of the Print dialog box, you can click the Save Settings button to save the current settings and assign them as the defaults. (You can't create a special Custom set of options, as you can in native Mac OS X Print dialog boxes.)

Finally, when you're ready to print, click the Print button. You'll see a status window appear while your document is either sent to the printer (if you're printing in the foreground) or sent to a spool file (if you're printing in the background). For foreground printing, you'll now wait until the entire document is sent to the printer; for a long document, it can be many minutes, depending on the speed of your printer and the number of print jobs that the printer or print server is trying to manage.

Classic Print Dialog for Non-Postscript Printers

If you've installed a non-PostScript printer that supports access from the Classic environment, you'll find that the Print dialog box for your printer is likely very different from anything you've seen elsewhere in this chapter. That's because non-PostScript printer drivers in Mac OS 9.1 and before (and, hence, the Classic environment) actually create a Print dialog box completely on their own, eschewing, for the most part, any standard Mac OS interface element. That means that each printer's Print dialog box can be very different from another (see Figure 13.13).

 NOTE You'll find that the Page Setup dialog box for non-PostScript printers also varies from model to model. In most cases, though, the options are very similar to those offered in standard Page Setup dialog boxes.

Although they are different, you'll find that these print dialog boxes are familiar enough to get the job done. You'll find copies, paper type, print quality, layout, color, and other choices. Make your selections and click the OK or Print button to begin printing.

FIGURE 13.13

The Classic Print dialog box for my HP DeskJet printer

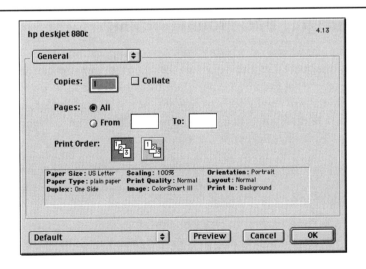

PART

III

Getting Things Done with Mac OS X

TIP Getting errors when printing to ink-jet printers from the Classic environment? One solution (according to postings in Apple's online help forums) appears to be to increase the memory allocation for the PrintMonitor application, which is located in the Extensions folder inside the Mac OS 9.1 System Folder. Highlight the PrintMonitor icon and select File ➢ Show Info. Choose Memory from the Show menu. Set the Minimum Size to at least 300KB. Click the Close button in the Show window, then try printing again.

Changing Printers in Classic

Some Print dialog boxes in the Classic environment will allow you to choose between different PostScript printers, as long as they all use the LaserWriter 8 driver. Those printers will appear in the Printer menu in the Print dialog box, enabling you to send a particular print job to a particular printer.

If you're switching between PostScript and non-PostScript printers, though, you'll need to choose a different printer before you invoke the Print command. You'll do that by returning to the Chooser and selecting the new printer. Then, open Page Setup in the application and make any settings changes that are necessary. (In fact, you should open the Page Setup dialog box in any Classic applications that were running at the time you changed the printer, so that the applications can be made aware of the changes.) Finally, invoke the Print command to print a document using the newly chosen printer.

Managing Background Printing

For background printing from Classic applications, you wait until all pages are sent to the spool file; then you have control over your application again. You'll notice, however, that even background printing doesn't add the job in the Print Center. Instead, you won't really see any progress indicators regarding your print job—at least, not by default. If you encounter an error, you'll likely see a floating alert box that you can dismiss by clicking its Close box.

The other way to check progress is by switching to the PrintMonitor, using Classic's Application menu at the top-right corner of the screen. (You can see this menu only when a Classic application is active.) Select PrintMonitor, and you're switched to the PrintMonitor, where you can see the current printer's queue (see Figure 13.14).

FIGURE 13.14

*The Classic environ-
ment's PrintMonitor*

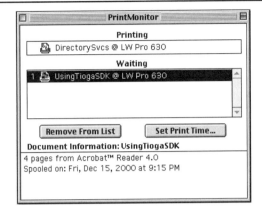

You can stop the currently printing document by selecting that document and
clicking Cancel Printing or choosing File ➤ Stop Printing. Select a print job in the
Waiting area to delete it (click Remove from List) or to set a certain time when it
should print (Set Print Time). To close the PrintMonitor, click its Close box or select
File ➤ Close; or you can simply wait until all queued documents have printed, when
PrintMonitor will close itself.

 TIP   The PrintMonitor has a File ➤ Preferences command that you can use to change
the way PrintMonitor behaves.

What's Next?

In this chapter, you saw the basics of setting up a printer and configuring it in the
Print Center. You also saw the Page Setup and Print dialog boxes in Mac OS X and the
Classic environment, as well as the Chooser and PrintMonitor in the Classic environment. In the next chapter, we'll move on to advanced printing and imaging issues,
including saving print jobs as PDF documents, installing and managing fonts, and
dealing with ColorSync, Apple's color-matching technology.

CHAPTER 14

Advanced Printing: PDF, Fonts, and ColorSync

C hapter 13 covered installing your printer, selecting drivers, and printing from your applications and from within the Classic environment. In this chapter, you'll see some of the more advanced issues that augment Mac OS X's sophisticated printing capabilities.

Because of Mac OS X's advanced Quartz engine, you'll find that your Mac is actually very capable when it comes to one advanced printing issue in particular: creating Portable Document Format (PDF) files. In fact, the Print Preview function is based on the PDF concept, enabling you to view pages exactly as they'll appear once printed. But Preview goes a step further by allowing you to save that previewed document as a PDF file. The resulting PDF file can then be viewed later in Preview or transmitted to others, who will be able to view or print the file on their computers in applications such as Adobe Acrobat Reader.

Mac OS X also has an entirely new approach (compared to older Mac OS versions) to managing fonts. Now fonts can be installed while applications are running, and those applications, in some cases, are automatically updated so that they can use the fonts. As with many other aspects of Mac OS X, you can manage fonts at both the system and user levels, such that individual users can have their own fonts, if desired. Also, most Mac OS X applications have access to the special Font panel, which can be customized so that collections of fonts can be managed on the fly.

Finally, Mac OS X incorporates ColorSync, a technology that enables you to create device-independent color schemes so that colors on your screen look like the colors in your printed documents.

Previewing and Creating PDFs

One of the tangible benefits of Mac OS X's Quartz graphics environment is a great deal of support for the Portable Document Format throughout the Mac OS. What PDF does, basically, is enable you to create documents that include fonts and layout information that can then be used on other computers or even other computing platforms. This may not seem like a big deal. But suppose, for instance, that you create a document in TextEdit, like the one shown in Figure 14.1. If you send that file as a Rich Text document, what your recipients see will vary wildly. Other Mac OS X users, of course, will see something similar to what you've created; but on other computing platforms, the results may be quite different. And if you happen to use fonts that the remote user doesn't have, your document will change even more (see Figure 14.2).

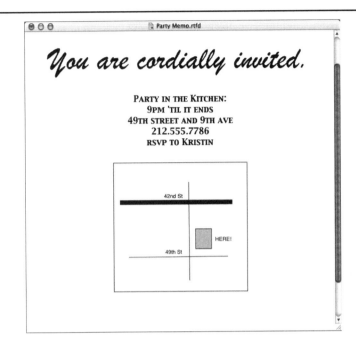

What Mac OS X includes, however, is a built-in capability that enables you to create PDF documents from nearly any Mac OS X application that supports printing. Because a PDF file maintains the layout of your document and even embeds special fonts, your recipients will see a document that's nearly (if not completely) identical to the document you created (see Figure 14.3).

As you can see from Figure 14.3, saving directly to PDF is a powerful feature. First, it enables you to save documents in such a way that the vast majority of computer users can see your file. Second, it doesn't require a special application to do the saving, as PDF creation required in the past. So nearly any application that takes advantage of Mac OS X's native printing capabilities should be able to create PDF documents. Third, saving to PDF is a way to make it possible for others to print out your document from their computers, and have it look exactly as you intended it to look. That makes for a printer-independent, platform-independent document that you can shoot across the Internet to, say, your pre-press shop, your printer, your boss, or a client.

FIGURE 14.3

Here's the document saved as a PDF file and viewed in Adobe Acrobat Viewer on a Mac OS 9 machine.

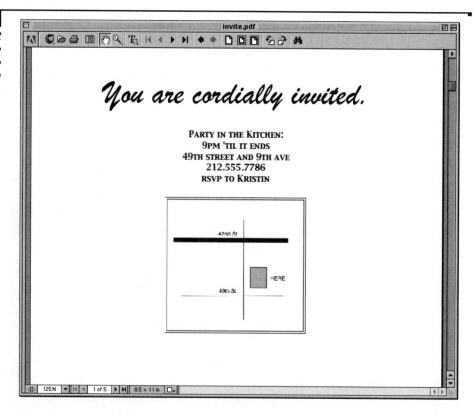

Creating a PDF

To create a PDF, you first build your document in a Mac OS X native (Carbon or Cocoa) application. You can't create PDFs from Classic applications unless those applications are specifically designed for creating PDFs (such as Adobe Acrobat Distiller). In Mac OS X, you don't need a special application to create PDFs.

NOTE In fact, Mac OS X application developers can add a special Print to PDF command or Save as PDF command within their applications, if desired. If you see such a command (probably in the File menu), you can use it to create a PDF directly instead of using the Preview application as an intermediary. You may also find it as an option in some Print dialog boxes. From the unnamed pop-up menu, select Output Options (if you have that choice), then turn on the Save as PDF File option. The Print button changes to Save; click Save to save the PDF file.

Once you've put together the document you'd like to save as a PDF, you should open the Print dialog box by selecting File ➢ Print or pressing ⌘+P. In the Print dialog box, click the Preview button.

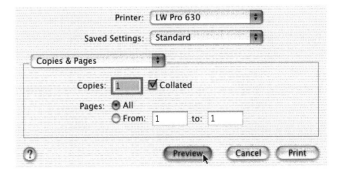

This creates a preview of the document and launches the Preview application so that you can view the PDF.

Now, in the Preview application, you can elect to save the file as a PDF. Choose File ➢ Save as PDF. In the dialog sheet that appears, enter a name for your document (you don't need to type the .pdf filename extension, as it will be added for you). Then choose a location for the file and click the Save button (see Figure 14.4). The PDF document is saved; you can now open it in the Preview application or transfer the PDF to others for viewing in PDF-aware applications.

FIGURE 14.4

A standard Save As dialog sheet in Preview lets you save the document as a PDF file.

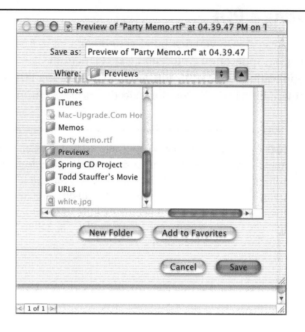

 TIP When transferring PDF documents to others, make sure you keep the filename extension .pdf intact so that other computing platforms will know what type of document they're dealing with.

Printing PDFs

The capability to save your print preview documents has another level of usefulness. It's possible to save documents in such a way that you're creating a "printed image" of sorts; the PDF stands in as an electronic version of the printed document. This means two things. First, you can create a "paperless archive" of documents in PDF format, making it possible for the documents to be viewed later without requiring them to be printed. For instance, a group of PDF documents could be archived to a recordable CD; then those documents could be retrieved later and viewed easily, even on other computing platforms.

Second, you can defer printing a document by saving it as a PDF. Then it can be printed at a later date, on a different printer, or it can even be transferred to some other computer or output center for printing. This built-in capability to save PDF documents, in fact, will likely lead many third parties (like printing and copy shops) to encourage Mac users to save documents as PDFs, which can then be printed and/or copied at the store to create the highest quality publications.

So how do you print a PDF? From within Mac OS X, you simply locate the saved PDF and double-click it to launch the document in Preview. (Or launch Preview and use the File ➢ Open command to locate the PDF document.) With the document open, choose File ➢ Print. Now you can make choices in the Print dialog box just as you normally would; the quality of the printed PDF page should be no different from the quality of the same page printed directly from the original application.

 NOTE Printing saved preview PDF documents isn't quite magical, particularly if you attempt to print the same document on different printers. The reason for this is simple— the preview was created by the original application with particular settings in the Page Setup dialog box. For instance, if you created the document originally with a LaserWriter printer selected in Page Setup and the Print dialog sheet, and you subsequently print the resulting PDF to an ink-jet printer, you may have trouble getting the margins and sizing to work. In some cases, accessing Page Setup in the Preview application can help. In others, however, you need to have saved the original preview document with the specific Page Setup and Print dialog settings for the ultimate target printer (see Chapter 13).

Working with Fonts

Another aspect of creating documents and printing from the Mac OS is dealing with *fonts*, or files that describe a typeface and set of attributes that make up printed and on-screen characters. Common typefaces are Times New Roman, Arial, and Helvetica; combine those typefaces with attributes such as size, pitch, and spacing, and you've come up with a font.

As far as the Mac OS is concerned, fonts are special files that you install in particular folders. Mac OS X is capable of dealing with three different types of fonts: True-Type, OpenType, and PostScript Type 1. Here's a quick look at each type:

GalaxBTReg

Type 1 PostScript Type 1 was the original *outline font* technology, developed by Adobe Systems. Outline fonts are those that can be scaled to different sizes when they're printed. In fact, PostScript fonts were originally designed as printer fonts, and couldn't be displayed on computer screens without some additional software. (In earlier Mac OS versions, that was Adobe Type Manager.) Now, thanks to Quartz, PostScript Type 1 fonts can be used easily both on-screen and for printed output. PostScript fonts can have differently shaped icons, but will often look like printer icons, as pictured.

Galaxy BT

TrueType   TrueType is a technology that Apple and Microsoft created together in the late 1980s as a competitor of Adobe's PostScript. TrueType has become enormously popular for all but the most professional uses of fonts; in publishing, PostScript still reigns supreme. For day-to-day documents and on-screen text, TrueType is what most of us use; in fact, all the fonts that come with Mac OS X are TrueType fonts. (Not all TrueType fonts have a distinctive icon; instead, some have simply a .ttf filename extension or, in some cases, no extension at all.)

ヒラギノ角ゴ Pro W3.otf

OpenType   OpenType is a more recent technology that has been developed by—who else?—Adobe and Microsoft. Although OpenType fonts aren't specifi-cally an Apple technology, Apple supports them within Mac OS X. They're as easy to work with as TrueType fonts, but OpenType is really a superset of True-Type and PostScript Type 1 fonts—an OpenType font can contain either type of font data or both. OpenType fonts are also particularly "downloadable" (espe-cially in applications such as Web browsers), so this technology is an exciting new approach to fonts. If you have OpenType fonts, you can install them easily in Mac OS X. (OpenType fonts are generally denoted by an .otf filename extension.)

Apple, in Mac OS X, has switched its underlying font technology completely to a new approach, called *Apple Type Services*. Along with support for TrueType, OpenType, and Type 1 fonts, Apple Type Services includes more built-in capabilities and better performance than the system used for fonts in older Mac OS versions. If you're famil-iar with those older versions, you'll be happy to know that Mac OS X's built-in *raster-izer*, or font-drawing engine, means you don't need to worry about add-ons like Adobe Type Manager. Likewise, you don't need to worry about installing screen and printer fonts together—you simply install one font file, and the Mac OS performs the rendering and printing.

One difference from earlier Mac OS versions is that Mac OS X doesn't support fixed-pitch, or *bitmapped,* fonts, which were a holdover from the earliest Mac OS ver-sions. These fonts couldn't scale to different sizes—when printed, the font would look good only at its specified size. All fonts in Mac OS X are outline fonts, and they all scale equally well on-screen and on the printed page.

Installing and Using Fonts

The move to Apple Type Services has also changed the way fonts are installed and how they appear in applications. Mac OS X offers a number of different folders where fonts can be installed for particular purposes. And when a font is correctly installed, it becomes immediately available to open applications. Unlike earlier Mac OS versions, you don't have to quit all your applications before they will be able to access the new fonts. (At least, this is the ideal. In early versions of Mac OS X, and with most applications, you do still need to quit the application before fonts will properly appear in the Font panel.)

The Mac OS has three distinct places where fonts can be stored, with a fourth location possible. If you're installing new fonts, you'll want to pick the correct location. Here's a look at the locations:

`/System/Library/Fonts/`   Fonts stored in this location are those that are required by the Mac OS to display information on the screen. In this folder you'll also find the default fonts that are installed with Mac OS X, including some familiar typefaces (to users of previous Mac versions) like New York, Times, and Chicago.

`/Library/Fonts/`   In the root-level Library folder, you can install fonts that are made available to all users on this Mac. This folder can accept any type of font, and all applications can retrieve fonts from this folder.

`~/Library/Fonts/`   In the Library folder inside each user's home folder (~), there's a Fonts folder where you can install and keep personal fonts. These fonts are not available to others on your Mac; they're active only when the associated user is logged in.

NOTE   Actually, there's another location where fonts can be stored for use in Mac OS X applications—the Fonts folder inside the Mac OS 9.1 System Folder. Mac OS X automatically adds any compatible fonts in the Classic Fonts folder to the Font panel for use in Mac OS X applications. Plus, those fonts are also made available to Classic applications, as discussed later in the section "Fonts in the Classic Environment."

If your Mac is set up on a properly configured network, you may also find that your system administrator has installed fonts in a special Fonts folder inside the network hierarchy at `/Network/Library/Fonts/`. These are fonts made available to your entire network of Macs and, in general, cannot be altered by users (or even administrator-level users, in most cases). For personal fonts or fonts on your local Mac, you'll use the main Library folder or your personal Library folder inside your home folder.

To install fonts, simply drag them to one of the above directories. Fonts can be in the form of a TrueType suitcase (a common type of font folder used in earlier

Mac OS versions), a regular TrueType font (with a `.ttf` filename extension), an Open-Type (`.otf`) font file, or a Type 1 resource file (see Figure 14.5).

 NOTE Mac OS X supports a special type of TrueType suitcase that stores all font information in the data fork of the file, instead of using the resource and data forks of past True-Type suitcase formats. These TrueType font suitcases have the filename extension `.dfont`.

FIGURE 14.5

The different types of font files you'll encounter; these are installed in the /Library/Fonts/ folder for access by all local users.

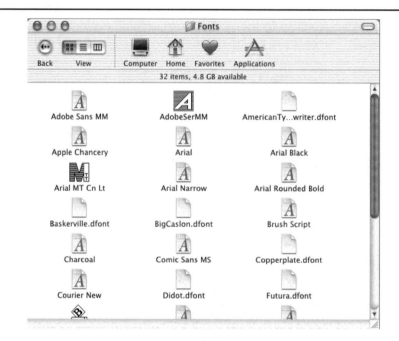

Once you've installed a new font, you'll need to restart any open applications so that the fonts can be recognized. (In some beta versions of Mac OS X, fonts were instantly recognized by the Font panel, so be aware that this capability may be added to new versions in the future.) In an application (such as TextEdit) that offers text-editing tools, select Format ➤ Fonts (or, in some applications, Format ➤ Show Fonts or Format ➤ Font Panel) so that the Font panel is revealed. Check the Font panel to see if the new font is available. If the font doesn't appear, it's possible that you've either installed an unrecognized font type or installed a font that's already installed in a different font folder (in which case you can access the font, but the Font panel doesn't change).

To remove a font, you can simply drag it from its current Fonts folder location to another folder. In fact, this is one way to manage your fonts per project, if desired. You can move fonts into and out of the font folders at any time, including entire groups of fonts that you use for particular projects (see Figure 14.6). To delete a font, you can drag it to the Trash. (In most cases you probably won't want to do this, however, because fonts are expensive! Make sure you have a backup of the font or the original installation CD on which the font came.)

NOTE If you move a font and forget to restart your applications, that font may still appear in the Font panel. When you attempt to access the font, however, any text that uses that font will either change to a more generic font or, in some cases, disappear from the document window.

FIGURE 14.6

Dragging fonts into the Library/Fonts/ folder for a particular project—in this case, a brochure

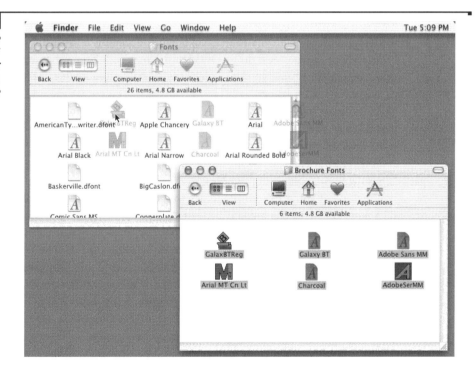

PART

III

Getting Things Done with Mac OS X

In most cases, if you're dragging fonts back and forth, the best plan is to drag them into and out of your personal Fonts folder (~/Library/Fonts/) instead of the main /Library/Fonts/ folder. That way, if you leave the fonts installed (or remove others), other users on the system won't be perplexed by a changing set of fonts in their applications. Plus, if you move a font out of its Fonts folder and then open a document that uses that font, the document will no longer have access to that font—a situation that may frustrate other users on your Mac.

Customizing the Font Panel

Another way to manage your fonts is to avoid swapping them in and out of the font folders and instead to rely on the Font panel interface. The Font panel (as discussed in Chapter 5) is a standard Mac OS X interface element that's included with many native applications. You can choose a font family, typeface, and size from the panel, as well as set favorite fonts. Another option, Collections, enables you to manage your fonts from within the panel. Also, you can determine which default sizes appear in the Font panel and how those sizes are chosen.

Font Collections

Collections of fonts allow you to quickly whittle the list of fonts down to something a bit more manageable. You do this by creating new collections that are task specific, such as a group of fonts you use for editing Web pages or a group of fonts you want to use on a particular project.

To create or edit a collection, you'll choose Edit Collections from the Fonts pop-up menu. That switches the Font panel around a bit so that you can create or edit collections, as shown in Figure 14.7.

You begin by creating a collection: Click the plus (+) button. Highlight the collection's name (it's something like **New-1**) and edit it as desired, pressing Return when you're done. If you'd like subsequently to rename the collection, highlight the collection name, click the Rename button, edit the name with your keyboard, and press Return when you're done.

The new collection will appear, by default, with no font families installed. In the All Families list on the right, select the name of a font family that should be part of that collection. Then, to add the fonts, click the left-pointing double-arrow button. This moves the selected font family into the Family list for the new collection. Continue selecting families and clicking the left-pointing double-arrow button until you've added all the families for that particular collection.

The new collection doesn't affect any other collections—that is, when you move a font from the All Families list to the Family list, you're not taking that font away

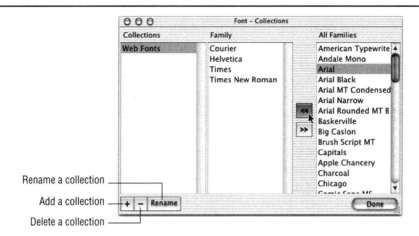

FIGURE 14.7

Creating and editing font collections

Rename a collection
Add a collection
Delete a collection

from any other collection. You can have as many collections as you wish, because they're designed to simply be a convenient way for you to view your fonts in different groupings.

When you've finished creating the collection, click the Done button. Now, back on the main listing of fonts on the left side, you'll see your collections, ready to be selected. Once you select a collection, you'll see a subset of all currently available fonts, making it easier to see the exact fonts you need to work with.

 TIP When you create a font collection, it's stored in a new folder inside your personal Library folder called FontCollections, in a file with a .fcache filename extension. If you like, you can share that font collection file with others. Just drop copies of the file in other users' Drop Box folders and tell those users to copy the font collection file to their own Library folders, creating a FontCollections folder if necessary. Now, when users open their own Font panels, the collection you've created will be available to them. (Note that if you've enabled the root account and you know the password, you can log in as root and copy the font collection file to your users' Library folders on your own.)

Font Sizes

The Font panel enables you to customize the default sizes that will appear when you're selecting fonts. Choose Edit Sizes from the pop-up menu at the bottom of the Font panel. The Font panel reconfigures to show you the font size options. To add a size to the fixed list, enter it in the New Size box and click the plus (+) button. To remove a size from the list, highlight it and click the minus (–) button.

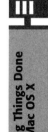

PART

III

Getting Things Done with Mac OS X

If you'd prefer to use a slider control to choose font sizes, click the Adjustable Slider radio button. Now you can enter minimum and maximum point sizes in the Min Size and Max Size entry boxes. Click Done, and the Font panel will now show a slider control for point size instead of the fixed list.

Fonts in the Classic Environment

Once again, the dual nature of Mac OS X means that the Classic environment has a slightly different approach to how it works with fonts. Fortunately, it isn't an overwhelmingly different system—at least, as long as you don't plan to tax Classic's capabilities with high-end design and layout applications—but it's different enough that it needs to be covered separately.

The Classic environment uses its own Fonts folder for all fonts to which Classic applications have access. That folder is inside the Classic environment's System Folder, which you'll find at the root level of whatever volume you used for your Mac OS 9.1 installation (see Figure 14.8).

FIGURE 14.8

The Fonts folder inside the Mac OS 9.1 System Folder is where fonts reside for Classic applications.

NOTE As mentioned earlier, Mac OS X can use fonts that are installed in the Mac OS 9.1 System Folder for the Classic environment. That road isn't two-way, however. The Classic environment can only use fonts that are installed in the Classic System Folder; it can't use fonts installed elsewhere in the Mac OS X hierarchy.

The Classic environment supports bitmapped, TrueType, and PostScript Type 1 fonts, although installation is a little different than in Mac OS X. Here's a look at each:

Bitmapped (fixed-width)   These fonts generally look and print well in only one point size; that point size is usually part of the font's name. If you happen to encounter a bitmapped font in a Classic application, you'll notice that many Classic applications will tell you which point size is supported, by outlining that point size in the application's font size menu.

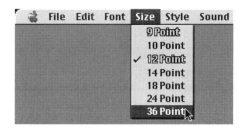

 NOTE Bitmapped fonts are a bit archaic, but important for one particular instance in the Classic environment: You must have at least one bitmapped version of any PostScript font you have installed on your Mac if you'd like to see and choose that PostScript font in your Classic applications.

TrueType   TrueType fonts can be installed either individually or in a special type of folder called a *font suitcase*. A font suitcase can hold any number of TrueType (or, for that matter, fixed-size) fonts, and these suitcases are useful for getting around an interesting limitation in Mac OS 9.1 (and the Classic environment): You can't have more than 128 items in the Fonts folder at once. The solution is to place multiple fonts within a font suitcase, then copy that suitcase file to the Fonts folder. Note that the easiest way to see font suitcases is to dual-boot into Mac OS 9.1 and manage them from within Mac OS 9.1's Finder instead of trying to use Mac OS X's Finder, which doesn't properly recognize font suitcases (see Figure 14.9).

PART III

Getting Things Done with Mac OS X

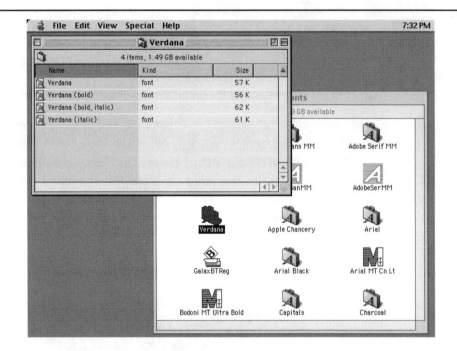

 NOTE A font suitcase isn't much more than a special type of folder that can hold multiple fonts. It's really just designed to be sort of "see-through" so that the fonts it holds are counted by the system as though they were directly installed in the Fonts folder. That notwithstanding, there isn't a convenient way to create a font suitcase; the only solution is to boot into Mac OS 9.1, duplicate an existing one (File ➢ Duplicate in the Mac OS 9.1 Finder), then clear out its contents and rename the suitcase. Note, also, that the name of the suitcase isn't important; all the valid font files inside that suitcase will appear in the font menus of your Classic applications.

PostScript PostScript fonts can be installed directly in the Fonts folder in order to make them available to Classic applications. (Indeed, PostScript fonts should not be stored in font suitcases.) However, PostScript fonts are a special case in Mac OS 9.1 and earlier: In order to display a PostScript font on the screen, Mac OS 9 must have available to it either a bitmapped font or a TrueType font of the same typeface. The reason for this is simple: Mac OS 9.1 (and hence the Classic environment) doesn't have a built-in rasterizer. So, instead of displaying the PostScript font, Mac OS 9.1 attempts to compensate by displaying a bitmapped or TrueType font instead. (Mac OS X *does* have a built-in rasterizer, which is why it doesn't have to jump through these hoops to display PostScript fonts.) Here, for instance, is an example of PostScript and TrueType font suitcases, stored together in the Fonts folder:

Galaxy BT

GalaxBTReg

 TIP There's another solution to the problem of getting PostScript fonts to appear on-screen: Install a rasterizer. One such rasterizer for Mac OS 9.1 (and hence the Classic environment) is the Adobe Type Manager Lite utility, which you can download directly from Adobe (www.adobe.com). Once installed, PostScript fonts can be used on-screen from within your Classic applications (as well as when you dual-boot into Mac OS 9.1). Note that version 4.6.1 (or higher) of Adobe Type Manager Lite is recommended for the best compatibility; older versions of ATM don't work properly in the Classic environment.

Whenever you install or remove fonts, you need to quit all active Classic applications and relaunch them before the fonts will be recognized in those applications.

So how do you install the fonts? Using Mac OS X Finder windows, it's possible to drag and drop font files and suitcases to the Fonts folder inside the Mac OS 9.1 System Folder. The problem is, the Mac OS X Finder application doesn't really recognize the differences between the different types of font files and suitcases. So the easiest way to add or change fonts in the Classic environment is to reboot your Mac into Mac OS 9.1. Once there, you can see and work with font suitcases with relative ease. When you return to Mac OS X, the Classic environment will work as expected with your new fonts.

 TIP In Mac OS 9.x, you can double-click individual font files (TrueType and bitmapped only) to display a little window that shows what the font looks like.

Working with ColorSync

One problem for users of any operating system is matching colors on the screen to colors from input and output devices. Different devices—monitors, printers, scanners—view colors in different ways, from the method used (such as RGB and CMYK)

PART

III

Getting Things Done
with Mac OS X

to the range, or *gamut,* of colors that the device can deal with. Most computer monitors use red-green-blue (RGB) color information to create the image on the screen. Yet most printers use cyan-magenta-yellow-black (CMYK) to create colors, and printers can vary significantly in the range of colors supported due to the variety of printer types (ink-jet, laser, dye sublimation, and so on).

In Mac OS X, this problem is solved by ColorSync, Apple's color-matching technology. ColorSync enables you to choose different color *profiles* for the devices connected to your Mac. Once a profile for a particular device is set, your Mac (and any Color-Sync-compatible applications that you use) has a good idea of how that device deals with color, making it easier for ColorSync technology (and applications that support ColorSync) to match the color from two or more devices. The result: What you see on the screen matches the scanned input or printed output you're trying to create.

You can configure ColorSync in the System Preferences application by choosing the ColorSync pane. You can then make your choices, including individual profiles for your devices or entire *workflows*—that is, series of settings for all the devices you'll use in a given project. We'll take a look at each of these settings in this section. You'll also see how to calibrate your Mac's monitor using the color calibration tool in the Display pane of System Preferences.

 NOTE Inside the main Library folder on your startup disk is the ColorSync folder, where profiles are stored. There, you'll also find a Scripts folder, which includes a number of AppleScripts that are useful for various ColorSync-related tasks—including getting information about documents with embedded ColorSync information or automatically changing your display for different calibration scenarios. Most of the scripts are "droplet" scripts that accept a dragged document.

Creating Workflows

Usually, workflows are of interest to creative professionals who might have a number of different input and output devices. For instance, you might create one workflow to help you manage projects in which you use a flatbed scanner, an LCD display, and a laser printer for the final output. And you might create another workflow for projects involving a 35mm slide scanner, a CRT, a color laser printer for the final output, and a color ink-jet printer for "proofs" or test output.

By default, you have one workflow created in the ColorSync pane, and it's creatively named Default. If you'd like to change that name, click the Info tab in the

ColorSync pane. Now you can edit the name and add any comments that you think are appropriate.

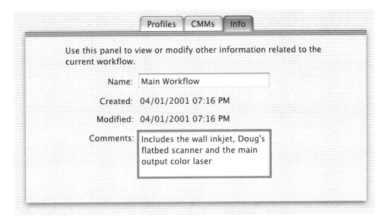

Creating a new workflow requires a few steps. First, select Edit Workflows from the Workflow pop-up menu. Now the Edit Workflows sheet appears from the title bar. To create a new workflow, you actually highlight an existing workflow and click Duplicate.

In the Duplicate dialog box, enter a name for your workflow and click OK. Now you'll see your new workflow appear in the list, just below Default.

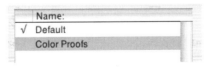

The Edit Workflows dialog sheet includes other options, too, including Import and Export. Choose Import, and you'll see an Open dialog box that you can use to find the workflow you want to import. This is a great way to work with workflows that other users have created. (For instance, you might have a particular workflow used by your entire office.) Once a workflow is imported, you don't have to worry about individual settings, assuming they all match the devices attached to your Mac. Obviously, that's most likely in a corporate or computer lab environment where all of the production Macs are basically the same model and configuration.

To export a workflow, select it and click Export. A Save dialog box appears, enabling you to choose a location for your workflow and save it to disk. Now others can import it and use it in their own ColorSync pane.

When you're finished in the Edit Workflows sheet, click the Done button and you're back in the main ColorSync pane. Now you can select from any new workflows you've created by choosing a new workflow in the Workflow pop-up menu.

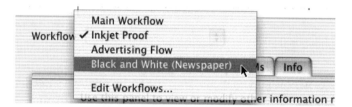

With a workflow set up and selected, you're ready to make individual choices for your devices.

 NOTE When you choose to change workflows or to close the ColorSync pane (or the System Preferences application), a dialog sheet will appear, asking if you'd like to save changes to the current workflow. You can rename the workflow, if desired (to create another entry in the Workflow menu) and/or click Save to save changes.

Choosing Profiles

The next step in completing your ColorSync configuration is to select profiles for all your devices and/or default profiles for documents. Normally, you'll need to change these settings only if you're not working with imported workflow files; if someone has already created the workflow for you, you can likely just switch to that workflow using the Workflow pop-up menu, and profile settings will change automatically. (You may still find it useful to calibrate your display and alter your Display Profile.)

Standard Device Profiles

If you're setting up your profiles by hand, though, click the Profiles tab in the Color-Sync pane. Then choose Profiles for Standard Devices from the unnamed pop-up menu. You'll now see options for Input, Display, Output, and Proofer profiles (see Figure 14.10).

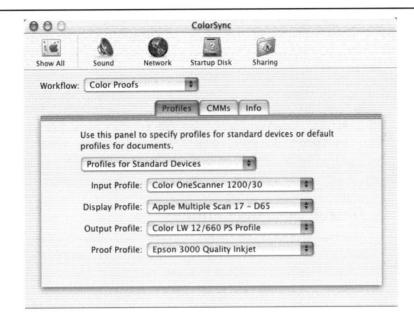

Set the profile for each item, as necessary:

Input Profile   Choose a profile that corresponds to the input device you're using in the workflow—usually a scanner, digital camera, or similar device.

Display Profile   Choose the profile that matches the display you're using. If you don't see a match, you can choose Generic RGB Profile, or you can create a calibrated display profile as discussed later in the section "Color-Calibrating Your Display."

Output Profile   Choose the profile that matches your final output device, usually a printer.

Proofer Profile   Choose the profile for the output device you use for proof or test copies of your output. This is usually an ink-jet or ink printer that's used for less expensive printouts before you send your job to the main output device.

PART

III

Getting Things Done
with Mac OS X

As you're setting these profiles, you'll notice that the built-in profiles are limited to Apple devices. If you have third-party monitors, scanners, printers, and other color devices, you'll need to install profiles that match them. Most of the time, the ColorSync profile for a particular device should be installed automatically when you install the drivers for that peripheral. In some cases, the ColorSync profile will be created by a utility application that's designed to help you calibrate the color of your devices. Whichever is the case, the profiles themselves need to be stored in the folder /Library/ColorSync/Profiles/. So, if you've got a profile document that you want to install, you can put it in this folder to make the profile available to all users on this Mac. (Note that you may need to restart your Mac before the profile will be available in the ColorSync pane.)

 NOTE There is also a /System/Library/ColorSync/Profiles/ folder, where some basic profiles (the generic ones) are installed. Of course, you should avoid altering these, and install your own profiles in the main Library hierarchy.

Default Document Profiles

When an application is ColorSync-aware, it will often embed ColorSync data within documents themselves. When you're creating a new document or working with one that doesn't have color information already specified, default settings can be assigned by ColorSync. With the Profiles tab selected, choose Default Profiles for Documents from the unnamed pop-up menu. Now you can choose options for the RGB, CMYK, Gray, and Lab color spaces. In most cases you can stick with the default; if you're supposed to be working with other settings, you'll know it, because they need to be created by your applications or otherwise installed in the folder /Library/ColorSync/Profiles/.

Repairing Profiles

If you have installed a profile that doesn't seem to appear in the ColorSync pane, it may be damaged; ColorSync profiles can become corrupted fairly easily, through normal use. Mac OS X includes the ColorSync Utility (see Figure 14.11), an application that you can use to verify and repair ColorSync profiles on your Mac. Launch the ColorSync Utility (in the Utilities folder inside your main Applications folder) and click the Verify button to have ColorSync Utility quickly check for problems. If you find any, click the Repair button to repair those problematic profiles.

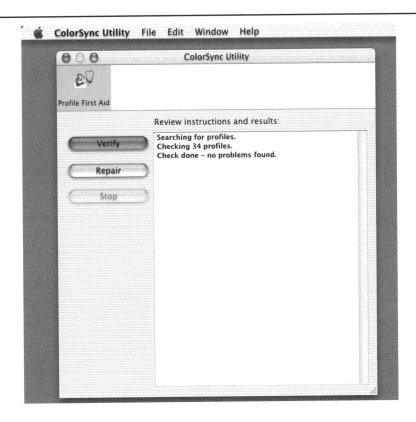

FIGURE 14.11

The ColorSync Utility is used to repair corrupt ColorSync profiles.

Choosing the CMM

ColorSync can be set to use different color-matching methods, if desired. Select the CMMs tab in the ColorSync pane, then use the Preferred CMM pop-up menu to select a CMM. By default, you can choose either Automatic or Apple CMM. (Choosing either one results in the Apple CMM being used unless you've installed additional CMMs.) If you'd like to install additional CMMs, you can do so in the folder /System/Library/ColorSync/CMMs/ if you have access to it, or you can create a folder in the /Library/ColorSync/ hierarchy called CMMs. (If you're installing a third-party CMM, it may create the appropriate folders for you.)

Color-Calibrating Your Display

Whether or not you're a serious graphics professional using your Mac for extraordinary color-matched undertakings, you'll probably find it useful to color-calibrate your

PART
III

Getting Things Done
with Mac OS X

Mac's display. Display calibration is a pretty important step to getting good color matching, even for simple output to a color ink-jet printer. Mac OS X has ColorSync technology turned on by default, so you'll find that a calibrated display will better match the output sent to your color printer (or the output received from your color scanner) than will an uncalibrated display.

Fortunately, calibrating is easy. You'll need to launch the Display pane of the System Preferences application and click the Color tab. Now you can select a prebuilt Display Profile from the list, or you can click the Calibrate button to launch the Display Calibrator Assistant.

 NOTE If you're calibrating a PowerBook or an LCD display, you won't see all of these steps.

Here are the steps for monitor calibration:

1. Begin with the Introduction screen, where you can read about the steps. If you're a color professional (and/or you know a little something about monitor technology), turn on the Expert Mode option toward the bottom of the screen. To move on, click the right-arrow button.

2. On the Display Adjustments screen, you'll see instructions regarding the setting of Contrast and Brightness for your monitor, so that the image appears as described. With third-party monitors, you'll set Contrast and Brightness manually. If you have an Apple-branded monitor (or an integrated display), you'll see sliders that enable you to set Contrast (top) and Brightness (bottom) right on the screen. Set Contrast to the highest setting, then move the brightness up to the point where you see the circle, but a solid-colored background. Click the right-pointing arrow when you're done.

3. On the Native Gamma page, move the slider around so that the Apple logo shape seems to disappear into the background (see Figure 14.12). If you chose Expert Mode on the Introduction screen, you'll see three different colors to blend. When you're done, click the right-arrow button.

4. On the Target Gamma page, select the gamma setting at which you'd like your monitor to be set. Regular options are simply Standard, Television, and No Correction. Television is good for testing Web sites; you can see how images will appear on PCs. No Correction is generally recommended only if you're working with a high-end graphics application that manages its own gamma settings. (Expert Mode users will see a slider that enables you to pick a more exact gamma number.) Click the right-arrow button to continue.

FIGURE 14.12

To choose the native gamma, move the slider until the Apple logo blends fully into the background.

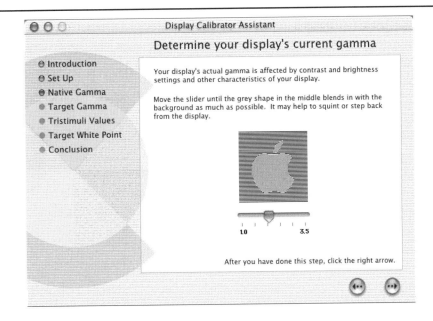

5. On the Target White Point page (see Figure 14.13), you'll select the white point setting for your monitor; in essence, you're choosing a color temperature for white, which will determine how all other colors appear. D50 (5000 degrees Kelvin) is the standard white point for matching internal lighting, so it's often chosen by graphics professionals, particularly for photo manipulation. Higher color temperatures give your display a brighter effect overall but may lead to less accurate color choices in your applications for printed output—but more accurate for Web or TV output. (Expert Mode users see a slider that enables you to choose an exact color temperature, if desired.) When you're done, click the right-arrow button.

6. Now, type a name for the profile in the entry box and click the Create button to create the profile.

That's it—the profile is created and added to the list that appears on the Color tab in the Display pane of the System Preferences application, as well as in the Color-Sync pane, where it can be selected when you're creating a workflow. With a calibrated monitor, what you see on-screen should hopefully match what you see as color printed output, particularly when you're working with ColorSync-aware applications and devices.

PART

III

Getting Things Done
with Mac OS X

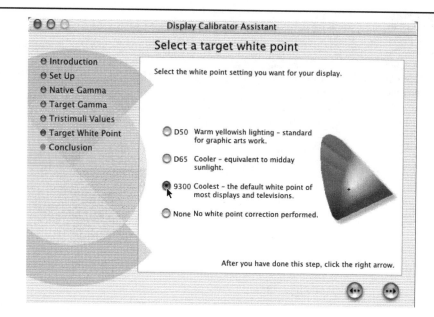

What's Next?

In this chapter you've seen some discussion of advanced printing topics, including creating PDF documents, installing and managing fonts, and working with Color-Sync. In the next chapter we'll move on to multimedia playback and creation—working with Apple's QuickTime technology to view and edit movie files.

CHAPTER **15**

QuickTime and QuickTime Pro

One of the true advantages of the Mac OS is the level at which QuickTime technology is integrated into the operating system. QuickTime is a far-reaching multimedia technology that makes a number of fun and useful tasks possible, including the playback, translation, and editing of Quick-Time movies. QuickTime is more than skin-deep, however: It not only incorporates obvious tools like the QuickTime Player application but also works at the programming interface level, making it possible for application developers to include quite a few QuickTime capabilities in their programs, utilities, and games.

In this chapter we'll take a look at QuickTime from a user's perspective—watching and playing back movies and compatible files—as well as from a technology perspective, including a discussion of QuickTime's ability to translate between various file formats. Then, later in the chapter, you'll also see the capabilities that the QuickTime Player offers for editing and exporting movie files, especially after you've upgraded to the QuickTime Pro version.

Introducing QuickTime

Apple calls QuickTime a "software architecture," suggesting that QuickTime is much more than what it might seem at first glance—a movie player application. Indeed, QuickTime is a major technical pillar within Mac OS X, responsible for a lot of the Mac OS's inherent ability to deal with multimedia. At its essence, QuickTime enables the Mac OS and its applications to work with *time-based data*—often audio and/or video data. Like the flipbook animations you may have sketched for yourself on the edge of each page in your notebook or textbook, QuickTime can display a series of images or sounds quickly enough to give the illusion of continuous playback.

Of course, QuickTime is much more sophisticated than a flipbook. QuickTime movies can have a number of different *tracks*, so that audio, video, and even text or still graphics can have a time-based relationship to one another. QuickTime movies are generally highly compressed, with different *codecs* (compressor/decompressors) being processed for different parts of the playback. And QuickTime ties all this together with a special file format—the QuickTime Movie format—that enables you to distribute time-based data to other computer users. Here's a quick look at the different elements that constitute QuickTime:

> **The QuickTime Movie file format** The QuickTime Movie file format enables users to deal with movie and/or audio "documents" just as they might deal with Microsoft Word or AppleWorks documents. QuickTime Movie documents often have the filename extension `.mov` or `.qt`. Note also that "movie" is something of a misnomer, because a QuickTime movie, if desired, can contain only audio data or only text tracks, sprites, or other non-"movie" data.

QuickTime translation capabilities   QuickTime gives the QuickTime Player or other QuickTime-enabled applications the ability to translate to and from a number of different video and audio formats, including popular formats for Microsoft Windows and other computing platforms.

The QuickTime APIs   QuickTime is an underlying technology that's part of Mac OS X, so it isn't just the QuickTime Player that can play back, edit, or translate to and from the QuickTime Movie format. All sorts of applications can work with the QuickTime system software in any way the developer sees fit. So, as you're working with Mac applications, you may come across similar Quick-Time interfaces and commands (such as the QuickTime Export dialog box or the QuickTime playback controls) in different applications (see Figure 15.1).

QuickTime Movies

To us as users, QuickTime movies seem pretty straightforward. You double-click or otherwise launch a QuickTime movie, an audio file, or some other compatible document, and it appears in the QuickTime Player. There you can play it, fast forward through it, pause it, and so forth. The fact is, though, that there's quite a bit of magic that goes on behind the scenes with QuickTime.

FIGURE 15.1

Since QuickTime is a technology that's part of Mac OS X, even Finder windows can play back QuickTime movies.

Getting Things Done
with Mac OS X

First, QuickTime is doing something that's fairly close to impossible: playing full-motion video by placing one image after another, up to 30 times per second, on the screen while synchronizing a soundtrack and (depending on the movie) other types of data as well. The reason that's nearly impossible is that individual, full-color image files can take up lots of storage space—multiple megabytes in some cases. Macs are pretty sophisticated, but it's still a stretch to ask them to load and process 30MB to 40MB of data per second, especially if you're also asking them to do anything else, like respond to user input, check your e-mail in the background, and so on.

And yet, QuickTime seems capable of doing this, thanks to a few tricks. Most QuickTime movies are actually quite heavily compressed using the aforementioned codecs. These codecs enable a QuickTime movie to store and process much less data than might seem necessary at first blush. That's because the codecs toss out a lot of redundant information; for instance, if the sky is blue, you don't need to store each pixel when a simple instruction such as "paint the next 300 pixels blue" would suffice. Such compression schemes are called *lossy* schemes because the more you compress, the more image quality you lose (see Figure 15.2), often in the form of *artifacts*, or glitches, in the image playback. Audio portions of a QuickTime movie can also be compressed.

Besides compressing each image, QuickTime movies also save storage space and processing time by changing only those parts of the image that need to be changed. Each movie has multiple *keyframes*, special frames that are fully updated every second or so. Then each non-keyframe image is used to update the changes between it and the previous keyframe. For instance, in a QuickTime movie showing a person talking, perhaps only the areas around that person's mouth and eyes need to be updated as they speak; at least, maybe those are the only parts that need to be updated during the fraction of a second between keyframes. If that's the case, the QuickTime movie can be smaller, and playback smoother, because there's less data to process.

Finally, another trick employed by QuickTime is one that cuts down on the amount of data needed for a movie by fooling the eye a bit. Although television generally uses about 30 frames per second to show motion (actually, NTSC, the North American standard, uses 29.97 frames per second, and the European and Asian PAL standard uses 25 frames per second), that many frames per second (*fps,* or the *frame rate*) isn't always necessary. Film, for instance, shows 24fps; for CD-ROM or Internet-based video, you can often get away with as few as 12fps and still show acceptable video quality. With fewer frames stored, QuickTime files are smaller and QuickTime doesn't have to work as hard to render the motion on-screen.

Besides all this video magic, the QuickTime Movie format is capable of storing audio data, text data, and other elements (such as animated graphics and even Macromedia Flash buttons and animations), all of which can be held together by that common QuickTime Movie file format. So QuickTime movies can be interactive, they can be sound-focused, and they can even include different tracks in various languages, with text-based subtitles or even different chapters that you can move between. The QuickTime file format is versatile enough to deal with pretty much everything that's considered "multimedia" in today's computing environment. And it's only one part of QuickTime.

What Can QuickTime Play?

So QuickTime can deal with QuickTime Movie files—that much is evident. But a big advantage of the application is that its underlying technology also makes it possible for a Macintosh to work with a variety of other file formats that fit into the general heading *multimedia.* That technology includes the ability to translate between file formats common to Microsoft Windows, Unix, and other computing platforms. What's more, these translations don't have to take place within the QuickTime Player—application developers are free to add these translation capabilities to their applications.

Besides video and soundtracks, QuickTime movies can incorporate text tracks, animated elements, and even clickable controls, thanks to Macromedia Flash support. QuickTime can also play back QuickTime VR (virtual reality) scenes, which are special panoramic or 3D-image "movies" that you can rotate or move around in (see the section "Playing QuickTime VR Movies" later in this chapter).

PART

III

Getting Things Done with Mac OS X

That covers the native formats. Here's a quick look at some of the other video file formats that QuickTime can play back and translate:

AVI (.avi)   AVI (Audio Video Interleaved) is a popular format used on Microsoft Windows computers. QuickTime can also work with the OpenDML extensions to the AVI format.

OMF   Avid Technology, a developer of high-end video editing applications and hardware, created the Open Media Format specification for exchanging high-end video data. QuickTime supports that format, so Mac applications can exchange data with Avid and similar systems.

MPEG (.mpg or .mpeg)   The MPEG (Moving Picture Experts Group) format (actually MPEG-1) is popular for CD-based and Internet-based movies. You can load an MPEG-1 file into the QuickTime Player and play it back or even translate it to QuickTime Movie format. MPEG-2 is the standard for DVD movies, and it can't be played back in the QuickTime Player. (Other, higher-end applications can be used to translate to and from MPEG-2.)

DV Stream (.dv)   Digital camcorders store images in a computer file format rather than on analog tape in VHS or Betamax formats. This computer file is a digital video (DV, or DV Stream) file, which QuickTime can launch and play back directly. If you work with iMovie or other Apple movie-editing software, you may find yourself exporting DV Stream files, using the QuickTime Pro Player for some editing, then re-importing the DV Stream file into iMovie or Final Cut Pro. One word of caution: DV Stream files are *huge*, requiring up to 3.5MB per second of video.

QuickTime can handle more than just video formats, however. It can also launch, play back, and translate between a number of audio formats, such as these:

AIFF (.aif or .aiff)   The Audio Interchange File Format has been an Apple standard for a number of years and is still very popular for recording and playing back sounds and music.

WAV (.wav)   WAV (short for *wavetable*) is a common format on the Microsoft Windows platform, used much the same way as AIFF—for recording small sound files, sound effects, and occasionally longer sound bites.

AU (.au)   AU (short for *audio*) is a common Unix-based audio format, originally developed by Sun Microsystems.

Sound Designer II   Many Mac-based sound-editing applications can work with the file format that was once the most popular among them: Sound Designer II. The QuickTime Player and applications based on QuickTime technology can work with such files, too.

MPEG-3 (`.mp3`**)**   The hottest new audio file format in quite some time is MPEG-3, also called MP3. This format offers a high level of compression while still maintaining almost CD-quality sound, resulting in files that require only about 1MB per minute of playback. These features have made MP3s popular for Internet downloads and swaps, and that popularity has encouraged Apple to include the ability to play back MP3s in the QuickTime Player.

MIDI (`.mid` or `.midi`**)**   MIDI, which stands for Musical Instrument Digital Interface, is a special case. A MIDI file is actually a set of instructions to MIDI-capable musical instruments—it's not a digital audio format as much as it's a special format all its own. Still, QuickTime includes a MIDI Musical Instruments library that enables QuickTime to play MIDI files directly and save MIDI information as a QuickTime movie.

Want more? QuickTime can also translate between various still-image formats. (This capability isn't built directly into the QuickTime Player, but it's available to other graphical applications that are based on QuickTime technology.) The possible formats include TIFF, PICT, PDF, Windows Bitmap (BMP), Adobe Photoshop, Portable Network Graphics (PNG), JPEG, and GIF files. QuickTime can even work with Macromedia Flash data and import and export some data as FLC animation documents.

As mentioned, all these capabilities are found in QuickTime technology, where application developers can get at the APIs and make the tools available to users. One such application is the QuickTime Player (particularly the Pro version), which is described in the following section.

The QuickTime Player

Mac OS X includes the QuickTime Player, an application designed not only as a showcase for QuickTime technology but as a practical little application in its own right. The QuickTime Player can be used immediately to play back just about any type of QuickTime-compatible file you can throw at it, including audio, movie, and text-only documents and files. If you've got something that you think is time-based and you're trying to "play" it, the QuickTime Player is where you should start.

Playing QuickTime Movies

You can open a QuickTime-compatible file in any of the standard ways: Double-click the file, drag and drop the file onto a QuickTime Player icon (or the Player's tile on the Dock), or use the File ➤ Open command in the QuickTime Player's menu. Note that some files—images, audio files, and non-QuickTime video files—won't always open directly in the QuickTime Player when you double-click them. (They may be associated with other applications, as discussed back in Chapter 5.) If that's the case, drag and drop the file onto the QuickTime Player icon or tile, or use the File ➤ Open command.

Once you have a file open in the QuickTime Player, you'll see the QuickTime Player interface. This interface is the same, whether you're dealing with audio or video (remember, QuickTime documents are collectively called "movies," even if they don't have a video track). The Player includes a number of controls that should be fairly familiar—they're based on the typical controls one would find on a VCR or cassette player (see Figure 15.3).

To select one of the controls, you simply click the button using the mouse; for Review and Fast Forward *while* the movie is playing, you need to click and hold down the mouse button. To select a volume level, click and drag the small Volume slider.

You can also use the keyboard to control some commands with the QuickTime Player:

- Press the spacebar to toggle between Play and Pause.

- Press the left and right arrows to move back one frame or forward one frame, respectively.

- Press ⌘+left arrow to watch the movie backward; press ⌘+right arrow to watch it forward.

- Press Option+left arrow to move to the beginning of the movie; press Option+right arrow to move to the end.

- Press the up and down arrows to change the volume level.

If you'd like to go directly to a particular part of your QuickTime movie, you can drag the small *playhead* around on the *scrubber bar*, which is the small scrolling area that shows you where you are currently while you're playing your movie. You can also simply click on the scrubber bar to place the playhead.

You can move the playhead to a new position to immediately move to a different part of the movie. If you do so while the movie is playing, the QuickTime Player won't miss a beat—it'll pick up and continue playing from that point.

FIGURE 15.3

The QuickTime Player offers the same controls for audio and video playback.

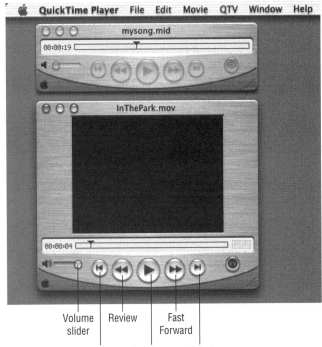

Volume slider   Review   Fast Forward

To Beginning   Play/Pause   To End

As in many Mac OS X windows, you can drag the bottom-right corner (the resize area) of a QuickTime movie window to change the size of the window. Because it's a QuickTime movie, you'll also notice that the size of the video track (if you have one) changes as you drag. By default, the video image will maintain its current *aspect ratio*, meaning that the ratio of its width to its height will stay the same. If you'd like to distort that ratio so that the image is exactly the same size as the window that you drag to create, hold down the Shift key while you drag the resize area.

 TIP If you drag the image out of proportion and want it to snap back, select Movie ➢ Normal Size from the QuickTime Player's menu.

While you're viewing a QuickTime movie with a video track, you also have a few basic options for changing the size of the video. Select the Movie menu, and you'll see Normal Size, Double Size, and Fill Screen as options. Although a movie that's originally small usually won't look good if it fills the screen (it becomes very *pixelated*

with details that are difficult to make out), you can sometimes double some Internet- or CD-based QuickTime movies and have them look pretty good on your Mac's screen.

The QuickTime Player also has some hidden sound controls that you can access by selecting Movie ➢ Show Sound Controls. The controls will appear in the scrubber bar area, enabling you to set Balance, Bass, and Treble response.

To return to the scrubber bar interface, select Movie ➢ Hide Sound Controls.

QuickTime Player Preferences

Options governing how QuickTime movies play back can be found in the preferences (QuickTime Player ➢ Preferences ➢ Player Preferences). In the General Preferences dialog box, you can turn off the "Play sound when application is in the background" option if you want to hear movies only when the QuickTime Player is in the foreground. Turn off "Play sound in front-most player only" if you'd like to hear more than one movie's sound at once (or if you'd like to listen to one movie even while you're moving others around on the screen).

You'll also find options that control the automatic behavior of the QuickTime Player, including "Automatically play movies when opened" and "Open movies in new players," an option that opens each newly double-clicked movie in a new Player window. (Opening additional players can be particularly useful when editing Quick-Time movies, which is discussed later in the section "Editing in QuickTime Pro Player.")

The QuickTime Controller

You won't always be playing QuickTime movies in the QuickTime Player. Often you'll find yourself playing the movies in Finder windows to preview them or playing them in other applications where you've embedded the QuickTime movie in a document. You may even find yourself controlling a QuickTime movie that's playing over the Internet in a Web browser window. In those cases you'll see the somewhat simpler controller (compared to the QuickTime Player), shown in Figure 15.4.

FIGURE 15.4

The QuickTime controller within other applications, such as the Finder's Info window, offers simpler controls.

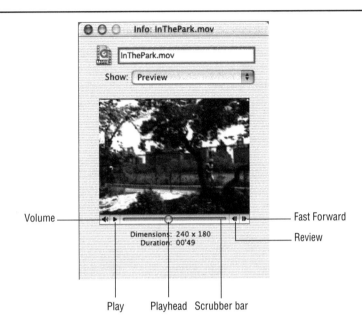

Volume — — Fast Forward

Dimensions: 240 x 180
Duration: 00'49

— Review

Play   Playhead   Scrubber bar

You may encounter another special case as well. In some documents and applications, you won't even see the simple controller. Instead, you'll see a *poster frame* (a single image from the movie, often the first frame) along with a small QuickTime icon in the bottom-left corner.

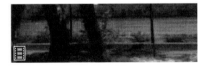

Click the movie once, and it should begin playing. If it doesn't, that may be because it's set to play automatically when the application enters a particular mode. For instance, in presentation applications such as Microsoft PowerPoint, QuickTime movies can be set to play automatically when a particular slide is displayed. (Remember, QuickTime movies can be audio-only, meaning that a PowerPoint presentation, for example, could be narrated using a voice recording saved as a QuickTime Movie file.)

Playing QuickTime VR Movies

QuickTime VR movies are a slightly different animal—actually two animals. QuickTime VR movies can take one of two forms: 360-degree panoramic views that you can maneuver by using the mouse, or 3-D views of individual objects that you can manipulate to see from all sides. QuickTime VR is a particularly popular technology with real estate agents, who use the scrolling panoramas to show entire rooms in for-sale houses, and car manufacturers, who use 3-D VR movies to show a car from all sides.

When you launch a QuickTime VR movie, you'll see a slightly different QuickTime Player window with different controls for manipulating the movie. Because you don't play a VR movie linearly, the Play button is grayed. Instead, you'll see buttons for zooming in and out, for returning to the "home" view of the movie, and for revealing *hot points*—points that can be clicked within the virtual reality scene. (These hot points can be clicked to move to a new scene—sort of like a 3-D action adventure game—or to view more information or even a Web page about the clicked item.) Figure 15.5 shows those unique controls used for QuickTime VR movies.

FIGURE 15.5

The QuickTime Player controls change when viewing VR movies.

To Home view

Zoom out   Zoom in

Show hot spots

Along with the new controls come new behaviors for the mouse. If you click and drag within the scene, you'll move it; either you'll move the panorama or you'll rotate the 3-D object, depending on what you're viewing. You'll note that clicking and dragging changes the mouse pointer to either a four-way pointer or a fist, depending on the type of movie you're viewing. You can also use keyboard keys and modifiers:

• Zoom in and out by pressing the Shift and Control keys, respectively.

- Use the arrow keys to move around in the scene.
- If you're viewing a panorama and the pointer turns into a forward-pointing arrow, you've found a hot spot. Click the mouse button to load the associated movie or Web document.

Registering QuickTime Pro

There is one dirty little secret about the QuickTime Player that you should know: It's hiding stuff from you. Specifically, it's hiding a number of commands, ranging from additional viewing options to commands that enable you to save and translate between different file formats. Why? Because Apple wants you to pay for those privileges. For $29.95 (at the time of writing), you can register QuickTime with Apple, which results in a registration code. Simply visit www.apple.com/quicktime/ and look for the registration link (or click the Register On-line button in the Registration dialog box shown below).

 NOTE Even if you already have a QuickTime Pro registration key for an earlier version (3.0 or 4.0) of QuickTime, you'll need to pay again for a QuickTime Pro 5.0 registration key. Apple has decided, with version 5.0, to charge all users again to upgrade. (Exception: If you paid for your key for QuickTime 4 after November 2000, it may still work.)

Once you have a registration code, enter that number (along with your name and the name of your organization, if applicable) in the Registration window within the Quick-Time Player (from the Application menu, select QuickTime Player ➤ Preferences ➤ Registration). Click the Edit Registration button to begin entering the items (note that the registration number in the following image is invalid):

Registration...

Registered to: Todd Stauffer

Organization: Mac-Upgrade.com

Number: AAAA-BBBB-CCCC-7777-FFFF

QuickTime Key: Standard Edition

Edit Registration

Register On-line...

Cancel   OK

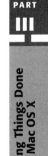

After you've entered the requisite information, click the OK button. If your registration is accepted, you'll now have the QuickTime Pro Player version, with all of its additional capabilities. They include:

- The ability to save, import, and export movies in various formats

- Additional movie sizes in the Movie menu, including the Present Movie command, which blanks the rest of the screen and shows the movie at the largest size possible

- The Movie ➤ Loop Back and Forth command, which enables you to play a movie forward, then backward, repeatedly

- The ability to select a portion of the movie by holding down the Shift key and dragging along the scrubber bar

- Hidden editing and special-effects commands, including the ability to selectively cut, copy, paste, enable, disable, or delete tracks within an individual movie file

You'll see more on the editing features of QuickTime movies later in this chapter. First, though, let's move on to some additional freebie capabilities: viewing streaming QuickTime movies and QuickTime TV over the Internet.

QuickTime on the Internet

As we discussed in Chapter 11, Microsoft Internet Explorer (the Web browser included with Mac OS X) contains a QuickTime plug-in that enables you to view QuickTime movies that are embedded in Web pages. This trick makes it possible for a basic QuickTime interface to appear right there in the browser window, where you can play, pause, review, and fast-forward a movie that's downloaded from a remote Internet server.

Beyond that capability, a few others are made possible by QuickTime's Internet awareness. One such feature is called *streaming*—the ability to display a QuickTime movie while the data for that movie is still being downloaded to your Mac. With a quick enough Internet connection, you can watch live events or view saved QuickTime movies almost immediately upon clicking the link. This differs from embedded and downloaded movies, as you must generally wait for the entire movie (or almost the entire movie) to download to your Mac before you can see it displayed.

This category of streaming movies has opened up another feature in the QuickTime Player: QuickTime TV. That's Apple's name for a number of "channels" of streaming video that can be accessed quickly via the QuickTime Player's special TV button. Click the TV button in the QuickTime Player window, then click one of the channels to begin viewing news, entertainment, and educational features right over the Internet. Better yet, all these capabilities are enabled in the basic, free version of QuickTime Player—no upgrade to QuickTime Pro is required.

 NOTE One thing that does require the upgrade to QuickTime Pro is the ability to save some Internet-based QuickTime movies to your local disk. If you've upgraded, you can hold down Control while clicking an embedded QuickTime movie, then choose Save as QuickTime Movie from the pop-up contextual menu. You'll then be able to give the movie a name and save it to disk for repeated viewing. (Note that some servers will use special commands to disable this feature, and you won't be able to save live, streaming movies.)

Streaming QuickTime

You can view a streaming QuickTime movie in one of two ways: in the simple Quick-Time controls of an embedded movie on a Web page or in the QuickTime Player itself. Generally, you won't have much control over which way you view—it's up to the Web developer who created the page where the movie is hosted. Click a link to a streaming movie, and either you'll see it appear on the page or you'll see the Quick-Time Player launched, in which case the movie will appear in a new QuickTime Player window.

 TIP QuickTime Streaming Server comes with Mac OS X Server and can be installed for free in some other situations. (There's an open-source version that Apple has released that has been turned into freeware ports to Mac OS 9.x and other operating systems.) Quick-Time Streaming Server is discussed in some detail in Chapter 25.

So how do you know that you're watching (or listening to, if the movie is audio-only) a streaming QuickTime movie? You'll know because you'll see special messages in the scrubber bar area of the window. First you'll see the Negotiating message, which means the QuickTime Player is determining what protocols and how much data your Internet connection can handle, which in turn determines the size and quality of the image. (The Connection Speed setting in QuickTime Preferences can affect this, as discussed in the next Note.) Then you'll see the Buffering message, which shows you how much QuickTime data is being temporarily stored on your hard disk so that the playback can be as smooth and "skip"-free as possible.

PART

III

Getting Things Done
with Mac OS X

There are two basic types of streaming video: stored video and live *webcasts*. You can't use the Review and Fast Forward buttons while viewing either type of streaming movie. With stored video, however, you can move the playhead around on the scrubber bar to start viewing the movie at a different point. When you do this, the Player is forced to reconnect to the server and renegotiate the connection, so it may take a few seconds before you're seeing the video.

With live webcasts, you generally can't move around in the streaming video at all, because you're watching the event as it's happening. With some webcasts, though, you can click the Pause button, which is really like pressing the power button on a TV. When you subsequently click the Play button, the webcast will pick up at the current moment in the webcast, as if you had turned a TV back on again.

Streaming movies act differently from regular Web movies because the QuickTime Player is actually connecting to a different type of Internet server. Instead of connecting to a Web server, it's accessing a special type of QuickTime movie (called a *hinted* movie) that has been stored on a QuickTime Streaming Server. The file is then accessed using a different Internet protocol, the Real-Time Transport Protocol (RTP). So, URLs to streaming QuickTime movies begin with `rtp://`. In fact, the QuickTime Player includes a File ➤ Open URL command, which results in an entry box where you can enter a URL for the streaming movie:

If the movie isn't a streaming movie, it can still be accessed directly via the File ➤ Open URL command, but with a conventional URL such as `http://www.mac-upgrade.com/movies/mymovie.mov`. (Note that some streaming movies can use the `http://` protocol, depending on the server.) In that case the movie will be downloaded to your Mac as usual, then played back in the QuickTime Player window.

NOTE You can set certain preferences for the way streaming movies are sent to your Mac. Select QuickTime Player ➤ Preferences ➤ QuickTime Preferences. In the QuickTime pane of the System Preferences application, click the Connection tab. Then, use the Connection Speed menu to tell QuickTime Player what sort of connection you have to the Internet. This enables it to automatically configure an optimum data stream whenever possible. Other options can be found by clicking the Transport Setup button; in the Streaming Transport Setup dialog box, you can choose a transport method and/or port. In most cases, you shouldn't need to set these preferences unless your ISP or system administrator tells you to. If you're not sure of the settings, you can leave them as they are, or click the Auto Configure button if you seem to be having trouble with streaming movies.

QuickTime TV

Once Apple added this streaming capability to QuickTime, the company seems to have realized that it had an interesting opportunity on its hands. The result was QuickTime TV, where media outlets from around the world can have an icon built right into your QuickTime Player interface. Click the TV icon in a QuickTime Player window (or select QTV ➤ Show QuickTime TV Channels), and the movie area is replaced with a screen full of icons, representing channels (see Figure 15.6).

FIGURE 15.6

The QuickTime TV lineup of channels

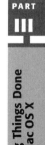

Click a channel, and the window will once again reconfigure to show you the options on that channel. In most cases you'll see a brief introductory movie that includes clickable Macromedia Flash buttons. (Sometimes you'll just go directly to a streaming feed, such as when you click the BBC World icon.) If you're seeing Flash controls, click a button or link, and the associated streaming audio or video will play in the QuickTime Player.

Once you've chosen a channel you like, you can assign it as a QuickTime Favorite. Choose QTV ➢ Favorites ➢ Add Movie as Favorite. That way, you can access it quickly by clicking the Favorites tab in the QuickTime Player window or by choosing it from the QTV ➢ Favorites menu.

 TIP While a movie is playing, you'll often be able to get a little extra information about it by selecting Window ➢ Show Movie Info, which will provide some vital statistics, including the file's name and copyright information, URL, data rate, and other interesting tidbits.

Advanced Topics with QuickTime Pro

In the earlier section "Registering QuickTime Pro," you saw some of the benefits that come from paying the $30 to register and upgrade your version of QuickTime. While some of those features are additional options for playing back and saving movies, the real benefits are found in some considerably more sophisticated tools that enable you to use the QuickTime Player as a QuickTime file translator and a movie editor of sorts. In this section I'll cover some of those capabilities in more depth.

Translating File Formats

QuickTime technology enables application developers to offer quite a few different translation capabilities between movie formats, audio formats, and even still-image formats. The free QuickTime Player doesn't give much access to these capabilities, but once you've upgraded to QuickTime Pro, you can access more of them. They break down into import and export features.

Importing and Saving Files

If you can't directly open a particular type of sound file or movie in the QuickTime Pro Player, try choosing File ➢ Import and opening the movie that way. A new

QuickTime Movie document will be created with the video or audio from the imported file. (QuickTime Pro can import the formats listed earlier in the section "What Can QuickTime Play?")

To save the imported movie as a QuickTime Movie file, choose File ➢ Save and use the standard Save dialog box to select a folder and give the file a name.

Before you click Save in the Save dialog box, you'll need to choose either Save Normally or Make Movie Self-Contained. Save Normally creates a QuickTime movie that doesn't necessarily include all of the translated movie's data in the new movie file. In other words, you'll still need to have the original movie file available on your disk—in fact, the original often needs to be in the same location. The Make Movie Self-Contained option is the better choice if you plan to place the QuickTime Movie file on a removable disk or network volume or if you intend to transmit the movie over the Internet, since all of the translated movie data is included in the newly created QuickTime Movie file.

Once you've made your choice, click Save.

Exporting Files

You use the Save command to save any sort of imported or edited movie as a Quick-Time Movie file. But what if you want to save a QuickTime movie in some other multimedia file format? In that case you need to export. With the movie open that you'd like to export, choose File ➢ Export from the menu.

PART

III

Getting Things Done
with Mac OS X

 NOTE   Actually, there are two reasons to export your movie. The first is to get the movie into a different file format; you can export QuickTime movie data as a Windows-friendly AVI movie, for instance, or you can export an MP3 audio file as an AIFF file for easy editing in Macintosh sound editors. Second, you can export data from a QuickTime Movie file to another QuickTime Movie file. This might seem redundant, but performing this export gives you the opportunity to make some advanced choices—you can select a different codec and quality levels via the Options button discussed in this section.

You may notice that the dialog box, shown in Figure 15.7, looks a little different from the standard Save dialog box. The Save Exported File As dialog box includes some additional menus as well as an Options button.

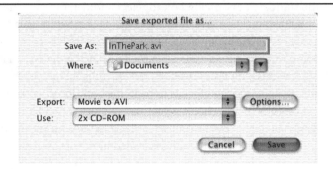

In the Export menu, choose how you'd like the movie to be exported. You'll find two basic types of options: Movie To and Sound To. If you're exporting a QuickTime movie that has both video and audio components, you'll see both types of options. If your movie has only a soundtrack, you'll see only Sound To options; if your movie has only a video track, you'll see only Movie To options. The Movie To options include a number of file formats—both video formats and still-image formats—that were discussed in the earlier section "What Can QuickTime Play?"; likewise, the Sound To options include many of the audio file formats discussed in that section. You'll notice that not *all* of the file formats are discussed; that's because QuickTime can read and play back more formats than it can export to. For more export options, you generally need to turn to a third-party application such as Terran Interactive's Movie Cleaner series of applications. (Terran's Web address is `www.terran.com`.)

Once you've chosen an option in the Export menu, you select, from the Use menu, *how* the movie will be exported. The options you see in the Use menu depend on the type of export you're performing. If you're exporting a movie that includes video to the AVI format, you'll see a few preset options for the compression and frame rate for that particular movie:

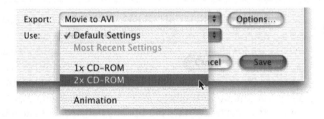

If you export the audio within your movie to an audio file format, you'll see options in the Use menu for selecting the quality of the sound file, such as "44.1kHz 16-Bit Stereo" (CD quality) or "11.025kHz 16-Bit Mono" (approximately AM-radio quality). Make your selection in the Use menu, then click Save to save the exported file.

Before you click the Save button, however, you may want to dig even deeper into the compression settings. The Options button gives you access to the advanced settings that are possible for audio and video compression and quality levels. You'll need to know a little something about codecs and other settings in order to make sense of these options. (That's why the Use menu is there; it offers simpler preset codec and quality settings.)

After you click the Options button, the particular Movie Settings dialog box you see depends on the type of file you're exporting to. If you're exporting video and audio to a movie format, you'll see a Movie Settings dialog box that includes controls for both video and sound settings. Select either the Video Settings button or the Sound Settings button to dig deeper into those settings (see Figure 15.8). Note that if you've chosen to export to QuickTime Movie format, you can also choose to Prepare for Internet Streaming. (If you're exporting to other formats, you won't see this option.)

FIGURE 15.8

Select Options when exporting to a movie format, and you can then select both the Video and Audio Settings buttons to set quality levels.

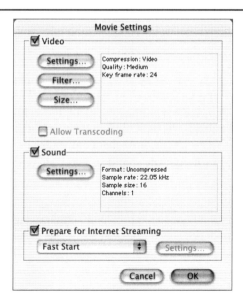

PART

III

Getting Things Done
with Mac OS X

If you're exporting directly to a still-image format, clicking Options brings up the Compression Settings dialog box. Here you can select the type of compressor to use for the image you're creating. For most still images you'll use a compressor that matches the image file format, such as TIFF for TIFF files and JPEG for JPEG files, with the exception of Picture, which can also use JPEG compression. You may also find other settings such as a color depth menu and a Quality slider. The higher the quality, the larger the exported image file will be.

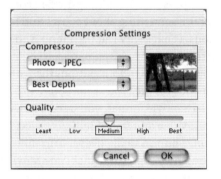

 TIP This Compression Settings dialog box is also what you'll see if you've chosen Options for exporting to a movie file format and then clicked the Video Settings button (shown in Figure 15.8). For video, however, you'll often have additional options in the Motion section, including the number of frames per second and the data rate for the movie.

If you're exporting directly to an audio file format, you'll see the Sound Settings dialog box. Here you can choose a compressor (codec) for the audio file, along with a *sample rate* (the kHz number that contributes to sound quality), a *size* (either 8-bit or 16-bit), and whether the sound should be exported as mono or as stereo.

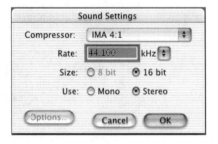

TIP This Sound Settings dialog box is what you'll see if you've chosen Options for exporting to a movie file format and then clicked the Audio Settings button (shown in Figure 15.8).

So what do you select for all these settings? Unfortunately, that's a bit outside the scope of this book. For QuickTime movies, either the Sorensen or Cinepak codecs are recommended for hard-disk and CD-ROM playback; if you intend to save a QuickTime movie for playback over the Internet, the Use menu in the Export dialog box offers some good presets. As noted, still images are best compressed with the codec that matches the file format, e.g., TIFF codec for TIFF file format. For a quick discussion of audio quality, see the sidebar "Understanding Audio Quality."

Understanding Audio Quality

While video quality is a function of codecs, frame rate, and keyframes, audio quality is measured by some different standards. The key factors for audio quality are the sample rate (measured in kilohertz), the sample size (either 8-bit or 16-bit), and the number of channels (mono or stereo).

When a computer stores a digital-sound file, it does so by creating thousands of *samples* of that sound per second. Unlike a cassette tape or similar analog device, a computer can't simply record the analog source; instead, it takes samples of the sound and records them digitally. The more samples per second, the more "true" the reproduction of the sound is. But more samples mean a larger computer file, so there's some balancing to be done.

A digital recording at CD quality has a sample rate of 44.1kHz, or 44,100 samples per second. FM-radio quality is about 22kHz, and AM-radio quality is about 11kHz. Much lower than that, and the sound file approaches the quality of a telephone call.

The next indicator of audio quality is the *sample size*, which is usually either 8-bit or 16-bit, meaning that either 256 numbers can be used to represent the sample or 65,536 numbers. 16-bit is much preferred in this case, because the human ear can distinguish more than 256 sounds; in an 8-bit sample, a lot of the quality of the sound is lost by "rounding" the sound down to those 256 numbers. 8-bit sound files require a lot less storage space, but it's an extreme compromise.

Finally, the *channel depth,* or number of channels used, means simply that you can select mono or stereo sound for your exported sound files. Mono takes up less storage space, while stereo, of course, offers better sound quality.

PART

III

Getting Things Done
with Mac OS X

TIP Apple offers additional information about codecs and file formats for QuickTime "authors" at www.apple.com/quicktime/products/tutorials/ on the Web.

Editing in QuickTime Pro Player

Once you've upgraded to QuickTime Pro, you'll find that you're free not only to save and export your movies but to edit them as well. Using the scrubber bar and play-head, you can select portions of your QuickTime movies, then copy and paste them between other movies. You can also enable and disable tracks within movies and paste one track over another, if desired.

 TIP With a movie open in QuickTime Player, select Movie ➢ Get Movie Properties or press Shift+⌘+I to see the Movie Properties palette. You'll find a number of properties settings you can play with, including some that let you adjust the volume and quality settings and even perform a special effect or two.

Selecting Movie Portions

You begin editing in QuickTime Player by selecting part of a movie that you'd like to copy or cut from the current movie. You can do this in a few different ways. One way is to place the playhead on the scrubber bar at the point in the movie where you'd like to begin the selection. Then hold down the Shift key and drag the playhead to the end point of your selection. When you've done that, a portion of your movie will be grayed (selected) in the scrubber bar.

 TIP Hold down the Shift key while pressing the left and right arrows to fine-tune your selection with the playhead.

You can also make a selection (or change an existing one) by dragging the small selection triangles that appear beneath the scrubber bar. The triangles represent the "in" and "out" points on your selection, so you can drag them around to make a more exact choice.

Once you've made a selection, you may wish to clear that selection so you can try again. To do that, select Edit ➢ Select None or press ⌘+B. Notice also that you can select the entire movie by choosing Edit ➢ Select All or pressing ⌘+A.

Editing Commands

With a portion of your movie selected, you're ready to issue a command. Using the Edit menu, you can choose Edit ➢ Copy to place that selection on the Mac's clipboard or Edit ➢ Cut to place the selection on the clipboard and remove it from the current movie. Then you can move to another QuickTime movie window, place the playhead, and select Edit ➢ Paste to paste the selection into the target movie (see Figure 15.9).

 NOTE Remember that you can opt to have QuickTime automatically open new movies in their own Player windows, which is convenient for editing work. Select QuickTime Player ➢ Preferences ➢ Player Preferences and turn on the Open Movies in New Players option in the General Preferences dialog box.

As you might guess, it's best to copy and paste between movies that are the same size (in width and height). If you paste together movies of different sizes, you'll end up forcing portions of the movie to play with large borders so that the largest of the clips can be accommodated in the Player window.

Besides Copy and Paste, you can use some other special commands in the Edit menu to do some editing. Begin by selecting a portion of your movie, then do the following to perform some interesting edits:

- Select Edit ➢ Clear to delete that selection from the movie.

- Choose Edit ➢ Trim to crop the selection. (Only the selected clip will remain, and the rest of the movie will be cleared out.)

- The Edit ➢ Add command adds the copied material to the second movie as another track, beginning at the point where the playhead has been placed in the

PART

III

Getting Things Done
with Mac OS X

target movie. This is particularly useful for adding other *types* of tracks to a movie; for instance, you could copy music from an audio-only movie and then use the Edit ➤ Add command to add that audio as a soundtrack in the second movie.

- The Edit ➤ Add Scaled command is similar, except that it makes the track it creates exactly as long as the selection in the target movie. For example, if you copy 4 seconds worth of audio from one movie, then select 2 seconds' worth of the target movie and click Edit ➤ Add Scaled, QuickTime will squeeze that audio down to 2 seconds. Of course, sound played at double time isn't terribly useful, so the Add Scaled command is normally used for adding still images. Select an image that's the same size of your movie, copy it, and then choose Edit ➤ Add Scaled to add it to your movie. (Note that when you add images in this way, you're not replacing part of the existing movie—for instance, you will still hear the audio portion of the target movie while you're viewing the still image.)

- The Edit ➤ Replace command is used to replace the selected portion of the target movie with the copied clip.

Selecting Tracks

With QuickTime Pro Player you can turn on and off the tracks individually within your movie. You can also extract individual tracks from a movie (such as the video track or the soundtrack) into new one-track QuickTime movies, which you can then use with the Add and other editing commands to add video over the soundtrack of another movie, for instance. The extracted track is copied from the original and placed in a new movie file, while the original movie is left untouched (it still has all its tracks intact).

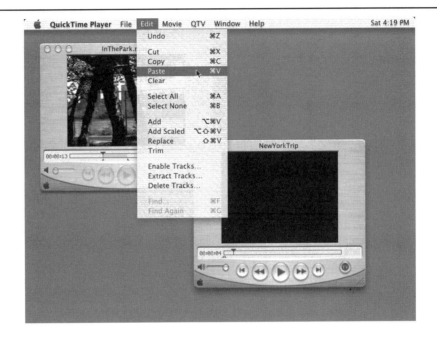

FIGURE 15.9

Copy a portion from the first movie and paste it into the second.

With a QuickTime movie open in a Player window, select Edit ➤ Extract Tracks if you'd like to extract a track. In the Extract Tracks dialog box, select the track you'd like to extract and click Extract. Once extracted, the new track appears in its own untitled Player window. Figure 15.10 shows a soundtrack that has been extracted from the movie behind it.

Besides extracting tracks, you can also delete them by selecting Edit ➤ Delete Tracks. In the Delete Tracks dialog box, select the track you want to delete and click Delete. It will be removed from the movie.

To turn tracks on and off, select Edit ➤ Enable Tracks. In the Enable Tracks dialog box, select the track you'd like to turn on or off as the case may be. A small icon next to each track shows its current state.

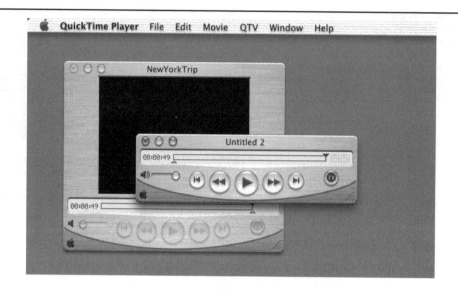

When you've finished enabling or disabling tracks, click the OK button.

QuickTime Preferences

Throughout this chapter you've seen the preferences you can set in the QuickTime Player application, and you've seen how to enter registration information for Quick-Time Pro. QuickTime also stores another set of preferences in the System Preferences application.

Launch System Preferences and select the QuickTime icon to open the QuickTime pane. There you'll see a number of tabs for setting QuickTime preferences, including Plug-In, Connection, Music, Media Keys, and Update. You've already seen the Connection options (in the section "Streaming QuickTime"), but you may find some of the others interesting as well.

Plug-In

On the Plug-In tab, you'll see options for the QuickTime plug-in—the software that makes it possible to view QuickTime movies in a Web browser window. Place a check mark next to any of the options that you'd like to turn on.

Play Movies Automatically   This option causes movies to be played as they're downloaded to your Web browser, without requiring you to click the Play button in the QuickTime controller.

Save Movies in Disk Cache   When this option is turned on, some movies, when viewed, will be stored in your Internet browser's cache. That means that returning to the movie might be easy; since it's already stored on your hard disk, the movie should play more quickly than if it's downloaded. QuickTime movies tend to be large files, however, so you may want this option turned off to prevent your Web browser's cache from filling with the movie (and, hence, very little else).

Enable Kiosk Mode   When this option is turned on, it isn't possible to Control+click a movie to see a contextual menu that enables you to save the movie.

Music

On the Music tab you can select a MIDI synthesizer to make it the default. This is useful if you've installed additional MIDI synthesizers that you'd prefer to use over QuickTime's included Music Synthesizer.

Media Keys

Media keys are special codes that you can use to access movies, sound files, and other multimedia files that require confirmation of your identity. Some QuickTime movies can include "secured" tracks that require a special key for playback, generally in exchange for having paid for the movie or song.

Update

On the Update tab, you can choose to manually update QuickTime or to turn on the option "Check for updates automatically," which will cause QuickTime to look for updates whenever it accesses the Internet for some other reason. To update manually, select one of the two choices at the top of the screen—"Update or install Quick-Time software" or "Install new 3rd-party QuickTime software"—and then click the Update Now button. If new QuickTime components are available, you'll see the QuickTime Updater appear, ready to walk you through the update process (see Figure 15.11).

PART

III

Getting Things Done
with Mac OS X

FIGURE 15.11

The QuickTime Updater will tell you whether or not new QuickTime components are available.

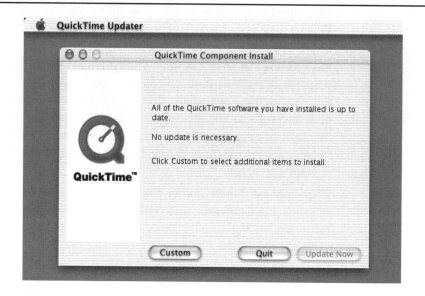

What's Next?

In this chapter you saw how to work and play with QuickTime, both in the QuickTime Player and in other applications. You learned what types of multimedia files can be imported and played back by the QuickTime Player and other QuickTime-enabled applications. You also saw how to work with streaming Internet and QuickTime TV. Next, you saw the power of the QuickTime Pro edition, which enables you to import, export, and edit QuickTime movies. Finally, you saw some of the QuickTime preference settings in the System Preferences application.

In the next chapter we'll move on to some of the other applications bundled with the Mac OS that allow you to work with CD, MP3 audio, and even DVD movies. Plus, you'll get a look at some of the technologies that enable you to use speech commands to communicate with your Mac.

CHAPTER <u>16</u>

Music, DVD Movies, and Speech

Although Mac OS X is a fully multimedia-ready and savvy OS, thanks to the inclusion of QuickTime and OpenGL technologies, the 10.0 version of the operating system is hit or miss for some of the basic multimedia tasks that you may want to perform with your Mac. At the time that Mac OS X shipped, no software for playing CDs and MP3s (digital music files) was available as part of the base installation. Another feature lacking in the original Mac OS X release is the ability to play DVD movies.

iTunes, Apple's CD/MP3 player and Internet music application, was made available for immediate download when Mac OS X was released, and it should be included with later Mac OS X installation CDs. So, if you have something other than the earliest release of Mac OS X, you may have iTunes; otherwise, you can download it. As of this writing, no Mac OS X native DVD player is available, but you can boot into Mac OS 9.1 (which does include the ability to play DVD movies on most Mac models that support DVD playback) to play back DVD movies, if desired.

Mac OS X includes an implementation of Apple's PlainTalk technology, which allows for Text-to-Speech and Speech Recognition—at least, on a limited basis. Again, this is new technology (for Mac OS X), which was included late in the development process. Not many Mac OS X applications support speech technology, but it is something you can play with, if you like.

In this chapter, we'll take an in-depth look at iTunes, as well as how to watch DVD movies from Mac OS 9.1 and use Mac OS X's text-to-speech and speech-recognition features.

 NOTE If and when Apple ships a DVD player with Mac OS X, check the Sybex Web site (www.sybex.com) for up-to-date information about playing DVDs. Just go to the search area and type the ISBN code **2581** or **Mastering Mac OS X**.

Playing CDs and MP3s

If you're interested in playing music CDs and/or MP3 files on your Mac, then you'll want to get to know iTunes. iTunes is a neat application that Apple has written in the spirit of some of its other consumer offerings, such as iMovie, to help you accomplish music-related tasks using a friendly, simple interface. iTunes enables you to create libraries of music, arrange your songs into custom playlists, and generally turn your Mac into a capable little stereo system.

MP3 (which is short for MPEG3) is actually a special compression scheme that results in high-quality audio files, almost indistinguishable in sound quality from CD audio. The size of an MP3 file is only a few megabytes for a standard-length song. That means MP3 files are easy to transmit across the Internet, which is exactly why they've ushered in a mini-revolution of sorts, including Napster "peer sharing" and other schemes (legal and otherwise), that have made MP3 audio popular. Apple jumped on this bandwagon by releasing iTunes, which can play CDs and MP3 files, as well as AIFF (the Mac audio standard) and WAV (the Windows audio standard) files.

If you don't already have iTunes as part of your Mac OS X installation, you'll need to download it. Visit www.apple.com/itunes/ and locate the latest version. After you've downloaded iTunes, install the application by mounting the disk image, then dragging the iTunes folder (not just the application, but the entire iTunes folder) to your Applications folder. If you don't have administrator privileges, you can drag the iTunes folder to your home folder. (If you downloaded iTunes using the Software Update pane in the System Preferences application, Mac OS X may have already installed it in the Applications folder for you.)

 NOTE iTunes 1.1 for Mac OS X doesn't currently support the ability to burn CDs from the playlists you create, which is a feature of the software under Mac OS 9.x. If you're interested in this capability and iTunes for Mac OS X hasn't yet been updated, you'll need to boot back into Mac OS 9.x to create a CD. iTunes 1.1 for Mac OS 9.1 includes the ability to burn audio CDs using both Apple's built-in CD-RW drives (in many of Apple's latest models) as well as many third-party CD-RW drives.

Launching iTunes

Once you've installed the iTunes folder, you can double-click its icon to launch it. The first time you launch the application, the iTunes Setup Assistant appears, asking you some basic questions about whether you would like to use iTunes for Internet playback (for playing MP3 audio streams that you access via the Web) and whether iTunes should automatically connect to the Internet when it wants to access online information. (For instance, iTunes can look up the name and playlist of your CDs using a standard online database, so that it can accurately report the artist and names of the songs on most audio CDs.)

Once you've made those decisions, the Assistant will ask if you would like to have iTunes search for MP3 files on your hard disk. If you select this option and click Next, the iTunes interface will appear and the application will begin searching the local volume for any MP3 files to which you have access.

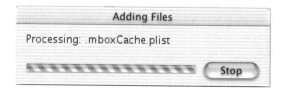

After iTunes is finished searching, any found MP3 files will be displayed in the main iTunes window. By default, all MP3 files are listed in the iTunes Library (see Figure 16.1), which can be selected in the Source list on the left side of the iTunes window. If you prefer, you can organize MP3s in other ways, as you'll learn in the next sections.

FIGURE 16.1

iTunes after your MP3s (if you have any on your hard disk) have been imported

Adding and Deleting Songs in the Library

After you have iTunes up and running, you may want to add new music files (in MP3, AIFF, or WAV format) to the Library or delete files from the list.

You can add music files in two ways:

- Select File ➢ Add to Library and, in the Choose Object dialog box, locate either a song file or a folder of song files that you would like to add; then select Choose. The songs will be added to your Library.

- Drag a song file or a folder of song files to the iTunes window. Drop the file or folder, and the song(s) will be added to the Library.

Realize that iTunes doesn't actually copy or move the files. (In fact, you'll see a dialog box with a message to that effect.) So, if you add files from another user's folder or across a network connection, iTunes may not always be able to play those songs. The easiest solution is to copy the files to your personal Music folder or the iTunes Music folder, and then add them to the iTunes Library.

To delete a song from the Library, select it in the song list and press the Delete key on your keyboard. You'll see a dialog box asking you to confirm the deletion; click Yes if you really want to delete the song. Note that the song is not deleted from your hard disk; it is just removed from the Library. If you want to add it again, you'll need to drag the song to the iTunes window or use the File ➢ Add to Library command.

Playing Songs

Once iTunes has imported your song files into the Library, you can immediately begin playing them. To play a song, simply double-click it in the Library listing. You'll see a small speaker icon appear next to that song's entry, and you'll hear the song begin to play through your speakers. With the song playing, you can use the controls at the top-left corner of the window to control the playback.

These controls work much like those on a CD player:

- Click the Rewind button once to move to the previous song. If the current song has already played for more than a few seconds, clicking Rewind will start the song over at the beginning. If that happens, click it again to move to the previous song in the Library.

- While the song is playing, click and hold the Rewind button to move backward in the current song.

- Click the Forward button once to move to the next song.

- Click and hold the Forward button to move forward within the current song.

- Click the Pause button to pause playback.

The slider below these controls changes the volume of the playback. You can also use the slider in the information area (where the song's title is shown at the top of the iTunes window) to move forward and backward within a song.

 TIP The Controls menu duplicates many of the playback controls with menu commands. And, in many cases, there are also keyboard shortcuts for controlling song playback.

Playing Audio CDs

If you would like to play songs from an audio CD, insert the CD in your Mac's CD (or DVD) drive. The audio CD should be recognized and, after a few seconds, the songs will be displayed in the iTunes window. You'll also see a CD icon appear in the Source list of the iTunes window (under the Radio Tuner icon). If you've opted to allow iTunes to access the Internet, it will attempt to access an online database (the CDDB) to learn the name of the CD and the names of the songs on that CD's playlist (see Figure 16.2).

 NOTE CDDB (www.gracenote.com) is a database of CD names and playlists that is made available to software developers, such as Apple, for inclusion in their CD-playing applications. Your Internet connection must be active before a CDDB lookup can be performed.

The controls for playing an audio CD are the same as those for playing songs in the Library. To eject a CD, click the small Eject button in the very bottom-right corner of the iTunes window.

FIGURE 16.2

iTunes has recognized an audio CD.

Managing Playback

Whether you're playing songs from the Library or from a CD, you can use three other CD player–like commands to manage the way songs are played:

- Controls ➤ Shuffle plays the songs in random order.
- Controls ➤ Repeat All causes the entire playlist or CD to be repeated indefinitely.
- Controls ➤ Repeat One causes the currently selected song to be repeated indefinitely.

You'll also find buttons for these commands on the bottom-left side of the iTunes window, next to the Add Playlist button. Click the Shuffle button (on the left) to play songs in random order. Click the Continuous button once to play the entire CD or playlist (or Library, if that is what is selected) continuously; click it again to play only the currently selected song continuously.

TIP iTunes has a fun little feature called Visuals, which changes the iTunes window into sort of a psychedelic music visualizer of sorts—it's great for parties. To turn on the effect, click the small eight-point-star-shaped icon in the bottom-right corner of the iTunes window or select Visuals ➤ Turn Visual On. (You can also press ⌘+T.) As a song plays back, the graphics follow it, making for an interesting effect. (In iTunes 1.1 for Mac OS X, visuals can't be full-screen size, as they can in iTunes 1.1 for Mac OS 9; if you have a later version, you may be able to see the visuals full-screen.)

Sorting, Searching, and Browsing

Whether you're viewing the Library or a CD list, you can sort the song list by clicking the headings at the top of the list: Song, Time, Artist, and so on. Note that the wider the iTunes window is, the more information you can see about individual songs, including the artist, album name, and genre.

You can also use the small Search entry box to search for a particular song, either in the Library or on a selected CD. To search, simply click in the Search entry box and begin typing your search text. You'll notice that iTunes begins finding matches as you type each letter, so you don't need to press Return after you've finished your keyword typing. In fact, you don't even need to finish your typing.

iTunes will attempt to find *all* entries that match the search text you enter. For instance, if you enter "blue" as your keyword, you'll see not only entries that are in the blues genre, but also any that have "blue" as part of the name of the song or album (or the artist, if that's relevant).

You'll likely find that searching is more useful once you've amassed a large collection of MP3 files in your Library. If you do have such a collection, you may also find that Browse mode is useful. With the Library icon selected (you can't browse a CD), click the Browse icon in the top-right corner of the iTunes window. Now you'll see the iTunes window reconfigure to help you dig through your collection of MP3s by artist, album, or both (see Figure 16.3). When you're finished browsing, click the Browse button again to return the window to its upright and locked position.

Trim down your Library listing by selecting an artist or album.

Creating a Playlist

If you have a fairly sizable collection of MP3 songs, you may find that you're interested in playing only subsets of those songs at different times. You might want to collect some of the songs for lazy afternoons and others for all-nighters of coding, studying, or trying to keep the baby quiet. Whatever your plan, you can most easily accomplish it by arranging the songs in your Library into a playlist.

There are two ways to create a new playlist:

- Click the Add Playlist button at the bottom-left side of the iTunes window. (It's the left-most icon next to the Shuffle and Continue buttons.) You can also select File ➢ New Playlist. This creates an empty playlist.

- Select songs in the Library first (you can use Shift+click to select a range of songs or ⌘+click to select multiple, noncontiguous songs), then choose File ➢ New Playlist from Selection or hold down the Option key while clicking the Add Playlist button. This creates a playlist that includes all the songs in your selection.

When the new playlist appears in the Source list on the left side of the iTunes window, it's immediately highlighted so that you can type in a name for it. Give your playlist a name and press Return.

Now you can add songs to the playlist simply by dragging them from the Library's song list to the playlist's entry in the Source list on the left side of the iTunes window. This allows you to organize the songs however you would like—by artist, by mood, and so on. The same songs can be added to multiple playlists, if desired; songs remain in the Library no matter how many playlists you add them to.

To play from a playlist, simply select the playlist from the Source list. Just as with a CD, the song list will change to display only the songs you've added to that playlist. Use the controls and/or the Shuffle and Continue buttons to play the songs on your playlist.

To remove a song from a playlist, select it and press the Delete key. It will be removed only from the playlist; it remains in the Library.

To delete a playlist, highlight the playlist in the Source list, then press the Delete key. If the playlist has songs in it, you'll see an alert box asking you to confirm that you want to delete the playlist. Click Yes if you're sure that is what you want to do. The playlist is deleted, although, as mentioned, the songs will remain in the Library. (Playlists without songs are deleted immediately.)

 TIP iTunes keeps track of the number of songs, the amount of time they take, and their approximate size in megabytes at the bottom of the iTunes window when a playlist is selected. If you have a version of iTunes updated to burn CDs (and you have a compatible CD-RW drive that shipped with your Mac), you can click the Burn CD icon at the top-left side of the iTunes window to create an audio CD with this playlist. After clicking Burn CD, insert a CD-R disc in your drive, and then click Burn CD again. The CD will be created.

Importing from a CD

Playing a CD is certainly easy with iTunes, but it's a bit more limited than working with MP3s in the Library. After all, once you take the CD out of your Mac, you won't have access to the songs. Also, you can't mix the songs on a CD with the songs in your Library to create a custom playlist that includes both.

The solution is to import (often called *ripping*) songs from audio CDs into your Library. The import process reads the songs from the CD and turns them into MP3 files. Then you will be able to browse them in the Library, add them to playlists, and, best of all, listen to them when the audio CD isn't in your CD-ROM drive.

 WARNING As with copying any commercial music, you should use iTunes for creating MP3s only for the music that you already own or have otherwise licensed. Ideally, that means using only CDs that you've purchased and plan to keep.

You can import songs from a CD or an entire CD to the iTunes Library. To import a single song, simply drag it from the CD's song list to the Library icon in the Source list on the left side of the iTunes window. You can drag multiple songs if you first select them by Shift+clicking or ⌘+clicking. When you drag a song (or songs), you'll see a small orange icon appear next to the selected song. You'll also see the top indicator change to show the song that's being imported and the time remaining for the import process to complete. (Note that iTunes can import songs faster than it can play them, so the import process may finish before the song does.)

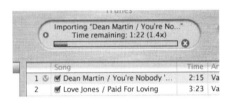

When the song is finished importing, you'll hear a tone and the small icon will change to a green check mark to indicate that the song has been imported. It's now an MP3 file, and you'll find it in the Library.

To import an entire CD of songs into your Library, select the CD's playlist in the Source list, then click the Import button at the top-right side of the iTunes window. iTunes will begin importing the CD into your Library. When it's finished, you'll hear a tone and see a small green check mark next to each song on the CD.

Importing Preferences

By default, iTunes imports sounds as MP3 files at an intermediate quality setting. You can change this in the iTunes Preferences dialog box. Select iTunes ➤ Preferences, then click the Importing tab in the Preferences dialog box (see Figure 16.4).

PART

III

Getting Things Done
with Mac OS X

FIGURE 16.4

The iTunes Preferences dialog box lets you change how songs are imported.

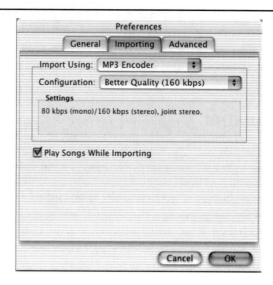

In the Import Using pop-up menu, you can select the type of file that should be created when you import: MP3, AIFF, or WAV. In the Configuration menu, select the quality level for the songs. Be aware that the higher the quality setting, the larger the resulting song file will be and the longer it will take to import. The Play Songs While Importing option at the bottom of the dialog box is checked by default. You can turn it off if you would prefer to have the songs imported in silence.

Retrieving Imported Songs

Once a song is imported, you may want to do something other than play it back in the Library or add it to a playlist—you may want access to the song file (MP3 or otherwise) itself. MP3s are generally only a few megabytes in size, making it possible to upload them to your iDisk for access from other Macs or to send them to a friend through e-mail (after considering the copyright implications of doing so!). To work directly with the MP3 file, you'll need to find it.

By default, iTunes stores ripped song files in the iTunes Music folder, which is inside an iTunes folder that is created in your personal Documents folder (that is, ~/Documents/iTunes/iTunes Music). There, you'll find the MP3 or other types of song files that are created whenever you rip songs from a CD. (Note that the songs may be in their own subfolders, sometimes named for the artist or album.) The songs are regular files that can be copied, attached to e-mail messages, or moved (although you may need to re-import them into the Library if you move them).

The folder that iTunes uses for its music files is something of an odd choice, considering that each user's home folder includes a Music folder that is created automatically by

Mac OS X. If you would prefer to use the Music folder—or any other folder, such as a Public folder where multiple users access MP3 files—you can change that setting in the iTunes Preferences dialog box. Select iTunes ➤ Preferences, then click the Advanced tab.

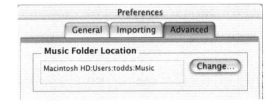

Click the Change button in the Music Folder Location area, then select the folder you would like to use for your music files in the Choose A Folder dialog box that appears.

Synching with an MP3 Player

iTunes can act as an interface to your MP3 player if you happen to have a USB-based MP3 player that's compatible with iTunes. MP3 players have become a popular (if still somewhat expensive) alternative to Walkman-style portable stereos. You simply download MP3 songs to the player, which can then play them back via headphones.

To manage your MP3 player from iTunes, connect it via its USB cable while iTunes is running. You should see the device appear in the Source list on the left side of the iTunes window (see Figure 16.5). Select the device, and you'll see a list of songs that are currently on the device.

FIGURE 16.5

If iTunes recognized your MP3 player, it will show up in the Source list.

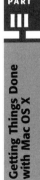

PART

III

Getting Things Done
with Mac OS X

To delete a song that is currently on the device, select the song and press the Delete key on your keyboard. In the alert box that appears, click Yes if you want to delete the song. It will be removed from the device. The small indicator at the bottom of the iTunes window will change to reflect the free space available on the device.

To add songs to the device, select the Library icon in the Source list. Locate the songs you want to add and drag them to the device's listing in the Source list. If all the songs can be copied to the device, they will be; if you don't have enough room, you'll see a warning and only the songs that will fit will be copied.

That's it. When you're finished adding and deleting songs, unplug the device. Now you're ready to listen to a new set of MP3s from your Library.

Listening to Internet Radio

If you're connected to the Internet (and have a fairly speedy connection), you may enjoy iTunes' Radio Tuner feature, which enables you to listen to Internet radio stations. The tuner works by accepting streaming audio from Internet sites, then playing it back as it arrives at your Mac. Note that this can affect other Internet operations (surfing in a Web browser or downloading e-mail), but shouldn't be much of a problem for high-speed and broadband connections.

To listen to an Internet radio station, make sure that your Internet connection is active, then select the Radio Tuner icon in the Source list on the left side of the iTunes window. You'll see a list of music genres. Click the arrow next to a genre that you would like to explore. When you see a show that interests you, double-click it to begin listening to that show (see Figure 16.6).

If you have a modem connection, you'll get your best results if you select a stream that is about the same speed as your modem connection, such as 56Kbps for a high-speed modem or 32Kbps for a slower-speed modem. Some shows have two or more connection options; select the lower-speed connection if you're having trouble listening to the show. Lower-speed connections also generally mean lower quality.

You can't record or save songs that you hear on Internet radio stations, but you can save the stations for quick access by dragging them to a playlist in the Source list. Save a list of your favorite stations, and you won't need to hunt them down each time.

 TIP If you note that iTunes often pauses while playing back music, you may want to try increasing the streaming buffer—the amount of music that is downloaded to your Mac before it begins trying to play continuously. Select iTunes ➢ Preferences and click the Advanced tab. Select Large from the Streaming Buffer Size menu.

FIGURE 16.6

Listening to an Internet radio show

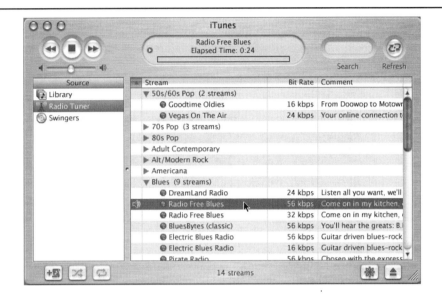

Playing DVD Movies

It's a little odd to put a section on playing DVD movies in this book because, in its first release, Mac OS X isn't actually capable of playing back DVD movies. That's right—even though DVD playback hardware is built into many popular Mac models—including iMac DV, PowerBook, and many Power Macintosh models—Mac OS X was released without this feature. You can't run the DVD player from the Classic environment either.

While DVD playback is likely slated for an interim release (and may be available for download by the time you read this, perhaps via the Software Update pane of System Preferences), the current solution is a simple workaround: Boot into Mac OS 9.1. If your Mac is set up for dual-booting, you can start up your Mac in Mac OS 9.1 and use the DVD player from there.

NOTE Your Mac must have an internal DVD-capable drive and the proper internal circuitry for DVD playback, which is generally present in any Mac model that offers DVD drive. (The exception is some early PowerBook G3 models, which require a special PC card for DVD movie playback.) If your Mac doesn't have an internal DVD drive and the appropriate circuitry (for instance, if your Mac has a CD-ROM or CD-RW drive), you will not be able to view DVD movies.

Once you're in Mac OS 9.1, insert a DVD movie in your DVD drive and launch the DVD Player, located in the Applications (Mac OS 9) folder. You should see a display screen and the DVD controller (see Figure 16.7).

FIGURE 16.7

The DVD Player in Mac OS 9.1

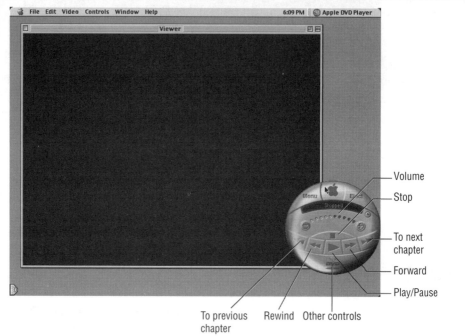

If the DVD movie appears with on-screen controls, you can use your mouse to click in the different regions and see different parts of the DVD. For instance, many DVDs offer outtakes, theatrical trailers, and interviews with the cast and crew, which you'll find behind multimedia-style buttons that you click to navigate.

To play a DVD movie, you can use the controller. The controller offers all of the features you would typically find on a DVD player or VCR, including Play, Pause, Rewind, and Fast Forward, as well as controls to take you to the previous chapter and to the next chapter. At the top of the controller, you'll also see controls for moving directly to the Menu screen and for ejecting the disc. In the middle of the controller is a volume control you can use to change the volume of the movie. (You can also press the + and – keys to change volume settings.)

At the bottom of the controller is a small area that you can click to reveal other controls. These other controls enable you to choose different language tracks, subtitles, camera angles, and other features that may or may not be built into the movie.

To play the movie at different sizes, pull down the Video menu and select a size. Select Video ➢ Present Video on Screen if you would like to see the movie at the full size of your screen. Move the mouse up to the top of the screen to make the menu bar visible once again so that you can change the video settings.

Working with Speech

Mac OS X includes some interesting technologies that have been brought along from earlier Mac OS versions: the ability to speak text aloud and to recognize, in a limited way, voice commands. While this technology certainly isn't yet up to science-fiction standards, if you would like to toy with your Mac's ability to speak and be spoken to, it's there for the testing.

The speech technologies are divided into two distinct areas: Text-to-Speech and Speech Recognition. Text-to-Speech technology is used to enable your Mac to speak text aloud—whether that speech occurs in Apple's applications, third-party applications, or Mac OS X itself. For example, you may find commands in some applications that enable you to select text and have it spoken aloud. Speech Recognition refers to the Mac's ability to listen for and recognize certain commands that you speak into the Mac's microphone.

Using Text-to-Speech Technology

Text-to-Speech technology requires two components. First, you enable and configure Text-to-Speech using the Speech pane of the System Preferences application. Then you'll need to get your hands on an application that actually supports Text-to-Speech technology; at the time of this writing, few Mac OS X native applications do. Once you have such an application up and running, though, you're ready to listen.

To configure Text-to-Speech, launch the System Preferences application and open the Speech pane. On the Text-to-Speech tab, you'll see an option for choosing the voice that you want your Mac to use for speaking, and you can use the small slider to select the rate at which that voice speaks. To test your selections, click the Play button.

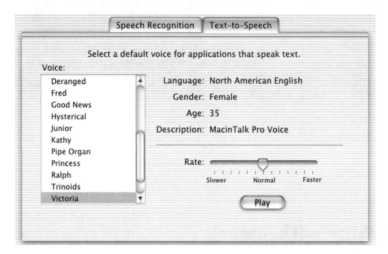

To work with Text-to-Speech, you'll need an application that supports it. Unfortunately, none of the applications that ship with Mac OS X support Text-to-Speech—at least, at the time of this writing. However, some third-party applications will offer a Speak Text command or something similar. For instance, iCab (www.icab.de), a third-party, shareware Web browser, will speak the text of a Web page when you select View ➤ Speak All. The browser will then speak aloud all the text on the page until you select View ➤ Stop Speaking.

Using Speech Recognition Technology

Speech Recognition technology is the flip side of Mac OS X's Text-to-Speech technology: It listens to your voice commands. In order to use Speech Recognition, you need to have a microphone attached to your Mac—either a PlainTalk microphone (designed to accept voice commands) or a microphone that's built into your Mac, such as the one in iMac and PowerBook models. If your Mac doesn't have a PlainTalk microphone port, you may need to buy a USB microphone. Shop for one that's specifically compatible with PlainTalk and/or Speech Recognition.

 NOTE Speech Recognition automatically selects the microphone by determining what microphone(s) you have plugged in. If you've installed a USB or PlainTalk microphone, it will be selected. If you haven't installed any microphones, the Mac's built-in microphone will be used.

With your microphone plugged in, you're ready to dig into the Speech Recognition settings. Launch the System Preferences application and select the Speech pane. On the Speech Recognition tab, you can begin by selecting the speech technology you want to use from the Recognition System pop-up menu. By default, you'll see only Apple Speakable Items in this menu, but the system has been designed to accept third-party recognition engines as well (see Figure 16.8).

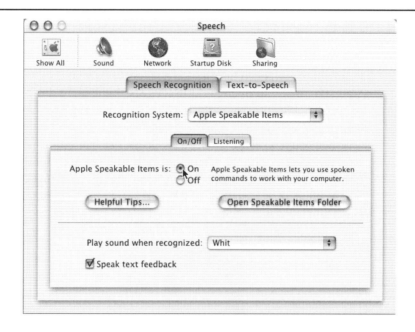

On the On/Off tab, you can turn on Apple Speakable Items by clicking the On radio button. When you do, you'll see the small Speakable Items disc appear on your desktop.

This is the interface to Speakable Items. When you hold down the Escape key, Speakable Items will begin listening to the microphone. You can then speak commands. You'll see the small color bars on the disc light up to let you know that your

PART

III

Getting Things Done with Mac OS X

speaking is being heard. If a command is recognized, you'll hear a small tone and the command will be put into action.

 TIP It's recommended that you hold down the Escape key for a full second, then speak the command, then wait another second before releasing the Escape key. For other hints, click the Helpful Tips button on the On/Off tab of the Speech Recognition tab.

The Speakable Items commands are stored in the Speakable Items folder, which you can open by clicking the Open Speakable Items Folder button on the Speech Recognition tab. If you have additional Speakable Items you would like to add to your Mac, you can install them in this folder. Speakable Items can be aliases to applications or even AppleScripts that perform tasks. As long as the item has a unique name and is launchable, you can add it to the Speakable Items folder.

While you're working with the Speakable Items interface, you may find it handy to have the Speech Commands window open. You can open it by clicking the small arrow at the bottom of the Speakable Items disc and selecting Open Speech Commands Window. You can then use the Speech Commands window to notice when a command is recognized (recognized commands appear at the top of the window) as well as to see the currently installed commands.

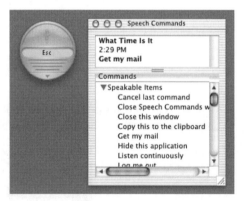

 NOTE Speech commands can be specific to the Finder or to individual applications (such as Mail), or they can be general Speakable Items commands that work anywhere.

If you're not pleased with the hold-down-Escape system of speaking to your Mac, you can change that. With the Speech Recognition tab selected in the Speech pane, select the Listening tab.

Now, you can change the alert key by clicking the Change Key button. In the dialog box that appears, you can press another key that should take the Escape key's place, and then click OK.

You can also change what the alert key does. If you switch the Listening Method option to the Key Toggles Listening On and Off radio button, then pressing the alert key will simply make the Speakable Items interface active or inactive.

Another option lets you edit the name for your computer in the Name entry box and select a frequency from the Name Is pop-up menu. For instance, if you name the computer Hal and select the Required Before Each Command setting from the Name Is menu, then you'll need to say, "Hal, what time is it?" and "Hal, get my mail" and so on in order to invoke your voice commands.

All in all, Speakable Items can be somewhat hit and miss. You'll find that the better your microphone, the better the overall recognition will be. Built-in microphones tend to offer the worst recognition, although later Macintosh models with quiet internal fans or no-fan operation seem to work fairly well with the built-in microphone. If you can get an external microphone—particularly a USB microphone that's designed for speech—you may have better luck. I tested with all three types and found that a USB headset-style microphone designed specifically for Speech Recognition offered somewhat better results.

If you're intent on experimenting with Speakable Items, you may want to try it out using the Chess application that's included with Mac OS X. That application is capable of receiving voice commands for playing the game, such as "Knight B1 to C3." In my experience, it works very little of the time, but you might have fun with it for 10 minutes or so. (Or, if you figure it out and get Speech Recognition to work well, more power to you!)

TIP Other companies are working on speech-recognition solutions that are more robust than Apple's built-in Speakable Items (although Speakable Items may continue to improve with age). In particular, third parties tend to focus on *dictation* software, meaning you can actually compose letters and reports by speaking aloud. Look for products from Mac-Speech, Inc. (www.macspeech.com) and IBM's ViaVoice group (www.ibm.com/viavoice/) for Mac OS X–related updates and releases.

What's Next?

In this chapter, you learned about some of the multimedia features that are built into (or, in some cases, *not* built into) Mac OS X. For playing MP3 songs and audio CDs, early Mac OS X users can download iTunes (it should be included with later Mac OS X releases). iTunes is a great little program that enables you to turn audio CDs into MP3s so they can be organized in your Library, added to individual playlists, and even exported to some portable MP3 players.

For DVD playback, Mac OS X isn't quite as promising. At the time of this writing, the solution for a DVD-compatible Mac is to boot into Mac OS 9.1 and use the Apple DVD Player from within that operating system. Still, if you plan to settle in with a movie for a few hours, it could be worse.

Finally, Mac OS X offers Text-to-Speech and Speech Recognition technologies that, while included with Mac OS X, haven't quite caught on yet. (In fact, similar technologies have been in the Mac OS since the early 1990s, but they may yet catch fire.) If you would like to experience talking to and listening to your Mac, you can.

In the next chapter, you'll see how to automate tasks on your Mac using another important technology that has been brought to Mac OS X from previous Mac OS versions: AppleScript. Some commands have changed and been updated, but AppleScript remains an interesting and powerful way to get your Mac to perform repetitive tasks via an easy-to-learn scripting language.

CHAPTER 17

Automating the OS and Applications: AppleScript

One of the most distinct carryovers from early Mac OS versions to Mac OS X is AppleScript, Apple's unique approach to automating tasks within the Finder and other AppleScript-aware applications. AppleScript is a technology that enables you to create scripts, or even small applications, that automate tasks on your Mac.

With Mac OS X, Apple has included the Script Runner, an application that's able to quickly run a few built-in scripts that Apple has also included. These built-in scripts are a great way to get started using AppleScript, even if you don't want to create your own scripts.

The heart of AppleScript is the Script Editor, which you can use to record actions, thus creating scripts of actions without actually writing code. You can also use the Script Editor to write your own original AppleScript scripts. And the Script Editor can be used to view any AppleScript-capable application's dictionary, where you'll find listings and explanations of the AppleScript commands and objects present in that application.

Once you've explored the Script Editor, you'll be ready to learn some of the basics of AppleScript. AppleScript is an English-like language that offers a fairly easy-to-grasp syntax. Once you've gotten to know the basics of AppleScript, you'll find that it can be easy to master new concepts and put them to use.

 NOTE If you've already spent some time with AppleScript in the past, I recommend that you launch the Help Viewer and choose the AppleScript Help module from the Help Center. There you'll see some fairly good information regarding differences and workarounds between Mac OS 9.x's and Mac OS X's support for AppleScript. I also recommend www.apple.com/applescript/ on the Web for more information, documentation, and some good beginner tutorials covering AppleScript.

Understanding AppleScript

AppleScript is a programming language that's built into Mac OS X. It's considered a *human-readable* language, meaning that you can figure out what it's doing most of the time simply by reading the commands. AppleScript uses a technology called Apple Events, which are messages passed between Mac applications, to enable you to send commands to one or more applications from within a script. That script then gets information about the settings for various objects within the application, and, if you wish, it changes those settings, invokes commands, or otherwise automates some processes.

Applications must be written to support Apple Events. Most applications understand at least a few events, such as open, quit, and print. Other applications support the standard suite of recommended Apple Events such as cut, copy, save, count, and delete. Still others take AppleScript very seriously, offering application-specific events such as a command that launches a URL in Internet Explorer or one that creates a new message in Mail.

Using Apple Events, then, you can send commands from the script to applications to get them to do things automatically and, in some cases, together. For example, an AppleScript script could:

- Rename, move, delete, or otherwise alter all (or some) of the files or folders in a particular folder

- Copy text from one application and automatically send it as an e-mail message to a predetermined recipient using an e-mail application

- Launch a series of applications (such as your Web browser, e-mail application, and address book application) and have them launch commands (open a particular Web site, check for e-mail) automatically

- Gather files with certain attributes into a particular folder

Beyond these, AppleScript can be implemented by an application developer to pretty much any extent that the developer desires. So you can do very specific things in some applications that support AppleScript, such as Mail, Internet Explorer, and Microsoft Word.

As you'll see later in this chapter, most of what you're doing with AppleScript is telling applications (including system applications like the Finder) to do particular things, in a particular order, and sometimes many times in a row. The more redundant the task, the better.

The Script Runner

For some Mac users, what's really cool about AppleScript is that you don't even have to write the scripts yourself. Instead, you can install and run scripts without worrying about their proper syntax and construction. In fact, some scripts are included with Mac OS X for you to play with.

In the Applications folder, open the AppleScript folder. There you'll see the Script Runner. Script Runner is a small application designed to run compiled scripts—scripts that have been saved as AppleScript scripts but not as applications. (Scripts can be saved as applications and double-clicked from within a Finder window, just like regular

PART

III

Getting Things Done with Mac OS X

applications.) Double-click the Script Runner to launch it, and you'll see a small palette window.

Click the icon, and a pop-up menu appears, although it probably has only one item on it: Open Scripts Folder. The Script Runner works by looking in your personal Scripts folder, which is stored at ~/Library/Scripts/. Whatever scripts you place in this folder will appear on the Script Runner menu. You can also add folders inside the Scripts folder, and they will become submenus in the Script Runner. So the Open Scripts Folder command is there on the menu to give you quick access to that folder.

You'll find a folder called Example Scripts in the /Applications/AppleScript/ folder. So here's what you do: Open the Example Scripts folder, then copy the contents of that folder to your personal Scripts folder. (If you can't find your Scripts folder, you can have the Script Runner create the folder by choosing the Open Scripts Folder command from the Script Runner's pop-up menu.)

After you've copied all those folders full of scripts to your Scripts folder, quit and relaunch the Script Runner. Click its icon again, and the menu is now filled with submenus and scripts.

Now you can run some scripts, just to get a sense of how AppleScript works. To run a script, simply select its name from one of the submenus. Note that there are a few different types of scripts that are found among the example scripts, including these:

Finder scripts   The example scripts (in the Finder Scripts and Navigation Scripts menus) include a number of scripts that work within the Finder. In most cases you need to have a Finder window open and/or an item (or more) selected in a Finder window before these scripts will work correctly. Other scripts, such as those in the Navigation Scripts folder, simply give a quick command to the Finder.

AppleScript scripts and code snippets   In the Info Scripts menu you'll find Current Date and Time, which simply uses some built-in AppleScript commands to get those items and return them to you. Some other scripts (under Script Editor Scripts) are really just portions of sample code that the intrepid script author can use to get started on advanced scripts.

Application scripts   These are the bread-and-butter scripts—code that tells applications what to do, automatically. The example scripts include scripts that send commands and exchange information with Mail, Internet Explorer, Sherlock, and even the Help Viewer application.

So, as you can see, these scripts are a fairly decent representation of some of the tasks that can be accomplished with AppleScript. For instance, AppleScript scripts can do things on their own with built-in commands from AppleScript itself—things like retrieving the date and time or allowing the user to enter data via a dialog box.

Second, scripts can send commands to objects in the Finder, meaning that you can do everything from moving windows around to copying files, renaming files, and, yes, deleting files. For instance, the script Add to File Names in the Finder Scripts menu simplifies the task of adding filename extensions to a folder full of files that don't have them.

When Add to File Names is launched, a dialog box appears. In it, enter the file-name extension you'd like to add (including a period, as this script takes things very literally).

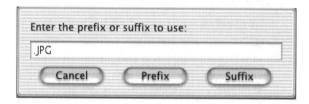

Now, click the Suffix button to add the filename extension to each filename in the folder. (Note also that you could choose Prefix, if desired, to add "proj1" to the beginning of each file's name, for instance.) The script goes into action, appending the suffix to each file in the folder. The result:

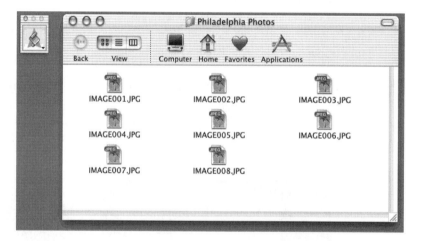

Third, scripts can send commands to applications, as long as they accept them. While most applications will accept four basic commands (open, print, quit, and run), others are specifically designed to accept a wide range of commands from Apple-Script scripts. As you'll see, each application can have its own AppleScript dictionary full of commands and objects that it will understand and respond to from a script.

Scripts as Applications

The Script Runner is there to run compiled scripts that you've placed in a special folder in your home hierarchy. But AppleScript code can also be distributed as an application (or an *applet*, a term that's meant to suggest "small application"). These

AppleScript applications work pretty much like any other applications: You can double-click them, they have menus (although usually with very few options), and in some cases you can even drag and drop files to the script applications. AppleScript applets have slightly different icons from the basic compiled scripts:

Connect To Web Site   Internet Launch

Update FTP Server

Such applications can be handy to have, because you can put them on your desktop or on the Dock; you can even add them to your Login Items list in the Login pane in System Preferences and have the applets launch automatically when you log into your Mac. Script applications can also be designed to stay open as a background process, enabling them to monitor the time or date, for instance, and to execute when something in particular happens. Later in this chapter you'll see how to save scripts as applications.

If you're not much of a programmer, though, and don't want to learn, you can focus on simply adding scripts to your Mac. If they're compiled scripts (not applications), you can store them in your personal Scripts folder and use the Script Runner to access them. If the scripts are applets, you can store them anywhere and launch them like any other application. You'll also find that many applications have their own script folders and AppleScript menus. If you add scripts for such an application to that application's script subfolder, you'll be able to access scripts from within the application.

 TIP   Want to download more scripts? Using the Script Runner, select URLs, then Apple-Script Related Sites. Select one of those URL scripts to automatically launch and access the Web site in Internet Explorer. You'll also often find extra AppleScript scripts that can be downloaded from Apple's site (`www.apple.com/applescript`), and scripts that support your applications may be found at the application publisher's Web site.

First Script: Recording and Saving

If the first level of AppleScript commitment is running scripts from the Script Runner or as applications, the second level isn't much tougher. The Script Editor—an application included with Mac OS X for the express purpose of creating and editing scripts—has a fun little function you can play with called Record. You turn on the Record function, then switch to applications and perform tasks that you'd like to script. When you switch back to the Script Editor, you'll see the scripting steps there in the Script Editor window (see Figure 17.1).

One of the major benefits of recording a script is that it can give you some idea of the commands that are available within an application (such as the Finder) as well as *how* that application prefers to receive instructions. As noted previously, many AppleScript scripts are geared toward individual applications. When you record an application scripting itself, you may be able to gain a bit of insight into how it likes to be scripted.

Not all applications are *recordable applications* that send AppleScript commands to the Script Editor while it's in Record mode. (In fact, given the relative immaturity of most Mac OS X applications, it's possible that very few applications will be recordable for the foreseeable future. For instance, even most of Apple's own bundled applications aren't recordable, and the Finder and Help Viewer offer only basic recordability.) That doesn't necessarily mean that the application isn't *scriptable;* an application can offer very sophisticated AppleScript support without offering recordability. So, if you find that an application doesn't seem to record script commands well, you can check for an AppleScript dictionary that's related to that application, as discussed later in the section "Application Commands."

FIGURE 17.1

Here's the Script Editor recording the steps I'm taking in the Finder.

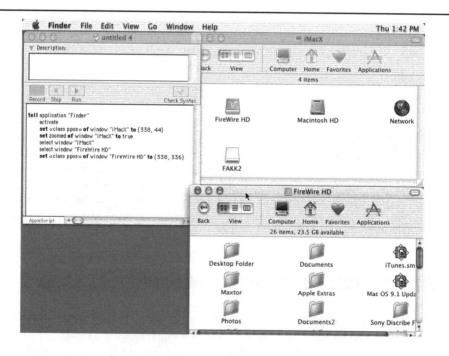

Recording Actions as a Script

In order to record the actions you perform in an application and turn those steps into a script, you need to do two things. First, you need to launch the Script Editor, which is located in the AppleScript folder inside your Applications folder. Second, you need to be working with a recordable application. If the application isn't recordable, you'll know soon enough, as you'll get little-to-no response from your actions in the Script Editor. In some cases the Script Editor will still record a few commands from non-recordable applications (like closing or moving windows) but won't know how to record more-detailed commands.

Now you're ready to begin recording. Here's how:

1. Launch the Script Editor and the application(s) you want to work with. (In most cases you don't want to record them being launched.)

2. Click the Record button in the Script Editor or select Controls ➤ Record.

3. Switch to the application(s) you're recording and perform actions that you'd like the Script Editor to record.

 NOTE If you hear a beep after the first action you take, the Script Editor may need your attention. It may need to know what application you've just selected if it isn't able to figure it out on its own. It will let you know that by causing the Choose Application dialog box to appear. Highlight the application in the Choose Application dialog box and click Select. Now, return to the recordable application and begin performing actions.

4. Switch back to the Script Editor and click Stop when you're done.

When you click Stop, you'll notice that an end tell command appears in the window. Now you can click the Run button to run the script again and test it to see if it works as you had hoped. (Chances are, it will require some tweaking, but you might have recorded something useful.)

Saving Your Scripts

After you've recorded your first script (and later, when you're creating scripts from scratch), it's important to save the script. There are a few different ways you can save a script from within the Script Editor. First, you can choose whether the script will be saved as Run Only (meaning it can only be run, not opened and edited) or saved as an editable script. To make that choice, select either File ➤ Save Run Only or File ➤ Save.

Second, you'll see the Save dialog box, shown in Figure 17.2, where you'll make choices about the type of script or applet you want to create.

FIGURE 17.2

The Save dialog box in the Script Editor

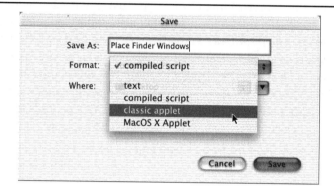

The Save dialog box is fairly standard, but you should note that the Format menu gives you some interesting options for saving:

Text   Save as a Plain Text file when you're in the middle of editing the script and it doesn't yet work. You can also easily edit these files in text editors other than the Script Editor.

Compiled Script   A *compiled script* is one that needs to be run from within the Script Editor, the Script Runner, or an application that includes the ability to launch scripts. This is a full-fledged (and ideally, working) script, but you can't just double-click it in a Finder window. (If you do, you'll launch the Script Editor, not the script.)

Classic Applet   Now you're creating a double-clickable (or drag-and-drop-capable) application icon, but this one will launch in the Classic environment.

Mac OS X Applet   With this option, you're creating a full-fledged Apple-Script applet that launches as a native Mac OS X application.

Choosing one of the applet options gives you two more check boxes to consider:

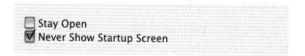

Select Stay Open if this script is designed to launch and then wait, as a background process, for other things to happen. Such scripts are more complex (and outside the scope of this book). Turn on Never Show Startup Screen if you'd prefer that the applet not show a startup, or "splash," screen when it launches. If you leave this option on, the startup screen will appear when the applet is launched:

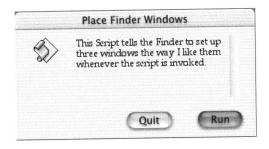

> **TIP** The startup screen for an applet includes any comment text you've typed in the top of that script's window in the Script Editor.

Creating Original Scripts

Now that you've seen how to record a script, perhaps you've learned a little about how the Finder and other applications like to be scripted. Next, you're ready to create your own script, from the bottom up. To begin, launch Script Editor and choose File ➤ New Script. A New Script window appears. At any time, you can decide to save the script, giving it a name and choosing whether it will be saved as text or a compiled script. You can then save your changes as you work to improve the script.

Let's start with a script that's considered an old standard in the programming universe: the Hello World script. It's customary whenever you learn a new language to first create a quick program or script to say "Hello world." In the case of AppleScript, this script is easy.

Entering the Script

Begin by entering some information about the script in the Description area at the top of the Script Editor window. It may seem like a silly thing to worry about for a short script, but it's worthwhile to *document* your scripts as much as you can—including information about who you are, why the script was written, and what it's supposed to do.

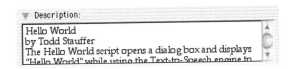

TIP The Description area has a disclosure triangle, which you can click if you'd like to hide the description and see more code in your script's window.

In the script below, you'll see a couple of special commands that AppleScript installations generally offer through something called *scripting additions,* which we'll discuss later.

```
display dialog "Hello world."
say "Hello world."
```

Simply type those lines into the Script Editor window, pressing Return after each line. Now you can click the Run button to see (and hear) the result. You'll notice that the font of the text in the Script Editor window changed immediately after you clicked Run. That's because the Script Editor recognized the text as valid after putting it through a quick check system.

In fact, you can initiate that check yourself any time you want to make sure you're formatting something correctly, but before you run the script. (This way, you can check the syntax quickly without having to actually execute the script over and over again.) Click the Check Syntax button in the Script Editor window to have the Script Editor check your syntax. If it's happy with what you've typed, it will change the font of the text (and may even make some words boldface). If the Script Editor doesn't like something you've scripted, it may return an error message.

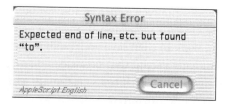

When you receive such a message, you'll have to dig back into the script and see what you may have mistyped or what commands you're using incorrectly.

 NOTE Whenever you click the Check Syntax button or the Run button, your script is automatically reformatted in a way that makes it acceptable to the AppleScript *compiler* and easy to read. You can change this formatting, if desired, by selecting Edit ➢ AppleScript Formatting and changing the defaults. You should also note, for the record, that even if the compiler accepts the words and constructs you've used, your script *may* not work correctly.

Commenting the Script

While you're entering commands, you have another option that's important to take advantage of: You can add *comments* to the script. Comments are useful for reminding yourself of what you're doing in longer scripts; likewise, comments can be used to tell future readers of your script what the script (or portions of it) was meant to do. Though some people feel that AppleScript is easy enough to read on its own, that really isn't always the case. Sometimes the comments are very important.

You can add comments to your script in two ways. The first way is to add the comment text at the end of a command line within the script. You do that by adding two hyphens, or dashes (--), before typing the comment, as in:

```
display dialog "Hello world." -- pops up a dialog box
```

You can also use the double-hyphen approach to place a comment on its own line, such as:

```
-- The following displays and speaks "Hello world."
display dialog "Hello world." -- dialog box
say "Hello world." -- spoken
```

In all these cases, the double hyphens simply tell the AppleScript compiler (the engine that's turning your commands into reality) to ignore anything that comes after them on that single line of text. In fact, you'll note that once you've clicked either Run or Check Syntax, the comments will be changed to italic, and a space will be added in front of the double hyphens if you didn't already type a space there. That indicates that the text has been recognized as a comment. (Note, incidentally, that you don't have to type a space after the hyphens, as in my examples, although I recommend it for easier reading.)

Do you have longer comments to add? Another way to enter them is to place the comments (particularly if they are paragraph-length) between a combination of parentheses and asterisks, such as:

```
(*
This script is designed to display a dialog box. Once the user has clicked
OK to dismiss the dialog box, the computer will speak the same text aloud,
using Apple's Text-to-Speech technology. The Text-to-Speech voice can be
selected in the Speech pane of System Preferences, and the audio volume must
be above 0 for the speech to be heard.
*)
display dialog "Hello world."
say "Hello world."
```

Formatting Issues

The Script Editor is good at reformatting your script—whenever you click either the Run or Check Syntax button—so that the script is more readable. For instance, the Script Editor often boldfaces words that are recognized as AppleScript language keywords, while leaving other words in a plain style. In fact, the formatting doesn't matter much to the compiler; you can even select Edit ➤ AppleScript Formatting to change the default way that scripts are auto-formatted.

One special formatting problem, however, occurs when a line of commands or operators is becoming so long that it's difficult to see in the Script Editor. By default, the script line won't automatically wrap itself to the window; it simply continues forever, forcing you to scroll right and left to see the results.

The solution is to press Option+Return in the middle of a command line to insert a *soft break,* represented by the *continuation symbol* (¬). Essentially, you're telling AppleScript that this single line of commands continues logically, but you'd like some of it to appear on the next line for the sake of readability.

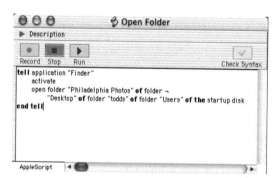

The only caveat is that you shouldn't break a string (text between two straightened quotation marks) using the continuation symbol. If you have a particularly long string, it can either continue past the bounds of the screen, or you can use the *concatenation symbol* (&) to take a single string and format it so that it's on two lines in the Script Editor, as in this example:

```
display dialog "Hello to the world. " & ¬
"This is my first script."
```

Note that when you *concatenate* (which simply means to link two or more strings together into one), you are responsible for making sure the spaces appear correctly, which is why the first string in the example above has a space after the period.

Checking Results

Finally, there's one other element of the Script Editor that's useful to know about—the Result window. The Result window is designed to show the resulting values from calculations and assignments as they occur during your script. In practical applications, most of what you'll see in the Result window will be the final result of your script, since the script will usually execute too quickly for you to see any results that occur in the middle of your script.

Still, the Result window can be useful for giving you a sense of what your script is doing and what values it's dealing with. To view the Result window, choose Controls ➢ Show Result. The small window will appear. Now, run your script to see what the final assigned or computed result is (see Figure 17.3).

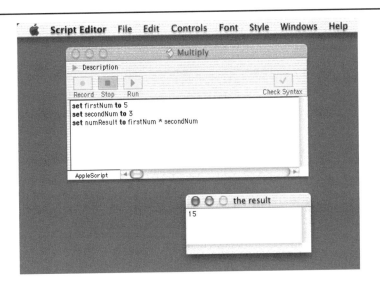

As your scripts get more complicated, the results that you see will get more complicated as well. But while you're learning to script, you may find it helpful to leave the Result window open to see what results, if any, are being recognized and returned when the script runs.

Scripting Concepts

AppleScript is *object oriented*, which means that it's designed primarily to deal with objects and their properties. In the real world, the main items you deal with are *objects*—a chair, a room, a house. Those objects are composed of *elements*—a room might have a wall, a window, and a light switch (among other elements). And those objects and elements can have *properties*—a light switch is in the "on" position, and a wall has certain width and height dimensions.

Within the AppleScript world, many of the main items that you work with in applications or the Finder can be considered objects. That includes folders, files, windows, disks, and documents, among others. A window can have many elements—a title bar, a Close button, a scroll bar. And the objects and elements can both have properties: A file has a modification date, and a window has a title.

Objects, References, and Properties

In AppleScript, objects can have both *containers* and properties. Containers are important for dealing with items in the Finder as well as in other applications.

For instance, if you're dealing with folders located on your hard disk, the container might be obvious, as in this command:

```
open the folder "Users" in the startup disk
```

The Users folder has a container, the startup disk. The relationship between objects and their containers can be more complicated, such as:

```
open the folder "Backup" in the ¬
    folder "Documents" in the folder "todds" ¬
    in the folder "Users" in the startup disk
```

When you're creating one of these long paths, you can truncate it a bit, if you like, by using colons to divide portions of the path, as in:

```
open the folder "Users:todds:Documents:Backup" ¬
    in the startup disk
```

For other disks, all you need to do is name them, as in:

```
open the folder "Documents:CD Movies" in the disk "Firewire HD"
```

You'll come across many other types of objects as you explore the scriptable parts of both the Finder and other AppleScript-aware applications. As you'll see later in the section "Application Commands," your applications can have their own objects—windows, documents—that you address in a similar manner.

 NOTE If you're following along in the Script Editor, you should know that the examples shown so far regarding containers will work only within a tell...end tell construct, as shown in the next example and discussed in the later section "AppleScript Commands."

So that's how you dig down through the containers to an object. But what do you do once you get there? What's often more important in scripting is the fact that that object has properties. These are the attributes of the object—its height, weight, and shoe size. Using AppleScript, a fair number of the commands you'll give will be to learn, compare, and change the attributes of objects, both in the Finder and in applications. For example:

```
tell application "Finder"
    get owner of startup disk
    set bounds of window 1 to {20, 60, 700, 500}
end tell
```

In this example we're "getting" the value of the startup disk's owner property (if you've got the Result window open, you'll likely see "root" as the result) and assigning ("setting") a value to the bounds property (the position on-screen) of a window.

That's a good deal of what you'll be doing in AppleScript—learning and setting the properties of objects. One way you'll do that, though, is through another special type of entity—the variable.

Working with Variables

When you're working with an object's properties in a script, you'll often want to take the value of a particular property and assign it to a temporary holding area. You'll find this useful for any number of reasons, not the least of which is convenience. These temporary holding areas are called *variables,* which are named areas of memory where AppleScript lets you temporarily store values. Here are two examples:

```
set x to 10
set myDisk to name of startup disk
```

Both statements use the AppleScript set command to set a value to a variable. In the first instance, the variable is named *x*; in the second, it's named *myDisk*. (For the record, this second command won't work unless you use a tell statement to send the command to the Finder. See the section "AppleScript Commands" later in this chapter.) Those variable names represent the customary way in which AppleScript variables are named. If you need a quick variable for a number or numeric evaluation, it's fairly common to use a simple letter such as *x* or *i*. If you're creating a more permanent variable for use later in your script, it's common to give it a compound name that suggests that variable's purpose. Examples might be *myCounter, docFolder,* and *fileCount.*

NOTE How you name your variables doesn't actually matter—the suggestions here are just following AppleScript custom. There's a good reason for the custom, though: Using these types of variables can improve the readability of your script (e.g., *fileCount* makes more sense than *xyz*). Also, a compound or one-letter approach is more likely to keep you from accidentally using an AppleScript command as a variable name, which will confuse the AppleScript compiler and create an error in your script.

If you're used to almost any other type of programming or scripting, you may be surprised at the flexibility of variables in AppleScript. Any variable can hold pretty much any sort of value, regardless of the variable's *type*. In other words, there's nothing special you have to do to create a variable that can hold a number, as opposed to a variable that can hold text or even a list. They're basically the same. Here are a few ways you can set variables:

```
set x to 1.5
set y to 5 + 6 -- evaluates to 11
set firstName to "John"
set filePath to {Users:todds:Documents:Memo1.rtf}
```

Note that you're seeing a few of the various types of values that AppleScript can work with, including integers, strings (text between straightened quotation marks), real numbers (numbers with decimal places), and file paths. You can also set variables to Boolean values (true or false) as well as to lists of other value types, which are placed between braces (curly brackets) and separated by commas, such as in these examples:

```
set classList to {"Julie", "Tom", "Eric"}
set numList to {1, 3, 5, 7, 9, 11, 343}
```

You'll find that this listing approach to variables is also useful for such things as storing all the values in a particular folder to a single variable, as in:

```
set fileList to name of every item in folder "Documents" ¬
    in disk "Firewire HD"
```

One more note on variable type: You may sometimes find it necessary to change one type of value (an integer, string, or real) into another type of value. In Apple-Script, you do that with a system called *coercion*, which simply causes a variable to be of the new type (if possible). You do that using the *as* keyword:

```
set x to 5
set numText to x as string -- assigns value as a string
```

Now *numText* has the value *5,* but it's considered a string, not an integer. (So you could concatenate it to another string, for instance.) Other *as* options include *as real* (decimal number), *as integer,* and *as list.*

Finally, it's interesting to know that there's another important variable that's built into AppleScript: *result.* Immediately after performing some sort of operation or command, you may have already seen that the result of that operation can appear in the Result window in the Script Editor. Whatever is placed in that Result window is also placed in the *result* variable. It's not a good idea to rely on the *result* variable, because it changes after each new assignment and after many commands. Still, it's possible to do something like this:

```
get 5 + 5
set numTotal to result
```

The get command adds 5 and 5, assigning the result, 10, to the special *result* variable. Then, the set command assigns the current value of *result* to the named variable *numTotal,* making *numTotal*'s value 10.

Loops and Conditionals

Hand in hand with variables come the ideas of *loops* and *conditionals,* which are simply ways to control the *flow* of your script from one command to the next. Sometimes, you'll want a particular command to be executed only if a certain criterion has been met. That's a conditional. Other times, you'll want a particular command (or group of commands) to execute a certain number of times or *until* something else happens. That's a loop.

AppleScript allows you to accomplish this type of flow control with two different statements: the *if...then statement* and the *repeat statement.* If...then statements are used to evaluate conditionals; repeat statements are used for looping.

If...Then Comparisons

An example of an if...then statement follows.

```
tell application "Finder"
    set numItems to the number of ¬
    items in the folder "Desktop Junk"
        if numItems > 10 then display dialog ¬
        "Time to clean out the Junk folder."
end tell
```

Note that the if...then construct always includes a portion that needs to be evaluated as either true or false (Boolean). In the example, that portion is numItems > 10, where *numItems* is a variable that was created immediately before the if...then statement.

NOTE In the previous example, AppleScript will look for the folder Desktop Junk on the current desktop. (The desktop is the first place a script will look for a folder if you don't specify any other containers.) If you wanted the script to look in a different folder, you'd want to include a full path to that folder, as discussed earlier in the section "Objects, References, and Properties."

Other types of comparisons are possible, too, such as these:

```
if x > 5 …
```

```
if x <= 4 …
```

```
if numItems is equal to 5 …
```

```
if totalFolders is greater than numFolders …
```

The common comparison operators include =, ≠, >, <, >=, and <=. (You can produce the ≠ symbol by pressing the Option and = keys together.) If you'd prefer to use actual words as your comparison operators, you can experiment a little with the text that AppleScript recognizes (it recognizes quite a few variations beyond those outlined here), along the lines of *equals, does not equal, is greater than, is less than, is greater than or equal to, is less than or equal to,* and so on.

You'll find that it's also possible to compare other items; for instance, you can use certain operators to determine whether a list or string variable contains a particular item or bit of text. For instance:

```
if (fileList contains ".txt") then …
if (myString starts with "Hello") then …
```

Containment operators include the words *contains, doesn't contain, starts with,* or *ends with,* among others.

An if statement that has more than one command as part of the statement needs to have an end if at the end of the string of commands so that the script knows what commands to avoid if the comparison is false. Here's an example:

```
set x to 3
if x is less than 5
    set lessTrue to 1
    display dialog "It's lower than five."
end if
```

In the example, if *x* happened to be *higher than* 5, neither the set nor the display dialog command line would be executed, because the script would immediately skip to the end if and move on to the rest of the script.

Any if statement can also have an *else* statement as part of it. The else statement is used to specify what the script should do in case the condition isn't true. Here's an example:

```
tell application "Finder"
    set numItems to the number of ¬
    items in the folder "Desktop Junk"
        if numItems = 0 then display dialog ¬
        "There are no items in the Junk folder."
        else display dialog "The Junk folder has items in it."
        end if
end tell
```

Note that incorporating an else statement also means that you need to include the *end if* statement to complete the if...then...else construct.

Repeat **Statements**

Repeat statements are used to perform tasks repeatedly until some condition is met. Repeat statements can use the same kinds of comparisons as if...then statements, although they don't have to, depending on how you create the repeat loop. For instance, you can use the *repeat...exit repeat* construct to leave an "endless loop," as in this example:

```
set x = 0
repeat
    set x = x + 1
    if x = 10 then exit repeat
end repeat
```

In its current form, this script doesn't do much good; but in other ways, it can. For instance, you could use this construct for a fun little script that asks the user to specify the correct number:

```
repeat
    display dialog "Enter a number between 1 and 50:" ¬
    default answer ""
    set numChosen to text returned of result
    if numChosen = "10" then exit repeat
end repeat
```

PART

III

Getting Things Done
with Mac OS X

Hopefully, you can see through the additional commands how the `exit repeat` command is used when the desired value is entered.

 TIP The `default answer` attribute is used in conjunction with the `display dialog` command to cause the dialog box to show an entry box for text. See the later section "Scripting Additions" for more details.

Other repeat constructs work differently. For instance, you can have a certain loop repeat a certain number of times using the `repeat x times` construct, such as:

```
set x to 0
repeat 10 times
set x to x + 1
end repeat
display dialog box "Total equals: " & x & "."
```

In this case, the repeat loop will continue until the number of times has been exhausted. (You can also use an `exit repeat` command if you need to have the loop end before the specified number of loops is completed.) Another repeat construct is the *repeat until*, which you can use as sort of a combination of an if...then and a repeat, because you're using a condition:

```
set x to 0
repeat until (x=5)
set x to x + 1
end repeat
```

In `repeat until`, the loop continues as long as the condition is false. *Repeat while* is similar, but the loop continues as long as the condition is true.

Commands in AppleScript

Now that you've seen some of the basics of AppleScript programming, as well as how to record, create, and save your AppleScript scripts, it's time to explore the commands that AppleScript has to offer. The best way to learn AppleScript is a combination of looking at the various AppleScript dictionaries (discussed in the section "Application Commands") and opening up other prewritten scripts or recorded scripts to get a sense of how they work. In this section, then, we'll focus on how to find the various commands you'll have at your disposal.

AppleScript really works on three different levels. Some (in fact, very few) commands are built right into AppleScript itself. The second group of commands comes from applications themselves, where the bulk of new and interesting commands are found. The third group of commands comes from scripting additions, which are special AppleScript add-ons that add important and very useful commands to the AppleScript vocabulary.

AppleScript Commands

AppleScript commands are very basic commands that are used, along with other commands and constructs, to learn property values and to set new property values to objects. These commands can be used for some basic programming and mathematical tasks. Built-in AppleScript commands include `activate`, `copy`, `count`, `get`, `launch`, `run`, and `set`.

Activate, `launch`, and `run` all have to do with starting up applications; `run` and `launch` are similar, while `activate` is generally used to make an application come to the front, as in these two examples:

```
activate application "Finder"
```

```
tell application "Finder"
    activate
end tell
```

Get, `set`, and `copy` are the really special commands within AppleScript, as they're used for learning and changing the values of object properties. You've already seen some of them in action, as in these examples:

```
get bounds of window 1
```

```
set bounds of window 1 to {20, 50, 600, 700}
```

```
copy {20, 50, 500, 700} to bounds of window 1
```

Perhaps one of the most important commands in AppleScript isn't technically a command, but rather a statement. The `tell` statement is used to focus a script on a particular application, such as the Finder. It's a *statement* because it has a beginning and an end, between which you place commands that you want the AppleScript to pass on to the targeted application. For instance, the following line has AppleScript contact the Finder, load the Finder's AppleScript dictionary (in which the Finder's AppleScript commands are stored), and prepare to send commands to the Finder:

```
tell application "Finder"
```

PART

III

Getting Things Done
with Mac OS X

The commands then follow, with a trailing end tell command to close the tell statement:

```
tell application "Finder"
    open folder "Applications" of the startup disk
end tell
```

You can have repeated tell statements, if desired, which allow you to have a script work with two different applications, such as:

```
tell application "Finder"
    open folder "Applications" of the startup disk
end tell
tell application "Internet Explorer"
    activate
    OpenURL "http://www.mac-upgrade.com/"
end tell
```

And, for the record, you don't need the end tell statement if you keep the entire tell construct on a single line:

```
tell application "Finder" open folder "Applications" on the startup disk
```

But clearly, it's important to have the end tell if you have more than one command's worth of instructions for the application.

 TIP A tell statement can be used to send commands to a Classic application, if desired, even if the script itself is compiled as a Mac OS X applet.

Application Commands

The second type of AppleScript commands we can talk about are those that are built into Mac OS applications themselves. Most applications that are AppleScript-aware include a few different sets of commands. The Required Suite of commands are those that any Macintosh application needs to adhere to: run, open, print, and quit. It's not a long list, but you can be fairly confident that any native Macintosh application that launches and runs on your Mac will respond to one or more of those four Apple Events, such as in this example:

```
tell application "TextEdit"
    print window 1
    quit saving yes
end tell
```

The print command will actually open a Print dialog box where the user can make additional choices before printing; then, once the print job has been sent to the printer, the application will receive the quit command along with the *saving yes* option, which means the application will quit and automatically save changes in any open documents.

Beyond these basic commands, applications are free to add their own commands for you to use in scripts; in fact, most of your scripting will use application-specific commands. In order to use them, though, you'll need to know them. Although a particular application's printed or store-bought manual might include such information, the easiest way to see the commands available to you is through the Script Editor's Open Dictionary command. If an application is AppleScript-aware, it will have a special AppleScript dictionary that's part of it. Using the Open Dictionary command, you can view that dictionary and, hence, the commands in it.

To view an application's dictionary, select File ➤ Open Dictionary. Now, in the Open Dictionary dialog box, locate the application you'd like to use with your script. Select that application and click Open in the dialog box. (If you don't see the application in question, you can try to locate it by clicking the Browse button in the Open Dictionary dialog box and locating the application using a typical Open dialog box.) Once opened, the dictionary appears in its own window in the Script Editor, as shown in Figure 17.4.

FIGURE 17.4

An application's AppleScript dictionary

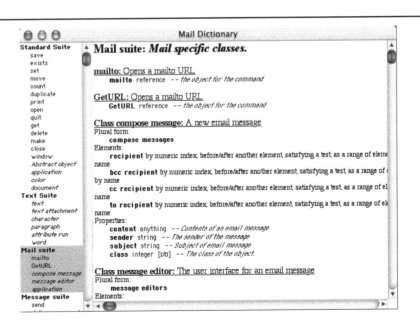

PART

III

Getting Things Done
with Mac OS X

The dictionary for an application is written by that application's developer, so it can vary in exactly how comprehensive, useful, or understandable it is. In most cases you'll need to take a little time to understand how items are presented in the dictionary; and after that, some additional experimentation will often be needed before you'll get the true sense of the application's scriptability.

That said, you'll notice some constants in almost any AppleScript dictionary. The dictionary is there basically to show you what items the application considers to be scriptable objects, what attributes those objects have, and additionally what commands the application will recognize in a `tell` statement. Putting these things together (objects, attributes, and commands) along with standard AppleScript commands, you can begin to build a script to control that application.

How do you use the dictionary? Simply click on an item on the left side of the window, and the definition of that item will appear on the right. Here's a look at the way the left side is organized:

Suites   In most cases the objects, attributes, and commands are stored in suites of related items. By selecting the name of one of the suites listed down the left side of the window, you can see all the items that are considered part of that suite. Sometimes seeing the whole suite can give you an idea of how the elements interact; other times, it's a bit too wordy.

Commands   Commands appear on the left side, under their suite heading, in regular text. Select a command, and you'll see a quick reference for how that command is supposed to be structured. In most cases the commands are meant to act on the objects that are also in the suite.

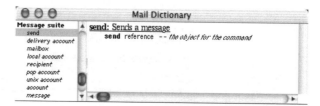

Objects   The objects in a given suite appear in italics. Select an object, and you'll see the attributes related to that object. Often you can change those attributes through a script (as mentioned, that's one main reason to create a script). So, as part of the object entry, you'll see the attributes and the type of data that each attribute expects. Attributes that can't accept changes from a script have "[r/o]" after them, meaning that they're read-only. In that case, you can only retrieve the value of that attribute, not set it. Still, that can be very useful in a script.

The first area where you might find the dictionary particularly useful is where most people start scripting—the Finder. The Finder has its own dictionary, which can be selected the same way other applications' dictionaries are selected, via the Script Editor. Opening the Finder's dictionary can be pretty revealing—the Finder offers a number of suites, including commands that affect your Mac, Finder items, folders, files, windows, and other objects. Spend a little time exploring the Finder dictionary, and you'll see some amazing options for scripting the Finder. Experiment!

Scripting Additions

The third group of commands comes from *scripting additions*, which are special command libraries that can be added to a Macintosh to expand AppleScript's capabilities. Scripting additions can be added to your Mac, then used for a variety of purposes to extend the usefulness of scripts that you create. Some of them help you build advanced interfaces (dialog boxes and windows) for your scripts, while others add commands that enable you to access network resources, special database backends, and other items from your scripts. In most cases you'll use scripting additions only for scripts you don't intend to distribute to others, because you can't assume those other folks will have the same scripting extensions that you do.

There's a special case—Apple's own Standard Additions, which are included with all Macs. These commands are safe to use on any Mac having a compatible version of AppleScript, including Mac OS 9.*x* or Mac OS X. In fact, you've already seen some of the Standard Additions commands, such as `display dialog` and `say`. Others offer even more powerful features, such as `choose file`, which enables you to get input from the user via an Open dialog box.

When Apple engineers decide to add commands to newer implementations of AppleScript, they generally do so by adding commands to the Standard Additions scripting extension. These are commands that can be used throughout your scripts to perform special tasks that aren't built into AppleScript and aren't included with most applications. In fact, you don't have to put these commands between `tell` statements (that's true of any scripting extension command).

You can view the Standard Additions the same way you view other applications' AppleScript commands: Open the dictionary. Using the Script Editor's File ➤ Open Dictionary command, locate the file Standard Additions. Open it, and you'll see the Standard Additions' dictionary.

As far as other scripting additions go, you'll need to check out AppleScript-related Web sites in order to obtain native Mac OS X scripting additions files. Scripting additions from Mac OS 9.*x* cannot be installed in Mac OS X—you'll need native (or, in some cases, hybrid) versions. Once you've downloaded a scripting additions file, you can install it in a folder called ScriptingAdditions in the main Library folder if you have an administrator account. (If the ScriptingAdditions folder doesn't exist, you can create it.) If you don't have an administrator account, you can create a folder called ScriptingAdditions in your personal Library folder and store the scripting additions file there—but remember that other users on your Mac won't be able to use any scripts that you create using commands from that scripting additions file.

Once ScriptingAdditions is installed, the Script Editor should be able to find it whenever you access the File ➢ Open Dictionary command. You can then open the new ScriptingAdditions' dictionary in the Open Dictionary dialog box to see the new commands it offers.

 TIP Don't forget the URLs menu in the Script Runner, where you'll find links to some popular AppleScript Web sites. Check them out for news on third-party scripting additions for Mac OS X.

What's Next?

In this chapter you learned a little bit about AppleScript, the built-in programming language for Mac OS X. You saw how to launch AppleScript scripts, how to record them, and how to save scripts as text, compiled scripts, or applications. You also saw the basics of the AppleScript language, and you saw how to learn the commands that are available to you from AppleScript, your applications, and scripting additions.

In the next section of the book, you'll learn how to install peripherals, troubleshoot applications, and recover from trouble with the Mac OS itself.

PART IV

Installing, Maintaining, and Troubleshooting

LEARN TO:

- *Install and troubleshoot internal and external devices*

- *Partition and initialize hard disks*

- *Troubleshoot applications and the Classic environment*

- *Troubleshoot the Mac OS X system and Internet connections*

- *Solve common problems encountered with Mac OS X*

- *Enable and work with the root account*

- *Back up and maintain your files and disks*

CHAPTER **18**

Peripherals, Internal Upgrades, and Disks

Mac OS X is a completely new operating system in terms of how it deals with hardware. In some cases, hardware will be easier to install and often a little easier to configure than it was with Mac OS 9.*x* and earlier. In other cases, it may be difficult to get existing peripherals to work with your Mac.

In general, hardware compatibility with Mac OS X is a moving target. As the months wear on after Mac OS X's release (as well as interim releases expected throughout 2001 and beyond), more and more hardware should be supported. That doesn't necessarily mean that all hardware will be totally supported by Mac OS X, even if the hardware was compatible with a Mac OS X–capable Mac model under Mac OS 9.1. Some compatibility issues will need to be resolved by the device manufacturers, who may not release new drivers or other fixes in a timely manner.

In this chapter, we'll take a look at some of the issues involving getting Mac OS X to work with both new and existing peripherals. You'll also learn how to use Apple System Profiler for troubleshooting peripherals and Apple's Disk Utility application to partition and format hard disks.

Adding External Devices

Thanks to Mac OS X's newness, one of the really sticky parts of using it (particularly for those upgrading from an earlier Mac OS version) is dealing with peripheral hardware. For a while after the introduction of Mac OS X, there will likely be many external peripherals that don't work well with the operating system. For instance, while Mac OS X supports many FireWire and USB hard disks, you may find that your external CD-RW drive fails to be recognized without a third-party driver update.

If you're lucky, you'll find a driver for your device built into Mac OS X. On the other hand, you may be forced to rely on the manufacturer of a problematic drive to release a driver update—assuming that the manufacturer has the interest and resources to develop a Mac OS X–compatible driver. In the case of peripherals that have been purchased in the past few years, manufacturer updates are fairly likely. However, for older peripherals, you may need to hold out hope for a third-party solution.

Drivers for hardware generally come in the form of a kernel extension (with a .kext filename extension), which is stored in the System/Library/Extensions folder on your hard disk. You'll need a special installer (and an administrator account) to install kernel extensions; then you'll need to restart the Mac. You should rarely, if ever, need to install a kernel extension by hand. However, you can do this by activating the root account (see Chapter 20) and copying the kernel extension into the System/Library/Extensions folder.

NOTE If you need to remove an extension, you should check the Read Me file associ-ated with the extension's installer—the package installer for your driver may have an option to remove the extension. If you can't find any instructions, you can try the following: Boot into Mac OS 9.1 and remove the .kext driver file from System/Library/ Extensions. In some cases, you may also need to remove the associated .pkg file from the /Library/Receipts/ folder. Next, restart your computer in Mac OS X.

Here, we'll take a look at some specific categories of devices, including external disks, CD-R and CD-RW drives, USB devices, keyboards, mice, Palm OS devices, modems, and serial devices. Also discussed is how to configure an AirPort Base Station, which must be done from Mac OS 9.1 (at least, at the time of this writing).

 NOTE One thing to remember if you're having trouble with an external device is that there may be an internal culprit as well. If you're using a PCI adapter card for SCSI, USB, or FireWire connections, remember that the adapter card, too, may require an update. See the "Adding Internal Devices" section later in this chapter for details.

External Disks

External disks—both hard disks and removable drives—vary widely in their ability to work with Mac OS X. Mac OS X has the built-in ability to deal with some models of external USB, FireWire, and SCSI hard disks, without requiring any additional drivers. Whether an external disk works depends, in part, on how the drive's interface with the Mac has been implemented.

Users of external SCSI hard disks and removable drives report reasonably few prob-lems working with them in Mac OS X. Iomega Zip and Jaz drives are supported by generic drivers that shipped with Mac OS X (version 10.0 and later). Some other SCSI removable drives may require driver updates. As always, SCSI isn't hot-swappable (meaning that you need to shut down the Mac before altering your SCSI chain of external devices), and it generally isn't recommended that you change the SCSI ID numbers on your peripherals often. Also note that the Apple Ultra Wide SCSI PCI card in the Power Macintosh G3 (beige) model can require a firmware update before it works correctly, which may also affect your ability to work with external SCSI drives.

One issue that can apparently crop up in odd ways with Mac OS X is "SCSI voodoo," a common term for the ways in which SCSI configuration sometimes does not seem to make much sense. If you're dealing with an external SCSI device and you believe it should work, you can try shutting down your Mac, removing all external SCSI devices but the one you're troubleshooting, and then restarting Mac OS X. If that doesn't work, shut down your Mac again, try a different SCSI ID number for the device (usually via a switch on the back of the device), and restart. If that again fails, shut down, try a different termination setting for the device, and start up again, and so on. If you're able to get the device to function, then you can attempt to rebuild your SCSI chain from there.

USB and FireWire disks should be hot-swappable, meaning that you can attach them to the Mac while it's running. If you plug in a USB or FireWire hard disk and it isn't recognized by your Mac, you may want to try restarting. (You should also ensure that the drive is properly plugged in, the power is turned on, and the USB or FireWire cable is attached correctly.)

 TIP Sometimes, Mac OS X can have trouble starting up with an external FireWire device attached, so you may wish to start up Mac OS X, then attach the FireWire drive. Bring the Finder to the front, then connect the FireWire cable first to your Mac, then to the drive. It seems to help, too, if you connect external devices while the Classic environment is not running.

If the drive requires a special driver to be installed in order for the drive to be recognized, you may need to get that driver from the manufacturer. In Mac OS 9.*x*, for instance, some external drives require a "shim" of sorts in order for the drive to be recognized as a true USB or FireWire drive. Such drives may have more trouble working in Mac OS X. Others, such as the Maxtor model, mount automatically on the desktop without problems (as shown below).

It's also possible that you will have problems with any external drive (USB, FireWire, or SCSI) that was formatted with a third-party formatting utility. If that's the case, your solution is either to obtain an update to the formatting software or to reformat the disk using Apple's Disk Utility (assuming Disk Utility can recognize the drive). Of course, this isn't a terribly appealing solution because you'll lose all of the data currently on that drive. (You can avoid data loss by backing up the drive fully, but that can be quite a task with a large hard disk.) See the "Partitioning and Formatting Disks with Disk Utility" section later in this chapter for more on formatting hard disks.

CD-R and CD-RW Drives

There's nothing nicer than being able to burn data and audio CDs when you need to, but the first release of Mac OS X doesn't exactly shine in this area. In order to work correctly, an external CD-R or CD-RW drive (I'll refer to both as CD-RW drives, for simplicity's sake) needs two things: a CD driver to recognize and mount media that has already been created, and an application that can recognize the drive well enough to burn data to recordable CDs.

Currently, few CD-RW drives are supported by Apple's built-in CD driver, so if you're able to hook up your external CD-RW drive and get a disc to appear on the desktop, you're ahead of the game. It's also possible that Apple will add more drivers and more capability by the time you read this, as it's something of a priority for the company. In fact, late in the writing of this book, Apple announced iTunes 1.1.1 for Mac OS X, which now includes the ability to burn music CDs using Apple's own built-in CD-RW drives in some Power Macintosh G4, iMac, and iBook models.

NOTE Mac OS 9.1 already has the ability to burn a CD directly from its Special menu in the Finder (if the CD-RW drive is supported). You simply drag files to the CD's icon to add them, then select Special ➢ Burn CD in the Finder. This feature isn't available in the 10.0 version of Mac OS X, but it should be available fairly soon.

In order to create a recordable CD, you'll need an application that is updated for Mac OS X. Some third-party CD-RW drives (and, ideally, all Apple CD-RW drives that shipped with new Mac models) should be supported by Mac OS X itself in an interim release beyond 10.0.

Other options for burning CDs include Roxio's Toast (`www.roxio.com`, formerly Adaptec Toast) and Charismac's Discribe (`www.charismac.com`). Both are anticipated to appear as Mac OS X native applications, able to recognize CD-RW drives and burn data to recordable CDs. If you have an external CD-RW drive and you wish to use it to burn data, check Apple and the other companies regularly for updates. In the meantime, you'll need to boot into Mac OS 9.1 to create CDs, because (at the time of this writing) CD-burning software doesn't work from the Classic environment.

WARNING The next section details particular problems with USB-based CD drives. You may not wish to use USB-based CD drives with the 10.0 version of Mac OS X at all, until interim releases are available from Apple.

USB Devices

Some users of the initial release of Mac OS X have reported that hot-swapping a USB device (connecting an external device while the Mac is on and operating) can result in a *kernel panic*—a Mac OS X crash that freezes the system, forcing a restart. Kernel panics are usually obvious, because command-line text appears on your screen, along with, in many cases, the option to press R to restart the Mac. If you press R, your Mac restarts in Mac OS X, and you see your USB device, you may have gotten around the problem. (Kernel panics are discussed in Chapter 20.)

Apple warns that many external USB devices—particularly CD-ROM, CD-RW, and magneto-optical drives—not only aren't supported in Mac OS X, but can cause problems. If you experience repeated problems with your USB drives, you'll need to unplug them before starting up Mac OS X and stop using them until you can obtain a driver and/or Mac OS X update that addresses the issues.

Mac OS X seems to work somewhat erratically with external USB hubs. Although USB hubs generally don't require special driver software, a hub is something to suspect if you're having trouble getting a USB device to be recognized. Try shutting down your Mac, unplugging the hub, and then connecting the USB device directly to a USB port on the side or back of the Mac. If the USB device is recognized on startup, you should consult the USB hub's manufacturer to see if workarounds or drivers are available for the hub.

Floppy Drives

A special case involves floppy drives—the 10.0 release of Mac OS X doesn't support the *internal* floppy drive in Power Macintosh G3 (beige) models. Some (but not all) external USB floppy drives reportedly work with Mac OS X, however, so if you have an external model (or plan to purchase one to deal with floppy diskettes), you should have luck using it.

 NOTE Apple produced two distinctly different Power Macintosh G3 models. The Power Macintosh G3 (beige) computers are early, cream or beige colored, models. They came in both desktop and mini-tower forms and included a floppy disk drive, an external SCSI port, and an Apple Desktop Bus (ADB) connector for keyboards and mice. The Power Macintosh G3 (blue and white) computers are one of the early "candy-colored" professional Mac models. These models came in only a mini-tower design, and they included USB and FireWire ports instead of ADB and SCSI ports.

Apple's workaround for the internal floppy drive is to boot into Mac OS 9.1 and copy the files to your hard disk. Alternatively, you can use Mac OS 9.1's version of the Disk Copy application to create a disk image. (The initial release of Mac OS X's Disk Copy can't create floppy disk images, but you can use it to mount disk images that you create in Mac OS 9.1.)

To create a disk image, first boot into Mac OS 9.1, and then follow these steps:

1. Insert the floppy disk from which you want to create an image.

2. Launch Disk Copy, which is likely found in the Utilities folder of your Applications (Mac OS 9) folder, assuming that you installed Mac OS X over Mac OS 9.1. (If not, you may simply have a Utilities folder on the root level of your Mac OS 9.1 startup disk.)

3. From the Disk Copy menu, select Image ➢ Create Image from Disk.

4. In the Select the Source Disk dialog box, locate the disk that you want to copy.

5. In the Save Disk Image As dialog box, give the disk image a name in the Name entry box.

6. Select a format from the Format menu (likely Read-Only Compressed, unless you would like the option of writing to the image; in that case, choose Read/Write). The Size menu should already have the size of the disk you're planning to create, but you can create a larger one if desired (particularly for a Read/Write image).

7. Click Save to create the disk image.

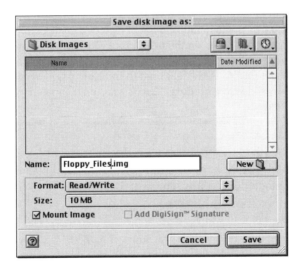

Now you have a disk image that can be double-clicked from within Mac OS X and mounted on your desktop like any other removable disk, thus giving you access to the contents of your floppies.

 TIP Need to take the "floppy" image with you? One solution is to create a CD-RW that includes a number of disk images, which you can then access using any other computer running Mac OS X (or, for that matter, any older Mac OS versions).

Keyboard and Mice

Mac OS X has built-in drivers for dealing with most USB keyboards and mice, giving them basic capabilities. If your keyboard offers special abilities, such as special "launcher" keys or other keys that can be custom configured, you'll need a special Mac OS X driver before you'll get full functionality.

Mice with two buttons are automatically supported by Mac OS X. (In fact, mice with more than two buttons are also supported, but only two buttons will work without a third-party driver.) While one button will operate as usual, the second button will be mapped to the Control+click combination, so that you can bring up contextual menus without being forced to hold down a key while clicking.

 NOTE Some manufacturers of high-end configurable mice will likely offer Mac OS X–compatible drivers in the near future. One manufacturer, Kensington Technology Group (www.kensington.com) has released its MouseWorks software for Mac OS X at the time of writing. This software is used to configure programmable buttons for some of the company's mousing products. Check your mouse manufacturer's Web site for updates and details.

The 10.0 version of Mac OS X doesn't support (or, in some cases, only erratically supports) the Volume, Brightness, and CD Eject keys that are available on some recent Mac models' keyboards. This will likely be corrected by the time you read this, in an interim release for Mac OS X.

Mac OS X also works with Apple Desktop Bus (ADB) keyboards and mice that are plugged into Mac models that support ADB, including Power Macintosh G3 (beige) and most Power Macintosh G3 (blue and white) models. ADB keyboards are generally fully functional, although you may sometimes have trouble with some boot-key sequences (such as holding down the Option key during restart to bring up the boot picker screen).

Palm OS Devices

At the time of this writing, Palm Computing had not yet released a native Mac OS X version of the Palm Desktop software necessary for HotSync operations. According to the company's Web site, however, it is possible to use the Palm Desktop (version 2.6.*x*) in the Classic environment for data entry, managing your calendar, and so on. Also, although it's not supported by Palm, users have had success synchronizing their Palm devices with the Palm Desktop software running under Classic. The company notes that this works with the Palm Connect USB Kit (or other USB-based connectors, such as the Handspring Visor's USB cable), but not with serial-based connectors or Palm's Universal USB cradles.

In order to perform the HotSync operation by pressing the button on the Palm's cradle, you also need to have the Classic environment preloaded. If you would like to be able to perform HotSync operations without first launching Palm Desktop, start the System Preferences application, select the Classic pane, select the Start/Stop tab, and turn on the Start Up Classic on Login to This Computer option. If you don't want Classic running all the time, then you'll need to launch the Palm Desktop application first, before attempting a HotSync. When the Classic environment is running, you can press the HotSync button to begin the HotSync process.

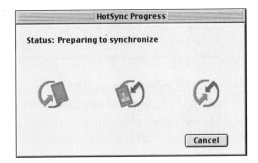

Modems

Mac OS X should work with all internal Apple modems that shipped with OS X–compatible Macs. It should also work with many external modems, including serial modems that are compatible with Power Macintosh G3 (beige) models and Power-Books that include serial ports. In fact, the "printer" port on Power Macintosh G3 (beige) can't actually be used for serial printers in OS X, but it can be used for modem connections.

You configure a modem through the Network pane of the System Preferences application. If your modem is recognized, you should be able to select it from the Configure menu in the Network pane. The example below shows the Configure menu choice for a Ricochet USB Wireless Modem. Note that the recognized device won't necessarily have the correct name, so you may need to figure out which device is which if you have more than one.

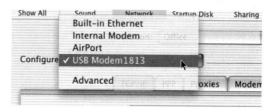

 NOTE Once an external modem (or similar USB device) has been recognized, it will remain as an entry in the Network pane, even if you unplug the device. So, if you're not careful, you may find yourself configuring a modem or networking device that isn't connected. If you've successfully connected in the past and you're suddenly having trouble, don't forget to make sure that the modem is actually plugged into a USB port on your Mac. You can disable and/or delete ports from the Network pane menu by choosing Configure ➢ Advanced, as discussed in Chapter 8.

Most external USB modems should be recognized and usable in Mac OS X, although standard modems (56Kbps models) seem to install more successfully than ISDN and other specialized modems. If you have a specialized modem and it doesn't appear in the Configure menu of the Network pane, try restarting your Mac while the modem is attached. You can also try plugging the USB modem directly into a USB port on the side or back of your Mac instead of into your keyboard, monitor, or an external USB hub. If restarting and replugging doesn't work, you may need to obtain a driver from the modem manufacturer. (Note that this doesn't apply to DSL or cable modems, which connect to the Mac via Ethernet, not USB.)

Once the modem is recognized, you should be able to configure it by selecting the Modem tab in the Network pane. In the Modem menu, you'll see entries for a variety of manufacturers' modems. These actually correspond to special modem script files, which are stored in the Modem Scripts folder inside the Library folder on your Mac's startup disk. If you need to add a modem script for your modem (if your modem's manufacturer makes one available), you can copy it to the Modem Scripts folder.

TIP Modem script files are the same in Mac OS X as they were in Mac OS 9.x and earlier. If you have a modem script file that you've used with an earlier Mac OS version, you should be able to copy that script file to the Modem Scripts folder inside the Library folder on your startup disk. Then your modem should appear in the Modem menu on the Modem tab in the Network pane.

Serial Devices and Adapters

Mac OS X is designed to work with relatively few serial devices, partly because all Mac models now offer USB ports in place of the older serial ports (called modem and printer ports by Apple). Serial printers aren't supported in Mac OS X, although, as explained in the previous section, some serial modems are supported. Serial devices such as a Palm cradle, digital camera, or serial scanner are not supported and aren't likely to be supported. (It should be technically possible for a third-party manufacturer to support such serial devices, but it's unlikely this will happen, because those devices haven't been available at the retail level for months or years.)

If you have a serial device that you would like to use with your Mac, you may still have an option. USB-to-serial adapters are available (in fact, they've been a mainstay for many Mac users in the past few years), and some of those manufacturers are offering Mac OS X drivers, with Keyspan (www.keyspan.com) leading the pack. Users have reported success in connecting some serial devices to their Mac via a USB-to-serial adapter. Note that two components are necessary for this to work: a Mac OS X driver for the USB-to-serial adapter and software that recognizes the adapted device.

Once you have the adapter's driver installed (the drivers I've seen are kernel extensions, which require an administrator's password to install), you should be able to access the serial device as if it were a USB device. Then, if you have the application necessary to work with that device, you may be able to access it. This can be a fairly big *if*, because most applications designed to work with serial devices aren't going to be Mac OS X native applications. You may be stuck in the Classic environment, where USB connections are shaky at best. If you can't seem to use the device from within Mac OS X, your only solution may be to boot into Mac OS 9.1 and use it from there.

AirPort Base Station

Although not technically an external peripheral in the classic sense, an AirPort Base Station is an important component of many Mac networks. The Base Station is a small device (the current version looks like a small flying saucer) that acts as an AirPort networking hub, enabling multiple AirPort-enabled Macs to communicate with one another through a wireless connection. At the same time, the Base Station is an Ethernet router, making it possible for AirPort and Ethernet Macs to share data and/or a broadband Internet connection. The Base Station has a built-in modem as well, enabling the network to share a modem-based Internet connection.

At the time of this writing, the AirPort Base Station wasn't configurable from Mac OS X. You can configure individual AirPort-enabled Macs to connect to an AirPort network (as discussed here and in Chapters 8 and 9), but you must configure the Base Station from Mac OS 9.1. (You can download the latest AirPort configuration software from `http://asu.info.apple.com/`.) Once you're working in Mac OS 9.1, you can configure the AirPort Base Station by launching the AirPort Setup Assistant. The Setup Assistant walks you through the process of configuring an AirPort Base Station (see Figure 18.1). Note that if you configure your Mac to *be* an AirPort Base Station, it will be able to act as a Base Station only while it's running Mac OS 9.1, not if you boot back into Mac OS X.

When you set up the Base Station, you give it a name and make some choices about security. You'll also be setting up Internet access. The AirPort Setup Assistant works by transferring the Internet settings from the Mac that is setting it up to the Base Station itself. So, if your Mac is configured for modem access in the TCP/IP and Remote Access control panels, those settings will be transferred to the Base Station. If you want the Base Station to be configured for Internet access in some other way, you'll need to set up the Mac with those settings before configuring the Base Station.

FIGURE 18.1

Configuring an AirPort Base Station

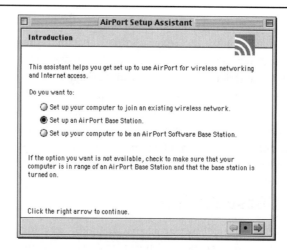

TIP Are you having trouble connecting to the Base Station? If your AirPort card seems to be working and the Base Station is turned on, but the two aren't communicating, you may need to check the AirPort card again. One of the most common goofs with AirPort is forgetting to plug the tiny antenna wire into the AirPort card. If you don't do this, it can't communicate with other AirPort devices, even though the Mac will report that it has found and configured the AirPort card.

Once the Base Station is set up properly, you're ready to select it for networking in Mac OS X. Back in the Network pane of the System Preferences application, select the AirPort tab. Choose the AirPort network you want to connect to and, if appropriate, enter the network password. Next, you can configure the rest of the Network pane to use AirPort for Internet access (if appropriate), and you can turn on AppleTalk, if desired (see Chapters 8 and 9). As long as your password for the network is correct, you should have a wireless online connection.

WARNING Apple notes that the Network pane doesn't give you a warning if you enter an incorrect password for the AirPort network—it simply won't work. This may be addressed in an interim update, but for now, you should be careful about entering the correct password for a network.

Adding Internal Devices

If you have a Power Macintosh model (as opposed to an iMac, iBook, or PowerBook), you might want to install internal hardware, such as additional hard disks or PCI cards. For other Macs, you may want to add an AirPort card (if your Mac supports AirPort) internally. You can also add RAM to your Mac.

Internal components that shipped with your Mac should be fine. If you've added secondary hard drives or if you've installed PCI cards, you may find that you need to do some tweaking to get Mac OS X to work correctly.

Internal Hard Disks

In most cases, you shouldn't have trouble with internal hard disks that are installed in your Power Macintosh. Mac OS X can't be installed on an ATA/IDE drive that is configured as a slave, although it can see and work with such drives. It may eventually allow you to install onto the slave drive, in some configurations, but early reports are that such installations are problematic.

As with external hard disks, you may need to update the hard disk driver software for a hard disk if it was formatted with a third-party utility such as Lacie's Silverlining (www.lacie.com) or FWB's Hard Disk Toolkit (www.fwb.com). If you can't get an update to the hard disk driver, your best solution may be to reformat the disk using Mac OS X's Disk Utility, discussed later in this chapter.

If you're working with internal SCSI drives, you may encounter a bit more trouble. First, you need to make sure that your SCSI adapter card is compatible with Mac OS X (assuming that you're using a SCSI adapter card, which is mandatory in Power Mac G3 and G4 models). Apple has a firmware fix for its Ultra Wide SCSI adapter installed in some Power Mac G3 (beige) systems. If you have a different Apple SCSI adapter or a third-party adapter, you may need to install a driver in order to access the drive. Adaptec (www.adaptec.com), one of the most popular vendors of Mac SCSI cards, has released beta drivers for many of its SCSI cards at the time of this writing. Also check the Mac OS X downloads Web site (www.apple.com/downloads/macosx/).

If you believe your SCSI card is compatible and/or you've updated the driver and you're still having trouble, you may be encountering SCSI voodoo (discussed in the "External Disks" section, earlier in this chapter). Try removing any external SCSI devices and restarting your Mac. If that doesn't work, you may need to check (or experiment with) the termination of the internal drives and make sure that you don't have any snagged or poorly connected cables inside the machine.

 NOTE Other hard disk issues are noted in Appendix A, including a problem where you may not be able to install Mac OS X onto a hard disk if its first (or only) partition is larger than 8GB.

Internal PCI Cards

In general, a PCI card needs a driver to work properly. If that PCI card originally shipped with your Mac, then the driver is most likely installed with Mac OS X. For instance, most video cards and SCSI cards that have been sold as part of various Mac models have drivers that are built in and support Mac OS X. So, your first step is to install Mac OS X and try the card out. It's possible that some internal PCI cards will simply work, particularly if they find generic drivers within Mac OS X that make them effective. In other cases, the cards might work, but not optimally. For instance, some third-party video cards are reportedly working with early Mac OS X installations, but not at the fully accelerated specifications of the card (particularly for 3D and gaming).

If you've added third-party video, Ethernet, video-capture, audio, or other PCI cards, you'll need Mac OS X drivers in most cases. Apple is fairly diligently tracking driver updates on its Mac OS X download site (`www.apple.com/downloads/macosx/drivers/`), which is one place to start looking. You should also consult the manufacturer of the device in question to see if the company is offering a Mac OS X driver.

If you have an immediate issue with a PCI card, it will likely be with a third-party Ethernet or SCSI card, many of which require drivers to work with Mac OS X, or with a specialized PCI card, such as a video-capture card. Asante (`www.asante.com`), Farallon (`www.farallon.com`), and other manufacturers of Mac-specific Ethernet cards are quickly updating their drivers; others may take more time, particularly manufacturers of more generic Ethernet cards designed for use in PCs and Macs.

Makers of PCI cards that add FireWire and USB ports to Macs seem to be having some luck with Mac OS X compatibility, including Sonnet Technologies (`www.sonnettech.com`) and Promax (`www.promax.com`), who have both made statements regarding Mac OS X compatibility. Again, check the manufacturer's site for upgrades and updates.

RAM

RAM is solid state—it either works or it doesn't. It doesn't require special driver software, either, although it does need to be recognized correctly by the Mac. Most Macs have guides to RAM installation in their user's manual.

To check whether the RAM you installed is being properly recognized, choose the About This Mac command in the Apple menu to see if the total amount of RAM is being accurately reported. You can also consult the Apple System Profiler, discussed in the next section, to see if RAM is being properly recognized.

If you think you've installed RAM that isn't being recognized, you should shut down your Mac, reopen its case, and ensure that the RAM is properly aligned and seated in its slot. If that doesn't appear to be the problem, you may have a firmware issue. On the weekend of Mac OS X's debut, Apple posted firmware updates that caused trouble with some types of RAM suddenly being unrecognized. Visit http://asu.info.apple.com and download the most recent firmware update for your Mac model. Run the installer to make sure your firmware is up-to-date.

NOTE In some cases, RAM that has worked in the past in your Mac model may suddenly stop working after you've installed a firmware update. This is a known issue; Apple has reworked the firmware so that RAM that is "out of spec" for Apple systems is disabled, preventing it from causing trouble in Mac OS X. (Mac OS X, apparently, is more finicky about installed RAM than is Mac OS 9.x.) If you install a firmware update and suddenly note that you have less RAM, contact the RAM vendor to see if there is a solution for the problem.

Troubleshooting Hardware with Apple System Profiler

Mac OS X includes Apple System Profiler (ASP), a great utility for learning more about your Mac in general, but particularly useful when you're having trouble with hardware. ASP can tell you exactly what the Mac OS is recognizing about your hardware, making it easier for you to determine where the problem might be if you can't seem to get a particular piece of hardware to work correctly. If ASP is able to show you the device, you know that it's installed properly. You can then determine whether there is a driver associated with the device. If not, you will need an updated driver or application to deal with that peripheral.

NOTE ASP should be located in the Utilities folder inside your main Applications folder. For more on the basics of using ASP, see Chapter 12.

When you're dealing with hardware, you'll focus on the first two tabs in the Apple System Profiler:

- The System Profile tab is useful for seeing whether RAM and network devices have been recognized.

- The Devices and Volumes tab is useful for seeing the USB, FireWire, PCI, and storage devices attached to your Mac.

System Profile Tab

Select the System Profile tab to check a few important facts. First, toward the top of the screen, you'll see a disclosure triangle next to Memory Overview. Click that triangle, then click the Built-in Memory triangle to see how much RAM is installed in your Mac and how it's installed. If you suspect that Mac OS X is underreporting the amount of RAM you've installed, you can check here to see which RAM modules are being recognized.

In the Hardware Overview section, the Keyboard Type entry shows the type of keyboard that has been recognized. If this entry doesn't match your actual keyboard, it may be a sign that you need an upgraded driver. This section also displays the type of Mac, processor, and processor speed. This information may be helpful if you're using a processor upgrade inside your Mac with Mac OS X. While processor upgrades are unsupported by Apple, several third-party companies, including Sonnet Technologies (www.sonnettech.com) and XLR8 (www.xlr8.com), have declared their upgrades Mac OS X–compatible. You can check ASP to see what CPU speeds are being registered by the Mac, which may be helpful if you're troubleshooting the processor upgrade.

The Network Overview section shows the Ethernet and/or other networking interfaces that are recognized and configured for your Mac. This can be useful if you're wondering whether an Ethernet PCI adapter or an internal AirPort card is being recognized. You can also learn the Ethernet adapter's MAC address (a number such as 00.00.00.AA.0F.AA), which you may need to know for some broadband modem setup or to track down which of your Ethernet devices (if you have more than one) is experiencing trouble.

Devices and Volumes Tab

The Devices and Volumes tab is useful for troubleshooting other internal and external peripherals, including USB and FireWire devices, PCI adapters, and your hard disk volumes. Using the information on this tab, you can determine whether certain devices are being recognized and whether they seem to have a particular driver associated with them. If you find that a problematic device is listed on the Devices and Volumes tab, then you know that the connection is being made, the cable is probably good, and the device is operational. That means that you're probably encountering a driver issue— either you need a driver or the current driver isn't performing correctly.

NOTE Devices in ASP aren't always updated correctly "on the fly." If you eject or unmount devices and they still appear in ASP, quit ASP and relaunch it to see your changes. Also note that ASP is a little buggy in Mac OS X 10.0. You may sometimes need to relaunch the application or even restart your Mac to get it to work correctly and recognize all devices. This may improve in later updates.

At the top of the tab's screen, you'll see the USB devices that have been recognized by the Mac. Clicking a disclosure triangle next to a particular device can tell you more about the device, the driver that is associated with it, and some other information, such as the device's power consumption.

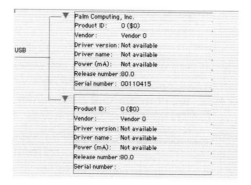

In this example, two USB devices have been recognized. Most Macs will also show their USB keyboard and mouse as recognized, but this test Mac, a Power Macintosh G3 (blue and white), happens to have an ADB keyboard and mouse attached. The top device is a Palm Computing cradle, which has been recognized by the Mac. It doesn't require a special driver, so no driver version is listed. The bottom device is recognized as connected to the Mac, but it doesn't appear to have any type of driver associated with it. This device is a Newer Technology iFloppy drive, which, as it turns out, isn't working properly. The suggestion here is that it could use a driver, which might not be forthcoming because Newer Technology is out of business.

If you have FireWire ports and FireWire devices attached to the Mac, next will be the FireWire entry. Select the disclosure triangle next to a FireWire device to see information about it.

In this example, the device recognized is an external FireWire hard drive that is functioning normally. Missing from the list is any indication of a second device I have attached—an external FireWire CD-RW drive. The drive will definitely need a third-party driver simply to be recognized, along with a third-party application (or a Mac OS X interim release) for burning CDs.

Next up are the PCI slots. Again, select the disclosure triangle next to one of the entries to see information about the card.

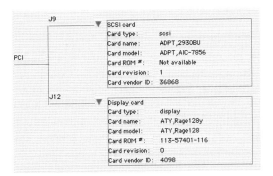

Here, both of my cards are recognized and functioning normally. The top entry is an Adaptec SCSI adapter that is working correctly, allowing an internal SCSI drive to appear on the desktop. The bottom entry is the standard Rage 128 Pro video card that shipped with the Power Macintosh G3 (blue and white) series.

Finally, at the bottom of the Devices and Volumes screen, you'll see information about all attached disk volumes, including hard disk partitions, removable media (Zips, CDs, and so on), and even mounted disk images.

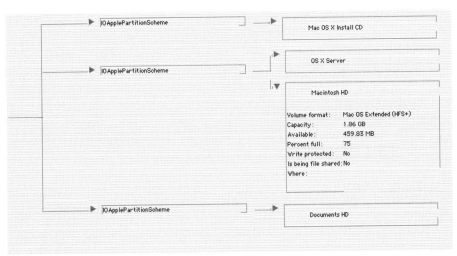

In this example, you see a CD and two hard disks that have been recognized. The first entry is the CD, which is recognized as the Mac OS X Install CD. The first hard disk has two partitions: one called Mac OS X Server and one called Macintosh HD (my main startup volume for Mac OS X). The second disk has a single partition, called Documents HD. Each entry includes information about the volume's format, capacity, and so on. This can be useful for learning whether or not a particular volume is being recognized, how it's formatted, and, in the case of multiple partitions, the disk on which a particular partition is located.

 TIP Want to dig even deeper? Select the Extensions tab in ASP to see all of the kernel extensions (and, thus, many of the drivers) that are installed on your Mac. If you've recently installed a driver that you don't believe is working, you can search through this list to see if it was properly installed and seems to be functioning. You can also use this list to see if a particular device would *seem* to have support. For instance, you'll find drivers for specific vendors (ATTO, nVidia, ATI, Sony, Adaptec, and so on) and devices that may mean that you can plug in a particular third-party device and use it successfully with Mac OS X.

Partitioning and Formatting Disks with Disk Utility

Mac OS X includes an application called Disk Utility, which incorporates the functionality of two utilities found in Mac OS 9.1 and earlier: First Aid and Drive Setup. Some of First Aid's capabilities (verifying and repairing disks) are discussed elsewhere in the book, including Chapters 20 and 21. Drive Setup can come in handy when you're dealing with new hard disks—internal or external—that you've added to your Mac. You can use Disk Setup to partition your disk, which erases and reformats it in the process. You can also use Disk Utility to simply and quickly erase all of the data from a disk and give it a new file system format, if desired.

Partitioning a Disk

In Mac OS X, partitioning a disk isn't particularly necessary. However, you may find disk partitioning convenient, because it allows you to install different OS versions on different partitions while minimizing the chance that they will interfere with one another. You may also want to partition your drives if you would like to use two different file systems—Unix File System and Mac OS Extended Format, for instance—on the same physical hard drive.

NOTE In certain cases, you may need to partition a disk before you can install Mac OS X. See Appendix A for details.

You may also wish to partition disks for simple efficiency. For instance, a partition that is dedicated completely to scratch video or audio files can be erased quickly and completely after a project has been properly saved and backed up, and you're ready to move on. Using the Erase Disk command in Disk Utility, you're able to not only remove all of the data you're finished with, but also start over with a completely defragmented drive. This works well with partitions for multimedia work, file sharing, Web serving, gaming, document files, or other data. Having two different volumes on the same disk offers a level of convenience in these situations.

What is inconvenient about partitioning a drive is the fact that the partitioning process will destroy all of the data on that drive in all partitions. Therefore, it's important that you partition a drive when you first add it to your Mac or after you've backed up all of your important data and you're willing to erase everything.

You can't partition disks that can't be written to, such as CD-ROMs or DVDs. Likewise, there's generally very little reason to partition removable media, because they are generally not large enough to warrant two volumes. (In almost all cases, you'll want each volume to be at least a few gigabytes in size to be useful.) In most cases, you'll opt to partition secondary external and internal hard disks, if you decide to partition at all.

 NOTE If you need to partition your startup disk, you can start up your Mac using the Mac OS X CD-ROM and launch Disk Utility. Note that doing so will erase all data from the startup disk, meaning that you'll need to reinstall Mac OS X (and any documents, applications, and utilities you've created or installed) after creating the partitions.

You use Drive Setup to partition disks. Launch Disk Utility, which is located in the Utilities folder inside the main Applications folder on your startup disk. Next, click the Drive Setup button in the Disk Utility window. The interface changes to the Drive Setup controls, and all attached disks appear at the top of the window, as shown in Figure 18.2.

Select the disk you want to partition from the Select Disk to Initialize portion of the window. If you're not logged in as an administrator, or if you're not the owner of the disk and don't have full privileges to access it, the disk may appear with a small lock as part of its icon and you may see the message "You don't have the privileges to edit this disk" on the Info tab. In that case, click the small padlock icon and enter either an administrator's name and password or the name and password of an administrator who has privileges for this disk.

FIGURE 18.2

The Drive Setup tools
in Disk Utility

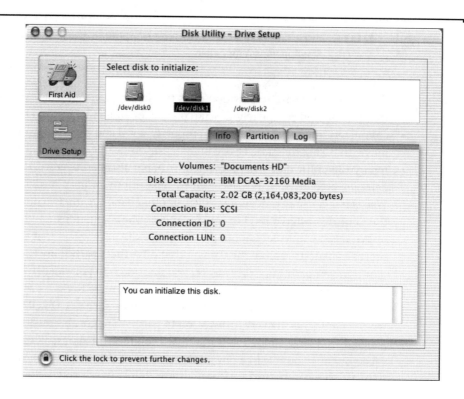

Once that's out of the way, you can click the Partition tab to begin partitioning the disk, as follows:

1. On the Partition tab, select the number of partitions you would like this disk to have from the Partition Scheme menu. You'll see the Volumes area change to represent that number of partitions.

2. Select one of the partitions in the Volumes area.

3. Click in the Name entry box and type a name for this volume.

4. From the Type menu, select the type of file system you want this partition to use. Mac OS Extended (HFS+) is recommended unless you have good reason to use Unix File System. Mac OS Standard isn't recommended unless you're dealing with removable media that needs to be compatible with Mac models running system software older than Mac OS 8.1.

5. Resize the partitions. You can do this one of two ways. First, you can drag the small resize bar that sits between two partitions to change the percentage of the drive

that is dedicated to a particular volume (see Figure 18.3). Alternatively, you can select a volume in the Volumes area, then enter a precise size for that volume in the Size entry box.

TIP You can use the Split button to further split a particular partition. Select a partition in the Volumes area, and then click the Split button. You can also delete a partition by selecting it and clicking Delete.

6. If you want the volume to be locked, or read-only, turn on the Locked option. (I'm hard-pressed to come up with a good reason for this, but you may have one.)

7. If you change your mind and want to revert the partition scheme back to the original settings, click the Revert button. Otherwise, if you're ready to go forward with the partitioning (and initialization) process, click the Partition button.

FIGURE 18.3

You can drag in the Volumes area to resize your partitions.

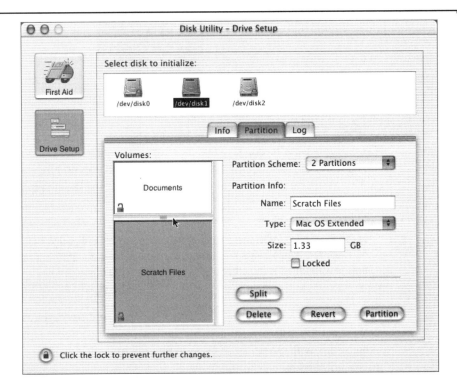

8. You'll see an alert box appear from the title bar of the Disk Utility window. If you're absolutely sure that you want to go forward with the partitioning—you'll lose *all* data currently on the drive—click Partition. Otherwise, click Cancel.

 WARNING Just for the record, I'll warn you again. You'll erase all of the files currently on your disk when you proceed with partitioning and initialization.

Once you click Partition, Disk Utility will spring into action. First, it unmounts the disk from the desktop, then it partitions the disk and replaces it with the number of volumes you created. The volumes are formatted and ready to use.

Erasing a Disk

If you simply want to quickly erase an entire disk—also called *formatting* the disk—you can do that from within Disk Utility. This is useful if you no longer need any of the data on a particular disk and/or you want to change the file system that the disk uses.

 NOTE Erasing individual partitions will not erase the entire disk that the partition is part of. Once a disk has been partitioned, each partition is a separate *volume*, which can be erased without affecting other partitions on the same physical drive.

To erase a disk, launch the Disk Utility program and select the First Aid button. Next, select the disk (or volume) you want to erase and choose Options ➢ Erase Disk. A dialog box will appear, asking you to rename the volume (if desired) and choose a file system format.

When you've made your selections, click Erase to proceed. You'll see the message "Erasing disk…" appear in the First Aid message area, and the formatting process will continue.

 WARNING   When you click Erase in the dialog box, the erase process begins immediately. All of the data on the drive will be lost (and only possibly recoverable with some third-party disk utilities). Double- and triple-check to make sure that you've selected the right volume and that you really want to erase every file on that volume.

What's Next?

In this chapter, you learned some of the specific issues concerning adding hardware under Mac OS X. It discussed the types of hardware that are supported by Mac OS X, as well as hardware that requires a workaround or third-party drivers. Also discussed were internal upgrades—such as hard disks, expansion cards, and RAM—and how you can get those upgrades working from within Mac OS X.

This chapter also covered two other utilities that are useful for dealing with hardware: Apple System Profiler and Disk Utility. Apple System Profiler can be used to examine and troubleshoot the internal and external devices that Mac OS X recognizes. Disk Utility can be used to partition and format disks.

In the next chapter, you'll learn how to troubleshoot application crashes and errors. You'll find steps for handling problems with both native and Classic Mac OS X applications.

CHAPTER 19

Fixing Trouble with Applications

Although Mac OS X itself is much more "crash-proof" than any previous version of the Mac OS, that doesn't necessarily mean you won't encounter *crashes*, which are simply problems with applications that cause them to stop running. After all, applications in Mac OS X are pretty much free to crash all they want; bugs and corruption, the main causes of application crashes, can still occur.

So you should be ready. While application crashes are much less likely to affect your entire Mac OS X session (for instance, in most cases, you can continue computing after an application crash without a restart), you'll still want to look into some strategies for dealing with crashes when they occur. Afterward, you'll want to troubleshoot to see why applications are crashing and what you can do to stop it.

If you work with Classic applications, you'll find that some of the limitations of earlier versions of the Mac OS are still around in the Classic environment. Classic applications can not only crash like any other application, but they can actually affect other Classic applications that are running at the same time—indeed the entire Classic environment. So, if you're having trouble with Classic applications, you'll want to troubleshoot those applications separately. We'll cover that later in this chapter.

Understanding Crashes and Errors

Mac OS X native applications—those written in Cocoa or Carbon—are likely to crash for three different reasons: bugs, conflicts, or corruption. *Bugs* are problems with the way an application is written—usually a mistake or oversight by the programmer. A *conflict* occurs when an application and a Mac OS component have trouble communicating; although this (ideally) occurs less frequently in Mac OS X than it did in earlier Mac OS versions, it's still a possibility.

Corruption happens when files contain errors in their data. This corruption can occur in the application file itself, but it's more likely to occur within the documents and preferences files that the application attempts to work with. Many applications are designed to create and edit text or image documents, and errors can creep into those files in a number of different ways. When such errors are encountered by an application, the application may respond with an error message or something more drastic, such as a crash.

More to the point, though, is the issue of what actually constitutes a crash and then what you can do about it. In general, you'll encounter a few different types of crashes and similar problems with applications in Mac OS X, each of which may have a different approach for rectifying it. They are:

> **Error message** If you encounter an error message but the application continues to function, that most likely means that the application has recovered and will continue to work properly. To be safe, you should save changes to any

documents in which you're currently working. You should also consider quitting and restarting the application, particularly if you suspect that the application has encountered corruption—for example, it reported an error with a document it attempted to open or a preference setting it tried to write.

Crash with error message   In this case, an application crashes and you see an alert message from that application; sometimes the alert message is helpful, but at other times it's less so. Sometimes an alert message can give you a hint that the problem is a bug, because the application has encountered a problem with an internal process and crashed. Error messages occasionally come from the application itself, but you're more likely to see standard Mac OS error messages:

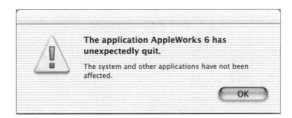

Crash without message   Sometimes you'll see an application that crashes and simply disappears; this is often the result of the program encountering corruption, as some programs have a tendency to just give up when they're fed erroneous data. This is especially true if you've just opened a new document or you suspect that the application is accessing a settings or preferences file.

Hang   A *hang* occurs when the application appears to stop responding. Often the spinning disk mouse pointer will appear when you're trying to work with the hung application. In most cases a hang is the result of a bug in the application: Either the application has entered an *endless loop,* or it has encountered corruption and doesn't know how to deal with the problem gracefully.

Freeze   A *freeze* is something you're much less likely to encounter in Mac OS X, but it happens from time to time. A freeze is like a hang, but you can't switch to other applications; in fact, you may not even be able to move the mouse pointer or get any response from the keyboard. In some cases freezes require a *hard restart* of the Mac, but there are some steps you can take before that to make sure.

NOTE In most cases any sort of crash, freeze, or hang will result in lost changes in any documents that you haven't recently saved. The best defense against lost work is to save often and, if possible, to turn on auto-save and auto-recovery features in your individual applications.

Recovering from Crashes and Hangs

If you encounter a crash, there isn't too much you have to do to recover—you'll usually be returned to the Finder or another open application after the crash. You can then relaunch the offending application (if you want to) or continue to work with other applications. You may want to troubleshoot the application following the crash; see the section "Diagnosing Application Troubles" later in this chapter.

 NOTE One other key to ultimately fixing a problematic application is to make a note of crashing behavior, including what you may have done immediately before the crash occurred. Whenever you're experiencing recurring crashes, jot down the circumstances on a pad of paper or in a Mac OS sticky note to help you remember the steps. You can then use the discussion in "Diagnosing Application Troubles" to try to determine why the crash is occurring. Also, for a more advanced approach, see the discussion of Crash Reporter in Chapter 20.

If you have a hang or freeze on your hands, there are some additional steps you'll need to take to determine what the problem is and resolve it. In most cases you should be able to stop the offending application and recover to the Finder; in other cases you may even be able to save data.

Of course, what steps you take with an unresponsive application depends on whether or not you have unsaved changes in the application. Here are some steps you should take if you encounter an unresponsive application in which you want to save data:

1. *Switch to another application.* Using either the Dock or the ⌘+Tab keyboard combination, try switching to another application. (You can also try clicking on the Mac's desktop to switch to the Finder.) If you switch successfully, you'll know that the Mac OS itself isn't responsible for the hang. If you can't seem to switch, then you either have a problem with your entire Mac or you have a physical problem with an input device.

2. *Check your keyboard and mouse connections.* If you've kicked or pulled your mouse or keyboard cable out of its port on your Mac, all of a sudden the mouse pointer and/or keyboard will stop responding. It may seem like you're encountering a software crash when, in fact, the problem is physical. Plug your mouse or keyboard back into the appropriate port, and see if your applications are responding correctly.

3. *Return to the application and wait a moment or two.* If your mouse and keyboard are connected and you can switch to other applications, then the next step is to wait for at least a few minutes before taking any more-drastic steps. An individual application can get caught in a seemingly endless loop, waiting for something to "time out" so that the application can return to normal. During this time, it's important not to press too many keys on the keyboard or click the mouse too often; you'll simply fill up the input buffer with stray key presses, which could cause more trouble.

4. *Save the document.* Press ⌘+S. If this saves the document, you may be able to keep working (the application may have sprung back to life), or maybe a particular thread of the application is hung. Once saved, though, you may be able to force-quit the application (see the next section, "Using Force Quit") without worrying about the document.

5. *Move the window, or switch to another window.* Sometimes an application pops up a dialog box or error message that inadvertently becomes hidden behind other windows. If you can't seem to get the application to work correctly (particularly if you hear beeps whenever you click the mouse button on a document window), try moving or minimizing the front-most window to see if another window or dialog box is behind it. The dialog box may be halting other operations in the application.

6. *Unplug external devices.* It's possible that an external FireWire, USB, or SCSI device is causing the application to hang while the application is trying to figure out how to work with that device. If you've recently plugged in a device or if you're seeing activity with a particular device, or if you simply want to be thorough in your troubleshooting, you should unplug or cut power to any suspect devices (or *all* of them, particularly "hot-swappable" USB and FireWire devices) to see if that frees up the application. (Don't unplug or cut power to a device that you know *another* application or the Finder is actively accessing; in that case you should wait as long as possible before giving up and unplugging the device.)

7. *Quit the application.* If you can't save your document (or if you don't have a particular document with changes), you can try accessing the application's Quit command via its application menu or by pressing ⌘+Q. Do this only once, though; if you aren't successful, continue to wait for a little while.

8. *Quit other applications.* If you have other applications open—particularly if you have *many* other applications open—you should close one or more of them. Doing so may free up system memory for the hanging application, just in case that application has encountered trouble because your Mac's system memory is being taken up by too many open applications at once.

9. *Log out.* Another solution to a hung application is to attempt to log out and see if the application will quit and enable you to save the document.

If none of these steps works, you may have encountered an application that is truly hung. (But if you've succeeded in switching to other applications, you can be fairly certain that the Mac OS itself isn't frozen.) The next step in dealing with a hung application will, unfortunately, cause you to lose unsaved data: Force Quit.

 NOTE If it does appear that the Mac itself has hung (you can't move the mouse pointer or you can't seem to switch to other applications), you'll need to move on to some lower-level recovery options, discussed in Chapter 20.

Using Force Quit

The Force Quit command enables you to do just that—force an application to quit. Under almost all circumstances, an errant application will receive the Force Quit command and dutifully shut down. The command tells Mac OS X to stop the running of the underlying application *processes*. This step cuts the application off from the other side, so to speak, causing it to quit.

To force-quit an application, you launch the Force Quit Applications window. You can do this in one of three ways:

- Pull down the Apple menu and select Force Quit.
- Switch to another application (by using the Dock, pressing ⌘+Tab, or clicking on the desktop background), then select Force Quit from the Apple menu.
- Press ⌘+Option+Esc.

Any of these three options (whichever one will work for you) will bring up the
Force Quit Applications window:

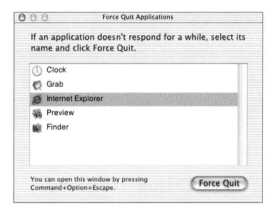

 TIP The Force Quit Applications window can actually be used to switch between open
applications as well—simply double-click one of the applications in the list. This might come
in handy on the off chance that the Dock is the application that you're having trouble with.

Now, in the Force Quit Applications window, select the application that you want
to stop from running; then click Force Quit. You'll see a dialog sheet, asking if you're
sure you want to force the application to quit. If you're sure, click the Force Quit button in the dialog sheet. The application should be forced to close without attempting
to save any changed data; it will disappear from the screen (if any windows are open),
and its application icon will no longer be on the Dock. (If the application has its icon
on the Dock permanently, the icon won't disappear; instead, the running indicator
will no longer appear under the icon.)

 NOTE If you select the Finder in the Force Quit Applications window, you'll notice that
the Force Quit button will change to Relaunch; you can, in fact, relaunch the Finder if it
seems to be having trouble. In many cases it will recover without further problems—you
can continue computing after the relaunch.

The Force Quit Applications window stays floating over all other windows so that
you can force any other applications to quit, if desired. If you're done with the Force
Quit Applications window, click its Close button to dismiss it.

WARNING Generally, it's not recommended that you restart your Mac by pressing the power button or plugging and unplugging the Mac from your surge protector or wall plug. Instead, if Force Quit doesn't seem to be able to stop an application, check Chapter 20 for other tips on restarting the Mac in an emergency.

So what do you do if Force Quit doesn't work? At that point, it's time to put on your system administrator's hat and dig into some of the more complex tools for troubleshooting and recovery. See Chapter 20 for tips on managing and killing processes as the administrator.

Diagnosing Application Troubles

Once you've gotten past the initial problems with your application and recovered or forced the application to quit, you can dig in and begin to figure out the root cause of the problem.

The first step in diagnosing problems is to note the symptoms. The key to this is probably to keep a notebook next to your computer when you begin to experience repeated trouble. Note the exact circumstances of a crash: what you were doing, what files or documents you were working with, and what button you clicked or other action you took. If you're experiencing chronic crashing in your applications, simply noting when and how the trouble occurs may help you begin to uncover the source.

The second step is to determine whether or not the error is reproducible. This can be the most important factor in helping you diagnose trouble. As you log symptoms, you may begin to see a pattern with that application—for example, it crashes every time it loads a particular document, it hangs when accessing a certain Web site, or it disappears from the screen without warning whenever you print. Now you should try to purposefully reproduce the circumstances within which the crash occurs. Go back through the steps you've logged and see if the problem happens again. If it does, you'll get a better sense of the type of problem you're having and what the solution may be. If it doesn't, you may need to continue logging symptoms until you get another idea for reproducing the problem.

Once you've successfully noted the symptoms and reproduced the problem, you can move on to deciding why the problem is occurring—whether the symptoms seem to suggest a bug, corruption, or conflict—and then taking some steps to resolve the problem.

Diagnosis: Bug

If you notice that a crash occurs every time you try to access a particular command in your application, that's a sign that you're dealing with a bug. Bugs can be generally characterized as "the application doing something wrong." This can be different from trouble with a particular document or preference setting; if you can focus in on a problematic document, the issue might be corruption. But if the problem happens in many different documents, it's possible you're dealing with a bug.

The solution for most bugs is to either update the offending application or figure out how to work around the problem. If your application came with a Read Me file or similar document in its installation folder or on its CD-ROM, read that document to see if any "known issues" are discussed. Sometimes application developers are already aware of the bugs and have offered ways to work around them.

You should also consult the application developer's Web site to see if an update has been made available that addresses the bug. If not, you should look to see if the Web site offers troubleshooting or workaround advice for dealing with the bug. If you still don't find any information, you may want to report the bug to the software manufacturer's technical support staff; the company may have a workaround they can tell you about. Even if they can't solve the problem immediately, hopefully they'll appreciate the information to help them track the problem down.

If the application's developer isn't particularly helpful, your solution will likely be to simply stop using the application or stop using the feature that's buggy. Just to be sure, though, check the next sections to make sure you aren't really encountering corruption or conflicts.

Diagnosis: Corruption

Corruption can sometimes be easy to diagnose, particularly if you notice problems when you're opening a particular document or set of documents. However, most applications are also often writing data to their preferences files, loading and working with fonts, and accessing underlying parts of the Mac OS. Others may have internal documents that they store and constantly retrieve information from (such as e-mail or address book databases, and cache files in an Internet browser). Any type of document file that is often left open and is constantly read or written to is susceptible to corruption. This is especially true if an application crashes while working with a particular file, or if the Mac itself hangs, loses power, or shuts down abruptly.

Tracking down corruption requires that you carefully note and document the circumstances of each crash. If you notice that a particular document seems to cause the crash, that document is likely corrupt. If that's the case, you should stop using the document and see if crashing persists. If that document is the culprit, you might want to attempt to recover the data from the document, if you can, or run a disk doctor utility to see if the file can be fixed. Otherwise, stop using it.

Preferences Files

You'll sometimes find corruption in the preferences files that applications create and store in your Preferences folder, which is located in the ~/Library/Preferences/ hierarchy on your hard disk (see Figure 19.1). If you notice that your application crashes when you access its Preferences command, or that it crashes when you launch or quit the application, it's possible that you've run into some corruption.

FIGURE 19.1

Every time you launch a new application, a preferences file is created in your personal /Library/ Preferences *folder.*

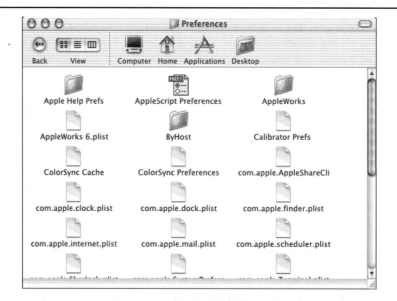

If you suspect that an application's preferences file is corrupt, you should begin by quitting the application. Next, drag the file out of the Preferences folder and place it in another folder, perhaps a subfolder of your Documents folder. (Or you could drag the file to your desktop for temporary safekeeping.)

Now, launch the application and test it again. In most cases applications aren't adversely affected by the absence of a preferences file; the application will simply create a new one. (Of course, you may need to reset some preferences, if you've customized them.) If the same crashing continues, the preferences file may not have been the culprit; if you feel you need to, you can return the original file to the Preferences folder. (If you're okay with the newly created preferences file, there's no need to return the old one.)

Once you've fully tested the suspected preferences file and you're sure you no longer need it, you can toss it in the Trash.

 NOTE Not all applications follow the convention, but Mac OS X introduces a special way for preferences files to be named. The name follows the pattern domain_type .domain.application.plist. This is intended to be useful to the user, because it gives you some hints for locating the Web site of the software publisher responsible for a particular preferences file, as in com.apple.clock.plist or com.microsoft.explorer.plist. Also note that many preferences files are simply Plain Text or, in some cases, XML (Extensible Markup Language) files. While it isn't a great idea to go playing with your preferences files, if you're the intrepid type, you may find interesting information within a preferences file by opening it (or, better yet, duplicating the file and opening the duplicate) in a text editor. Shareware and freeware utilities such as Marcel Bresink's PrefEdit (www.bresink.de/osx/) can also help you peek into and edit your preferences files.

Database Corruption

Along with documents and preferences files, other important files may sometimes become corrupt. For instance, if your application is based on a large database (such as Mac OS X's Mail application), portions of that database can become corrupt (or simply fragmented, thanks to repeated deletions or changes) and eventually cause problems. For this type of application, you'll probably need to look for a solution within the application. Most applications that are based on databases also have a built-in way to rebuild those databases. (For instance, Mail has the Mailbox ➤ Rebuild Mailbox command, which can be used to increase the speed and reliability of a particular mailbox's database.)

Internet Cache Corruption

Another area of trouble can be crashing within Internet applications. Web browsers and some other Internet applications rely on cache, history, and similar files that are written to and read from repeatedly. If you notice that your Web browser is crashing often, you may want to test the different files in which the browser stores links and data. Internet Explorer, for instance, stores important files in a folder called Explorer in your ~/Library/Preferences folder; there you'll find a number of files including those where History and Favorites links are stored. Internet Explorer also, by default, stores cached pages and images in a database file called IE cache.waf that's stored in the folder MS Internet Cache, which is also inside your ~/Library/Preferences folder. Other Web browsers will likely store their own cache files in folders that those applications create in your personal Preferences folder.

When you have trouble with a Web browser, you should consider shutting down the browser and moving the cache file to another folder on your Mac. (You can simply drag the cache database file to the Trash if you don't mind losing the images and Web pages that are stored in it. Removing the cache means that some pages you've visited recently will need to be completely downloaded again the next time you attempt to access them.) Restart the browser and see if the problem disappears. If it's still there, or if you notice that you have trouble specifically when you attempt to access your history or bookmarks files (Favorites in Internet Explorer), you can quit the browser again and move those files to a new folder. It's possible that one of them has become corrupted and is causing the browser to choke on bad data, resulting in an error or crash.

If you're having trouble with a number of different Internet applications, it's possible that your main Internet preferences file has become corrupt. Troubleshoot the file `com.apple.internet.plist` by removing it from your Preferences folder (place it in another folder) and retesting your Internet applications. If that solves the problem, you should delete the Internet Preferences folder and reset preferences in the Internet pane of the System Preferences application.

Font Corruption

If you notice trouble with your application as it starts up or when you select a particular font, that font may be corrupt. You may also encounter the trouble when you're printing a particular document that contains a corrupt font. Or, if you're experiencing crashes when attempting to print from a number of different applications, you should at least consider whether a particular font is being used in all of those various applications. If so, remove the font from its folder (either `/Library/Fonts/` or your personal `~/Library/Fonts/` folder, depending on where the font is installed) and check to see if the crashing continues. If the problem seems solved, you'll need to either avoid using the font or reinstall it.

 NOTE Trouble with printing from multiple applications could also suggest a problematic printer driver. If you don't seem to find a corrupt font as the culprit, you might visit your printer manufacturer's Web site to see if troubleshooting information or a new printer driver has been made available.

Diagnosis: Conflict

Conflicts between the Mac OS and your applications aren't as likely in Mac OS X as they are in earlier versions of the Mac OS, mainly because Mac OS X acts as a barrier between your applications and the driver software you install with Mac OS X. As you'll see in the section "Troubleshooting Classic Applications," previous versions of the Mac OS are capable of accepting *extensions,* which can alter the capabilities of the Mac OS but can also prove problematic with some applications. Mac OS X doesn't support extensions in this way.

In fact, the newness of Mac OS X makes it difficult to know exactly what conflicts may arise, and how. In most cases problems between Mac OS X and applications will likely be very similar to bugs; the application will simply need to be updated to deal with any underlying issues it has with the Mac OS.

If you suddenly begin having trouble with an application after you've installed new system software, new driver software, or a hardware device, that may indicate a conflict. In this case, the best plan is to attempt to uninstall the device or software. Once it's uninstalled, if the application works correctly again, you may have found the culprit. At that point, though, you may have to decide which is more important—the application or the component you just installed.

If you notice that crashes occur with specific applications when they interact with specific system software, that may suggest a conflict. For instance, if you notice crashing when an application attempts to access system dialog boxes (Print, Save, Open) or underlying technology like ColorSync, QuickTime, or graphics acceleration routines, you may have a conflict. This is particularly true if you're working with a newer version of the system software than the application was originally tested against, or if you've recently updated the Mac OS via the Software Update pane in the System Preferences application. (See Chapter 20 for details on using Software Update.)

So what can you do? Aside from not using one or the other of the items that are in conflict, your best approach may be to check the Read Me files, Web sites, and documentation of each application/device that's involved. You may find that you're dealing with a known issue or a conflict that has previously been reported and identified. In that case you may find a fix for the problem or a workaround of some kind. If not, you should contact customer service for one or more of the devices and let them know what problems you're having.

Troubleshooting Classic Applications

Aside from outward appearances—Classic applications look a little different from native applications—the most significant difference is that Classic applications don't offer the same robust defenses against crashes and conflicts that Mac OS X applications do. Although any application can crash, in Mac OS X, such crashes are far less likely to affect other applications that are running at that time. In the Classic environment, however, the crashing of a Classic application can easily affect others—or even the entire Classic environment itself, which can also freeze or crash. So, in this section we'll take a look at troubleshooting some of the issues that can specifically affect Classic applications.

Recovering from Crashes and Freezes

If a Classic environment application crashes or freezes, you can begin by trouble-shooting the problem in the same way that you troubleshoot crashes and freezes with native Mac OS X applications. If you receive an error message in a dialog box during a crash, it may point you in the right direction. If you don't get an error and the application simply disappears, you have less indication.

If a freeze or hang occurs, you'll want to take the same steps you use in combating a freeze or hang in a native application. In particular, you should wait a few minutes, check to see if you can switch to other applications, and make sure you aren't experiencing a problem with an unplugged keyboard or an errant peripheral device.

If you've encountered a problem that you believe requires you to force the application to quit, the solution is the same: Simply press ⌘+Option+Esc, which should bring up the Force Quit Applications window. Select the Classic application and click Force Quit. The application should stop running.

Now, once a crash or Force Quit has taken place, it's important to restart any *other* running Classic applications, along with the Classic environment itself. That's because of the shared nature of the Classic environment's memory space (Classic applications can conceivably overwrite portions of each other's memory, causing problems) as well as the fact that, once a Classic application has crashed, the Classic environment is simply less stable.

Here are the steps to take after you've used Force Quit to stop a crashed or hung Classic application:

1. Immediately save changes to any other documents that are open in Classic applications, then quit those applications.

2. Open the System Preferences application and select the Classic pane (see Figure 19.2).

3. On the Start/Stop tab of the Classic pane, you have a number of options for managing the Classic environment, including these:

   Stop   If you see the Stop button, that means that Classic is currently running. You can click the Stop button at any time to shut down the Classic environment. This is similar to selecting the Shut Down command in the Finder, except that it will shut down only the Classic environment, not your entire Mac. It will also shut down any Classic applications that are running, and it will ask you to save changes in any documents that are currently open and unsaved.

FIGURE 19.2

The Start/Stop tab of the Classic pane in System Preferences

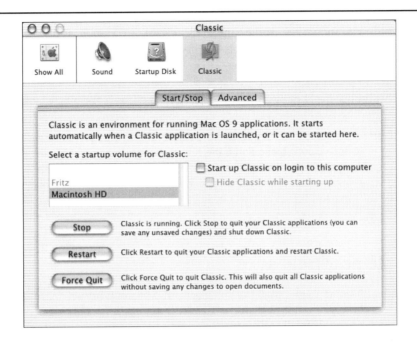

Restart   You can select the Restart button if you'd like to shut down and then restart the Classic environment. This is a good idea if you've had a Classic application crash or encountered memory errors. In fact, it's a good idea to restart the Classic environment periodically before trouble strikes, especially if you've been running many Classic applications and/or if the Classic environment has been running for a few days.

Force Quit   If you can't seem to get the Classic environment to shut down or restart, you may need to force it to quit. You can do that by clicking the Force Quit button. This will kill the Classic environment processes, and any unsaved document changes will be lost. Also, if Classic won't quit and won't allow your Mac to shut down or restart, a Force Quit will allow you to shut down your entire system.

4. Once you've made your choice, close the System Preferences window and continue computing, using native applications. If you like, you can restart any Classic applications from the Finder, or you can launch and troubleshoot the Classic environment as detailed in the later section "Managing Classic Conflicts."

After you've recovered from the problem and restarted the Classic environment, you should take some time to troubleshoot the application itself, if you can. Check the sections earlier in this chapter for tips on troubleshooting bugs in native applications. Those same ideas apply to Classic applications.

 NOTE For troubleshooting corruption, you'll find that the process is the same, but the location of some system-level files is different. For instance, if you suspect that the preferences file for a Classic application is the culprit, you may need to look in the Preferences folder of the System Folder that you use for your Classic environment. Likewise, fonts for the Classic environment are stored in the Fonts folder inside Classic's System Folder; if you suspect font corruption, you'll need to head to that Fonts folder to remove those fonts for troubleshooting.

Memory Issues

In the Classic environment, memory is handled differently than it is in the native Mac OS X environment. With native applications, Mac OS X is able to allocate memory dynamically, meaning that memory is given to applications as they need it. With Classic applications, memory can be allocated dynamically to the Classic environment, but individual applications are allocated memory in a more primitive, fixed way. So, if you're having trouble with an application that runs out of memory (or if you notice that crashing occurs when the application is asked to open a large number of documents or deal with a computing-intensive task), you may need to change the application's memory allocation.

Memory allocation is managed through the Info window in the Finder. Here's how:

1. Quit the Classic application whose memory allocation you'd like to alter.

2. Locate the application in the Finder.

3. Select the application's icon, and choose File ➤ Show Info or select ⌘+I. This brings up the Info window.

4. In the Info window, select Memory from the Show pop-up menu. You'll see three items listed: Suggested Size, Preferred Size, and Minimum Size (see Figure 19.3).

The numbers in the Info window represent the amount of RAM, in bytes, that the Classic environment attempts to allocate to the application when it launches. If the Classic environment doesn't have at least the minimum amount available, you'll see an error message telling you that the application can't be launched. If the Classic environment has more than the minimum available, it will give the application as much memory as it can, up to the preferred size.

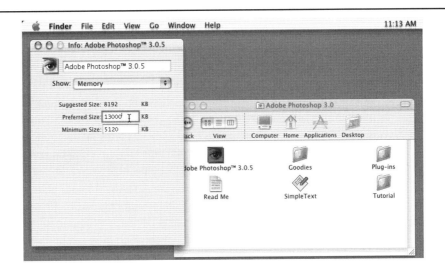

FIGURE 19.3

In the Info window, you can set your minimum and preferred memory sizes.

If you suspect that the application is crashing often and chronically due to memory problems, particularly if the application has trouble even starting up and warns of a memory problem, it's possible that the application's minimum size is too low. Click in the Minimum Size entry box and edit the amount of RAM allocated. You don't want to set the minimum size too high; consider bumping it up one megabyte (approximately 1,024K) or so.

 NOTE Although a megabyte of RAM is technically 1,024K and you'll often see RAM minimums expressed as multiples of that number (for instance, 8,192 or 10,240), it isn't mandatory that you set the preferred and minimum sizes at those levels; you can enter 8,000 or 10,000 if you like.

You should set the preferred memory size to at least the suggested size, which is the recommendation built into the application by the application developers. If you notice that the application still runs into frequent memory errors, or you can't seem to open as many documents as you'd like, you can set the preferred size higher by a few megabytes. Note that some applications, particularly graphics and multimedia applications, work particularly well with a large preferred size setting.

Remember, though, that the amount of RAM that's allocated to one application will take away from the amount of RAM that can be allocated to another application, whether it's a Classic or native Mac OS X application. This means that setting a particularly high preferred memory number can affect your ability to run other applications while that memory hog is running.

The Classic environment can run into another problem: memory fragmentation. When a number of Classic applications are started, quit, and started—while the Classic environment runs continuously—those applications can leave fragments of memory behind, which make it more difficult for the Classic environment to allocate RAM effectively. If you notice memory errors with your Classic applications that just don't seem to make sense (for instance, you can't launch a Classic application even though you have no or very few other applications running), you may need to restart the Classic environment. Restarting clears out Classic memory and enables it to begin allocating with a fresh block of available memory.

 NOTE In general, you'll have trouble working with the Classic environment and Classic applications if you have less than 128MB of RAM installed in your Mac. Although Mac OS X and native applications can get by with less, the RAM requirements of launching both the Classic environment and a few Classic applications can double the amount of RAM required for decent performance on your Mac. So, if you plan to work with Classic applications, you should upgrade your Mac to *at least* 128MB, and preferably 256MB or more, for best performance.

Managing Classic Conflicts

As mentioned before, earlier Mac OS versions and applications are much more apt to encounter conflicts than is Mac OS X. The Classic environment, because it's based on Mac OS 9.*x*, is more susceptible to conflicts between it and Classic applications. So, if you find yourself having trouble with Classic applications, a conflict may be one issue to consider, after you've ruled out bugs and corruption.

In the Classic environment, conflicts can occur between two different applications; so, if you notice crashing or freezing, you should also note whether the problems occur when a particular pair or group of applications are open. If that's the case, you can test to see if the conflict is reproducible: Launch both (or all) applications on their own, then reproduce the steps that caused the crash. If the crash happens every time (or if it happens with some frequency), you may have your conflict. You'll need to consult the applications' developers to see if they've developed a fix or workaround.

Most of the time, however, conflicts occur between *extensions* to the Classic environment and applications. These extensions, created by either Apple or third parties, augment the capabilities of the basic Classic environment by *patching* portions of it with new bits of code. (If you've worked with Mac OS 9.*x* or earlier, you're probably very familiar with extensions.)

So, if you're having trouble with a Classic application and it doesn't appear to be a bug, corruption, or a conflict with another Classic application, it may be a conflict with an extension to the Classic environment.

 NOTE Conflict Catcher by Casady and Greene (`www.casadyg.com`) has long been considered the ideal tool for managing conflicts in Mac OS 9.*x* and earlier. The latest versions (Conflict Catcher 8.0.8 and higher) have boasted additional features to help deal with the Classic environment under Mac OS X. If you're having Classic conflict troubles and you don't feel like troubleshooting manually, you might consider purchasing Conflict Catcher.

Testing for Extension Conflicts

Testing for extension conflicts can be tiresome. You first have to determine if an extension (or group of extensions) is causing the problem. Then you have to determine *which* extension or group of extensions is causing the problem. Finally, you have to decide what to do about the fact that an extension or group of extensions is causing the problem.

 TIP Some conflicts are known issues. Consult the Read Me file or customer support of the publisher of the crashing application to see if any extension conflicts have been identified. If so, and if you have the extension loaded, you may be able to stop the crashing immediately by disabling the extension.

There's a method to this madness of extension troubleshooting. Generally, you begin by turning off all extensions and launching the Classic environment. You then test the application to see if it has a problem. If it doesn't, you can move on to the next step. In the next step, you enable only the extensions that are native to the Classic environment, to see if the application is in conflict with a "built-in" extension—one that Apple includes or has updated. If there's no trouble with built-in extensions, the final step is to enable third-party extensions and determine which of those are causing the conflict.

Fortunately, the Mac OS has tools available for troubleshooting extension conflicts. Launch the System Preferences application and open the Classic pane. Click the Advanced tab, and you'll see some options that enable you to troubleshoot conflicts (see Figure 19.4).

FIGURE 19.4

The Advanced tab of the Classic pane offers options for trouble-shooting conflicts.

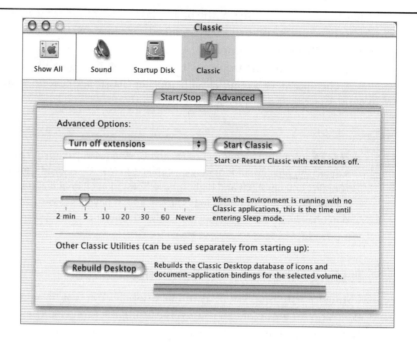

From the Advanced Options pop-up menu, you have two choices for testing extensions:

Turn Off Extensions   If you choose this option and click Start Classic (or Restart Classic, if the environment is already running), the Classic environment will launch with no extensions active. You can then test your application again to see if the application isn't really conflicting with an extension, but rather encountering a bug or corruption. If you start up Classic with extensions turned off and your application encounters the same trouble as before, you probably aren't seeing a conflict.

NOTE   If the application is encountering *different* trouble, the problem may be that the application requires some extensions to function properly. If that's the case, you'll need to enable at least the required extension(s) and then test again.

Open Extensions Manager   Select this option and click Start Classic. The Classic environment will start up and then display the Extensions Manager (see Figure 19.5). It's within the Extensions Manager that you'll find the tools for activating sets of extensions or individual extensions.

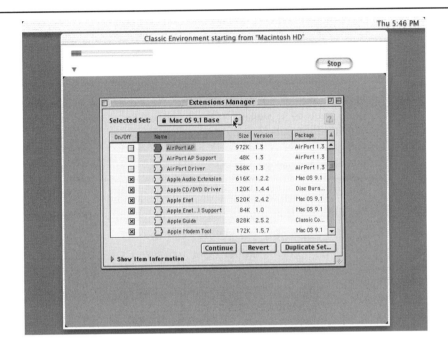

FIGURE 19.5

In the Extensions Manager, you can enable and disable extensions by clicking the check boxes next to them.

For instance, if you've determined that the application isn't having trouble when no extensions are enabled, you can select the Mac OS 9.1 Base option from the Selected Set pop-up menu, then click the Continue button to allow Classic to continue starting up. Once Classic is started up, you can test to see if the conflict occurs. If it doesn't, then you've eliminated the possibility of a conflict with Apple's base set of extensions.

 TIP   Actually, you have a third choice in the Advanced Options pop-up menu: Use Key Combination. If you'd like to start the Classic environment so that it believes certain keys are being held down (for instance, the Shift key to bypass all extensions or any keystroke combinations recognized by third-party extensions), select the Use Key Combination option, then press up to five keys. Press the Clear key to reset the key combination.

From here, you can use the Extensions Manager to enable individual extensions, in addition to the Classic Extensions set. You then systematically restart the Mac and add to the extensions until you locate the conflict. Here's how:

1. Enable the Classic Extensions set, then place a check mark next to a few of the third-party extensions. (If you actually have a particular extension or set of extensions that you suspect as being the problem, you can enable those first.) The first time you do this, you'll be asked to create a new set of extensions. Name the set and click Save.

 NOTE You can arrange items in the Extensions Manager in alphabetical order, by type of extension, or by package. You may find package order the most useful if you have some idea of what may be causing the conflict (for instance, if you suspect a particular manufacturer's extensions). Otherwise, enabling the control panels first, then the extensions, alphabetically, may be the best approach.

2. Click the Continue button. When the Classic environment finishes starting up, launch the application and test it.

3. If you don't encounter trouble, restart Classic again with the Open Extensions Manager command, then add three to five more extensions to your new set. Continue into the Classic environment and test your application. Keep doing this until you encounter trouble.

4. Once you encounter trouble, restart Classic with the Open Extensions Manager option once again; then, in the Extensions Manager, *disable* all but the first extension in your most recently added set of extensions. Continue into the environment and test the application.

5. Repeat step 4 with all the extensions in that final set until you find the extension that caused the problem.

Now you may have isolated your conflict. If you notice that removing the extension from your startup set causes the trouble to stop with the problematic application, that extension may be all you need to worry about. Try to determine where the extension came from, and contact that software publisher to see if an update, workaround, or any other information is available.

 NOTE Finding one problematic extension isn't always the end of your troubles. For one thing, you may have identified an extension that's crucial to your Classic computing. If that's the case, it's possible that *two or more* extensions are in conflict and are causing trouble. If you suspect that the problem is with more than one extension, you may need to add the problematic extension to your base Mac OS set of extensions, then begin testing again at step 1 above.

Faster Classic Startup: Manage Extensions

If you use the Classic environment only on a limited basis, or only for a few applications, you may find it useful to customize the number of extensions that are enabled in the Extensions Manager. If you choose a limited number of extensions, the Classic environment will launch more quickly, and, once launched, it will require less overall system RAM.

The easy way to accomplish this is to launch Classic from the Advanced tab in the Classic pane of System Preferences, with the Open Extensions Manager option turned on. When the Extensions Manager appears, choose Mac OS 9.1 Base. Now, in the Extensions Manager, you'll want to enable the additional items required by Mac OS X in order for the Classic environment to run: Classic RAVE, Classic Support UI, and ProxyApp. (Technically these last two aren't extensions, but they are required for the Classic environment to function properly.)

Note that the first time you attempt to click one of these items to enable it, you'll be asked to create a new set. In the alert box, click Duplicate Set, give the set a name in the dialog box that appears (perhaps "Fast Classic" or something similar), and click OK. Now you can enable those important Classic extensions. Then, continue into the Classic environment by clicking Continue in the Extensions Manager. The launch should take between 30 and 45 seconds—faster than the typical startup time by a minute or more.

If you're feeling intrepid, you can dig in and disable other extensions as well, depending on what tasks you tend to attempt in Classic. Again, with the Fast Classic set you created in the Selected Set menu, begin turning off items. Turn off some of the items in the Control Panels folder, for instance, if you don't use the Appearance, Control Strip, and similar control panels.

If you don't use games or other 3D applications, you can turn off ATI extensions; if you don't print from Classic, you can turn off the various printer drivers (other than the LaserWriter 8 and PrintingLib) as well as the Desktop Print Spooler, the Desktop Print Monitor, and the regular PrintMonitor. In any case, you can turn off DVD extensions, since they aren't used in the Classic environment, anyway. Note that the Classic environment requires all of the following in order to launch without complaint:

- General Controls and Startup Disk (in Control Panels)
- Apple Guide, AppleShare, CarbonLib, Classic RAVE, File Sharing Extension, LaserWriter 8, Open Transport, Open Transport ASLM Modules, OpenTpt Remote Access, PrintingLib, and QuickDraw 3D RAVE (all in Extensions)
- Classic Support UI and ProxyApp (both in the System Folder)

Continued

CONTINUED

When you're finished configuring, you can click the Continue button to launch the Classic environment; hopefully it happens very quickly. Now, the next time you launch Classic or a Classic application, it should seem like only a slight pause before the Classic application appears.

If there's a downside to this tweak, it's that you'll run into many applications that won't run without associated extensions or control panels. If that's the case, you'll have to relaunch Extensions Manager and enable the necessary components—and they may not be particularly easy to figure out.

One other thing: If you boot into Mac OS 9.1 using the same System Folder that you use for Classic, you should hold down the spacebar while Mac OS 9.1 starts up. You'll see the Extensions Manager again, enabling you to select a different set of extensions in the Selected Set menu—preferably one you've created specifically for booting into the full Mac OS 9.1 operating system. In this case you probably will want many or most of your extensions enabled so that you can get the most out of your sessions in the Mac OS 9.1 environment.

Noting Problem Extensions

In the Classic window, extensions are represented by small icons that crawl along the bottom of the screen, appearing as they're loaded by the Classic environment.

If an extension appears with an X through it, it means that the extension isn't loading correctly. In the Extensions Manager, you can disable that extension to make sure it doesn't try to load in the future, which could cause instability. Note, however, that the extension may be necessary for booting into Mac OS 9.1. In that case it's a good idea to use the Extensions Manager to create two different sets of extensions— those for loading with the Classic environment and those that should be loaded when you're booting directly into Mac OS 9.1. You can then use the Extensions Manager to switch between the two sets, depending on which is appropriate.

 TIP To launch the Extensions Manager when you're booting into Mac OS 9.1, hold down the spacebar as the Mac is starting up, until you see the Extensions Manager window. Then you can change the set you want to use by choosing it in the Selected Set pop-up menu.

What's Next?

In this chapter you saw some of the problems that can affect applications in Mac OS X and how to troubleshoot them. Included was a discussion of recovering from crashes and hangs and forcing applications to quit, when necessary. You also saw how to troubleshoot bugs, corruption, and conflicts. In the second half of the chapter, you saw how to troubleshoot the Classic environment as well as conflicts and problems encountered by Classic applications.

In the next chapter you'll see how to deal with problems that arise with Mac OS X itself, including some tips for low-level troubleshooting and recovering from major problems with the operating system.

Troubleshooting
Mac OS X

Not that you'd know it from the hype, but sometime, somewhere, Mac OS X might not perform the way you want it to. Apple has been working on Mac OS X for some time, but it's just now being released "into the wild." The way it behaved under laboratory conditions may not be the way it will behave for every user. Each user has a particular combination of software, hardware, and usage patterns.

But there's good news. Thanks to Mac OS X's protected memory and file-level permissions, Mac OS X will probably crash less often than earlier versions of the Mac OS. So you should spend much less time troubleshooting Mac OS X. The bad news is that fallible humans make software, and operating systems are made by legions of humans.

Any experience you have from troubleshooting Mac OS 9.*x* will still generally be relevant for Mac OS X. You will still need to know the expected behavior and recognize deviations from it. You will still need to gather information, isolate a problem, and try some solutions, depending on the symptom. How you perform these tasks will be different.

 NOTE Dan Nolen, a technical writer and consultant based in Austin, Texas, contributed this chapter. Dan can be reached through his Web site at http://macmastery.com.

Dealing with Problems

If you're reading this chapter to prepare for when something goes wrong, you're ahead of the game. There are things you can do (or avoid doing) right now to stay out of trouble. If you're reading this after running into problems, you can learn here what to do next time, after you fix the problem.

 TIP You can conduct some Mac OS X diagnosis and troubleshooting at the Terminal command line. If you aren't yet familiar with Terminal (or the Unix command line), you should read Chapter 22 to get a sense of how to work with the command line in Mac OS X.

Before Problems Occur

The most important step you can take to avoid problems is to regularly back up your data. You should do so anyway, even if you weren't installing the first commercial release of an entirely new operating system. You have insurance on your home and car, perhaps even on your business. So it only makes sense to have at least a little insurance on your Mac by backing up. (See Chapter 21 for more on creating a backup strategy.)

If you're responsible for a large installation of computers, you should proceed cautiously before installing Mac OS X. Test one installation with a representative computer (with typical speed, RAM, hard-drive size, etc.) and the applications you require. Have some of your more advanced users run Mac OS X exclusively for a week, if possible. Run it yourself for your day-to-day work. Don't upgrade everybody over the weekend with no warning. Above all, research the experiences of others using the same applications and devices that you plan to use.

Mac OS 9.1 was designed to coexist well with Mac OS X and is in fact the Classic environment in Mac OS X. So you should upgrade your Mac(s) to Mac OS 9.1 before installing Mac OS X. (See Appendix A for details.) Mac OS 9.1, when installed, adjusts some of the default names and locations of root-level folders that it creates, to minimize confusion with folders installed by Mac OS X. For example, both Mac OS 9.1 and Mac OS X have a folder called Applications. The Mac OS 9.1 installer renames Mac OS 9's Applications folder to Applications (Mac OS 9) and moves other folders, like the Internet and Utilities folders, there.

However, the renaming works only if you install Mac OS 9.1 before Mac OS X. If you install Mac OS X first, Mac OS X will create an Applications folder, and then Mac OS 9.1 will rename it. You'll have both Mac OS X and Mac OS 9 applications in one folder called *Applications (Mac OS 9)*. At first glance, that may seem desirable; but remember, only Mac OS 9.*x*–compatible applications will work when you boot into Mac OS 9.1. Then, native Mac OS X applications will appear as a single file as `Calculator.app` or something similar. (The file represents a Mac OS X *application package*, which appears as a valid application only when you're running Mac OS X.)

If you can, you might consider installing Mac OS X on a second partition of your main hard disk or a different hard drive. Although you won't necessarily have problems with Mac OS X on the same volume as Mac OS 9.1, allocating a separate partition or physical drive will simplify removing the operating system and reformatting the partition, should your installation encounter critical trouble.

One key bit of advice, particularly for experienced Mac OS 9.1 (and earlier) troubleshooters, is to avoid logging in as root and/or fiddling with the files in Mac OS X's System folder hierarchy. In Mac OS 9.1 and earlier, troubleshooting system-software problems was cumbersome and time-consuming, as both Apple and non-Apple components belonged together in the System Folder. Even if you knew which items in every System Folder subfolder were installed by what programs, picking the bits out after a clean install was tedious.

In Mac OS X, what gets installed in System is meant to be unaltered by a user via the Finder. If you're used to earlier Mac OS versions, think of the System folder in

Mac OS X as similar to the System *file* in earlier Mac OS versions. If you alter the contents of the System folder, the Mac might fail to start up correctly. On the bright side, the mostly Apple-only nature of the System folder means, at worst, you simply replace the Mac OS X System folder to bring your Mac back online after a severe problem. The only non-Apple components that might need to go in the System folder are third-party drivers, in the form of kernel extensions. In that case, the drivers should come with an installer that puts them there for you; you shouldn't drag the files into the System folder yourself.

Know Your System

Another safety measure you should take is to learn about the underlying Mac OS X file system. Before you perform any system-level troubleshooting, you should be somewhat familiar with the hidden files and folders in Mac OS X, particular for command-line troubleshooting. In this section, I'll show you some fundamentals of the Mac OS X system.

Hidden Files and Directories

Aside from the folders you see and work with in the Finder, Mac OS X also has a number of hidden directories that are generally visible only from the command line and, in some cases, visible only while you're logged into an Admin account.

 NOTE As discussed in Chapter 22, it's common to refer to *folders* in the Mac OS, but *directories* when you're discussing the underlying Unix directory structure. Remember that they refer to the same basic concept, but Unix commands in the Terminal often use a d (as in cd for change directory) for directory-related commands.

Here's a quick look at some of the directories that might appear at the root level of your hard disk (/) if you are in the Terminal:

/bin　This directory is short for *binaries*. System-level command-line scripts and compiled programs are stored here. Most of the folder contents have names that can be typed in a Terminal window. At the command line you can also type man *command*, (where *command* is the command you want to learn about) and press Return. (See Chapter 22 for details.)

/cores　This directory appears at root level of your hard disk, but it's really a link to the /private/cores directory. The directory is for *core dumps*, a snapshot of memory saved to disk during a crash. Core dumps would be only useful if you're developing software, so it's turned off by default.

/dev   The /dev directory contains the files that act as interface to your devices, including the drives, keyboard, mouse, display, ports, and so on. You can look at these files, but I don't advise altering them.

/etc   The /etc directory appears at the root level, but it's actually a link to the /private directory, which contains miscellaneous configuration and startup files. Many of these files aren't really used in Mac OS X, unless the computer starts in single-user mode (described later in this chapter). You can inspect most of the miscellaneous configuration and startup files while in TextEdit or by using the command-line command more.

/private   This directory contains the real folders of several of the traditional Unix-like folders mentioned here.

/sbin   This directory contains the system binaries, including many of the processes that run the system. It is similar to /bin.

/tmp   This directory is really a link to the /tmp subdirectory of the /private directory, which holds temporary files. The contents of this directory are deleted at startup, so don't put anything here you care about. This is like Mac OS 9's hidden Temporary Items Folder.

/usr   The /usr directory contains user-level items for a command-line user. Here you'll find less important commands and utilities and also pieces for command-line programming.

/var   This directory is really a link to the /private/var directory. It contains some of Mac OS X's log files, the NetInfo databases, root's home directory, and other important items accessible for Unix system administration.

The Library Folders

Mac OS X logically divides the file system into four distinct domains, based on their function and scope. (The *file system* is the collective name for all the volumes available to the computer, including the boot volume, other local fixed and removable drives, and network volumes.) The four domains are User, Local, Network, and System. You'll notice that most of the domains correspond to folders you'll see in the Finder window.

The Library folders in the User domain (~/Library) are for files that should be available for only the logged-in user. Preference files, for example, belong in each individual user's Library folder. What one user has in the Dock should be (and is) specific to that user and should not be changed by another user's (normal) use of the computer. The folders named for each user, which contain their personal documents, are stored in the Users folder on your startup disk.

The Local domain (which includes the root-level Library and Applications folders) is for files that should be available to everyone on the computer but that are not required for the computer to run and are not considered part of the core operating system. Fonts, screen-saver modules, printer modules, and many other such items go in the root-level Library folder on your startup disk. Similarly, the Applications folder is in the Local domain. Only an administrator-level user can modify items in this domain. (In the case of only one system user, that user is the administrator.)

The Network domain is for applications, resources, and other items shared among all users on a network. This information is normally stored on a file server, and the most common use is on a network that includes a NetInfo server. In general, however, most users won't have anything in this domain, unless your Mac is set up specifically to access servers and other resources from a central Unix or Mac OS X Server computer. (For instance, for day-to-day file sharing discussed in Chapter 8, you don't have to access the Network domain. The Network domain is accessed by first clicking the Computer button in a Finder window, then double-clicking the Network icon.)

The System domain (everything inside the System folder that you see on your startup disk when viewing in a Finder window) is for system software installed by Apple and is only on the boot volume. As noted previously, unlike for Mac OS 9.1 and earlier, users are not meant to modify this folder. (In fact, the only way to alter the folder is to enable the root account, log out, and log back in.) Long-time Mac users may be slow to get used to the idea that the System domain is simply not meant for user or even administrator changes. Instead, most noncore items will be installed in the Local domain, generally in the /Library folder (when viewed in the Terminal window) or by accessing the root-level Library folder on your startup disk.

What's in System/Library?

The System/Library hierarchy is the exclusive domain of Apple's installers. Unless otherwise noted, an administrator-level account cannot delete the files and folders—only the root account has write permission in this hierarchy. However, it should not normally be necessary to alter any files there.

If you suspect these files are causing problems, try the typical troubleshooting step: Simply rerun the Mac OS X installer program, which will replace corrupted files or files whose permissions, owner, or group are wrong.

It should never be necessary to add files to these folders, except by using an installer that puts them there automatically (such as drivers for a device). If you have a configuration file, plug-in, or similar system-level file you want to add to your Mac, you'll almost certainly use one of the other Library folders. Which Library folder you use depends on the domain into which you're installing the file. If the file should be installed for all users of your Mac, install it in the main Library folder. For network-wide changes, you'll install files in Network/Library—but only if you're the system administrator for a network of

Macs using shared resources in the Network hierarchy. For items that will affect only a specific user's Mac experience, files should be installed in the Users/current_user/ Library folder (where *current_user* is the home folder of the specific user).

Finding the Cause of the Problem

The first step in finding a problem's cause is to determine if the situation is in fact a problem. This spiffy new OS will probably necessitate a period of adjustment; you'll find small differences between Mac OS 9.*x* and Mac OS X that may seem like problems.

OS Peculiarities

Aside from how the operating system looks and feels, other behaviors may seem like problems at first. Consider the following:

- File sizes shown in the Terminal are different from those shown in the Finder— and may even be zero bytes. The reason is simple: Terminal shows only the file size of the data fork of a file. Files that have nothing in the data fork and everything in the resource fork will always show zero bytes. The listing is a limitation of the FreeBSD portion of the operating system; the Finder displays the proper sizes. (See Chapter 22 for more discussion of dual-fork files.)

 TIP If you installed the developer packages for Mac OS X, a program called CpMac (in the CpMac folder of the Tools folder of the Developer folder) will copy a dual-forked file. In Mac OS X, resource fork-type information is stored in a separate file but managed properly by the Carbon Resource Manager.

- The cp (copy) and mv (move) commands at the Darwin command prompt will correctly move an application package (files that end in .app) but, for all other files, will move only the data fork. (Note that the difference is often relevant only for files specific to Mac OS 9.1 and earlier—cross-platform documents and files are generally unaffected.)

 NOTE In general, Apple is moving away from dual-forked files. Although it is a good idea to hide file metadata (file type, file creator, whether a file is visible or locked), no other mainstream operating system uses a dual-forked system. The dual-fork approach causes difficulty when transferring files between platforms. Chapter 22 has more information on the differences between earlier Mac OS versions and the Darwin/Mac OS X file system.

- Volumes other than the one you used to start the computer are really "mounted" in an invisible folder, at the root level of your startup disk, called Volumes. Although you won't see this folder in the Finder (unless you make it visible), you may need to be aware of it when you're working with the Terminal. The Volumes folder contains other partitions of the startup disk that you may have, other disks, removable volumes, network volumes (like volumes you mounted using the Connect to Server command in the Finder), and even volumes mounted from Disk Copy Images.

Symptoms: Gather Information

If you've determined that you really do have a problem, you need to gather information about the symptoms. First, you may want to consult Chapter 19 if the problem you're having is with a particular application or document—your issue may not be at the system level at all. If you believe you have a system-level problem, answer the following questions:

Is the symptom reproducible on that computer?   If not, then trouble-shooting may be a big waste of time. If the time lost by encountering and recovering from the situation is less than the time and effort you would spend troubleshooting, it may not be worth it.

Is the symptom reproducible on another computer with the same version of Mac OS X?   If so, it may be a bug. If it is a bug, all you can do is report it to Apple's support staff and work around it while you wait for the fix. The odds of two separate computers developing the same problem at the same time are low enough that you can be fairly confident that a system-level problem on both is not a problem specific to your computer, and therefore not something you can fix.

NOTE To report bugs to Apple, either call in, if you're within your complimentary support period, or post it on its discussion boards. Apple provides no formal way to submit bug reports, and, truth be told, many people who submit a bug report do not include sufficient relevant information to be useful. When reporting an issue, you should tell the service representative the corrective steps you took, their results, and exact error messages or steps to reproduce the issue. You should also try to determine whether the error happens with more than one computer (if you can) and more than one application and whether it's a problem with only Classic applications or the Classic environment.

When did the symptom start?   Note whether anything in particular happened before the problem appeared, particularly if anything *automatic* seemed to take place. If you noted trouble with the interaction of your applications or if the computer went into sleep mode or did something similar before trouble struck, that may help you find the cause. When answering this and the next question, it will be worthwhile to have a notepad handy to jot down the circumstances surrounding any problems.

What was the last action you took?   This is the corollary to the above question—did the problem occur after you did something? Did you install a new application, try a new feature, install a peripheral device, or undertake some particular task before the problem occured?

You can also take a few active steps to learn more information about your Mac as it starts up. Obviously, doing so is most helpful if you're having trouble during startup, but it can also be helpful if certain underlying components, such as servers, networking, printing, or peripherals, don't seem to be working correctly. You take these steps by holding down keyboard combinations immediately after your Mac has restarted and you've heard the restart chime. You can try the following:

Boot in verbose mode.   While your Mac starts up, hold down the keyboard combination ⌘+V. *Verbose mode* displays detailed text messages about each step of the booting process. You'll want to use verbose mode any time your computer is not getting to the login window, so you can see where it's stopping. You can also use verbose mode if there is a long delay during startup. You might also use it if you are looking for a specific piece of information. The information displayed in verbose mode is not stored in any one place. Some of it is stored in `system.log`, and some of it is stored in the system message buffer. Some of it is not captured at all.

Boot in single-user mode.   Hold down ⌘+S while your Mac starts up, and you'll boot into *single-user mode*. With that mode, you can start the computer *part* of the way so you can gather information or fix the problems that keep it from starting the rest of the way. Single-user mode does not have a graphical user interface, networking, and multiple users. However, if you ever have to perform major command-line surgery, single-user mode gives you an option for recovery and repair.

 NOTE   If you have severe directory damage, the Mac OS may drop you into single-user mode automatically and display a message to that effect. Such an occurrence should be rare. If it does happen, read the section "Fixing File and Directory Corruption" later in this chapter.

Checking the Logs

Mac OS X does not always display a message in the Finder or elsewhere when something has gone wrong. However, a *log file*, a plain-text document in which information about a particular activity gets saved, can provide useful information for determining the cause, extent, and duration of a problem. Mac OS X logs information to a number of such files. Checking these files periodically, whether or not you encounter trouble, is a good idea.

Console

A good early troubleshooting step is to look in the Console. Console is an application that displays the contents of the file /private/var/tmp/console.log, which is created every time you log in. This file is deleted when you log out or restart the Mac because the directory /private/var/tmp is flushed. If you can't easily reproduce a problem, you should check the Console before you log out or restart. You may also find it useful to leave the Console application running in the background. Applications can send several types of messages to the file read by Console; some types are error, warning, status, and debugging messages.

To launch the Console, you can double-click its icon in the Utilities folder of the Applications folder. Then, as you work in the Mac OS, actions and issues are logged constantly in the Console window, as shown in Figure 20.1.

FIGURE 20.1

The Console window gives you a look at the items being logged to /private/var/tmp/console.log.

```
  ● ● ●                          console.log
Mac OS X Console
*** CFLog (21):
/System/Library/CoreServices/DocklingServer.app/Contents/MacOS/DocklingServer[245] dyld
cannot find symbol _DocklingToggle in CFBundle 0x7ec70 </Applications/Dock
Extras/Displays.dock> (bundle, loaded)
*** CFLog (21):
/System/Library/CoreServices/DocklingServer.app/Contents/MacOS/DocklingServer[245] dyld
cannot find symbol _DocklingTerminate in CFBundle 0x7ec70 </Applications/Dock
Extras/Displays.dock> (bundle, loaded)
DOCK: CFMessagePortSendRequest returned -2


May 22 14:06:57 System Preferences[249] Could not get value for Organization from _dict
May 22 14:06:57 System Preferences[249] Could not get value for Password from _dict
May 22 14:06:57 System Preferences[249] Could not get value for Organization from _dict
May 22 14:06:57 System Preferences[249] Could not get value for Password from _dict
May 22 14:07:22 BlueG3 ipconfigd[137]: MANUAL en0: 192.168.1.3 in use by 0:a:27:83:9d:7c

May 22 14:07:31 BlueG3 nibindd[186]: Shutting down NetInfo servers

May 22 14:07:31 BlueG3 nibindd[186]: Restarting NetInfo

May 22 14:07:32 BlueG3 niutil: NetInfo connection failed for server 127.0.0.1/local
```

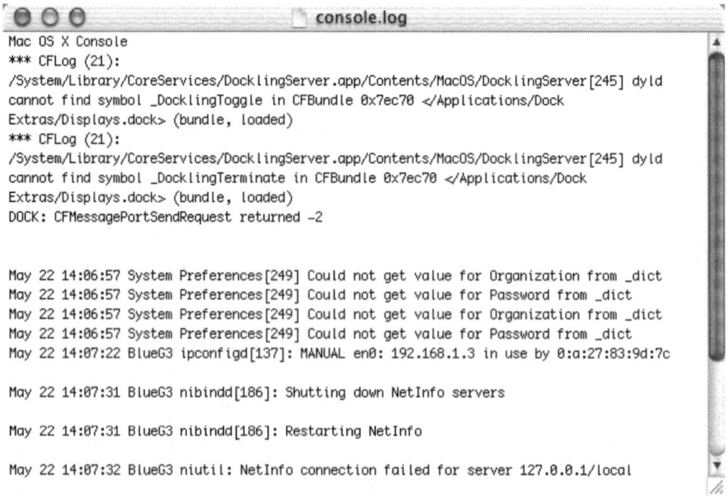

Reading Log Entries

The format of the messages in the Console window will usually be as follows:

Date   Time   Host name   Process name [Process ID]:   Message

Not every message will include all the variables. Here's a quick look at what items in a log entry mean:

Date and time   These variables can help you target the timing of a problem. You might have to compare these variables against a time stamp in other log files.

Host name   This shows the name of your computer, as reported by the Domain Name Service (DNS), but without the domain. So, if an IP address in the DNS server is 1.2.3.4 and it represents foo.bar.com, then foo will be displayed as the host name. If you move a log file to another machine later, you'll have some idea of where the log file came from. However, if the host name is listed as localhost and you have a real domain name, you might infer that network services or DNS were down. (In many cases, stand-alone Macs won't have a domain name, so localhost might be correct in those situations.)

Process ID (PID)   The value of PID is the unique number of the process (program) that generated the log entry. When the computer starts, the first process is 0 and each subsequent process is the next higher number. Generally, the larger the number, the longer the computer has been running without restarting. More to the point, you can tell the order in which processes have been launched, and you can see if a particular process seems to be quitting and relaunching on its own, perhaps in response to an error. If you quit a program and start it up again, it gets a new process ID.

Process name   This is more useful than PID—exactly how much more depends on the process. If you know what the process does, it is most helpful. (For instance, if the process is System Preferences or NetInfo, you can infer that something might be wrong with a configuration setting that you can access from one of those applications.) Even if the process name isn't familiar, the text that comes after it might be useful. In some cases, you'll see an entry like CFMessagePortSendRequest. You'll note that many of these *API calls* include two of three letters at the beginning of their name that may help you begin to track down the issue. Here's a look at some of the letter combinations you may encounter:

CG (CoreGraphics)   These letters designate information about the operating system drawing things on the screen (windows, menus, icons).

CF (CoreFoundation)   CF is a symbol for low-level string-handling routines.

LS (LaunchServices)   LS describes routines that control which applications can open which documents.

ATS (AppleTypeServer)   These letters signify what handles fonts and font rendering.

NS (NextStep)   These letters describe low-level operating-system routines that have been around since Mac OS X's earlier life as OpenStep and NextStep. They simply refer to low-level operations that don't involve the high-end graphics and other Mac OS X services and applications.

IO or IOKit (Input/Output Kit)   Typically, these letters signify driver-level information for any sort of device.

 NOTE   A *process* is another name for an application program. Just like in Mac OS 9.1 and earlier, many processes run in the background, without a user interface.

Message   The message field contains the substantive information. Remember, the messages can be warnings, errors, or just notes.

Many log entries will mean very little to you. They are often useful only to programmers troubleshooting their applications. But you may pick up on certain malfunctions—for instance, your network settings may be reported as inaccurate, applications may have trouble completing a task, or many errors may occur within a particular process. So the Console log may at least give you a hint for locating the problem.

Other Log Files

The Console application by default opens any .LOG file. To open a file in the Console application, do this:

1. Open the Console application from the Utilities folder of the Applications folder on your hard drive.

2. Choose Open Log from the File menu. The window to select a file will appear.

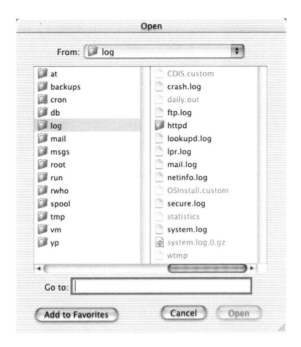

3. Choose the file you want to open. Console cannot open the files listed in light gray and will give you an error if you open a file you don't have permissions to open (like secure.log).

Once the log file is open, you can scroll backward and forward. The latest entries show up at the bottom.

The */private/var/log* Files

The /private/var/log folder is invisible by default, because its contents won't be that useful to most Mac OS X users. The files in this folder report problems with services that the typical user may not even be running (FTP, LPR, Sendmail). However, if your computer is a server with many remote users and if you're planning to connect your Mac to the Internet full-time, more of these files may be more useful. To see private/var/log in the Finder, choose Go to Folder from the Go menu. Then type **/private/var/log/** (or just **/var/log/**, which is a link to the same folder) in the box and press Return. You should see a window like the one that follows.

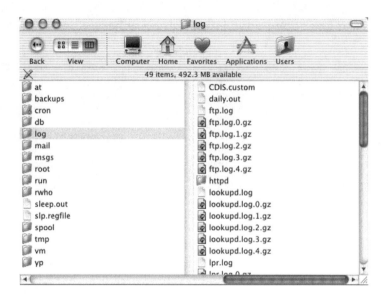

In general, errors or messages from the FreeBSD levels of Mac OS X are sent to a process called `syslogd`—the system-logging *daemon* (background process). The daemon `syslogd` diverts the messages to different files depending on the kind of message and its severity. Some information is more sensitive than others, so some of the files are readable only by root. You can examine the default settings for Mac OS X by looking at the file `/etc/syslog.conf`. Reconfiguring the file is beyond the scope of this book, but any good Unix system-administration text should cover it.

So which log files do what? Here's a quick look at each:

ftp.log   This file shows connections and successful and failed logins.

access_log   The `access_log` file is the standard Apache access log in the `httpd` directory. If you are using Mac OS X Personal Web Sharing (which is powered by the industrial-strength, open-source Apache Web server), the file will contain the information about each "hit" to your Web site. For more on Personal Web Sharing and Apache, see Chapter 24.

error_log   This log is the standard Apache error log in the `httpd` directory.

lookupd.log   This optional log file can be configured for the `lookupd` background process to use. Messages about `lookupd` are stored in `system.log` if you don't set a custom log in NetInfo Manager.

lpr.log   Messages found here are about LPR printing, mostly from the `lpd` (line printer daemon) process. You are using only `lpr` and `lpd` if you have set up a printer with the LPR Printers Using IP option in Print Center. If you are using a USB or AppleTalk printer, this log file will probably not be used.

`mail.log` Messages from command-line mail programs like `Sendmail`, the command-line mail-sending program, are contained here. The file is not used by the Mail application that comes with Mac OS X. So it would be only useful if you were sending or checking mail on the command line. The log would report problems mailing automated reports.

`netinfo.log` This log file stores messages about processes relating to NetInfo, mostly `lookupd` and `nibindd`.

`secure.log` The file logs messages relating to security. Failed logins from `login` and messages from /System/Library/CoreServices/SecurityServer are stored here. The log might be of value if you believe users are trying to access your Mac without a proper username and password or if you'd simply like to see who attempts to log in. Because of the sensitive information that this file might contain, it cannot be opened in Console. Only the root user can read it.

`system.log` This is one of the important log files, containing much information. After `console.log`, `system.log` is most likely to be helpful. Most of the information shown at startup is logged here. Some of the information stored in other log files is also duplicated in `system.log`. If you're worried about redundant information that appears in other log files, double-check the times when each message is logged.

`wtmp` This file stores information about who has logged in to the computer recently. It is not a text file and cannot be read by a normal application; you can read it with the Terminal command `last`. That command lists the user, terminal, originating host (if remote), time logged out, time logged in, and whether the user is still logged in or was disconnected by a crash. Unless you allow many people to log in to your computer, `wtmp` will probably not be that useful. This file also shows when the computer was rebooted or shut down, although such messages are also duplicated in /var/log/system.log.

Logs Folder

You'll find log files about AppleFileService (also known as Personal File Sharing) and Directory Services (which includes LDAP, NetInfo, and Kerberos) in the Logs folder inside the Library folder. You'll find these log files for the Apple-specific services particularly useful when you're encountering local networking problems. I'll describe the files here:

`AppleFileServiceError.log` The file shows when File Sharing was started. It logs a warning that AppleTalk is not active. (Regrettably, System Preferences does not display an alert to warn you.)

DirectoryService.server.log This file reports whether Directory Service plug-ins (NetInfo, LDAP, Kerberos) have loaded.

DirectoryService.error.log Errors with the Directory Service plug-ins are reported here.

/sbin/dmesg

In the Terminal window, type **/sbin/dmesg** and press Return to display the system-message buffer, which contains information about Ethernet, FireWire, and PPP, among other protocols. Some messages here are similar to what is displayed as your Mac starts up. You can read the message (use the `more` application, if desired) to see many of the basic settings your Mac is using for startup configuration. For instance, you may note in this log that certain drivers fail to load or are unloaded by the Mac OS, perhaps because the devices that they drive aren't found due to faulty installation.

Mac OS X Diagnostic Utilities

If the log files don't provide an answer for you—or if they've pointed you in a direction that you'd like to test further—your next step might be to fire up one of Mac OS X's troubleshooting utilities. In this section, you'll see the Apple System Profiler and the Network Utility, two utility applications that may help you track down problems.

Troubleshooting with Apple System Profiler

Apple System Profiler is a good tool for gathering information about many different subsystems of your computer, which is particularly useful in Mac OS X if you are not yet familiar with the operating system. If you have a device that you can't use under Mac OS X, Apple System Profiler can help you see whether the device is recognized by the system itself, even if a particular application program does not recognize it. The graphical version of the Apple System Profiler is discussed in Chapters 12 and 18.

You can access a nongraphical version of Apple System Profiler from the command line, whether via single-user mode or in the Terminal. Type **/usr/sbin/ AppleSystemProfiler | more** and press Return. (If you've read Chapter 22 and/ or you're familiar with the Unix command line, you'll notice that the contents are being fed to `more` so that only one screen of text appears at a time. Press the spacebar to move to the next screen.) If you'd like to output the Apple System

Profiler's findings to a text report, type **/usr/sbin/AppleSystemProfiler > /Users/** **user_name/Desktop/ASP.txt** and press Return. The report will be placed in the file ASP.txt on the desktop of the user specified in *user_name*. Change the user folder and report filename as you desire.

So how can the Apple System Profiler be useful in troubleshooting? You can see what devices are on each hardware bus. In some cases, you can see very specific information about the ROM and firmware versions of your devices (though Apple System Profiler in Mac OS 9 and 9.1 reports more of these details than the Mac OS X version). The Apple System Profiler shows, in one place, a summary of all your networking connections and volumes; that's not possible elsewhere in Mac OS X. The command-line version of Apple System Profiler in Mac OS X shows more general, device, and volume information than the graphical Mac OS X version.

Test with Network Utility

Mac OS X ships will a full-fledged utility, called Network Utility, for testing networking and internetworking connections. With Network Utility, you can get basic information about your network connections easily, test your Mac and other devices, trace the path between you and servers you're interested in, and even look up information about other servers on the Internet. Figure 20.2 shows the Network Utility interface. In this section, I'll look at each of the tabs in the Network Utility interface.

FIGURE 20.2

Network Utility enables you to test and troubleshoot a variety of TCP/IP networking issues.

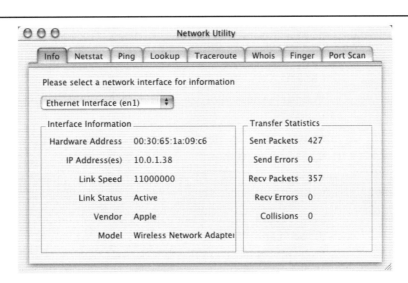

TIP Some features of Network Utility require the BSD Package, which is optional in the Mac OS X Installer. If you did not install it, Network Utility will alert you when it starts, and you will not have all of the tabs described here. If you would like to work with a tab not available, relaunch the Mac OS X Installer and install the BSD Package. (See Appendix A for more on installing Mac OS X components.)

Info

On the Info tab, you'll find general information and statistics about your connection and your network hardware:

Hardware address   This is your Ethernet chip's MAC (Media Access Controller) address. A unique 48-bit number identifies each Ethernet chip; the number is normally written as six pairs of hexadecimal numbers. A hexadecimal number has 16 possible values (0–9 and a–f) instead of 10 (0–9). The first three pairs uniquely identify the vendor of the chip. For more information on which vendors have which codes, see `http://standards.ieee.org/regauth/oui/index.shtml`.

Link speed   *Link* is simply a physical connection to another device. The speed will normally be 10Mb, 100Mb, or 1Gb (as negotiated with the switch, hub, router, or other machine). If you have an AirPort wireless networking card, the speed will be 1Mb, 2.5Mb, 5Mb, or 11Mb. (Note that AirPort connection speeds may be displayed unabbreviated—that is, 11000000 instead of 11Mb.)

Link status   The value shows whether the connection is currently active or inactive.

Vendor   The vendor listed is the company that manufactured the network interface.

Model   Here, the model name of the network interface (according to the manufacturer) is shown.

Sent packets   Sent Packets shows how many pieces (packets) of information have been sent.

Send errors   Errors are rare, but possible. You should be concerned only if the Send Errors number is constantly climbing. But you'll probably have other problems before you notice the relatively high number. The variable measures an error known as *dropped frames*.

Received packets   Received Packets shows you how many pieces (packets) of information have been received.

Receive errors   Here also, errors are reasonably rare, but possible. You should be concerned only if the number shown here is constantly climbing. If you notice problems with your networking applications, you might also check this number to see if you're encountering receive errors. The value here also measures *dropped frames*.

Collisions   A collision occurs when two computers are "talking" at the same time. Computers on a network take turns communicating with each other. If two computers talk at once, that's a collision. You will see proportionally more collisions on networks with more computers or with heavy network usage. You should be concerned only if the number here is high (as in more collisions than sent packets).

 TIP   At the command line, you can get information similar to what is displayed on the Info tab by typing `ifconfig` **–a** and pressing Return.

Netstat

Netstat gives you information about the way network information is routed through your computer. Such information will probably be useful only for troubleshooting multiple, simultaneous connections to a network. For example, if you have a connection to your ISP over AirPort and also a connection to a local Ethernet LAN, then Netstat may come in handy. If needed, you can give this information to a network administrator or to an ISP technician who requires specific, detailed information about your problem.

 TIP   At the command line, type **man** **netstat** and press Return for more information on using a command-line version of Netstat.

Ping

On the Ping tab, you can test whether your computer can communicate using TCP/IP at the most basic level. Ping sends a special kind of message (an ICMP Echo_Request packet) to the host name or IP address you specify. If a computer responds, you can infer that the computer is active on the network, responding at least on some level, and that the physical connection between your two computers is good.

You should use Ping when you want to test minimal TCP/IP connectivity. You can even ping yourself (that is, your own IP address) to make sure a round-trip communication exists between the TCP/IP networking part of Mac OS X and your networking hardware.

Because pinging yourself almost always works, you should start with pinging something else. What you ping depends on what you're testing. If you can't get to a certain Web site with your browser, you can try pinging the same Web site or another machine in that site. For example, if www.apple.com doesn't come up in your Web browser but you can send and receive e-mail, your own network configuration is probably functional. So you might ping www.apple.com or ftp.apple.com to see if anything in the apple.com domain responds (see Figure 20.3). The connection from your ISP might be down, or Apple may have trouble with its servers (however unlikely that might be).

FIGURE 20.3

Using Ping to test your connection to a remote (in this case, Apple's) Web server

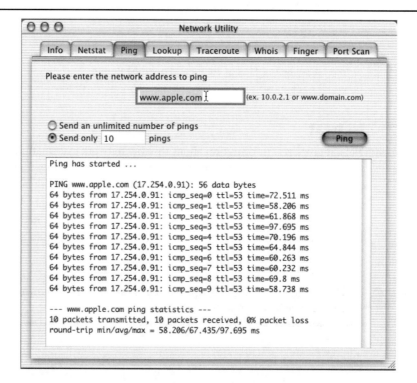

If you can ping the remote Web server but you can't get Web pages from it, then either the Web-server software on that machine or your Web browser is not working. Try another Web browser or another page or site in the same domain. For instance, you could try to load developer.apple.com if www.apple.com is not responding.

TIP Type **man ping** in a Terminal window for more information on the command-line equivalent of Ping.

Lookup

The Lookup tab allows you to convert a TCP/IP machine name (host name) to its IP address and back. If you need to test whether you have incorrect DNS information or your DNS server went down, you can use the Lookup tab from another computer to get an IP address. Then take the IP address to the computer you're troubleshooting to try that IP address with the Ping command or in a Web browser (if it is the IP address of a Web server).

Also, if you have an IP address and you want to see if it has a host name associated with it, you can type in the IP address and get back a name. However, not all IP addresses have a corresponding host name. Some ISPs have a generic host name that includes the IP address; for example, cs6668170-19.austin.rr.com would be the same as 66.68.170.19. Remember, a DNS server translates an easy-to-remember name into an easy-to-compute number.

You can use the dig command instead. It is just another tool to find the same information that nslookup provides.

 TIP Type **man nslookup** in a Terminal window for more information on the command-line equivalent of Lookup. The command-line version allows you to look up information in a name server other than the one for your ISP. Doing so would be useful for diagnosing a name server with incorrect information.

Traceroute

As the name suggests, this tab offers a tool that traces the route your packets take between your computer and any other computer. You can use Traceroute whenever local network services work (the previous commands, such as Ping and Lookup, are successful for machines on your network) but multiple remote services are unavailable. For example, if your local mail server works at your ISP but neither www.apple.com nor www.yahoo.com responds, then Traceroute might help you figure out where the problem is.

Here's how to use Traceroute:

1. Enter the computer (host) name or IP address of the machine to which you wish to map the route.

2. Click the Trace button. The results will be displayed.

3. The results are displayed in the following format:

Host name (IP address of host name); maximum, average, minimum millisecond times

---

 TIP Type **man traceroute** in a Terminal window for more information on the command-line equivalent of Traceroute.

Whois

The Whois tab contains the whois command; it looks up records in the database of the domain-name registrars to see who owns a domain. You can also type part of a domain name and see what domains contain that part. Besides simple ownership questions, whois can give you an administrative contact for a domain when a Web site you expected to be up is unavailable. Or, if you find that you're being harassed by traffic from a certain domain, you can look up the owner of the domain to complain.

 TIP One technique that harassers use to avoid getting caught is to fake another domain. So if you are going to complain, be polite because you might be contacting another victim.

Here's how to use whois:

1. Click the Whois tab.

2. Type the domain or IP address in question.

3. Change the Whois server, if desired.

4. Click the Whois button. The information about who the domain is registered to will be displayed.

 TIP Type **man whois** in a Terminal window for more information about the command-line equivalent of whois.

Finger

The Finger tab shows information about user(s) logged in to a machine. It also displays a file named .PLAN in the user's home directory.

 WARNING Many server administrators turn off the Finger server process (technically, the fingerd daemon) on their servers because they consider it a security hole. If crackers can find out the names of people logged into a machine, then they only have to guess passwords, not names and passwords. (In Mac OS X, fingerd is disabled by default.) Also, people who put extensive info in their .PLAN file make the *social engineering* approach to cracking easier. That approach is used by a person who calls a company and, through charm and guile, gets a representative to reveal information about internal systems or operations that can be used later for cracking.

You can use Finger when you want to see if a specific person is logged into a specific machine or to see what users are logged into a specific machine. Here's how:

1. Type a user in the entry box to the left of the @ symbol.

2. Type a domain in the entry box to the right of the @ symbol.

3. Click the Finger button.

Any information available from the host domain will be returned.

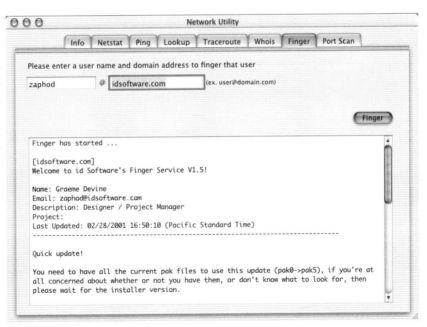

TIP Type **man finger** in a Terminal window for more information about the command-line equivalent to Finger.

Port Scan

The Port Scan tab has a utility that scans the TCP ports (not the physical ports on the outside of your computer) that are open (listening for connections) on a machine. An Internet server will often use different port numbers to receive different types of clients—for instance, the same computer can accept Web, FTP, Telnet, and other clients, all by using different port numbers for each type of connection.

If a Web server on a remote computer has a problem and you want to see if that machine supports AFP, FTP, SMB (Server Message Block, discussed in Chapter 25), or some other connection, Port Scan could be useful. It can also be useful for finding out what services are running on your own computer.

 WARNING Using Port Scan on a machine you don't own may trigger an alert if that machine is monitoring for such behavior. Be aware that some crackers use Port Scan to look for ways to break into a machine. You may be presumed to be a cracker, so let that guide your behavior. Your network administrator or Internet service provider may have rules against scanning, so check before you scan anyone other than yourself.

You can scan yourself by entering **localhost** or **127.0.0.1** as the address to scan. This reserved address, called a *loopback address*, always refers to the machine you're on.

The list of well-known ports for TCP and UDP is in a document called RFC 1700 (www.freesoft.org/CIE/RFC/1700/4.htm). You can see some of the most common ports in the file /etc/services in Mac OS X or most Unix-like operating systems. To reveal this file in the Finder, choose Go to Folder from the Go menu. In the sheet that pops down, type **/private/etc/** and press the Return key.

Where to Look for Solutions

You can attack problems in Mac OS X a few different ways. For some problems, it may be easiest to stop and start again, if you can. Quit and restart the application, log out and back in again, or just restart the computer. Restarting won't fix anything, but if the problem is sufficiently intermittent, it may be the most efficient way to handle the situation.

Obsolete Troubleshooting

If you're an old hand with Mac OS 9.1 or earlier, understand that some types of trouble-shooting are obsolete in Mac OS X—that is, for troubleshooting that doesn't take place in the Classic environment. Here are some obsolete troubleshooting steps (note that many of them that *are* still appropriate for Classic are discussed in Chapter 19):

Extension conflicts Troubleshooting extensions for Mac OS 9.1 and earlier are necessary when a carelessly programmed or malicious extension has changed the way part of the system software works and resulted in a side effect. Mac OS X has abandoned, for the most part, third-party operating-system extensions. You may still have to troubleshoot extensions in the Classic environment, but that should be increasingly less frequent.

Clean install A clean install in Mac OS 9.1 and earlier is a technique to disable (but not delete) the System Folder so that you can install an Apple-only System Folder not tainted with non-Apple pieces. Mac OS X has well-documented ways for developers to modify Mac OS X, and the old, unstable ways are no longer possible. Any unstable non-Apple software should only affect itself and not the rest of Mac OS X.

Rebuilding the desktop You don't have to rebuild the desktop for Mac OS X. You can still rebuild the desktop for Mac OS 9 in the Classic pane of System Preferences, as discussed in Chapter 19.

Adjusting memory allocation/virtual memory In Mac OS X, the kernel allocates any available memory that an application asks for. Applications do not have to reserve up-front the amount of memory they need. Also, Mac OS X users are no longer expected to toggle virtual memory on and off or adjust its settings. Again, Classic applications can still benefit from manually allocating memory.

Missing application files Most Mac OS X applications are delivered as packages. That is, they come in a special package folder with a name ending in .APP; the folder (which looks like a regular application icon in the Finder) contains versions for different languages or different platforms (such as OS X and Mac OS 9.1). You can just drag-copy applications in the Finder, and all the supporting files should just come along for the ride. Gone are the days of digging around in the System Folder and guessing which programs install what files.

If a particular program keeps the computer from responding in a timely manner or at all, you may need to force applications or parts of the operating system to quit. Of course, you'll have to identify the offending component first.

To minimize problems caused by bugs in software, you should always install software updates for Mac OS X, whether you use the Software Update pane of System Preferences or you download individual updates from `http://asu.info.apple.com` on the Web.

Performance Problems

Some tasks may be faster in Mac OS 9.1 than in Mac OS X. Not every feature is optimized for performance or takes full advantage of acceleration (in graphics hardware, for example). The earlier versions of the Mac OS have had a number of years to tune for performance. In general, for Mac OS X, the newest hardware will run better because of faster processors, processor speeds, bus speeds, hard disks, more and faster memory, caches, and video hardware. If you think you're encountering some severe performance issues, you can take several steps to find the problem:

Measure performance. Processes using most of the CPU will usually cause a slowdown. The symptom will usually be the spinning rainbow optical-disc cursor. A single application can become unresponsive because of bugs or other limitations in the way it was written. You can test for that by clicking on another application's window or moving the mouse toward or over the Dock (if the hiding or magnification options are on). If other applications pop up and seem to perform well, you know that the performance issues are confined to the problematic application. If you have the CPU Monitor visible, it may be full before you even notice a slowdown. (See "Measuring Performance" for more on performance-monitoring tools.)

Identify the culprit. Common culprits for performance slowdowns are the Classic environment, Apple File Server (the background process for Personal File Sharing), and ContentIndexing (used by Sherlock to index documents so you can search the contents of your files). Depending on your usage patterns and software, you may find other culprits.

Get more memory. If you have only the minimum amount of RAM installed in your Mac, you will notice seriously downgraded performance. Just like in Mac OS 9.1 and earlier, when the computer runs out of memory, it allocates available hard-drive space to store unused items it transfers from memory. Hard-disk access is much slower than RAM, so when RAM is used up, you will feel the pain when virtual memory kicks in. Because no (easy) way exists for the user to control virtual memory in Mac OS X, the best you can do is to have enough real memory so that virtual memory will rarely be used. Keep in mind that software ported from Mac OS 9.1 and earlier may still reserve memory that it doesn't need. So programs may actually use less memory in the future than they require now!

Report problems.   Due to the magnitude of changes in applications and operating systems, the companies that make them (Apple and application developers) are going to need your feedback about what bothers you the most so they can prioritize their work accordingly.

Troubleshoot the Spinning Cursor

If you notice the cursor spinning continuously, be patient. Then troubleshoot for application problems, as discussed in Chapter 19. If the problem doesn't seem to be application specific (for instance, the cursor spins even before the Finder appears at startup), you might need to consider what the OS is trying to accomplish. Here are some thoughts:

- If you can hear nearly constant clicking from your hard drive, you know something is going on. When you don't have enough RAM, and virtual memory needs to rearrange RAM contents, you may hear the drive *thrashing*. Generally, the solution is to run fewer applications, disable any network services (such as the Web server or AFP server), and, as soon as you can, install more RAM.

- If you're seeing the spinning cursor while your network activity lights are active on a network card, transceiver, hub, switch, or router, there may be a networking issue, particularly if you don't have a large network copy operation (or something similar) going on at that time. You may be having trouble with a name server, Directory Services, or a bootstrap (BootP or DHCP) server on your network. Also consider the possibility that someone else has logged into your Mac and is performing a large network operation, if you have File Sharing turned on.

- If you are using Network File Services (NFS) disks (if you don't know, your network administrator will) and the servers are hard-mounted, then any time the server has problems, you will too. If you're using NFS and the remote drive has become unavailable, it can be quite some time before your Mac allows you to work in the Finder again. You may need to ensure that the remote server is back online and restart your Mac before you can work without delay in the Finder.

In Mac OS X, the spinning cursor does not necessarily mean that the whole operating system is unresponsive; usually, it's just one particular program (or the whole Classic environment). Again, consult Chapter 19 for more on troubleshooting apparent hangs and freezes.

Measuring Performance

Three basic tools in Mac OS X measure how busy your computer is. *CPU Monitor* lets you see at a glance how busy the computer is but not what processes are causing the activity. *Process Viewer* shows the processes and the corresponding amounts of processor time. *Top* is essentially a command-line version of Process Viewer.

CPU Monitor

Through CPU Monitor, you can keep an eye on how busy your computer is. Three kinds of CPU Monitor windows are shown in Figure 20.4.

FIGURE 20.4

Three kinds of CPU monitor windows

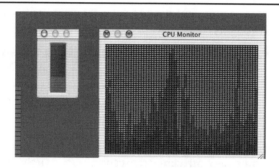

If you leave the monitor open at all times, you might prefer the floating window that is a single bar, flush with the corner of your screen. It's unobtrusive and shows high CPU activity so you can investigate performance problems. To pick this one, choose Toggle Floating Window from the Processes menu in CPU Monitor.

Realize, however, that even when the CPU Monitor is full, you don't necessarily have a performance problem. The first test should be the responsiveness of your computer. If the computer is responsive, it doesn't matter what the CPU Monitor shows. CPU Monitor gives you the option of opening the other two tools from its menu.

Process Viewer

When the computer becomes less responsive, you can launch the Process Viewer. You can then get a sense of which processes are using the most CPU time.

Here's how to use the Process Viewer:

1. Launch Process Viewer by double-clicking its icon in the Utilities folder inside the main Applications folder. (You can also open Process Viewer by selecting Processes ➤ Open Process Viewer in the CPU Monitor's menu bar.)

2. Click on the % CPU column heading. Doing so will sort the list by percentage of the processor(s) used.

3. You may find it useful to change the Sample Every X Seconds to 1 second. It's interesting to watch the Process Viewer change, but note that Process Viewer uses more of the processor when you sample every second—which may defeat the purpose. Be sure to quit the Process Viewer when you've determined which processes are monopolizing the processor.

4. Find the offending process. If it is a program you're running (as opposed to something that the OS is running), then see if you can quit it normally. If you need to use it, try starting it right back up again. If you see no change, try quitting other programs that don't need to be open.

5. If the culprit is not a program you're running, you may need to log out and log back in. All of the user processes that are running, but not the administrator (system) processes, will quit.

6. If step 5 doesn't work, you have to restart your computer to get all of the system processes to start from scratch.

Occasionally, you will have a process that you cannot stop from within the program or by using the Force Quit window, as discussed in Chapter 19. Sometimes, such a process can even prevent you from restarting. Or, restarting may be something you want to avoid at all costs. Process Viewer may then be the only way to quit the program without going into the Terminal.

To quit a process, double-click on it. You will get a dialog asking if you want to Quit or Force Quit. The former is a request and the latter is a demand. Always try Quit before Force Quit.

 WARNING If you kill the ATSServer or Window Manager process, Mac OS X will quit all of your graphical applications with no chance for you to save any unsaved work.

Just because a process uses much CPU time doesn't mean that it uses much memory (and vice versa). The percentage of memory column (% Memory) can show you if a particular process is using quite a bit of memory.

A program can have a bug called a *memory leak*, which is when an application takes memory but does not properly release it after it is done using it. The symptom is that over time, that process's memory usage can grow. If you find a pattern of memory gobbling by a certain process, be sure to report it to the developer.

When using Process Viewer, you may want to note the following:

- Processes running because of something you did are (mostly) running as the user you are logged in as (the user's short name). Processes running whether or not you are logged in will be running as root. They don't quit when you log out. Note that if you have Web Sharing turned on, you will see one or more copies of httpd running as the user www, a special user only allowed to run the Web server.

- Having more than one of the same process is not usually bad. Some processes are used within other programs. So for every Terminal window you have open or for every remote user connected with Telnet or SSH, you'll see a copy of tcsh (or whatever your shell is set to be). For every log you have open in Console, you'll see a copy of tail. Other processes have one copy that launches a second copy. The first one watches the second one. If the second one has a problem, the first one can relaunch it.

- Occasionally, the status of a process will be listed as *zombie*. A zombie process is one that is no longer running but did not successfully quit. Although listings of zombie processes look strange, the processes should not cause any problems because they use no CPU time or memory.

- The TruBlueEnvironment process is the heart of the Classic environment. If you ever need to force Classic to quit from the Process Viewer, TruBlueEnvironment is the process you need to kill. (Note that the Force Quit window from the Apple menu shows *Classic Environment* instead of *TruBlueEnvironment* and also shows each individual Classic application, which Process Viewer doesn't.)

- You can't quit any process owned by another user, even if you're the administrator. You also cannot quit a couple of the processes launched by the system when you first log in (and are running "as you"). If you try to quit pbs or loginwindow, you may see an error message such as "WARNING: Quitting pbs will log you out."

NOTE Any LaunchCFMApp processes are usually Carbon applications. At the time of writing, Process Viewer has a bug in getting the names of Carbon applications. If you're having a problem with an application with this name and you have more than one application with this name in Process Viewer, quit your Carbon applications using their Quit commands one at a time. When you encounter a Carbon application that won't quit, that's your culprit.

Top and Kill

If you ever need to check, from the command line, the performance of all processes running on your computer, use top. The top tool is basically a command-line version of Process Viewer. Having such functionality from the command line is handy when you have to kill a process, a particular application—or the whole Mac OS X Aqua interface—is hung up, and you want do everything possible to avoid losing unsaved info.

To use top, simply open a Terminal window (or log in remotely using Telnet or SSH) and type **top -u**. This will give you a listing of all of your processes, with the one using most of the processor at the top. The list will refresh itself every second. Though the list has eleven columns of information, the first three are the most relevant here.

In order, the first three columns show the process ID (described earlier in this chapter), the name of the process, and the percentage of the CPU it's using. Using the same criteria as with Process Viewer, decide what process you want to quit. If you are connected via Telnet or SSH, you can even log out from the computer and stay connected from the other machine, watching how top changes.

If you are not able to quit a process, you can force a process to quit on the command line using kill as follows:

1. Write down the process ID of the process that you want to quit.

2. Type **q** to cancel top.

3. Type kill *process_ID*, inserting the process ID you just wrote down.

4. If the process you want to kill is not a program you started, you will need to type this command with sudo in front of it: **sudo kill** *process_id*. Remember, when you type **sudo** followed by a command, you will be prompted for your Admin password.

5. If the regular kill command doesn't work, you can try substituting kill -9 instead of kill in the commands in step 4. The -9 attribute is the equivalent of a force quit.

 WARNING The sudo kill version of the kill command will kill just about any process. Killing processes required by the system can have severe and immediate effects. If you kill the ATSServer, pbs, loginwindow, or WindowServer process (and possibly others), Mac OS X will quit all of your graphical applications with no chance for you to save any unsaved work.

If you'd rather avoid command-line procedures, simply force the computer to restart if it doesn't catch up with itself after a reasonable time (a few minutes).

For more information, type **man top** or **man kill** in the Terminal.

Updating with Patches

Unlike many Unix-like operating systems, one company makes most of Mac OS X; therefore, most of your software updates are going to come directly from Apple. However, with Apple's foray into open-source software, you have some interesting options for updating the open-source pieces of Mac OS X.

Software Update

In the System Preferences application in Mac OS X, you'll find the Software Update pane. If your computer is connected to the Internet (and you don't pay a per-minute charge for Internet access), you can schedule the computer to look for updates sometime when you're away from the computer.

Software Update communicates only with Apple servers and sends only enough information about your computer to determine what software updates are relevant. No cases of security breaches through Software Update have been reported. Almost immediately after releasing Mac OS X, Apple released small updates to the operating system as they were ready. (In fact, by late in the writing of this book three updates to Mac OS X had already been released via Software Update.) Large numbers of new features will probably be restricted to major, boxed versions of Mac OS X that you have to buy. However, if a bug results in data loss or major instability or if a serious security hole exists, Apple will have an extra incentive for sending an update to all Mac OS X users.

In contrast to other Unix-like operating systems, you are not expected to download the source code to an update and custom-compile your own version (although you can do that if you choose).

Some updates are prerequisites for other updates, so always run Software Update a second time and make sure it finds no further updates. So far, Apple has also been posting these software updates at `http://asu.info.apple.com`, so you can download them there if you have trouble getting them through Software Update.

If you ever need to reinstall from your Mac OS X CD after applying these updates, you should reinstall any available software updates so you don't have a strange mix of newer and older pieces that might behave unpredictably together.

 NOTE See Chapter 21 for more on using Software Update.

Darwin

Apple has made Darwin, the core of Mac OS X, freely available (`www.opensource`
`.apple.com`), both in source code (modifiable text that can be changed by programmers) and in binary (ready-to-install) formats. Darwin does not include Aqua (the

graphical user interface), QuickTime (for playing rich media like movies), OpenGL (for 3D games), Quartz (for 2D graphics), Cocoa, Carbon, or Classic. So basically you will have a command-line operating system like DOS, CP/M, or Unix.

The stripped-down OS will mainly appeal to computer science students or control freaks. Now, it is theoretically possible for someone to make changes to low-level parts of the operating system and redistribute those changes. If you add those changed parts to your copy of Mac OS X, you will be not only a groundbreaker but also totally at the mercy of the programmer.

Open Source

Some components of Mac OS X came from open-source software—Apache (the Web server), for instance, as well as the whole BSD layer that underlies Mac OS X. If you encounter a problem in the version of some particular open-source component that Apple includes with Mac OS X, you may be able to get a newer version of that component more quickly by installing it yourself than by waiting for Apple to roll its own software update. You may only need to download some files and run an installer (depending on how user-friendly the originators are), or you may need to download the source code and custom-compile your own copy. You will have to weigh the benefit versus your tolerance for getting under the hood of Mac OS X.

Keep in mind that Apple will likely not be of much help for software that you obtain and integrate directly, so be prepared to support it yourself or to revert to the Apple-supplied version. Also, a reinstall of Mac OS X might conceivably downgrade something to its original version, depending on how the Mac OS X installer is designed to treat that component. If you patch those components, you would do well to keep backup copies of them and instructions for reapplying them. If simplicity is your game, just opt for things that show up in the Software Update application from Apple. You can hope that Apple will respond quickly if a severe stability or security issue in some component of Mac OS X surfaces.

 TIP Chapter 22 discusses Darwin in detail, including the installation of Darwin applications and components.

Getting Help and Information

At the time of this writing, no one is an expert on Mac OS X yet. Even the Apple engineers that worked on Mac OS X don't necessarily know anything about the parts of the operating system outside of the ones they worked on. Don't be shy about looking for and asking for help, particularly in the early days (and months and years) of Mac OS X.

Web Resources

Here are some resources on the Web that you can use to learn more about Mac OS X troubleshooting:

Apple TIL/Knowledge Base   Apple has two interfaces to the same database of information. The Technical Information Library (TIL) is the old-style interface that Apple has had for some time. Apple seems to be moving toward a Knowledge Base (KB) that has a more user-friendly interface but may not contain all the articles. The TIL is located at `http://til.info.apple.com`, and the Knowledge Base can be found at `http://kbase.info.apple.com`.

Apple discussion boards   Though Apple moderates the discussion boards, you are as likely to get answers from another helpful person as from Apple. Nevertheless, Apple employees have been known to read messages here to keep a pulse on user sentiment. Just stay on the topic and be constructive. If you make inflammatory posts, expect them to disappear like Houdini in the Witness Protection Program. (You can find the discussion boards at `http://discussions.info.apple.com`.)

Apple Mac OS X Feedback page   Apple has a feedback page for Mac OS X just like it had for Mac OS X Public Beta. Apple does not want bug reports here, but if you have some feedback about Mac OS X, this is probably the most direct way to get it into Apple's ear without waiting on hold. You can find the Mac OS X feedback page at `www.apple.com/macosx/feedback/`.

MacFixIt.com   This is a popular site for researching issues with the Mac OS and with non-Apple products. It includes not only daily reports but also extensive discussion between users and moderators on Mac OS X as well as other troubleshooting topics (hardware, peripherals). The MacFixIt Mac OS X forum is at `www.macfixit.com/reports/macosx.shtml`.

Usenet newsgroups and mailing lists   Whatever your favorite Mac-oriented site, expect Mac OS X to be the hot topic for months after release. Not everyone will upgrade at the same time, so early adopters will likely identify issues that will be documented or even fixed by the time Mac OS X starts shipping preinstalled on computers. Usenet appears not to have any Mac OS X newsgroups at the time of this writing. Check Google (`www.google.com`) for any that might start after this book is published. In the meantime, you might try `nntp://comp.sys.mac.system` (a Usenet newsgroup). Several good mailing lists can be found at `www.themacintoshguy.com/lists/X4U.html`.

Typical Problems and Solutions

Although it's impossible to cover every conceivable problem here, particularly at this point in Mac OS X's early life, beta testers and early adopters are already encountering some common problems with Mac OS X. Check this list for answers to frequently encountered problems. If you don't see what you need, check Apple's Knowledge Base and Discussion areas, discussed in the previous section.

Can't Boot into the Right OS

Some users report trouble simply getting their Mac to boot into the correct OS, particularly if they dual-boot frequently between Mac OS 9.1 and Mac OS X. You might see your jagged fonts in the Finder and your Apple Menu Items disappear when you are changing the startup disk in Mac OS 9.1. You may also get the message at shutdown that you no longer have a valid system folder. If you ignore it and reboot, then Classic may fail to start; the error message will read "This System Folder will not work on this Macintosh model."

If you have these problems, make sure you're using the right tool. The Startup Disk control panel from Mac OS 9.1 doesn't always work reliably. Mac OS X includes version 9.2 of the Startup Disk control panel on the installation CD. Startup Disk 9.2.1 is available from the Apple Software Update Web site (www.asu.info.com). Remember that if you ever reinstall Mac OS 9.1, you should reinstall Startup Disk 9.2.1 to continue to boot reliably. The Startup Disk preference pane in the System Preferences application in Mac OS X will also work.

On Macs built in 1999 or later, if you hold down the Option key at startup, you can bring up a list of volumes to boot from. The list is sometimes called the Startup Manager, System Picker, or Boot Picker. When the screen appears, you'll see icons representing each possible startup disk—select one and click the right-facing arrow icon to begin the boot process. You might do this if you intend to boot into the other OS (9.x to X or X to 9.x) but forgot to make the change in the Startup Disk control panel or in the Startup Disk pane in System Preferences. Be aware that using the Boot Picker is a one-time change and will not change which OS you will boot into the next time. To make a lasting change, use Startup Disk.

 NOTE The Boot Picker never shows you more than one OS per volume. If you have more than one (two or more Mac OS 9.x System Folders or a Mac OS 9.x System Folder on the same volume as Mac OS X), the Boot Picker will show you only the default OS.

Application Has Unexpectedly Quit

If an application quits unexpectedly, you do not have to restart your computer. The Mac OS and other applications will not have been affected. The error message in Mac OS 9.1 and earlier might have indicated that other applications or the OS could crash at any time, which is why it recommended that you restart. In Mac OS X, the application will likely be at fault either directly or via some loaded framework (supporting code). The program will have either attempted to do something forbidden (like modifying another user's memory) or failed to properly handle an unexpected condition (a bug).

The quick fix is to try it again. If you get the same problem, see if you can reproduce it on another computer running Mac OS X. If you get the same result, see if a later version of the software is available. If so, obtain and install the new version. If not, report the bug to the manufacturer of the software. (You can also see Chapter 19 for more in-depth coverage of application crashing and hanging resolution.)

If you've moved past the troubleshooting discussion in Chapter 19 and you'd like to further troubleshoot a crash, you can use an advanced tool called Crash Reporter to capture much programmer-helpful information. It is included with Mac OS X but turned off by default. To turn it on, follow these steps:

1. Open the Terminal program.

2. Type **sudo pico /etc/hostconfig** and press the Return key. This command lets you edit the file /etc/hostconfig using the command-line text editor pico as if you were the root user.

3. Type in your Administrator password.

4. Using the keyboard arrows to navigate, add the line **CRASHREPORTER=-YES-** or **CRASHREPORTER=-LOGONLY-**. YES will display an alert for every crash and log the crash to a file. LOGONLY will only record the crash, not display an alert.

5. Type Control+O to save the file and press the Return key to save the file with the same name.

6. Type Control+X to exit pico.

7. If you want Crash Reporter to be available right away, restart the computer. Otherwise, it will be available the next time you start your computer.

8. If you like, use Process Viewer to verify that Crash Reporter is running.

9. Wait for your computer to crash or perform the operation that makes it crash.

With Crash Reporter on, you will get a second alert in addition to "Application Has Unexpectedly Quit," as shown in Figure 20.5.

FIGURE 20.5

The Crash Reporter dialog

Once Crash Reporter is running, you can access the report by opening the /var/log/crash.log file in the Console application, as discussed earlier in this chapter. The report may not help you much, but it can be invaluable to the application developer's support technician.

Mac OS X Is Frozen

If you've completed the troubleshooting steps in Chapter 19 and have come to the conclusion that the Mac OS itself is frozen (you can't access any other applications, can't access the Dock, and can't bring up the Force Quit Applications box), you may still have another option. It may be that the Aqua interface is frozen or encountering trouble, while the underlying system can still be accessed. If your Mac is connected to a network and has remote access enabled, you can attempt to access it using Telnet or an SSH application.

 NOTE See Chapter 23 if you're unfamiliar with remote access.

From another Mac OS X machine on the network, launch Terminal. Then use telnet or ssh to log in to the problem Mac using an administrator account on that Mac. At the command line, enter the command **sudo shutdown -h now** and press Return. You'll be prompted for your password again. Enter it. If the command succeeds, you'll see a message stating that the problem Mac is being shut down—you'll also be logged out of the remote Mac.

If the command doesn't shut down the frozen Mac, your only choice will be to hard reset the Mac. How you do that depends on your Mac model—you either press the Power key on the front of the Mac for 5 to 10 seconds, press the reset button (on some Power Macintosh models), or press Control+⌘+Power on the keyboard. After a hard reset, it's a good idea to run Disk First Aid or fsck, as discussed in the section "Fixing File and Directory Corruption."

Fixing Problems with Privileges

Because Mac OS X is a multiuser operating system to the core, you can't turn off multiple users, even if you're the only person working on your Mac. It's difficult to say how privileges problems will manifest themselves. When an action is disallowed, you may have a privileges problem.

To act on a file or folder, the action must be permitted at the user, group, or global level. The possible privileges are Read, Write, and Execute (run an application or script or open a folder). If you're an Admin user, you are automatically in the Admin group and the Wheel group. Any user on the computer is automatically in the Staff group. When the Finder shows *system*, that is a less scary term for root. You will see both an Unknown user and an Unknown group.

The Finder lets a user change privileges only for files owned by that user. However, if you change privileges on files and folders as root in the Finder or the Terminal, you can cause quite a bit of trouble. You shouldn't experiment with changing the privileges of anything as root unless you're prepared to reinstall programs or undo changes.

Ignore Permissions on This Volume

If you move portable media between two computers running Mac OS X, you may run into a privileges problem. The first time you use a piece of removable media on a Mac OS X machine, any files you copy to it are copied complete with their privileges. However, the user on the first machine will not be recognized as the same user on the second machine. To get around this, you can force Mac OS X to "adopt" the removable disk and let you access the files on it as if you were the owner. The Ignore command is available to both Admin and non-Admin users. You can also use the Ignore option on nonremovable volumes, and the changes take effect right away. But, if you leave the Ignore option on, it can cause other problems, so you should consider it only as a stopgap measure (for copying files to another volume that has correct privilege settings, for instance). And, regardless of the disk in question, remember that turning on the Ignore option is a security risk because any user, even a non-Admin user, will have full access to the volume.

To force Mac OS X to ignore privileges on a volume, perform the following:

1. Choose Show Info from the File menu.

2. On the desktop, click the volume whose privileges you want to ignore.

3. Choose Privileges from the pop-up menu in the Info window.

4. Check the box Ignore Privileges on This Volume. A note appears just below the check box: "Changes take effect on restart." (See Figure 20.6.)

5. Restart the computer.

FIGURE 20.6

Ignore privileges on this volume.

You should now be the owner of everything on the volume. Note that ignoring privileges does not work for network volumes. The server administrator determines those privileges.

Fixing Privileges in the Terminal

Once you discover a privileges problem, you can make permissions fixes through the Terminal. If you must change the owner or group assigned to a file or folder, you can do so only on the command line. Although the Mac OS X installer will fix permissions problems, it's quite time-consuming if you have only one permissions problem to fix. If you know what the problem is and you know how to fix it, then just do that instead of reinstalling.

For more information about permissions fixes, you can type **man chown**, **man chgrp**, and **man chmod** in a Terminal window. You can also consult Chapter 22, which offers more information on chown, chgrp, and chmod.

When You Can't Log In

If you're having trouble at login, you can use a couple of techniques to get around the trouble and get your Mac up and running again, depending on when the trouble occurs.

At the Login Window

If after normal startup messages, you have a blue screen with an alternating spinning wheel and cursor, you may have a font problem. The ATSServer process scans your font directories on startup, including the Fonts folder of your Mac OS 9.1 System Folder. If the ATSServer doesn't like a font there, that font could be causing the symptom.

As a workaround, you can boot into Mac OS 9.1, either from the hard drive or a CD, and move or rename the Fonts folder. (You'll have to force OS 9.1 to boot, perhaps by holding down the Option key at startup.) After taking care of the Fonts folder, try rebooting back into Mac OS X.

The next time you boot into Mac OS 9.1, all your menus will look jagged and ugly. If the problem persists, just troubleshoot your fonts and put the Fonts folder back. If that doesn't work, try deleting the file ~/Library/Preferences/com.apple .loginwindow.plist.

 TIP You can try the workaround in single-user mode if you prefer, as it's more efficient. You must know what you're doing, however; otherwise, single-user mode could give you a headache.

Finder Crashing on Login

Finder is set to be the first application to start when you turn on your computer, and it allows you to start other programs. If you suspect that the Finder is damaged and you need to attempt repairs instead of reinstalling, you can tell Mac OS X to start some other program by default. From any command-line prompt (including the Terminal, single-user mode, or >console, described in the next two sections), type:

```
defaults write com.apple.loginwindow Finder /applications/utilities/
Terminal.app
```

This command sets Terminal as the default application instead of the Finder the next time you log in. (For other applications, substitute the full path to the application after the Finder entry.) To change it back, use:

```
defaults write com.apple.loginwindow Finder /system/library/coreservices/
Finder.app
```

When you once again log out and log in, the Finder will be active again.

Stop Auto-Login in Single-User Mode

If your computer is set to log in automatically but you have a crashing Finder, you won't be able to try any of the troubleshooting steps for Finder crashing at login.

However, you can force it to display the Login window at startup; that requires single-user mode. Note that many techniques used by logging in as >console (discussed next) or used remotely with Telnet or SSH can be performed in single-user mode as well. To force the computer to display the login window, do the following:

1. In single-user mode, make sure you already mounted the hard drive with the command /sbin/mount –uw / and press Return.

2. Type **nicl –raw /var/db/netinfo/local.nidb delete /localconfig/autologin** and press Return.

 WARNING Warning, if you're trying to force the computer to display the Login window over the network instead of in single-user mode, replace nicl –raw with sudo nicl. The first version of this command could damage your NetInfo database if you run it outside of single-user mode.

Log In as >*console*

Another way to get to the command line in Mac OS X (as if you didn't already have enough ways) is to type **>console** in the user field in the login window and press Return. Doing so will shut down all graphical parts of Mac OS X and give you a text-only login prompt.

If your computer is not set to log in automatically and crashes when you log in, you can try a couple quick fixes.

If the problem is caused by the Finder or Dock (two programs that always start up when you log in), you can move aside the preferences files for those two programs. The files are com.apple.finder.plist and com.apple.dock.plist, respectively, and are located in your home directory in ~/Library/Preferences/.

Assuming you're already logged in at the command line, here's how to reset the preferences files:

1. Type **mv ~/Library/Preferences/com.apple.dock.plist ~/Library/Preferences/com.apple.dock.plist.old** and press Return. To move the Finder's preference file, just substitute com.apple.finder.plist in place of com.apple.dock.plist.

2. Type **exit** to log out of the text-only mode.

3. Log in as the user having the problem. If the problem is fixed, you can continue computing. If the problem isn't fixed, the preferences files weren't the issue—you should restore them by typing the command in step 1 again with the paths reversed, as in **mv ~/Library/Preferences/com.apple.dock.plist.old ~/Library/Preferences/com.apple.dock.plist**.

Crashing Because of an Auto-Launched Item

If your problems at startup are caused by a program other than Finder set to launch when you log in, you can stop the program from a command line. Log in as the user having the problem and, at a command line, type `rm ~/Library/Preferences/loginwindow.plist`.

This one command will delete the `loginwidow.plist` file. Then, using techniques outlined in Chapter 19, troubleshoot the problematic program. If you have more than one program, after troubleshooting, add them back one at a time in the Login Preference pane of System Preferences.

Problems with User Accounts

If your user account information becomes confused or corrupted, particularly if you've been attempting to alter it using NetInfo Manager, you will not be able to fix it by reinstalling Mac OS X. User account information is stored in the NetInfo database. The NetInfo database is not installed by the installer but is created when the computer starts up for the first time. The NetInfo database is first created without any users that can log in. (If it created an account and logged you in with some default password, that would be a big security hole.) To create all of the information needed to log in, you should re-run the Setup Assistant.

If you get into a situation that requires you recreate the NetInfo database (by typing **root** as the name of the user in the Setup Assistant, for example), you have to force the computer to create a new NetInfo database and force it to re-run the Setup Assistant. To do this:

1. Boot the computer in single-user mode.

2. If the computer was not shut down cleanly, run `fsck` (covered in the next major section, "Fixing File and Directory Corruption").

3. Make sure to mount the file system as specified by typing `mount -uw /` and pressing Return, so you can make changes to the disk. At this point, you are root, so be careful what you type.

4. Type `mv /var/db/netinfo/local.nidb /var/db/netinfo/local.nidb.old`. This will rename your NetInfo database that contains your user and group information.

5. Type `rm /var/db/.AppleSetupDone` to force the Setup Assistant to run again.

6. Type **exit** to continue booting. You should now boot into the Setup Assistant. Proceed normally through the Setup Assistant to create a new user.

Forgotten Password

If you can't log in because you forgot your password, see "Resetting Passwords" later in this chapter.

Stalling When Starting Network Services

If the computer stalls when network services starts, disconnect the Ethernet cable. Network operations may then time out faster and allow the startup process to continue.

Fixing File and Directory Corruption

What is *corruption*? In short, corruption is unexpected information or information in an unexpected format. For example, in Mac OS 9.*x*, because the memory a program was using could be modified "behind its back," when a program saved its memory to disk, that information would not necessarily be the information that should have been saved. The result was corrupted information on disk.

Directory Corruption

Just like in Mac OS 9.*x*, incorrect information about hard-drive contents can exist on the hard drive. The incorrect information can result from a freeze, power outage, or other forced reboot.

As a program makes changes to a file in memory, the changes are normally saved often, but not immediately. If the Mac OS X does not shutdown properly, it checks the directory structure on the boot volume when it starts up (using fsck, the command-line File System Check utility).

If the directory structure is really damaged, it's rare but possible for Mac OS X to stop loading and drop you into single-user mode (covered earlier in the section "Symptoms: Gather Information"). If that happens, you should follow the instructions that appear on screen. You'll type **/sbin/fsck –y** and press Return to run fsck. The information displayed about what fsck is checking and fixing will be very similar to what you see in Disk Utility in Mac OS X. When the check and any repair are done, you can just type **exit** to continue starting up the computer.

If the problem can't be fixed by fsck, you may need to use other disk-repair utilities like Symantec's Norton Disk Doctor or AlSoft's Disk Warrior. (See Chapter 21 for more on these utilities.)

 WARNING Always run Mac OS X's Disk Utility instead of Mac OS 9.1's Disk First Aid, if you can. To work with the startup disk, boot from the Mac OS X CD to run the Mac OS X Disk Utility and make repairs; otherwise, problems reported may not really exist, and Disk Utility won't be able to repair your main startup disk unless it's run from the CD.

If none of your disk utilities can repair the directory damage, your only option is to back up what you can and to reformat the hard disk. If your data is so valuable that reformatting (and, hence, losing some of that data) is not an option, your option may be to have the drive looked at by an Apple-authorized dealer or service center or by a drive-recovery company like DriveSavers (www.drivesavers.com). Bringing in the big guns can be costly, but it might be worth it.

File Corruption

The easiest way to fix a single corrupted file is to replace it. If a file is auto-generated, like a preference file in ~/Library/Preferences, you can simply move or rename it, and a new one will be created the next time that preference file is needed. It might be necessary to relaunch the application or even to log out or restart the computer. Try to avoid the temptation to delete the suspect file until it's clear whether or not it was causing the problem.

Even then, it's worth keeping the file if you plan to contact Apple or another software vendor. The representative might ask for an auto-generated file. If the representative can't reproduce the issue, your file will be the only record of what happened.

Because every file and folder in Mac OS X has privileges assigned and just about every program you run has the same privileges as you do in the Finder, any problems should be limited to files you could corrupt manually in an administrator or root account. The kernel prevents unauthorized access to memory or files. Any program that tries to access a file it doesn't have privileges to modify will fail and probably display a privileges-related error message. The kernel will force any application to quit if an application tries to touch memory other than its own. You should therefore much more easily identify problematic programs under Mac OS X than under Mac OS 9.*x*.

 NOTE Evidence suggests that the rules of creating applications in Mac OS X will make programs much more robust in the future. In Mac OS 9.1 and earlier, it was possible for the cause of program bugs to go unnoticed for a long time. Developers have commented that porting their programs to Mac OS X has resulted in easily discovering the subtle memory-corruption bugs that they had been chasing through many versions.

Troubleshooting with Installer

The Mac OS X Installer can be quite useful in fixing most operating-system problems. When reinstalling the OS, the Installer looks at the receipts in the main Library folder and compares the files listed there to the files it has to install. If the file has been moved, renamed, modified, or corrupted, it will be replaced under most conditions.

Unless you select the Erase option—which erases the target disk and starts over with a new installation—the Installer will not alter your data files. So reinstalling OS X is the easiest way to correct widespread OS file corruption. Also, if you have no interest in command-line tools and workarounds, rerunning the Installer is your best troubleshooting fix when you've run out of GUI options. Reinstalling is overkill for fixing privileges problems, but the command line is currently the only other way to fix them. I hope that Apple will remedy this deficiency in a future version.

When you're reinstalling over an existing Mac OS X installation, the installer doesn't replace everything it installed before. To retain files that most users would not want reset to their default state, the Installer checks a list of certain files that it treats specially. This checking can make a reinstallation take up to twice as long as a first-time installation. The file (the list) is called `default.hints` and is located in `/System/Library/PrivateFrameworks/Installation.framework/Resources/`.

You can open `default.hints` in TextEdit and inspect its contents. (If you do so, copy the file to your home folder first so that you don't accidentally overwrite it. If you're signed into the root account, make sure you *copy*—as opposed to *move*—the file.) The list is self-explanatory about what files would be replaced and why. Most notably, your user and group information, stored in the NetInfo (`/private/var/db/netinfo/local.nidb`), will not be replaced. So when you restart after the reinstall, the computer won't restart the Setup Assistant and so on. Most files on the list are traditional Unix files that are hidden by default.

Boot with Mac OS 9.1

Mac OS X is different and, in some respects, a little younger and less experienced than Mac OS 9.*x* and earlier. Although Mac OS X is based on time-tested technology, the interface itself—Aqua, the Finder, the organization of folders—is brand new. So, if you're used to earlier versions of the Mac OS, you may encounter some growing pains with Mac OS X.

Some problems have a low-tech workaround. For instance, in Mac OS 9.1, you can have more than one Info window open in the Finder. In Mac OS X, the Show Info window, for the sake of reducing window clutter, shows only information for the active item, and you can't open more than one window. When you click on another item, the information for that item is displayed automatically. So you can't compare two files at once. It's not worth booting back into Mac OS 9.1 for that capability. The solution might be old-fashioned, but it works: You can write on paper the information you wish to compare.

With other problems, you will have no choice but to boot back into Mac OS 9.1. For example, some installers (particularly for older Classic applications) expect to install their files at the root level of the hard drive and don't let you modify where they install files. In Mac OS X, nonroot users cannot modify the root level of the hard drive. So a nonroot user using an installer with this limitation will have problems. You will probably get an error message such as "access denied" or "you do not have privileges to install here." In that case, you'll need to boot directly into Mac OS 9.1 to work with that installer application or find a more recent version of the installer that's designed to be aware of Mac OS X's privilege restrictions.

For all of its nice features, the first release of Mac OS X doesn't perform some tasks that Mac OS 9.1 does. Mac OS X doesn't:

- Play DVD movies (though DVD-ROM data discs, rare as they are, should work just fine).

- Configure an AirPort Base Station (though version 1.3 and later of the AirPort Admin Utility should work in the Classic environment).

- Use program linking (AppleEvents between machines). Program linking is used mostly for AppleScript-based remote control.

- Use LocalTalk, the old AppleTalk-based communication that works over serial ports. These days, LocalTalk mostly just connects to older, network-based printers. The printers can be bridged to Ethernet or replaced with a better, cheaper USB printer.

You should be aware of important limitations in the Classic environment. For all of its magic, the Classic environment is not a 100% identical replacement for Mac OS 9.1. For instance, some programs behave erratically in Classic because they assume that they have exclusive access to the computer's hardware as in Mac OS 9.

Virus-checking programs may well check for viruses in your Classic applications but have no idea how to check Mac OS X applications and OS components. Luckily, Unix-like operating systems aren't quite as popular a target for virus writers because the structure of the operating system makes viruses less effective.

Anything that depends on the Mac OS 9.1 desktop (like desktop printing) is simply not relevant in Classic. (See Chapter 19 for more on troubleshooting Classic applications and Chapter 13 for a discussion of printing from the Classic environment.)

Resetting Passwords

If you forget your password and can't log in, the password must be reset. For security reasons, you can't recover a lost password—passwords can only be replaced. You have three different password-replacement scenarios:

- The easiest way to reset the password of a regular (nonadministrator) user is to have the administrator reset the password in the Users pane of the System Preferences application. Once logged in, regular users can reset their own passwords in the Password pane of the System Preferences application, but they can't replace a forgotten password without an administrator's help.

- If the system has more than one administrator, a second administrator's account can be used to reset the first administrator's account in the Users pane of the System Preferences application. If no other administrators are available, you must use the root account (if active) or the Mac OS X CD, discussed next.

- The easy way to change an administrator account is to boot from the Mac OS X CD. After you pick your language, choose File ➢ Reset the Password. Keep in mind that anyone with a Mac OS X CD can reset your passwords, so it's important to keep your Mac OS X CD in a secure place. If the security issue worries you, secure your system physically. (That is, put it in a locked room and lock it to the furniture using the connector built onto the machine.)

As a last resort, follow these steps if you don't have the Mac OS X CD and you need to reset the administrator's password:

1. Restart the computer.

2. After you hear the startup tone but before you see the spinning rainbow-wheel cursor, press ⌘+S. Your computer will start in single-user mode. You'll know you've properly pressed the keys if you see scrolling text messages. If you see the spinning rainbow-wheel cursor, you were too late—restart and try again. If you press the keys too early (before the tone), you'll see a normal graphical startup, which you'll also see after the spinning cursor if you were too late.

3. If you successfully started in single-user mode, the computer will start part of the way and then give you the following prompt localhost#.

4. At this point, you are root with no other users and no networking; the hard drive is mounted as read-only. Don't be surprised if you see messages like "kmod_destroy: com.appledriver.AppleCore99PE (id 16), deallocating 8 pages starting at 0x721f000." Such messages, though scary-looking, are innocuous; they are sent from the kernel as it conserves memory by unloading drivers for hardware that does not exist on the machine.

5. If the computer was not previously shut down properly, type **/sbin/fsck** **-y** and press Return. The fsck program in the /sbin directory will run. Answer **yes** to all questions it asks you about whether you want it to fix any problems it finds.

6. In order to make changes to the hard drive, you have to mount the drive so that it can be written on. Type **/sbin/mount** **-uw /** and press Return to mount the hard drive to be written on at the root level.

7. Type **/usr/bin/nicl** **-raw /var/db/netinfo/local.nidb** **-create /users/** ***username* passwd** but replace *username* with the user's short name. Press Return.

This sets the user's password to be blank. The `nicl` command allows you to edit the NetInfo database of settings for the machine. You are editing it in raw mode, without the help of daemons (which aren't running now anyway).

 WARNING Do not use `nicl` with the `-raw` tag on a computer that is booted all the way up and running with the NetInfo daemons (server processes) `netinfod` and `lookupd` running. Modifying a database in raw mode when NetInfo is running can cause corruption of the NetInfo database, where all your user and group information is stored. For more information about `nicl`, type **man nicl** in a Terminal window.

8. Type **exit** and press Return to allow the computer to continue starting up.

9. Log in as the user whose password you just reset. (You won't need to enter a password in the login window.)

10. Open the System Preferences application from the Apple menu.

11. Click Show All if needed.

12. Click Password pane's icon.

13. Change the password for the user (remember, it's currently set to blank), following the on-screen instructions.

The user's password is reset, and that user will be able to log in successfully with the new password.

Getting Past a Kernel Panic

What is a *kernel panic*? According to Apple's TIL article number 106076 (at the time of writing), "A kernel panic is a type of error that occurs when the core (kernel) of an operating system receives an instruction in an unexpected format or that it fails to handle properly." When a kernel panic occurs, you will see a message of white text on a black background drawn on top of whatever was on the screen at the time.

A kernel panic is the most severe software problem you can have in Mac OS X. The machine will basically be unusable at that point and, aside from restarting the Mac, you can do nothing to get out of it.

If you think you know what caused the kernel panic, try to avoid it. The cause might be related to your hardware (video cards, accelerator cards). Try removing such devices and see if you can cause the kernel panic to recur. Also, if you were doing several device-level operations at once, try doing them one at a time. For example, if you were waking up a PowerBook from sleep while ejecting a PC card, hot-plugging a media bay, and attaching a string of six FireWire devices, you tested the limits of how much the system can keep track of at once.

 TIP During a kernel panic, note the steps that lead up to the problem, as developers and tech-support staffers find them valuable for troubleshooting. Note the complete error message and report it to Apple or another appropriate developer. Future software updates may fix such conditions or at least provide better handling of the error. And, in fact, Mac OS X 10.0.3 fixes several causes of kernel panics in earlier versions.

If you've recently installed a kernel extension and encountered a kernel panic while starting up, the extension may be buggy or corrupt. The solution is to boot into *safe mode* and remove the extension. Safe mode is a special startup that loads only the kernel extensions absolutely required to start the computer. So you can see video on your screen, mount the hard drive, and have basic mouse and keyboard functionality.

To invoke safe mode, restart your Mac. After hearing the startup tone, hold down the Shift key. You'll have no visual indication that depressing the key has worked unless you boot in both safe mode and verbose mode (by holding down Shift+⌘+V). In that case, you will see "configuring kernel extensions for safe mode." (Mac OS 9 displayed "Extensions Off" when a restart in safe mode was successful.)

Safe mode is useful only if you have installed non-Apple software kernel extensions. Although the non-Apple extensions use the same key for turning off extensions in Mac OS 9.1 and earlier, you'll find that safe mode is used considerably less often in Mac OS X because kernel extensions do not compromise stability like Mac OS 9 system extensions.

In fact, the easiest way to fix a kernel extension problem is to boot into Mac OS 9.1 and manually delete the appropriate folder from /System/Library/Extensions. Alternatively, you can enable the root account and log in as root to delete the wayward kernel extension, as discussed in the next section.

Much Ado about Root

There is also much legend and fable about the root account. "I hear that logging in as root makes it just like Mac OS 9," say some. Others say, "*Never* log in as root. You might accidentally hit the wrong key and blow up your processor!" So what are we poor Mac users to do about the root account and the command line?

Never fear. Using the command line is totally optional for troubleshooting Mac OS X, just as it is for *using* Mac OS X. If you know what you're doing, the command line can be more efficient. If you're not comfortable with the command line, you can still get everything done; you will just have fewer tools to choose from. Over time, you power users will probably add command-line use to your toolkit.

It's just like being able to work on your own car. Nearly everyone can check the oil and the tires' air pressure. However, if you understand the engine well enough to take it apart, you may be able to fix it yourself. Even if you can't, you can take it to a mechanic and be back on the road in short order.

People used to operating systems with a root account hasten to use it. However, before you "root" around where you shouldn't, consider the discussion in the following section.

Do You Actually Need to Be Root?

Some users falsely believe that they must be logged into the root account to be able to see hidden files and folders. For simplicity's sake, the Finder hides certain items from all users, even root. (Note that this is also true in Mac OS 9.1 and earlier.) However, for any user, you can force Finder to show all files. In the Terminal, type **defaults write com.apple.finder AppleShowAllFiles true**. The command will take effect the next time you log in (or you can just relaunch the Finder using the Force Quit command in the Apple menu).

To show a hidden directory in the Finder, use the Go to Folder command in the Finder's Go menu. For example, to show the hidden directory /var/log/, type **/var/log/** in the Go to Folder box and press return. (The method works only if you know the name of the folder.)

Users might believe they need the root account to access the /System/Library hierarchy. That's true, but for good reason. You shouldn't be changing or adding *anything* in the Library subfolder of the System folder. In general, items that you think should go in the System/Library folder hierarchy actually belong in the root-level Library in subfolders of the same name. If those folders do not exist, you can create them. Their contents will be scanned and included. (For Mac OS 9.1 and earlier experts: Imagine never having to sort through the hundreds of files Apple installs to find one or two items of which you don't have a backup copy!)

Alternatives to the Root Account

One way you can get around logging into the root account is by temporarily giving yourself root privileges at the command line. To execute a single command as root,

PART

IV

type **sudo** *command* and press Return at the command line in a Terminal window. The computer will prompt you for the administrator's password. The sudo *command* performs the *command* as root and brings you right back to your user prompt. The method here is best when you have only one or two commands to type.

To get a command-line prompt where you don't have to type this before every command, type **sudo** **-s** and the Admin password when prompted in a Terminal window and press Return. This gives you a new shell, where you're logged in as root until you close the window or type **exit**.

 WARNING The fact that you recently authenticated as the super user (root) using sudo will be remembered for 5 minutes. So, if you type more than one sudo command in that time, commands after the first one won't prompt you for your password. If that bothers you, just close the Terminal window.

Reenabling the Root Account

When the root account is disabled (including by default when you install Mac OS X), you can't log in as root at the login window or connect via SSH (Secure Shell). Normally, this isn't a big deal because of the alternatives just discussed. Even if you reenable the root account, you still won't be able to log on using Telnet, FTP, or AFP without additional steps. However, if you have to delete files or folders that no other user has permissions to delete *and* you don't want to use the command line, your only option short of booting into Mac OS 9.1 or reformatting would be to reenable the root account and log in as root. You can reenable the root account as follows:

1. Open NetInfo Manager from the Utilities submenu of the Applications folder.

2. Choose Domain menu ➣ Security ➣ Authenticate, then type in an Admin password (and Admin name, if needed). Note that unlike most other places in Mac OS X, NetInfo Manager does not automatically authenticate you even though you're the Admin user.

3. Select Domain ➣ Security ➣ Enable Root User. If this is the first time you have set up the root account, you will be warned that the root password is blank, and you'll be forced to change it to a nonblank password. You should now be able to log in from the loginwindow or SSH (but not Telnet, AFP, or FTP).

4. If you change your mind or want to undo the process when you're done rooting around, select Domain ➣ Security ➣ Disable Root User.

What's Next?

In this chapter you saw the many approaches you can take to troubleshooting Mac OS X at the system level. Mac OS X is a very robust operating system, which will hopefully translate into fewer OS-level troubles than in previous versions of the Mac OS. But when trouble does strike, the steps to correct the trouble can, in some ways, be more confusing than with past versions. Using a combination of graphical and command-line tools, however, you can get your Mac up and running in most cases.

In the next chapter, you'll learn some of the basics for maintaining a healthy Mac system, including tools and ideas for backing up important files, avoiding and dealing with virus infections, and troubleshooting your disks when corruption or inefficiency sets in. You'll also see ideas for a regular schedule of Mac maintenance to keep performance up and problems at bay.

CHAPTER 21

Hard Disk Care and File Maintenance

One of the keys to a happy Mac OS X system is maintenance. In most cases, maintenance means managing your hard disk to keep files from fragmenting, fighting viruses, and checking for software updates. Many of these tasks can be easily automated, so you'll only occasionally need to dive into the System folder on purpose.

Perhaps the most important part of preventive care is backing up your hard disk. Third-party utilities offer the best solutions for backup, although any strategy—even a manual strategy or one automated by AppleScript—is better than none. Fortunately, because of Mac OS X's hierarchical nature, creating a backup strategy is fairly straight-forward, especially when it comes to securing important documents and data files created by your users.

Beyond backup, Mac OS X has built-in applications for basic disk functions, including the Disk Utility program, which works both as a diagnostic utility and as a utility to enable you to format and partition your hard disk. Mac OS X also includes the Apple System Profiler and the Software Update panel, which can be used to help with maintenance tasks. Along with these tools, third-party utilities can be added to the mix to keep your disks in good shape and virus-free.

In this chapter we'll discuss all of these approaches to maintaining a Mac OS X system, including a list of issues you should address on a regular basis (do's and don'ts) for keeping your Mac OS X system up and running well as you work with it.

Backing Up Your Mac

Although Mac OS X is designed to be a fairly stable and problem-free environment for computing, the fact is that things happen. It's important to perform some occasional maintenance tasks on any computer, regardless of the operating system, if only to ensure that your important files are always backed up and that the computer hasn't encountered any data corruption or other such errors that could cause harm to data. And for any computer connected to a network and/or the Internet, protection against viruses is always a concern.

As it turns out, your first line of defense against all these problems is a good backup. If you work with your Macintosh for a living—or if you use it at home or in the home office for managing money, taxes, and investments—then it's likely that your data is worth more to you than the actual, physical computer. I personally would rather have a CD with my important data on it than an entire roomful of Macs, because I really hate to rewrite book chapters and articles that I've already written. And I'd hate to have to re-enter all of last year's checkbook data.

So you create a *backup*, which simply means that you copy important files to some form of secondary media on a regular basis. The secondary media should be something that isn't fixed—that is, you don't just copy files to another hard disk in your office, but rather to a disk or tape of some sort that you can store in another location. Ideally, this means using *removable media* (recordable CDs, Zips, Jaz, tape) that allows you to transport the media and swap in new media whenever necessary.

The same basic process also enables you to create *archives* of your important data, meaning backup disks that are dropped out of the rotation. An archive is a copy of your documents and other files that represents a particular moment in time—for instance, it's a snapshot of how your documents and other files were on March 15th. Creating an archive gives you two advantages. First, it lets you avoid backing up files (or you can even opt to delete files) that don't change subsequent to that archive. Second, having an archive makes it possible for you to turn to that archive if you ever need a file that has since changed. That includes files that change because a user saved the wrong data to the file, files that have been infected with a virus, and updated files that you'd like to revert to a former state.

In addition to having your backup data safe, a proper backup routine can help guard against problems such as data corruption and virus attacks. In fact, the most clever backup schemes will help you not only recover lost or corrupted files but actually retrieve earlier copies of files if you ever need to "revert" to a former version of a document. And, perhaps most importantly, a smart backup scheme makes you—if you're the system administrator—look like a hero.

What You Need for Backing Up

To back up your Mac effectively, you'll need an external removable drive that's compatible with Mac OS X. The drive should support media that can store enough space in one setting to make the backup process worthwhile. With today's modern hard disks, that means the removable drive should probably be capable of storing 700MB (such as a CD-RW disc) or greater, such as the 2GB or 2.2GB supported by the Iomega Jaz and Castlewood Systems Orb drives, respectively. Some Macs come with DVD-RAM (DVD-random-access memory) or DVD-R (DVD-recordable) drives preinstalled; they're an excellent choice for large-scale backup tasks, especially if you use your Mac in a creative environment to produce large graphics or multimedia documents.

For a professional-level backup solution, you may want to use a tape drive. Travan tape drives are inexpensive solutions, while DLT (digital linear tape) and DAT (digital audio tape) are faster, but more expensive. A tape drive is often called a *near-line solution* because the disk itself doesn't mount on your desktop (or in the Computer view of a Finder window). In order to access the tape, you have to use a special program—and that program needs to be Mac OS X–compatible, unless you run your backups by booting into Mac OS 9.1. Tape is also linear, so you have to fast-forward or rewind through a tape to find a particular file. Still, it's a good solution for backing up many, many gigabytes of data on a regular basis.

Along with hardware, you'll likely want to use software to help you back up your files. For very infrequent backups, it's possible to simply drag and drop items from your Mac's disk to the removable disk; this isn't the most advised course of action, but it's something. You can even use Sherlock to help you seek out recently changed files if you're following a manual backup routine.

Backup software, however, enables you to automate the process, creating schedules for your backups as well as game plans for rotating your backup media and creating archives that you drop out of your rotation and store in a secure location. Backup software ranges from personal versions for individuals to network versions that back up an entire network at once.

 TIP At the time of writing, few companies offer native versions of their backup software for Mac OS X. Dantz (www.dantz.com) has announced beta testing of a Mac OS X–compatible backup client that interacts with its professional-level backup server software, and will hopefully offer its consumer-level software (Retrospect Express) for Mac OS X as well. Mac OS 9–compatible backup software can also be used under some circumstances, although for best results you should boot into Mac OS 9.1 and run backup utilities only on HFS+ volumes (not UFS volumes, if you created any when you installed Mac OS X).

What to Back Up

One important consideration is what, exactly, needs to be backed up. On most Macs, it may be less than you think—which is good, because you likely have a hard disk that's quite a bit larger than the disks that your removable drive supports. So you'll want to avoid backing up your entire hard disk every few days.

For the most part, you probably don't need to back up your applications, as long as you have access to the original CD-ROM or other disks used for distribution. If you've downloaded applications or application updaters from the Internet, those should be backed up (or, more to the point, archived and stored somewhere safe).

You probably don't need to back up most system files, especially those that you haven't touched since you installed the Mac OS. (Ideally, you won't need to touch much of anything in the System folder, because it's supposed to be changed only by

PART

IV

Apple's official installer programs.) You can, however, make a point of backing up any additional installers that you've used to augment your system—for example, any peripheral drivers, downloads from Apple, or other system-level tools you've used to upgrade your Mac over time. If you should ever need to reinstall Mac OS X, you'll be able to start from the Mac OS X CD, then add the other drivers and updates that you've downloaded and stored in a safe place.

NOTE If you're a system administrator for a number of Macs, however, you may find it more convenient to download and archive Mac OS X system updates individually, so you won't have to sit through the Software Update process every time you restore a Mac to a CD version of the Mac OS X. Those updates can be downloaded individually at http://asu.info.apple.com on the Web.

If you have administrative responsibilities for your Mac, you'll want to back up the Mac's main Library folder hierarchy, where you're more likely to have system-related files that change frequently. Remember that drivers, fonts, Web pages, and other common files are stored in the main Library hierarchy; if you have overall responsibility for the Mac, it's a good idea to back up those files.

NOTE If you're the type who likes to tweak, it's important to remember to back up any files that you plan to change manually, especially configuration files such as those used by Apache (see Chapter 24) and other low-level servers, applications, and tools. At the command line, the /etc hierarchy is where you'll find many of the configuration files for your Mac that you may have altered, thus making it a good candidate for backup. If you've worked at all in the root account, remember that the root account's home folder is /private/var/root. (See Chapter 20 for more on the root account, and Chapter 22 for more on the command line.)

In fact, most of the files you'll want to back up will be in the Users hierarchy; long-time Mac users will note that this is one of the areas where Mac OS X's new file-system hierarchy can really be helpful. Since most Mac users have little choice but to store files in their home folders, it's much easier for you, as an administrator, to back those folders up. As an administrator, you'll probably opt to back up the entire Users folder and all its subfolders. Doing so not only creates a backup of all users' personal files but also the Shared folder, where users may be exchanging files with one another.

TIP File privileges can make backing up the Users hierarchy from a regular Admin account tricky at best. If you have a graphical backup application, it may allow you to authenticate so the backup program can read and copy other users' files. Otherwise, you might consider enabling the root account and logging in as root so that you can copy the Users folder to another disk or disks. Note also that Admin accounts have greater file privileges when logged in from a remote Mac, so you can log in (via Apple File Protocol or FTP) and back up the Users folder to another Mac that way.

Even if you're backing up only personal files, it may be tempting to focus solely on the Documents folder inside the home folder. This is probably a mistake, however, since important files are often stored in the Desktop folder inside the home folder, particularly recent downloads and any document folders that have been created or dragged to the desktop. Likewise, the Library folder in each home folder is an important repository of preferences files, fonts, Internet plug-ins, and other items that may have been installed by that user. And, within each user's Library folder is a Mail folder, which you may wish to back up (and even archive) regularly in order to restore e-mail in case of a disk failure or other problem. Even the Public and Sites folders may be important if the user has shared files or a personal Web site.

So the best plan is to back up your entire home folder if you're backing up your own files, or the entire Users hierarchy if you have administrator responsibilities. Although that may sound like a lot of files, a system of rotation and incremental backups, as discussed next, should make creating regular, useful backups fairly painless.

Backup: Rotating and Archiving

Correctly backing up your Mac means following a routine. That routine may be helped along by your backup software, if you have such an application, or it may be a routine you enforce on your own. (You could conceivably use AppleScript or another scheduling application to help you with backup tasks.) Part of that routine is regular *rotation* and archiving. By rotating your backup media, you ensure against two problems: bad media and corrupt files. If you're regularly backing up to different disks, if one disk goes bad, the other can be used to recover files. Also, if a file becomes corrupt on one disk, a proper rotation and archiving scheme may allow you to recover an earlier version of that file.

 TIP If you're interested in working at the command line in the Terminal application, you can use a combination of rsync (which synchronizes files in remote directories) and cron, a scheduling program, to automate the backing up of files. Use the man command (e.g., man rsync and man cron) to learn more about them, and see Chapter 22 for more on the command line and Terminal.

A proper rotation of media can also enable you to make use of *incremental backups*, meaning you can back up only those files that have changed since a recent backup. Incremental backups are convenient because they require less time than a complete backup. If, for example, I perform an incremental backup to a disk I created last Wednesday, only the files that have changed since Wednesday need to be included on the disk. But an incremental approach is only part of the solution. If you consistently make incremental updates to the same disk, you risk data loss if that one disk fails. So you rotate media to avoid the possibility that a single media failure will leave you without your data.

Here's a typical rotation scheme:

1. Begin with three fresh removable disks or tapes.

2. On Monday, perform a full backup to disk A.

3. On Wednesday, perform a full backup to disk B.

4. On Friday, perform a full backup to disk C.

5. On the subsequent Monday, perform a full backup to a new disk, disk D. Disk A used on the previous Monday can become an archive—stored off-site or in a fireproof box, safe, safety deposit box, or something similar.

6. On Wednesday, perform an incremental backup to disk B. All data changed or added since the previous Wednesday will be added to this backup. This backup should take place more quickly than the previous backup.

7. On Friday, perform an incremental backup to disk C. All data changed or added since the previous Friday will be added to this backup.

8. On the next Monday, perform an incremental backup to disk D.

9. On Wednesday, perform a full backup to a new disk, disk E. Drop disk B out of the rotation and store it as an archive.

The process continues rotating from there. Note that this isn't the only solution; you might opt to use two disks for your rotation, or you may decide to drop out an archive less often—for example, every few weeks or once a month instead of once a week.

For a fairly bulletproof corporate or organizational rotation, the approach outlined above is hard to beat. For instance, if the Mac (or the network or network server, if that's what you're backing up) fails on Tuesday, you have a recent backup from Monday, a backup from the previous Friday, and an archive that's less than a week old. Likewise, other archives are made every 10 days or so, so you can revert to a previous version of a file if necessary. And disks are used as archives fairly quickly to help ensure that they don't get worn out or begin to fail.

WARNING Even with a good rotation scheme, it's still important to test your backup disks or tapes on a regular basis, especially if you, your mission, or your organization is relying on those disks to secure your data.

Personal Backup

You may not always desire a high-end backup system using software and rotation plans. In some cases you may not even be the administrator of your Mac, and your only desire is to back up your own personal files. In that case, regularly copying folders from your Mac to a removable disk is the best course of action.

One solution in this case, however, is to use Sherlock to locate files that have been created or updated since your last backup. This can be helpful, as it enables you to perform a sort of manual incremental backup. Incremental backups are best done with add-on software, but you can use Sherlock and the Finder to approximate it. Using Sherlock, you can create a custom search that locates files that have a "date modified" since a particular date.

First, launch Sherlock and choose the Files channel. Select Edit from the Custom pull-down menu, and you'll see the More Search Options dialog box. Here you can select Date Modified (turn on its check box) and use the other options to determine what Sherlock should search for.

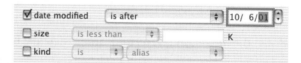

You can customize the search even further; for instance, you can look for all items modified since a particular date with a "kind" that "is not folder."

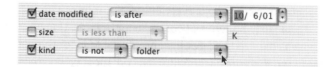

Now, click OK. Then, back in the main Sherlock window, click the large magnifying glass icon to invoke the search.

If you searched only your home folder (remember that Sherlock can search individual folder hierarchies, if desired, as discussed in Chapter 6), you should see only the files and/or folders that have changed since a particular date. You can create a folder on your backup disk with today's date and then drag those files to that new folder, thus creating an incremental backup.

NOTE There's one limitation to this approach: You can't drag two files with the same name from a Sherlock window to a single folder. So you may need to page through the files quickly to make sure there are no duplicate names. Or you can drag files a few at a time so that if two files *do* have the same name, you'll be prompted by the Finder.

For simple, personal backup rotation, you might opt to back up using two different disks, performing the backup once a week:

1. In the first week, create a full backup of all the files and folders you want to safeguard to disk A.

2. In the second week, create a full backup to disk B.

3. In the third week, create an incremental backup to disk A.

4. In the fourth week, create an incremental backup to disk B.

5. In the fifth week, increment disk A.

6. In the sixth week, increment disk B.

7. After the sixth week's backup to disk B, turn disk A into an archive disk (store it somewhere safe). In the seventh week, create a full backup to disk C.

8. Keep rotating until the eleventh week. When you've made that incremental backup to disk C, turn disk B into an archive disk. In the twelfth week, create a new backup to disk D.

And so on. With a rotation like this, you're never more than one week out from a complete backup, and at all times you have an archive that's only a few weeks old. Also, you're still rotating disks so that they don't get too old and worn before you retire them as archives. You get longer life out of each disk.

You may find that a shareware solution is a convenient way to quickly back up your personal files to removable media. One such utility is FoldersSynchronizer X, a $30 shareware application from a company called Softobe (www.softobe.com). FoldersSynchronizer X, shown in Figure 21.1, offers a number of options to help you automate synchronizing or backing up folders in one location to folders in another location. (Synchronizing will make each of two folders an exact mirror image of the other, so that changes in each folder are duplicated in the other. Backing up makes the target folder identical to the source folder, but not vice versa.) The program includes the ability to schedule regular backup sessions to take place automatically, as well as options to filter certain types of documents and folders, back up multiple folders, and purposefully exclude certain files or folders.

PART IV — Installing, Maintaining, and Troubleshooting

FIGURE 21.1

FoldersSynchronizer X is a convenient shareware tool for personal backup tasks.

 TIP Another shareware program, Synk X (`mypage.uniserve.ca/~rvoth/synkx.html`), is in beta testing at the time of writing. It's also useful for quickly synchronizing two folders for personal backup.

Virus Detection and Avoidance

A *virus* is a program designed to replicate itself as much and as often as possible. Viruses aren't always designed to cause data loss or other problems, but they generally end up causing trouble of some kind, whether maliciously or not. Viruses can vary in their intent from popping up messages on your screen to destroying low-level information on your disk drive in order to render it unusable. Poorly written viruses may not set out to be malicious but may still crash your applications, the Classic environment, or your entire Mac OS X environment.

Worms and Trojan horses are often lumped in the general category of "viruses," although they aren't technically the same thing. A *Trojan horse* is a program that masquerades as something else—a malicious program disguised as something you might want to double-click and play with. (They often have "love," "free," or "money" in their name.) A *worm* is actually more similar to a virus; it can replicate itself and use system memory, but it can't attach itself to another program. Instead, it needs to be run on its own (often as a Trojan horse).

Special Variants: E-Mail Viruses

So far, no one has come up with a way to infect an e-mail message with a virus, partly because e-mail messages are always ASCII (plain-text) documents. Virus authors have created the next best thing, though—e-mail attachment viruses.

Viruses such as Melissa and the Love Bug work by attaching themselves to an e-mail message. Then, when the attachment is double-clicked by a recipient, the virus does two things. First, it sends itself to everyone in the user's e-mail address book. Then it does whatever else it was designed to do: delete files, change settings, or whatever the virus author could envision.

The reason it *can* do these things is that Microsoft has built-in scripting commands to Outlook Express, Microsoft Outlook, and Microsoft Entourage that the virus authors take advantage of. The scripting is (ideally) designed to help automate tasks in the same way that AppleScript helps automate tasks in the Mac OS. Unfortunately, a few security holes in the design of Microsoft's scripting makes it fairly easy to exploit for evil. Fortunately (for Mac users, at least), most virus authors write their viruses to do damage to Microsoft Windows computers because there are many more of them to infect. Still, at least one Mac-specific strain of the Melissa virus has popped up recently, and others may be coming.

The solution is to avoid *ever* launching an attachment that you're not familiar with; this is especially true if the attachment seems very enticing (using the aforementioned target words *love, free,* or *money*). Also, remember that an attachment from a friend isn't necessarily a good thing; these viruses are designed to appear to be from your friends and colleagues, which is why they exploit the address book feature in the affected e-mail programs. Instead, you should only launch and work with attachments that you were specifically expecting to receive. When in doubt, contact the person who sent you the message (by phone, if possible) and confirm that they meant to send the attachment. If they didn't, that's a good sign that you should delete the attachment and let them know that a virus may be at work on their computer.

Mac OS X presents some interesting issues when it comes to viruses. The majority of computer viruses are written for Microsoft Windows computers, with far fewer written for Macs. Mac OS X, then, would ideally have very few viruses written for it. However, Mac OS X installations will often use the HFS+ hard-disk format that's common to both older versions of the Mac OS and Mac OS X, meaning that some earlier Mac viruses can still infect the computer. Because you're likely to use some files created on older Macs, and the Classic environment is still there, the potential to be affected by "Classic viruses" still exists. Plus, Mac OS X is built on top of FreeBSD (as part of the Darwin underpinnings), meaning that it's also possible for Mac OS X to contract viruses and other malicious programs that are common to FreeBSD and similar operating systems.

Some Mac OS X applications are also susceptible to *macro* viruses—those that rely on built-in scripting behavior in certain applications. Common culprits are Microsoft applications, such as Microsoft Word and Excel, which are incredibly popular and also happen to have built-in scripting mechanisms that virus authors exploit. Likewise, e-mail attachment viruses (popular strains have been called "Melissa" and "I Love You," or "the Love Bug") replicate themselves in Microsoft Outlook Express and similar applications such as Microsoft Entourage. So far, these viruses generally haven't caused damage to Macs and the Mac OS. They can, however, be replicated by the Mac versions of Microsoft programs, so you should be aware of them (see preceding sidebar).

Avoiding Viruses

So how do you get a virus? Like human viruses, computer viruses generally require contact with the outside world. Computer viruses are small programs that attach themselves to other programs or documents and then spread when those programs are shared, whether it's via the Internet, a local area network, or a removable disk.

To avoid viruses, the most reliable solution is not to share files with others. That includes downloading files from online sources, working with attachments, and even copying files from CD-ROMs that are distributed with your favorite Macintosh magazines. In most cases, though, that's impractical. So you need to take some middle steps:

- Never launch an attached document or application that you've received in e-mail—even from a friend or colleague—unless you fully expected to receive the attachment.

- Download files and applications from the most reputable sources possible. Major download sites (Apple, Download.com, AOL.com) make a point of checking files for viruses before they are posted. (That's not a guarantee, but it helps.) Check other sites for indications that the owners scan for viruses and take other steps to avoid malicious code.

- Pay close attention to warnings you receive from applications immediately after launching documents. This is particularly true of Microsoft applications, which now attempt to detect attached macros before allowing a document to appear in the application. If you don't believe a particular document is supposed to contain a macro (or if you're not sure), cancel the loading of that document and contact the document's author to see if it's supposed to have a macro.

- Avoid using removable media from noncommercial sources. Don't swap programs, utilities, and documents with friends via Zip disks, CDs, or other removables. Of course, this is of limited effectiveness, because even commercial CDs can accidentally distribute viruses.

- Avoid the Package Installer, if possible. As noted in Chapter 7, early versions of the Package Installer have a few security holes that could make it easier for viruses to spread and for root or administrative privileges to be accessed. If you have the option, don't use the Package Installer, or use it only to install applications from very reliable vendors. Also, keep watching Apple and other Mac news sites for discussions about updates and fixes to the Package Installer.

- Stay out of the root account, if it has been enabled. If you happen to set off a virus while you're logged in as root, you may be giving that virus much more free reign over the files on your Mac, thanks to the root account's privileges. Instead, work in a user account when you're doing anything other than system maintenance and management.

And the number one way to avoid viruses? Catch them before they enter your system. Buy and use a virus protection program, as discussed in the next section.

What *Isn't* a Virus?

Internet hoaxes may be just about as popular as viruses when it comes to malicious little ways that some people like to have "fun." Some e-mail hoaxes are just stories or urban legends—the one about the cookie recipe, the alligators in the sewers, or the little boy who wants to set a Guinness record for postcards received while in the hospital.

Other e-mail hoaxes are virus alerts from supposedly credible sources. In most cases these cause no more harm than prompting naïve or cautious users to forward the message to everyone they know, alert the IT department, and take an early lunch just in case the building comes crashing down.

The fact is, most of these hoaxes are fairly easy to spot. The regular text of an e-mail message can't transmit a virus (only an attachment can), so simply *reading* a virus-infected e-mail can't cause it to spread. (This may change someday when someone exploits a particularly stupid hole in an e-mail program's scripting implementation, but it hasn't happened yet.)

Finally, breathless e-mail messages warning of viruses will pretty much never be released by Microsoft, "the U.S. government," or any major, official-sounding body—especially if that group's name is misspelled in the warning. If you'd like to check an official source, try HoaxBusters (hoaxbusters.ciac.org), a service of the Computer Incident Advisory Capability, which is a part of the U.S. Department of Energy. There you'll find a roundup of common hoaxes and suspected hoaxes, and you can learn what's real, what's not, and what may have been real three years ago and is still circulating as junk mail.

Identifying and Removing Viruses

You won't always know immediately when your Mac has contracted a virus; after all, part of the point of a virus is that it replicates beneath the surface before causing any damage. Still, there are "viral symptoms" that you can look out for on your Mac:

- Files that suddenly appear or disappear, folders that move on their own, or files and folders whose size or modification date has changed could indicate trouble. If an entire folder or hierarchy appears to disappear or to be deleted, you should immediately suspect a malicious program.

- Trouble opening or saving documents, particularly in Microsoft applications, or documents that, once saved, cannot be opened again for editing are possible symptoms. Also, if commands disappear or menus move in Microsoft applications (and the behavior is not expected macro behavior), you may have a virus.

- Dialog boxes that appear on their own, particularly with odd, malicious, or nonsensical text, could indicate some sort of infection. This is particularly true if the dialog box appears immediately after something else has changed, such as starting up your Mac, installing an application, or inserting a removable disk into the Mac or an attached drive.

- Any other automatic behavior—such as colors or screen resolution changing, the mouse pointer disappearing or moving on its own, or anything else that seems to happen without your input—could suggest a malicious or prank application. These behaviors are tougher to pin down, however, since some applications change screen resolutions and an errant driver could cause issues with the mouse pointer. Still, it's a good time to run a virus-checking application.

None of these is a surefire sign of virus infection. But if you note one of them and suspect foul play, the first thing you should do is stop working with other applications and documents. You want to avoid allowing the virus to spread to other files. This is especially true of macro viruses; once you have an infected Microsoft Word or Excel document, the Normal template in your Office application is infected. Documents that you subsequently create or open to edit might also be infected.

If you note odd disk activity, files disappearing as you watch, unfriendly dialog boxes flashing on the screen, or similar problems, you should shut down your Mac. If you can't seem to get the Shut Down command to work—and you absolutely suspect a damaging virus—pull the plug.

Then the next solution is to get an antivirus software package as soon as you can. At the time of writing, there are no antivirus applications that are completely native to Mac OS X, so you'll need to stay on top of the news to see when that changes. As of now, you need to run Norton AntiVirus 7 (www.norton.com/mac/) or higher from within the Classic environment (see Figure 21.2) or by booting from the included CD-ROM. This virus checker can check Mac OS X HFS+ disks and will catch many "Classic" viruses. Dr. Solomon's Virex (www.drsolomons.com) is another popular virus-checking application for Mac OS 9.*x* that may be updated for Mac OS X. Check those companies' Web sites or other materials to see if they recommend running their products from the Classic environment. In some cases you may need to boot into Mac OS 9.1 before running the application. And if an antivirus software wasn't written to at least be aware of Mac OS X, you should avoid using it at all on your Mac.

As time wears on and Mac OS X becomes more and more popular, you should start to see commercial antivirus software available for it. Such applications can be set up to run in the background, always checking when you download items from the Internet, receive e-mail attachments, and insert removable media. Antivirus software also generally allows you to manually scan your hard disk, removable disks, or particular files and folders to see if an infection has occurred. If an infected file is found, the application will let you know about it and isolate the file, often by moving it to a new folder.

FIGURE 21.2

At the time of writing, the only solution for antivirus software is to run Norton AntiVirus 7 or higher in the Classic environment (or boot into Mac OS 9.1).

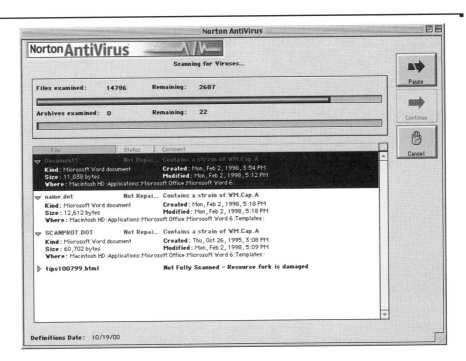

WARNING You may need to log in as an administrator and/or authenticate your antivirus application so that it has the correct permissions for accessing files and scanning them for viruses. See your antivirus application's instructions for details.

If you need the data from the file, you may be able to save it, depending on the type of virus; your antivirus application may have the ability to inoculate the file and remove the virus. If so, you can recover the file (see Figure 21.3). (If it's a text-based file, you might be able to load it into TextEdit or a similar program and retrieve portions of the file.) Most of the time, though, the safest course of action with an infected file is to inoculate it with your antivirus program (if possible), then delete it.

Also, most virus applications have a regular schedule on which their virus definitions are updated. These applications make updater files or libraries available, which you can download from the virus application's Web site. (The ability to download the updaters may also be built into the application.) You should make a point of updating your antivirus application whenever possible so that you can be assured of catching the very latest viruses if they've infected your files or disks.

FIGURE 21.3

Although the recommended course of action is deleting the infected file, in some cases you may be able to repair it.

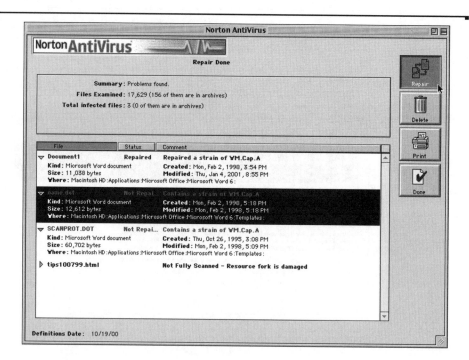

WARNING Some users automatically think the best solution for a virus infection is to format the hard disk and reinstall the Mac OS. While this may be appropriate in some cases, you're better off running an antivirus application before doing any reinstallation. Some viruses (especially those that attack the boot sector of a disk) can actually survive a reformat and still be there to cause problems. Other viruses may have already infected files that you've backed up; if you add those files back to your reinstalled system, you'll simply infect it again.

Disk First Aid and Maintenance

A modern computer ends up working with a lot of files. For instance, as I wrote the virus section of this chapter, I ran an antivirus application on one of my test computers and noticed that it had over 23,000 files stored on one of its three attached disk drives. And I don't even use that Mac every day. What with the Internet browser application's cache files, tens or hundreds of e-mail messages a day, large multimedia files, fonts, system files, and an entire underbelly of Darwin and Unix-like files beneath your Mac's glossy veneer, your disks have a lot of work to do.

The more a disk works, the more it's susceptible to errors, whether they're small problems in the way the files are recorded and details are maintained or they're larger problems with the way files are stored. In order to keep your Mac humming along nicely, it's important to maintain the disks. This maintenance is done in a two-step process: first aid and disk "doctoring."

Disk First Aid

Actually, first aid is more than a technique; First Aid is the name of a utility that comes with Mac OS X. In the Utilities folder inside your Mac's main Applications folder, you'll find the Disk Utility. Launch it, and you'll see the First Aid option on the left side of the window. (Users of earlier Mac OS versions will note that this is similar to the stand-alone application Disk First Aid that shipped with previous Mac OS releases.)

 NOTE If you need to repair the startup disk, you should begin by booting your Mac from the Mac OS X CD-ROM. When the installer appears, choose Open Disk Utility from the Installer menu. Now you can use First Aid to repair the startup disk.

First Aid can verify all the different types of disks (Mac OS Standard, Mac OS Extended, UFS, CD-ROM, and so on) that you might have attached to your Mac. First Aid checks to make sure the disk's file-tracking databases have entries that match the files that are stored on that disk. Minor errors can be caught and corrected by First Aid. Larger problems need to be tackled by a third-party disk doctor application.

To use First Aid, open the Disk Utility application and then select the First Aid button on the left side of the Disk Utility window. At the top of the window, you'll see all the volumes that are currently connected to your Mac, including hard disks and removables. Select the disk that you would like to check, then click Verify or, if the Repair button is available, click Repair. Clicking Repair causes any errors to be fixed immediately, if First Aid is capable. This is usually preferable, but the Repair button will sometimes be grayed out because either the disk can't be altered (such as a CD) or it's the current startup disk (such as your main hard disk). Once you've clicked either Verify or Repair, First Aid starts checking the drive (see Figure 21.4).

FIGURE 21.4

First Aid is verifying the disk.

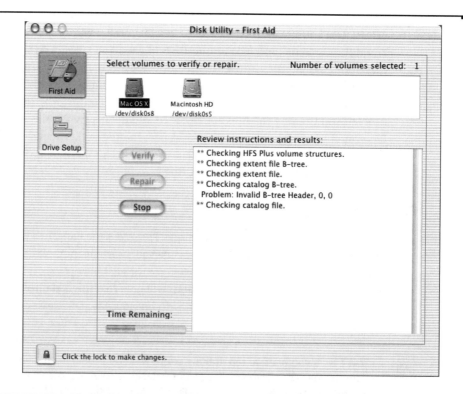

NOTE If you have disk images that are mounted on the desktop, you may see them in the First Aid window as well. These generally don't need to be verified by First Aid.

While First Aid is scanning the disk, it will report any errors and whether or not it was able to fix them. If it was unable to fix them, you may need to run a third-party disk doctor application, as described in the next section. If First Aid finds errors on your startup disk, you may need to restart your Mac using the Mac OS X CD-ROM. Then you can run First Aid from the CD and attempt to repair items on your main hard disk. (Because you started up from the CD, First Aid will be able to fix the startup hard disk. Then you can restart your Mac once again from its main hard disk.)

 NOTE If you're working in Classic or in Mac OS 9.1, note that the Disk First Aid application that ships with Mac OS 9.1 or higher (it's Disk First Aid version 8.6 or above) can also be used to check your Mac OS X disk, assuming it's in HFS+ format. If you don't have that version, you can download the latest Disk First Aid from `asu.info.apple.com/` on the Web.

Disk Doctors

When First Aid can't help with a problem, you need to turn to a disk doctor application. Common disk doctor applications include Norton Utilities and Alsoft Diskwarrior (`www.alsoft.com`). At the time of writing, Micromat (`www.micromat.com`), the publisher of TechTool Pro, has announced a disk utility that specifically runs in Mac OS X, called Drive 10.

You can run Norton Utilities 6 to fix HFS+ volumes used with Mac OS X, although it runs by booting from the Norton CD; but Symantec hasn't yet released a Mac OS X native utility. (I'm sure they will, if they haven't by the time you read this.) Diskwarrior 2.1 has also been rated to recover HFS+ volumes used with Mac OS X.

 WARNING Do not run a disk utility on a Mac OS X disk (or any disk connected to a Mac OS X–based Mac) if that utility wasn't written specifically with Mac OS X in mind. (It doesn't have to be a Carbon or Cocoa application, but if it's a Classic-only or Mac OS 9.x–only application, it needs to be designed to work in a Mac OS X environment and/or with Mac OS X volumes and files.) A good deal about the file system has changed between Mac OS 9.1 and Mac OS X, and an older utility could cause serious damage to your files.

Whatever the name of your disk doctor utility, its function is to find fairly serious problems with individual files and folders, compare them with the disk's database, and fix those anomalies. That will help the Mac run more efficiently and make sure that corruption isn't creeping into your files, causing trouble with saved files or causing crashes within applications. (Diskwarrior works its magic by rebuilding the disk directory from scratch. This approach sometimes saves entire disks that appear to have been erased or destroyed by corruption.)

Most disk doctor utilities work best if you reboot your Mac from the recovery CD-ROM itself. This will allow you, among other things, to make low-level repairs to your main startup disk. You can restart from the CD-ROM in one of three ways:

- Insert the CD-ROM and select it from the Startup Disk pane within the System Preferences application.

- Insert the CD-ROM, restart your Mac, and immediately after your Mac chimes, hold down the C key on the keyboard until the Mac begins to start up from the CD-ROM.

- Insert the CD-ROM, restart your Mac, and immediately after the chime, hold down the Option key. You'll see a special screen that enables you to select the CD-ROM (among other options) as the startup disk. Select it and click the right-arrow icon to begin the startup process.

Once you've finished running the program, you may have the option of launching the Startup Disk application or control panel from the CD, selecting your main startup disk, and then restarting. If that doesn't work, you can hold down the Option key once again after the startup chime, then use the special startup screen to select your main Mac OS X startup disk.

Besides fixing disks, many disk doctor programs have utilities that can stay "resident" in the background, always watching for problems with the disk (or checking periodically when you're not actively using the computer). Other programs offer additional tools that save information about your disk while it's still in good shape, making it easy to recover the disk later, if something has gone wrong.

Perhaps the most important additional feature you can look for, though, is the disk doctor's ability to *defragment* a disk. When a disk is used repeatedly, files have a tendency to fragment; as files are deleted from the drive, others are stored in their place. Eventually, even if you have quite a bit of free space on your hard disk, that space may be subdivided into much smaller blocks where earlier items were deleted. If the disk doesn't offer enough *contiguous* space for a large file, the file is broken up and stored as separate fragments. Usually, this isn't a problem for the OS, which can handle the different file fragments without losing them. But it does slow down the retrieval of the file a bit, and, over time, increased fragmentation can lead to unnecessary complications, slowdowns, and a higher likelihood of errors.

The solution is to occasionally move the files around so that they're stored contiguously again. That's what a defragmenting utility does—it rearranges the files on the disk so that they are stored without fragmentation and all the open, available space is on one part of the drive. That means that, at least for a while, new files will be saved contiguously and the disk will be able to locate and load files a bit more quickly.

You should defragment occasionally (I'd recommend about once a month, if you have a good defragmentation utility) to keep your drive in top performance, with one caveat: The process of defragmenting can result in data loss. So before defragmenting, you should make sure you have a good, current backup of your important files. Then, go for it.

 NOTE Mac OS X includes a command-line utility, called *fsck*, which can be used to clean up the underlying file system. You must enter single-user mode to use fsck, along with a few other requirements. Single-user mode and using fsck are covered in Chapter 20.

Other Maintenance Tasks

Aside from a good backup, the best way to keep your Mac humming along happily is a little preventive medicine. If you create and stick to a schedule for regularly updating, checking, and cleaning up your system, you'll be much less likely to run into unforeseen errors. Mac OS X, unlike almost any other consumer-oriented operating system, should be able to keep running for months and months without troubleshooting-related shutdowns or restarts.

You've got an even greater chance of keeping the Mac trouble-free if you follow a regular schedule of maintenance to keep your disks and files in top shape. In this section, I'll quickly cover some important do's and don'ts of Mac OS X maintenance. Then I'll discuss the Software Update pane of System Preferences, which you should check regularly (or schedule for automatic checks) to keep Mac OS X and your applications as up-to-date as possible.

Do's and Don'ts

Mac OS X changes the way some tasks are handled and approached—especially things like when and how you should shut down your Macintosh. With Mac OS X, your Mac is designed to run as continuously as possible, with the Sleep command used to put your Mac into a low-power mode. You should also perform some particular maintenance tasks regularly and avoid some other situations that can get you into trouble.

Don't turn your Mac on and off repeatedly.   Remember that all modern Macs have sleep functions and other automatic energy-saving components that help the computer conserve power even while the Mac is still "on." Turning your Mac on and off shuts down servers and automated tasks and forces the Mac to go through the startup process repeatedly. (It's a minor issue, but repeatedly turning a Mac on and off could potentially shorten its life or cause internals to fail a bit more quickly.) If you like to turn your Mac off completely, shut it down once at the end of the day, then start it up again the next morning. There's no reason to shut it down when you go to lunch or take a break—just log out and/or put your Mac to sleep.

NOTE In fact, Mac OS X, more than any previous Mac OS version, is really designed to run continuously. This not only makes it easier for you to start up and work with your Mac whenever you want, but it also allows the Mac OS to perform important low-level maintenance tasks that it schedules for times with the Mac isn't in use. To save energy, you should use the sleep function whenever you walk away from your Mac for more than a few minutes; but otherwise, you should rarely need to shut down your Mac. You should also turn off your monitor if it doesn't power down automatically when your Mac is asleep. (You may also want to lock your keychain, implement the screen saver with a password, and/or log out for security reasons.) But sleep mode is very energy conscious, while allowing you to resume work within a few seconds.

Do use the Shut Down command.   When you do opt to turn your Mac off, you should avoid pulling the plug at all costs. (In fact, you should never just "pull the plug" or turn off your surge protector before shutting down your Mac unless you're sure your files are being attacked by a destructive virus.) If you don't use the Shut Down command, the Mac doesn't properly go through the logout and shutdown sequence, leaving files open to corruption, which could result in a less stable Mac. On all modern Macs, you can press the power button to get a dialog box that enables you to shut down properly and quickly.

TIP Need to shut down, but you can't see the screen? Sometimes this happens—a monitor fails, it's pulled from the Mac, or you've somehow lost access to the Apple menu while using two different monitors. In any case, you can press the power button on your Mac to bring up the Shut Down dialog box, then press Return to select Shut Down.

Do check storage space and organize your files.   You should check your Mac regularly to make sure it has plenty of disk space available; if necessary, toss items in the Trash and empty it to make more space. When your Mac begins to run low on disk space, odd errors can begin to crop up.

Do back up and archive.   As discussed earlier in this chapter, backing up in an organizational setting should be done every other day or even more frequently. Personal backup can take place a little less frequently. Every four to six weeks, you should also create an archive of important files on your Mac and store that archive in a safe place—preferably not in the same place as your Mac. This should be part of your regular backup rotation; in fact, for organizational use you should create an archive more frequently. (See the earlier section "Backing Up Your Mac" for a detailed discussion.)

Don't forget your disks.   You should regularly run First Aid, part of Disk Utility, at least once a month, if not more often—and, if you have a good disk doctor program, run it as well. (Some disk doctor programs are designed for recovery only, but if they have special tools that aid recovery, you should use them.) And don't forget removable and external disks; even if they're connected via USB or FireWire, they still need regular checkups. Many Mac users are willing to go months or even years without maintaining their disks, which is a mistake, since corruption and inefficient disk management can slow down the Mac and create problems.

Do update applications.   In the near future, many applications will likely update themselves over the Web, as Mac OS X does with the Software Update pane (discussed next). In the meantime, it's important that you keep on top of updates yourself, particularly as Mac OS X and Mac OS X applications mature. Because the Mac OS X environment is very new, applications will tend to have more bugs and problems out of the starting gate. So you should regularly launch your Web browser and surf for possibilities. Visit www.versiontracker.com and www.softwatcher.com/mac/ for starters, as well as the sites of the companies that publish your software, to see if they've posted any updates.

Software Update

Software Update is an important tool for keeping your Mac running as efficiently and effectively as possible. Although Apple has had Software Update technology built into Mac OS versions for a few years now, the Mac OS X implementation is the strongest thus far. You'll find that Apple offers regular updates to both the Mac OS in general and the company's own applications—iTunes, iMovie, and others—via Software Update. In fact, it will likely become the primary mechanism for Apple's software update distribution as Mac OS X gains popularity.

More to the point, Software Update is a pane in the System Preferences application. It automatically checks special server computers at Apple to see if any updates for the Mac OS or other Apple software have been posted. If so, the update is downloaded to your Mac so that you can install it. To use Software Update at any time, click the Update Now button (see Figure 21.5).

FIGURE 21.5

Click the Update Now button in the Software Update application to check for updates from Apple.

It's important to check Software Update regularly, or to schedule it to check automatically, particularly if you have an "always-on" Internet connection. Apple distributes new updates to Mac OS X whenever they're needed and completed by the engineering team, thus getting the latest possible version to Mac users quickly. Instead of waiting for a CD to arrive or heading to Apple's Web site to download an update, you can use Software Update to retrieve new updates immediately and install them painlessly.

When Software Update locates a new update, you'll see the Install Software window (see Figure 21.6), which enables you to select the software updates that you'd like to install. After making your selections, click the Install button and you'll be asked to enter an Admin username and password; although any user can check for new updates, Software Update requires an Admin password to download and install them. Once you're authenticated, the download begins.

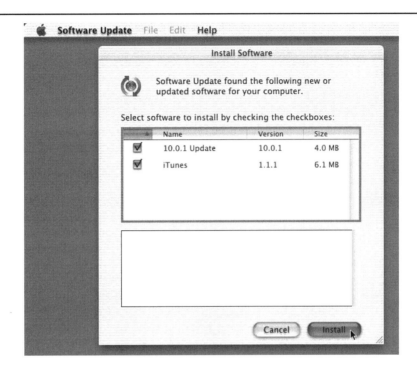

FIGURE 21.6

When Software Update locates an update, you'll see the Install Software window.

You can automate the Software Update application so that it checks for software automatically at regular intervals. If you're interested in having Software Update adhere to a schedule, you need to first authenticate yourself as an administrator. Next, select the Automatically button in the Software Update pane. Now you can select how often you want to check for updates from the Check For Updates pop-up menu: Daily, Weekly, or Monthly. You can also check the Ask Me Before Installing New Software option if you'd like Software Update to confirm with you that it's okay to install any updates it finds; otherwise, the update installation will take place automatically, too.

Seasonal Cleaning and Sweeping

Over the long term you'll want to set aside a little time every six months to do some fairly serious maintenance. During these sessions, you should consider doing a full scouring of your disks, during which you'll go through many of the folders on your disk that you have permission for and remove old, outdated, redundant, or archived files that you no longer need on the Mac. In conjunction with a disk-fixing session, this can help you free up wasted disk space for new files.

 NOTE If you want to dig through the entire disk (particularly the Users hierarchy), you might want to enable the root account, as discussed in Chapter 20. An administrator account may be able to perform some of this file maintenance, but you may not have the file privileges to alter files in the Shared folder or elsewhere in other users' folders.

One place to focus your efforts is the Library folder in your (and in other users') home folder. There you should check for old preferences files created by applications that are no longer installed, as well as fonts and other personal add-ons that are no longer necessary. You should also regularly check Public and Shared folders for files that were placed in them and later abandoned or forgotten, and remind yourself and others to purge e-mail regularly to minimize disk-space usage.

 TIP Remember the Preferences folder that's in the System Folder for your Classic (or Mac OS 9.1 dual-boot) environment. You'll often find old preferences files there, especially if you use Classic applications often.

You can use utilities to help you with spring cleaning tasks. OmniGroup (www .omnigroup.com) makes a product called OmniDiskSweeper that you can use to see, at a glance, what portions of your disk are taking up the most space. If you suddenly see anomalies—such as a particular user who is storing a gigabyte's worth of files, or an inordinate amount of storage space being taken up by Public and Shared folders—you may be able to plan your cleaning a bit more efficiently (see Figure 21.7).

 NOTE Aladdin Systems (www.aladdinsys.com) has updated its own rival utility, called Spring Cleaning, for Mac OS X. Spring Cleaning performs a number of cleaning tasks including locating outdated preferences files, Internet files, and multiple applications. It's also useful for uninstalling Mac OS X applications.

FIGURE 21.7

OmniDiskSweeper enables you to see how much space certain folders and folder hierarchies are using.

You should also hunt down duplicate files that aren't necessary—for instance, Classic applications have a tendency to install the application SimpleText repeatedly. You may also find multiple copies of Read Me files for applications you've deleted or PDF files that have been created as saved print jobs and that no longer need to be stored. Likewise, if you're an administrator, you may come across a font that multiple users have installed in their user folders; if that's the case, you can consolidate that font by installing it in the main /Library/Fonts/ folder on your hard disk.

One way to track down files that may be ripe for pruning is with Sherlock. Select all available volumes, search for common filename patterns—.rtf, .pdf, .ttf, .pref, SimpleText—and look to see if any might be duplicates that are no longer necessary (see Figure 21.8). As with any maintenance task, you should be cautious, as you don't want to get rid of files that are important to the Mac or to your users.

If you use a special folder for downloads from your Web browser or FTP application, you should sift through it regularly to see which files can be tossed. Often, downloading creates a few different files: a binary file (.bin, .hqx, .uu), a compressed version (.sit, .zip, .gz), and a final folder or a disk image (.img, .dmg). You need to keep only the uncompressed, final versions of your downloads. The others can be thrown away in the Trash (although you might want to first archive the compressed versions to a removable disk for safekeeping).

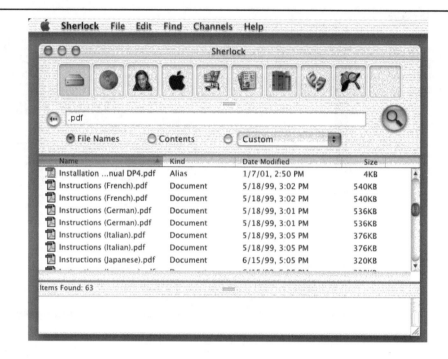

FIGURE 21.8

Sherlock can find duplicate or unnecessary files that are stored in different folders on your Mac's disks.

TIP Another way to find archives and compressed files you may no longer need is to search in Sherlock for files that end in `.hqx`, `.bin`, `.sit`, `.zip`, `.tar`, `.gz`, and other common filename extensions.

What's Next?

In this chapter you saw some of the maintenance tasks associated with keeping your Mac's files and disks up and running. Those tasks include backing up your Mac, detecting viruses, and fixing disks. Once you know the basics of each, the whole thing comes together as part of a maintenance routine—regular tasks that you should perform as you work with your Mac, as well as special "seasonal cleaning."

In Part V, we'll move on to advanced Mac OS X topics, where you'll learn more about Mac OS X's Darwin underpinnings and some of the powerful features of the built-in Web server, the FTP server, and command-line applications. You'll start with Chapter 22, which gives an overview of the Terminal application and working at the Darwin command line.

PART V

Advanced Mac OS X Topics

LEARN TO:

- *Work with Darwin in the Terminal application*

- *Activate remote login services and access remote servers from the command line*

- *Serve Web and FTP content and configure Apache*

- *Add third-party Internet and local networking services*

CHAPTER 22

Terminal and the Command Line

When your Mac OS X system boots up, it starts by loading Apple's Darwin operating system. Darwin is a nongraphical, Unix-based operating system with a long, rich history. It provides the powerful and robust foundation upon which the rest of Mac OS X is built. Darwin is also available for free as an independent operating system—in fact, it's *open-source,* meaning it can be downloaded, installed, and even modified by developers. Darwin lacks much of the user friendliness and functionality of Mac OS X, however, making it mostly the domain of programmers and hobbyists.

All of Mac OS X's graphical programs and tools, including Sherlock and Explorer, run on top of Darwin; Darwin is always there, running silently in the background, and there are several ways to reach it. The easiest is the Terminal program that Apple includes in Mac OS X. Another way is to type >console instead of your username in the Mac OS X login window. This brings up a text-only Darwin command-line interface, which is much less flexible than using Terminal to access the command line.

With Mac OS X, Apple has put a lot of work into making sure you don't have to use Darwin directly, so that you can stay in the more-familiar graphical areas of the OS. There's a great deal of power "under the hood," though, if you're interested in exploring a bit.

 NOTE This chapter was contributed by Chris Pepper. Chris is a system administrator, writer, and programmer. He is actively involved in the Apache documentation project and has ported several Unix tools to Darwin, including analog, zlib, libpng, and mrtg. You can find Chris on the Web at www.reppep.com/~pepper/.

Aqua vs. Darwin: Why Use Terminal?

Aqua is a brand-new interface, but with a rich heritage (Mac OS through 9, NextStep/ OpenStep, Java, and Unix). Darwin is a much simpler beast, directly descended from BSD Unix with Apple/NeXT modifications. Because Unix and the Mac OS have such different histories and emphases, the applications available for them are very different. Compared to Mac OS, Unix lacks productivity applications (such as Microsoft Office) but is rich in networking and security software and in experimental programs. Additionally, a great deal of free software is available for Unix systems.

Using Darwin, you can download and install free open-source programs like the following:

Apache   The world's most popular Web server (already included in Darwin/ Mac OS X and discussed in Chapter 24)

analog   A powerful, flexible program to analyze Web logs, telling you who's been accessing your Apache Web sites

Samba   A full-featured Windows file server and client, which lets a Unix/Darwin/Mac OS X computer participate in a Windows network just like a Windows computer (for more on Samba, see Chapter 25)

mrtg   A charting program that monitors and graphs network activity

Additionally, shells like `tcsh` offer a great deal of power for automating tasks. Wildcards and loops (see the section "Shell Scripting and Behavior") turn many time-consuming operations from the Mac into single commands or simple combinations. Another major benefit of shell scripts is that they don't require physical proximity. Unix systems are designed to be usable and manageable from anywhere on the Internet. This offers a great deal of power, from the ability to access home files while at work to full-featured remote troubleshooting, without additional software.

Perhaps best of all, working at the command line can be a much faster way to do things. For instance, if you accidentally download a bunch of MP3s into your Documents folder, you could quickly make a new folder in your home folder by typing the command `mkdir ~/mp3` and pressing Return. Then, one more typed command, `mv ~/Documents/*.mp3 ~/mp3`, would move all those MP3 files to the new folder. Once you get used to the command line (assuming you *do* get used to the command line), you may never want to go back.

There are some rough edges in Mac OS X. If you have a permissions problem, or if Apple hasn't yet provided a graphical tool to manage something you need to do, you may appreciate the ability to log into Darwin, use the `sudo` (superuser do) command to gain root access, and fix the problem directly. Apple has done a great job of insulating the Aqua experience from the underlying nuts and bolts, but the command line still offers some capabilities that aren't yet mature on the graphical side.

Using Terminal

To access Darwin on a Mac OS X system, first log into Mac OS X, just as you would to use Mac OS X normally. Then go to the Utilities folder inside the main Applications folder, find the Terminal icon, and double-click it to launch Terminal.

When you open Terminal, you'll see a simple window containing a *prompt* and a cursor. The standard prompt shows your Mac's name, the directory you're in (analogous to the front window in the Finder), and your username. As you type commands, they'll appear after the prompt, and, once you press Return, the system's responses will follow your commands. When execution is complete, the system will show another prompt so that you'll know you can type another command. Figure 22.1 shows what a Terminal window looks like.

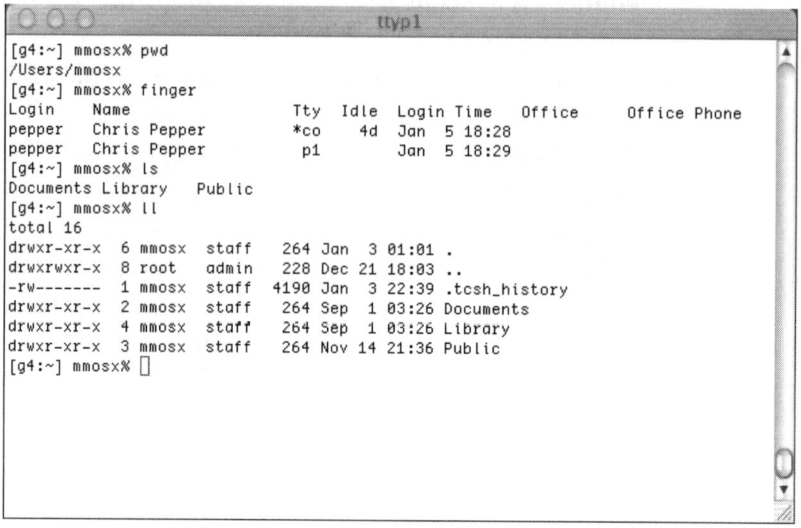

FIGURE 22.1

A Terminal window showing some simple commands and their output. Note the prompt [g4:~] mmosx% followed by typed commands.

```
                                        ttyp1
[g4:~] mmosx% pwd
/Users/mmosx
[g4:~] mmosx% finger
Login     Name                    Tty  Idle  Login Time    Office      Office Phone
pepper    Chris Pepper            *co   4d   Jan  5 18:28
pepper    Chris Pepper            p1         Jan  5 18:29
[g4:~] mmosx% ls
Documents Library    Public
[g4:~] mmosx% ll
total 16
drwxr-xr-x   6 mmosx    staff     264 Jan  3 01:01 .
drwxrwxr-x   8 root     admin     228 Dec 21 18:03 ..
-rw-------   1 mmosx    staff    4190 Jan  3 22:39 .tcsh_history
drwxr-xr-x   2 mmosx    staff     264 Sep  1 03:26 Documents
drwxr-xr-x   4 mmosx    staff     264 Sep  1 03:26 Library
drwxr-xr-x   3 mmosx    staff     264 Nov 14 21:36 Public
[g4:~] mmosx% []
```

Quitting Terminal

To leave Terminal, type **exit** and press Return to log out of the Terminal session, then close the window (if Terminal doesn't automatically close it for you when the session is ended). If you're using other programs with their own command-line interfaces, such as telnet, ssh, and ftp, you may have to exit multiple times to get all the way out. You can also use the Window ➤ Close Window command or the Terminal ➤ Quit Terminal command, or their standard keyboard shortcuts (⌘+W and ⌘+Q), but you should be careful not to break a connection without logging out first. By doing so, you could leave a login session open, which another user might be able to hijack. This is unlikely, but it's still good practice to log out before closing shell windows.

Useful Terminal Tricks

You can resize Terminal windows just like other Mac windows. When resizing, you'll see that the title bar shows two numbers separated by an X; these are the width and height of the window, in characters. It's often convenient to make Terminal windows wider for certain commands so that you can see more text without wrapping, or taller, to see more text without scrolling.

Terminal supports the standard Edit ➤ Copy and Edit ➤ Paste commands to move text into and out of the Mac Clipboard. You can drag an item from a Finder window into Terminal—the path to the dragged item is appended to whatever you've typed at the command line—but you can't drag text out of Terminal windows.

Terminal's Edit ➤ Find command searches the window buffer (the area you can scroll back through to see a history of your actions) for any text you specify. When you close the window, though, this buffer is lost unless you save it first. The Shell ➤ Save as Text and Shell ➤ Save Selection as Text commands also allow you to save the whole session or selection as a text file. This is useful for keeping track of what you've done or for recording interesting program output. The Shell ➤ Save command can be used to store the positions and settings of one or more open windows. By checking the Open This File When Terminal Starts Up check box, you can save your preferred layout for future use.

 NOTE Wondering about the word *shell?* At the Darwin command line, you have the option of using different *shell interpreters*, all of which offer slightly different features and commands. A shell is responsible for displaying the command-line prompt, accepting your input, and returning results. As you'll see later in this chapter, you can change your shell and even program it to perform commands automatically.

Keyboard shortcuts for scrolling are plentiful: Press ⌘+up arrow and ⌘+down arrow to move by line, press Page Up or Page Down to move by screen, and press Home or End to go to the top or bottom of the scroll buffer.

Terminal can use any installed font, but monospaced fonts, such as Monaco and Courier, generally work best. (To change fonts, select Terminal ➤ Preferences and click the General button.)

Terminal is a minimalist program; its purpose is to be a window or portal of sorts that enables you to see and interact with Darwin, not to be interesting itself. Terminal's features are focused on connecting the shell and the rest of your system, and on being unobtrusive.

Terminal will happily open multiple windows for you; this is often useful for reading directory listings or documentation with the man command (Unix's basic help tool) in one window, while acting on this information in another. It's also often convenient to dedicate one window to the local shell and to use other windows for commands that work on other machines, such as telnet, ssh, and ftp, or on other users, perhaps using sudo.

To switch between windows, press ⌘+*number,* where *number* is the number of the window (normally visible in its title bar), or press ⌘+left arrow and ⌘+right arrow to cycle through open windows in numerical order.

Using Darwin: A Quick Tour

If you aren't familiar with shells, try following these steps to get a feel for some basic commands and how Darwin works. More explanation of these commands appears in the sections that follow this one. For now, though, you can perform this quick run-through.

First, open Terminal, and then type these commands:

ls   Shows (lists) the contents of a directory. If you've just started a Terminal session, you'll see the contents of your home directory.

ll   Shows more information about the items in the current directory, along with some additional items that don't show up when you use the normal `ls` command.

pwd   Shows you where you are currently in the hierarchy of directories. (For now, this is probably your home directory.)

cd Documents   Moves you into your Documents directory.

ll   Now this command lists the contents of your Documents directory. (There may not be anything here yet, particularly if you've just installed Mac OS X.)

cd ../..   Moves you up two levels—first, to the parent of the current direc-tory (your home directory is the parent of your Documents directory), then to its parent (the Users directory is the parent of your home directory).

pwd   Shows you where you are, which is now the Users directory.

ls   Shows all user home directories (except root's, which is located in a differ-ent part of the file system at `/private/var/root`).

That's all it takes to move through your folder hierarchy using typed commands. Next, we'll move on to explain some of those commands and see what else can be accomplished.

 NOTE   It's conventional in Unix-based environments to use the term *directories* to refer to what the Mac OS calls "folders." We'll use that convention here, because many com-mands (such as `pwd` and `cd`) have "directory" as part of their name or definition. Just remember that the terms *directory* and *folder* refer to the same thing.

Using Commands in Darwin

To use Darwin, you'll probably want to memorize a few commands. (You could con-ceivably post the commands on a sticky note next to your monitor, but you'll find that they become natural the more you use the command line.) Basic commands include pwd (print working directory) to tell you where you are, finger to see who's currently using the machine (logged in), cd (change directory) to move around, ls to list the files in a directory, and exit to log out (finish using Terminal and disconnect). Darwin includes hundreds of commands, including telnet and ftp, as described in Chapter 23. Because Darwin uses standard Unix-based commands, a large number of reference books for these commands are available (for instance, Wrightson and Merlino's *Mastering™ Unix,* Danesh's *Mastering™ Linux,* and Pfaffenberger's *Linux Command Instant Reference,* which are published by Sybex).

As a general rule, whenever you type something at a shell prompt, the first word you type on the line is a command, and the rest of the line consists of arguments and options. Most commands, including telnet and ftp, are actually names of programs. When you type such a command, Darwin finds the program you've named and starts it—like double-clicking a program in the Finder.

To give these programs additional information, you can add *arguments* after the command's name. Any arguments you type are passed on to the program, which then tries to figure out exactly what you wanted from the arguments. For example, if you type ls /, the ls program displays the contents of /, which is the system's root directory. Programs also take options, which modify the processing of arguments and normally start with a hyphen (-). For instance, ls -l / shows a longer listing because of the -l option. To find a program from its name, use the which command, which accepts a command name as its argument and responds by showing you its location, called a *path.* For more on paths, see the later section "Darwin File System Differences."

As mentioned earlier, the program that accepts your typing and invokes other commands is called the shell. It's similar to the Finder in Mac OS X, in that its main purpose is to control other programs. And, like the Finder, shells have commands built into them for managing files and folders. Many of the simplest and most-used commands, such as cd and alias, are *builtins.* To see a list of builtins, use the builtins command. Figure 22.2 shows the response to the builtins command from Darwin's default shell, which is named tcsh. (Note the two which commands, which identify cd as a builtin and ftp as an independent program.)

WARNING Some builtins are different from shell to shell. In particular, the csh-style and sh-style shells use different loop keywords and syntax to set variables. (For instance, bash, an sh-style shell, is common in Linux releases. Although tcsh is the default in Darwin, several other shells are also available.) The builtins command itself is available only in csh-descended shells. More information is available in the later sections "Terminal Preferences" and "Shell Scripting and Behavior."

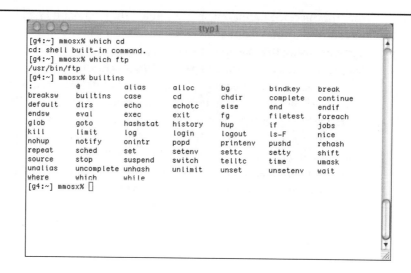

```
                                     ttyp1
[g4:~] mmosx% which cd
cd: shell built-in command.
[g4:~] mmosx% which ftp
/usr/bin/ftp
[g4:~] mmosx% builtins
:            @           alias       alloc       bg          bindkey      break
breaksw      builtins    case        cd          chdir       complete     continue
default      dirs        echo        echotc      else        end          endif
endsw        eval        exec        exit        fg          filetest     foreach
glob         goto        hashstat    history     hup         if           jobs
kill         limit       log         login       logout      ls-F         nice
nohup        notify      onintr      popd        printenv    pushd        rehash
repeat       sched       set         setenv      settc       setty        shift
source       stop        suspend     switch      telltc      time         umask
unalias      uncomplete  unhash      unlimit     unset       unsetenv     wait
where        which       while
[g4:~] mmosx% ▯
```

Some Basic Commands

Along with programs like telnet and ftp, Darwin includes commands to help you
navigate around your Mac (and, in some cases, other computers on a network). In fact,
these commands all together constitute something comparable to the Mac Finder—
they're how you move to different folders, and copy, delete, and remove files and
directories. Here are a few basic commands:

pwd   Print working directory. pwd shows you where you are, and is most useful
in conjunction with cd.

cd   Change directory. cd moves to the specified directory (see the later section
"Darwin File System Differences"). With no arguments, cd moves to your personal home directory. An example with arguments is cd /Applications, which
would move you to the main Applications directory on your startup disk.

ls   List files and directories. This command offers extensive options, which you
can see by reading its manual page (type **man ls** and press Return). Apple makes
the most popular sets of options for ls available with the aliases l and ll.

cat   Display one or more files. cat is a simple command; it spits out the whole
file on-screen, and if you provide multiple files, it displays them all consecu-
tively. Example: cat file.txt.

more   Display a file on-screen, pausing after each screen of text. Press the
spacebar to page through the file, and press Q to stop. Additionally, if you type
a slash (/) followed by some text, and then press Return, more will search for

the text you've typed. The more command is much more convenient than cat for reading long files. Example: more README.

man   View online documentation (the manual) on a command. man requires an argument—the command to read about. man is based on more (or sometimes its more powerful cousin, less), and it includes more's commands for paging through the file. Examples: man ftp and man man, which shows information about the man command itself.

cp   Copy files. To copy directories and all files inside them, use cp -R (recursive). If the last argument is a directory, copies of the files specified by the other arguments are created in that directory. If not, the first argument is copied to the path specified by the second argument. Examples: cp *.txt ~/Documents/ and cp readme.txt info.txt.

TIP   The example above uses the asterisk (*) as a *wildcard*, which means simply that the shell fills in any results that match the rest of the filename as entered. For *.txt, all files that end in .txt, such as readme.txt, notes.txt, and memo.txt, would be selected. Similarly, * would select all the files in the current directory. Wildcards can be used with many commands, such as ls *.txt or l mem* (which would return memo.txt, memory, and so on).

mv   Move and/or rename files and directories (uses source and destination arguments, like cp). Darwin's mv is a bit odd; if you have trouble moving directories, remove any trailing slashes from the path arguments and try again. Example: mv storytext.rtf ~/web.

WARNING   If the second argument for mv (or cp, for that matter) isn't a valid folder (for example, mv memo.rtf memos, where memos is not a valid folder name), the file will be "moved" into a *file* named by that second argument. If a file with that name already exists (in the example, if there is already a file called memos), it will normally be replaced with the file you're moving (in the example, memo.rtf) without warning.

rm   Remove files and directories (be careful with this one!). Examples: rm memo.rtf and rm *.rtf.

mkdir   Make a directory. Examples: mkdir Movies and mkdir ~/Documents/Movies/.

PART

V

Advanced
Mac OS X Topics

rmdir   Remove a directory. (The rmdir command works only on empty directories, but rm -R directory removes a directory and all its contents. Again, be careful!) Example: rmdir ~/Documents/Movies/.

exit   Logout. (Many programs use exit, and some use quit.)

Try using these commands to explore your system a bit. Once you're familiar with them, we'll examine some more.

More Commands

After you've familiarized yourself with the basic commands above, try these. A bit more involved, the following commands allow you to customize your environment, selectively extract information from files, find files, examine volumes, and do a bit of account management.

alias   Allows you to create your own commands. With no arguments, alias shows you aliases that have already been defined; with one argument, alias shows what the specified alias is defined to do; and with two arguments, alias defines the first argument as a private command to execute the full command line specified by the second argument. Figure 22.3 shows the creation of an alias, the use of that alias, and then a listing of aliases.

 WARNING   The alias command works slightly differently under shells descended from sh, such as bash.

FIGURE 22.3

Defining an alias, using that alias, and listing all defined aliases

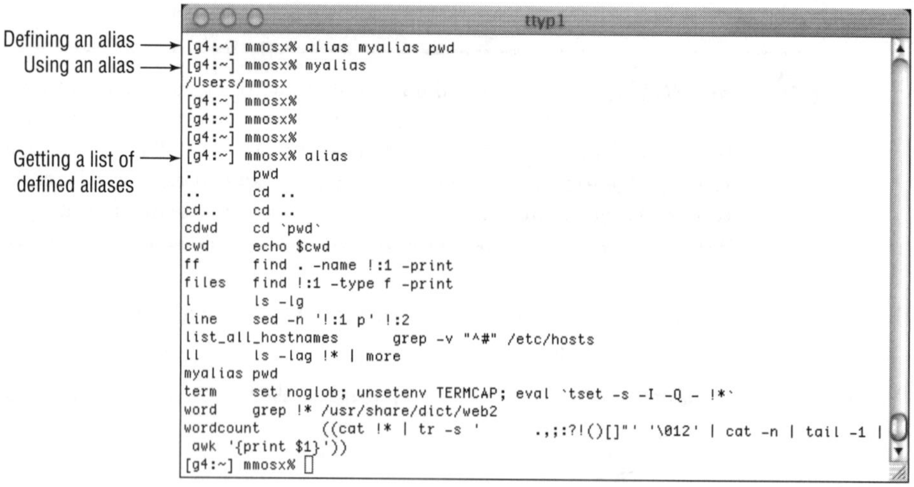

Defining an alias ⟶
Using an alias ⟶

Getting a list of ⟶
defined aliases

```
                                           ttyp1
[g4:~] mmosx% alias myalias pwd
[g4:~] mmosx% myalias
/Users/mmosx
[g4:~] mmosx%
[g4:~] mmosx%
[g4:~] mmosx%
[g4:~] mmosx% alias
.           pwd
..          cd ..
cd..        cd ..
cdwd        cd `pwd`
cwd         echo $cwd
ff          find . -name !:1 -print
files       find !:1 -type f -print
l           ls -lg
line        sed -n '!:1 p' !:2
list_all_hostnames    grep -v "^#" /etc/hosts
ll          ls -lag !* | more
myalias pwd
term        set noglob; unsetenv TERMCAP; eval `tset -s -I -Q - !*`
word        grep !* /usr/share/dict/web2
wordcount   ((cat !* | tr -s '    .,;:?!()[]"' '\012' | cat -n | tail -1 |
 awk '{print $1}'))
[g4:~] mmosx% []
```

head   Display the first few lines of a file. The syntax is head *-10 myfile*, and the number (after the hyphen) specifies how many lines to display.

tail   Display the last few lines of a file. Its syntax is very similar to that of head. The tail command is particularly useful for displaying recent events in log files, many of which reside in the directory /var/log.

grep   A powerful and flexible search command. In the simplest case, grep searches a single file for a specified string. It can also search multiple files, search for lines that don't match the search string, search with or without case sensitivity, and do wildcard searches. grep's syntax is complicated, but is explained by man grep; it may be familiar to you if you've used other programs that support grep syntax, such as the popular Macintosh text editor BBEdit.

locate   A simple tool for finding files. Unix has a powerful and confusing find command to search for specified files, but Darwin also includes the simpler locate command, which uses a pregenerated search database and works much more quickly. Just provide part or all of a file path as an argument, and locate will list all files on the system that match. Be careful with locate, though; it can return a lot of matches, especially if your search string matches a directory containing many files. The command locate mystring | more will pass the output from locate to more, letting you page through the results and quit when you're done. Pipes (|) are discussed in the later section "Shell Scripting and Behavior."

WARNING   The locate command uses a database that's automatically updated every week. This means that it won't find files added since the last update, and if you don't leave Mac OS X running overnight, the database won't get updated. For more on scheduled tasks, use man cron crontab and try more /etc/crontab /etc/weekly.

df -k   Show all mounted disks and how much space they have free in kilobytes. Without "-k," df will show you how many 512-byte blocks each disk has free.

du   Show disk usage for the specified item(s) and each item inside any directories. You'll generally want to use du -ks *directoryname* for total usage for the directory in kilobytes.

passwd   Change the password for the account that's currently logged in.

sudo   Execute a command as another user. Using sudo, you can execute commands as though you had logged in as someone else (normally root). When you use sudo, you'll be asked for your own password, and sudo will then run the rest of the command as root. See the later section "Unix Philosophy" for more on when to use root access. In the default configuration of Mac OS X, only administrators can use sudo.

Advanced Commands

The following commands are a bit more involved and powerful. (In fact, they're all applications instead of shell builtins.) They allow you to manage files and archives and to connect to other machines. You may be familiar with these capabilities from Macintosh programs with similar capabilities.

telnet   Log into another computer. The telnet command is normally used with a single argument—the host name of the computer to connect to. See Chapter 23 for more on this command.

ftp   Connect to another computer to transfer files. Like telnet, ftp typically takes a host name as an argument. See Chapter 23 for more on ftp.

ssh   Establish an encrypted connection to another computer. The ssh command is basically a secure version of telnet, but it can also be used to provide encryption capabilities to other programs. You should use ssh instead of telnet whenever possible, and scp or sftp instead of ftp. These two commands are part of the ssh package, replacing rcp and ftp, respectively, with secure commands that take advantage of ssh encryption. The ssh tools are also discussed in Chapter 23.

pico   Edit the specified file. The pico command is a simple Unix text editor, with all the basic features. It's roughly comparable to TextEdit in that it's fine for simple writing or editing tasks, but is much less powerful than other programs like BBEdit and the notoriously complicated emacs editing environment. One of the good things about pico is that it always shows basic Control+*key* shortcuts at the bottom of the screen, which makes it much easier to use than emacs or vi.

tar   Tape archive command. A complex but powerful tool for combining multiple files into a single archive (like StuffIt, but without compression). To "untar" an archive, first copy it into its own subdirectory, then "cd" into that subdirectory and use tar -xf *archive.tar* to unpack the contents into the subdirectory (where *archive.tar* represents the name of the archive to unpack).

gzip   GNU compression program. The gzip command compresses individual files (but be forewarned that it removes the original). Darwin's tar command includes a very useful -z option to compress or uncompress archives with gzip.

Compressed TAR files are also called "tarballs," and they usually have either .tgz or .tar.gz as a suffix. To uncompress a tarball, use the command tar -xzf *archive.tgz*. The tar and gzip commands are important for two main reasons. First, they are standards for compressing and uncompressing Unix freeware and shareware software that you'll find on the Internet. Second, as command-line utilities, they can be controlled remotely; so you can log into another computer, "tar up" a directory you want, and "ftp" the tarball to your own Mac—or "untar" a tarball on a remote system. This is important when you work with more than one machine. The command to uncompress a gzipped file is gunzip.

 TIP The combination of tar and gzip can be very convenient for creating archives of important files quickly. For instance, you could type tar -czf backup.tgz ~/Documents to create a compressed archive of your Documents folder. You could then copy that archive to a remote server or external disk as a backup.

Unix Philosophy

Unix has been around much longer than the Mac OS, and, like the Mac, it has a rich history and some basic philosophy that's common among its users. Here are some of the highlights, to help you understand the concepts and attitudes behind Darwin:

Programming is good for you.   Unix was originally a research project and software development environment. The creators were all programmers, who believed programming was good mental exercise. This is part of the reason so many good compilers and software development tools exist for Unix, and why the shell is fundamentally a programming environment, unlike the Finder or Windows Explorer.

The shell is an interpreter.   Each shell can run interactively to process commands one at a time, or as an interpreter to process files of commands, called scripts. This makes programming the same as daily use, which encourages people to program.

The shell is a launcher.   The shell has lots of built-in commands, but it's fundamentally an interface that enables you to run other programs. Builtins have been added where appropriate to facilitate use of these external programs and to manage shell features (such as command-line editing and the command history).

Wasted time is bad. The original Unix machines were much slower than current systems, and, as you may have noticed, command-line computing requires a lot of typing. As a result, and with the realization that Unix users use the same commands over and over, the developers abbreviated many command, file, and directory names. Thus "list" became 1s, "user" became usr, and "temporary space" became tmp. Although it's a bit harder to learn the abbreviations, with serious use, the time saved becomes significant.

Don't assume high-end hardware. Many Unix systems were used primarily through paper-based terminals—there were no graphics, and not even backspacing! As a result, the most basic tools are line-based. vi (the "visual interactive editor") and sed (the "stream editor," a find-and-replace tool) are derived from ed, a line-based editor; ed required the user to specify one line to be edited at a time. While Unix systems now assume that terminals have cursor control, and line printer support isn't a major issue, Unix has retained support for very basic interfaces. This provides great power without requiring much bandwidth or a complicated interface.

Root is unrestricted and dangerous. Unix administrators have both a personal account and a separate root account. Personal accounts are for general day-to-day use, and the root account is used for system management. Root has few or no restrictions on its capabilities, which means that it's easy to destroy a system as root, and root access must be protected from malicious users.

Simple tools can be connected for complex tasks. The pipe (|) allows chaining several simpler programs to perform complex actions. The simple tools are easier to use and maintain than custom programs written for each task, and shell scripting gives them great power and flexibility.

Don't second-guess the user. The Mac OS includes lots of warnings— before erasing a disk, after a crash, before overwriting files, before emptying the Trash, and so on. Unix systems have fewer warnings. As a result, it's easier to destroy files irrevocably or (as root) to damage your system. Be careful not to misspell filenames, and avoid mistyping any commands that remove or move files, as it's easy to "rm" a file you need or to "cp" one file over another one you want, inadvertently replacing the second file.

Computers are good; networks are great. One of the reasons the Internet is largely based on Unix programs and technologies is that Unix has long been network-friendly, and Unix users have understood that networked computers are much more useful than isolated ones. Mac OS X's fundamental orientation toward TCP/IP, options like File Sharing (now based on Apache), and the inclusion of Software Update show progress in this direction, but Unix systems have historically made much heavier use of networks.

Everything is a file. Files are used to represent disks, directories, data streams, and even running programs under Unix. This improves consistency and flexibility, since the same commands apply to "regular" files, directories, devices, input and output, and other file-system objects.

Useful Shell Tricks: *tcsh*

The oldest Unix shell in active use is sh. There are several later shells, such as bash, that attempt to be backward compatible, meaning that anything that works in sh should work in its descendants. The other major family of shells is derived from csh (the "C shell"), and its descendants, including tcsh, are generally backward compatible with the original csh syntax.

 NOTE Linux systems use the bash shell, which has a different syntax from tcsh. If you use Linux frequently, you can switch to tcsh on Linux or install bash on Darwin. See the later section "Installing Darwin Programs" for more on getting bash for Darwin.

Darwin uses tcsh as its default shell. Major enhancements in tcsh since csh include the following:

- Command history, allowing you to repeat previous commands without retyping them.
- Command-line editing, allowing you to fix typos and edit commands.
- Spelling correction: If you type a command that tcsh can't recognize and process, it will make an (often correct) guess as to what you really wanted to type, and offer to do that instead.
- Filename completion, which lets you press the Tab key to have the system finish commands and arguments, or list available choices.
- More flexible prompts (so that you can see the directory you're in and machine you're on).

Because the shells and the command line are the primary interface to Unix-based systems, a lot of work has gone into making shells like tcsh powerful, fast, and convenient.

You can see the complete reference for the tcsh shell by typing the command man tcsh at a command prompt and pressing Return. Some highlights follow.

- *Command-line editing* allows you to make changes, such as fixing typos and changing arguments, using the arrow keys and Delete key on your keyboard. There are also several keyboard shortcuts to facilitate editing: Control+A moves the cursor to the beginning of the line, Control+E moves it to the end, and Control+U clears everything back to the beginning of the line. These conventions are available in many different programs.

- The *command history* stores the last 150 commands. You can use the up arrow to view previous commands, and the down arrow to move forward (back toward more recent commands). Once you find the desired command, you can press Return to execute it again, as though you'd typed it from the keyboard, or you can edit the command to do something slightly different. To see saved commands, use the history built-in command. This lists all saved commands, along with the times they were executed and an identifying number for each line. You can use these command numbers, rather than press the up arrow dozens of times, to invoke saved commands. For example, an exclamation point followed by the number 50 (!50) would repeat command number 50 from the history. An exclamation point followed by letters repeats the most recent command that started with those letters—for example, !ft would repeat the last ftp command. Figure 22.4 shows part of a history listing, with command numbers and times.

FIGURE 22.4

The end of a history listing

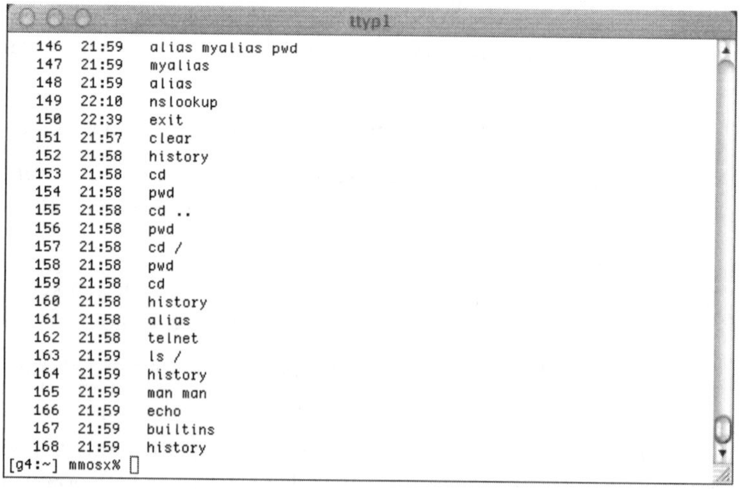

```
     146   21:59   alias myalias pwd
     147   21:59   myalias
     148   21:59   alias
     149   22:10   nslookup
     150   22:39   exit
     151   21:57   clear
     152   21:58   history
     153   21:58   cd
     154   21:58   pwd
     155   21:58   cd ..
     156   21:58   pwd
     157   21:58   cd /
     158   21:58   pwd
     159   21:58   cd
     160   21:58   history
     161   21:58   alias
     162   21:58   telnet
     163   21:59   ls /
     164   21:59   history
     165   21:59   man man
     166   21:59   echo
     167   21:59   builtins
     168   21:59   history
[g4:~] mmosx%
```

- *Spelling correction:* If you type a command that `tcsh` can't find (see "File Paths" in the "Darwin File System Differences" section), `tcsh` will try to find a similarly spelled command that you might have misspelled and offer to execute that one for you instead. If you type y in response to the prompt, the corrected command will be used; if you type n, `tcsh` will try (and fail) to execute the command exactly as you typed it. As an example of spelling correction, if you typed `telnt`, which isn't a valid command, `tcsh` would suggest `telnet`, which *is* valid.

```
[g4:~] mmosx% telnt lynx.org

OK? telnet lynx.org? yes
Trying 209.167.201.2...
Connected to lynx.org.
Escape character is '^]'.
```

- In addition to spelling correction, `tcsh` offers *filename completion*. This is a tremendous timesaver. When you type the beginning of a word and press the Tab key, `tcsh` will look for complete words you might have started. If it finds a single match, it fills in the rest; if it finds multiple matches, it fills in the rest until they diverge; and if it doesn't know which match is desired, `tcsh` lists the possible matches. Automatic completion works with commands (first word on the line), files and directories (one directory level at a time), and variables. For more detail on how filename completion works, use `man tcsh` and see the "Completion and listing" section of the man page.

- The `tcsh` shell uses several special characters in addition to the space. Sometimes it's necessary to use one of these characters as itself instead of for its special function; this is called "escaping" or "protecting" characters. To tell `tcsh` to ignore the special meaning of such a character, precede it with a backslash (\). In some cases double straight quotes (") and single straight quotes (') work as well, but a backslash is the most reliable.

Terminal Preferences

The Terminal ➢ Preferences menu command provides a great deal of flexibility. Apple provides good defaults for these options, but several may be worth adjusting.

Click the General button in the Terminal Preferences dialog box, and you'll see the Set Font button, which you can click to change the font used in Terminal windows. The default is Monaco 10, which fits four windows on a 1024×768 display with minimal overlap. If you spend a lot of time in Terminal, you will probably find such a layout very useful; additional windows might be logged into another computer, or displaying

PART

V

**Advanced
Mac OS X Topics**

documentation, or logged into another account. If you find a layout you really like, save it with Shell ≻ Save and use the Open This File When Terminal Starts Up check box to make it your default configuration. If you do this, be sure to change the Save pop-up dialog from Main Window to All Windows.

The Window Size boxes enable you to set the size of new windows by entering their width in characters (Columns) and height in characters (Rows). 80×24 is the standard width and height for a Terminal window. Since it's easy to resize windows after opening them, you probably won't need to change these settings.

Figure 22.5 shows the layout of Terminal's Preferences. Note the buttons along the top, which you can click to change to a different panel of options. When you've finished making changes, click the OK button.

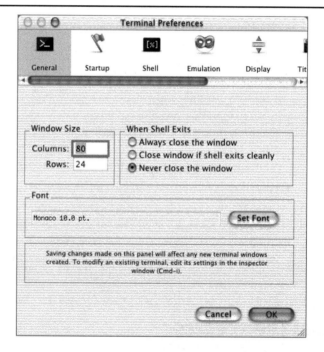

If you want to use a shell other than tcsh, you can click the Shell button in the Terminal Preferences dialog box and then type the path to another shell. Why do this? Most likely, you'll feel the urge if you're familiar with bash from Linux and you're getting confused or annoyed by the differences in tcsh. Be careful when changing this setting, though; if you put the wrong path here, Terminal can become unusable until it's fixed.

NOTE The bash shell for Darwin is available at `http://osx.macnn.com/features/installbash.phtml`.

Darwin File System Differences

Darwin is basically a current Unix-like system, with lots of enhancements to make it suitable as the foundation for an advanced Mac OS. Because of its Unix heritage, Darwin has several differences from earlier versions of the Mac OS that should be explained.

As noted earlier, one basic but minor difference is in terminology: What Mac OS calls "folders," Unix calls "directories." They're the same thing, but the terminology is different. In this book, the two terms are interchangeable.

File Paths

The Mac file systems, HFS and HFS+, allow any characters except colons in filenames. Colons (:) are not allowed because they're *delimiters*—they separate directories in paths. If you type a colon when naming a file or folder in Mac OS 9's Finder, the Finder inserts a dash instead. The HFS path `Macintosh HD:System Folder:Preferences:Interarchy:` refers to a folder named Interarchy inside a folder named Preferences, inside System Folder, on the disk Macintosh HD.

In Unix file systems, the slash (/) is the delimiter, so the path above would appear as `/Macintosh HD/System Folder/Preferences/Interarchy/`. The slash at the beginning means that this is an *absolute* path—expressed in terms of the root (top level) of the file system. Paths that *don't* start with a slash are *relative*—expressed in terms of the current working directory (this directory is what the `cd` command controls). When you log in, the current working directory is set to your home directory—normally something like `/Users/pepper/` or `/Users/amy/`. This means that if you type `ls Documents` when logged in as user pepper, you get back a listing of `/Users/pepper/Documents`. In contrast, `ls /Documents` would attempt to list a directory named Documents in the root directory on your disk.

Unix has several other useful filename conventions you should know about. Since spaces normally separate arguments, but filenames can contain spaces, we need a way to "protect" spaces. Without such protection, `ls System Folder` would try to list two items—System and Folder.

There are two ways to protect or escape actual spaces in pathnames and elsewhere on command lines. One way is to put a backslash before the space, and the other is to put quotes around the whole path. Thus, both `ls System\ Folder` and `ls "System Folder"` list a single folder named System Folder in the current directory.

Fortunately, `tcsh` can handle spaces in filenames, so if you type part of a filename that contains spaces, and then use filename completion with the Tab key, `tsch` escapes the spaces for you (see the earlier section "Useful Shell Tricks: `tcsh`" for more on filename completion).

The dot-slash combination (`./`) refers to the current directory; this is useful for being clear about where a file is and for running programs not in your path (see the next section). The dot-dot-slash combination (`../`) refers to the parent of the current directory; it's essential for navigating around software packages that use multiple directories (see the later section "Aliases vs. Links" for more on `./` and `../`).

The tilde (`~`) is used to refer to user home directories, so `~amy/Documents` represents the Documents folder inside user amy's home directory, wherever that may be on the system. It's more common to use paths like `~/Documents`, which means *my* Documents folder (equivalent to `/Users/amy/Documents/` if you're logged in as user amy).

Shells also do wildcard expansion, which can save a lot of typing. If you put an asterisk (*) in a path, the shell replaces that path with all the filenames that match the specified pattern. This is very convenient for interactive use but critical for shell scripting, because it enables scripts to selectively and intelligently specify files to process at runtime, even if those files don't exist when the script is written. The other wildcard is the question mark (?), which matches against any single character, but not more than one or no characters.

 TIP If you have a file that's visible in a Finder window and you want its path, you can drag it to the Terminal, and the file's path will be inserted at the cursor.

The *PATH* Variable

Mac OS 9.*x* maintains an invisible desktop database of all available application programs and what types of files they can handle, so when you double-click a Word document, it automatically opens in Word. Unix systems, including the Darwin layer of Mac OS X, use an older mechanism called the *PATH variable* (Carbon/Cocoa programs in Mac OS X use another new mechanism for tracking applications and what documents they handle).

In Mac OS X, the `ls` program is installed as `/bin/ls`, the `more` program is `/usr/bin/more`, etc. Obviously, typing full paths for every command would be inconvenient, so each shell maintains a PATH variable containing places to look for programs.

For a user named amy, the predefined PATH variable might be the following list of directories separated by colons:

```
/Users/amy/bin/powerpc-apple-macos:\
/Users/amy/bin:\
/usr/local/bin:/usr/bin:/bin:\
/usr/local/sbin:/usr/sbin:/sbin
```

If a string is too long to fit on a single line, carriage returns can be escaped by a backslash as the *very last* character on the line, which negates the carriage return. That's why you see a backslash as the last character on each for the first three lines. If you use echo PATH, the PATH variable will be a single long "word," but it might appear this way (with the backslash) in a shell script for readability.

TIP By default, there is no *bin* (short for "binary" and meant to suggest applications) directory in your home directory. So, if you want to install personal command-line applications that can be run from any directory (using the PATH variable), you'll need to create the bin directory (mkdir ~/bin) and install your Darwin applications there. You'll also need to make sure ~bin appears somewhere in the PATH variable stored for your account. Shared programs will have to go in a system-wide directory that appears in each user's PATH variable—not inside a user's home directory. (See "Installing Darwin Programs" later in this chapter.)

When you type ls and press Return, tcsh goes through these directories, in order, looking for a program named ls, and then executes it. If you look at the PATH variable above, you'll note that personal directories (inside /Users/amy/) are present at the beginning of the list. This hierarchy makes it possible for you to use your own versions of programs instead of the standard ones, because /Users/amy/bin/ls would be found before /bin/ls.

NOTE Actually, it's a bit more complicated. The csh and tcsh shells scan the directories in your PATH variable ahead of time, so they don't have to scan each time you type a command. Because of this, if you add a new program and want it to be immediately accessible, you must use the rehash command to make your shell "notice" the new program.

To view your own PATH variable, type **echo $PATH** at the shell prompt and press Return. If you want to execute a command not in your path (if you're testing it, for example), use its full path. First, make sure you have execute ("x") permission on the program file. If you'd like to add a new directory to your PATH variable, type **setenv PATH=$PATH:newdir** and press Return, where *newdir* is the full path to the new directory.

 NOTE Unix systems don't deal with file types and creators (or even suffixes) at the most basic level; that's left to users and graphical add-on layers, like Mac OS X and file manager applications. Although you can name programs and documents anything you like, file suffixes are useful for exchanging files with others and quickly identifying your own files—so you may find yourself using .mp3, .txt, and .sh (for sh shell scripts) even though Darwin itself doesn't care what you call your files.

Permissions and Ownership

Another difference between Mac OS and Unix systems is in permissions. In Mac OS 9.*x*, folders have permissions only if File Sharing is turned on, and then only for remote users. In Unix (along with Mac OS X and Darwin), every file and directory always has permissions. To see permissions, use ls -l or just ll, which generates a long listing. Figure 22.6 shows such a listing.

FIGURE 22.6

Long listing of a sample /Users/ Shared directory showing permissions and ownership

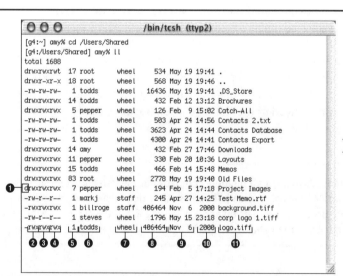

1. Type
2. Owner permissions
3. Group permissions
4. Other permissions
5. Links count
6. Owner
7. Group
8. Size
9. Month and day
10. Time or year
11. Filename

NOTE As with folders and directories, the Mac OS and Unix-like systems differ in how they refer to privileges (Mac OS) and permissions (Unix). They are essentially the same, with the exception that Unix offers an "execute" permission, which Mac OS X (in the Show Info window of the Finder) ignores.

In long listings the first character represents the type of the item: a hyphen (-) for regular files, d for directories, and l for symbolic links (see the later section "Aliases vs. Links"). The next three characters are the owner's permissions. If an r, the owner can read the file; if a w, the owner can write the file; and if an x, the owner can execute the file. If one of these permission characters is a hyphen (-), it means that that category of user doesn't have that particular permission. There are additional permissions and letters listed under man chmod.

The second group of three characters represents the same three permissions for members of the file's group, and the last group of three characters shows permissions for everybody else.

The second column, after the 10-character permission column, is the link count—normally 1 for files and 2 or more for directories (see the later sections "Aliases vs. Links" and "Invisible Items" for more on link counts). The third column identifies the owner of the file, and the fourth column is the file's group. The fifth column is the file's size in bytes; for directories, this doesn't include files inside the directory.

After that come two columns for the month and day the file was last modified, and the next column shows either the modification time (if within the past year) or the modification year (if older). The last column is the file's actual name.

 WARNING When you install Mac OS X, the installation process automatically sets up appropriate permissions for the Mac OS X partition. It does *not* set permissions for other volumes (partitions and disks). As a result, any other users to whom you give access to your system are likely to have much more access than they should to any other volumes on your Mac. Be very careful when creating other user accounts on your system; you should definitely review ownership and permissions on all your partitions with ls -l /Volumes before creating accounts.

The system considers *any* file for which you have execute permission a valid command, so be careful not to make files executable if they aren't actually programs. If you want to protect a file from being accidentally corrupted or deleted, you can turn off your own write permission. Assuming you have write permission to the file's parent directory, you can give yourself write permission again later if you need to change the file.

If your system has any other users, you should give some thought to who (if anyone) should have permissions to see or change your files and directories—primarily inside your home directory, but also in any other directories you control.

The ability to "ls" or "cd" into a directory is governed by the directory's x permission. The ability to create new files within a directory is controlled by the parent directory's w permission.

Besides ls -l, there are three main commands for managing file permissions: chmod, chown, and chgrp.

> **chmod** Change permissions on files and directories. This command has two main modes of use, numeric and symbolic, and it can be very complicated; but for starters you can use commands of the symbolic form chmod u+w filename. The first argument has three parts. The first part indicates whose permissions will change; the options are u, g, o, and a, representing user (owner), group, other, and all three, respectively. The second part is either + or -, for adding or removing the permission. The third part is r, w, or x, for read, write, or execute, respectively. The second argument is the file (or directory) to change; additional filenames may follow as additional arguments. For more possibilities, see the man page on chmod. (For instance, you'll see that you can use numbers to choose different levels of permissions, where chmod 755 ~/Sites would assign read, write, and execute permissions for the owner and read and write permissions for the group and everyone.)
>
> **chown** Change the ownership of a file or directory. The first argument is the new owner (or *owner:group,* to change both the owner and the group), followed by the file(s) to change. Example: chown amy /Library/WebServer/Documents/amy.

 NOTE In most cases you'll need to use the sudo command to actually change the owner of a file or directory, unless you're logged into the root account. Thus, the above example would actually read: sudo chown amy /Library/WebServer/Documents/amy. You'd then be prompted for an administrator's password in order to perform the change.

> **chgrp** Change the group associated with a file or directory, similarly to chown. Example: chgrp authors *.html.

All three of these commands support -R as an option (before the arguments). This option makes these commands recursive, meaning that if you use them on a directory, they will also process all of the directory's files and subdirectories, and all their files and subdirectories. Be careful when changing execution permissions recursively, as it's easy to accidentally scramble directory permissions this way.

Aliases vs. Links

Mac OS aliases are similar to Unix links, but there are subtle differences in how they work. A Mac *alias* is a special file that provides information referring to another file or folder. Unix systems use *hard links* and *symbolic links* (also called *symlinks*) instead of aliases. Darwin doesn't recognize or resolve aliases (they're visible but useless from the command line), but the Mac OS X Finder treats symbolic links as aliases and resolves them normally. Classic applications don't understand symbolic links, but if you double-click or drop them in a Finder window, the original file is opened just as with an alias.

One of the main differences between aliases and symbolic links is that aliases are based on file IDs; so if you move or rename the file that an alias points to, the alias still points to the file (as long as it remains on the same disk). Symbolic links, however, are based on file paths; so if you move the destination file, the link fails until you put it back or put a different file in the original location. Both methods have advantages; aliases are more robust, but can cause trouble when there's a newer version of a file but the alias to the old version still works.

Another issue concerns the handling of directories. If you double-click a directory alias in the Mac OS, the Finder jumps to the new location. If you move into a directory symlink, the system may show your path as inside the symlink or inside the linked-to directory. This can be confusing, so be careful.

Aliases and symlinks are similar ways of accomplishing the same thing. Hard links, though, are different. With hard links, a file system object can have multiple valid names or paths, all independent and equally "real"; by contrast, with symlinks or aliases, there's a single original, and one or more references to that original. With hard links, two or more paths point to the same file system object, whether a file or directory. Deleting a hard link just removes one of the valid paths to an object; when the last link is deleted, the item itself is removed. The link counts shown in the second column of ls -l listings increase as hard links are added, and decrease as they're removed.

 WARNING Shells use the alias command to define shell shortcut commands. Be careful to avoid confusion around the different meanings. The alias command is described in the earlier section "More Commands."

File Forks

Mac files can have three parts, called *forks:* data, resource, and info:

- *Data forks* contain fundamental information, such as text, Word documents, Photoshop images, and so on.

- *Resource forks,* if present, contain Mac-specific information: fonts, icons, system sounds, and such.

- *Info forks* contain type and creator codes and a bit of other administrative information.

As cross-platform programs and data exchange between Macs and other computers have become prevalent, emphasis has gradually shifted away from resource forks, because they're useless on other platforms. To simplify all this and make compatibility easier, Apple now encourages developers to store resource information in data forks. With a data-fork-only file, MacBinary, AppleDouble, and AppleSingle (all ways of maintaining a Mac file's resource fork when storing the file on a foreign file system) encodings are unnecessary.

The UFS file system, supported by Mac OS X, doesn't support forks directly; when you store a file with a resource fork on a UFS volume, Mac OS X actually creates two files. The data fork is stored under the specified filename, and the resource fork is stored in the same directory with a "._" prefix, which prevents the resource fork from showing up normally (see the later section "Invisible Items" for more on how this is handled).

Since HFS+ supports forks, Mac OS X stores both forks under the specified name on HFS+ volumes. On either UFS or HFS+, the Aqua side of Mac OS X handles all the fork "magic" invisibly. Unfortunately, the standard Unix commands under Darwin don't understand forks, so resource forks on HFS+ volumes aren't easily accessible from the Darwin command line or through Unix-based servers like Apache or ftpd.

 TIP If you need to work with resource forks from the command line, you can append /rsrc to a filename to refer to the resource fork–for example, ls -l MyProgram/rsrc. To copy Mac files with forks intact, use CpMac (/Developer/Tools/CpMac). Note that in order to work with CpMac, you must have the optional developer tools installed using the Developer Tools CD that ships with Mac OS X.

Case Sensitivity

HFS and HFS+ are case-insensitive, case-preserving file systems. This means that if you save a file named myfile.txt and then save another file named MyFile.txt in the same directory, you get a warning, and the newer file replaces the older one; but when you look at the file, you'll see the name you specified.

Unix file systems are normally case-sensitive, meaning that a single directory can simultaneously contain distinct files with names that are spelled the same but capitalized differently. On HFS or HFS+, if you try to open `myfile.txt` but the file is actually named `MYFILE.txt`, there's no problem—the system understands that the names are equivalent, and `MYFILE.txt` opens. But under Unix, since these are distinct filenames, you get an error message instead.

Because HFS+ is case-preserving, Unix programs generally run fine on HFS+ file systems. Some programs may be confused by the case insensitivity, though. One example is filename completion in `tcsh`. Because `tcsh` assumes that `myfile.txt` and `MYFILE.txt` are distinct filenames (even though both are actually names for the same file under HFS+), if you miscapitalize the beginning of a file path, `tcsh` doesn't understand which file you're referring to and can't complete the path for you.

Invisible Items

Under Unix, files whose names start with a period are special. Most commands ignore them, and these "dot files" often contain special administrative information.

In addition to its main path or name, such as /Users/amy, every directory contains two additional items: a directory called "." that's a hard link to the directory itself (yes, this is recursive) and ".."—a hard link to its parent directory. In other words, /Users/amy/ and /Users/amy/. are the same directory, as are /Users/amy/Documents/.. and /Users/amy/Library/... (In fact, they are *all* the same directory.)

Since these additional directory entries are usually more confusing than useful, `ls` generally doesn't display them; but its -a option (part of the `ll` alias) shows invisible items, including these special directory entries. This is also why link counts (see the "Permissions and Ownership" section above) for directories are greater than one; directories always have at least two valid paths or hard links.

 TIP The links are useful when you want to move *up* in hierarchies, as in `cd ..` or `cd ../`; both will move you to the parent of the current folder.

HFS and HFS+ file systems have an invisibility *bit*, or setting, for each file and folder. Unfortunately, Apple makes many of the standard Unix directories invisible in Mac OS X, so that the Aqua environment looks simpler and more familiar to Mac users. If you look inside your Mac OS X system disk in a Finder window, you'll see much less than if you type `ls -l /` in a Terminal window, because most of the standard Unix directories are invisible from the Mac side. Thus, to view or edit many Unix-based configuration files using a Mac OS X (or Classic) application, you may need to use a Unix-based tool like more or pico; or copy the files into a visible directory from the command line, edit them, and then put them back.

Shell Scripting and Behavior

Shell scripting offers two major advantages over AppleScript. The first is that shell scripts can be more flexible than AppleScript, because shell scripts work without requiring additional features in the target program. Programmers have to add AppleScript capabilities to applications, and many applications have little or no scripting support. By contrast, shell scripts have as much flexibility as a person typing commands. In the Unix world, almost anything can be controlled from the command line or a script, and graphical interfaces, as a rule, are purely optional.

The second major advantage of shell scripting is familiarity. Many advanced Mac users have never used AppleScript, and you can't figure it out from the everyday experience of using a Mac normally. But shell scripts use the same commands and facilities that you use all the time when typing commands at a shell prompt—there's not much new to learn. As a result, anyone who has spent some time working at the command line has almost all the knowledge necessary to write scripts. All you need to know is how to put together the script file and how to get it to perform all those commands that, after a few months, you've begun to memorize (if not dream about).

Although this section can't give you much more than a brief overview of shell scripting and some advanced command-line controls, you'll see that shell scripting is fairly easy to pick up. Then, in the future, when you're working at the command line and think to yourself, "I wish I could automate this tedious process," maybe you'll realize that you can, with a quick script.

Shell Scripts

A *shell script* is a series of commands, just as you'd type them at the prompt, saved in a file. There are two main differences. First, shell scripts contain blank lines and comments. Any line starting with a pound sign (#) is ignored by the shell, except the first line—and the first line itself is the other difference.

Each script starts with a line specifying the path to the shell for which the script is written. Because different shells have different syntax and features, a script, to work properly, must be executed by the shell it's written for. Since sh is the oldest shell in active use and the most widely available, most scripts are written for it. Scripts intended for sh on Darwin-based systems should start with #!/bin/sh. Some downloaded scripts specify the wrong location for the shell, so this is a good thing to check if a new script doesn't work.

WARNING Remember that each shell has a slightly different syntax. In this section, when you're writing scripts, you'll need to use sh syntax; when you're entering shell commands (at the prompt), you'll need to use tcsh syntax. Shells derived from sh, including bash, use the sh syntax for loop control and setting variables, and have their own set of builtins; but csh-descended shells, including tcsh, use a different syntax and slightly different builtins. See the man pages (man sh and man tcsh) for details.

Unix shells are also called "interpreters," since they interpret and execute commands and scripts. Generally, the term *shell* refers to interactive use, and *interpreter* is used for script processing. The same program performs both functions, though.

 NOTE Some newer shells have sh compatibility modes, which disable new features so they can be used in place of the "real" sh. Under Darwin, /bin/sh is actually the same file as /bin/zsh, using a hard link. Under Red Hat Linux, /bin/sh is a symbolic link to /bin/bash; and when bash is invoked with the name sh, it runs in compatibility mode.

Scripts use the same commands and syntax as the command line, which means that writing scripts is easy to pick up, once you're familiar with the command line. If you want to put two different commands on a single line, you can separate them with a semicolon. This is equivalent to typing the first command, pressing Return, and then typing the second and pressing Return; but it's more compact and sometimes more convenient.

Figure 22.7 shows an example of a script that runs every month to do automated maintenance—mostly log file management. In /etc/monthly, you'll see many of the same commands you've used yourself. This script starts with a specification of the interpreter, comments, variables, a pipe (|), and several standard commands (see the section "Pipes: Connecting Programs" later in this chapter).

Creating a Script

To create a script, simply create a text file, then give yourself execute permission for that file. You can create the script in a regular text editor in Mac OS X, if you like, or you can use a command-line editor such as emacs or vi. In this example, we'll use pico.

If you use a Mac OS–based text editor, such as BBEdit, you'll need to make sure your saved files use Unix-style line breaks; that's because Darwin and Unix use different characters to identify line endings than does the Mac OS, and the Mac-style endings will confuse interpreters. In BBEdit and other programs that support Mac and Unix-style line endings, this is controlled through the Save or Save As dialog box.

FIGURE 22.7

/etc/monthly, *a script that runs on the first of every month*

```
[g4:~] mmosx% more /etc/monthly
#!/bin/sh -
#
#       @(#)monthly     8.1 (Berkeley) 6/9/93
#

PATH=/bin:/usr/bin:/sbin:/usr/sbin
host=`hostname -s`
echo "Subject: $host monthly run output"

echo ""
echo "Doing login accounting:"
ac -p #| sort -nr +1

echo ""
echo -n "Rotating log files:"
cd /var/log
for i in wtmp; do
        echo -n " $i"
        if [ -x /usr/bin/gzip ]; then gzext=".gz"; else gzext=""; fi
        if [ -f "${i}.3${gzext}" ]; then mv -f "${i}.3${gzext}" "${i}.4${gzext}"
; fi
        if [ -f "${i}.2${gzext}" ]; then mv -f "${i}.2${gzext}" "${i}.3${gzext}"
; fi
        if [ -f "${i}.1${gzext}" ]; then mv -f "${i}.1${gzext}" "${i}.2${gzext}"
; fi
        if [ -f "${i}.0${gzext}" ]; then mv -f "${i}.0${gzext}" "${i}.1${gzext}"
; fi
        if [ -f "${i}" ]; then mv -f "${i}" "${i}.0" && if [ -x /usr/bin/gzip ];
 then gzip -9 "${i}.0"; fi; fi
        touch "${i}" && chmod 640 "${i}"
done
if [ -f /var/run/syslog.pid ]; then kill -HUP $(cat /var/run/syslog.pid | head -
1); fi
echo ""

if [ -f /etc/monthly.local ]; then
    echo ""
    echo "Running monthly.local:"
    sh /etc/monthly.local
fi
[g4:~] mmosx% 
```

Here's how to create a basic script entirely within Darwin:

1. Make the directory ~/bin with **mkdir ~/bin** (if it doesn't already exist).

2. At the prompt, type **cd ~/bin** to enter the directory, then press Return.

3. Type **pico *myscript*** and press Return. (Replace *myscript* with the name you'd like to give the script in this step and in steps 6 and 8.)

4. Type the script. In this example, the script will simply use the **echo** command to return text to the screen.

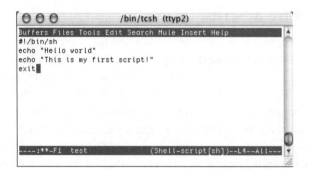

```
                    /bin/tcsh  (ttyp2)
Buffers Files Tools Edit Search Mule Insert Help
#!/bin/sh
echo "Hello world"
echo "This is my first script!"
exit
```
```
----:**-F1   test              (Shell-script[sh])--L4--All---
```

5. Type **exit** as the last line of your script, then press Control+X. The status line at the bottom of the screen asks if you'd like to save your changes. Press Y and then Return to save your work.

6. Type **chmod u+x** *myscript*. Now you have execute permission. Without this step, it's just a text file that lists some commands.

7. Type **rehash**. This will make tcsh recognize that there's another command in your PATH.

8. Type *myscript* at the command line, and your new script will run.

```
[g4:~/bin] todds% myscript
Hello world
This is my first script!
[g4:~/bin] todds% []
```

In the next few sections, you'll find information on some more-advanced shell features that are particularly useful for scripts.

 TIP   Since the script is in your personal ~/bin directory, it's automatically in your PATH variable. The result is that you can type this script name from any directory, and it will execute.

Filters: Standard Input, Standard Output, and Standard Error

Filters are a key concept in Unix-based operating systems. A *filter* is a program that takes input, processes it in some way, and emits processed output. Many command-line utilities, including grep, head, tail, and tar, can be used in this way. These utilities can accept input in any of three ways: text typed by the user, file(s) specified on the command line, and *standard input* (also called stdin). Output is to the screen or to *standard output* (stdout). By chaining one program's output to another's input, it's possible to do very complex processing using simple component programs. In addition to input and output, there's a third stream, *standard error* (stderr).

File Redirection

To make a program read a file from standard input, use the < (less than) character. This isn't terribly important for interactive use, since most of the standard commands also accept filenames as arguments, but it becomes useful in scripts; it allows you to control input and output of your own scripts without adding code to do argument processing or file management directly.

To make a program record its output in a file, use the > (greater than) character. An example using both < and > is grep 212 < phonebook.txt > ny-pb.txt. This would copy all the lines containing "212" from the file phonebook.txt into the file ny-pb.txt.

Pipes: Connecting Programs

Unix gains much of its power and flexibility from the ability to chain simpler programs together to perform processing that's more complex than any of the programs can do alone. To make one program's output go to another's input, use the pipe character (|). This is useful for programs that generate lots of output; results might be sent to more, grep, head, or tail, to get just the relevant bits. A simple example is ls -l | more, which sends the output from ls -l to the more program as input.

You can use more complex "pipelines" to create long chains of commands and to process data through multiple steps. Pipes often start with commands that provide large amounts of data, such as cat (to bring files into a pipe) and man. The highly flexible commands sort and grep, with their many options, often go in the middle, to extract or prioritize the relevant bits; and more, head, and tail often go at the ends of pipes, to facilitate reading the output. Another useful command for pipes is tee, which copies its input into one or more files, and also passes it along to stdout for additional processing.

Internal and Environment Variables

Shells, including tcsh and sh, work with two different kinds of variables: *internal variables* and *environment variables*. Environment variables are important because they are passed to other programs launched from the shell. To see all the current internal variables, use the set builtin with no arguments (type **set** and press Return); use setenv to see the current environment variables. To set variables for tcsh, use set or setenv with one or more arguments of the form *variablename=value*, as in this example:

```
set foo="Hello World"
```

For sh (and hence for scripts using sh), the set command isn't required, so you would use:

```
foo="Hello World"
```

Once a value is assigned to a variable, you'll use that value via *variable substitution*. When the shell sees a variable name starting with a dollar sign ($), it replaces the whole word with the variable's value before processing the command. In a script, it might look like this:

```
#!/bin/sh
foo="Hello World"
echo $foo
exit
```

As you can see, to send a single variable's value to standard output (usually the screen), you can use the echo command. Figure 22.8 shows the procedure to set and use an internal variable, as well as environment variables from printenv.

FIGURE 22.8

Setting and using an internal variable, and output from printenv

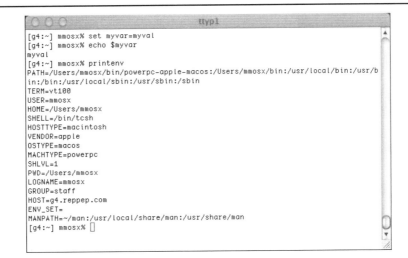

```
[g4:~] mmosx% set myvar=myval
[g4:~] mmosx% echo $myvar
myval
[g4:~] mmosx% printenv
PATH=/Users/mmosx/bin/powerpc-apple-macos:/Users/mmosx/bin:/usr/local/bin:/usr/b
in:/bin:/usr/local/sbin:/usr/sbin:/sbin
TERM=vt100
USER=mmosx
HOME=/Users/mmosx
SHELL=/bin/tcsh
HOSTTYPE=macintosh
VENDOR=apple
OSTYPE=macos
MACHTYPE=powerpc
SHLVL=1
PWD=/Users/mmosx
LOGNAME=mmosx
GROUP=staff
HOST=g4.reppep.com
ENV_SET=
MANPATH=~/man:/usr/local/share/man:/usr/share/man
[g4:~] mmosx% 
```

NOTE To use a literal dollar sign in a command, you need to *escape* it with a backslash. The backslash protects special characters from being immediately interpreted, so that they can be passed along to the next program intact. For example, echo \$foo would avoid variable substitution and would return "$foo" regardless of what the variable foo was set to.

You can use a couple of special variables to receive command-line arguments within a script (e.g., myscript somefile). The variable $# is used to determine the number of arguments the user entered, while $*n*, where *n* is an integer, is used to refer to a particular argument, such as $1 for the first argument or $0 for the script's name. $* is used to display all of the arguments. For example:

```
#!/bin/sh
# This script demonstrates argument variables.
echo "You typed $# arguments."
echo "This script is $0"
echo "The first argument is $1"
echo "A list of the arguments is: $*"
exit
```

Getting argument variables this way enables you to create your own shell commands! For instance, you could create a script called *lsize* that uses the argument variables to perform `ls -lS | more` so that a long listing, sorted by size, is piped to the more command:

```
#!/bin/sh
# lsize: long listing sorted by size, using more.
ls -lS $* | more
exit
```

Save the script as ~/bin/lsize (with the proper permissions), and you'll be able to easily list long directories, sorted by size, with the help of the more command, as in lsize ~/Documents.

Flow Control

When a program finishes running, it returns an exit status. This is 0 if the program succeeded, or a positive or negative number if it failed. (Depending on the program, the number might provide more information about the failure. Check the program's man page.) This exit status is stored in the variable status. Many programs also send error messages to standard error, which normally appears on the screen—so the errors show up in your Terminal window. Many programs also record error messages in log files (use `ls /var/log` to see the standard log files).

 NOTE Be careful with the status variable, because commands (including echo $status) will change its value to their *own* exit status after they complete. The trick is that if you need to use status more than once, you must first copy it into another variable, and you can then use the copy as much as you want.

The basic *conditional test* in tcsh is if. It can be used on the command line in conjunction with a command, using the return value to determine what to do next. The syntax is if *test command*—if *test* returns true (0), then *command* is executed. To run a command and use its status value as the conditional, the command must be surrounded by braces (curly brackets, {}) and spaces.

Here's an example of a couple of tests. The user "root" does appear in /etc/passwd, so that test is successful, and the conditional command runs and says "Matched!" But "gates" isn't present, so that test fails and the echo command is never executed.

```
[g4:~] mmosx% if { grep -q root /etc/passwd } echo Matched!
Matched!
[g4:~] mmosx% if { grep -q gates /etc/passwd } echo Matched!
[g4:~] mmosx% []
```

 NOTE The grep command's -q option puts it into quiet mode: It returns status but doesn't list matches on standard output (normally the screen).

In addition to normal shell commands, tests may use special, dedicated comparison operators. Tests using these operators must be enclosed in *square brackets*, and *each* bracket must be preceded and followed by a space, as in this example: if [$# -lt 1] . Note that normal commands used as conditionals must be enclosed in braces, but tests using the comparison operators below use square brackets—and the spacing is crucial.

When you're scripting, you'll often use conditional tests to determine whether something is true. Conditional tests, like programs, return exit status of 0 for true or any other number for false. Table 22.1 shows some common conditionals. (There are others, and they can become rather complex, especially if you're dealing directly with the tcsh shell. See man test and man tcsh for details.)

TABLE 22.1: SOME COMPARISON OPERATORS

Operator	Test
-eq	equal to
-ne	not equal to
-lt	less than
-gt	greater than
-le	less than or equal to
-ge	greater than or equal to

If you want more, the if structure can be more elaborate—perhaps familiar to you if you've done other programming:

```
if [ test ]
    then command
elif [ test ]
    then command
else command
fi
```

Note that everything between the first then line and fi is optional, including the elif line, its then line, and the else line.

Here's an example that elaborates on some ideas you've already seen—it lists directories but uses a test:

```
#!/bin/sh
# Return sorted listing of specified directory
if [ $# -lt 1 ]
then
    echo "This script requires one or more arguments."
    exit -1
fi
ls -lS $* | more
exit
```

Now, if the user doesn't enter any arguments, the error message is returned and the script aborts (returning –1 to signify failure, so it can be used by another script that needs to know if this one succeeded).

And that's just one way to test! You can also use while, for, and case. See "Flow-Control Constructs" in the sh man page for more on conditionals and loops.

Shell Configuration Files

On startup, each shell reads in a few configuration files, if they exist. The tcsh shell starts by reading in two shared configuration files of standard commands: /etc/csh.cshrc and /etc/csh.login. When you install Darwin, these two files do nothing themselves; instead, they use the source command to read in the "real" configuration files located in /usr/share/init/tcsh. These files, in turn, do fairly involved initialization on each tcsh invocation. Next, tcsh loads personal configuration files: ~/.tcshrc (or ~/.cshrc if ~/.tcshrc is missing), then processes ~/.history, ~/.login, and ~/.cshdirs. Non-login shells (when tcsh is executing scripts, instead of taking input from a user at the terminal) process only the first global and first personal configuration files.

NOTE For more on initialization, see "Startup and Shutdown" on the tcsh man page.

In Figure 22.9, you can see that /etc/csh.login just uses the source command to read in /usr/share/init/tcsh/login, which sets the special path local variable (corresponding to the PATH environment variable, but in a different format) and then does additional configuration.

FIGURE 22.9

Darwin's system-wide login files for tcsh

```
[g4:~] mmosx% cat /etc/csh.login
source /usr/share/init/tcsh/login
[g4:~] mmosx% cat /usr/share/init/tcsh/login
##
# LOGIN FILE
#
# Wilfredo Sanchez Jr. | tritan@mit.edu
# Dec. 5, 1998
#
# MIT Project Athena
#
# ORIGINAL SOURCES: /usr/athena/lib/login
#                   and /usr/prototype_user/.login (ATHENA REL 7.2)
##

##
# Set paths
##
set path = (                                              \
               ~/bin                                       \
               /usr/local/bin /usr/bin /bin                \
               /usr/local/sbin /usr/sbin /sbin             \
           )

if ($?version) then
  if ("$version" =~ tcsh*) then
    set path = ( ~/bin/${MACHTYPE}-${VENDOR}-${OSTYPE} $path )
  endif
endif

setenv MANPATH "~/man:/usr/local/share/man:/usr/share/man"

if (-r ${tcsh_initdir}/path) source ${tcsh_initdir}/path

##
# Read user's login
##
if (-r ${tcsh_initdir}/login.mine) then
  source ${tcsh_initdir}/login.mine
endif

[g4:~] mmosx%
```

Advanced Mac OS X Topics

Installing Darwin Programs

You can install Darwin applications in a number of ways. The easier methods involve simply decompressing an archive that includes an application that has already been compiled to run in Darwin. But the easiest way isn't always the most interesting, because there are lots of great programs available as Unix source code that aren't packaged for Darwin. We'll cover both types of installations in the following sections.

Darwin Binary Installation Example: Analog

Analog is a fast and free Web traffic analyzer. It reads server logs from Web servers such as Apache, analyzes them, and generates HTML reports showing traffic levels broken down in several ways. Analog is a pure command-line program—its configuration is stored in `analog.cfg` and optional additional configuration files, or provided at the command line when starting the program. Analog is available in source form, as a precompiled Darwin/Mac OS X binary package, and as a Carbon or Classic application with a minimal interface, from `www.analog.cx/download.html`.

The Darwin binary distribution of analog uses a very simple installation procedure: After downloading and unpacking the tarball, the user moves the unpacked files into place, and the package's Web page lists additional command-line steps to complete the setup. One problem with this installation procedure is that the packager must keep the instructions script in sync with the official `Makefile` from the source package, and the user must perform several steps manually.

This Darwin binary package is less important now, because every copy of Mac OS X and Darwin is shipped with the developer tools. As a result, it may be replaced by an automated system like fink (`http://fink.sourceforge.net`), which can download the analog source package, compile it, and install it automatically.

Compiling Code for Darwin

Unix and Unix-based systems normally include compilers and software development tools. This is partially because Unix was designed as a programming environment, and also because so much software is available in source form for Unix systems, including excellent free tools.

Mac OS X, however, with its user-friendly Aqua focus, doesn't contain these tools as part of its base installation. Instead, Apple includes them in `Developer.pkg` on the Developer Tools CD, included with the Mac OS X installation CD. Because these tools are open-source as part of the Darwin project, they should always be freely available, but exactly how they're distributed may change over time. Carbon and Cocoa programs tend to follow their Mac OS (and NextStep) heritage and be precompiled so that users can just install them without any need for compilers. Unix programs, however, are often available only in source form. Supporting Mac OS X/Darwin for a Unix program may consist of making sure that the default compilation and installation procedure works, rather than precompiling and packaging the software, as you might expect for a Carbon application. To install Unix programs from source, then, you'll need to have the Developer Tools installed.

Here's the process for compiling freely available source code into a Darwin application:

NOTE This is the standard procedure; application authors often use slightly different steps. Check for instructions in README or INSTALL files included with the software, or on the software's Web site.

1. Download the file (using `ncftp`, `ftp`, `wget`, or a graphical FTP client or Web browser). The filename is likely to be something like `package.src.tgz`.

2. Use `tar` to unarchive (and decompress) the file. To continue the example above, type **`tar -xzf package.src.tgz`** and press Return.

3. Change to the directory created by the unarchiving process. Type **`cd package`** and press Return.

4. If the archive has a `configure` script, run it. This script, if present, inspects the system environment and determines how to compile the included source code. To run `configure`, type **`./configure`** and press Return.

TIP If you get an error from the `configure` script that gcc can't be found, it's because the program expects the C compiler to be called gcc, but Apple installs it as cc. To fix this, do **`sudo ln -s /usr/bin/cc /usr/bin/gcc`**. After you do this once, you'll have a symlink named gcc in your PATH, where `configure` can find it. You only have to perform this fix once.

5. Next is the `make` command. This command reads its instructions from `./Makefile`—another file included with the program source code—and compiles and installs software. With no arguments, `make` generally just compiles. Any additional arguments desired may be defined in the `Makefile`, to compile or delete files or to install files to appropriate places on the system. Type **`make`** and press Return.

6. The final `make` command finishes the installation by copying files to their intended locations and possibly creating symlinks in standard directories to the actual executable programs, so files are effectively included in the PATH. Type **`sudo make install`** and press Return.

PART

V

Advanced
Mac OS X Topics

WARNING OK—here comes another sudo/root warning. In Unix, regular users usually have permission to make changes only within their own home directories. So, in order to install software for general use, you'll need to install using sudo, which asks for your administrative password and then runs the rest of the command with elevated permissions. As a rule, you should be very careful with any new software, but this warning is even more important when you're using sudo. Whether you're compiling source code or installing binary files, you should consider how much you trust the author or packager of the software, as well as your own knowledge of Unix. If you're concerned, don't use sudo to install; just install the program for inside your home directory for private use.

Compiling Darwin Programs

Aside from the general ./configure, make, and make install steps outlined above, there is no universal method for compiling and installing Unix programs from source. With each program, you'll have to read the included documentation (generally in a README or INSTALL file or on the program's Web site). There are a few useful tidbits to keep in mind, though, when compiling software for Darwin and Mac OS X:

- Mac OS X's command-line environment is basically the same as the stand-alone Darwin open-source operating system, so Unix programs written for Unix or Darwin normally run on Mac OS X as well. Because Mac OS X has many features not in Darwin, though, most Mac OS X programs can't run in Darwin.

- Darwin is based on BSD Unix. This means that generic Unix software should work as well, possibly with minor tweaking to accommodate Darwin idiosyncrasies. Developers often build these workarounds into their installation procedures, so that the next version compiles and installs without any manual intervention.

- Apple includes a great deal of software in Mac OS X, so don't compile new software without checking first to see if it's already present. Among the major packages that Apple installs are OpenSSH, Perl, Java 2, emacs, and pico.

- If you're stuck, try online Mac OS X and Darwin resources. There are strong online communities for both Mac OS X and Darwin, and you may find instructions or help on a Web site or mailing list.

TIP Some good starting points for Mac OS X/Darwin tips and discussions are `www.stepwise.com`, `osx.macnn.com`, and `www.omnigroup.com/community/ mailinglists/`.

Types of Darwin Programs

Darwin has several types of programs you can use, just like the Mac OS. It's worth defining them here so that you can decide what to install on your own system.

First, there are command-line applications, such as `cat`, `ls`, `tar`, `analog`, and many of the other commands discussed earlier. These are generally controlled by command-line options and/or configuration files.

Interactive programs, like `more`, `ftp`, `ssh`, and `tcsh` (when used as an interactive shell), have their own text-based interfaces available while the programs are running. These interfaces allow such programs to be more complicated.

Some programs are actually libraries—pieces of code that may not do anything by themselves but can be used by other programs to perform useful functions; examples are `libm`, `zlib` (a compression library), and `libgd` (a graphics-generation library). You probably won't need to install any libraries unless they're required by other software you're installing, such as `mrtg`, a network utilization program that requires `zlib` and `libgd` to function.

Stand-alone daemons (also called servers) run continuously, waiting to respond to requests from other programs. Apache is such a server—it constantly waits for requests from Web browsers. Even when idle, it keeps running, waiting for new requests to handle.

Unix has another type of daemon, though, which has no direct counterpart on the Mac. The servers for Telnet, FTP, and Finger (`telnetd`, `ftpd`, and `fingerd`, respectively) don't run when no connections are open. These daemons are controlled by `inetd`, the Internet "super server," which runs all the time, awaiting requests for any of the services it manages. When `inetd` receives such a request, it starts a copy of the appropriate daemon and passes the connection over to the new copy. This is much more flexible and efficient than keeping all those programs running all the time, since one `inetd` manages all the ports for all its subsidiary services, potentially starting hundreds of services as needed. The cost is performance; having `inetd` receive each Web request, start an Apache process, and then pass control over would cause a significant delay, so Apache normally keeps several idle processes waiting for new requests, and completely eschews `inetd`.

What's Next?

In this chapter you learned quite a bit about the Terminal application and how to access the underlying Darwin command line. You saw reasons to learn the command line, basic and advanced commands, command-line applications, and basic Unix philosophy. You also learned about the different shells that are available, including tricks for the default tcsh shell. Then you saw the basics of shell scripting and configuration. Finally, you saw how to install and use new programs at the command line.

In the next chapter you'll take a closer look at command-line tools for transferring files and accessing remote computers, as well as how to activate the remote login servers built into Mac OS X.

CHAPTER 23

Remote Access and FTP

As discussed in Chapter 22, Mac OS X's command line is accessed through the Terminal application, a utility that's included with every installation. It's worth noting that you don't ever *have* to use the command line, at least not in day-to-day activities. Mac OS X is designed to be a fully graphical operating system, with commands generally accomplished using the Finder and graphical applications managed from the Dock and other interface elements. Indeed, Apple doesn't really encourage daily users to access the command line, partly because it's a bit more complex and confusing and partly because intricate typed commands aren't really the "Macintosh way."

That said, the command line is a convenient way to perform a number of tasks, including Telnet (or SSH) and FTP, Internet protocol–based applications designed to enable you to access remote computers, either over a LAN or over the Internet. While you may opt to use third-party applications for Telnet, SSH, and FTP access, those capabilities are also built into the Terminal application, giving you an instant solution.

 NOTE SSH is the secure version of Telnet and is included in Mac OS X 10.0.1 and later versions. The original Mac OS X 10.0 shipped with standard Telnet, which is less secure but commonly used. I'll cover both in this chapter (they're similar). Note, though, that you'll use SSH to connect to most Mac OS X machines; Telnet can be used with many Unix-based and other computers on the Internet.

In this chapter you'll see what remote access is and how to turn it on in the Mac OS so that you (or others) can access your Mac remotely. You'll then see how to get started with the Terminal application, including the basics of using the Terminal for both FTP and Telnet/SSH access. Throughout, I'll discuss the security implications of turning on these remote-access features.

 NOTE If you want to get serious with the command line—using it to work day-to-day with your Mac—you may wish to begin with Chapter 22, which covers the Terminal and the command line in depth.

Understanding Remote Access

Telnet and SSH are standard protocols for *terminal emulation*, a method by which an application can pretend to be a command-line terminal, like those used to access mainframes and minicomputers in large-scale computer centers. Unlike a desktop computer or personal computer (such as a Macintosh), terminals are screens and keyboards that don't do their own processing. Instead, they're used to connect to a remote computer, where the processing, storage, and other tasks generally considered "computing" take place. For this reason, such terminals are often called "dumb terminals."

Of course, your Mac is fully capable of some impressive computing on its own. For that reason, the Terminal application is simply used to emulate a terminal for the purpose of connecting to other computers and accessing them as though your Mac were a dumb terminal. In practice, the Terminal application is really used for three different tasks: accessing *your own* Mac using a command-line interface, accessing remote Macs using a command-line FTP application, and accessing remote Macs using a command-line Telnet or SSH application.

When you're using Telnet or SSH, you sign into the remote computer using a username and password. Then, just as with Mac OS X, you'll have access to your home folder on the remote computer, as well as certain command-line applications that are accessible on that remote computer. In fact, there's a whole underbelly of command-line applications that are installed with any Unix variant—even Mac OS X, via its version of FreeBSD—that you can access using Telnet.

But Telnet isn't limited to other computers running Mac OS X. You can use the Terminal application and the `telnet` command to access any Unix or Unix-like computer for which you have a user account and password. That might include university computers, your ISP's Web server computer, or any number of command line–based public servers and BBSs, or bulletin board systems. All you have to know is the correct Telnet address (see Figure 23.1).

FIGURE 23.1

Here's one use of Telnet–logging into the New York Public Library's computer system to check on available books.

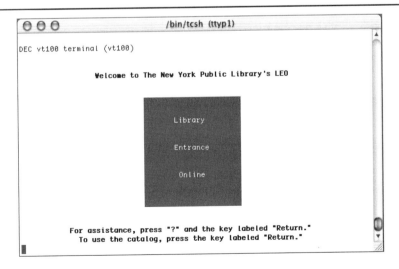

In summary, both Telnet/SSH and FTP are command-line applications that you can use from within the Terminal application to access remote computers. In the case of Telnet/SSH, you're logging into the remote computer to access command-line applications or manage files. In the case of FTP, you're logging into the remote computer to transfer files between the remote computer and your own. We'll discuss both later in this chapter.

Turning on Remote Access

Mac OS X enables you to turn on SSH access (Telnet access in Mac OS X 10.0) so that you and others can log into the Mac from a remote computer. Before doing so, however, it's important to consider the implications of this sort of access. Enabling remote access is a security risk, because it means that anyone who has a connection to your Mac—on the local network, on a wide area network, or via the Internet—can potentially log into your Mac, access files, and conceivably do some damage. Although both Telnet and SSH require that remote users have a valid account on your Mac, it's conceivable that remote access could be exploited by knowledgeable individuals.

Enabling remote access also means that, once your Mac is accessed by a remote user (even if the user is valid and authorized), it's possible for that account to be compromised. If you have users with the unfortunate habit of getting up and walking away from their computers while they're still logged into your Mac, there's the potential that someone else could come along and do some harm.

 WARNING If your Mac is directly accessible on the Internet via a fixed IP address and/or a host name and domain name combination, you should seriously consider whether the benefit of turning on remote access outweighs the risks. This is especially true if your Mac contains sensitive data or is connected to your business's or organization's network.

Obviously, though, the ability to log into your Mac remotely can be a considerable benefit, too. For one, it's an important tool in the arsenal of a Mac OS X administrator who needs to troubleshoot a Mac. Even if a Mac OS X–based computer seems frozen or unresponsive, you can often access that Mac remotely in order to attempt to shut it down or otherwise troubleshoot it (see Chapter 20 for more on this technique).

Enabling remote access for your users can also be a useful touch, as it allows them to access their personal account from anywhere in the world. While Mac OS X is primarily geared toward the use of graphical applications (those that rely on a mouse and menu commands using the Aqua interface), a number of commands and programs can be accessed by a remote user logged in via remote access. So, if you'd like users to be able to access their accounts remotely, you can enable remote access to make that possible.

Enabling remote access is actually quite easy:

1. Open the System Preferences application.

2. If necessary, launch the Network pane and configure your Mac for TCP/IP access (see Chapters 8 and 9).

3. If TCP/IP access is configured, open the Sharing pane.

4. Click the padlock icon and sign in as an administrator (if necessary).

5. Click to place a check mark next to Allow Remote Login (see Figure 23.2).

Remote access is activated immediately; if you have no further business in the System Preferences application, you can close it. You needn't even restart your Mac; once remote access is activated, the Mac can immediately be accessed by remote Telnet client applications (if you're running Mac OS X 10.0) or SSH client applications (if you're running Mac OS X 10.0.1 or higher).

PART

V

Advanced
Mac OS X Topics

FIGURE 23.2

Enabling remote access so that remote users can access your Mac

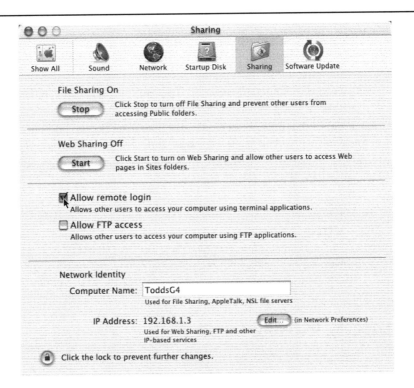

NOTE As with FTP serving (discussed in Chapter 24), other File Sharing settings aren't relevant to remote access, even though the File Sharing Start/Stop button appears in the Sharing pane. If remote access is turned on, files can be accessed by remote users (according to their file privileges) regardless of the File Sharing state. That said, users allowed to access your Mac remotely must have a valid user account set up in the Users pane of System Preferences.

If your Mac has a host name and is part of a named domain, users will be able to access the remote-access server by entering that named address (e.g., mymac.mac-upgrade.com) in their Telnet or SSH applications or when using the command-line version of Telnet or SSH in a Terminal window. If you don't have such an address, users will access your Mac using its IP address—whether it's a public IP address (one that's fixed on the Internet) or a private IP address (one used exclusively for local LAN access and/or behind a firewall or router).

Accessing Computers Remotely

Got a Mac you'd like to log into using Telnet or SSH? You can accomplish that easily using the Terminal application that's built into Mac OS X. As mentioned, Terminal is a multipurpose application designed to give you access to Mac OS X's command line. Once you've launched Terminal, you can then access the Telnet or SSH application and use it to log into remote-access servers.

This also works for any Unix-like operating system on which you have a username and password. The process is a little different for accessing remote Telnet and SSH servers (such as, for instance, an automated library catalog), as discussed later in the section "Accessing Telnet Applications."

 NOTE Even if you've enabled the root account on your Mac (as discussed in Chapter 20), you can't log into your Mac via Telnet or SSH using that root account. You can, however, use an administrator account and the sudo command to gain root privileges.

Logging In Using Telnet

To begin, you'll need to know the address for the remote Mac that you plan to access. It can be either an IP address or a machine-name address including the host name, domain name, and three-letter extension. If you know the address, here's how to open a Telnet session using the Terminal application:

1. Launch the Terminal application. You should find it in the main Applications folder inside the Utilities folder. Once launched, you'll see the main prompt, which should look something like this:

```
[localhost:~] todds%
```

2. Enter **telnet** *xxx.xxx.xxx.xxx* (where each series of *xxx* represents a portion of the remote Telnet server's IP address) or **telnet** *hostname.domain.tlx*, where *tlx* stands for the three-letter extension—com, net, org—of the remote server. (An example might be telnet toddsmac.mac-upgrade.com). Press Return after entering the address. (Note that if the Telnet session requires a different port number, you enter that after the host address, as in telnet toddsmac.mac-upgrade.com 3000.)

```
[localhost:~] todds% telnet 192.168.1.2
```

3. What happens next depends, in part, on what sort of computer you're logging into. In most cases you'll see a little information about the computer you're signing into (the "connect message"); then you'll see a Login prompt. Shown here is the typical message generated by a Mac OS X system:

```
[localhost:~] todds% telnet 192.168.1.2
Trying 192.168.1.2...
Connected to 192.168.1.2.
Escape character is '^]'.

Darwin/BSD (localhost) (ttyp0)

login: []
```

4. Now, at the Login prompt, enter your username on the remote system. Once you've entered the username, press Return.

 TIP On Unix and Unix-like systems, usernames and passwords are case-sensitive.

5. Next, you'll see a Password prompt (at least, in many cases). Enter the password for your remote account and press Return. If you're logging into a user account and your username and password are recognized, you should see a welcome message followed by a prompt:

```
[localhost:~] todds% telnet 192.168.1.2
Trying 192.168.1.2...
Connected to 192.168.1.2.
Escape character is '^]'.

Darwin/BSD (localhost) (ttyp0)

login: todds
Password:
Welcome to Darwin!
[localhost:~] todds% []
```

Once you're logged in, you'll see the Telnet prompt. Now you can access the remote Mac by typing commands at the prompt and pressing Return. Of course, you'll need to know what some of those commands are before you can accomplish very much.

There's another way to log in using Telnet: You can type `telnet` at the command prompt, then press Return. Now you're in the Telnet application without being connected to a host. Type ? and press Return to see a listing of commands. Typing `open` *host_address* will open a new connection.

 TIP Want to customize the welcome message that appears on your own Mac when you're hosting remote access? You can do it using the Terminal application and a text editor, such as pico, described in Chapter 22. The file you need to edit is called `motd`, and it's stored in the `/etc/` folder. Note that you may need to use the `sudo` command (`sudo pico /etc/motd`) in order to edit and save the file, as it requires root access (and hence an administrator's password if you're using the `sudo` command).

Logging In Using SSH

An SSH connection can go a little differently, as it requires a bit more security. For the most part, the steps are the same, but you may need to jump through additional hoops to get signed in correctly. Here are the steps:

1. With the Terminal open, type **ssh** *xxx.xxx.xxx.xxx* (where the *xxx*'s represent the remote SSH server's IP address) or **ssh** *hostname.domain.tlx*, where *tlx* is the three-letter extension for the host's domain—com, net, org. (An example might be `ssh toddsmac.mac-upgrade.com`). Press Return after entering the address.

NOTE If you're logging into the remote computer using a different username than your current Mac account (for instance, if you're logged into the account "stevej" on your Mac but you want to use the username "sjobs" on the remote machine), then you need to enter the command as follows: ssh -l *username xxx.xxx.xxx.xxx*, such as ssh -l sjobs 192.168.1.4. The -l argument tells SSH to override its built-in behavior, which is to automatically attempt to log into the remote server using the current account's short username.

2. In some cases, the next message you see may begin "The authenticity of host..." and continue with a warning message. If you're sure that the host you're connecting to is valid (for instance, if you're connecting to a Mac on your local network), you can enter yes at the prompt and press Return. The machine will then be remembered as valid when you log into it in the future.

3. Now, enter your password on the remote machine and press Return.

If the password is accepted, you'll see the welcome message; if not, you'll be asked to enter it two more times before the connection will drop.

 NOTE In the Terminal, type **man ssh** to learn more about the different authentication methods and arguments you can use to alter SSH's behavior. They can get somewhat complicated, trust me.

Basic Remote-Access Commands

The commands you'll use in a remote-access session, whether Telnet or SSH, are actually very similar to the commands used at any Mac's command line, including your own. For a more complete overview, you can consult Chapter 22, which includes details about accessing your Mac via the Terminal application.

These commands are all typed commands, which you'll enter at a prompt, followed by pressing the Return key. Once you press the Return key, the command is executed.

 NOTE If you've read Chapter 22, these commands may be familiar to you. Note that Telnet and SSH applications generally support a subset of all the commands that are available in a Darwin command-line session. You can experiment with others from Chapter 22, if desired, but here I'll cover the basic commands used to get around in a Telnet or SSH session.

PART

V

Advanced Mac OS X Topics

As an example, when you first log into a remote Mac, you'll be taken to your home folder on that Mac. This is the same folder where, if you had logged into the remote Mac physically using the Mac OS X prompt, you would have found your personal Documents, Library, and other folders. They look a little different from the command line, but they're the same folders. To see them immediately, type the letters ls and press Return.

```
[localhost:~] todds% ls
Desktop               Music                 Sites
Documents             Network Trash Folder  TheVolumeSettingsFolder
Library               Pictures
Movies                Public
[localhost:~] todds% []
```

The ls command is the "list" command, which enables you to list the contents of a folder. In the example above, you're seeing a mix of subfolders and documents.

When you use the basic ls command, though, it can be a bit tough to tell exactly which listed items are folders and which are files. One way around this is to add a special *argument* that modifies the ls command: ls -l. Type that at a prompt and press Return. The result should look something like this:

```
[localhost:~] todds% ls -l
total 0
drwx------  12 todds  staff  364 May  8 17:34 Desktop
drwx------   9 todds  staff  262 May 15 19:04 Documents
drwx------  25 todds  staff  806 May  2 14:54 Library
drwx------   4 todds  staff  264 Apr  1 19:31 Movies
drwx------   4 todds  staff  264 Apr  1 19:31 Music
drwx---rwx   2 root   wheel  264 Apr 29 18:13 Network Trash Folder
drwx------   4 todds  staff  264 Apr  1 19:31 Pictures
drwxr-xr-x   3 todds  staff  264 Nov 15 17:09 Public
drwxr-xr-x   4 todds  staff  264 Feb 13 19:31 Sites
drwxrwxrwx   2 root   wheel  264 Apr 29 18:13 TheVolumeSettingsFolder
[localhost:~] todds% []
```

Now it's a little easier to tell the types of files apart. Thanks to the argument, the list now shows quite a bit of information about the files and folders, including a giveaway: the letter d that appears in the left-most column for the listed items. The d actually stands for *directory*, which is the standard way that Unix-like operating systems refer to folders. (The use of "directory" is important to note because many of the commands, which are often abbreviations, will make more sense in this context.) When you see items listed that have a - (hyphen) instead of a d, those are regular files.

Many commands accept path statements as arguments. You may have noticed, for instance, that by default you're able to see only the listing of your home folder when you access a remote Mac via Telnet or SSH.

To work with the contents of another folder, you'll need to change to that folder. You do that by entering the cd (change directory) command, followed by the directory to which you'd like to change. For example, you could enter cd Documents and then press Return. As a result, the prompt would change to indicate that you've moved to the new directory:

[localhost:~/Documents] todds% []

The portion of the prompt that shows ~/Documents indicates that you're now in the Documents folder that's a subfolder of your home folder. If you invoke the ls command, you'll now see a listing of that Documents folder. (Note that you can also use ls with a path statement, such as ls ~/Documents, if you'd like a listing of a folder without first changing to that folder.)

NOTE As you may recall from Chapters 3 and 22, the tilde (~) is a shortcut character used to represent your home folder. You can use that character (press Shift+`, which is the key immediately above your Tab key) in Telnet/SSH commands, such as cd ~, to change to your remote home folder. Also noted in Chapter 3 is the leading slash (/) character. When used alone or at the beginning of a path statement, the slash represents the root folder on the remote disk.

As I've discussed elsewhere, the folders on a Mac OS X machine are part of a hierarchy of folders that can be represented as their names separated by slashes, such as /Users/Documents. Using this hierarchy and format, you can change directly to a completely different folder on your Mac, as long as you enter the path correctly. As an example, you can change immediately to the main Applications folder by entering cd /Applications and pressing Return. That causes you to change to the root folder, then the subfolder Applications. The prompt should now indicate that you're in that subfolder.

TIP A special directory command can also be used with cd: two periods (..). Type **cd ..** and press Return to change to the parent folder of the current folder. For instance, if you're currently in the folder /Documents/Memos, then typing **cd ..** and pressing Return will take you to the /Documents folder.

You'll find that many of the most common command-line commands can be used while you're accessing a remote computer. They include:

mkdir Make a directory (a subfolder) within the current directory (folder). Enter mkdir Memos within the Documents folder, for instance, to create a subfolder called Memos.

TIP Unix and Unix-like operating systems weren't designed with the idea that folder names would include spaces, but it's fairly common with Mac OS X. To enter a folder name with a space at the command line, you have to jump through an odd hoop. Use a back-slash character (\\) before typing the space, as in `mkdir New\ Folder`. This will create a folder called "New Folder" with the space properly placed. In some cases you can also use quotes, as in `mkdir "New Folder"` and `cd "New Folder"`, to refer to a folder name that includes spaces. (This won't always work, as some non-Mac systems may prefer the back-slash character.)

mv Move a file to another location. For instance, `mv Memo.rtf ~/Documents/Memos` would move the file `Memo.rtf` to the Memos subfolder of the Documents folder in my home folder.

cp Copy a file. For instance, `cp Memo.rtf MemoCopy.rtf` would create a copy of `Memo.rtf` called `MemoCopy.rtf`. Or `cp Memo.rtf ~/Documents/Memos` would create a copy of `Memo.rtf` and place it, with the same name, in the Memos folder. Alternatively, `cp Memo.rtf ~/Documents/Memos/MemoCopy.rtf` would copy the file to the Memos subfolder but also rename the file as `MemoCopy.rtf`. In all cases the original stays the way it was—this is like the duplicate command in the Finder. (Be careful about how this command works; if you mistype the name of a destination folder—e.g., "Memo" instead of "Memos" in the above examples—the command will assume that you want to copy the file's contents to a *new* file with that accidental name. A file is copied to a folder only if the folder already exists.)

TIP You can use an asterisk (*) as a wildcard character with many commands in a Telnet session. Among other things, this enables you to copy more than one file at a time. For instance, the command `cp *.* ~/Documents/Memos` would copy all the files in the current folder to the Memos folder. You can also use the wildcard in other ways, such as to view only the files and folders that start with certain letters in a particular folder. For example, type `ls doc*` and press Return to see a listing of files and subfolders that start with "doc" in the current folder.

rm Remove a file. For example, `rm Memo.rtf` would delete that file if it's in the current folder.

rmdir Delete an empty directory (folder). Once you've used the `rm` command to clear out a folder, you can use `rmdir` to remove the directory (folder) from existence. For example, `rm ~Documents/Memos` will remove the subfolder Memos if it's empty.

man   Display a manual ("man") page. This is a special command that's used to give you help regarding commands in Unix-like operating systems. Type `man rmdir` and press Return, for instance, to see the man page regarding the `rmdir` command.

more   Display a text file. Using the `more` command not only displays the file but shows the More bar at the bottom of each screen of text. Press the spacebar to advance to the next screen. An example would be `more text.txt` if the file `text.txt` is in the current folder.

Other command-line commands work as well—for instance, the `chmod` and `chgrp` commands for altering file privileges will work in remote sessions, assuming your remote user account has the correct privileges for altering files. This can be useful if, for example, you're creating shell scripts on the remote computer (see Chapter 22) or you need to change privileges on a remote Web server so that others can properly view files (see Chapter 24 for more on Web server files and privileges).

So what about running actual programs? To launch a program, you can simply type its name (if it's in the current directory) and press Return. If you're launching an application that's not in the current directory (folder), you can type a full path statement to the program, such as `~/bin/myprog`, and press Return.

Note, however, that only command-line applications will launch correctly while you're accessing a Mac via Telnet or SSH; graphical applications (those that use the standard Mac OS X Aqua interface) can't be launched. There's actually a set of typical programs that ship with Unix-like applications that you can access from the command line, such as *mail, grep, finger, emacs,* and *pico.* Simply typing their names at any prompt can launch most of those programs.

As an example, you could send an e-mail message from the remote account, if desired. Type `mail` *e-mail_address*, where *e-mail_address* is the address to which you want to send the message. You'll be prompted for a subject; type one and press Return. Now, type the body of your message. When you're done, press Control+D on a blank line. If the remote computer is set up to properly send e-mail using Sendmail (most Mac OS X machines aren't set up by default, but other Unix machines may be), then the message is sent.

NOTE   Command-line applications (along with command-line commands and syntax) are discussed in more detail in Chapter 22. Also, Chapter 20 provides some commands for troubleshooting your Mac using Terminal and remote access—for instance, using the `shutdown` command to shut down a Mac that you can't otherwise access.

Logging Out

If you're connected to a remote machine via Telnet or SSH, you can log out in most cases by typing `logout` and pressing Return. You'll be returned to your original prompt in the Terminal application—you'll be back on your own Mac's disk, probably viewing your local home folder (as opposed to the remote folders you just left).

With Telnet, you may be able to use the commands `close` or `quit` to end the Telnet session and return to the Telnet prompt. The Telnet prompt suggests that the Telnet application is still running but that you're no longer connected to the remote server.

```
telnet> []
```

If you encounter the Telnet prompt, either you can enter `quit` and press Return or you can enter `open hostname.domain.tlx` to open a new Telnet connection to a remote host.

Accessing Telnet Applications

Not all remote-access connections are designed simply for managing files and running remote programs. Some are designed specifically for running a particular program, such as a database lookup application or an information server of some kind. In those cases you may still log in with a username and password, if you have them, or you may log in as an anonymous user.

You'll begin the session the same way you begin any Telnet session: At a prompt in the Terminal window, enter `Telnet hostname.domain.tlx`, which can be either an IP address or a host- and domain-name combination, where *tlx* is the three-letter extension such as `com`, `net`, or `org`. (In most cases, you'll use Telnet to access a public server, particularly if you don't have a user account on that server. If the server supports SSH, however, you can use it at the command line instead.) Press Return and the Telnet program will attempt to access the remote server. Once it's found the server, you should see a Login prompt. If you don't have an account for accessing the application, you'll likely be prompted with the correct username for entering the system; otherwise, you'll need to contact that server's administrator for assistance.

 TIP Sometimes you're asked for a terminal type when logging into a Telnet application. Choose VT100.

When you've successfully logged in, you likely won't see a command-line prompt—in most cases you'll navigate menus by typing numbers that represent commands and pressing Return (see Figure 23.3). Most Telnet applications offer a help feature of some sort, usually responding to your typing help or ? and pressing Return.

FIGURE 23.3

Here's a menu from the New York Public Library's Telnet application (nyplgate.nypl.org).

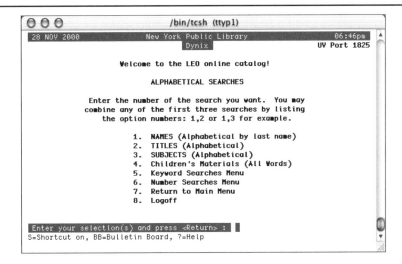

Most Telnet applications also have an exit or logout command; try typing either of those commands and pressing Return if you need to leave the session. (If typing commands doesn't work, you may have to find a numbered "logout" command.)

Sometimes a Telnet application will hang or you'll otherwise appear to be stuck. If that's the case, you can try sending an escape character to the remote computer, which will often reset it and return you to some predetermined menu. (Or it may log you out of the application and server immediately.) To send an escape character, press Control+C or select Control ➢ Send Break from the Terminal's menu.

NOTE The Terminal application window has a scroll bar and scroll arrows, which enable you to return to previous screens that you've seen during that Terminal window's session. Before you assume that a command prompt is missing, make sure you haven't accidentally scrolled back a bit in your session.

Most of the Telnet applications I come across these days are library catalogs, although government offices, universities, and some companies and other organizations use them extensively. In any case you may often find it useful to save the text of a Telnet session as a file for later review or for printing. You can do that by selecting Shell ➤ Save Text As and using the Save dialog box to save a text file record of your session. You can also use the Shell ➤ Print command to print your current session. When you select that command, you'll see the Print Attributes dialog box, where you may select the text attributes (underlining and highlighting) and text range that you'd like to print.

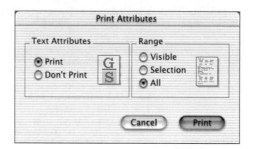

FTP via the Terminal

Another of Mac OS X's included command-line applications is an FTP client that you can use to transfer files to and from your Mac. The FTP client works a little like accessing a remote volume via Telnet or SSH, although you're never really *on* the remote server as you are with remote access. Instead, you're able to access listings from the remote server while downloading them back to your home folder (and subfolders) on your local Mac.

In order to access the remote computer, it must have an FTP server running. Depending on the type of server, you may also need to have a username and password in order to access the computer; this is particularly true if you're transferring files between machines on your local network or between yourself and a corporate or organizational FTP server.

Another type of FTP server, called a *public FTP* server or *anonymous FTP* server, doesn't require a user account and password. Instead, you enter the word anonymous as your username, and traditionally you enter your e-mail address as your password. (Most anonymous FTP servers don't actually require that you enter your e-mail address as a password, but it's considered a common courtesy.) Entering your e-mail address as a password stores the e-mail address in the FTP server's logs, so that that Mac's administrators can look up users if necessary when there's a problem or concern.

Anonymous FTP servers abound—you'll find that they're still very popular and common for trading shareware and freeware applications, as well as being available for a variety of other purposes. To get started, you can check out Apple's own anonymous FTP servers at `mirrors.apple.com`. First, though, you'll need to know how to log into a remote FTP server.

Logging In

Logging into a remote FTP server is very similar to logging in via Telnet or SSH, with one particular difference: You should use the Terminal application to first switch to the folder where you plan to store your downloaded files. At the command prompt, you can use the `cd` command to change to a different directory (folder). For instance, to change to the folder "downloads" located in your home folder, type `cd ~/downloads` and press Return. (It actually is possible to change your local folder while you're connected via FTP, but it's easier if you start by simply changing to the folder where you'd like to store downloaded files and/or where you have files that you'd like to upload.)

 NOTE At the main prompt in the Terminal, you can also use the commands discussed in the earlier section "Basic Remote-Access Commands" on your own folders. You can create directories, remove them, and so on. This is also discussed at length in Chapter 22.

Once you're in the correct folder, you're ready to log into the remote FTP server. Type `ftp remote_server`, where *remote_server* is either the IP address or the host and domain name of the FTP server to which you'd like to connect. Then press Return. The FTP command-line application is launched and will attempt to connect to the remote server. Now, if the server is found, you're ready to log in. Here's a typical prompt from a remote Mac OS X FTP server:

```
[localhost:~] todds% ftp 192.168.1.4
Connected to 192.168.1.4.
220 localhost FTP server (Version 6.00LS) ready.
Name (192.168.1.4:todds): []
```

At the Name prompt, enter your username or anonymous if the remote server supports anonymous access, and press Return. (If the name shown as part of the prompt is also the username you want to use on the remote FTP server, you can simply press Return.) You'll then see the Password prompt; enter your password and press Return. (If you're logging in anonymously, either enter your e-mail address at the Password prompt and press Return or simply press Return.)

Now you'll see a message welcoming you to the system (if it's a public server, it may be a rather long message detailing the rules, hours, and limitations of the system), and you'll be presented with the FTP> prompt. This is your indicator that you're signed into the remote server and ready to begin transferring files.

```
230- Welcome to Darwin!
230 User todds logged in.
Remote system type is BSD.
ftp> []
```

Basic FTP Commands

At the FTP> prompt, you can use the same, familiar Unix-like commands that work during Telnet sessions, such as ls (for listing the contents of remote directories) and cd (to change to a new remote directory). If you have the correct privileges, you can also use mkdir to create remote directories.

Other commands differ, however; some are similar to Telnet/SSH commands, while others specifically enable you to take special advantage of the FTP program's abilities to transfer files to and from your Mac.

For instance, two commands right up top are important to understand: ascii and binary. These commands put FTP in certain *modes*, which determine how files are transferred. If you're transferring text files or files that have been encoded using a text-encoding format (such as BinHex, MacBinary, uuencode, or base64/MIME encoding), you can type ascii and press Return to place FTP in ASCII mode. (Actually, it's in ASCII mode by default when you initially connect to most FTP servers, so you can probably skip the command unless you've previously set the mode to binary.)

 TIP Common filename extensions for textual files include .txt, .html, .bin, .hqx, .uu, and .mim.

Binary mode is used to transfer nontext files; binary files are those that use 1s and 0s to represent computer data. This includes any sort of program, document, or archive that's compressed using StuffIt or ZIP formats. If you're transferring a Word document, a PDF document, an image file, a QuickTime movie—anything that isn't in Plain Text format—you'll need to type binary at the FTP> prompt and press Return to put the server in binary mode.

Here's a look at those and the other FTP commands:

ascii   Set the file transfer type to ASCII for transferring text-based files.

binary   Set the file transfer type to support binary file transfer.

bye   End the FTP session and close the FTP program. You're returned to the main Shell prompt in Terminal.

close   End the FTP session with the remote server, but leave you at the FTP> prompt. You can then use the Open command to open a connection to a new remote server.

delete   Delete a file on the remote machine. For example, `delete memo.rtf` will delete the file `memo.rtf` on the remote server (assuming you have the file privileges to do so).

dir   Display a listing of the contents of the specified folder on the remote server. (By itself, it lists the contents of the currently selected folder; you can also type `dir` *path*, such as `dir /users/todds/documents`, to see the contents of a folder that isn't currently selected on the remote server.) Note that `dir` is a special FTP command that displays a content listing in whatever way the remote server thinks is appropriate; so the listing can vary from server OS to server OS.

get   This is the command to download a file from the remote server to your Mac. Type `get` *full_filename* and press Return to retrieve a particular file, such as `get memo.rtf` if `memo.rtf` is in the currently selected folder. (If it's not, use the `cd` command to change to that folder.) You can also type `get` *path/ filename* to download a file that isn't in the current folder, such as `get /users/todds/documents/memo.rtf`. Note that this will download the file according to the current type setting (binary or ASCII), so make sure you change the type setting before transferring the file, if necessary.

TIP   Again, the common use of spaces in Mac OS X filenames can rear its ugly head here. In many cases you should be able to use quotes with the `get` command (such as `get "My File.txt"`) when dealing with filenames that have spaces. You can also use the escape character, as in `get My\ File.txt`, and press Return.

lcd   Change the selected folder on your local machine. If the command is used by itself, you're changed automatically to your home folder. Otherwise, include a path statement, such as `lcd ~/todd/documents`, and press Return.

lpwd   Display the current folder on your local machine.

mget   This is a "multiple get" command, which enables you to download more than one file at a time. You specify the multiple files using wildcard characters.

For instance, type `mget doc*` to attempt to download all files and/or folders that start with doc. You can use `mget *.*` to download all *files* in the currently selected remote folder. You'll then see a prompt that lets you step through which files you'd like to download by typing a y or n next to each (and pressing Return after each). You can also type a and press Return to download all matching files. (A similar command, `mdelete,` can be used to delete multiple files on the remote server if you have the file privileges.)

```
ftp> mget *.*
mget Favorites.html? y
200 PORT command successful.
150 Opening ASCII mode data connection for 'Favorites.html' (15948 bytes).
226 Transfer complete.
16228 bytes received in 0.00293 seconds (5542350 bytes/s)
mget Mac-Upgrade.Com Home Page? n
mget MemoCopy.rtf? n
mget create_keychain.tiff? y
```

 TIP You can type `prompt` and press Return to toggle the level of prompting that FTP uses with your commands. If you toggle prompts off, then `mget` will automatically retrieve all files that match the wildcard items you type (and `mput` will upload all matching files).

mput This is the "multiple put" command. As with `mget`, you can use wildcards with `mput` to upload multiple files to the remote server at once (see "put"). For example, `mput *.*` would upload all files in your current local folder to the currently selected remote folder.

newer This command is identical to `get` except that it compares the modification date of the remote file to the date of the same file on your own Mac. If the file doesn't exist in your local Mac's currently selected folder, or if it does exist but it's older, the file is downloaded from the remote server. If the file exists on your local Mac but its modification date is more recent, the download doesn't occur.

open Open a new FTP remote connection. This works only from the FTP> prompt after you've issued the `close` command (or if you've launched FTP by simply typing `ftp` and pressing Return). To open a new server, type `open` *server_address*, where *server_address* is the IP address or the host name and domain of the remote server; then press Return.

progress This toggles on an active progress bar to show you the progress of downloads. (It also doesn't always work.)

put   Upload the specified file from your local Mac to the currently selected folder on the remote server. For example, type put `memo.rtf` and press Return to upload that file to the remote server. You can also specify a path, as in `put ~/documents/memos/memo.rtf,` to upload a file from a particular folder on your local Mac to the remote server. Remember that `put` uses the current setting for type (ASCII or binary), so you'll need to set it appropriately.

pwd   Display the name of the currently selected folder on the remote machine.

quit   Works just like `bye`, signing off from the remote server and closing FTP.

size   Display the size of a file on the remote server. For example, type `size memo.rtf` to see the size of that file.

That's most of them. You can see a quick listing of FTP commands by typing `help` or ? and pressing Return at the FTP> prompt. At a Shell prompt (not the FTP> prompt), you can type `man ftp` and press Return to see the man page on the FTP application, including additional commands and different ways you can use FTP and special arguments to alter the way FTP works.

To sign out of FTP, simply type `bye` or `quit` at any FTP> prompt and press Return. That's it—you're returned to the main Shell prompt in Terminal.

What's Next?

In this chapter you saw the basics of turning on remote access to your Mac via Telnet or SSH. You then saw how to connect to remote Telnet and SSH servers via command-line applications in the Terminal, as well as how to access remote applications. You also learned how to use the command-line FTP application via the Terminal window and how to access both private and public FTP sites.

In the next chapter you'll see how to turn on Mac OS X's other Internet servers: Web and FTP. You'll see how to post Web pages, add CGI scripts, and check the Web server's log files. And you'll see how to turn FTP serving on and off, check the log files, and consider some of the security implications of turning on Internet servers.

PART

V

Advanced
Mac OS X Topics

CHAPTER 24

Serving Up Web and FTP Content

In previous chapters, you've seen how to get on the Internet and access various types of servers and content. But what about creating and serving some of that content yourself? Mac OS X comes with some serious and sophisticated built-in servers that enable you to do just that. What's more, the servers are surprisingly easy to start up and work with online.

Mac OS X includes Web and FTP server capabilities. Turning them on and off is simple: Like other server functions, you access these in the Sharing pane of the System Preferences application. Managing these servers isn't much more difficult; you'll need to assign some privileges and locate the correct folders, but it's not much more difficult than any other administrative task. You'll also find special log files that enable you to see who is accessing your Mac via these Internet protocol servers.

The fact that these servers are built on top of the Darwin underpinnings of Mac OS X, however, makes them more powerful than they might seem at first blush. The Web server in Mac OS X is a version of the well-known Apache Web server, the most popular on the Internet. What that means is that it's possible—and fairly easy—for you to customize the servers with performance tweaks and additional features and settings.

In this chapter we'll also discuss the security of using these servers, which is an important consideration for almost any Mac OS X user. But once you've made your security decisions, if you've got a Mac with a direct Internet connection—or if you'd like to create an intranet for file and information sharing between your Macs—you're ready to turn on your Internet servers and get started.

Serving the Web

As mentioned, Mac OS X includes a built-in Web server based on the popular and venerable Apache Web server, an open-source Web server application that's available for most Unix and Unix-like operating systems (along with others). It's been ported to Mac OS X and, what's more, been made exceptionally easy to work with.

What Is a Web Server?

A *Web server* is an application designed to respond to requests by remote client applications (usually Web browser applications) by sending documents to those clients using the HyperText Transfer Protocol (HTTP). The client applications make the request by asking for a particular URL, which includes both the Web server's IP (or domain name–based) address and a path to the particular document that the Web browser would like to see. As you saw in Chapter 11, such URLs can be manually input by the user, or they can result from the clicking of a hyperlink. In most cases the Web server will do one of three things:

- It will send an HTML document to the client application (including any other items, such as images and embedded multimedia files that are also part of that request).

- It will process a request for an unrecognized file, which will generally result in that file being downloaded by the client application. For instance, this would work if the user clicked a link to a StuffIt archive, which would then be downloaded to the user instead of being displayed in that user's browser.

- It will process an HTML form request by passing important data to a script or program through the Common Gateway Interface (CGI). Once the data is passed to a CGI script, the server will wait for a response from that script, usually in the form of an automatically generated HTML document.

That, in a nutshell, is what a Web server does. And Mac OS X provides for all of these possibilities, enabling you to turn on the Web server and add files (HTML, image, and other downloadable files) that can be served by the Web server to remote clients. Mac OS X also offers a special folder for CGI scripts, which you can create and store so that they may be accessed by an HTML form request.

Web Serving Schemes and Security

Now that you know what a Web server does, you may wonder why you should care. One reason may be obvious—to serve files on the World Wide Web. But there are other reasons, too, that can be added to that one:

Serving on the Web   This is the most obvious reason. If you have a direct connection to the Internet and a static IP address, you can turn your Mac into a Web server. (Even if you *don't* have a static IP address, you can turn your Mac into a Web server temporarily, if necessary.) This enables you to serve HTML documents and other files to anyone with Web access.

Serving an intranet   If you have a LAN, you may wish to use the Web server to disseminate files and other information. An *intranet* is an private network that uses Web servers and other Internet-protocol servers to create an "internal Internet" of sorts. An intranet is a great means for updating your medium-to-large organization on regular news items, as well as a way to distribute Web-based forms (human resources, mailings, important documents) and to offer feedback (people can e-mail the CEO or access a chat room or bulletin board). You can serve that intranet easily using the built-in Web server features.

PART

V

Advanced
Mac OS X Topics

Cross-platform file sharing   If you need to share files on a LAN with Windows-based PCs—and you don't have third-party add-ons to make the Windows PCs compatible with Apple File Protocol servers—you can solve the problem using a Web server. Just turn on the Web server, place the files you want to share in the Web Documents directory, and access the Web server from the PCs. Now you should be able to download the files easily. (You can also use FTP to solve this problem, which could prove even easier.)

Which of the above you're capable of doing can depend, in some cases, on the type of connection you have to the Internet. For instance, if your LAN doesn't have an Internet connection at all, then only users on your local network will be able to see your Web server—and they'll do that by entering the local IP address for your Mac in their Web browser, as in `http://192.168.1.4`. That would apply for both Mac users and users of other types of computers, as long as they have access to your local IP subnet.

If you'd like to make your Web site available on the Internet itself, you'll need a publicly available IP address. This will usually be a fixed IP address, provided by your ISP. Once you have that IP address, users anywhere on the Internet will be able to enter that IP address in their Web browser to access your Mac's Web server. If the address is fixed, those users will always know how to access your Mac.

You can serve Web pages using a dynamic IP address, but it's less convenient—you'll have to tell users the address for your Web server every time you sign onto the Internet. This makes it possible to serve Web pages over modem and dial-up DSL connections. (Ideally, you'd want to limit this to single-session sharing where you call a friend or colleague and say, "Head to my IP address and download the file," or a similar scenario.)

Of course, the ideal approach for a public Web server is an actual domain name address that your users can easily remember, such as `www.mac-upgrade.com`. Getting such a domain name requires three things:

- You need to register the domain name with a domain name registration service such as Register.com or Network Solutions (`www.networksolutions.com`). Your ISP can also register a new domain name for you.

- You need a static IP address for your Mac (in most cases). If you don't have a fixed IP address, you can conceivably use a special registration service to forward Web requests to your dynamic IP address.

- DNS (Domain Name Service) computers around the world need to recognize that your domain name is associated with your static IP address.

For most of these things, you'll consult your ISP. The ISP can register your domain name, if necessary, then create a DNS record that associates your fixed IP address with that particular domain name. Once the DNS record has had a chance to replicate itself to DNS computers around the Internet (this usually takes a few days), users anywhere will be able to access your Mac by name.

Whenever your Mac has *any* IP address on the Internet, you've created a security risk, particularly if you have servers, including Web Sharing, enabled. That risk is lessened when the IP address is dynamic; if you sign onto and off the Internet and regularly get a different IP address from your ISP, you're less likely to run into any trouble.

With a fixed address, particularly if your Mac has an "always-on" connection to the Internet, you need to be especially security-conscious. Whether or not your Mac has a domain name associated with it, that fixed address makes your Mac an enticing target for hackers, crackers, or any other malicious beings on the Internet, including automated *sniffer* applications that troll the Web looking for machines that are on the Internet.

In most cases, I wouldn't recommend running a Web server with a fixed IP address from your personal computer—at least, not without a *firewall* of some sort in place. A firewall (or an Internet router with network address translation and a "virtual server" function) is designed to block all requests from the Internet other than those requesting Web pages. This is possible because Web requests generally come in on a particular Internet *port* (Port 80), enabling the firewall or router to block other types of access. Firewalls can also be configured for other, more-specific types of access blocking, including blocking of certain types of requests and attacks or blocking access from certain IP address ranges and domains.

If you do opt to use your Mac as a Web server and you don't have a firewall in place, I'd definitely recommend that you turn off other servers, such as File Sharing, FTP, and remote login. If you choose not to turn these off, then keep in mind that other Internet users may be able to access the servers in ways that you don't intend, and could conceivably gain access to your Mac and its files and applications. (They may also be able to gain access to other computers on your local network, if you have one.) That means you need to be vigilant about user accounts, passwords, and privileges on your Mac, so that anyone who *does* gain access can't do any major harm.

Turning on the Web Server

If you've decided to turn on the Web server in Mac OS X, doing so is fairly simple. First, you'll want to have set up TCP/IP networking in the Network pane, as detailed in Chapter 8. If you're planning to use your Mac as a server on the Web (as opposed to simply serving Web pages on your local network), you'll also need to configure Internet access for your Mac (see Chapter 9). Then, turning on the server is a simple matter:

1. Launch System Preferences.

2. Open the Sharing pane.

PART

V

Advanced
Mac OS X Topics

3. Click the padlock icon and sign in as an administrator (if necessary).

4. Click the Start button under Web Sharing.

That's it—you don't even have to restart for the setting to take effect. You've turned the Web server on. (Figure 24.1 shows the Sharing pane.) It will remain on until you shut down the Mac (or turn the server off); and if you shut down the Mac while the Web server is still on, the server will be restarted the next time you start up the Mac.

FIGURE 24.1

Turning on the Web server

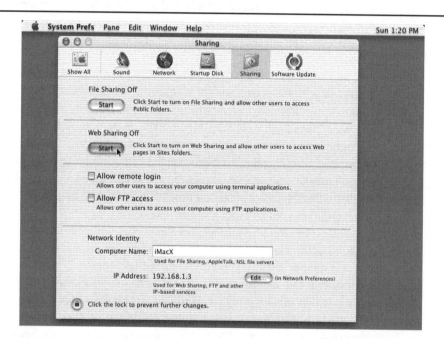

 NOTE To turn off the Web server, just click the Stop button under Web Sharing. There's no need to restart the Mac—the server is turned on and off immediately.

At the bottom of the Sharing screen, you'll see the Network Identity section, where your Mac's current IP address is displayed. That's the address at which your Mac can be reached via Web browser applications. If you'd like users to see your main Web site, tell them to enter that IP address in their Web browsers, unless you have a DNS record assigned to your Mac's fixed IP address, as discussed in the previous section. In that case, Internet-based users should be able to access your Web server by entering your domain name address. If you don't see an IP address and you use a dial-up connection to the Internet, you may need to sign onto the Internet first. Then you should see the IP address.

Serving Web Documents

Once you've got the Web server up and running, you may wish to test it. You can do that from the same Mac, if desired, or from another Mac, depending on the type of access that's available. If your Mac has a fixed IP address on the Internet, you can access it by entering that IP address in any Web browser that's also connected to the Internet. If your network (or your particular computer) has its own domain name, you can access the server by entering its server name (e.g., www) and domain name (e.g., mac-upgrade.com) together (e.g., http://www.mac-upgrade.com).

If your Web server isn't connected to the Internet (or if you're connecting to it from behind a firewall on a private IP network), you can enter the server's private IP address from either your own Mac or from another Mac on your local network. The result, if all goes well, will be the Apache default document, downloaded to your client Mac from the Web server (see Figure 24.2).

PART

V

Advanced
Mac OS X Topics

FIGURE 24.2

The default page served to a remote Mac by the Mac's built-in Web server

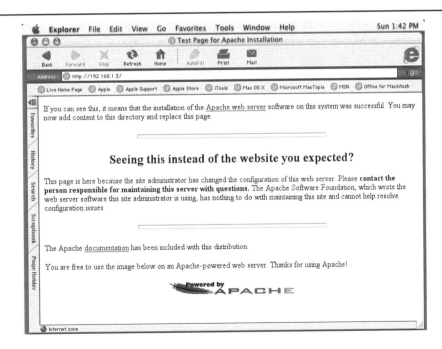

NOTE If your server name isn't www, you don't need to use www as part of the server name. For example, if my Mac's name were ads, accessing it via ads.mac-upgrade.com would cause the default Web page on the server to load, if Web Sharing is enabled.

This default page is actually somewhat informative, telling you not only what type of server (Apache) is being used to serve your Web documents, but also providing links that explain more about the server application. For instance, the page offers hyperlinks to Apache documentation, FAQs, and related Web sites. It also offers a *badge*, or small image, that you can use on your own Web site to advertise that you're using Apache. You can add that image to your own pages if desired.

 TIP A couple of additional badges can be found in the /Library/WebServer/ Documents/ folder, including GIF images called PoweredByMacOSX.gif and Powered-ByMacOSXLarge.gif. You can use these images to proclaim your loyalty to Mac OS X on your pages.

Of course, you probably don't want to display this default Apache page forever. Web pages are stored in the Documents folder inside the WebServer folder that's inside the main Library folder on your startup disk. (The full path is /Library/WebServer/Documents/, and I'll refer to it as the Web Documents folder for simplicity's sake.) So, to replace the default index page, you'll need to create and store a new index.html file in the Web Documents folder. Once you copy that file to the Web Documents folder—naming it index.html and replacing the current index.html— your new index page will be served to visitors who access your Web server.

 NOTE If you delete the index.html file that exists in the Web Documents folder and don't replace it, you'll cause the server to display the directory of files in your Web Documents folder, enabling the remote user to see and download all files in that directory. If that isn't your intention, then remember that it's important to keep an index.html document in your Web Documents folder at all times. Otherwise, you're free to delete the default pages that are stored in the Web Documents folder and replace them with your own.

You can add subfolders to your Web Documents folder, which are then accessed as part of the URL. For instance, if you add a subfolder called "files," that folder would be accessed using a URL such as `http://192.168.1.4/files/` or `http://www.mac-upgrade.com/files/`. If that subfolder has a document in it called `index.html`, that document will be sent to the user's Web browser automatically when a URL pointing to the folder is accessed. Other files can be accessed directly, such as `http://www.mac-upgrade.com/files/listing.html` or `http://www.mac-upgrade.com/files/download.sit`, and then either displayed in the Web browser (if they're HTML files or browser-compatible image files) or downloaded to the remote computer.

By default, you must have an Admin-level account to create folders within the Web Documents folder. You should note, however, that if you create a subfolder within that folder, it will likely have different privileges than the Web Documents folder itself: Instead of being writable by all Admin users, it may have write status assigned only to you, the owner.

In most cases you'll probably want to change the privileges on any subfolders that you create in the Web Documents folder so that the Admin group has write access as well. (You don't have to do this if you want to be the only user who can add files to this folder.) Here's how:

1. Select the subfolder and choose File ➢ Show Info or press ⌘+I.

2. In the Info window, select Sharing in the Show pop-up menu.

3. Using the Privileges menu, select Read & Write privileges for the Admin group (see Figure 24.3).

FIGURE 24.3

Changing the privilege level for a subfolder within the Web Documents folder

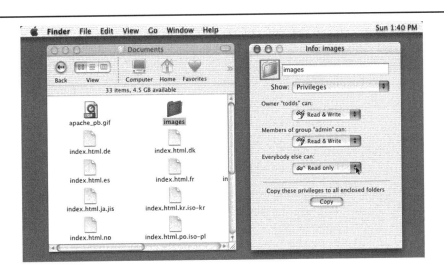

You'll also need to have Read Only privileges assigned for Everybody Else, but you should be very careful not to set Read & Write privileges for Everybody Else. If you do, others on the Internet who access your site could conceivably delete files or upload files to your server, which you definitely want to avoid, since those files could be viruses, worms, or others of malicious intent.

Adding CGIs

As mentioned earlier, one of the interesting capabilities of the Web server is that it can be extended somewhat to provide a level of interactivity via the Common Gateway Interface. CGI is a method by which applications can be run on the Web server so that your server can respond, in real time, to data and other input provided by the user. This can range from a CGI script designed to send HTML form data as an e-mail (see Figure 24.4) to an entire Web shopping application written so that user feedback (for instance, the user clicks a "buy" link on the page) results in a personalized response (that item is added to the user's virtual shopping cart).

FIGURE 24.4

One use of CGI scripts is to gather data from a simple form, then send that to a back-end application or e-mail it to a particular address.

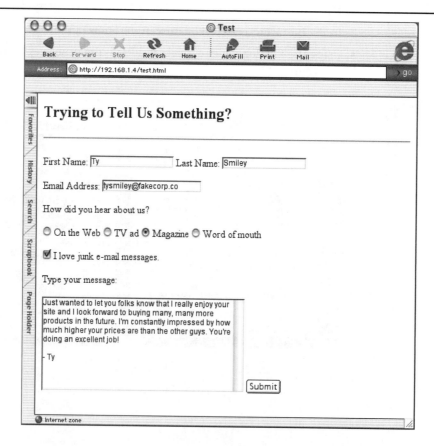

The built-in Apache Web server, by default, can support CGI scripts and applications. *CGI scripts* are small programs that are used to accept data entered by users into HTML forms, process that data, and return dynamic HTML documents to the user in response. CGI scripts (also called just "CGIs") are used for everything from accessing databases of Web documents to accepting Web-based e-commerce orders or tallying votes in an online poll. In Mac OS X, you can write CGIs in any number of languages, including Perl, AppleScript, C, Objective C, Java, and others.

 NOTE If you're creating a script in Perl and saving it to the CGI-Executables folder, you'll need to remember two things. First, you'll need to set execute privileges for that script, as detailed later in this section (as well as in Chapter 22). Second, you'll need to save the Perl script using a text editor that supports Unix line feeds for text documents; if you save the script using Mac or PC line feeds, the script probably won't execute correctly.

Writing the scripts is up to you—it's outside the scope of this book. Once you've written the script so that it properly handles data from the Web server, you can store the script in the CGI-Executables folder found inside the WebServer folder on your Mac. The CGI-Executables folder is mapped to the standard URL path `/cgi-bin/` (you don't have to use "CGI-Executables"). For instance, if you've stored a CGI script called "count" within the CGI-Executables folder, and your server is named `http://www.mac-upgrade.com`, you can access that CGI with this URL:

`http://www.mac-upgrade.com/cgi-bin/count`

The script is then executed, and, if so designed, it will return HTML feedback to the browser. As an example, Mac OS X includes a script called "test-cgi" that you can access directly on your own server just to make sure the CGI feature is functioning appropriately.

Before a script in your CGI-Executables folder will execute correctly, however, you need to change the privileges for that file. Interestingly, Mac OS X doesn't really offer a graphical tool for enabling this privilege—partly because what we're worried about here is the Unix-style *execute* privilege (in Unix parlance, privileges are *permissions*), which is something that Mac OS X's File Sharing (and, hence, the Privilege window in the Finder's Show window) doesn't really worry about.

In any case, you're going to need to dig into the Terminal application to get CGI scripts working correctly. Here's how:

1. Locate and launch the Terminal application.

2. At the command line, type **cd /Library/Webserver/CGI-Executables** and press Return. That will move you to the CGI-Executables folder.

3. Now, you're going to need to change the permissions for each CGI script that you want to make active. You'll do this using the chmod command described in Chapter 22. If you aren't logged into the root account, however, you'll also need to use the sudo command (which enables you to assume a different user account for a single command) in order to execute the chmod command. Here's what the command looks like for changing the permissions associated with the CGI script "printenv":

`sudo chmod 755 printenv`

4. After typing this command, press Return. Now, you'll see a password prompt—enter your Admin account password. If the password is correct, the command is executed. Now, proper permissions have been set and you should be able to access the CGI script. (Try `http://localhost/cgi-bin/printenv` to see if it works on your own Mac. If your Mac has a host name other than "localhost," enter it instead of *localhost* in the URL. You can also enter your IP address, if desired, as in `http://192.168.1.3/cgi-bin/printenv`.)

The *755* argument tells chmod to assign read and execute privileges for the Group and Everyone, but without giving them write privileges. This is the proper privilege level for a CGI script. Note that you'll need to perform this modification for any script you place in the CGI-Executables folder, replacing *printenv* in the command with whatever names you give the CGI scripts you place in the folder.

WARNING One issue to note when dealing with CGIs in Mac OS X is that it's fairly important to make sure you don't change the access privilege settings on the CGI-Executables folder itself unless you're sure of what you're doing. That's because changing the write privileges so that others can write to the folder is a security risk. (You don't want unauthorized users to be able to add executable scripts to your server, as they could be viruses, worms, or other malevolent bits of code. In fact, you may not even want any other Admin users to add scripts to the folder, as those scripts may have security holes in them as well.)

User Sites

By default, Mac OS X enables individual users to have a personal Web site via Web Sharing. As a user, you can place HTML documents in your Sites folder, making them accessible by simply appending *~username/* to the URL of your Web server, using the short username that's assigned to you. For instance, if my Web server's IP address were 192.168.1.3, the URL `http://192.168.1.3/~todds/` would cause the page `index.html` to be loaded from my Sites folder. By default, that page looks like Figure 24.5. Scroll down the page to see Apple's discussion of turning on the Web server and making pages available on an intranet or the Internet.

FIGURE 24.5

The default page for
an individual
Mac OS X user's site

If your Mac's Web server is accessible via a domain name address, such as www
.mac-upgrade.com, then user sites can be accessed with an address like http://
www.mac-upgrade.com/~todds/. Users are able to place new pages in their Sites folder
and to create subfolders within the Sites folder. As a user, you can't, by default, store CGI
scripts in a subfolder of your Sites folder, although you can link to CGI scripts stored
in the CGI-Executables folder, using a full URL such as http://www.mac-upgrade
.com/cgi-bin/myscript or a relative URL such as ../cgi-bin/myscript.

Again, subfolders must have the correct privileges if they are to be accessible by
other users. The subfolder should have read-only access assigned for both the Admin
group and Everyone; don't assign write privileges, as that may enable visitors to copy
and delete files in your folders.

 WARNING You should also avoid placing aliases or symbolic links in your Sites
folder, as those links may allow a user to gain access to other locations on your Mac.

Examining the Logs

Apache keeps logs of activity involving the Web server, including an access log that
tracks how often pages and files are accessed and an error log that tracks problems the
server has had with requests from Web browsers or other client software. These logs

are somewhat hidden, in the `/private/var/log/httpd/` folder, which you can't access directly in a Finder window. In order to view the logs, you'll need to use the Terminal application to "cd" to the folder, or, if you're logged into an Admin account, you can use the Go ≻ Go to Folder command in the Finder to move directly to that folder.

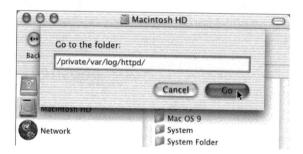

In the folder you'll find two log files, `access_log` and `error_log`. The `access_log` keeps track of every "hit" that your Web server receives, while the `error_log` makes a note of every problem that the Web server encounters.

Now, the best plan is to copy the log files to another location (in the Terminal, use the `cp` command), preferably in your home folder hierarchy, where you can analyze the Web site traffic and problems that have been logged to those files. (You don't want to open the files for viewing while they are still actively being used as the log files.) If you'd like to see the raw contents of the `access_log` file, for instance, drag the copy's icon to a text editor such as TextEdit, which enables you to view information about recent access to your Web server (see Figure 24.6).

Viewing the error log directly can be somewhat informative, but you may quickly find that viewing the access log directly in a text editor doesn't do you much good. Instead, it's generally more useful to use a special application to view the access log. Third-party applications are available that can process the log and return more meaningful statistics to you, generally via an automatically generated HTML document. The result gives you a summary of access to your site and a better idea of some relevant statistics, such as which pages were accessed the most and on which days of the week or month.

 TIP One of the more popular tools, analog, is currently available for use in the Classic environment and may well be ported to Mac OS X. See `http://summary.net/soft/analog.html` for details and downloading. A command-line version of analog has been ported to Darwin (Mac OS X's Unix-like underpinnings) by Chris Pepper, the author of Chapter 22; see that chapter for details.

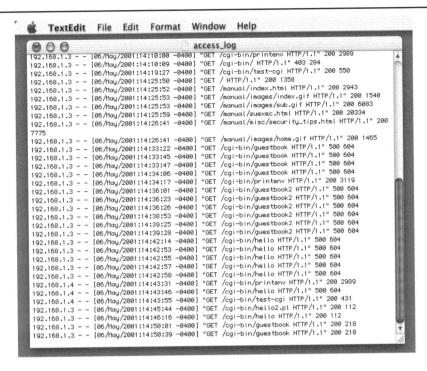

FIGURE 24.6

*A quick look at the
Apache access log*

Another important step in dealing with your Apache logs is to *rotate* them occasionally. By default, logs are rotated automatically, but you may occasionally find that a log file has become very large and that you'd like to start over again with a fresh file.

Rotating the logs is essentially a process whereby you remove the current log file(s), ideally by moving them to another folder on your Mac, then restart the server so that the log files are re-created and begun again. This is important to do occasionally because the larger the log files become, the more inefficient they are. Depending on how busy your Web server is, the log files can grow to many megabytes—even gigabytes—in size. So it's a good idea to rotate them on a regular basis. Here's how:

1. Log into your Mac so that you have the proper privileges to move and delete the log files. (This will usually require a root login, unless you intend to use the sudo command in the Terminal.)

2. Launch System Preferences, open the Sharing pane, and click the Stop button under Web Sharing to turn off the Web server.

3. Open the /private/var/log/httpd/ folder and move the files access_log and error_log to another folder on your Mac. (If this only duplicates the files instead of moving them, you should also delete the original log files by dragging

PART

V

**Advanced
Mac OS X Topics**

them to the Trash. Double-check the copied files and make sure they were successfully duplicated, however, before deleting the originals, or you'll lose that log data for future analysis.)

4. In System Preferences, turn Web Sharing back on.

As a result of turning the Web server back on, it's started up and new log files are created in the /private/var/log/httpd/ folder. Those new log files begin with the first entry and will slowly, once again, gain in size as new access and error messages are added. You'll need to check in occasionally and rotate them regularly, depending on how busy your Web server gets.

The Apache Configuration File

If you decide to dig deeper into the customization of Apache, you'll most likely do so in the Apache configuration file. This is the file read by Mac OS X's file server whenever it starts up, receiving its preferences and settings. It has a decidedly "Unixy" flavor, but you'll get used to it after a little experience.

 TIP You can read about the Apache configuration file in numerous Apache and Unix-oriented books and at Web sites (for instance, www.apache.org) dedicated to discussing Apache and how it can be configured. For Mac-specific Apache discussion, I've found www.macosxhints.com to be a great place to find interesting tweaks and tricks, including such things as tweaking Apache for speed and for password-protecting documents and subfolders on your Web sites.

The configuration file is stored in the folder /private/etc/httpd/ and it's named httpd.conf. Unless you're logged into the root account, you can't point and click to this folder in the Finder; instead, you'll need to open a Terminal window and use the cd command to access the folder. (With an Admin account, you can also use the Go ➤ Go to Folder command in the Finder and enter **/private/etc/httpd/** in the Go To Folder dialog sheet.)

Once there, you should copy the httpd.conf file to another folder on your hard disk (probably somewhere in your home folder) before attempting to alter it. This gives you a chance to look at it and play with it without potentially messing up the working version.

Drag the copied file to TextEdit or another graphical text editor that's capable of saving documents with Unix line feeds. Or, at the command line in Terminal, type **pico httpd.conf** to edit the file in the pico editor.

The configuration file is well documented, and you'll likely find that you'll get a sense of what some things do just by reading through it. You should absolutely avoid changing things in the file that you don't understand (particularly if you plan to implement this configuration file at some point). In most cases, working within the configuration file involves adding and removing the # sign in front of commands to enable or disable them. The # sign is the *comment* character for the log files (as it is in shell and Perl scripting), so placing the # sign in front of a configuration line effectively turns that line off. If there's no sign in front of a setting, then it's activated.

```
#
# ServerType is either inetd, or standalone.  Inetd mode is only supported on
# Unix platforms.
#
ServerType standalone
```

The other thing you'll often do in the configuration file, if you're customizing things, is change values. Some of the configuration lines in the file have a range of numerical values, while others have Boolean values of On or Off. In most cases, the commented description that precedes a configuration line should make the range or type of acceptable values clear.

Once you've edited the configuration file, you can save it. To replace the current Apache configuration file, you'll need to either log into the root account (if enabled) or use the sudo command at the Terminal command line to copy the file to /private/etc/httpd/. Here's how:

1. Open the Sharing pane of System Preferences and click Stop under Web Sharing to stop the Web server.

2. In /private/etc/httpd/, rename the current apache.conf file to apache.conf.myback or something similar. It's important to do this so that you can recover the current, working apache.conf file if necessary. (At the command line, if you're not in the root account, type **cd /private/var/httpd** and press Return; then type **sudo mv apache.conf apache.conf.*myback*** and press Return again. You may be asked for your password—enter it and press Return.)

3. Copy your altered copy of apache.conf to /private/etc/httpd/, making sure to name it apache.conf exactly.

4. Restart the Web server by opening the Sharing pane, and click the Start button under Web Sharing.

That's it. Apache will restart, read the new apache.conf file, and, hopefully, start up with your new setting and preferences intact. To make sure everything went well,

PART
V

Advanced
Mac OS X Topics

you can take a look at the Apache `error_log` file discussed earlier in the section "Examining the Logs."

 NOTE The default Apache configuration is stored in a file called `apache.conf` `.default`. If you ever need to revert Apache's configuration to its original (for instance, if you mess up the configuration file you're customizing), you can simply shut down Web Sharing, copy this file to `apache.conf` (`cp apache.conf.default apache.conf`), and turn Web sharing back on.

Serving FTP

Mac OS X also features a built-in FTP, or File Transfer Protocol, server, which enables it to share files using the Unix-standard method of logging into and out of individual computers. In a way, FTP is very similar to Apple File Protocol (AFP), in that it enables you to use a username and password to log into a remote computer and copy files to and from that remote computer, according to the file privileges you have on the remote computer.

One real difference is that FTP is a multi-platform standard that's commonly used over the Internet as well as on a LAN; although AFP can be used in the same way, it's primarily used for Mac-to-Mac connections on a LAN or over the Internet. Another difference is that you can't mount FTP volumes on your desktop as you can AFP volumes. Instead, you'll generally use either a third-party FTP application (such as those discussed in Chapter 11) or Mac OS X's built-in Terminal (discussed in Chapter 23) to access remote FTP servers.

Turning FTP On and Off

As for turning your own Mac into an FTP server, the decision is up to you (assuming you have administrator or root access to your Mac). Once the server is enabled, anyone with an account on your Mac can access the Mac using an FTP client application. Once that user has gained access, they can read and write files according to their file privileges, exactly as if they were physically sitting at your Mac. (The user cannot execute applications on your Mac, however—that's reserved for Telnet or SSH access, which is discussed in Chapter 23.)

WARNING Turning on FTP access is a potential security risk, as it opens up your Mac to remote access over a network, via either your LAN or the Internet (or both) if your Mac is networked to other computers. By default, Mac OS X's FTP doesn't allow anonymous or guest access via FTP, so the risk is limited to the possibility that a remote user will "crack" the password of an existing user account. As always, encourage your users (and yourself) to use difficult-to-guess passwords. Also, if you have a fixed IP address and your Mac isn't guarded by a firewall or similar router protection, consider carefully whether it's appropriate to turn on FTP access. Finally, you should make sure that you haven't created a user called "ftp" in the Users pane of System Preferences, since creating such a user could allow anonymous FTP access to your Mac.

The process of turning on FTP access is simple:

1. Open the System Preferences application.

2. If necessary, launch the Network pane and configure your Mac for TCP/IP and, if appropriate, Internet access (see Chapters 8 and 9).

3. If TCP/IP access is configured, open the Sharing pane.

4. Click the padlock icon and sign in as an administrator (if necessary).

5. Click to place a check mark next to Allow FTP Access.

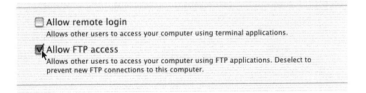

FTP access is actually turned on immediately; if you have no further business in the System Preferences application, you can close it. You needn't even restart your Mac—once FTP access is activated, the Mac can immediately be accessed by remote FTP client applications.

 NOTE Other File Sharing settings aren't relevant to FTP access, even though the File Sharing Start/Stop button appears in the Sharing pane. If FTP access is turned on, files can be accessed by remote users (according to their file privileges) regardless of the File Sharing state. Note that file and folder privileges are relevant, however.

Once FTP is turned on, remote users, including your own account, can access this Mac using an FTP client elsewhere on your LAN. If your Mac is connected to the Internet and has a fixed IP address, you can use an FTP client to log into it from anywhere on the Internet. Just launch the FTP application and enter your Mac's IP address or, if appropriate, the machine name, domain name, and three-letter domain extension. (Chapter 11 discusses FTP clients in more detail, and Chapter 23 discusses using the Mac OS X Terminal to access FTP servers.)

 WARNING FTP usernames and passwords sent to your Mac from a regular FTP application are sent in "clear text," meaning they could conceivably be intercepted and read easily because they aren't encrypted. At the time of this writing, Mac OS X doesn't currently support more secure methods of FTP (such as SFTP), but it may in the future. Check Apple's Web site and technical information for updates.

One account isn't allowed to access the Mac remotely: the root account, if it's enabled. You can't sign in as root via an FTP client—which is a good thing, because it means that no one can have root's file privileges and access the Mac from a distance. If it's you who is logged into your Mac, however, don't forget to sign out of your FTP application whenever you leave it unattended, just to make sure that unauthorized users can't get even limited access to your Mac remotely.

To turn the FTP server off, simply reopen the Sharing pane, log in as an administrator via the padlock icon (if necessary), and click to remove the check mark next to Turn on FTP Access. When you uncheck the server, it's immediately turned off and further access by remote FTP applications is denied.

Accessing FTP Logs

The FTP logs, like the Web Sharing logs, are stored away in the /private/var/log/ folder on your hard disk, but the FTP log is more easily accessible because you can read it using Console. Launch Console (located in the Utilities folder inside the Applications folder) and choose File ➢ Open Log. In the Open dialog box that appears, select ftp.log and click Open. You'll see the FTP log appear in the Console window.

```
                              ftp.log
May  7 15:48:13 localhost ftpd[934]: connection from 192.168.1.2
May  7 15:48:13 localhost ftpd[934]: FTP LOGIN FAILED FROM 192.168.1.2, todds
May  7 15:48:17 localhost ftpd[935]: connection from 192.168.1.2
May  7 15:48:17 localhost ftpd[935]: FTP LOGIN FROM 192.168.1.2 as todds
May  7 15:49:15 localhost ftpd[943]: connection from 192.168.1.2
May  7 15:49:16 localhost ftpd[943]: ANONYMOUS FTP LOGIN REFUSED FROM 192.168.1.2
May  7 15:49:36 localhost ftpd[945]: connection from 192.168.1.2
May  7 15:49:36 localhost ftpd[945]: FTP LOGIN FROM 192.168.1.2 as alex
```

In the Console window you can view the log file, which shows you successful and unsuccessful attempts to access your Mac via FTP. If you'd like to view the file at the command line, first type **cd /private/var/log/** and press Return; then type **cat ftp.log** or **more ftp.log** and press Return again to view the file. (If you plan to work with the file any more than simply viewing it, you should probably copy it to a folder within your home folder, where you can analyze it with third-party applications and so on.

What's Next?

In this chapter you saw how to activate the Web server that's built into Mac OS X, as well as how to manage that server's logs and to add CGI scripts to augment the server's functionality. You also learned how to enable the FTP server and to check its log file.

In the next chapter you'll see a few server add-ons you can add to Mac OS X, including the QuickTime Streaming Server and Samba, a server that enables Mac OS X to share files with Microsoft Windows–based computers. You'll also see some interesting third-party applications available for extending Mac OS X's Internet- and LAN-serving capabilities.

PART

V

Advanced
Mac OS X Topics

CHAPTER 25

Adding Internet and Network Services

As you saw in Chapter 24, Mac OS X has a few built-in Internet services, such as the Apache Web server and the ability to act as an FTP server. Likewise, Chapter 8 covers the basics of creating connections between Macs and sharing files using TCP/IP and personal File Sharing.

If you'd like to go beyond those services, you can do so. A number of third-party applications are available that enable you to augment Mac OS X's ability to serve files remotely. Those capabilities include free (and sometimes open-source) add-ons such as Apple's QuickTime Streaming Server and Samba for sharing files with Microsoft Windows–based computers. Also, if you've got some cash to throw around, you can consider some wonderful server application packages from commercial third-party publishers.

In this chapter we'll take a look at a few server add-ons, including what they do and what it'll take to install them.

QuickTime Streaming Server

One of the more exciting Internet server options for Mac OS X is the QuickTime Streaming Server (QTSS), which makes it possible for you to use your Mac to serve QuickTime movies that arrive and play "on the fly" in your recipient's browser. This makes it possible to send longer movies over the Internet without requiring the recipient to wait for the entire download before the movie can be viewed.

The streaming server takes portions of a QuickTime movie, separates them into packets, and transmits those packets over the Internet to the QuickTime Player. When the packets arrive, they're pieced back together by the QuickTime Player, which then plays them as a QuickTime movie.

QTSS can be used for two different types of streaming—a unicast or a multicast. A *unicast* is a simple situation where a single stream is sent from the server to the client. For instance, a user has requested to see an archived QuickTime movie, and clicks a link to that movie. The movie is then sent to the user by QTSS over the Internet.

In a *multicast*, multiple client computers receive the same QuickTime movie. In some cases this may even be a live broadcast, where you are using one Mac to capture audio or video, then using QTSS to send that stream to multiple clients. QTSS can handle both of these tasks, although it will require more setup and equipment (microphones, cameras, and a second Mac, at a minimum) before you can create a multicast.

NOTE Apple makes QTSS available for other platforms as well, including computers running the open-source (non-Aqua) version of Darwin. QTSS is also offered as open-source software, so developers are free to modify it and even port it to other operating systems, including the earlier Mac OS and Linux.

Installing QTSS

Before you can use QuickTime Streaming Server with Mac OS X, you'll need to install it. You can download QTSS from Apple's Web servers; head to `http://asu.info` `.apple.com` and search for "QuickTime Streaming Server." Once you've downloaded the archive file, it should expand itself (or you can drag it to StuffIt Expander to expand it). You'll then have the package file available, which you can double-click to begin the installation process.

Here's how the rest of the installation goes:

1. On the first screen of the QuickTime Streaming Server installation assistant, you'll be asked to authenticate as an administrator if you aren't currently logged into the root account. Click the padlock and enter an administrator's name and password. (The installation adds files to the main Library hierarchy on the drive, so you need an administrator account to install those files.)

2. Once you're authenticated, you'll see the Introduction screen. Click the Continue button to move to the next screen.

3. Now you'll see the Read Me screen. Scroll through it to learn the latest issues regarding QTSS, including any troubleshooting tips or known problem areas. When you've finished reading, click the Continue button.

4. Read the Software License agreement and, if you agree with it, click Continue. A dialog sheet will appear from the title bar, asking if you disagree or agree with the license. If you agree, click the Agree button to move on.

5. On the Select Destination screen, select the hard disk where you'd like QTSS installed. In most cases you'll select your main Mac OS X disk. Once you've selected a disk, click Continue.

6. Click Install to perform the basic installation. When the installation is finished, click the Close button to exit the QTSS installer.

PART

V

Advanced
Mac OS X Topics

Configuring QTSS

Once QTSS is installed, you might be surprised to see that you actually don't have any applications or control panels to access. Instead, you'll configure QTSS using your Web browser. To access the configuration screen, enter the URL of the server where QTSS is installed, plus the port number 1220, as in `http://192.168.1.4:1220` or `http://www.ourserver.com:1220`. You'll see a dialog box requesting a username and password; in current versions, the default user ID is **streamingadmin** and the password is **default**. (If these don't work, consult the Read Me screen in the Installer. Note also that you'll want to change the user ID and password later.) Type those and click OK. If the username and password are accepted, the Server Snapshot page will appear, as shown in Figure 25.1.

TIP Because you access the QTSS administration screen from a Web browser, you can access and alter the server from anywhere on the Internet. This also means that you should keep the administrator account and password secret. Note that they're *not* the same as the root account and password for the rest of your Mac OS X system; it's advised that you use a different password for the QTSS administrator account.

FIGURE 25.1

The Server Snapshot page shows you the current status, settings, and log settings for QTSS.

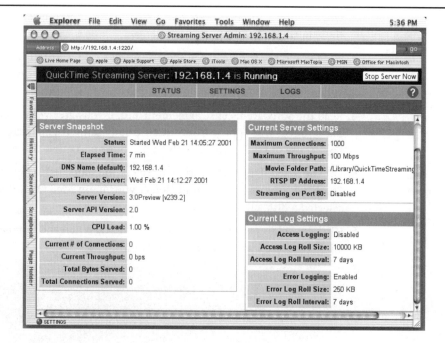

At the top of the page, you'll see a status line that includes the current address of the server and its status—whether or not it's running. You'll also see the Stop Server Now (or Start Server Now) button, which enables you to start and stop the server with a simple click.

 TIP In the top-right corner, just beneath the Stop/Start Server Now button, is a small question mark icon. Click that icon to access the QTSS Help system.

The lower portion of the screen contains some panes of information, including these:

Server Snapshot Here you'll find information about the current status of the server, including when it was started, how long it has been running, its current IP address, and the current time on the server. You'll also be able to check other information, such as what portion of your Mac's CPU resources the server is requiring (the *CPU load*) and information about the current number of connections, the *throughput* (the amount of data being served to those connections), and totals of how much data and how many connections have been served.

Current Server Settings In this section you'll see the current settings for the server, including the maximum number of connections allowed, the maximum throughput allowed, the current path for movie documents, and whether or not streaming is allowed on Port 80.

Current Log Settings Here you'll be able to quickly see how the server is keeping its *log files* (records of all transactions, stored in special files) and how those files are being managed.

To change settings, see additional information, or make preference choices, click one of the three buttons that appear immediately below the status line: Status, Settings, and Logs.

Check Status

Click the Status button, and two new options appear beneath it—Server Snapshot and Connected Users. Since you're currently viewing the Server Snapshot page, you'll notice it isn't a hyperlink; so it can't be clicked. If you'd like to change the display to show how many users are currently connected, click the Connected Users link.

PART

V

Advanced
Mac OS X Topics

Once you've chosen this link, the Connected Users page is loaded. This page is helpful for learning more about the people who use your server. You can see how many people are taking advantage of your server, what sort of connections they're getting (under the Bit Rate column, which shows the *bits per second* level at which they're receiving data), whether a large percentage of packets are being lost, and what movies or streams the users are currently viewing.

On this page, you can set two options:

Number of URL entries to display   You can use this pop-up menu to limit the number of IP addresses that are resolved, via a DNS server, to the actual URLs they represent. The more IP addresses that are resolved, the longer it will take to update and refresh the page.

Update interval for this page   Use this pop-up menu to determine how often the page will refresh itself. The more often it refreshes, the more current the information will be. At the same time, constantly refreshing the page could slow down your ability to take in all the information, and page updates may be slow if many users are connected.

You can sort the display by selecting either Ascending or Descending from the Sort Order pop-up menu. Then, within the list of connected users itself, you can click any of the topic headings to change the column by which the entries are sorted.

To return to the Server Snapshot status screen, click its hyperlink at the top of the page. To change other settings and preferences, click the Settings or Logs buttons.

Change General Settings

Click the Settings button below the status line, and you'll see a new page: General Settings (see Figure 25.2). On this page you can make some basic decisions about your server, including which directory to use for movies, the name of the streaming server, and some other low-level settings.

Here's a quick look at the settings on this page:

Movies Directory   In this entry box, you can edit the path to the folder where movie files are to be stored. Note that, according to Apple, anything in that folder is available for streaming, so you may want to avoid placing aliases, folders, and other items in the movies folder, unless you intend to stream them. You probably won't need to change this location.

Server Name   You can give the server a distinct name here, if desired.

Streaming on Port 80   If enabled, users will be able to access the streams on the HTTP port—the port that's typically used for Web pages. This can be important if the user is behind a firewall that doesn't allow access to other ports for other types of data.

FIGURE 25.2

The General Settings for QuickTime Streaming Server

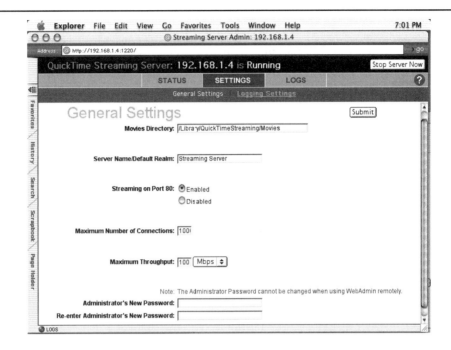

Maximum Number of Connections   You can limit the number of connections so that the server doesn't become bogged down or overloaded by users viewing streaming movies. By default, the number is 1,000, but you may want to experiment with that, particularly if your Mac is used for other tasks. When the maximum number of connections is reached, subsequent attempts to connect by users will result in an error message, until another user stops their connection.

Maximum Throughput   This is another setting you can make to ensure that QTSS doesn't bring your Mac to its knees. Setting a limit for the Mbps number will help your Mac cope with large loads. You could set the maximum throughput to 10Mbps, for instance, to limit the amount of data that is dedicated to streaming. Of course, the number you choose for this setting would depend on the type of connection your server has to the Internet (or the bandwidth of your local area network, if that's where your streaming client computers will be).

Administrator's Password   Here is where you can change the password to something more secure than "default." As noted on the screen, you can change the administrator's password only by accessing the server from a Web browser that is physically running on that same Mac. You can't access it remotely. To change the password, enter the new password twice in the two entry boxes provided.

Whenever you make any change on the General Settings page, you have another step before that change takes effect: You have to click the Submit button on that page. Once you click Submit, the changes will be made immediately; there's no need to stop, start, or restart the server.

Change Log Settings

Below the Settings button and next to the General Settings hyperlink, you'll find another hyperlink, Logging Settings. Click it, and the page will change to display the Log Settings page, as shown in Figure 25.3.

These settings essentially enable you to decide whether or not you want to log errors and access and how those log files should be *rolled*. After a certain amount of time or after the file reaches a certain size, you can have QTSS automatically rename the log file, store it as an archive, and then start a fresh, new log file. This approach keeps the file from becoming too unwieldy, which could make it difficult to read, slow down the server, and increase the possibility that the file will become corrupted.

To enable one of the types of logging, click the Enabled radio button in that log's pane. You can specify how often, in days, the log file should be rolled into a new file or how large, in kilobytes, the file should be allowed to become before it is rolled. Then click the Submit button to send the changes and update the server.

FIGURE 25.3

The Log Settings page

NOTE Log files can be viewed within the Web interface by clicking the Logs button under the status bar at the top of the page. In case you'd like to access the logs directly, they're stored in /Library/QuickTimeStreaming/Logs by default.

Serving Streaming Movies

You can serve two types of streaming movies—broadcast movies and archived movies. Archived movies are far easier, since they simply need to be saved in a certain format and then placed in the movies folder. From there, you give your users a URL (or enable them to click a hyperlink) for accessing the movie stream with their QuickTime Player. Broadcast movies are tougher, since they require additional software and, usually, additional hardware, such as a second Mac and recording hardware (cameras or microphones). They also require special software that can receive the audio and/or video in real time, process it, and send it on to the Mac that's running QTSS.

Serving Archived Movies

If you plan to serve archived QuickTime movies to your visitors, the process is really pretty simple. First, you need to create and save the movie in the correct format. For streaming, that means saving the movie as a *hinted movie*. A hinted movie includes information that QTSS can use to properly split the movie into packets and send it to remote users.

 NOTE QuickTime Pro Player is part of the QuickTime Pro upgrade, which requires a small payment (currently $30). You can upgrade your current version of QuickTime to QuickTime Pro at Apple's QuickTime Web site: www.apple.com/quicktime/. QuickTime Pro is discussed in Chapter 15.

QuickTime Pro Player can create hinted movies from regular movies, as can most commercial QuickTime movie applications. (Although, at the time of this writing, none are available for Mac OS X, a number are available for Mac OS 9.*x*.) In Quick-Time Pro Player, you can simply open an existing QuickTime movie, then select File ➤ Export. In the Save Exported File As dialog box, select Movie to Hinted Movie from the Export pop-up menu.

PART

V

Advanced
Mac OS X Topics

Save exported file as...

Save As: | stream.mov |

Where: | 📁 Documents |

Export: | Movie to Hinted Movie | Options...

Use: | Default Settings |

Cancel   Save

Once you've selected Movie to Hinted Movie and given the movie a name, you can click Save to save the movie. Now you have a hinted movie, which you can move to the folder that you've set for QTSS movies (if you didn't already save it there when exporting).

 TIP Before saving your movie, you can click the Options button to dig deeper into the options for exporting to a hinted movie. One option in particular, Optimize Hints for Server, is recommended for best performance, although you should be aware that it can make the hinted movie file much larger than the original movie file.

After you've placed the hinted movie in the QTSS movies folder, your users can access it remotely (assuming the server is turned on). The URL for accessing the movie is rtsp://*www.yourserver.com/movie.mov*, where *www.yourserver.com* is the URL to your server and *movie.mov* is the name of the movie file to be streamed. Note the use of *rtsp://* as the protocol for accessing the streaming movie. (It's the Real Time Streaming Protocol, which is how such streamed movies are sent over the Internet.)

So how do your users access the movie? You can create a link on a Web page that includes that full URL to the movie, which should cause the movie to be loaded in your user's QuickTime Player, assuming the user's computer is configured correctly. The user can also enter the URL directly, using the File ➢ Open URL command in the QuickTime Player. This brings up the Open URL dialog box, where the user can type the URL for the movie:

Open URL

Enter an Internet URL to open:

| rtsp://movies.mac-upgrade.com/hinted.mov |

Cancel   OK

TIP You can also *embed* a QuickTime movie in a Web page so that the QuickTime plug-in for Web browsers becomes responsible for playing back the movie. To learn more about embedding QuickTime movies, see Apple's QuickTime tutorials page at `www.apple.com/ quicktime/products/tutorials/`.

Serving Broadcasts

If your goal is to serve live broadcasts from your QuickTime Streaming Server machine, you'll need to take some special steps that fall outside the scope of this quick introduction. Generally, you'll need to have software, usually on another computer, that's designed to accept input from a video camera or microphone while the live broadcast is happening. (Sorenson Broadcaster, `www.sorenson.com`, is one such application.) Then the broadcast software is used to create a Session Description Protocol (SDP) file, which is stored in your QTSS movies folder. Once that file is on your server, you tell users to direct their QuickTime Player software to connect to your server using the File ➤ Open URL command. They enter a URL like `rtsp://www.yourQTserver.com/livefile`, where *www.yourQTserver.com* is the address for your server and *livefile* is the name of the SDP file that's stored there. (You could also link to this file in a Web page, if you'd like to make it more convenient for your users.) From there, the broadcast software receives the signal and sends it to QTSS, which then broadcasts it to all users who are connected to that SDP file.

Samba: Services for Windows

Another area of interest for Mac OS X users might be networking with Windows machines. Most Microsoft Windows–based computers work with the Server Message Block (SMB) protocol for sharing files and print services. Samba is the open-source version of these services, which you can add to your Mac OS X machine, giving it the ability to act as a server for Windows clients. Those clients can then access your Mac through their regular networking control panels.

The nice thing about Samba is that it's available for free, enabling you to implement Windows sharing without additional cost. The less-than-nice thing about Samba, though, is that configuring it and getting it to work with Mac OS X is difficult. If you're not interested in performing all the installation and configuration steps yourself, you might opt instead to buy Apple's Mac OS X Server package. Apple has done its own port of Samba, including an Aqua-based interface for making it easier to serve files to Windows clients. But if you'd like to avoid that expense, you can dig in and add Samba to Mac OS X yourself.

 NOTE Third-party applications are also available to do the opposite of what we're discussing here—enabling your Mac to access a Windows server computer. A popular open-source option is Sharity Light, offered by Objective Development (www.obdev.at), which also offers a commercial version that's called simply Sharity. Likewise, Thursby Software, makers of MacSOHO and DAVE for older Mac OS versions, has announced DAVE for Mac OS X, which is also a peer-to-peer networking client that you install on the Mac to access services from Windows machines.

Installing Samba

Installing Samba isn't much tougher than installing an Apple-provided server such as QuickTime Streaming Server. Derick Jan-Hartman has ported Samba to Mac OS X, and his version, along with installation instructions, is available at http://xamba .sourceforge.net/sambax/index.shtml. From his Web site, it appears that Jan-Hartman is also working on a GUI interface for Samba (called Xamba), which may be available by the time you read this.

Once you have the Mac binary of Samba (which you can download from the site mentioned above), you need to unarchive it, if it isn't unarchived automatically. Double-click the file to launch StuffIt Expander and automatically decompress the archive. If that doesn't work, you can drag the file to StuffIt Expander. When Expander is finished, you'll have a new Samba disk image.

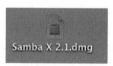

Double-click the disk-image icon to mount the image on your desktop. You'll see the Samba window appear in the Finder, including two Read Me files and the Samba package file. Once you've read the Read Me files, double-click the Samba.pkg file to launch the Package Installer. The Samba package is installed in the same way that any Package Installer application is installed—you'll authenticate, read the Read Me documents and license agreement, select a target disk for installation, and then click the Install button. Once the software is installed, you can click the Close button to close the Package Installer.

Configuring the Server

The next step is to configure the server. You can do this in one of two ways. The hard way is to directly edit the file smb.conf, which is located at /usr/local/samba/lib/smb.conf on your Mac. To do so, you'll want to open a Terminal window, then copy the above file to your desktop or another location. (For instance, you could type the command cp /usr/local/samba/lib/smb.conf ~/Desktop and press Return to copy the file to your desktop.) Then open TextEdit or a similar text editor, load the configuration file, and edit the file. (You could also use pico at the command line if you're comfortable with it as a text editor. See Chapter 22 for more on pico.) When you've finished editing the configuration file, you can save your changes and then copy the changed file back to the original location. (I'd also recommend that you keep a backup of the original configuration file somewhere safe so that you can replace the edited configuration file in the future if necessary.)

What you put in that configuration file is the next problem; you can find instructions for those settings at the main Web site for the Samba project (www.samba.org). Choose a local server, then locate the links to Samba FAQs, documentation, and forums for discussion and help.

 NOTE At the time of this writing, sharing printers via Samba seems to be a little beyond the scope of this book, if such sharing is possible at all. The problem is that Samba relies on the file printcap, which is a standard Unix file for locating printer information. However, Apple's use of NetInfo for storing printer information means that the printcap file is circumvented and regular printers don't appear to be added to that file. You'll often find, however, that you can still share a printer on a network without a server like Samba, particularly if the printer is accessible via TCP/IP and/or if the printer has a built-in print server.

Accessing SWAT

The easier way to configure Samba is to use SWAT (Samba Web Administration Tool), a browser-based configuration application that's included with the Samba distribution that we're discussing here.

There's one important trick to using SWAT: You need to log into SWAT using the root account on your Mac. By default, the root account isn't even enabled in Mac OS X, but it's required before you can see the full functionality of the SWAT interface. To enable the root account, refer to Chapter 20, which walks you through the steps in detail. (You'll launch NetInfo Manager, authenticate, and then choose Domain ➢ Security ➢ Enable Root User.)

Once you have the root account enabled, you're ready to access SWAT and configure Samba. To launch SWAT, open your Web browser and access your own Mac's Web server at Port 901, as in `http://www.myserver.com:901`, or `http://192.168.1.4:901` if you want to use the server's IP address. You'll be asked for a username and password; log in as root. (If you log in using another administrator account, you won't see the full functionality of SWAT.) Now you'll see the SWAT browser screen, shown in Figure 25.4.

FIGURE 25.4

Configuring Samba from the SWAT browser interface

Once you're logged into SWAT, you'll see a number of buttons across the top of the screen, each of which leads you to a new page of options and settings. In essence, SWAT breaks down the process of editing the `smb.conf` file into multiple Web pages with HTML forms, controls, and links to definitions and help for each entry. The pages are fairly full-featured, enabling you to set options, check status, and even get help on individual items. In this section we'll walk through the basic setup of the server, and you'll see each of the pages offered by SWAT.

Home

Select this button to see the main welcome screen for SWAT. For the most part, it's useful for seeing different Web-based documentation links for the Samba installation, as well as information about the different command-line tools that are included with the Samba distribution.

 TIP One of the last links on the home page points you to *Using Samba*, the free, online version of a popular and useful book written by Robert Eckstein, David Collier-Brown, and Peter Kelly. If you're serious about Samba, you'll find this a convenient resource while you're working in SWAT. If you'd prefer an actual, bound book, try Sybex's *Linux Samba Server Administration* (Craig Hunt Linux Library) by Roderick W. Smith.

View

You'll most likely want to start getting to know SWAT by clicking the View button, which presents an overview of the current setup of your server. If you've just installed everything, you'll see only a single entry, *[global]*. It will show the current name assigned to this Mac and the version number of the server. If you'd like, you can also view the entire configuration file by clicking the Full View button on the View page.

As you update other items throughout SWAT, you can return to this page to get a sense of the overall changes you've made to the settings.

Globals

On the Globals page, you can set a number of global variables, including perhaps the most important setting, the workgroup name. If you don't already have a Windows workgroup that this server will be part of, you should enter a new workgroup name here, which you'll use to configure your Windows clients. You can also enter a name for your particular Mac in the Netbios Name entry box. If your Mac has a host name (configured via DNS or the `etc/hostconfig` file on your Mac's startup disk), you should use that name here.

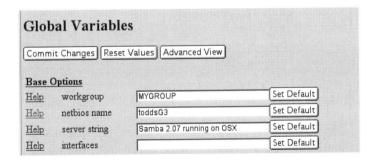

Note that to change any setting, you either enter the new value in the entry box next to that setting's label, or you select the setting from the pop-up menu. Then you click the Commit Changes button at the top of the screen in order to actually write those settings to the `smb.conf` file on the server. If you opt to return to a default setting, you can do that by simply clicking the Set Default button next to the entry and then clicking Commit Changes again.

The Globals page is used for a variety of other settings, including security options, logging options, and browsing options. Of particular importance while you're testing is to turn on the Encrypt Passwords option (select On from its pop-up menu) if you will be dealing with clients using Windows 98, Windows NT Service Pack 3, or higher.

The other important setting is the WINS Support option, found at the bottom of the screen. If your network doesn't already have a WINS (Windows Internet Naming Service) server, you should turn WINS Support on; if the network does already have such a server (most likely another Samba server or a Windows NT server), then you should enter the IP address of that server in the WINS Server entry box. When you've finished with the changes, click Commit Changes at the top of the screen.

Shares

The next step is to click the Shares button, which loads the Share Parameters page. As mentioned, a share is simply a folder you make available to SMB clients. To configure an existing share, select it in the pop-up menu and click Choose Share.

Alternatively, you can enter the name for a new share point on your server and click Create Share if you'd like to begin sharing that new folder. (You should avoid naming shares after their actual path; a short name like Shared or Documents is better.)

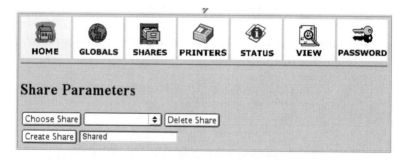

Once you click either Choose Share (if you've selected an existing share from the pop-up menu) or Create Share (if you've typed a share name), you'll see more options appear at the bottom on the screen. If you're creating a new share point, you should enter the path to that share point in the Path entry box, then make choices in the Security Options area, such as whether the share point should be read-only and whether guest access is appropriate. Once you've made your choices, click the Commit Changes button to write the changes to the smb.conf file. At this point, you can also click the View button to return to the View page and quickly confirm that the share point has been added.

 NOTE You can delete share points from this same screen by selecting the share in the pop-up menu and clicking the Delete Share button.

Password

Once you've finished setting globals and creating shares, you can move on to creating a user or two for your testing. Click the Password button, and you'll see an interface that enables you to create new users. Note that these users actually need to have accounts on your Mac (discussed in Chapter 7)—you'll enter their names and passwords again to add them as remote Samba users. If you want to add a user who doesn't have an account on your Mac, you'll first need to head to the Users pane in System Preferences and add that user.

To add a Samba user, enter the username in the first entry box and then enter the password in the two password boxes. Finally, click Add New User. If the add is successful, you'll see a message to that effect immediately below the entry boxes and buttons:

Server Password Management

User Name : `todds`
New Password :
Re-type New Password :
[Change Password] [Add New User] [Delete User] [Disable User] [Enable User]

Added user todds.

You can also use the entry boxes and buttons on this page to change the existing password for a Samba user or to disable, enable, or delete a user.

 NOTE If you're changing information about a user from a browser that isn't located on the Samba server, use the Client/Server Password Management tools. All you can do, in that case, is change the user's password. You'll need to enter the IP address of the main server computer in the Remote Machine entry box.

Status

When you've finished with all your configuration (at least far enough for testing purposes), you can click the Status button to switch to the Status page. Here you'll be able to confirm that the server is running, and in the future you'll be able to note active connections to the Samba server.

Setting Up the Windows Client

Once you've got the server configured, you're ready to configure a Windows client. In this section we'll briefly discuss what you need to do to set up a Windows 98–based computer; others versions of Windows are outside the scope of this book.

To set up your Windows client, you'll need to focus on two things. First, you need the Windows login feature activated, so that you sign into the Windows machine using the same username and password that you've set up on the Samba server. Second, you need to have Windows networking correctly configured so that it can locate the Samba server and mount it in the Network Neighborhood.

Windows Password

To enable password access on your Microsoft Windows PC, you should open the Control Panel and double-click the Passwords icon. Click the User Profiles tab in the Passwords Properties window. Now, make sure you've selected the option that begins, "Users can customize their preferences..." In addition, turn on both options under User Profile Settings.

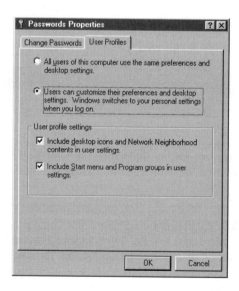

If you see the Change Passwords tab, you should select it and change your password to the password that you'll use to log into Samba. When you're done, close the Password Properties window; you'll probably be asked to restart Windows. Click Restart. When Windows has finished restarting, you'll be presented with a login window; enter your username and password, then press Enter to log into Windows.

 TIP If the username you use in Windows isn't the same as the username you have set up for Samba on the Mac OS X computer, you can click the Users icon in the Control Panel in Windows to create a new username. Create a user with the same username and password as you've set up on the Samba server.

Windows TCP/IP Settings

The next step is to set up Windows so that it's properly able to access the Samba server over TCP/IP. Obviously, you'll need to have the two computers (the Windows client and the Samba server) on the same Ethernet network. (If you happen to be using some other type of networking scheme, you're on your own, but you may be able to figure this out.) Then, once they're connected through an Ethernet hub, you can assign IP addresses and set some options to make sure they're communicating.

On the Windows client, begin by opening the Control Panel and double-clicking the Network icon. If the client is already configured for LAN-based TCP/IP access, you should see an entry that shows the TCP/IP protocol bound to a particular Ethernet adapter, as with the "TCP/IP -> PCI Fast Ethernet DEC 21140 Based Adapter" entry shown here:

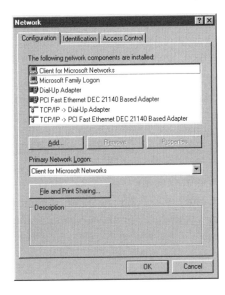

NOTE If you don't see any such entry for TCP/IP and your Ethernet adapter, you'll need to add the TCP/IP protocol; then you'll select the Ethernet adapter, click Properties, and use the check boxes on the Bindings tab to bind TCP/IP to that adapter.

Select the appropriate TCP/IP -> *Ethernet device* entry and click Properties to see the TCP/IP properties associated with that Ethernet port. You'll need to focus on three of the tabs in the TCP/IP Properties window:

IP Address Click this tab and make sure that the PC is properly configured with an IP address. If the PC can receive an IP address automatically (from a DHCP server, for instance, if you have such a server or router on your network), select Obtain an IP Address Automatically. Otherwise, select Specify an IP Address and enter the IP address and subnet mask.

WINS Configuration For the networking to work correctly, you should have WINS Resolution enabled. Click Enable WINS Resolution and enter the IP address for your WINS server. If your Samba server is the only such server on your network (that is, you don't have other Windows NT or other WINS servers running), enter the IP address for your Samba server. (Also note that WINS Support needs to be enabled in SWAT, as discussed earlier in the section "Globals.") You can ignore the Scope ID entry box, and should choose Use DHCP for WINS Resolution only if it's recommended by your system administrator.

DNS Configuration Again, you may have a DNS configuration already entered if your PC is set up for Ethernet-based Internet access. If not, you should enter a DNS server here, based on the DNS server you use for other Ethernet-based Internet connections on your network. You'll also need to enter a name for this Windows machine in the Host entry box; remember this name, since you'll need to enter it again in a moment.

Once you're finished with this configuration, you may want to click the Bindings tab and make sure Client for Microsoft Networks has a check mark next to it. (It likely does.) If it doesn't, click to place that check mark, then click OK to close the TCP/IP Properties window.

Finally, you'll need to click the Identification tab in the Network window. In the Computer Name entry box, enter the name for this client—the same name you entered in the Host entry box on the DNS Configuration tab previously. Then, in the Workgroup entry box, enter the name of your local workgroup; this is the same workgroup name you entered on the Globals page in SWAT when you configured your Samba server.

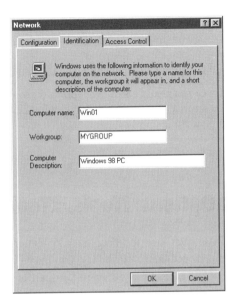

Enter a computer description, if desired, and then click OK. You'll be asked to restart the PC. Click Restart.

Accessing the Server

Once you've set all the TCP/IP and network settings, and the PC has restarted, you're ready to see exactly how lucky you are. After all of this configuration, you may actually be able to access the server.

From the Windows login prompt, enter the proper username and password. Once you're signed in and the desktop appears, double-click the Network Neighborhood icon on the desktop. You should see an entry for the Samba server; double-click that entry, and you'll see any share points you've set up—they'll appear as folders.

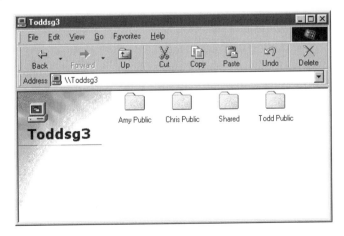

Finally, double-click a folder, and you'll see the contents of that folder in the window. You're connected!

 NOTE Once again, I encourage you to dig into a more complete Samba reference to learn more about security, user issues, and other management tasks such as log management and rotation.

Commercial Options: iTools, xTools, and Communigate

If you're interested in extending Mac OS X even further into the world of Internet services and Unix-like functionality, you may want to consider a commercial application. Out of the gate, a few different companies have promised Mac OS X versions of popular server applications and add-ons, most notably Tenon Intersystems (www.tenon.com), which makes xTools and Tenon's iTools, and Stalker Software (www.stalker.com), publishers of Communigate Pro.

Communigate Pro

Communigate Pro is a server application that focuses on adding complex mail-serving capabilities to your Mac. If you'd like your Mac OS X Server computer to act as a mail server for a local network, Communigate Pro offers those tools. Following are some of the features:

- POP3 server for Internet e-mail addresses
- IMAP server for "live" e-mail accounts
- Web-based e-mail retrieval for accessing e-mail accounts when the user is away from their computer
- Mailing list management, enabling groups to communicate via group mailing lists (often called "listservs")
- SMTP server for managing outgoing e-mail
- Hooks for anti-spam and antivirus applications

Communigate Pro is generally offered as a limited-license download from the Stalker Software Web site, so you can try the software before purchasing it.

iTools

Tenon's iTools (as distinguished from Apple's iTools, which are something else entirely) is a suite of Internet applications, including a mail-server application and tools to augment Mac OS X's built-in FTP and Apache Web servers. The tools include these:

- Secure Sockets Layer 3.0 (SSL) support for secure Web transactions
- A Web-based interface for configuring and customizing Apache for better performance
- Virtual host support, enabling a single Mac to host both multiple Web addresses and multiple FTP addresses, so that remote users can directly access their own Web server spaces
- Cacheing of HTML files to improve Web performance
- DNS support for your local network
- A built-in search engine for adding searches to your Web site
- An e-mail server that includes POP, IMAP, SMTP, and Web-based e-mail options

iTools—carrying a retail price of $495 at the time of this writing—isn't cheap. (Like Communigate, there's a free demo of iTools that you can download from Tenon's Web site.) Still, it's a nice add-on for hosting and managing professional-level Web sites, including FTP and e-mail service, from a single Mac OS X server. In fact, the tools are ideal for companies, other organizations, or even small Internet presence providers that want to offer Web hosting to multiple clients.

iTools requires a Mac that has a static IP address and a broadband connection to the Internet. You'll also need to have the Mac properly configured with a domain and host name. Once you've installed iTools and logged in with a new username and password (these are unique to iTools and not based on your Mac OS X account name), you'll be able to configure the additional capabilities from within a Web browser window.

 WARNING Tenon notes that iTools may alter your apache.conf configuration file. If you've altered it yourself in the past (perhaps with guidance from Chapter 24), you should make a backup of the file before installing iTools.

xTools

Another offering from Tenon Intersystems is xTools ($199), which adds the ability to deal with X Window applications from within Mac OS X's Aqua interface. (xTools is an X Window server, meaning it makes it possible for X Window applications to appear on your Mac OS X desktop.) X Window is a Unix-world standard for graphical applications; you may have heard of some popular X Window applications such as The GIMP or the X Window version of the Mosaic Web browser. X Window enables you to work with these applications in one of two ways.

First, it's common in the Unix world to actually run an application on another computer in your local network, but have the graphical results of that application displayed on your computer screen. That's one thing that xTools enables you to do on a Mac OS X machine—you could run an X Window application on another Unix computer on your network, and view that application on your Mac OS X desktop.

Second, you can compile and run X Window applications directly on your Mac OS X machine, thanks to the compilers and other tools included with xTools. Figure 25.5 shows some typical X Window applications and tools that have been compiled to run on Mac OS X (technically, they're running on Darwin), and displayed using xTools.

FIGURE 25.5

Here is xTools running the familiar xterm, xclock, and xlogo applications.

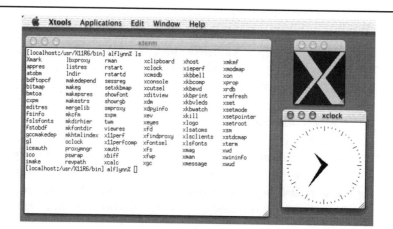

What's Next?

In this chapter you saw some server products you can add to Mac OS X, including two free options: QuickTime Streaming Server and Samba. QuickTime Streaming Server gives you the ability to stream hinted QuickTime movies using the Real Time Streaming Protocol from your Mac OS X computer. Users will be able to access, over the Internet, QuickTime movies that play in "real time," while the data is downloaded to their computers, instead of being forced to wait for the entire QuickTime movie to transmit completely before it can be viewed.

Samba gives your Mac the ability to act as a file server for Windows 95, 98, 2000, NT, and other compatible clients. With Samba installed, you can create share points that show up in the Windows computer's Network Neighborhood, making it easy to share files between the Mac and Windows clients on your network.

A few commercial server options are available at the time of this writing, including iTools and xTools from Tenon Systems, as well as Communigate Pro from Stalker Software. Communigate is a high-end mail-server application, offering features like IMAP support, Web mail, and other interesting add-ons. iTools is a suite of tools for improving on the Apache Web server that's built into Mac OS X. xTools is a very interesting tool, giving you the ability to run X Window applications directly on your Mac OS X desktop.

In Appendix A, you'll see instructions and advice for installing Mac OS X, including installation and configuration of Mac OS 9.1, enabling you to boot between the two OS versions.

PART

V

Advanced
Mac OS X Topics

APPENDIX <u>A</u>

Installing and Setting Up Mac OS X

FEATURING:

I f Mac OS X isn't yet installed on your Mac, then you'll need to do a little planning before you get started. If you've used a Mac before, you'll find that Mac OS X is different from Mac OS 9.*x* and earlier versions. First, you'll need to consider how you're going to set up your hard disk to accommodate Mac OS X. You may want to run both Mac OS X and Mac OS 9.1, allowing you to dual-boot between the two of them. To use Mac OS X in a dual-boot environment, you may decide to partition your disk.

In this appendix, you'll take a look at the requirements for Mac OS X. Then you'll learn how to plan your Mac OS X installation, including how to initialize and partition your hard disk, if necessary. Finally, you'll learn how to run the installer and set up Mac OS X for the first time.

Reviewing Mac OS X Requirements

Before you install Mac OS X, you should know its requirements. On the Mac OS X CD, you'll find a PDF document called READ ME BEFORE YOU INSTALL.pdf. From Mac OS 9.*x*, you can open this file and examine its contents using Adobe Acrobat Reader.

Mac OS X requires 128MB of RAM (according to Apple). More RAM is recommended if you plan to run many background services (such as Apple File Sharing and Web Sharing) and use the Classic environment extensively.

Mac OS X can be installed on the following Macintosh models:

- All Power Macintosh G3 and G4 models

- All iMac models

- All iBook models

- All PowerBook G3 and G4 models, with the exception of the original PowerBook G3 (sometimes called the PowerBook 3500)

You can't install Mac OS X on an external FireWire or Universal Serial Bus (USB) hard disk, although you should be able to use most such disks for data and application files, if desired, once Mac OS X is booted up. Also, some early Apple technical information suggests that once you've installed Mac OS X on an internal SCSI hard disk, you should make sure that you don't change the SCSI ID number of that disk, because that may cause Mac OS X to fail to boot. (You would need to dig around in your machine to change the ID number, so it's unlikely you would do this, but it's important to avoid.)

Mac OS X uses either the Unix File System (UFS) or HFS+ format as the disk format for its volumes. Earlier Mac OS versions use the HFS (Hierarchical File System) or HFS+

format, also called Mac OS Standard and Mac OS Extended, respectively. Although Mac OS X can read and write data to a Mac OS Standard volume, it can't be installed on one. It must be installed on either a Mac OS Extended or UFS volume.

Preparing to Install Mac OS X

Before you install Mac OS X, you'll need to carefully consider how you want to install it and complete some preparatory steps, as follows:

- Decide whether you want to use the Classic environment and if you would like to be able to dual-boot between Mac OS X and Mac OS 9.1.

- Back up all the important files on your hard disk.

- Partition your disk into multiple volumes, if desired, and initialize those volumes.

- If necessary, install or update to Mac OS 9.1 (unless you do not plan to dual-boot into Mac OS 9.1 and/or use the Classic environment).

- Update you Mac's firmware, if necessary, as well as the firmware for any of your internal cards and other devices, particularly if the device's manufacturer has a special firmware update that supports Mac OS X.

Choosing an Installation Option

One of the main considerations for installing Mac OS X is whether you want to use the Classic environment and/or whether you would like to be able to dual-boot between Mac OS X and Mac OS 9.1. If you have both operating systems installed on your Mac, then you have the option of booting the Mac (starting it up) in either of those operating systems, depending on the task you're trying to accomplish. If you install only Mac OS X on your Mac, you won't have the option of booting into Mac OS 9.1, and you won't be able to run Classic applications within the Classic environment.

If you do opt to dual-boot and/or run Classic, then you have another decision to make: whether to install Mac OS X and Mac OS 9.1 on separate volumes or disks. If you have more than one disk drive installed in your Mac, you may be able to install Mac OS 9.1 on one and Mac OS X on another, which is a good solution, particularly if you're not completely sure you're committed to working in Mac OS X. But even if you have only one hard disk in your Mac, you can opt to partition your disk, thus dividing it into multiple volumes. Each volume acts more or less as a separate disk. You can initialize volumes using different file systems, for instance, and each can have a different name.

APP

A

Getting Installed and
Set Up

Partitioning a disk is a bit tricky, though, because it requires you to erase the entire disk, thus losing any data that's currently stored on the disk. If you can fully back up your important files, however, partitioning your disk and installation Mac OS 9.1 and Mac OS X can have some advantages.

Here's a summary of the installation options:

Mac OS X and Mac OS 9.1 on the same disk   You can install Mac OS X on the same disk as an existing installation of Mac OS 9.1. This is the easiest way to install Mac OS X, because it probably won't require you to do any low-level reinitializing of the hard disk. In some ways, it's a bit risky, though, because it makes it more difficult to remove Mac OS X from your Mac if you encounter problems or decide to delete it for some other reason. It also requires that the disk already be formatted in the HFS+ format.

Mac OS X and Mac OS 9.1 on different disks or partitions   You can install Mac OS X on a separate disk or on a different partition of your main hard disk from Mac OS 9.1. In this case, you can still dual-boot between the two operating systems and you can use the Mac OS 9.1 installation for the Classic environment in Mac OS X. The advantages include the fact that the Mac OS X partition or disk can be formatted as a UFS volume (if you have a good reason to do this, such as integrating your Mac into a Unix environment more easily) and the Mac OS 9.1 volume can be formatted as HFS+. Also, with Mac OS X on its own partition, it's easier to troubleshoot and, if you decide it's necessary, to remove and/or reinstall Mac OS X.

NOTE   Some beta versions of Mac OS X had trouble booting properly from IDE hard disks configured for slave mode, so you may want to make a point of installing Mac OS X on an IDE drive configured as master, if you have a choice.

Mac OS X and Mac OS 9.1 on the same disk and on different disks
You can install Mac OS 9.1 or lower on a separate disk or partition, then install Mac OS 9.1 *and* Mac OS X on another disk or partition. This has the advantage of enabling you to dual-boot into a fully customized version of Mac OS 9.1 or lower, while using a "clean" version of Mac OS 9.1 for the Classic environment within Mac OS X.

Apple has designed Mac OS X to coexist on the same HFS+ partition as a previous installation of Mac OS 9.1. Mac OS X's installer program will recognize the Mac OS 9.1 installation and properly install its files *over* that installation, moving some of the Mac OS 9.1

files to different folders, such as the Applications (Mac OS 9) folder that the installer will create. So, using one partition is certainly possible, and it still allows you to dual-boot between Mac OS 9.1 and Mac OS X. However, if you're serious about testing Mac OS X before you fully adopt it as your day-to-day operating system, you should take the more careful approach of working with two or more partitions. Which you do depends on how eager you are to switch completely to Mac OS X as well as *when* you're reading this book. If Mac OS X has been updated beyond the 10.0 stage by Apple, you may feel better about installing Mac OS X on the same partition as Mac OS 9.1. In the early months, though, Mac OS X is likely to have some bugs to work out, so a two-partition approach may be warranted, especially on "mission-critical" computers.

Backing Up Files

Before you install Mac OS X, you may want to use a backup utility on your Mac to make sure you create a complete backup. Ideally, you should always have a current backup of your important data files. For the purpose of this installation, though, you can simply copy your files to an external hard disk, a removable disk, or other media you have available. Mac OS X will be able to read those disks after installation, and you'll be able to copy applications and documents back to your Mac OS X machine for future use.

Partitioning and Initializing

As noted early, you can opt to install Mac OS X in one of two basic ways: on the same volume as an existing Mac OS 9.1 installation or on a separate volume. If you plan to install Mac OS X on a separate volume, you may need to create that volume by partitioning your existing hard disk into two or more volumes.

To partition your hard disk, start up from the Mac OS 9.1 CD that is included with your Mac OS X retail package. Place the CD in your Mac's CD or DVD drive, then restart the Mac. Immediately after you hear the startup tone, hold down the C key until the Mac begins starting up from the CD.

Then run Drive Setup, the Mac OS utility that allows you to initialize volumes and create partitions on those volumes. Double-click the Drive Setup icon in the Utilities folder on the Mac OS 9 Install CD. You should see the Drive Setup window, as shown in Figure A.1.

A

Getting Installed
and Set Up

 NOTE If your hard disk is already partitioned, you don't need to run Drive Setup. You can simply back up the data on the target volume and then use the Erase command under the Special menu in the Finder to erase the volume you want to use for Mac OS X. You can then move on to the section "Installing or Updating to Mac OS 9.1."

The Drive Setup window enables you to select and initialize your hard disks.

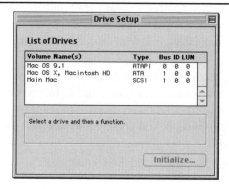

In the Drive Setup window, you'll see a list of drives you can select to initialize and partition. Select your Mac's internal hard disk, and then click the Initialize button. (If you plan to install Mac OS X on another internal hard disk, select that disk in Drive Setup instead, and then click the Initialize button.)

NOTE You can install Mac OS X on a secondary hard disk if you have one installed inside your Mac or attached via the external SCSI bus. (That said, installing Mac OS X on an external SCSI disk isn't a recommended setup, and there are some compatibility issues with SCSI controllers and Mac OS X.) You can't install Mac OS X on removable disks or external hard disks connected to your Mac via USB or FireWire ports.

In the Initialize window, you'll see a list of the volumes that are on the disk you're planning to initialize. Look at this list carefully—it's possible that you're not aware of or have forgotten the fact that the disk you've selected actually has multiple volumes on it. All of these volumes will be erased if you continue the initialization process, so make sure you've backed up all of them, if necessary.

Now, to set up your partitions, click the Custom Setup button. This brings up the Custom Setup window, as shown in Figure A.2.

In the Custom Setup window, you choose how many partitions you want on this disk after it's initialized. If you plan to use this disk for both a Mac OS 9.1 (or earlier) version and Mac OS X, then you'll want at least two different partitions. You can have more, if you like, as long as the volume you plan to use for Mac OS X has at least 1.5GB of available disk space. (Don't forget that you'll probably want more than this so you can store documents, new applications, and downloaded files on the Mac OS X partition.)

FIGURE A.2

The Custom Setup window allows you to create more than one partition.

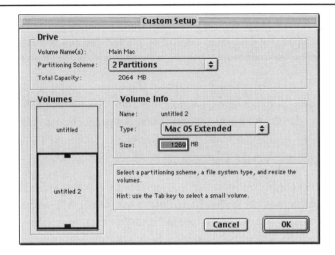

You can change the size of the partitions in two ways. Between each partition in the Volumes area you'll see a line with a small drag box; click and drag that box to change the size of the partitions using your mouse. You can also click a partition in the Volumes area and enter a numerical size for it in the Size entry box.

NOTE If you plan to have two partitions for dual-booting on an IDE drive, your best bet is to install Mac OS 9.x on the first partition and Mac OS X on the second partition. Be sure to plan the size of your partitions accordingly.

You should also choose the formatting type for each partition by selecting the partition in the Volumes area and choosing the type of format for that volume from the Type menu. For the Mac OS 9.x partition, you should choose Mac OS Extended (HFS+). For the Mac OS X partition, you'll need to format using Mac OS X Extended or UFS (although Mac OS X Extended is recommended for most installations, because it is more compatible with Classic applications and documents, as well as some Carbon applications).

Once you have your partitions set the way you want them, click the OK button. Return to the Initialize window and click the Initialize button to begin the formatting process. You'll see one more dialog box to confirm your decisions, and then the initialization takes place. This will erase all of the data on the selected drive (including all volumes on that drive) and create the new partitions on that disk.

APP

A

Getting Installed
and Set Up

WARNING Last warning! Don't initialize your disk without creating backups of important data. All of the data on the selected disk will be erased.

When Drive Setup is finished initializing, you'll see any Mac OS Extended partitions appear on the desktop as separate disk icons. (UFS partitions aren't recognized by Mac OS 9.x.) You can quit Drive Setup by choosing Quit from its File menu.

Updating Your Firmware

Another necessary task for some Mac OS 9.1 and Mac OS X installations (particularly on some of the earlier Mac models that Mac OS X supports) is the need to update your Mac's *firmware*. Firmware is an internal, rewritable snippet of code that is used to help the Macintosh when it's first powering up and recognizing its components. As time goes on, Apple often makes slight changes and fixes to the firmware code that can then be used to update your Mac to be fully compatible with new technologies such as Mac OS X.

All relevant firmware updates that were available at the time that Mac OS 9.1 was published are available on the Mac OS 9.1 CD. To determine whether your Mac requires a firmware update, you can open the Firmware Updates folder on the Mac OS 9.1 CD (in the CD Extras folder, inside the subfolder FirmWare Updates) to see if your particular Mac system has a recommended update.

You should also visit asu.info.apple.com in your Web browser and search for firmware updates for your Mac model, because subsequent updates may have been made available since the Mac OS 9.1 CD was created. (At the time of this writing, the Mac OS X CD didn't include firmware updates, but it may in the future, so check the CD as well as visiting Apple's support site to see if newer versions are available.)

 WARNING At the time of this writing, the latest round of firmware updates available from Apple's Web site for iMac and Power Macintosh G4 (and G4 Cube) models carry a special caveat: The updates can disable some third-party RAM modules. Apple has stated that the firmware update disables modules that aren't fully compatible with your Mac and Mac OS X, causing crashes and freezes. If you find you've installed the firmware update and suddenly your Mac seems to have less RAM available, the firmware update may have disabled a RAM module that it considered faulty.

Updating firmware is fairly painless. You begin by booting into Mac OS 9 (or higher) and launching the updater—double-click the updater's icon, whether it's on the Mac OS 9.1 CD-ROM or on a disk image that you've downloaded from Apple's

Web site. Note that if you've just formatted your Mac's hard disk and you have no version of the Mac OS on it, you'll need to install Mac OS 9 or Mac OS 9.1 first, because you can't start up from the Mac OS 9.1 CD and install the firmware update. You must start up from your hard disk.

If your firmware is up to date, you'll see a dialog box telling you that. If not, follow the on-screen instructions for the update. In most cases, the updater will tell you to shut down your Mac, then hold down the programmer's button on the back or side of your Mac while you press the Power button. Finally, you'll hear a long tone, which is your cue to release the buttons. Then your Mac should start up. In many cases (depending on your Mac model), you'll see a status bar and a success message. You may also see a blinking question mark before your Mac finds its startup disk—that's normal.

As part of the firmware update process, PRAM (Parameter RAM, a small portion of RAM reserved for system-level settings and the Mac's clock) is also reset, so you may need to reset your Startup Disk, Date & Time, Monitor, AppleTalk, and other control panels.

 NOTE As mentioned earlier, you should also visit the Web sites of the manufacturers of any third-party peripherals that you have attached to your Mac. Many of them will likely have both firmware updates and driver software updates designed to make their products compatible with Mac OS X. This is particularly true of internal PCI adapter cards, but it can extend to external devices as well. For instance, Apple makes a special note in the Mac OS X Read Me file concerning the Apple Ultra Wide SCSI PCI card in Power Macintosh G3 (beige) models. If you have such a card, make sure that you also update the firmware for the card. An updater is on the Mac OS 9.1 CD-ROM.

Installing or Updating to Mac OS 9.1

If you've opted to partition and initialize your hard disk, then your next step will be to install Mac OS 9.1 on one or both of those partitions. It's possible to run Mac OS X without installing Mac OS 9.1, but I don't recommend it for three reasons:

- Some Classic applications for the foreseeable future will simply work better when you dual-boot into Mac OS 9.1.

- Even if you don't plan to dual-boot, Mac OS 9.1 is required for the Classic environment in Mac OS X, and you'll likely find *some* reason to run a Classic application at some point.

- Mac OS 9.1 is sometimes required by Apple's updaters, installations, and for the occasional workaround when you're troubleshooting in Mac OS X.

If you already have another Mac OS version installed on your Mac, you can use the Mac OS 9.1 CD that is included with the retail Mac OS X package to update that installation to Mac OS 9.1. To start up from the CD, place the Mac OS 9.1 CD in your CD or DVD drive and restart your Mac. Immediately after hearing the startup chime, hold down the C key on your keyboard. After a moment, you'll see the Mac OS 9.1 startup screen and you should hear the CD/DVD drive whirring away. (If you've just partitioned and/or initialized your hard disk, then you probably already booted from the Mac OS 9.1 CD.)

When the desktop appears, you should see the Mac OS 9.1 CD window. Locate the Install Mac OS 9.1 icon and double-click it to launch the installer. Now, you'll walk through the steps of the Mac OS 9.1 installer:

1. The first screen is the Welcome screen. Click Continue to move to the next screen.

2. On the Select Destination screen, select the volume onto which you wish to install Mac OS 9.1 from the pop-up menu, then click Continue.

3. You see the Important Information screen, which includes the contents of the Before You Install file on the Mac OS 9.1 CD. Read through it to see if it addresses any particular issues that relate to your Mac, such as incompatibilities or warnings regarding firmware and other updates. When you're ready, click Continue.

4. The Software License Agreement screen appears. Page through the license agreement (you should read the whole thing). When you're finished, click the Continue button. A dialog box appears asking if you agree with the license agreement; if you do, click Agree. If you click Disagree, the installer application will quit.

5. Finally, you arrive at the Install Software screen, shown in Figure A.3. Here you have two choices. You can click Start to begin a standard installation on the specified volume (check to make sure the specified volume is correct), or you can choose Customize if you would like to customize the Mac OS 9.1 installation (and you know what you're doing).

 NOTE On the Install Software screen you can click the Options button if you want to turn off the installer's attempts to update the hard disk driver and/or create an installation report.

Once you click Start, the installer will begin the installation process by scanning the hard disk and noting any errors. In most cases, it will fix minor errors, but occasionally it will encounter one that it can't fix. If that happens, you'll need to either run a disk repair program or reinitialize the disk before installation.

FIGURE A.3

*The Install Software
screen*

Once the disk has been checked, the installer goes about installing (or updating) the System Folder on the target disk. After 15 to 20 minutes, Mac OS 9.1 should be installed. You can now restart into Mac OS 9.1, if desired, and complete the Setup and Internet Assistants. Those settings will be used whenever you boot into Mac OS 9.1 in the future.

Installing Mac OS X

With your drive partitioned and initialized, your firmware updated and Mac OS 9.1 installed (if desired), you're ready to install Mac OS X. First, you run the installer program, and then you set up Mac OS X using the Setup Assistant. In order to complete the Setup Assistant, you'll need to know some things about your Mac, so have the following information handy:

- The networking protocols (AppleTalk, TCP/IP, or both) that you plan to use on your network.
- The host name and router address for your TCP/IP network (unless you have a BootP server on your network).
- Your IP addressing scheme, unless you have a BootP server on your network. If you don't have a BootP server, you'll need to know the IP address and subnet mask for your Mac. (If you don't know this information, consult your system administrator.)
- Information provided to you by your Internet service provider (ISP) regarding dial-up account settings, phone numbers, and your e-mail accounts.

APP
A

Getting Installed
and Set Up

Running the Mac OS X Installer

Once you have Mac OS 9.1 installed (or updated) and you're ready to install Mac OS X, you should restart in Mac OS 9.1. When the desktop appears, insert the Mac OS X CD. Then double-click the Install Mac OS X icon. In the Install Mac OS X window, click the Restart button. Your Mac will restart, boot using the Mac OS X CD, and then launch the Mac OS X installer.

 NOTE If your Mac is currently shut down, you can boot directly into the Mac OS X installer by starting up your Mac, placing the Mac OS X CD in your CD or DVD drive, and holding down the C key on your keyboard. This is the approach you should take if you don't have Mac OS 9.1 installed and don't intend to install it.

Now, you're ready to install Mac OS X, as follows:

1. On the Language screen, select the language you want to use for Mac OS X's main language and click Continue.

2. The next screen is the Welcome screen. Click the Continue button after reading the welcome message.

3. On the Important Information screen, you'll see last-minute information about Mac OS X, such as computer models supported, information about software updates, and limitations of the current release. When you're finished scrolling through the message, click the Continue button.

4. The Software License screen appears. Read through the license, then click Continue. In the dialog box that appears, click Agree if you agree with the license agreement. (If you click Disagree, you won't move on in the installer.)

5. On the Select a Destination screen, select the hard disk where you want to install Mac OS X. You may also wish to choose the Erase Destination and Format As option, using the pop-up menu to select the disk format you would like to use. Use this option only if you're planning to initialize the target volume—it will be erased, so it shouldn't have important data on it. (If you're installing over Mac OS 9.1, you shouldn't select this option.) With the disk selected, click Continue.

6. The Easy Install screen appears. If you wish to customize the installation, click the Customize button and use the check boxes to determine which portions of the installation you want to install. Otherwise, click the Install button to begin the installation.

The installer will check your hard disk, then begin installing components. After about 10 to 15 minutes, the installation will complete. The installer will automatically restart your Mac and launch the Setup Assistant.

Trouble Selecting Volumes

At the time of this writing, the Mac OS X installer was still pretty young. If you have trouble selecting volumes in the installer, see if any of the following explanations help. If not, check Apple's Support site at www.apple.com/support/ or call Apple's 800 support number for help.

Volumes Are Gray in the Installer

- If the volume you want to install onto is gray in the installer, that volume is not able to contain Mac OS X. Possible reasons include volumes formatted as Mac OS Standard format (HFS), locked volumes (such as a CD-ROM), or FireWire and USB hard drives, which Mac OS X doesn't support in this release.

- On older PowerBook G3 (Wallstreet) models, tray-loading iMac models, and Power Macintosh G3 (beige) models, Mac OS X can be installed only on a partition that is entirely contained within the first 8GB of the drive. If your disk is larger than 8GB, you'll need to partition it, but you need to be careful that the first partition is smaller than 8GB. So, if you have a 12GB drive whose first partition is 10GB and second partition is 2GB, you won't be able to install Mac OS X on either of these. Both volumes will be gray in the Mac OS X installer. If you have the same drive with an 8GB partition and a 4GB partition, you can install Mac OS X on only the first partition.

- The Mac OS X installation cannot install to some UFS volumes that were created with Drive Setup 1.9.1 (the version included with some Mac OS 9.0 installations). If you expect to see a UFS volume and don't, you'll need to reformat the volume with the version of Drive Setup on the Mac OS 9.1 CD.

No Volumes Are Visible in the Installer

If you don't see any volumes in the installer, you will also get a warning about not having Mac OS 9.1 installed, just before the screen where your volumes would appear. The most likely cause of this is that your Open Firmware settings have gotten messed up. (Open Firmware is a low-level set of instructions that the operating system uses for communicating with the Mac's hardware.) Resetting Open Firmware may fix this problem. To reset Open Firmware:

1. Restart the computer (press ⌘+Option+O+F). When you've done this correctly, you will see a white screen that says Open Firmware.

2. Type reset-nvram and press Return.

3. Type reset-all and press Return.

The computer should restart. After you hear the startup chime, hold the C key to get the computer to start up from the CD. If Open Firmware was the problem, you should now see your volumes.

APP

A

Getting Installed
and Set Up

Using the Setup Assistant

The Setup Assistant, aside from being pretty and playing some jazzy music, walks you through the process of configuring your Mac for the first time with Mac OS X. You'll choose a number of settings, including an administrative password, the time and date, and information about your network and Internet connection. You'll also be able to create user accounts for users on this Mac OS X system. Follow these steps to configure Mac OS X with the Setup Assistant:

1. The first screen welcomes you to the Assistant. Select the name of the country you're in, then click the Continue button. (If you don't see the correct country, check the Show All option.)

 NOTE The Assistant includes both Continue and Go Back buttons. If, at any point, you want to go back one or more screens within the Assistant, click the Go Back button. You can then change settings and move forward again with the Continue button.

2. Select the keyboard layout you want to use and click Continue. Again, you can turn on the Show All option if you want to use a keyboard layout that isn't listed.

3. On the Registration Information screen, enter your personal information. The Assistant requires that you enter a name, address, city, state, Zip code, and phone number. If you would like to read Apple's privacy policy, click the Privacy button. Finally, click Continue.

4. On the next screen, answer the survey questions, select Yes or No regarding whether or not Apple and third-party companies can send you offers, and then click the Continue button. When you see the Thank You screen, click Continue once more.

5. On the Create Your Account screen, you can create the first user (and administrator) account for your Mac. Enter your full name in the Name entry box, then enter a shorter, one-word username (up to eight characters) in the Short Name entry box. Next, enter a password in the Password entry box and enter the same password in the Verify box so that the Assistant can ensure that you've typed the password correctly. Finally, enter a short hint that will help you remember your password (but that doesn't make it easy for others to guess). Click the Continue button, and your account will be created.

NOTE The best passwords are nonsensical to anyone but you, preferably composed of both numbers and letters, eight characters long. All passwords in Mac OS X are case-sensitive, so you need to remember exactly how you enter passwords, including upper-case letters and numbers that you use.

6. On the Get Internet Ready screen, choose either I'll Use My Existing Internet Service or I'm Not Ready to Connect to the Internet. Click Continue after you've made your selection. (If you choose not to set up Internet access, skip to step 9 below.)

7. If you chose to use your existing Internet service, you'll see the How Do You Connect screen. Select the type of connection you have and click Continue.

8. The next screen you see depends on the type of connection you are attempting to set up. For a dial-up modem connection, you'll enter account information for your ISP and your ISP's phone number, and then you'll configure your modem. For other types of connections, you'll set up TCP/IP access. (For more information about these settings, consult your ISP or system administrator; also refer to Chapter 9 in this book.)

9. Once you've configured your Mac for Internet access, the Get iTools screen appears. Here, you can sign up for an iTools account or enter information regarding an account that you've already set up. If you already have an account, select I'm Already Using iTools and enter your name and password. Otherwise, select either I'd Like to Create My iTools Account or I'm Not Ready for iTools and click Continue. (If you choose to skip iTools or if you enter your own iTools account information, skip to step 11.)

NOTE iTools are Apple's special online applications—iDisk, Mac.com e-mail, and Home-Page. They're discussed in more detail in Chapter 11 of this book.

10. To create an iTools account, enter a username to use for your iTools account (it does not need to be the same as your Mac OS X account username), then type the password you will to use for iTools twice. Next, enter a Password Question and Password Answer that the iTools server can use to confirm your identity if you need to ask for your password in the future. Use a question and answer that you'll remember but that isn't easily guessed and that has nothing to do with

APP
A

Getting Installed
and Set Up

your actual password. Something like "What is my favorite color?" or "Who was my childhood dog?" and the appropriate answer will work well. Finally, select your birth month and year (again, for confirmation when you need to retrieve your iTools password) and click Continue.

11. The Registration screen appears. If you've set up Internet access, simply click Continue to configure your computer for Internet access and to send your registration to Apple. If you haven't set up your Mac for Internet access, you'll be asked if you want to Register Now by modem. If you don't have a modem installed in your Mac, select Register Later. Make your choice and click Continue. If you've chosen to connect and register, your Mac will either connect to the Internet automatically or you'll be prompted to enter information about your modem.

12. If you've set up Internet access, the Set Up Mail screen appears. Here, you can opt to set up only your Mac.com e-mail account (which should be set up for you already if you previously entered iTools information) or you can add additional accounts by selecting Add My Existing Email Account. If you select the latter, you'll need to enter an e-mail address, incoming mail server address, account type, account ID, password, and an outgoing mail server. (See Chapter 10 of this book for more information about these settings.) Then click Continue.

13. The Select Time Zone page appears. Select your current time zone from the map and/or pop-up menu, then click Continue.

That should be it. You'll see a final congratulatory screen. Click Continue, and your Mac should boot up into Mac OS X. You'll see your desktop, ready for action.

 NOTE After you have completed the Startup Assistant and your desktop has appeared, you may find that Software Update launches automatically. If your Mac is connected to the Internet and Software Update finds updates, you can opt to download them so that Mac OS X and its components can be updated immediately to the latest version. Software Update is discussed in Chapter 20 of this book.

Dual-Booting

If you've installed Mac OS 9.1 and Mac OS X on the same disk, or if you've installed Mac OS X and an earlier Mac OS version on separate volumes, you now have the option of booting into different Mac operating system (OS) versions whenever you find it necessary. How you choose a volume depends on the OS that you're currently using.

If you're in Mac OS X, you can switch to another OS version by opening the System Preferences application and selecting the Startup Disk pane. Mac OS X will scan your volumes for valid System Folders. Once they've appeared, you can select the system you would like to use the next time you restart the Mac. (Note that you need to have an administrator's account or password to change the startup disk.)

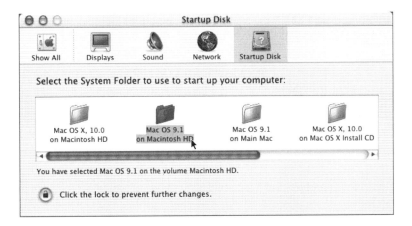

Once you've selected the startup disk, close the System Preferences application. Then restart your Mac (select Restart from the Apple menu). It should start up using the System Folder you selected.

If you're in Mac OS 9.1, you can decide to boot into a different OS by opening the Startup Disk control panel, which will show you each disk that is connected to the Mac. You can then click the disclosure triangle next to a disk to see the operating systems that are available for startup on that disk. Select the OS you want to use the next time the Mac is restarted. Then you can click the Restart button to restart the Mac into the selected OS.

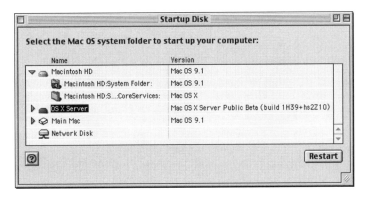

If you're currently using an earlier Mac OS version, its Startup Disk control panel may not recognize Mac OS X partitions. In that case, you have two options:

- You can use the Startup Disk control panel in that version to select a Mac OS 9.1 System Folder; then, once you're in Mac OS 9.1, you can use *its* Startup Disk control panel to restart again in Mac OS X.

- You can restart your Mac (Special ➢ Restart), then hold down the Option key after hearing the startup tone. Next, you should see the Startup Picker screen. Select the volume you want to use for startup (most likely the volume with a small OS X icon), then click the right-facing arrow to continue with the startup process.

Either way, your Mac should restart in Mac OS X.

INDEX

Note to Reader: **Bolded** page references indicate main discussions of a topic. *Italicized* page references indicate illustrations.